T0181165

Lecture Notes in Computer Science 14264

Founding Editors

Gerhard Goos
Juris Hartmanis

The series Lecture Notes in Computer Science (LNCS), including its subseries Lecture Notes in Artificial Intelligence (LNAI) and Lecture Notes in Bioinformatics (LNBI), has established itself as a medium for the publication of new developments in computer science and information technology research, teaching, and education.

LNCS enjoys close cooperation with the computer science R & D community, the series counts many renowned academics among its volume editors and paper authors, and collaborates with prestigious societies. Its mission is to serve this international community by providing an invaluable service, mainly focused on the publication of conference and workshop proceedings and postproceedings. LNCS commenced publication in 1973.

Ullrich Köthe · Carsten Rother
Editors

Pattern Recognition

45th DAGM German Conference, DAGM GCPR 2023
Heidelberg, Germany, September 19–22, 2023
Proceedings

 Springer

Editors
Ullrich Köthe 🆔
IWR, Heidelberg University
Heidelberg, Germany

Carsten Rother
IWR, Heidelberg University
Heidelberg, Germany

ISSN 0302-9743   ISSN 1611-3349 (electronic)
Lecture Notes in Computer Science
ISBN 978-3-031-54604-4   ISBN 978-3-031-54605-1 (eBook)
https://doi.org/10.1007/978-3-031-54605-1

This Springer imprint is published by the registered company Springer Nature Switzerland AG
The registered company address is: Gewerbestrasse 11, 6330 Cham, Switzerland

Paper in this product is recyclable.

Preface

On behalf of the organizers, we are happy to present the proceedings of DAGM-GCPR 2023, the 45th annual conference of the German Association for Pattern Recognition. It took place in Heidelberg from September 19 to 22, 2023.

The conference covered all aspects of modern data analysis, computer vision, and machine learning, from autonomous driving to large language models to medical diagnosis. Unsurprisingly, many papers took a deep learning approach, and it was interesting to observe that the questions of systematic validation, performance guarantees, robustness, and explainability of deep learning received considerable attention and played a prominent role within the conference presentations. Besides the established formats (talks, posters, young researcher forum – YRF), this year's edition offered a pre-conference workshop on "Scene Understanding for Autonomous Drone Delivery" (organized by Elisa de Llano, Amazon Austria), a tutorial on "Generative modelling in computer vision and the sciences" (presented by Felix Draxler, Peter Sorrenson, and Lars Kühmichel, Heidelberg University) and an Industry and Start-up Fair. An impressive number of renowned researchers – Lena Maier-Hein (DKFZ Heidelberg), Patrick Perez (valeo.ai Paris), Barbara Plank (LMU Munich), Michael Unser (EPF Lausanne), Anna Kreshuk (EMBL Heidelberg), Jens Kleesiek (University Hospital Essen), Christoph Lampert (IST Austria), Bernt Schiele (MPI Informatics Saarbrücken), and Daniel Cremers (TU Munich) – accepted our invitation for keynote and overview presentations, adding a most valuable complementary perspective on our field to the conference program.

The call for papers attracted 76 original submissions. All authors agreed to Spinger's Code of Conduct[1]. The program committee conducted a rigorous reviewing process with three double-blind reviews per submission and selected 11 papers for oral and 29 for poster presentation at the conference (acceptance rate 52%). We would like to thank all program committee members and external reviewers for their high-quality evaluations of the submissions and helpful feedback to the authors. Likewise, we thank the authors for choosing DAGM-GCPR as their publication venue, thus making the success of the conference possible in the first place. In addition to the regular articles published here, we accepted 45 articles for the nectar track, where authors can present work recently published elsewhere to the German-speaking community – a big thank you that so many people took advantage of this unique opportunity to discuss brand-new results.

As in previous editions, an independent jury – consisting of Christoph Lampert (ISTA Klosterneuburg), Margrit Gelautz (TU Wien), Felix Heide (Princeton University), and Björn Andres (TU Dresden) – awarded three prizes to outstanding conference contributions:

Best Paper Award: Sudhanshu Mittal, Joshua Niemeijer, Jörg P. Schäfer, Thomas Brox. "Best Practices in Active Learning for Semantic Segmentation"

---

[1] https://www.springernature.com/gp/authors/book-authors-code-of-conduct.

Honorable Mentions: Marvin Schmitt, Paul-Christian Bürkner, Ullrich Köthe, Stefan T. Radev. "Detecting Model Misspecification in Amortized Bayesian Inference with Neural Networks"

Lea Bogensperger, Dominik Narnhofer, Filip Ilic, Thomas Pock. "Score-Based Generative Models for Medical Image Segmentation using Signed Distance Functions"

The YRF award for an outstanding master's thesis was given to

Young Researcher Award: Felix Seegräber (with Patricia Schöntag, Felix Woelk, Kevin Koeser). "Underwater multiview stereo using axial camera models"

We would like to extend our sincere thanks to everyone who helped making DAGM-GCPR 2023 a success, most notably the local organizers Barbara Quintel, Jeannette Kautzmann, and Svenja Reith, as well as the volunteers from Heidelberg University and beyond. We want to thank the Interdisciplinary Center for Scientific Computing (IWR) and the Physics Department at Heidelberg University for generously offering their facilities for hosting the conference. Moreover, we express our gratitude to our sponsors Carl Zeiss AG (Gold), Bayer AG and Robert Bosch GmbH (Silver), and Quality Match GmbH and Copresence AG (Bronze). We appreciate their donations to our community, which recognize and reinforce the importance of our contributions to the advancement of machine learning, computer vision, and artificial intelligence. Finally, we thank the sponsors of the German Pattern Recognition Award (Mercedes-Benz Group) and the PhD thesis award (MVTec GmbH). These awards went to

German Pattern Recognition Award: Anna Rohrbach (TU Darmstadt) for her groundbreaking research on multimodal learning at the intersection of vision and language

Wieland Brendel (MPI Intelligent Systems Tübingen) for his exceptional contributions towards understanding, and closing the gap between, deep vision models and human visual perception

DAGM MVTec Dissertation Award: David Stutz (MPI Informatics Saarbrücken) for his dissertation "Real-time Human Performance Capture and Synthesis"

We were honored to host the 45th DAGM-GCPR conference in Heidelberg and are looking forward to the next edition, to be held in Munich.

November 2023

Ullrich Köthe
Carsten Rother
Bogdan Savchynskyy
Janis Keuper
Christoph Lampert
Karl Rohr

Organization

General Chairs

Ullrich Köthe   Heidelberg University, Germany
Carsten Rother   Heidelberg University, Germany

Program Chairs

Bogdan Savchynskyy   Heidelberg University, Germany
Christoph Lampert   Institute of Science and Technology Austria, Klosterneuburg, Austria
Janis Keuper   Hochschule Offenburg, Germany
Karl Rohr   Heidelberg University, DKFZ, Germany

Special Track Chairs

Pattern Recognition in the Life and Natural Sciences

Joachim Denzler   University of Jena, Germany
Xiaoyi Jiang   University of Münster, Germany

Photogrammetry and Remote Sensing

Helmut Mayer   Bundeswehr University Munich, Germany
Ribana Roscher   University of Bonn, Germany
Uwe Sörgel   University of Stuttgart, Germany

Program Committee

Aamir Ahmad   Max Planck Institute for Intelligent Systems, Germany
Andreas Maier   University of Erlangen-Nürnberg, Germany
Arjan Kuijper   Fraunhofer Institute for Computer Graphics Research IGD/TU Darmstadt, Germany

Bastian Leibe	RWTH Aachen University, Germany
Bernt Schiele	MPI Informatics, Germany
Bjoern Andres	TU Dresden, Germany
Bjoern Menze	TUM, Germany
Carsten Steger	MVTec Software GmbH, Germany
Christian Bauckhage	Fraunhofer IAIS, Germany
Christian Heipke	Leibniz Universität Hannover, Germany
Christian Riess	Friedrich-Alexander University Erlangen-Nuremberg, Germany
Christian Theobalt	MPI Informatik, Germany
David Stein	TU Dresden, Germany
Dietrich Paulus	University of Koblenz and Landau, Germany
Dorota Iwaszczuk	TU Darmstadt, Germany
Felix Heide	Princeton University, USA
Fisher Yu	ETH Zurich, Switzerland
Gernot Fink	TU Dortmund, Germany
Helge Rhodin	University of British Columbia, Canada
Helmut Mayer	Bundeswehr University Munich, Germany
Hilde Kuehne	Goethe University Frankfurt, Germany
Jannik Irmai	TU Dresden, Germany
Jens Behley	University of Bonn, Germany
Joachim Denzler	Friedrich Schiller University Jena, Germany
Josef Pauli	University of Duisburg-Essen, Germany
Julia Vogt	ETH Zurich, Switzerland
Jürgen Gall	University of Bonn, Germany
Kevin Koeser	GEOMAR Helmholtz Centre for Ocean Research Kiel, Germany
Marcus Magnor	TU Braunschweig, Germany
Margret Keuper	University of Siegen, Max Planck Institute for Informatics, Germany
Margrit Gelautz	Vienna University of Technology, Austria
Markus Ulrich	Karlsruhe Institute of Technology, Germany
Martin Weinmann	Karlsruhe Institute of Technology, Germany
Max Mehltretter	Leibniz Universität Hannover, Germany
Michael Moeller	University of Siegen, Germany
Michael Schmitt	Bundeswehr University Munich, Germany
Nina Shvetsova	Goethe University Frankfurt, Germany
Olaf Hellwich	Technical University of Berlin, Germany
Ole Johannsen	Helmholtz Imaging, Germany
Paul Roetzer	University of Bonn, Germany
Pauline Trouvé-Peloux	ONERA, France

Peter Eisert	Fraunhofer HHI/Humboldt University Berlin, Germany
Peter Ochs	University of Tübingen, Germany
Qichen Fu	Carnegie Mellon University, USA
Radu Timofte	University of Würzburg & ETH Zurich, Switzerland
Reinhard Koch	Kiel University, Germany
Ribana Roscher	University of Bonn, Germany
Roland Kwitt	University of Salzburg, Austria
Ronny Hänsch	IEEE GRSS, Germany
Shamit Lal	Carnegie Mellon University, USA
Shengxian Zhao	TU Dresden, Germany
Silvia Di Gregorio	TU Dresden, Germany
Stefan Harmeling	TU Dortmund, Germany
Stefan Roth	TU Darmstadt, Germany
Tarun Yenamandra	TU Munich, Germany
Thomas Brox	University of Freiburg, Germany
Thomas Pock	Graz University of Technology, Austria
Uwe Soergel	University of Stuttgart, Germany
You Xie	ByteDance, USA
Zhakshylyk Nurlanov	University of Bonn, Germany

Contents

Photogrammetry and Remote Sensing

Pattern Recognition in the Life Sciences

Interpretable Machine Learning

Weak Supervision and Online Learning

Robust Models

Segmentation and Action Recognition

Score-Based Generative Models for Medical Image Segmentation Using Signed Distance Functions

Lea Bogensperger[(✉)], Dominik Narnhofer, Filip Ilic, and Thomas Pock

Institute of Computer Graphics and Vision, Graz University of Technology, Graz, Austria

{lea.bogensperger,dominik.narnhofer,filip.ilic,pock}@icg.tugraz.at

Abstract. Medical image segmentation is a crucial task that relies on the ability to accurately identify and isolate regions of interest in medical images. Thereby, generative approaches allow to capture the statistical properties of segmentation masks that are dependent on the respective structures. In this work we propose a conditional score-based generative modeling framework to represent the signed distance function (SDF) leading to an implicit distribution of segmentation masks. The advantage of leveraging the SDF is a more natural distortion when compared to that of binary masks. By learning the score function of the conditional distribution of SDFs we can accurately sample from the distribution of segmentation masks, allowing for the evaluation of statistical quantities. Thus, this probabilistic representation allows for the generation of uncertainty maps represented by the variance, which can aid in further analysis and enhance the predictive robustness. We qualitatively and quantitatively illustrate competitive performance of the proposed method on a public nuclei and gland segmentation data set, highlighting its potential utility in medical image segmentation applications.

Keywords: Score-based generative models · image segmentation · conditional diffusion models · signed distance function

1 Introduction

Medical image segmentation approaches are often trained end-to-end in a discriminative manner using deep neural networks [3,18,29]. However, also generative models have emerged for image segmentation with the advantage of learning the underlying statistics of segmentation masks conditioned on input images [1,9,34]. Apart from generative adversarial networks (GANs), promising candidates in this field are score-based generative models [6,23,26], which learn the score of a data distribution to sample from the distribution in the framework

Supplementary Information The online version contains supplementary material available at https://doi.org/10.1007/978-3-031-54605-1_1.

of a stochastic differential equation (SDE). Herein, noise is gradually injected to smooth the data distribution until it resembles a simple, tractable prior distribution – a process which can be reversed with the corresponding time-reverse SDE relying on the learned score function.

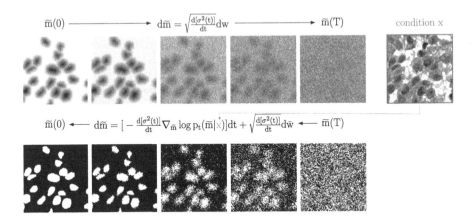

Fig. 1. Schematic of the corruption process (top row from left to right for different $t \in [0, T]$) on an SDF segmentation mask $\widetilde{m}$ for a given image x. The forward and reverse processes are governed by the variance-exploding SDE and its time-reverse SDE, respectively, where the latter uses the conditioned score of the distribution of SDF masks $\widetilde{m}$ given images x. The corresponding thresholded segmentation masks m are shown in the second row.

Diffusion models can be naturally incorporated to solving inverse problems in medical imaging [25], but they can also be extended to learn a conditional distribution, which makes them well suited for image segmentation. Their potential applicability has already been shown in works [1,30,31] using conditional denoising diffusion probabilistic modeling (DDPM). A significant drawback when directly injecting noise on segmentation masks is given by the fact that the distortion process is unnatural with respect to the underlying distribution. One could argue that the statistics of segmentation masks, which are bimodal or contain very few modes depending on the number semantic classes, are not easy to learn as there is no transition between class modes. A remedy is provided by recalling the SDF, a classic image segmentation technique [16], which has also regained attention within newer works on discriminative image segmentation using convolutional neural networks (CNNs) [4,15,33]. It is based on the idea that an implicit segmentation map is computed using the SDF for which at any given point in the resulting segmentation map the orthogonal distance to the closest boundary point is computed. Additionally, the distance is denoted with a negative sign for interior regions and a positive sign for the background regions. Thus, the SDF acts as a shape prior in some sense and it represents a smoother distribution of segmentation masks and thus a smooth transition in class modes. Moreover, it naturally promotes smoothness within the transformed binary segmentation map – which in return is obtained by thresholding the SDF map at the object boundaries.

In this work, we propose to fuse medical image segmentation using score-based generative modeling based on SDEs with a segmentation approach relying on the Euclidian SDF - thereby learning a smooth implicit representation of segmentation masks conditioned on the respective image. The noise-injecting data perturbation process in diffusion models thereby blends in canonically by gradually smoothing the distribution of the SDF mask. Since binary masks only provide a discrete representation of the object region, the score function can be highly sensitive to small changes in the binary mask, leading to segmentation errors and inconsistencies. On the other hand, the SDF provides a smooth and continuous representation of the object boundary, which can be more natural and better suited to model the shape and boundaries of objects in the image.

With this approach, the object boundaries are obtained from the sampling process, which can then be used to threshold for the binary segmentation masks, implying that the segmented objects will be smooth. Moreover, the segmentation uncertainty can be quantified by acquiring multiple segmentations given an input image due to its generative nature, thus further enhancing the robustness and interpretability of the approach and providing valuable insight into the segmentation process.

2   Method

2.1   Image Segmentation Using SDFs

Image segmentation is the task of finding a segmentation mask $m \in \mathcal{M}$ that assigns each pixel in an image $x \in \mathcal{X}$ a class, where $\mathcal{X} := \mathbb{R}^{M \times N}$ and $\mathcal{M} := \mathbb{R}^{M \times N}$. Using SDFs the segmentation problem can be rephrased in the context of (signed) distances with respect to the object boundaries, where we consider each pixel m_{ij} of the domain $\Omega = \{1, \ldots, M\} \times \{1, \ldots, N\}$ with the object $\mathcal{S}$ to be segmented. The SDF map then contains for each m_{ij} the distance to the closest boundary pixel $\partial \mathcal{S}$, where a negative/positive sign denotes the interior/outside of the object, respectively.

Mathematically, the SDF $\tilde{m}$ of a segmentation mask m can thus be computed using the Euclidian distance function for each pixel m_{ij}, which additionally can be truncated at a threshold δ to consider only a span of pixels around the object boundary $\partial \mathcal{S}$. Moreover, the truncation helps to remain agnostic with respect to higher positive distances belonging to the background, as they should not impact the resulting segmentation. The implicit, truncated SDF $\phi(m_{ij})$ is then obtained as follows (also see [16]):

$$\phi(m_{ij}) = \begin{cases} -\min\{\min_{y \in \partial S} \|y - m_{ij}\|_2, \delta\} & \text{if } m_{ij} \in \mathcal{S}, \\ \min\{\min_{y \in \partial S} \|y - m_{ij}\|_2, \delta\} & \text{if } m_{ij} \in \Omega \setminus \mathcal{S}, \\ 0 & \text{if } m_{ij} \in \partial \mathcal{S}. \end{cases} \tag{1}$$

Thus we can obtain the full segmentation map $\widetilde{m} = \phi(m_{ij})_{\substack{i=1,\dots,M \\ j=1,\dots,N}}$ by applying $\phi(\cdot)$ on the entire segmentation mask m, which is also depicted in Fig. 2.
Conversely, given $\widetilde{m}$ one can easily retrieve the binary segmentation map m by
thresholding at 0 to separate segmented objects from background.

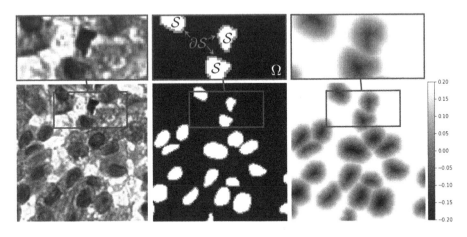

Fig. 2. Given an image x (left), its binary segmentation mask (center) can be transformed into a truncated, normalized SDF mask (right). The zoomed area shows some
segmentation objects in detail denoted by $\mathcal{S}$ and their boundaries $\partial\mathcal{S}$ embedded in the
domain Ω.

2.2   Conditional Score-Based Segmentation

In generative approaches for image segmentation the goal is to sample from the
conditional distribution $p(\widetilde{m}|x)$ to obtain a segmentation mask $\widetilde{m}$ given an input
image x. We frame this task in the setting of SDEs, which gradually corrupt data
samples from the data distribution $\widetilde{m}(0) \sim p_0$ until a tractable prior distribution
p_T is reached. There exists a corresponding time-reverse SDE which can then
be leveraged to transform the prior distribution back to the data distribution by
using the score of the conditional data distribution at time t, i.e. $\nabla_{\widetilde{m}} \log p_t(\widetilde{m}|x)$.
This score function can be learned using a training set of S paired data samples
of images and SDF segmentation masks $\mathcal{D} = \{(\widetilde{m}_s, x_s)\}_{s=1}^{S}$.

In general, SDEs have a drift term and a diffusion coefficient that govern its
forward and corresponding reverse evolution. Hereby, we solely focus on so-called
variance-exploding SDEs, as presented in [26], although our approach should
hold also for variance-preserving SDEs. Thus, for a time process with $t \in [0, T]$,
a sequence $\{\widetilde{m}(t)\}_{t=0}^{T}$ is generated by means of additive corruptive Gaussian
noise with standard deviation $\sigma(t)$. Using Brownian motion w to denote the
noise corruption, the corresponding SDE then reads as

$$d\widetilde{m} = \sqrt{\frac{d[\sigma^2(t)]}{dt}}dw. \tag{2}$$

The SDE in (2) can be reversed [2], which requires – when conditioning on images x – the score of the conditional distribution $\nabla_{\tilde{m}} \log p_t(\tilde{m}|x)$. Both the forward and the reverse process are illustratively demonstrated in Fig. 1, where the resulting thresholded segmentation masks also show the effect of the corruption process on the explicit binary segmentation mask (which is obtained by thresholding the SDF segmentation mask). The reverse SDE for $\bar{w}$, since time is now going backwards such that $t \in [T, 0]$, essentially reads as

$$\mathrm{d}\tilde{m} = \left[-\frac{\mathrm{d}[\sigma^2(t)]}{\mathrm{d}t} \nabla_{\tilde{m}} \log p_t(\tilde{m}|x) \right] \mathrm{d}t + \sqrt{\frac{\mathrm{d}[\sigma^2(t)]}{\mathrm{d}t}} \mathrm{d}\bar{w}. \tag{3}$$

The scores of the conditional distribution $\nabla_{\tilde{m}} \log p_t(\tilde{m}|x)$ can be estimated using either techniques from score matching [8,23,24] or from implicit score estimation such as DDPM [6,21]. Here, we choose to learn a noise-conditional score network $s_{\theta*}(\tilde{m}(t), x, \sigma(t))$ for the reverse-time SDE following the continuous formulation of denoising score matching with $t \in \mathcal{U}(0, T)$ for noise levels from $\sigma_{\min}$ to $\sigma_{\max}$ [26]. Thereby, using Tweedie's formula [5] we minimize the following objective:

$$\theta^* = \arg\min_\theta \mathbb{E}_t \left\{ \sigma^2(t) \mathbb{E}_{\tilde{m}(0)} \mathbb{E}_{\tilde{m}(t)|\tilde{m}(0)} \left[\|s_\theta(\tilde{m}(t), x, \sigma(t)) - \nabla_{\tilde{m}} \log p_{0t}(\tilde{m}(t)|\tilde{m}(0))\|_2^2 \right] \right\}. \tag{4}$$

The perturbation kernel $p_{0t}(\tilde{m}(t)|\tilde{m}(0))$ has the form of a standard normal distribution using $\sigma(t) = \sigma_{\min}(\frac{\sigma_{\max}}{\sigma_{\min}})^t$.

Once the learned scores $s_{\theta*}$ are available, they can be used to sample from the conditional distribution, where there exist several numerical solvers based on the time-reverse SDE. Here, we employ a predictor-corrector sampler as proposed by [26], which alternates between time-reverse SDE steps (the predictor) and Langevin Markov chain Monte Carlo (MCMC) sampling steps (the corrector), see Algorithm 1.

Algorithm 1: Predictor-corrector algorithm to sample from $p(\tilde{m}|x)$.

---

1 Choose conditioning image x, set number of iterations K, J, set $r \in \mathbb{R}^+$
2 $\tilde{m}_K \sim \mathcal{N}(0, \sigma_{\max}^2 I)$
3 **for** $k = K - 1, \ldots, 0$ **do**
4 $\quad z \sim \mathcal{N}(0, I)$;
5 $\quad \tilde{m}_k = \tilde{m}_{k+1} + (\sigma_{k+1}^2 - \sigma_k^2)s_{\theta*}(\tilde{m}_{k+1}, x, \sigma_{k+1}) + \sqrt{\sigma_{k+1}^2 - \sigma_k^2} z$;
6 $\quad$ **for** $j = 1, \ldots, J$ **do**
7 $\quad\quad z \sim \mathcal{N}(0, I)$;
8 $\quad\quad g = s_{\theta*}(\tilde{m}_k^{j-1}, x, \sigma_k)$;
9 $\quad\quad \varepsilon = 2(r\|z\|_2/\|g\|_2)^2$;
10 $\quad\quad \tilde{m}_k^j = \tilde{m}_k^{j-1} + \varepsilon g + \sqrt{2\varepsilon} z$;
11 $\quad$ **end**
12 $\quad \tilde{m}_k = \tilde{m}_k^J$;
13 **end**

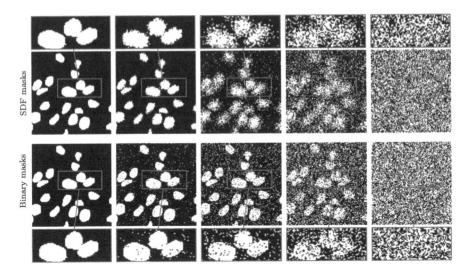

Fig. 3. Comparison of the effect of the corruption process on the resulting thresholded segmentation masks when using an SDF mask $\tilde{m}$ and a binary mask m for a given image x. Note that the SDF representation allows for a more natural distortion process in its thresholded masks, which evolves along the object boundaries instead of directly introducing "hole"-like structures at random pixel positions as it is the case in the thresholded masks when directly using the binary segmentation mask.

2.3   Motivation of the SDF in Conditional Score-Based Segmentation

The motivation of using the SDF in conditional score-based segmentation is due to the nature of the perturbation process in standard diffusion models, which consists of gradually adding noise to the sought segmentation mask in its SDF representation such that its distribution gets smoothed. The destructive process thus implicitly incorporates the boundary information of the segmented objects.

In contrast, if the binary masks are used directly in the perturbation process, the corruption yields "hole"-like structures in the resulting thresholded segmentation masks and there is no possibility to integrate the structure of the segmentation objects within the forward process. A comparison of effect of the destructive process on both variants of segmentation mask representations for varied time steps is shown in Fig. 3.

3   Experiments

3.1   Data Sets

For the experimental setting, we utilize two publicly available data sets. The first data set is MoNuSeg [12], which consists of 30 training images and 14 test images. Each image is of size 1000×1000 and overall they contain more than

21,000 annotated nuclei in Haematoxylin and Eosin (H&E) stained microscopic images. For data preprocessing we resort to a structure-preserving color normalization [27] as the different organ sites yield considerable intensity variations in the data. This is followed by a gray scale conversion and all images are subsequently resized to 500×500. During training, overlapping crops of 128×128 were used with random horizontal and vertical flips for data augmentation.

As a second medical data set, the Gland Segmentation (GlaS) data set [20] was used. It consists of 85 training and 80 test H&E stained microscopic images with annotated glands from colorectal cancer tissue. Again, a structure-preserving color normalization [27] is used also here for data preprocessing, which is followed by resizing all training and test images to 128×128 inspired by [28]. Data augmentation in training is done as with the MoNuSeg data set.

3.2 Architecture and Training

The architecture to learn the noise-conditional score function is adapted from [6, 26]. Further, a conditioning on the image x is required, for which we roughly follow recent works related to conditional generative modeling by concatenating the encoded conditioning image to the network input [7,17,19].

For the diffusion parameters we set $\sigma_{\max} = 5$ and $\sigma_{\min} = 1e-3$. Note that the latter is slightly lower than usually proposed in literature, which is due to the SDF data distribution, as denoising score matching requires a perturbation kernel at the lowest noise scale such that the input distribution remains more or less unchanged. For the learning setting we employ Adam's optimizer [11] with default coefficient values and a learning rate of $1e-4$.

3.3 Sampling

To obtain segmentation masks for test images x, we use the predictor-corrector sampler in Algorithm 1. The test images of the MoNuSeg data set are each divided into four evenly sized patches per image, whereas for the GlaS data set the entire test images are processed. In all sampling experiments we set $r = 0.35/0.15$ for the corrector step size scaling for the MoNuSeg and GlaS data set, respectively, as we empirically found this to work best in terms of evaluation metrics. Moreover, we use $K = 500/200$ predictor steps and $J = 2/1$ corrector steps for both data sets, respectively, as this setting revealed to yield best results, despite general low numeric fluctuations amongst different settings.

3.4 Evaluation

The resulting samples are SDF predictions which have yet to be converted to valid segmentation maps. Thus, they have to be thresholded at 0 which represents object boundaries to separate segmented objects (which have 0 at the boundary and negative distances inside assigned) and background (consisting of positive distances). However, due to the employed approach of denoising score matching we set the threshold to $3\sigma_{\min}$, since we have to assume that there is still remaining noise present at the scale of the smallest noise level. This is crucial to consider since we are interested in the exact boundary.

By leveraging the generative nature of our approach, we are further investigating the effect of averaging over 128 sampling runs. Thereby we obtain the minimum mean square error (MMSE) which gives a more robust prediction, which is shown in increased quantitative scores.

The obtained segmentation masks are then evaluated using the standard metrics F1 score and section over Union (IoU). We compare our method to commonly referred benchmark models, ensuring that both U-Net variants and attention/transformer mechanisms are considered. Moreover, we also consider [30] to obtain a comparison with a generative, conditional DDPM that predicts standard binary segmentation masks in the sampling process. The approach in [30] can also be viewed in the form of an SDE and its time-reverse SDE using a variance-preserving scheme.

3.5   Results

Table 1 shows quantitative results for both data sets with our method and comparison methods. To enable a fair comparison the benchmark results were taken from [28] where possible. The results indicate that our method outperforms the comparison methods on the GlaS data set, but also for the MoNuSeg data set competitive results can be obtained, although slightly worse than some of the comparison methods. For both data sets, using the MMSE by averaging over multiple sampling runs clearly gives a significant boost in quantitative performance. In comparison, the DDPM delivers slightly worse results, but we want to emphasize that they could also be increased by computing the MMSE over several runs before thresholding as it is a generative model – this was also shown in [30] where segmentation ensembles are computed to improve the results.

Table 1. Quantitative segmentation results on the MoNuSeg and GlaS data set.

Method	Metric			
	MoNuSeg		GlaS	
	F1 ↑	mIoU ↑	F1 ↑	mIoU ↑
FCN [3]	28.84	28.71	66.61	50.84
U-Net [18]	79.43	65.99	77.78	65.34
U-Net++ [35]	79.49	66.04	78.03	65.55
Res-UNet [32]	79.49	66.07	78.83	65.95
Axial Attention U-Net [29]	76.83	62.49	76.26	63.03
MedT [28]	**79.55**	**66.17**	81.02	69.61
DDPM [30]	76.03	61.42	76.81	64.15
Ours	78.13	64.19	82.03	71.36
Ours – MMSE	78.64	64.87	**82.77**	**72.07**

Figure 4 shows exemplary qualitative results for both data sets to further highlight the potential applicability of our proposed method. Note that although the evaluation metrics for our approach that can be found in Table 1 are obtained by evaluating the entire images, we show smaller crops here for the sake of a more detailed visual inspection of the segmented objects. One can clearly observe the smooth segmented objects m obtained from thresholding the SDF predictions $\widetilde{m}(0)$, which are in good agreement with the groundtruth segmentation masks m_{gt} for both data set samples.

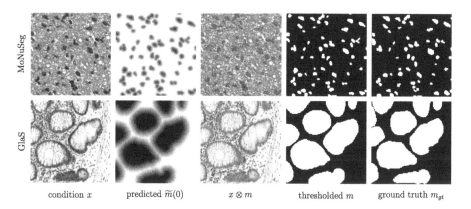

condition x predicted $\widetilde{m}(0)$ $x \otimes m$ thresholded m ground truth m_{gt}

Fig. 4. Exemplary sampled segmentation masks for both data sets. The predicted SDF masks $\widetilde{m}(0)$ are directly obtained from the sampling procedure, whereas the thresholded masks m are shown to additionally enable a visual comparison with the depicted ground truth m_{gt}. Furthermore, we provide the condition image with the overlaid thresholded mask $x \otimes m$.

A visual comparison is additionally depicted in Fig. 5, where we compare the thresholded segmentation prediction of our model of a MoNuSeg test image with its DDPM-based (generative) counterpart [30] and two discriminative models, namely U-Net++ [35] and MedT [28]. As can be seen in the provided zoom, the SDF representation of segmentation objects indeed seems to act as a shape prior and thus yields smoother segmentation objects while avoiding artefacts such as single pixels/small structures that are mistakenly classified as foreground objects.

3.6   Segmentation Uncertainty

Since the presented approach is based on a generative scheme, we can sample from the conditional distribution of the SDF given the conditioning image $p(\widetilde{m}|x)$. An advantage of this approach is given by the fact that the resulting statistical values allow for the quantification of segmentation uncertainties in the SDF predictions as well as the thresholded masks, which provide additional insights into the segmentation process that are not available with traditional

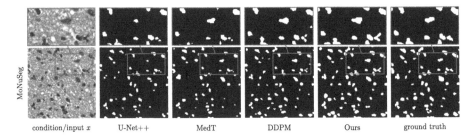

Fig. 5. Qualitative results for a test input image x for discriminative approaches resp. condition image x for the generative approaches. We compare our model with the generative DDPM [30] and two discriminative models, U-Net++ [35] and MedT [28]. Using the SDF in our conditional score-based segmentation approach shows that a shape prior is learned, thus preventing small pixel-wise artefacts in the resulting predictions and yielding smooth segmentation objects.

discriminative approaches. An illustration of the aforementioned property on a MoNuSeg data sample can be seen in Fig. 6, where the standard deviation maps associated with the SDF predictions and thresholded masks highlight the regions of uncertainty.

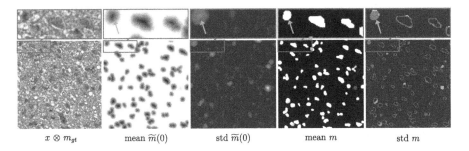

Fig. 6. Segmentation example with according statistical values for the SDF predictions $\widetilde{m}(0)$ respectively thresholded masks m. Notably, the image includes a region erroneously segmented as a nuclei, as indicated by the orange arrow. This region is highlighted in the standard deviation maps, which represent the associated uncertainty in the segmentation.

In general, we observe that the standard deviation appears high on transitions from nuclei to background as well as in wrongly detected nuclei or oversegmented parts of nuclei. This encouraging observation leads us to the hypothesis that the uncertainty may be associated directly with segmentation errors similar to what has been shown in [14], see also Fig. 7. Here, a visual comparison of the error and standard deviation (uncertainty) maps indicates that the latter very likely has high predictive capability. A detailed analysis including the mutual information of the two variables, however, is out of scope for this work and subject to future work.

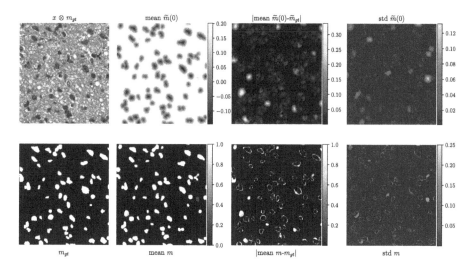

Fig. 7. Segmentation example with statistical values for the predicted $\tilde{m}(0)$ and thresholded masks m, along with the corresponding ground truth images and the absolute error between the predictions and the ground truth. The visual comparison of error and standard deviation maps (uncertainty) suggests that the latter has predictive capability for the error.

3.7 Ablation

As we rely on the standard noise-conditioned score network following [6] for the proposed method, it is more interesting to investigate the influence of the SDF. Therefore, we learn the conditional score function such that segmentation masks m can be sampled given x, where all other settings remain unchanged – including $\sigma_{\min}$ and $\sigma_{\max}$. Hereby, we obtain a mean IoU/mean F1 score of $51.72/67.80$ on the MoNuSeg data set, and $61.39/73.97$ on the GlaS data set, respectively.

Our approach should work reasonably well with other types of architectures suitable for learning the score of a data distribution. As the primary objective of this work was to introduce a novel concept rather than striving to surpass existing benchmarks, in future work, a more sophisticated network architecture could be considered to further improve the segmentation accuracy.

4   Discussion and Limitations

Generative approaches usually require an increased network complexity and are thus computationally more expensive than their discriminative counterparts. We believe that the advantages of having a generative model outweigh its potential drawbacks due to the possibility to evaluate statistical quantities, such as averaging multiple predictions and the generation of uncertainty maps, which may give valuable insights and might be crucial especially in medical imaging applications. While the sampling process itself still requires significantly more time than executing a single forward pass of a discriminative network, there is a variety of new methods available to speed up the inference stage of diffusion models [10,13,22]. For the sake of simplicity the standard method was chosen, however, there should be nothing to argue against incorporating a different sampling technique.

The proposed approach outperforms the comparison methods only on one of the two used data sets. However, also on the MoNuSeg data set competitive results have been presented that could potentially be improved with a further optimized network architecture. While a state-of-the art model based on U-Net or transformer architectures might in some cases outperform our quantitative results we still want to emphasize that there is no option of obtaining a segmentation uncertainty as in Figs. 6 and 7 with such discriminative approaches. Robustness and reliability should not be traded for minor quantitative increments and improvements.

Moreover, using SDF maps to represent the segmentation masks bears the advantage that a shape prior is learned which favors smooth segmentation objects. The resulting binary segmentation masks thus encompass a different characteristic than when using standard conditional DDPM based approaches [1,30]. Although the statistics of these underlying segmentation masks are properly learned, the quantitative results do not reflect those findings in the respective metrics.

Further, obtaining SDF predictions can generally offer other potential advantages such as obtaining instance segmentations as a byproduct. By using the watershed transform, the SDF maps could easily be turned into instance segmentation maps and the problem of touching instances is circumvented.

5   Conclusion and Outlook

In this work we proposed a generative approach for medical image segmentation by fusing conditional score-based methods with the concept of representing segmentation maps with the SDF. The potential applicability of the method was demonstrated qualitatively and quantitatively on two public medical data sets. The SDF provides a smoother and more continuous representation of object boundaries compared to binary masks, which makes it a more canonical choice for accurate and robust segmentation.

Furthermore, by leveraging the generative approach, statistical measures such as mean and standard deviation can be calculated to quantify the uncertainty in the segmentation results. This information is especially useful for medical diagnosis and treatment planning, where it is important to know the level of confidence in the segmentation results.

As an outlook for future research we will focus on the extension of the approach to multi-class segmentation by additionally incorporating the exclusivity of semantic classes per pixel into the predicted SDF maps. Additionally, fuelled by preliminary experimental successes, the possibility of learning the score of the joint distribution of images x and segmentation masks $\widetilde{m}$ will be explored. This would provide a powerful framework, where one could directly sample paired training data $(\widetilde{m}_s, x_s)$ from the joint distribution or condition on either one of them to sample from the conditional distributions $p(\widetilde{m}|x)$ or $p(x|\widetilde{m})$.

References

1. Amit, T., Nachmani, E., Shaharbany, T., Wolf, L.: SegDiff: image segmentation with diffusion probabilistic models. arXiv preprint arXiv:2112.00390 (2021)
2. Anderson, B.D.: Reverse-time diffusion equation models. Stoch. Process. Appl. **12**(3), 313–326 (1982)
3. Badrinarayanan, V., Kendall, A., Cipolla, R.: SegNet: a deep convolutional encoder-decoder architecture for image segmentation. IEEE Trans. Pattern Anal. Mach. Intell. **39**(12), 2481–2495 (2017)
4. Brissman, E., Johnander, J., Felsberg, M.: Predicting signed distance functions for visual instance segmentation. In: 2021 Swedish Artificial Intelligence Society Workshop (SAIS), pp. 1–6. IEEE (2021)
5. Efron, B.: Tweedie's formula and selection bias. J. Am. Stat. Assoc. **106**(496), 1602–1614 (2011)
6. Ho, J., Jain, A., Abbeel, P.: Denoising diffusion probabilistic models. In: Advances in Neural Information Processing Systems 33, pp. 6840–6851 (2020)
7. Ho, J., Saharia, C., Chan, W., Fleet, D.J., Norouzi, M., Salimans, T.: Cascaded diffusion models for high fidelity image generation. J. Mach. Learn. Res. **23**(47), 1–33 (2022)
8. Hyvärinen, A., Dayan, P.: Estimation of non-normalized statistical models by score matching. J. Mach. Learn. Res. **6**(4) (2005)
9. Iqbal, A., Sharif, M., Yasmin, M., Raza, M., Aftab, S.: Generative adversarial networks and its applications in the biomedical image segmentation: a comprehensive survey. Int. J. Multimedia Inf. Retr. **11**(3), 333–368 (2022)
10. Karras, T., Aittala, M., Aila, T., Laine, S.: Elucidating the design space of diffusion-based generative models. In: Advances in Neural Information Processing Systems 35, pp. 26565–26577 (2022)
11. Kingma, D.P., Ba, J.: Adam: a method for stochastic optimization. arXiv preprint arXiv:1412.6980 (2014)
12. Kumar, N., Verma, R., Sharma, S., Bhargava, S., Vahadane, A., Sethi, A.: A dataset and a technique for generalized nuclear segmentation for computational pathology. IEEE Trans. Med. Imaging **36**(7), 1550–1560 (2017)
13. Lu, C., Zhou, Y., Bao, F., Chen, J., Li, C., Zhu, J.: DPM-solver: a fast ODE solver for diffusion probabilistic model sampling in around 10 steps. In: Advances in Neural Information Processing Systems 35, pp. 5775–5787 (2022)
14. Narnhofer, D., Habring, A., Holler, M., Pock, T.: Posterior-variance-based error quantification for inverse problems in imaging. arXiv abs/2212.12499 (2022)
15. Naylor, P., Laé, M., Reyal, F., Walter, T.: Segmentation of nuclei in histopathology images by deep regression of the distance map. IEEE Trans. Med. Imaging **38**(2), 448–459 (2018)
16. Osher, S., Fedkiw, R., Piechor, K.: Level set methods and dynamic implicit surfaces. Appl. Mech. Rev. **57**(3), B15–B15 (2004)

17. Özdenizci, O., Legenstein, R.: Restoring vision in adverse weather conditions with patch-based denoising diffusion models. IEEE Trans. Pattern Anal. Mach. Intell. (2023)

18. Ronneberger, O., Fischer, P., Brox, T.: U-Net: convolutional networks for biomedical image segmentation. In: Navab, N., Hornegger, J., Wells, W.M., Frangi, A.F. (eds.) MICCAI 2015. LNCS, vol. 9351, pp. 234–241. Springer, Cham (2015). https://doi.org/10.1007/978-3-319-24574-4_28

19. Saharia, C., Chan, W., Chang, H., Lee, C., Ho, J., Salimans, T., Fleet, D., Norouzi, M.: Palette: image-to-image diffusion models. In: ACM SIGGRAPH 2022 Conference Proceedings, pp. 1–10 (2022)

20. Sirinukunwattana, K., et al.: Gland segmentation in colon histology images: the GLaS challenge contest. Med. Image Anal. **35**, 489–502 (2017)

21. Sohl-Dickstein, J., Weiss, E., Maheswaranathan, N., Ganguli, S.: Deep unsupervised learning using nonequilibrium thermodynamics. In: International Conference on Machine Learning, pp. 2256–2265. PMLR (2015)

22. Song, J., Meng, C., Ermon, S.: Denoising diffusion implicit models. arXiv preprint arXiv:2010.02502 (2020)

23. Song, Y., Ermon, S.: Generative modeling by estimating gradients of the data distribution. In: Advances in Neural Information Processing Systems 32 (2019)

24. Song, Y., Garg, S., Shi, J., Ermon, S.: Sliced score matching: a scalable approach to density and score estimation. In: Uncertainty in Artificial Intelligence, pp. 574–584. PMLR (2020)

25. Song, Y., Shen, L., Xing, L., Ermon, S.: Solving inverse problems in medical imaging with score-based generative models. In: International Conference on Learning Representations (2022)

26. Song, Y., Sohl-Dickstein, J., Kingma, D.P., Kumar, A., Ermon, S., Poole, B.: Score-based generative modeling through stochastic differential equations. In: International Conference on Learning Representations (2021)

27. Vahadane, A., et al.: Structure-preserved color normalization for histological images. In: 2015 IEEE 12th International Symposium on Biomedical Imaging (ISBI), pp. 1012–1015. IEEE (2015)

28. Valanarasu, J.M.J., Oza, P., Hacihaliloglu, I., Patel, V.M.: Medical transformer: gated axial-attention for medical image segmentation. In: de Bruijne, M., et al. (eds.) MICCAI 2021. LNCS, vol. 12901, pp. 36–46. Springer, Cham (2021). https://doi.org/10.1007/978-3-030-87193-2_4

29. Wang, H., Zhu, Y., Green, B., Adam, H., Yuille, A., Chen, L.-C.: Axial-DeepLab: stand-alone axial-attention for panoptic segmentation. In: Vedaldi, A., Bischof, H., Brox, T., Frahm, J.-M. (eds.) ECCV 2020. LNCS, vol. 12349, pp. 108–126. Springer, Cham (2020). https://doi.org/10.1007/978-3-030-58548-8_7

30. Wolleb, J., Sandkühler, R., Bieder, F., Valmaggia, P., Cattin, P.C.: Diffusion models for implicit image segmentation ensembles. In: International Conference on Medical Imaging with Deep Learning, pp. 1336–1348. PMLR (2022)

31. Wu, J., Fang, H., Zhang, Y., Yang, Y., Xu, Y.: MedSegDiff: medical image segmentation with diffusion probabilistic model. arXiv preprint arXiv:2211.00611 (2022)

32. Xiao, X., Lian, S., Luo, Z., Li, S.: Weighted Res-UNet for high-quality retina vessel segmentation. In: 2018 9th International Conference on Information Technology in Medicine and Education (ITME), pp. 327–331. IEEE (2018)

33. Xue, Y., et al.: Shape-aware organ segmentation by predicting signed distance maps. In: Proceedings of the AAAI Conference on Artificial Intelligence, vol. 34, pp. 12565–12572 (2020)

34. Xun, S., et al.: Generative adversarial networks in medical image segmentation: a review. Comput. Biol. Med. **140**, 105063 (2022)

35. Zhou, Z., Rahman Siddiquee, M.M., Tajbakhsh, N., Liang, J.: UNet++: a nested U-Net architecture for medical image segmentation. In: Stoyanov, D., et al. (eds.) DLMIA/ML-CDS -2018. LNCS, vol. 11045, pp. 3–11. Springer, Cham (2018). https://doi.org/10.1007/978-3-030-00889-5_1

A Trimodal Dataset: RGB, Thermal, and Depth for Human Segmentation and Temporal Action Detection

Christian Stippel$^{(\boxtimes)}$ ⦿, Thomas Heitzinger⦿, and Martin Kampel⦿

Computer Vision Lab, TU Wien, Vienna, Austria
{christian.stippel,thomas.heitzinger,martin.kampel}@tuwien.ac.at

Abstract. Computer vision research and popular datasets are predominantly based on the RGB modality. However, traditional RGB datasets have limitations in lighting conditions and raise privacy concerns. Integrating or substituting with thermal and depth data offers a more robust and privacy-preserving alternative. We present TRISTAR (https://zenodo.org/record/7996570, https://github.com/Stippler/tristar), a public TRImodal Segmentation and acTion ARchive comprising registered sequences of RGB, depth, and thermal data. The dataset encompasses 10 unique environments, 18 camera angles, 101 shots, and 15,618 frames which include human masks for semantic segmentation and dense labels for temporal action detection and scene understanding. We discuss the system setup, including sensor configuration and calibration, as well as the process of generating ground truth annotations. On top, we conduct a quality analysis of our proposed dataset and provide benchmark models as reference points for human segmentation and action detection. By employing only modalities of thermal and depth, these models yield improvements in both human segmentation and action detection.

Keywords: segmentation · temporal action segmentation/detection · scene understanding · video understanding

1 Introduction

RGB data is one of the most commonly used modalities for computer vision datasets [18,25]. However, this modality has a number of notable shortcomings. Firstly, RGB sensors are sensitive to lighting conditions, and their image quality can be compromised under non-optimal conditions. Secondly, the RGB modality can lead to the identification of individuals, posing potential privacy concerns in sensitive applications. Lastly, segmentation accuracy may suffer due to inadequate camera quality and intensity similarities between the foreground and background.

Integrating various modalities offers a more comprehensive and detailed scene representation: color modalities provide contour and texture details, depth data

ⓒ The Author(s), under exclusive license to Springer Nature Switzerland AG 2024
U. Köthe and C. Rother (Eds.): DAGM GCPR 2023, LNCS 14264, pp. 18–33, 2024.
https://doi.org/10.1007/978-3-031-54605-1_2

shows the scene geometry, and thermal imaging contributes temperature information.

This paper presents a unique trimodal dataset designed to address the limitations of existing single-modality datasets in semantic segmentation and action recognition. Our dataset comprises 101 registered sequences of RGB, thermal, and depth shots, captured in diverse office scenarios. The key dataset characteristics are listed in Table 1.

Table 1. Details of the Trimodal Dataset.

Content	Indoor Human Behavior
Modalities	Registered RGB, Depth, Thermal
Type of Data	Sequences
Resolution	640×480
Frame Rate	8.7 fps
#Offices	10
#Camera Angles	18
#Shots	101
#Frames	15,618
#Individuals	8
#Actions	14

Figure 1, shows samples of our trimodal dataset where we employ the registration methodology outlined by Stromayer et al. [31] to align the different modalities.

Fig. 1. Examples from our trimodal dataset, encompassing RGB, depth, thermal imaging, and human segmentation mask.

The second row emphasizes a potential limitation of relying solely on the RGB modality: the similar RGB intensities in the foreground and background make it challenging to precisely distinguish the person from the couch.

Our key contributions include a novel trimodal dataset consisting of varying office settings, that provides a resource for researchers focusing on multi-modal data fusion and related tasks, combined with human segmentation maps to aid with the task of, semantic segmentation, action labels that describe a wide range of activities, enabling the development and evaluation of temporal action detection models.

In addition, we train benchmark models on the task of human segmentation and action recognition and provide them as baselines for further research. These baselines demonstrate the effectiveness of complementing or replacing RGB with depth and thermal modalities.

The selection of segmentation and temporal action segmentation as our primary downstream tasks is based on several considerations. First, these tasks represent diverse levels of complexity, allowing us to demonstrate the utility of our trimodal dataset across a wide array of challenges. Second, both tasks have substantial real-world applicability, encompassing use-cases from autonomous driving to assistive technologies, underscoring the practicality of our research. Third, they particularly benefit from multimodal data, with depth and thermal information enhancing performance by offering structural context and distinguishing capabilities. Finally, as these tasks are commonly used for benchmarking in computer vision, they enable a direct and meaningful comparison of our work against existing methodologies and datasets.

The remainder of this paper is structured as follows: Sect. 2 presents a review of existing datasets and their limitations; Sect. 3 provides an overview of the system setup, including sensor configuration and calibration; Sect. 4 details the construction, analysis, and evaluation of our trimodal dataset; Sect. 5 outlines potential tasks and applications that benefit from the dataset; and Sect. 6 concludes the paper and discusses possible future work.

2   Related Work

Our efforts to build a trimodal dataset are based on an understanding of the existing literature on datasets, their limitations, and current methodologies employed for multimodal datasets. To provide a broader context for our work, we now delve into a review of existing datasets and their accompanying methodologies.

2.1   Datasets

Some notable examples of datasets for semantic segmentation and action recognition include PASCAL VOC [8], COCO [18], ADE20K [36], and the Charades dataset [28]. While these datasets played a vital role in advancing semantic segmentation research and action classification, they primarily focus on RGB data and lack the inclusion of additional modalities such as thermal and depth information.

Depth datasets provide information about scene geometry and can be used in a various domains, such as 3D reconstruction and scene understanding. Examples of outdoor depth datasets include KITTI [10] and Cityscapes [3], while the NYU Depth [30] dataset is a prominent example of an indoor depth dataset. Furthermore, IPT [13] is a depth dataset for tracking tasks in enclosed environments. Although these datasets provide depth information, they do not include thermal data, which can be crucial for addressing challenges posed by varying lighting conditions and ensuring privacy preservation. The follow-up MIPT dataset also includes a small number of depth and thermal sequences, but lacks RGB data [12].

Thermal imaging is acknowledged for its potential in a variety of computer vision tasks [12,13,17]. Unlike traditional RGB imaging, thermal imaging is less susceptible to illumination changes and provides additional information about the subject. Thermal data provides information of the temperature distribution, which proves particularly useful in scenarios with bad lightning and semantic segmentation of living objects. Several thermal image datasets have been introduced to promote research in this domain. One noteworthy example is the OSU Thermal Pedestrian Dataset [5], which includes a substantial number of pedestrian thermal images collected under different environmental conditions. However, this dataset is primarily used for pedestrian detection tasks rather than segmentation or action recognition. Another dataset, the Terravic Facial Infrared Database [21], contains both visible and thermal facial images. Kniaz et al. propose Thermagan for person re-identification and publish their dataset ThermalWorld alongside it [17]. Heitzinger et al. introduce an identity-preserving 3D human behavior analysis system that addresses privacy concerns in continuous video monitoring. They also release a public multimodal dataset composed of depth and thermal sequences, intended to support a variety of privacy-sensitive applications in ambient-assisted living and human security monitoring [12]. Brenner et al.'s survey [1] provides a systematic literature review of the fusion of RGB-D and thermal sensor data, highlighting the progress made in this area over the past decade. The PST900 dataset [27] is one resource that proposes long wave infrared (LWIR) imagery as a supporting modality for semantic segmentation using learning-based techniques. This dataset provides 894 synchronized and calibrated RGB and thermal image pairs with per-pixel human annotations across four distinct classes. In addition to presenting a unique dataset, the authors introduce a novel passive calibration target. Another notable resource is the InfAR action dataset [9], which focuses on action recognition using infrared data.

To the best of our knowledge, only a single dataset exists that combines RGB, thermal, and depth data [22] for human segmentation. This dataset consists of 5,274 frames recorded in three shots in three distinct office scenes.

Given the scarcity and potential benefits of trimodal data, we motivate the creation of our dataset; we provide 101 different shots recorded in 10 offices from 18 unique camera angles to provide a resource for researchers working on multi-modal data fusion and related tasks.

2.2   Methods

One of the earliest methods for human segmentation is the Histogram of Oriented Gradients (HOG) descriptor combined with a Support Vector Machine (SVM) for human detection, introduced by Dalal and Triggs [4]. However, this approach struggles with occlusions and variations in human appearance. To overcome these challenges, more recent works have leveraged the power of deep learning. Mask R-CNN, proposed by He et al. [11], extends Faster R-CNN [23] by adding a branch for predicting an object mask in parallel with the existing branch for bounding box recognition. DeepLabv3+ [2] is another method that employs an encoder-decoder structure with dilated convolutions and spatial pyramid pooling for semantic segmentation. Recent methods for segmentation have moved towards leveraging attention mechanisms and transformers, leading to the development of architectures such as Self-Attention Generative Adversarial Networks (SAGANs) [35], and Vision Transformers (ViTs) [7]. One particularly notable method is the Swin Transformer [19], which introduces a hierarchical structure with shifted windows to enable efficient self-attention over images. Finally, Segment Anything (SAM) paves the way for generalizable zero-shot segmentation that can be applied to RGB, thermal, or depth modalities [16]. These methods have primarily been developed and evaluated using RGB data. Their effectiveness with depth or thermal data is less explored, likely due to the scarcity of multimodal datasets that include these modalities.

In the domain of action recognition and classification long-term Recurrent Convolutional Networks (LRCNs) [6], 3D Convolutional Neural Networks (3D-CNNs) [14] and transformer-based approaches such as the Video Swin Transformer [20] are among the notable methods. These models primarily rely on RGB data, however, the exploration of action recognition in multimodal datasets combining RGB, depth, and thermal data is relatively limited, primarily due to the scarcity of such datasets. Although there are a few existing works like NTU RGB+D [26] that incorporate depth information, their ability to handle thermal data is limited.

In summary, while existing datasets and methods have significantly advanced semantic segmentation and action recognition, they predominantly focus on RGB data. The limited availability of multimodal datasets, particularly those combining RGB, thermal, and depth data, limits exploration into the potential benefits of these modalities.

3   System Overview

In light of the scarcity of RGB, depth and thermal datasets identified in the prior literature, we designed and implemented a system to capture and annotate data across these three modalities. This system includes a Compact Tri-Modal

Camera Unit (CTCAT) for data acquisition and implements a streamlined annotation process for data labeling [31]. Our approach is inherently scalable and capable of distributed operation, leveraging the novel zero-shot model Segment Anything [16] for effective object recognition and employing a distributed labeling system that allows for efficient, large-scale annotation tasks [32]. Annotators perform labeling on the RGB modality. However, to improve the accuracy of the labeling process, they are provided access to the corresponding thermal and depth data. These additional data are mapped to RGB using a color scale, as illustrated in Fig. 1.

3.1 Sensor Setup

We utilize the Compact Tri-Modal Camera Unit (CTCAT) described by Strohmayer et al. [31]. The CTCAT combines three types of cameras: RGB, a structured light depth camera with an operational range of 0.6–8 m, and a 160 × 120 uncooled radiometric thermal camera which allows us to capture across all three modalities at a rate of up to 8.7 fps. Although each camera has its unique resolution, we rescale all images to a standardized resolution of 640 × 480 pixels for consistency within the dataset. To align the RGB, thermal, and depth cameras, a custom-made, heated checkerboard calibration pattern is used.

Figure 2 illustrates our camera setup, a close-up view of the CTCAT unit and a sample trimodal shot, capturing the scene's diverse modalities. Mounted on a tripod, the camera and its accompanying portable monitor are powered by an affixed battery pack. Typically positioned on tables or countertops at a height between two and three meters, the setup allows for comprehensive capture of office scenes. Before recording, we optimize the camera perspective using the narrow field of view of the thermal sensor. Individuals are then filmed performing various actions, guided by instructions provided by a designated person. The action list includes tasks like picking up a glass, drinking, and typing.

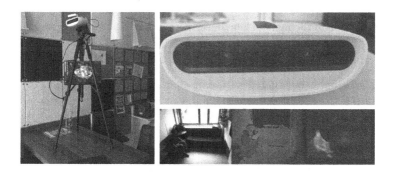

Fig. 2. The camera setup with the CTCAT unit and the captured scene.

3.2   Ground Truth Generation

We employ pretrained YoloV7 and YoloV8 models [15,34] to detect bounding boxes of humans based on the RGB modality of our trimodal dataset. These bounding boxes serve as input for the Segment Anything tool [16], allowing us to obtain preliminary human masks. The initial results obtained from Segment Anything form the foundation for the manual labeling process. A team of twelve annotators undertakes the task of labeling a total of 15,618 frames on the RGB modality. The generated masks are also used for the corresponding depth and thermal frames. While the labeling takes place directly on the RGB modality, the annotators are also provided access to the corresponding thermal and depth modalities, registered and color mapped, to use as reference in cases where the person is not clearly distinguishable from the background. To facilitate this large-scale task, we utilize a self-hosted Label Studio instance [32] which allows multiple annotators to work simultaneously. Figure 3 illustrates the human segmentation annotation process using Label Studio.

Fig. 3. Illustration of the manual human segmentation annotation process using Label Studio.

Action labeling is conducted with dense per-frame labeling of 14 classes, categorized into actions, states, transitions between states, and location of the person on the RGB modality. The labeling process is performed using a spreadsheet with the columns: original file name, person, shot, frame, actions, transitions, state, and location. If multiple labels were applicable within a single column, they are delimited with a space. The objective for this task is temporal action segmentation or action detection, which entails identifying the specific actions occurring within a given frame.

4   Trimodal Dataset

Building upon the groundwork laid out in the sensor setup, we now present our own multimodal dataset. Our dataset encompasses an array of office scenes recorded using a trimodal sensor arrangement integrating RGB, thermal, and depth data.

4.1   Dataset Design

In order to construct our multimodal dataset, we drew inspiration from notable contributions in the field. The Charades Dataset [29], shows humans in indoor environments and is densely labeled with activities. Meanwhile, the work of Palmero et al. [22] highlights the potential of multimodal datasets, albeit with a more limited scope and volume of data.

For our dataset we select an office environment, as it provides a variety of scenarios, activities, and lighting conditions. The selection of action labels is based on their occurrences in a real office setting. Table 2 presents a comprehensive list of the various actions, states, transitions, and locations that are represented in our dataset.

Table 2. List of Actions, States, Transitions, and Locations used for Labeling.

Label	Items
Action Classification	`put_down`, `pick_up`, `drink`, `type`, `wave`
State	`sit`, `walk`, `stand`, `lie`
Transitions	`get_down`, `get_up`
Location	`out_of_view`, `out_of_room`, `in_room`

Furthermore, our dataset includes different types of office spaces, namely open office environments, meeting rooms, and individual offices, each offering a different layout and set of interactions with surrounding objects. Figure 4 illustrates the variety of office locations and lighting conditions covered in our dataset.

Fig. 4. Variety of office locations and lighting conditions in the dataset.

Lighting conditions, a crucial factor in visual data, are also varied in our dataset ranging from bright daylight, and artificial lighting, to low-light conditions. Finally, our dataset encompasses object classes commonly found in office environments ranging from office furniture such as desks, chairs, and cabinets to electronic devices like computers, and phones, as well as various personal items.

4.2   Dataset Analysis

Our dataset comprises 15,618 annotated frames, recorded from 18 unique camera angles. It documents the actions of eight individuals within various office settings, as highlighted by the distribution in Fig. 5.

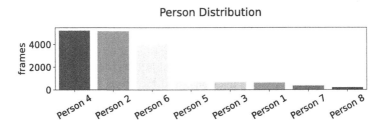

Fig. 5. Distribution of individuals in our dataset.

The action labels captured in our dataset showcase a diverse range of office activities. Actions such as `type`, `wave`, `drink`, `pick_up`, and `put_down` appear 1,420, 1,276, 1,129, 821, and 710 times, respectively as shown by Fig. 6a. In terms of states, labels such as `walk`, `sit`, `stand`, and `lie` are featured 4,855, 4,065, 4,036, and 578 times, respectively. Transition labels, namely `get_down` and `get_up`, occur 821 and 770 times, respectively. The states and transitions happen exclusively and their distribution is shown in Fig. 6b.

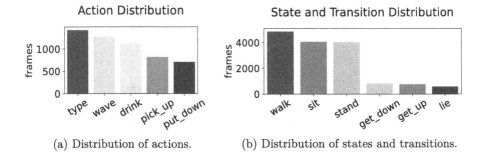

(a) Distribution of actions.   (b) Distribution of states and transitions.

Fig. 6. Distributions of actions, states, and transitions in our dataset.

Finally, location labels `in_room`, `out_of_view`, and `out_of_room` are marked in 14,211, 1,163, and 234 instances, respectively.

Considering human segmentation, our dataset includes approximately 14,000 instances where humans are segmented within the frames. These instances, captured under varying scenes and lighting conditions, provide a dataset for human segmentation.

4.3   Dataset Quality Evaluation

To assess the consistency of the human segmentation labeling process in our dataset, 1106 frames are annotated twice. The quality of the labels is quantified through the calculation of the Jaccardian Index, which measures the overlap between two sets. The average Jaccardian Index is found to be **0.948**, indicating a high level of consistency between the different labelers. A further investigate of the frames with the 20 lowest Jaccard Indices, reveals two sources of errors. The first case, as depicted in Fig. 7a, occurs when the labeled area is very small. This typically happens when the person is far away from the camera or mostly occluded. The second case, as shown in Fig. 7b, arises from suboptimal labeling quality.

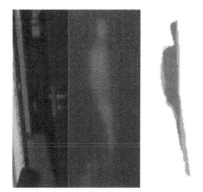

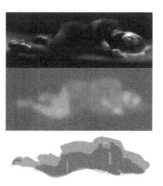

(a) First case: small labeled area due to a person leaving the room.

(b) Second case: discrepancy due to sloppy labeling.

Fig. 7. Visualization of RGB, thermal modality, and human segmentation masks. Violet, indicates an overlap between the two annotator's labels. Red and blue regions, signify areas of disagreement. (Color figure online)

For labels, we compute the label agreement by comparing the labels given in both versions for the same frames. A match is considered when the same set of labels for a frame are provided, irrespective of the sequence. The results indicate a strong agreement for actions (92.4%), transitions (98.0%), states (94.7%), and locations (99.1%), confirming the robustness of our labeling process.

Figure 8 presents a confusion matrix for state transitions, providing insights into the instances where discrepancies occurred between the two labels. Of particular interest are the transitions from the `get_down` state to either the `walk` or `stand` states. These transitions often cause confusion due to the difficulty in pinpointing the exact moment when an individual begins to sit down. As the process of transitioning from a standing to a sitting or lying position is relatively brief, it results in a higher degree of error.

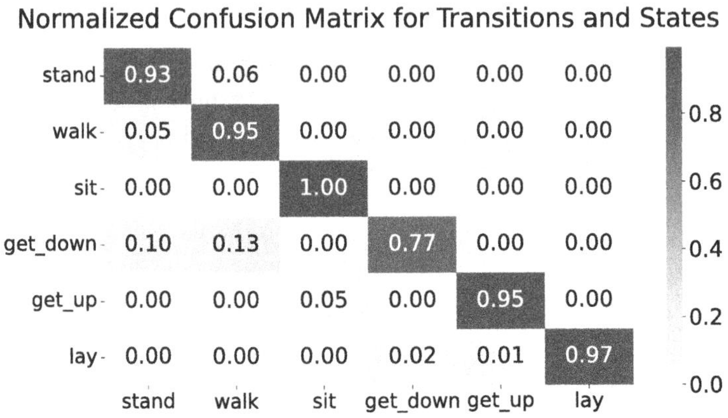

Normalized Confusion Matrix for Transitions and States

	stand	walk	sit	get_down	get_up	lay
stand	0.93	0.06	0.00	0.00	0.00	0.00
walk	0.05	0.95	0.00	0.00	0.00	0.00
sit	0.00	0.00	1.00	0.00	0.00	0.00
get_down	0.10	0.13	0.00	0.77	0.00	0.00
get_up	0.00	0.00	0.05	0.00	0.95	0.00
lay	0.00	0.00	0.00	0.02	0.01	0.97

Fig. 8. Confusion matrix for state transitions in our double-labeled dataset.

5   Benchmarking

In our evaluation, we train a UNet and DeepLabV3 for human segmentation and an action detection model. To enable comparisons across different modalities, we employ z-normalization based on each modality's training set mean and variance. We adjust the size of each model's input channels and concatenate the normalized frames as per the combination of modalities in use. For example, combining depth and thermal data results in an input channel size of two, while employing all modalities increases the input channel size to five. These adjustments aim to assess the performance and impact of individual and combined modalities in multimodal learning tasks.

5.1   Split

The benchmark performance of models trained on our dataset requires a training, validation, and test split. The structure of this split is on the shot level rather than the frame level. This ensures that every frame within a shot is assigned exclusively to a single set (training, validation, or test set). Additionally, the selection of shots minimizes the overlaps in terms of offices and subjects within training, validation, and test shots to prevent information leakage. The distribution the training, validation, and test sets, encompasses 63.77%, 18.23%, and 18.00% of the total data. This corresponds to 9,959 frames in the training set, 2,848 frames in the validation set, and 2,811 frames in the test set.

5.2 Human Segmentation

For the human segmentation task, we adopt the UNet [24] and DeepLabv3 [2] architectures, fine-tuning a model pretrained on the COCO dataset [18] for our trimodal data. We implement an early fusion technique, normalizing the input frames from each modality to a standard distribution via z-normalization, and then concatenating the respective modalities to form the multimodal input. To accommodate these inputs, the DeepLabv3 model-originally designed for RGB inputs-has an input channel added for thermal and depth modalities. When including the RGB modality, we copy the original RGB weights to the new input layer. Following this, the model undergoes ten epochs of training with a learning rate of 0.0001. The model yielding the lowest validation loss during this process is selected for testing. Interestingly, as revealed by Tables 3a and 3b, the best performing combination-yielding the highest Intersection over Union (IoU)-excludes the RGB modality. This finding underscores the value of thermal modality in achieving clear human visibility, especially in test scenes with RGB clutter.

Table 3. Results for Segmentation using UNet and DeepLabv3 on the test set. The input layers channel are updated to accommodate the concatenation of the models.

(a) Results for UNet.

RGB	Depth	Thermal	Loss	IoU
–	–	✓	0.040	0.659
–	✓	–	0.055	0.580
–	✓	✓	**0.020**	**0.775**
✓	–	–	0.147	0.356
✓	–	✓	0.062	0.673
✓	✓	–	0.071	0.553
✓	✓	✓	0.025	0.726

(b) Results for DeepLabv3.

RGB	Depth	Thermal	Loss	IoU
–	–	✓	0.041	0.660
–	✓	–	0.045	0.622
–	✓	✓	**0.023**	**0.806**
✓	–	–	0.050	0.586
✓	–	✓	0.041	0.670
✓	✓	–	0.086	0.494
✓	✓	✓	0.048	0.619

5.3 Action Detection

Our approach for temporal action detection builds upon the method presented in [33]. We employ the same early fusion technique as in the segmentation task to fuse the multimodal inputs. The model is initialized with random weights. Its input is a set of eight frames at a time: the first seven frames serve as temporal context, and the eighth frame is the prediction target. The model architecture includes four 3D convolution pooling blocks with ReLU for feature extraction, global average pooling, and two Multi Layer Perceptrons (MLPs) for classification. One MLP classifier with softmax and cross-entropy loss is utilized for mutually exclusive state, transition, and location labels. The second MLP with sigmoid and binary cross-entropy loss is employed for action labels, accounting for the possibility of simultaneous actions. As demonstrated in Table 4, the combination of depth and thermal modalities yields the highest performance for action classification. This finding underlines the results from the segmentation tasks, reinforcing the advantages of utilizing non-RGB modalities, particularly in complex scenes, for robust action recognition.

Table 4. Results for Temporal Action Detection using custom 3D Convolution Architecture on the test set.

RGB	Depth	Thermal	Loss	Accuracy	Precision	Recall
–	–	✓	2.367	0.903	0.796	0.620
–	✓	–	2.504	0.889	0.749	0.577
–	✓	✓	**2.347**	**0.907**	**0.813**	0.626
✓	–	–	2.659	0.876	0.704	0.537
✓	–	✓	2.346	0.904	0.799	0.623
✓	✓	–	2.465	0.897	0.758	**0.629**
✓	✓	✓	2.349	0.901	0.783	0.618

6   Conclusion

In this work, we have introduced a novel trimodal dataset that combines RGB, thermal, and depth data captured in diverse office environments. One finding from our experiments is the superior performance achieved by utilizing the depth and thermal modalities, even surpassing the combination of RGB, depth, and thermal data. This finding underlines the role that these less traditionally utilized modalities can play in enhancing the robustness and performance of machine learning models, particularly in environments with varying lighting conditions. Future research could exploit the temporal characteristics of our dataset. While UNet and DeepLabV3 architectures mainly focus on spatial features, incorporating temporal information could provide a richer context for the segmentation task. Leveraging Transformer models, which have demonstrated capability of capturing temporal dependencies in data, could also be considered.

Acknowledgments. This work was partly supported by the Austrian Research Promotion Agency (FFG) under the Grant Agreement No. 879744.

References

1. Brenner, M., Reyes, N.H., Susnjak, T., Barczak, A.L.: RGB-D and thermal sensor fusion: a systematic literature review. arXiv preprint arXiv:2305.11427 (2023)
2. Chen, L.-C., Zhu, Y., Papandreou, G., Schroff, F., Adam, H.: Encoder-decoder with atrous separable convolution for semantic image segmentation. In: Ferrari, V., Hebert, M., Sminchisescu, C., Weiss, Y. (eds.) ECCV 2018. LNCS, vol. 11211, pp. 833–851. Springer, Cham (2018). https://doi.org/10.1007/978-3-030-01234-2_49
3. Cordts, M., et al.: The cityscapes dataset for semantic urban scene understanding. In: Proceedings of the IEEE Conference on Computer Vision and Pattern Recognition, pp. 3213–3223 (2016)
4. Dalal, N., Triggs, B.: Histograms of oriented gradients for human detection. In: 2005 IEEE Computer Society Conference on Computer Vision and Pattern Recognition (CVPR 2005), vol. 1, pp. 886–893. IEEE (2005)
5. Davis, J., Keck, M.: A two-stage approach to person detection in thermal imagery. In: Proceeding of Workshop on Applications of Computer Vision (WACV) (2005)
6. Donahue, J., et al.: Long-term recurrent convolutional networks for visual recognition and description. In: Proceedings of the IEEE Conference on Computer Vision and Pattern Recognition, pp. 2625–2634 (2015)
7. Dosovitskiy, A., et al.: An image is worth 16x16 words: transformers for image recognition at scale. arXiv preprint arXiv:2010.11929 (2020)
8. Everingham, M., Van Gool, L., Williams, C.K., Winn, J., Zisserman, A.: The PASCAL visual object classes (VOC) challenge. Int. J. Comput. Vision **88**, 303–338 (2010)
9. Gao, C., et al.: Infar dataset: infrared action recognition at different times. Neurocomputing **212**, 36–47 (2016)
10. Geiger, A., Lenz, P., Urtasun, R.: Are we ready for autonomous driving? The KITTI vision benchmark suite. In: 2012 IEEE Conference on Computer Vision and Pattern Recognition, pp. 3354–3361. IEEE (2012)
11. He, K., Gkioxari, G., Dollár, P., Girshick, R.: Mask R-CNN. In: Proceedings of the IEEE International Conference on Computer Vision, pp. 2961–2969 (2017)
12. Heitzinger, T., Kampel, M.: A foundation for 3d human behavior detection in privacy-sensitive domains. In: 32nd British Machine Vision Conference 2021, BMVC 2021, 22–25 November 2021, p. 305. BMVA Press (2021). https://www.bmvc2021-virtualconference.com/assets/papers/1254.pdf
13. Heitzinger, T., Kampel, M.: IPT: a dataset for identity preserved tracking in closed domains. In: 2020 25th International Conference on Pattern Recognition (ICPR), pp. 8228–8234. IEEE (2021)
14. Ji, S., Xu, W., Yang, M., Yu, K.: 3D convolutional neural networks for human action recognition. IEEE Trans. Pattern Anal. Mach. Intell. **35**(1), 221–231 (2012)
15. Jocher, G., Chaurasia, A., Qiu, J.: YOLO by Ultralytics, January 2023. https://github.com/ultralytics/ultralytics
16. Kirillov, A., et al.: Segment anything. arXiv preprint arXiv:2304.02643 (2023)
17. Kniaz, V.V., Knyaz, V.A., Hladůvka, J., Kropatsch, W.G., Mizginov, V.: Thermal-GAN: multimodal color-to-thermal image translation for person re-identification in multispectral dataset. In: Leal-Taixé, L., Roth, S. (eds.) ECCV 2018. LNCS, vol. 11134, pp. 606–624. Springer, Cham (2019). https://doi.org/10.1007/978-3-030-11024-6_46
18. Lin, T.-Y., et al.: Microsoft COCO: common objects in context. In: Fleet, D., Pajdla, T., Schiele, B., Tuytelaars, T. (eds.) ECCV 2014. LNCS, vol. 8693, pp. 740–755. Springer, Cham (2014). https://doi.org/10.1007/978-3-319-10602-1_48

19. Liu, Z., et al.: Swin transformer: hierarchical vision transformer using shifted windows. In: Proceedings of the IEEE/CVF International Conference on Computer Vision, pp. 10012–10022 (2021)

20. Liu, Z., et al.: Video swin transformer. In: Proceedings of the IEEE/CVF Conference on Computer Vision and Pattern Recognition, pp. 3202–3211 (2022)

21. Miezianko, R.: Terravic research infrared database. In: IEEE OTCBVS WS Series Bench (2005)

22. Palmero, C., Clapés, A., Bahnsen, C., Møgelmose, A., Moeslund, T.B., Escalera, S.: Multi-modal RGB-depth-thermal human body segmentation. Int. J. Comput. Vision **118**, 217–239 (2016)

23. Ren, S., He, K., Girshick, R., Sun, J.: Faster r-cnn: Towards real-time object detection with region proposal networks. Advances in neural information processing systems 28 (2015)

24. Ronneberger, O., Fischer, P., Brox, T.: U-Net: convolutional networks for biomedical image segmentation. In: Navab, N., Hornegger, J., Wells, W.M., Frangi, A.F. (eds.) MICCAI 2015. LNCS, vol. 9351, pp. 234–241. Springer, Cham (2015). https://doi.org/10.1007/978-3-319-24574-4_28

25. Russakovsky, O., et al.: ImageNet large scale visual recognition challenge. Int. J. Comput. Vision **115**, 211–252 (2015)

26. Shahroudy, A., Liu, J., Ng, T.T., Wang, G.: NTU RGB+ D: a large scale dataset for 3d human activity analysis. In: Proceedings of the IEEE Conference on Computer Vision and Pattern Recognition, pp. 1010–1019 (2016)

27. Shivakumar, S.S., Rodrigues, N., Zhou, A., Miller, I.D., Kumar, V., Taylor, C.J.: PST900: RGB-thermal calibration, dataset and segmentation network. In: 2020 IEEE International Conference on Robotics and Automation (ICRA), pp. 9441–9447. IEEE (2020)

28. Sigurdsson, G.A., Divvala, S., Farhadi, A., Gupta, A.: Asynchronous temporal fields for action recognition. In: Proceedings of the IEEE Conference on Computer Vision and Pattern Recognition (CVPR), pp. 585–594 (2017)

29. Sigurdsson, G.A., Varol, G., Wang, X., Farhadi, A., Laptev, I., Gupta, A.: Hollywood in homes: crowdsourcing data collection for activity understanding. In: Leibe, B., Matas, J., Sebe, N., Welling, M. (eds.) ECCV 2016. LNCS, vol. 9905, pp. 510–526. Springer, Cham (2016). https://doi.org/10.1007/978-3-319-46448-0_31

30. Silberman, N., Hoiem, D., Kohli, P., Fergus, R.: Indoor segmentation and support inference from RGBD images. In: Fitzgibbon, A., Lazebnik, S., Perona, P., Sato, Y., Schmid, C. (eds.) ECCV 2012. LNCS, vol. 7576, pp. 746–760. Springer, Heidelberg (2012). https://doi.org/10.1007/978-3-642-33715-4_54

31. Strohmayer, J., Kampel, M.: A compact tri-modal camera unit for RGBDT vision. In: 2022 the 5th International Conference on Machine Vision and Applications (ICMVA), pp. 34–42 (2022)

32. Tkachenko, M., Malyuk, M., Holmanyuk, A., Liubimov, N.: Label studio: data labeling software (2020–2022). https://github.com/heartexlabs/label-studio

33. Tran, D., Bourdev, L., Fergus, R., Torresani, L., Paluri, M.: Learning spatiotemporal features with 3d convolutional networks. In: Proceedings of the IEEE International Conference on Computer Vision, pp. 4489–4497 (2015)

34. Wang, C.Y., Bochkovskiy, A., Liao, H.Y.M.: YOLOv7: trainable bag-of-freebies sets new state-of-the-art for real-time object detectors. In: Proceedings of the IEEE/CVF Conference on Computer Vision and Pattern Recognition (CVPR), pp. 7464–7475 (2023)

35. Zhang, H., Goodfellow, I., Metaxas, D., Odena, A.: Self-attention generative adversarial networks. In: International Conference on Machine Learning, pp. 7354–7363. PMLR (2019)
36. Zhou, B., Zhao, H., Puig, X., Fidler, S., Barriuso, A., Torralba, A.: Scene parsing through ADE20K dataset. In: Proceedings of the IEEE Conference on Computer Vision and Pattern Recognition, pp. 633–641 (2017)

Airborne-Shadow: Towards Fine-Grained Shadow Detection in Aerial Imagery

Seyed Majid Azimi$^{(\boxtimes)}$ and Reza Bahmanyar

German Aerospace Center, Remote Sensing Technology Institute, Wessling, Germany
{seyedmajid.azimi,reza.bahmanyar}@dlr.de
https://www.dlr.de/eoc/en

Abstract. Shadow detection is the first step in the process of shadow removal, which improves the understanding of complex urban scenes in aerial imagery for applications such as autonomous driving, infrastructure monitoring, and mapping. However, the limited annotation in existing datasets hinders the effectiveness of semantic segmentation and the ability of shadow removal algorithms to meet the fine-grained requirements of real-world applications. To address this problem, we present Airborne-Shadow (ASD), a meticulously annotated dataset for shadow detection in aerial imagery. Unlike existing datasets, ASD includes annotations for both heavy and light shadows, covering various structures ranging from buildings and bridges to smaller details such as poles and fences. Therefore, we define shadow detection tasks for multi-class, single class, and merging two classes. Extensive experiments show the challenges that state-of-the-art semantic segmentation and shadow detection algorithms face in handling different shadow sizes, scales, and fine details, while still achieving comparable results to conventional methods. We make the ASD dataset publicly available to encourage progress in shadow detection. It can be accessed via https://www.dlr.de/eoc/en/desktopdefault.aspx/tabid-12760.

Keywords: Shadow detection · Aerial imagery · Benchmark dataset

1 Introduction

Shadows are common in natural images taken from ground, aerial, and satellite imagery. When a light source is blocked by an object, as a result a shadow is created, causing colors to appear darker and textures to be less detailed. Therefore, shadow influences almost every Artificial Intelligence (AI) algorithms in the processing of image features. Since shadow can add information to images, such as the geometrical properties of the objects within the images, most of the existing AI-based computer vision and image processing algorithms work more

Supplementary Information The online version contains supplementary material available at https://doi.org/10.1007/978-3-031-54605-1_3.

Fig. 1. A cropped section of an aerial image from the ASD dataset with ☐ heavy and ■ light shadow annotations, covering $5.7\,\mathrm{km}^2$ of Munich, Germany. (Color figure online)

effectively on shadow-free images. For example, detecting an object is certainly easier if the illumination conditions remain constant over the object surface and within different images.

In this paper, we focus on shadow detection in high-resolution aerial images, which can lead to the development of more shadow-adapted AI algorithms that effectively handle shadowed areas for various applications such as semantic segmentation and object detection, where the existing methods often fail in the areas covered by the shadows of objects such as buildings and trees [1,15]. In the past few years, various data-driven methods have been proposed for shadow detection in ground imagery owing to the various shadow detection datasets. Although the authors tried to cover various scenes and object classes, these datasets mostly contain images from ground perspective. Apart from the Wide Area Motion Imagery (WAMI) [31] dataset introduced recently, existing shadow detection datasets offer only a limited number of aerial images, which inadequately represent the real-world challenges of aerial imagery. As a result, the number of data-driven shadow detection methods for aerial imagery is limited. To address this shortage, we present ASD, a novel and meticulously annotated aerial shadow detection dataset. To the best of our knowledge, it is the first dataset of its kind to include extensive and thorough manual annotation of natural shadows and to include two distinct shadow classes, heavy and light, providing a new level of detail. Figure 1 shows a section of a large aerial image with its shadow annotations overlaid. The large number of objects as well as their diverse sizes and shapes introduce significant challenge to the shadow annotation in aerial images. In order to assure the quality and validity of the annotations, a rigorous three-step review process involving remote sensing experts was conducted. The annotations were refined based on their feedback. To evaluate the impact of our dataset on the performance of data-driven shadow detection methods, we perform extensive evaluations by training and testing various semantic segmentation and dedicated shadow detection methods. The results highlight the persistent challenges that existing approaches face in accurately detecting and extracting the edges of very small shadows. Furthermore, we assess the generalizability of the trained models on our dataset to other shadow detection datasets. The results show that the model trained on ASD performs well on the aerial part of the other shadow detection datasets, while it has difficulties when applied to ground images, indicating the presence of different challenges in the two domains.

2   Shadow Detection Datasets

Over the past decade, numerous shadow detection and removal datasets have been introduced. In this paper, we present an overview of various shadow detection datasets, with a focus on the publicly available ones with aerial images.

The first shadow detection dataset is the dataset of the University of Central Florida (UCF) introduced by Zhu et al. [44]. It has 245 images and their shadow masks of size 257×257 pixels, selected from Overhead Imagery Research Dataset (OIRDS) [29]. The authors created the shadow masks through a manual image annotation. Most of the images in UCF are scenes with dark shadows and dark albedo objects. Guo et al. [9] introduced the University of Illinois at Urbana-Champaign (UIUC) shadow detection and removal dataset. This dataset is composed of 108 RGB natural scene shadow images as well as their corresponding shadow-free images and shadow masks. The authors took two images of a scene after manipulating the shadows by blocking the direct light source (to have shadow in the whole scene) or by putting a shadow into the scene. In this dataset, the shadow masks were generated automatically by thresholding the ratio between the shadow and shadow-free images. The authors claim that this approach is more accurate than manual annotation. In this dataset, a large number of images contain close shots of objects. Vicente et al. [34] introduced Stony Brook University (SBU) shadow detection dataset with 4,727 images. The authors collected a quarter of the images from the MS COCO dataset [19] and the rest from the web. The images include aerial, landscape, close range, and selfie images. The annotations were performed through a lazy-labeling procedure in which shadows were segmented by a geodesic convexity image segmentation and then were refined manually.

Wang et al. [35] generated Image Shadow Triplets Dataset (ISTD), the first benchmark dataset for simultaneous evaluations of shadow detection and removal. This dataset contains 1,870 image triplets including shadow image, shadow mask, and shadow-free image. Each shadow and shadow-free image pair was generated in a fixed exposure setup by inserting and removing an object in the scene. In order to have diverse scenes and shadow shapes, the authors considered 135 different ground materials and objects with various shapes. Hu et al. [12] introduced Chinese University of Hong Kong (CUHK) dataset for shadow detection in complex real-world scenarios with 10,500 shadow images and their manually labeled ground-truth masks. The shadow images were collected from a web-search, Google MAP, and three different datasets including the ADE20K [43], KITTI [6], and USR [11] datasets. Therefore, CUHK contains shadows in diverse scenes such as cities, buildings, satellite images, and roads with shadows cast by objects on themselves and the other objects. To leverage instance shadow detection, Wang et al. [36] generated Shadow-OBject Association (SOBA) dataset which include 3,623 pairs of shadow and object instances in 1,000 images collected through a web search and from the ADE20K,

Table 1. Statistics of the shadow detection datasets.

Datasets	# Imgs	Img Type	Shadow Casting	Aerial Imgs						
				# Imgs	Avg. Size	Shadow Quantity (px)		# Shadow Instances		Year
						Total Mean	Std.	Total Mean	Std.	
UCF [44]	245	Ground, Aerial	Natural	74	433×594	0.6M 2.1k	4.2k	275 3.72	1.86	2010
UIUC [9]	108	Ground	Artificial	0	-	- -	-	- -	-	2012
SBU [34]	4,727	Ground, Aerial	Natural	153	447×557	3.1M 2.7k	7.1k	1,088 7.11	5.21	2016
IDTD [35]	1,870	Ground	Artificial	0	640×480	- -	-	- -	-	2018
SOBA [36]	1,000	Ground	Natural, Artificial	0	-	- -	-	- -	-	2020
CUHK [12]	10,500	Ground, Aerial	Natural	311	455×767	23.8M 5.6k	17.7k	4,242 13.64	7.51	2021
WAMI [31]	137,180	Aerial	Artificial	137,180	660×440	- -	-	- -	-	2021
PISTA [40]	172,539	Ground	Artificial	0	-	- -	-	- -	-	2023
ASD	1,408	Aerial	Natural	1,408	512×512	72.7M 51.6k	26.1k	67,781 48.14	25.36	2023

SBU, ISTD, and MS COCO datasets. Yücel et al. [40] presented the Patch Isolation Triplets with Shadow Augmentations (PITSA) dataset, which contains 172k triplets derived from 20k unique shadow-free ground images. The dataset was created using a pipeline designed for generating large shadow detection and removal datasets, focusing on shadow removal. Shadows were superimposed using a shadow library.

Table 1 shows statistics of the reviewed shadow detection datasets. Among these datasets, UCF, SBU, and CUHK contain a few aerial shadow images; however, the number of samples and their diversity are very limited. Due to their coverage, aerial images usually contain large number of objects with diverse shapes and sizes which makes them different from the terrestrial images. Therefore, in order to develop efficient aerial shadow detection algorithms for real-world applications, large aerial image shadow datasets are crucial. The existing datasets are not appropriate for training Deep Learning (DL)-based algorithms for real-world aerial shadow detection applications. Dealing with this shortcoming, Ufuktepe et al. [31] introduced WAMI dataset containing 137k aerial images, which is the largest shadow detection dataset for aerial imagery. The shadows in the dataset were generated and superimposed using a 3D scene model approach, eliminating the need for tedious manual annotation. However, the generated shadows may contain imperfections due to inaccuracies in the 3D model and the superposition process. In addition, this dataset is currently not publicly available.

3 Airborne-Shadow Dataset

To address the limitations of existing datasets for shadow detection in aerial imagery and to promote the development of efficient and effective data-driven shadow detection and removal algorithms, we present the ASD dataset. It consists of 1,408 non-overlapping RGB images with dimensions of 512×512 pixels. These images were derived by splitting the 16 large aerial images (5616×3744

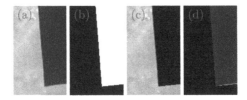

Fig. 2. Example of imperfection in shadow annotation at the shadow borders. Original image (a), binary shadow mask (b), shadow-free region (c), shadowed region in which some non-shadowed pixels are still present (d).

Fig. 3. A scene from the ASD dataset with its overlaid annotation for □ heavy and ■ light classes and sample zoomed areas. (Color figure online)

pixels) from the publicly available SkyScapes dataset[1] [1]. The images were captured using the German Aerospace Center (DLR)'s 3K camera system (three DSLR cameras mounted on an airborne platform) during a helicopter flight over Munich, Germany in 2012. The images are nadir looking and have been taken from an altitude of 1000 m where their average Ground Sampling Distance (GSD) is 13 cm/pixel. We split the dataset into training and test sets according to the train-test split of the SkyScapes dataset, where ten large images are assigned to train and six images to the test set.

3.1 Shadow Annotation

We manually annotated the shadowed areas by 2D polygons and classified them into light and heavy shadows. According to our annotation guidelines, shadows caused by objects that allow sunlight to pass through (such as tree crowns) are classified as light shadows. On the other hand, shadows caused by objects that completely block sunlight are classified as heavy shadows. Furthermore, if an area is partially illuminated by direct sunlight, it is called a light shadow, while if the entire area is illuminated by indirect sunlight reflected from other objects, it is called a heavy shadow. The annotation resulted in 67,781 instances with 72,658,346 annotated pixels, of which about 17.5% are assigned to the light shadow class and the rest to the heavy shadow class. Table 1 represents the statistics of the ASD and the other shadow detection datasets.

[1] https://eoc-datasets.dlr.de.

Annotating shadows in aerial imagery is challenging due to the large number of objects in each image and the wide range of shadow sizes and shapes. In our dataset, we aimed to provide shadow annotations with exceptional precision, which posed additional challenges, particularly when delineating shadow boundaries and shadows cast by small objects from an aerial perspective (e.g., lamps and poles). In addition, distinguishing between shadowed and non-shadowed pixels, especially along shadow edges, can be a complex task. Figure 2 illustrates an imperfection in the annotation of shadow borders. As another example, for objects such as trees, it is usually difficult to decide for shadow pixels in their border with the tree branches and leaves. In addition, it is not always easy to separate the shadows of densely packed objects, such as trees in a forest. Also, the heavy shadows are annotated more precisely than the light shadows because their boundaries were much clearer. For the light shadows, the annotations are made by drawing a polygon around the approximate boundary of the shadows. Our annotation process overcomes the challenges of shadow annotation, enabling high accuracy and consistency while reducing potential annotation errors. Validation by remote sensing experts at multiple levels ensures the quality and validity of annotations, resulting in refined annotations. Figure 3 shows an example scene from the ASD dataset along with its corresponding annotation. Zoomed areas highlight the precision of the annotations in capturing fine details.

3.2   Comparison to the Other Datasets

Except for the WAMI dataset, existing shadow detection datasets are primarily general-purpose and thus contain either no or only a limited number of aerial images. In addition, these datasets typically consist of images obtained through web searches or from publicly available sources such as OIRDS and Google Maps. Figure 4 shows some examples from the UCF, SBU and CUHK datasets. As can be seen in the examples, the GSDs, viewing angles, illumination conditions, and scene types of the images in SBU are very diverse. Given the limited number of samples in this dataset, this sample heterogeneity may prevent the algorithms from learning different features correctly. Regarding the CUHK dataset, since the images are taken from Google Maps as snapshots of the 3D reconstruction of the environment, they do not represent the true structures and reconstruction distortions are evident in the images. As a consequence, the shadows are also not real shadows. Therefore, a model trained only on these images may not be applicable to real-world scenarios.

In contrast, the images in the ASD dataset were acquired during an aerial campaign specifically designed for urban monitoring, which closely resemble real-world scenarios. In addition, the high quality and resolution of the images in our dataset allow algorithms to learn shadow features from objects of different sizes. The ASD dataset was developed to demonstrate practical applications of aerial image shadow datasets. Careful selection of images from the same flight campaign ensures a diverse range of shadow samples while maintaining consistency in parameters such as illumination, weather conditions, viewing angle, and GSD. Compared to the WAMI dataset, the manual annotation in ASD ensures precise

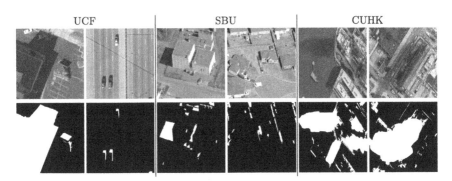

Fig. 4. Sample aerial images with their corresponding masks from the UCF, SBU, and CUHK shadow datasets.

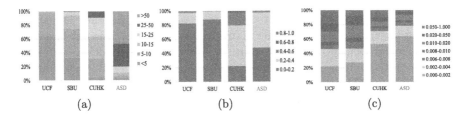

Fig. 5. Statistical properties of the aerial set of the UCF, SBU, CUHK, and ASD datasets. The number of annotated shadow instances per image (a), shadowed fraction of images (b), and the size of annotated shadow instances relative to image sizes (c).

annotation of small objects and shadow edges, which may be prone to errors in the automatic annotation of WAMI due to imperfections in 3D reconstruction and overlay techniques. In addition, ASD includes two shadow classes, which improves fine-grained shadow detection in aerial imagery. Furthermore, by building ASD on top of the SkyScapes fine-grained semantic segmentation dataset, it provides opportunities to explore shadow detection and removal on different objects and surfaces, as well as to investigate the impact of shadow removal on the segmentation of different semantic categories. In contrast to the WAMI dataset, our dataset will be made publicly available, fostering advancements in the development of shadow detection algorithms. We compare the statistics of our dataset with publicly available shadow datasets containing aerial imagery. As shown in Fig. 1, the total number of annotated shadow instances in ASD is about 16 times higher than that of CUHK. Also, according to the diagrams in Fig. 5, ASD contains a larger number of shadow instances, especially at smaller sizes, than the other datasets. According to Fig. 5-(a) most of the images in our dataset contains more than 25 instances in contrast to the other datsets which rarely have such images. Moreover, Fig. 5-(c) indicates that most of the annotations in our dataset are tiny shadows which could be caused by the fine looking objects in aerial images. This also shows the high quality and resolution of our images so that even such fine annotations could be provided. In addition, similar to the other shadow detection datasets, the number of shadowed and non-shadowed pixels is not balanced in our dataset. However, according to Fig. 5-(b) about half of the images in ASD are covered by 20% to 40% shadow pixels.

4   Shadow Detection Methods

Previous works in the field of shadow detection have primarily focused on the extraction of shadows using engineered feature descriptors, illumination models and physical properties of shadows [8,9,14,17,23,30,33,44]. The classification of shadowed pixels was often performed using algorithms such as Support Vector Machine (SVM) and decision tree. In the field of remote sensing, threshold-based methods have been proposed with promising results in [7], using Gram-Schmidt orthogonalization in the LAB color space. In addition, an image index has been developed in [21] that incorporates all available bands of multispectral images. Furthermore, the use of Principal Component Analysis (PCA) to detect shadows in multispectral satellite images was introduced in [5]. These methods are not specifically designed for shadow detection. Therefore, their results are not directly comparable with state-of-the-art shadow detection methods.

Inspired by the successful applications of Deep Neural Network (DNN)s in various image processing and computer vision tasks, a number of recent works have proposed to exploit the ability of DNNs to automatically learn relevant features for shadow detection. A structured Convolutional Neural Network (CNN) framework was used in [28] to predict the local structure of shadow edges, which improves the accuracy and local consistency of pixel classification. A CNN structure was proposed in [34] for patch-level shadow detection, which refines the detected shadow patches based on image-level semantics. A method called scGAN was proposed in [22], which uses a stacked Conditional Generative Adversarial Networks (CGAN) with a sensitivity parameter to both control the sensitivity of the generator and weight the relative importance of the shadow and non-shadow classes. The BDRAR method, introduced in [45], utilizes a bidirectional Feature Pyramid Network (FPN) with Recurrent Attention Residual (RAR) modules. It extracts feature maps at different resolutions using a CNN, enabling the capture of both shadow details and shadow semantics. Another method, called Direction-aware Spatial Context (DSC), proposed in [13], incorporates an attention mechanism in a spatial Recurrent Neural Network (RNN) with a newly introduced DSC module to learn spatial contexts of images and shadows. Despite its performance, DSC is unable to outperform BDRAR. The FDRNet method proposed in [46] uses a feature decomposition and reweighting scheme to mitigate intensity bias. It separates features into intensity-variant and -invariant components and reweights these two types of features to redistribute attention and balance their evaluation. The BDRAR method, introduced in [35], enables joint detection and removal of shadows in an end-to-end manner. It utilizes two stacked CGANs, with the first generator producing shadow detection masks and the second generator removing shadows based on the generated masks. A context preserver CNN called CPAdv-Net was proposed in [20], which is based on the U-Net [26] structure and trained by adversarial images. In [12], a fast shadow detection method called FSDNet was proposed. It utilizes the MobileNet-V2 [27] architecture and a novel detail enhancement module. FSD-Net achieves competitive results with state-of-the-art methods in a shorter time.

5   Evaluation Metrics

For the evaluations, we use commonly used metrics including mean Intersection over Union (IoU), Dice similarity coefficient, and Balanced Error Rate (BER). In the following equations, n_{ij} is the number of pixels of class i predicted as class j and n_{cl} is the number of classes, with $t_i = \sum_j n_{ij}$ representing the total number of pixels of class i. TP, TN, FP, and FN denote the number of true positives, true negatives, false positives, and false negatives, respectively. P and T refer to prediction and ground truth, respectively. For IoU and Dice, higher values indicate better results, while for BER, lower values show better results.

$$MeanIoU = \frac{1}{n_{cl}} \sum_i \frac{n_{i,i}}{t_i + \sum_j n_{j,i} - n_{i,i}},$$

$$Dice = \frac{2 \mid P \cap T \mid}{\mid P \mid + \mid T \mid},$$

$$BER = 1 - \frac{1}{2} \left(\frac{TP}{TP + FN} + \frac{TN}{TN + FP} \right).$$

6   Results and Discussion

In this section, we evaluate the performance of several DL-based semantic segmentation and shadow detection methods on the ASD dataset. We train and test them on the training and test sets of the dataset for three tasks: heavy and light shadow classes, heavy shadow class only, and merging the two classes.

Among the existing methods, we select methods with publicly available training source code, including the state-of-the-art InternImage [37] together with AdaptNet [32], BiSeNet [39], DeepLab [2], DeepLabv3+ [3], DenseA-SPP [38], Context-Encoding [41], FC-DenseNet [16], FRRN [25], GCN [24], MobileUNet [10,26], PSPNet [42], and RefineNet [18] for semantic segmentation, and BDRAR [45] and FDRNet [46] for dedicated shadow detection methods. Moreover, for semantic segmentation, we conduct experiments with multiple available variants and different backbones of each method. The best result for each method is listed in Table 2. We refer the reader to the supplementary material for the full set of experimental results.

For our experiments, we crop the images into 512×512px patches. The reason is the original size of images is 21 MP which does not fit into the GPU memory. We use Titan XP and Quadro P6000 GPUs for training of the semantic segmentation algorithms and A100 GPU for training the InternImage and shadow

Table 2. Benchmark on our dataset for multiple semantic segmentation and dedicated shadow detection methods for different class setups evaluated by IoU↑, Dice↑, BER↓, and Class IoU↑. B, H, L, and M denote background, heavy shadow, light shadow, and merged classes. The values are given in percent. In red and blue are the best and second best results. IoU is in %.

Method	Heavy and Light			Heavy				Merged			
	IoU	Dice	Class IoU [B,H,L]	IoU	BER	Dice	Class IoU [B,H]	IoU	BER	Dice	Class IoU [B,M]
AdapNet-Incep.V4 [32]	66.59	78.17	[89.36, 69.30, 41.12]	80.27	11.64	88.65	[91.23, 69.32]	79.02	12.91	87.91	[89.23, 68.80]
BiSeNet-Res.152 [39]	69.15	80.51	[89.70, 70.16, 47.60]	80.80	11.43	88.99	[91.52, 70.08]	80.02	12.24	88.58	[89.78, 70.27]
DeepLabv3 - Res.152 [2]	65.28	77.43	[88.24, 64.99, 42.62]	78.26	13.43	87.28	[90.38, 66.15]	77.20	14.24	86.69	[88.26, 66.13]
DeepLabv3+ - Res.152 [3]	68.45	79.81	[89.80, 70.62, 44.94]	81.22	11.19	89.27	[91.73, 70.71]	80.30	11.89	88.76	[89.87, 70.72]
DeepLabv3+ - Xcep.65 [3]	**71.00**	**81.88**	[90.67, 72.59, **49.72**]	82.57	**10.48**	90.13	[92.41, **72.73**]	81.84	**10.75**	89.76	[90.67, 73.02]
DenseASPP-Res.50 [38]	65.36	77.03	[88.76, 69.10, 38.23]	79.85	10.65	88.39	[90.67, 69.04]	78.68	12.89	87.70	[88.95, 68.41]
Encoder-Decoder-Skip	69.76	80.86	[90.23, 71.95, 47.10]	81.70	10.98	89.57	[91.98, 71.41]	80.37	11.78	88.81	[89.89, 70.85]
FC-DenseNet65	70.02	80.99	[90.62, **72.77**, 46.67]	82.02	12.04	89.76	[**92.45**, 71.59]	**81.88**	**10.75**	89.78	[90.70, **73.06**]
FRRN-A-Incep.V4 [25]	68.98	80.15	[90.24, 71.70, 45.00]	81.81	11.37	89.64	[92.15, 71.47]	80.92	11.47	89.16	[90.21, 71.63]
FRRN-B [25]	69.17	80.31	[90.25, 71.88, 45.37]	81.72	11.07	89.59	[92.02, 71.42]	80.78	11.85	89.07	[90.23, 71.33]
GCN-Res101 [24]	69.47	80.60	[90.31, 71.76, 46.34]	81.57	11.08	89.49	[91.93, 71.21]	80.84	11.89	89.10	[90.29, 71.40]
InternImage [37]	71.39	82.16	[91.00, 73.37, 49.79]	82.75	10.15	90.35	[92.45, 73.04]	82.51	9.95	**90.02**	[91.00, 74.03]
MobileUNet-Skip-Incep.V4 [10]	68.14	79.46	[89.87, 70.98, 43.56]	81.35	11.64	89.34	[91.93, 70.77]	80.38	11.55	88.82	[89.82, 70.95]
PSPNet-Res.152 [42]	68.13	79.50	[89.70, 70.77, 43.94]	81.12	11.65	89.19	[91.78, 70.45]	80.17	11.76	88.68	[89.72, 70.61]
RefineNet-Res.152 [18]	69.05	80.32	[89.85, 71.11, 46.21]	81.46	10.92	89.42	[91.82, 71.10]	80.51	11.20	88.91	[89.80, 71.22]
BDRAR [45]	68.01	79.33	[89.91, 71.05, 43.09]	81.84	10.99	89.69	[92.08, 71.60]	80.63	12.02	88.91	[90.05, 71.21]
FDRNet [46]	69.87	80.88	[90.69, 72.61, 46.33]	82.46	11.09	90.08	[92.42, 72.49]	81.68	10.95	90.14	[**90.74**, 72.98]

detection algorithms. Regarding data augmentation, we apply both horizontal and vertical flipping, as well as 50% overlap between neighboring crops. During inference, we apply 10% overlap to alleviate the lower performance at boundary regions. The learning rate is 0.0001 with the batch size of 1. We train the

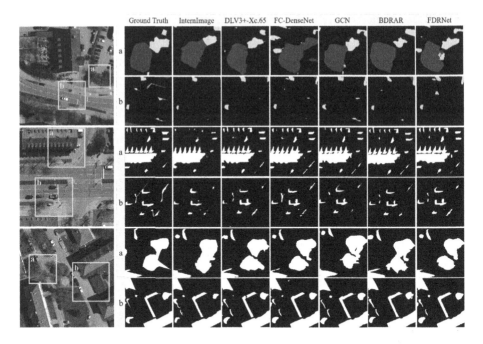

Fig. 6. Shadow segmentation results by six different methods for two class (first row), only heavy (2nd row), and the merged classes (3rd row). □ heavy and ■ light shadows. (Color figure online)

algorithms for 60 epochs to make the comparison fair with all algorithms converged until this step instead of using early stopping and learning-rate scheduling techniques. In total, there are 8820 training crops. For training InernImage[2], BDRAR[3] and FDRNet[4], we use the original implementations. As shown in Table 2, InternImage achieves the highest performance of 71.29 IoU and 10.15, 9.95 BER in ASD-two-classes, heavy(H) and -merged(M) respectively, closely followed by DeepLabv3+-Xcep.65 as the second best method for most of the evaluations. Notably, the results of InternImage, currently the state-of-the-art semantic segmentation method on the CityScapes dataset [4], are not significantly better than many of the earlier methods, indicating that the challenges in ASD are still affecting newer methods. Figure 6 demonstrates the qualitative performance of selected algorithms. InternImage and DeepLabv3+-Xcep.65 excel at extracting large shadow instances, while FC-DenseNet and GCN perform better on small shadow instances such as poles. In addition, FDRNet and BDRAR have comparable performance. Overall, the methods perform better with heavy shadows and face more challenges with light shadows. Light shadows often have lower contrast and can be more difficult to accurately detect than

---

[2] https://github.com/OpenGVLab/InternImage (accessed June 5 2023).
[3] https://github.com/zijundeng/BDRAR (accessed June 5 2023).
[4] https://github.com/rayleizhu/FDRNet (accessed June 5 2023).

heavy shadows, which tend to have more distinct boundaries and higher contrast. Therefore, methods that focus on edge refinement and enhancing contrast in light shadow regions could potentially improve the overall performance of shadow detection algorithms in real-world scenarios. Still almost all algorithms have a major difficulty in extracting shadows of tiny objects e.g., poles which is important in pole detection algorithms as poles normally appear as one point in ortho aerial images. With further investigation, as expected we notice that algorithms are under performing in edge areas. We contemplate that one of the reasons for the slight better performance of InternImage is due to the more extended extracted shadowed areas leading to higher quantitative performance especially in IoU. Overall, ASD shows that there is a significant challenge still remaining in the shadow detection task in aerial imagery which we hope this dataset could support further developments to shorten this gap.

Cross Validation. To assess the generalizability of the models trained on our dataset, we trained DeepLabv3+-Xcep.65 on ASD and tested it on SBU, CUHK, and ISTD datasets. Similarly, we tested models trained on these three datasets on ASD. The quantitative results are presented in Table 3, and Fig. 7 illustrates some qualitative results. The models trained on the heavy and merged classes of ASD performs significantly better on the aerial images of the SBU and CUHK datasets than on the entire dataset, which includes both aerial and ground images. Furthermore, the results on the ISTD dataset clearly show that the model trained on the aerial images does not generalize well to the ground images. This highlights the different challenges in different domains of shadow detection. BDRAR and FDRNet achieve 3.64 and 3.04 in BER on SBU dataset respectively while the trained algorithms on ASD-H and -M achieve 8.04. The reason is the significant change in aerial images of SBU such as oblique ones shown in Fig. 7. This justification is confirmed on CUHK dataset in which trained algorithms on ASD-H and -M achieve 11.79 versus the trained one on CUHK yielding 13.34 while tested on the aerial images in CUHK dataset i.e., CUHK-aerial(A). Interestingly, DeepLabv3+-Xcep.65 achieves 4.90 in BER when trained on SBU. We will further investigate the lower performance of BDRAR and FDRNet compared to DeepLabv3+-Xcep.65 when tested on ASD in the future. ISDT dataset has no aerial images, however, we can see that trained algorithm on ASD-H or -M can achieve better BER on ISDT with 25.49 and 24.67 than trained ones on ISDT, tested on ASD-H and -M with 27.16 and 26.50. The same phenomena occurs in the SBU and CUHK datasets. Therefore, ASD has a better generalization capability than the aerial images contained in SBU and CUHK dataset. Furthermore, the model trained on ASD performs significantly better on the SBU and CUHK aerial sets than the model trained on these two datasets and tested on ASD. This indicates that ASD generalizes better than the airborne parts of SBU and CUHK.

Table 3. Evaluation of the generalizability of models trained on ASD and tested on SBU, ISTD, and CUHK datasets, and vice versa, using the DeepLabv3+-Xcep.65 network. H and M refer to the heavy shadow and merged classes in ASD, and A denotes the aerial parts of the SBU and CUHK dataset. The results are in percent, with the best and second best results marked in red and blue, respectively. IoU is in %.

ASD vs. SBU					ASD vs. CUHK					ASD vs. ISTD				
Train	Test	IoU↑	BER↓	Dice↑	Train	Test	IoU↑	BER↓	Dice↑	Train	Test	IoU↑	BER↓	Dice↑
ASD-H	SBU	65.95	13.70	77.56	ASD-H	CUHK	44.22	22.56	59.07	ASD-H	ISTD	53.09	25.49	63.39
ASD-M	SBU	67.06	14.26	78.57	ASD-M	CUHK	45.25	22.82	60.27	ASD-M	ISTD	54.43	24.67	65.58
ASD-H	SBU-A	85.03	8.04	91.52	ASD-H	CUHK-A	70.27	11.79	81.80	ISTD	ISTD	91.47	6.62	95.46
ASD-M	SBU-A	85.29	8.72	91.69	ASD-M	CUHK-A	75.57	12.68	82.82	ISTD	ASD-H	61.21	27.16	74.46
SBU	SBU	90.17	4.90	94.73	CUHK	CUHK	83.55	9.07	91.03	ISTD	ASD-M	60.44	26.50	74.03
SBU	SBU-A	84.09	7.17	90.90	CUHK	CUHK-A	78.61	13.34	87.84					
SBU	ASD-H	69.77	15.55	80.96	CUHK	ASD-H	64.01	24.72	77.25					
SBU	ASD-M	64.41	17.29	76.80	CUHK	ASD-M	64.81	23.63	78.02					

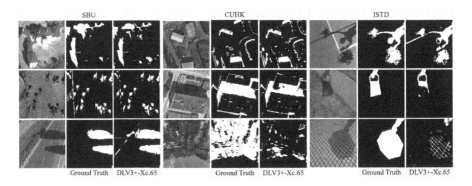

Fig. 7. Shadow segmentation results for DeepLabv3+-Xcep.65 trained on ASD (merged classes) and tested on SBU, CUHK, and ISTD test sets.

7   Conclusion and Future Works

In this paper, we present ASD, the first and largest publicly available dataset dedicated to fine-grained shadow detection in aerial imagery, including both heavy and light shadow classes. By evaluating and benchmarking state-of-the-art methods, we found that current algorithms struggle to achieve high accuracy on this dataset, highlighting the intricate details and complexity of ASD. In addition, the cross-dataset evaluation results show that the model trained on ASD performs well on the aerial set of the other shadow detection datasets, indicating the potential transferability of models trained on ASD to other similar aerial image datasets. Altogether, ASD will advance the development of efficient and effective shadow detection methods, ultimately improving shadow removal and feature extraction for various applications such as HD map creation and autonomous driving.

References

1. Azimi, S.M., Henry, C., Sommer, L., Schumann, A., Vig, E.: Skyscapes fine-grained semantic understanding of aerial scenes. In: Proceedings of the IEEE International Conference on Computer Vision, pp. 7393–7403 (2019)
2. Chen, L.C., Papandreou, G., Kokkinos, I., Murphy, K., Yuille, A.L.: Semantic Image Segmentation With Deep Convolutional Nets And Fully Connected CRFs. arXiv preprint arXiv:1412.7062 (2014)
3. Chen, L.C., Zhu, Y., Papandreou, G., Schroff, F., Adam, H.: Encoder-decoder with atrous separable convolution for semantic image segmentation. In: Proceedings of the European Conference on Computer Vision (ECCV), pp. 801–818 (2018)
4. Cordts, M., et al.: The cityscapes dataset for semantic urban scene understanding. In: Proceedings of the IEEE Conference on Computer Vision and Pattern Recognition, pp. 3213–3223 (2016)
5. Dharani, M., Sreenivasulu, G.: Shadow detection using index-based principal component analysis of satellite images. In: 2019 3rd International Conference on Computing Methodologies and Communication (ICCMC), pp. 182–187. IEEE (2019)
6. Geiger, A., Lenz, P., Urtasun, R.: Are we ready for autonomous driving? The KITTI vision benchmark suite. In: IEEE Conference on Computer Vision and Pattern Recognition (CVPR), pp. 3354–3361 (2012)
7. Guo, J., Yang, F., Tan, H., Lei, B.: Shadow extraction from high-resolution remote sensing images based on Gram-Schmidt orthogonalization in lab space. In: Urbach, H., Zhang, G. (eds.) 3rd International Symposium of Space Optical Instruments and Applications. Springer Proceedings in Physics, LNCS, vol. 192, pp. 321–328. Springer, Cham (2017). https://doi.org/10.1007/978-3-319-49184-4_32
8. Guo, R., Dai, Q., Hoiem, D.: Single-image shadow detection and removal using paired regions. In: CVPR 2011, pp. 2033–2040. IEEE (2011)
9. Guo, R., Dai, Q., Hoiem, D.: Paired regions for shadow detection and removal. IEEE Trans. Pattern Anal. Mach. Intell. **35**(12), 2956–2967 (2012)
10. Howard, A.G., et al..: Mobilenets: efficient convolutional neural networks for mobile vision applications. arXiv preprint arXiv:1704.04861 (2017)
11. Hu, X., Jiang, Y., Fu, C.W., Heng, P.A.: Mask-shadowgan: learning to remove shadows from unpaired data. arXiv preprint arXiv:1903.10683 (2019)
12. Hu, X., Wang, T., Fu, C.W., Jiang, Y., Wang, Q., Heng, P.A.: Revisiting shadow detection: a new benchmark dataset for complex world. IEEE Trans. Image Process. **30**, 1925–1934 (2021)
13. Hu, X., Zhu, L., Fu, C.W., Qin, J., Heng, P.A.: Direction-aware spatial context features for shadow detection. In: Proceedings of the IEEE Conference on Computer Vision and Pattern Recognition, pp. 7454–7462 (2018)
14. Huang, X., Hua, G., Tumblin, J., Williams, L.: What characterizes a shadow boundary under the sun and sky? In: 2011 International Conference On Computer Vision, pp. 898–905. IEEE (2011)
15. ISPRS: 2D Semantic Labeling Dataset. http://www2.isprs.org/commissions/comm3/wg4/semantic-labeling.html. Accessed 01 Mar 2023
16. Jégou, S., Drozdzal, M., Vazquez, D., Romero, A., Bengio, Y.: The one hundred layers tiramisu: fully convolutional DenseNets for semantic segmentation. In: Proceedings of the IEEE Conference on Computer Vision and Pattern Recognition Workshops, pp. 11–19 (2017)

17. Lalonde, J.F., Efros, A.A., Narasimhan, S.G.: Detecting ground shadows in outdoor consumer photographs. In: Daniilidis, K., Maragos, P., Paragios, N. (eds.) Computer Vision – ECCV 2010. ECCV 2010. LNCS, vol. 6312, pp. 322–335. Springer, Berlin, Heidelberg (2010). https://doi.org/10.1007/978-3-642-15552-9_24
18. Lin, G., Milan, A., Shen, C., Reid, I.: Refinenet: multi-path refinement networks for high-resolution semantic segmentation. In: The IEEE Conference on Computer Vision and Pattern Recognition (CVPR), July 2017
19. Lin, T.Y., et al.: Microsoft coco: common objects in context. In: Fleet, D., Pajdla, T., Schiele, B., Tuytelaars, T. (eds.) Computer Vision – ECCV 2014. ECCV 2014. LNCS, vol. 8693, pp. 740–755. Springer, Cham (2014). https://doi.org/10.1007/978-3-319-10602-1_48
20. Mohajerani, S., Saeedi, P.: Shadow detection in single RGB images using a context preserver convolutional neural network trained by multiple adversarial examples. IEEE Trans. Image Process. **28**(8), 4117–4129 (2019)
21. Mostafa, Y., Abdelhafiz, A.: Accurate shadow detection from high-resolution satellite images. IEEE Geosci. Remote Sens. Lett. **14**(4), 494–498 (2017)
22. Nguyen, V., Vicente, Y., Tomas, F., Zhao, M., Hoai, M., Samaras, D.: Shadow detection with conditional generative adversarial networks. In: Proceedings of the IEEE International Conference on Computer Vision, pp. 4510–4518 (2017)
23. Panagopoulos, A., Wang, C., Samaras, D., Paragios, N.: Illumination estimation and cast shadow detection through a higher-order graphical model. In: Conference on Computer Vision and Pattern Recognition (CVPR), pp. 673–680 (2011)
24. Peng, C., Zhang, X., Yu, G., Luo, G., Sun, J.: Large kernel matters-improve semantic segmentation by global convolutional network. In: Proceedings of the IEEE Conference on Computer Vision and Pattern Recognition, pp. 4353–4361 (2017)
25. Pohlen, T., Hermans, A., Mathias, M., Leibe, B.: Full-resolution residual networks for semantic segmentation in street scenes. In: 2017 IEEE Conference on Computer Vision and Pattern Recognition (CVPR), pp. 3309–3318, July 2017
26. Ronneberger, O., Fischer, P., Brox, T.: U-Net: Convolutional Networks for Biomedical Image Segmentation. In: Navab, N., Hornegger, J., Wells, W., Frangi, A. (eds.) Medical Image Computing and Computer-Assisted Intervention – MICCAI 2015. MICCAI 2015. LNCS, vol. 9351, pp. 234–241. Springer, Cham (2015). https://doi.org/10.1007/978-3-319-24574-4_28
27. Sandler, M., Howard, A., Zhu, M., Zhmoginov, A., Chen, L.: Mobilenetv 2: inverted residuals and linear bottlenecks. In: 2018 IEEE/CVF Conference on Computer Vision and Pattern Recognition, pp. 4510–4520 (2018)
28. Shen, L., Chua, T., Leman, K.: Shadow optimization from structured deep edge detection. In: IEEE Conference on Computer Vision and Pattern Recognition (CVPR), pp. 2067–2074 (2015)
29. Tanner, F., Colder, B., Pullen, C., Heagy, D., Oertel, C., Sallee, P.: Overhead imagery research data set (OIRDS) - an annotated data library and tools to aid in the development of computer vision algorithms (2009)
30. Tian, J., Qi, X., Qu, L., Tang, Y.: New spectrum ratio properties and features for shadow detection. Pattern Recognit. **51**, 85–96 (2016)
31. Ufuktepe, D.K., Collins, J., Ufuktepe, E., Fraser, J., Krock, T., Palaniappan, K.: Learning-based shadow detection in aerial imagery using automatic training supervision from 3d point clouds. In: 2021 IEEE/CVF International Conference on Computer Vision Workshops (ICCVW), pp. 3919–3928 (2021)
32. Valada, A., Vertens, J., Dhall, A., Burgard, W.: Adapnet: adaptive semantic segmentation in adverse environmental conditions. In: 2017 IEEE International Conference on Robotics and Automation (ICRA), pp. 4644–4651, May 2017

33. Vicente, T., Hoai, M., Samaras, D.: Leave-one-out kernel optimization for shadow detection. In: Proceedings of the IEEE International Conference on Computer Vision, pp. 3388–3396 (2015)

34. Vicente, T., Hou, L., Yu, C.P., Hoai, M., Samaras, D.: Large-scale training of shadow detectors with noisily-annotated shadow examples. In: Leibe, B., Matas, J., Sebe, N., Welling, M. (eds.) Computer Vision – ECCV 2016. ECCV 2016. LNCS, vol. 9910. Springer, Cham (2016). https://doi.org/10.1007/978-3-319-46466-4_49

35. Wang, J., Li, X., Yang, J.: Stacked conditional generative adversarial networks for jointly learning shadow detection and shadow removal. In: Proceedings of the IEEE Conference on Computer Vision and Pattern Recognition, pp. 1788–1797 (2018)

36. Wang, T., Hu, X., Wang, Q., Heng, P.A., Fu, C.W.: Instance shadow detection. In: Proceedings of the IEEE/CVF Conference on Computer Vision and Pattern Recognition (CVPR), June 2020

37. Wang, W., et al.: Internimage: exploring large-scale vision foundation models with deformable convolutions. In: Proceedings of the IEEE/CVF Conference on Computer Vision and Pattern Recognition, pp. 14408–14419 (2023)

38. Yang, M., Yu, K., Zhang, C., Li, Z., Deepmotion, K.Y.: DenseASPP for semantic segmentation in street scenes. In: CVPR, pp. 3684–3692. Salt Lake City (2018)

39. Yu, C., Wang, J., Peng, C., Gao, C., Yu, G., Sang, N.: Bisenet: bilateral segmentation network for real-time semantic segmentation. In: Proceedings of the European Conference on Computer Vision (ECCV). pp. 325–341, September 2018

40. Yücel, M.K., Dimaridou, V., Manganelli, B., Ozay, M., Drosou, A., Saa-Garriga, A.: LRA&LDRA: rethinking residual predictions for efficient shadow detection and removal. In: Proceedings of the IEEE/CVF Winter Conference on Applications of Computer Vision, pp. 4925–4935 (2023)

41. Zhang, H., Dana, K., Shi, J., Zhang, Z., Wang, X., Tyagi, A., Agrawal, A.: Context encoding for semantic segmentation. In: The IEEE Conference on Computer Vision and Pattern Recognition (CVPR), June 2018

42. Zhao, H., Shi, J., Qi, X., Wang, X., Jia, J.: Pyramid scene parsing network. In: CVPR. Honolulu (2017)

43. Zhou, B., Zhao, H., Puig, X., Fidler, S., Barriuso, A., Torralba, A.: Scene parsing through ade20k dataset. In: IEEE Conference on Computer Vision and Pattern Recognition (CVPR), pp. 5122–5130 (2017)

44. Zhu, J., Samuel, K.G., Masood, S.Z., Tappen, M.F.: Learning to recognize shadows in monochromatic natural images. In: 2010 IEEE Computer Society Conference on Computer Vision and Pattern Recognition, pp. 223–230. IEEE (2010)

45. Zhu, L., et al.: Bidirectional feature pyramid network with recurrent attention residual modules for shadow detection. In: Proceedings of the European Conference on Computer Vision (ECCV), pp. 121–136 (2018)

46. Zhu, L., Xu, K., Ke, Z., Lau, R.W.: Mitigating intensity bias in shadow detection via feature decomposition and reweighting. In: Proceedings of the IEEE/CVF International Conference on Computer Vision, pp. 4702–4711 (2021)

UGainS: Uncertainty Guided Anomaly Instance Segmentation

Alexey Nekrasov[1]([⊠]) [ID], Alexander Hermans[1] [ID], Lars Kuhnert[2] [ID],
and Bastian Leibe[1] [ID]

[1] Visual Computing Institute, RWTH Aachen University, Aachen, Germany
nekrasov@vision.rwth-aachen.de
[2] Ford Motor Company, Dearborn, MI, USA

Abstract. A single unexpected object on the road can cause an accident or
may lead to injuries. To prevent this, we need a reliable mechanism for finding anomalous objects on the road. This task, called anomaly segmentation, can
be a stepping stone to safe and reliable autonomous driving. Current approaches
tackle anomaly segmentation by assigning an anomaly score to each pixel and
by grouping anomalous regions using simple heuristics. However, pixel grouping is a limiting factor when it comes to evaluating the segmentation performance of individual anomalous objects. To address the issue of grouping multiple anomaly instances into one, we propose an approach that produces accurate
anomaly instance masks. Our approach centers on an out-of-distribution segmentation model for identifying uncertain regions and a strong generalist segmentation model for anomaly instances segmentation. We investigate ways to use
uncertain regions to guide such a segmentation model to perform segmentation
of anomalous instances. By incorporating strong object priors from a generalist
model we additionally improve the per-pixel anomaly segmentation performance.
Our approach outperforms current pixel-level anomaly segmentation methods,
achieving an AP of 80.08% and 88.98% on the Fishyscapes Lost and Found and
the RoadAnomaly validation sets respectively. Project page: https://vision.rwth-
aachen.de/ugains.

Keywords: Out-of-Distribution Detection · Anomaly Segmentation · Semantic
Segmentation · Instance Segmentation

1 Introduction

Current semantic segmentation approaches [7,8,51] achieve impressive performance
for known classes on driving datasets. However, in the context of autonomous driving, the real world is more complex than the test scenarios captured in today's benchmarks [47]. In particular, a wide variety of objects, *e.g.* wild animals or debris on
the road, can pose a threat to vehicles or passengers when encountered on the road.
Since individual objects may occur very rarely, learning to reliably detect such potentially dangerous objects in the long tail of the data distribution is a major challenge.
Even datasets with millions of images may only contain few frames with anomalous

U. Köthe and C. Rother (Eds.): DAGM GCPR 2023, LNCS 14264, pp. 50–66, 2024.
https://doi.org/10.1007/978-3-031-54605-1_4

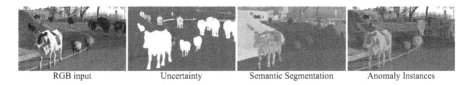

| RGB input | Uncertainty | Semantic Segmentation | Anomaly Instances |

Fig. 1. Instance prediction of anomalous objects. We propose UGainS, an approach for instance segmentation of anomalous objects. UGainS combines a strong generalist segmentation model (SAM [26]), and a strong out-of-distribution method (RbA [39]). This allows us to predict an anomaly instance segmentation, refined uncertainty maps as well as an in-distribution semantic segmentation.

objects [29]. Since modern roads are built according to well-defined rules, it creates a model bias towards regular road context. To make matters worse, deep networks tend to make overconfident predictions and often fail on out-of-distribution cases [16,25]. Together, rare occurrences of anomalous instances and model overconfidence, creates a need to address the problem of detecting anomalous road objects.

Most anomaly segmentation approaches focus on predicting a per-pixel outlier score to create an uncertainty map of the visible scene. Available approaches in this category are based on classification uncertainty [18,19,27], reconstruction errors [34,50], or they rely on data augmentation with synthetic outliers to regularize models [2,6,15].

In this paper, we propose an approach that addresses the anomaly instance segmentation problem. Our approach uses uncertainty maps to detect image structures that are not well captured by the given training data [39]. However, we then use the extracted outlier pixels as point guidance for a class-agnostic segmentation pipeline [26] to segment anomalous instances. The resulting out-of-distribution instance segmentations (see Fig. 1) can then be used for mining rare objects [23], which could be added to the training set to improve future model performance. When using such a point-guidance scheme, the key challenge is to decide how to sample and prioritize the guidance points in order to achieve a good coverage of the relevant anomalous regions with as few proposals as possible. We systematically explore this design space and present a detailed experimental evaluation of the different design choices.

Current anomaly segmentation benchmarks evaluate methods based on per-pixel or component-level metrics [5]. Per-pixel metrics make it possible to evaluate performance under large class imbalance, but they favor large objects. Component-level metrics are a proxy for object-level segmentation and evaluate the intersection between predicted and ground truth anomaly regions. To generate object instances, benchmarks often use the connected components algorithm in the metric formulation, which is a proxy for instance-level performance [5]. However, current benchmarks do not provide a clear way to evaluate instance prediction performance within anomaly regions and focus on finding the entire region. We argue that finding individual instances within large anomalous regions can be beneficial for downstream tasks such as object mining [29], tracking [35], or model introspection. Therefore we propose an anomaly instance segmentation evaluation measure (*instance AP* or *iAP*) and present experimental results using this measure, in addition to also evaluating on the standard per-pixel measures.

Our proposed approach achieves state-of-the-art per-pixel performance on the Road-Anomaly and Fishyscapes Lost and Found benchmark datasets. In addition, we demonstrate the utility of the extracted anomaly instances by visualizing cases where previous methods would not be able to recover separate anomalies.

Our Contributions are summarized as follows: 1) We propose UGainS, a novel approach for predicting anomalous object instances based on point-guided segmentation with points sampled from an epistemic uncertainty map. 2) We evaluate the design choices of performing uncertainty guidance for a generalist segmentation model and provide detailed ablations to highlight the influence of the different steps of our approach. 3) UGainS achieves state-of-the-art anomaly segmentation performance on the Fishyscapes Lost and Found [3] validation set with 80.08% pixel-level average precision, and on the RoadAnomaly [34] dataset with 88.98% pixel-level average precision. Notably, UGainS improves per-pixel performance compared with previous anomaly segmentation methods, while at the same time extracting interpretable instance segmentation masks.

2   Related Work

2.1   Pixel-Wise Anomaly Segmentation

The anomaly segmentation task has attracted attention in recent years, and is derived from the out-of-distribution classification task. Early approaches used probabilistic modeling directly to obtain outlier scores and did not require any special training procedures. These methods assume that anomalies should have high uncertainty values. Methods have approximated the epistemic uncertainty of predictions using deep ensembles [27], Monte-Carlo dropout [38], or directly using SoftMax probabilities [18]. Liang *et al.* [30] recently proposed to use Gaussian Mixture Models in a segmentation model to capture class conditional densities. In another line of work, methods focus on directly improving the predicted outlier scores [6,24].

Previous studies have relied on embedding space estimation [3,28] or direct classification of anomalous regions [3]. Reconstruction-based methods rely on re-synthesis of input images [10,33,34,40,50] and the assumption that anomalies cannot be reconstructed well. Other approaches train or fine-tune on images with artificial anomalies [2,5,14,15,18]. Following early methods derived from classification [31], recent methods focus on using adversarial examples on an unmodified in-distribution model [1,28]. While the majority of previous approaches use per-pixel prediction models [7], the most recent approach, Rejected by All (RbA), focuses on acquiring anomaly scores from a set of predicted mask-class pairs [39]. It assumes that pixels which are not covered by any masks correspond to anomalous objects. We follow this line of work and extend it to instance segmentation.

2.2   Anomaly Instance Segmentation

While the majority of anomaly segmentation approaches focus on a per-pixel anomaly classification, and thus ignore any instance information, several recent methods have attempted to address anomaly instance segmentation. MergeNet [17] uses two networks to predict anomalous regions. LiDAR-guided small object segmentation focuses on retrieving small objects [44]. Xue *et al.* [53] uses occlusion edges to represent anomalous instances and a sliding window approach to generate object proposals. These method use low-level heuristics, based on connected components or over-segmentation, to retrieve anomalous instances. The SegmentMeIfYouCan [5] benchmark suggests using component-level metrics to evaluate object segmentation performance, grouping anomalous pixels with connected components and evaluating component-level intersection over union. However, grouping multiple spatially close objects may hinder downstream tasks such as tracking, data collection, or model introspection. Treating multiple connected instances as a single object may furthermore be limiting for future advances in anomaly instance segmentation.

A few works tackle the problem of finding anomalous instances without such heuristics. OSIS [48] is an open-set instance segmentation work on 3D point clouds (which was adapted to images by Gasperini *et al.* [13]). It learns class-agnostic spatial instance embeddings that are clustered to predict an object. A more recent work, EOPSN [20], relies on existing unknown instances in the unannotated regions during training, which is a limiting factor for autonomous driving setups as training set are often close to densely annotated. The concurrent Holistic Segmentation U3HS approach [13] also uses uncertainty scores to obtain anomaly instance segmentations, however U3HS uses explicit clustering of learned instance features. In contrast, we use an uncertainty guided point sampling scheme with a generalist instance segmentation model to provide anomaly instance segmentation, which achieves a stronger instance segmentation performance in practice.

2.3   Promptable Segmentation Models

Recent advances in large-scale text-guided training for classification [22,42] are sparking interest in large-scale open-vocabulary and open-world segmentation [11,43,52]. XDecoder [55] addresses multiple segmentation tasks by combining the Mask2Former decoder [8] with text supervision. A recent extension, SEEM [56], extends the work to open-set segmentation using multiple prompt types. Our method uses the recent Segment Anything Model (SAM) [26]. Kirillov *et al.* propose the large-scale segmentation dataset SA-1B with class-agnostic mask annotations and SAM for interactive segmentation. SAM accepts prompts of different types, such as points, masks, boxes, or text. Several other works extend SAM to medical image segmentation [37,49], image inpainting [54], camouflaged object detection [45], industrial anomaly segmentation [4], and other applications [21]. The base SAM model is limited to prompted prediction and lacks query interaction for separate objects. As such it is difficult to use for general instance segmentation with a fixed set of classes. By first predicting general outlier regions, we can sample points and utilize SAM for anomaly instance segmentation though.

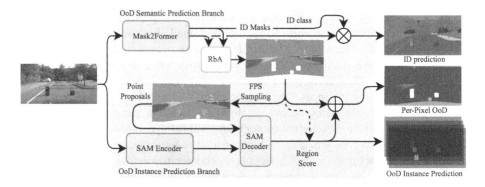

Fig. 2. Method Overview. UGainS consists of two main blocks: an OoD Semantic Prediction Branch (☐) and OoD Instance Prediction Branch (☐). We use the Mask2Former model [8] to get class and mask predictions for in-distribution (ID) classes. From these predictions we compute a per-pixel uncertainty map using RbA [39] . Using farthest point sampling (FPS) on the uncertainty map we generate point proposals for anomalous objects. These point proposals are then used as input for the Segment Anything Model (SAM) [26] to get anomaly instance predictions. The final prediction is an in-distribution semantic segmentation, instance-refined per-pixel anomaly scores, and a set of out-of-distribution anomaly instance masks. (Color figure online)

3   Method

UGainS combines a strong in-distribution segmentation model with a strong generalist segmentation model (see Fig. 2). At the core of our method is a Mask2Former [8] regularized to avoid predicting objects in unknown regions [39], and the Segment Anything Model (SAM) [26]. The semantic branch predicts masks for known semantic classes, such as cars or pedestrians, and avoids prediction in regions occupied by out-of-distribution objects. Based on the Reject by All (RbA) score definition [39] these unknown regions will have higher uncertainty values. We obtain point proposals for the out-of-distribution branch by sampling points in these regions. For each sampled point, the Segment Anything Model generates an instance mask. We average the anomaly scores under the mask regions to obtain the final prediction. To this end, we propose to tackle the problem of anomaly segmentation as segmenting *everything* we know and prompting to segment *everywhere* where we do not know. In this section, we provide a detailed description of each component of our approach.

OoD Semantic Prediction Branch. With the out-of-distribution (OoD) semantic prediction branch we predict in-distribution (ID) semantic segmentation and OoD per-pixel scores (see Fig. 2, ☐). Here we use the RbA adaptation of the Mask2Former model. The Mask2Former model consists of a backbone with a pixel decoder and a transformer decoder. For an image x, the Swin-B [36] backbone produces latent features at a coarse scale, and in combination with the pixel decoder, produces an L-layer feature pyramid $\{f_i(x)\}_{i=1}^{L}$. The transformer decoder processes these multi-resolution C-dimensional features together with the N learned object queries $\mathbf{Q}_0 \in \mathbb{R}^{N \times C}$. The object queries are sequentially updated by cross-attending the multi-resolution features in a round-robin fashion. The final set of object queries $\mathbf{Q}_i$ is then multiplied with the high-resolution feature map $f_L(\mathbf{x})$, generating $\mathcal{M} \in \mathbb{R}^{N \times H \times W}$ binary masks for an image of the size $H \times W$. In addition, class probabilities $\mathcal{L} \in \mathbb{R}^{N \times (K+1)}$ are predicted from queries, where $(K+1)$ are closed-set classes with an additional class to signal a query deactivation. During training we use the RbA approach, which regularizes Mask2Former to predict no in-distribution class or mask in an anomalous region. RbA uses a per-pixel negative sum of mask predictions to score anomalous regions, where every pixel in a mask is assigned a sum of predicted class posterior probabilities:

$$U(\mathbf{x}) = -\sum_{k=1}^{K} \sum_{n=1}^{N} \mathcal{L}_{k,n}(\mathbf{x}) \cdot \mathcal{M}_{k,n}(\mathbf{x}).$$

This results in per-pixel RbA scores $U(\mathbf{x}) \in [-N, 0]^{H \times W}$, where a low score indicates that a pixel is contained in one or multiple predicted masks for in-distribution classes. A high score indicates that the pixel belongs to no masks or all masks have a very low confidence for the pixel. We use the RbA method because it predicts low anomaly scores on semantic boundaries, *i.e.*, road-to-sidewalk boundaries (Fig. 1), and since it generally has a strong anomaly segmentation performance. However, in principle we could use any model that predicts a per-pixel anomaly score. For a detailed overview of Mask2Former and RbA we refer the interested reader to the respective papers [8, 39].

OoD Instance Prediction Branch. To get instance predictions we use an instance prediction branch that is based on semantic outlier scores (see Fig. 2, □). A naive approach to obtain instances would be to apply the connected components algorithm on a binary mask from outlier scores. However, as discussed earlier, this approach does not work when objects have an overlap or an intersection with known classes (see Fig. 3). We address this problem with a novel approach using a segmentation model promptable with point proposals. To convert the per-pixel anomaly predictions into instances, we prompt SAM to predict instance masks for a set of sampled anomalous points. However, there is no obvious way to create a prompt from a noisy and partially incorrect anomaly mask. While we could use all anomaly points as prompts, this would result in increased computational complexity and diminishing results (see Sect. 4.2). We therefore resort to farthest point sampling (FPS) which we run on the 2D coordinates of the thresholded anomaly points. (Ablations on hyperparameters and other sampling strategies can be found in Sect. 4.2.)

We then prompt SAM with the resulting anomaly point proposals to predict instance masks. SAM consists of an image encoder, a prompt encoder, and a lightweight mask decoder. The image encoder is a plain ViT-H [12] which extracts latent dense image features. During the prompting, we obtain a prompt embedding for each sampled coordinate, comprised of a positional and learned embedding. Finally, the lightweight mask decoder from SAM processes image features together with prompt embeddings to predict object masks. The mask decoder maps each prompt to a hierarchy of three masks with foreground probabilities. Based on the predicted foreground probability, the best of the three masks is selected to remove the ambiguity. To provide each mask with anomaly scores, we use an average of the uncertainty values in the mask region. After obtaining individual scores, we remove duplicate masks using non-maximum suppression (NMS).

Since we obtain high-quality object masks, we further combine them with the initial per-pixel anomaly predictions. Similar to the computation of the per-pixel anomaly scores in the semantic branch, we obtain the anomaly scores as a sum of individual scores. We add these new instance-based anomaly scores to the existing RbA scores to produce new per-pixel scores, which can be seen as a form of RbA ensembling. Effectively, we improve the per-pixel scores by using strong object priors from the instance predictions. In summary, UGainS predicts an in-distribution semantic predictions, a set of out-of-distribution anomaly instance masks, and an improved per-pixel anomaly score.

4   Experiments

Datasets. We use the Cityscapes dataset [9] for in-distribution training. We use 2975 training and 500 validation images with 19 labeled classes with instance and semantic labels.

To validate the quality of anomaly predictions we use the Fishyscapes Lost and Found (FS L&F) [3] and RoadAnomaly [34] datasets. Fishyscapes L&F [3] is a filtered and re-annotated version of the Lost and Found dataset [41]. The original Lost and Found dataset (L&F) was created by placing anomalous objects on the road in front of a vehicle. Lost and Found contains both semantic and instance annotations for anomalous objects, as well as a *road* annotation; it labels the rest as *ignore*. However, it contains noisy annotations, *e.g.* labeling bicycles and children as anomalies [3]. Thus, the FS L&F dataset has become a standard benchmark in the anomaly segmentation community. Fishyscapes L&F contains 100 images in the validation set and 275 images in the test set. However, the FS L&F dataset does not originally contain instance labels. To evaluate instance segmentation performance, we re-label objects in the validation set by applying connected components on semantic annotations. This works for FS L&F, since objects in the dataset are far apart. For comparability with pixel-level evaluation, we only use the newly generated instance for the instance-level evaluation.

The RoadAnomaly [34] dataset is an earlier version of the RoadAnomaly21 dataset, which is part of the SegementMeIfYouCan [5] benchmark. SegmentMeIfYouCan does not provide annotations for instance masks in the validation set. The RoadAnomaly dataset contains 60 images with semantic labels and partial instance annotations, as such we only evaluate pixel-level metrics on this dataset.

Dataset-Specific Adjustments. The RbA method has strong responses for the car hood and rectification artifacts at the image boundaries, since these areas are not labeled in the Cityscapes dataset. We create a dataset-specific ignore mask and do not sample points from the masked regions. While this is a heuristics, we argue such an ignore masks can easily be constructed during a calibration process and does not harm the generality of our method. Furthermore, common evaluation protocols exclude predictions from ignore regions, so we do not gain an unfair advantage over other methods.

Evaluation Metrics. To evaluate the out-of-distribution performance we use the standard community metrics *average precision* (AP) and *false positive rate at* 95% *true positive rate* (FPR_{95}). To distinguish these pixel-level metrics from our later instance-level metrics, we prepend a p: pAP and pFPR_{95}. Evaluating anomalous instances on

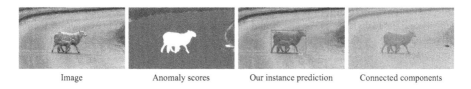

| Image | Anomaly scores | Our instance prediction | Connected components |

Fig. 3. Groups of anomalous pixels as instances. Current evaluation of methods do not distinguish object groups and individual objects to evaluate the quality of object retrieval. We argue that for purposes such as tracking, data mining, or model introspection, it is important to recover individual instances rather than groups of objects. Methods or metrics that rely on connected components are therefore not well suited for instance segmentation in practice.

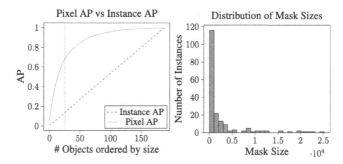

Fig. 4. Pixel-level vs Instance-level AP. The commonly used pixel-level AP metric favors large objects. We sort the 188 instances in Fishyscapes L&F in descending order of size and compute both pixel-level and instance-level metrics. By correctly predicting only 25 objects, we can achieve a pAP of 69.03%, while only getting an iAP of 13.82%. Since the majority of the objects in the dataset are small (as seen on the right), it is important to use a metric that does not favor large objects near to the ego-vehicle.

the other hand is not trivial. One approach is to use a component-level metric, such as the sIoU [5] evaluation protocol. In the sIoU formulation, the connected components method creates instances from predicted uncertainty maps and then scores them using the intersection-over-union metric. However, it does not penalize grouping of objects or prediction that overlaps with an *ignore* region. We argue that it is still important to segment individual instances for downstream tasks, such as data mining or model introspection. If an anomalous object appears in front of another anomalous region, the computation of component-level metrics will ignore grouping (see Fig. 3). For example, in the Cityscapes dataset tunnels or bridges are labeled as a *void* class, resulting in high anomaly scores. Therefore, to evaluate unknown instance segmentation we use the common AP and AP50 from the Cityscapes evaluation protocol, here refered to as iAP and iAP50. We argue that the instance-level AP metric is a harder metric since objects of all sizes are treated the same, while the pixel-level AP is dominated by large objects. This is visually demonstrated in Fig. 4. Unlike the default Cityscapes evaluation, we evaluate any instances larger than 10 pixels, using all objects in the Fishyscapes L&F dataset for evaluation.

Table 1. Comparison to State-of-the-Art. We report pixel-level scores for UGainS on the Road Anomaly and the Fishyscapes Lost and Found datasets. As can be seen, we obtain state-of-the-art performances, both with and without additional OoD training data. (*: RbA scores based on our re-implementation.)

Method	OoD Data	Extra Network	Road Anomaly		FS L&F	
			pAP↑	FPR₉₅↓	pAP↑	FPR₉₅↓
MSP [18]	✗	✗	20.59	68.44	6.02	45.63
Mahalanobis [28]	✗	✗	22.85	59.20	27.83	30.17
SML [24]	✗	✗	25.82	49.74	36.55	14.53
GMMSeg [30]	✗	✗	57.65	44.34	50.03	12.55
SynthCP [50]	✗	✓	24.86	64.69	6.54	45.95
RbA [39]	✗	✗	<u>78.45</u>	<u>11.83</u>	<u>60.96</u>	<u>10.63</u>
RbA*	✗	✗	74.78	17.83	59.51	11.34
UGainS (Ours)	✗	✓	**81.32**	**11.59**	**70.90**	**10.38**
SynBoost [10]	✓	✓	38.21	64.75	60.58	31.02
Maximized Entropy [6]	✓	✗	–	–	41.31	37.69
PEBAL [46]	✓	✗	44.41	37.98	64.43	6.56
DenseHybrid [15]	✓	✗	–	–	63.8	**6.1**
RbA [39]	✓	✗	85.42	**6.92**	70.81	<u>6.30</u>
RbA*	✓	✗	87.12	12.06	<u>75.61</u>	7.46
UGainS (Ours)	✓	✓	**88.98**	<u>10.42</u>	**80.08**	6.61

Models and Training. We follow the setup by Nayal *et al.* [39] for training and fine-tuning the Mask2Former. Initially, we train the model on the Cityscapes dataset. Then, we fine-tune the model for 5000 iterations on Cityscapes images with pasted COCO [32] objects as simulated anomalies. Differently to RbA, we fine-tune the full transformer decoder and use the entire COCO [32] dataset. We do not fine-tune or alter the SAM model.

4.1 Results

Comparison to State-of-the-Art. To validate the overall performance of our approach, we first compare it on a pixel-level to existing anomaly segmentation methods. We report performance on the FS L&F and RoadAnomaly datasets according to the common protocol, evaluating both a model without fine-tuning, as well as a fine-tuned version. These are shown above and below the dashed line in Table 1, respectively. On both the RoadAnomaly and Fishyscapes Lost and Found datasets we outperform other approaches in the pixel-level average precision (pAP) metric, with and without the use of additional training data. We attribute this performance to strong object priors from our OoD instance prediction branch.

Table 2. Upper and lower bound comparison. We show how our method compares to two important baselines, sampling points in an oracle way from the ground truth and simply using dense grid sampling as proposed by SAM. As expected we cannot match the oracle sampling, however, we do outperform the simple dense sampling strategy significantly.

Method	N samples	GT Data	Fishyscapes L&F			
			pAP↑	FPR$_{95}$↓	iAP↑	iAP50↑
Center Sampling (Oracle)	1 per object	✓	8.39	100.0	49.94	77.56
+ RbA [39] scoring	1 per object	✓	70.46	48.55	36.18	60.60
FPS Sampling + RbA Scoring	50 points	✗	63.70	99.91	6.12	9.20
+ NMS	50 points	✗	73.32	99.54	29.75	48.35
+ RbA ensemble	50 points	✗	80.08	6.61		
SAM [26] dense + RbA scoring	1024 points	✗	73.85	5.15	17.02	24.60

Lower and Upper Performance Bounds of UGainS. Since no other method has been properly evaluated for anomaly instance segmentation on the FS L&F or RoadAnomaly datasets using a standard average precision metric, we unfortunately cannot compare our method to other works, but we can create two baselines using the strong SAM model. For the first baseline, we can obtain instance predictions using the perfect sampling to define an upper boundary. For the second, we can get instance predictions from SAM based on the simple dense grid sampling approach to get instance masks. These two baselines can be seen as an upper and lower bound on the performance of our approach.

The upper part of Table 2 shows the upper-bound performance when we use ground-truth annotations to sample a single point per anomaly object. Note that such an oracle setting can only be considered for finding theoretical bounds and should not be considered as an actual performance of our approach. While this setting achieves a strong instance AP of nearly 50%, the pAP score is low. To address this, instead of using the IoU scores predicted by SAM, we use the average of the underlying RbA scores. This significantly improves the pixel AP, but also reduces the instance-level AP (iAP) by assigning a lower score to anomalies that were not well captured by RbA.

The other end of the spectrum would be to use SAM with the default automatic mask generation module, which samples 32×32 points in a dense grid and predicts three mask for each point, followed by a series of post-processing steps [26]. Since this sampling approach generates masks for the majority of objects, masks require anomaly scoring. Similar to the upper-bound baseline, we assign the average uncertainty score of the pixels inside a mask, since SAM does not provide any type of anomaly score out of the box. While, such an approach can be used in practice, it achieves a significantly lower iAP compared to our approach, indicating that sampling proposal points for the mask prediction in an informed way is beneficial (see Table 2). In addition, while low scores of dense sampling could be addressed by sampling a denser grid, the computational complexity increases quadratically.

To compare our approach, we look at the individual steps and indicate how they compare to the two upper and lower bounds. In the simplest case, where we sample only 50 points from the RbA pixel-level predictions, we cannot match the dense predictions

| Image | RbA scores | Instance segmentation | Updated scores |

Fig. 5. Qualitative results on Fishyscapes L&F. The third column shows the instance segmentations generated using RbA predictions in the second column. Note the prominent anomalous objects in the refined per-pixel anomaly predictions in the fourth column.

Fig. 6. Qualitative results on CODA. Our model also performs well even under a larger domain shift. We are able to segment the typical unknown dangerous objects on the road, but it also reveals other instances for which the model has no proper semantic knowledge, *e.g.* bridges.

of SAM. However, since we typically sample multiple points from the same object, a significant improvement can be gained with a simple non-maximum suppression step, which is also applied to dense point sampling. At this point, we can obtain an iAP that is significantly better than dense sampling, although there is still a gap to the oracle performance that could be attributed to incorrect sampling. As a final step, we ensemble the average uncertainty scores under each anomaly mask with the initial RbA scores, significantly increasing the final pixel-level AP of our approach, while also being able to predict meaningful instance segmentation of the anomalous objects in the scene.

Qualitative Results. We show qualitative results of our approach on the Fishyscapes L&F dataset in Fig. 5. It can be seen how our approach segments instances from the pixel-level anomaly score predictions. In addition, UGainS can further refine the initial pixel-level predictions using instance predictions. In Fig. 6 we show additional qualitative results on the more challenging CODA dataset [29]. Here we show that our method can capture interesting objects that are not well-covered in the training set. This ability is valuable for model introspection, providing insight into instances that the model may struggle with.

4.2   Ablations

In this section, we ablate some of our design choices. We focus on how pixel-level performance, the proposal sampling method, and the number of sampled points affect instance-level performance.

Table 3. UGainS improvements of several anomaly segmentation methods. Our method notably improves pixel-level AP results of several methods in addition to providing anomaly instance segmentations.

Method	UGainS	Fishyscapes L&F			
		pAP↑	FPR$_{95}$↓	iAP↑	iAP50↑
Max Softmax [18]	✗	4.58	40.59	–	–
	✓	10.31 ⟩+5.73	46.43	5.61	9.11
Mahalanobis [28]	✗	28.75	9.52	–	–
	✓	30.26 ⟩+1.51	13.27	2.69	4.18
Maximzed Entropy [6]	✗	41.31	37.67	–	–
	✓	47.98 ⟩+6.67	37.86	12.16	18.72
DenseHybrid [15]	✗	69.78	5.08	–	–
	✓	71.19 ⟩+1.41	5.77	27.49	44.07
RbA[39]	✗	75.61	7.46	–	–
	✓	80.08 ⟩+4.47	6.61	29.75	48.35

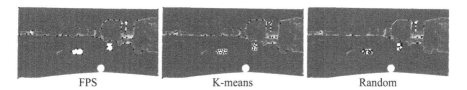

FPS   K-means   Random

Fig. 7. Visual comparison of different anomaly point sampling methods. Bright areas correspond to high RbA scores and black dots represent the sampled points. K-means estimates points mostly in the center of uncertain regions, while FPS generates most points at the boundary. Random sampling randomly selects points from the high uncertainty regions and thus often misses smaller objects.

Evaluation of Other Per-Pixel Methods. Although we get the best performance with the RbA approach, we want to note that we can get instance segmentation and per-pixel score improvements for other anomaly segmentation methods as well. Table 3 shows the performance differences and anomaly instance segmentation performance of our approach for several other per-pixel anomaly segmentation methods. In all cases, we can improve the per-pixel AP by quite a large margin, and we observe that higher pixel-level AP generally leads to higher instance-level AP. Since none of the other approaches achieve a similar or higher resulting instance-level AP, this indicates that all tested methods still have problems with small/far objects.

Sampling Methods. In Table 4, we evaluate farthest point sampling (FPS), K-means, and random sampling from uncertainty regions. We observe that K-means predicts

Table 4. Performance impact of the proposal sampling methods. On the left we report the typical metrics, whereas on the right we additionally report metrics of the sampled points, *i.e.* how many points fall on an anomalous object (precision) and how many anomalous objects are sampled at least once (recall). FPS and K-means performs roughly on par, while random sampling performs worse due to a lower recall on the point level.

Sampling method	Full Metrics				Point Level	
	pAP↑	FPR$_{95}$↓	iAP↑	iAP50↑	Precision	Recall
Random Sampling	79.81	5.97	25.82	40.45	57.22	60.11
K-means	79.92	6.60	29.04	46.23	47.51	70.74
FPS	80.08	6.61	29.75	48.35	35.30	71.81

Table 5. Performance impact of the number of sampled points. Considering there are often a few larger anomalous instances per frame, we see a diminishing return after sampling more than 50 points. While the recall of smaller instances might go up, we are also bound to segment false positive instances, thus reducing the precision.

# Points	pAP↑	FPR$_{95}$↓	iAP↑	iAP50↑
10	76.73	**5.89**	26.81	41.33
20	78.83	5.90	**30.82**	**49.14**
50	**80.08**	6.61	29.75	48.35
100	78.96	7.01	27.16	45.39
200	78.99	7.09	25.77	43.82
300	78.55	7.16	24.44	41.98

points closer to the centroids of the objects (see Fig. 7). In contrast, FPS generates proposals at boundaries and achieves higher recall. Due to the maximum recall achieved with the same number of points, we chose farthest point sampling as the best option. We also evaluate random sampling, but samples favor larger objects, resulting in a higher point-level precision, but a significantly lower recall compared to FPS and K-means.

Number of Samples. In Table 5 we evaluate the impact of the number of sampled point proposal used to generating instance masks. Since the FS L&F dataset typically contains several instances per scene, we observe diminishing returns as the number of samples increases. With increased number of samples, most of the predicted masks end up getting removed by non-maximum suppression, and the approach tends to predict multiple small boundary regions increasing the number of false positives.

5   Conclusion

We have proposed a novel approach for uncertainty-guided segmentation of anomalous instances. By combining anomaly object scores with initial per-pixel anomaly scores our approach shows consistent improvement on the task of anomaly segmentation. We show that UGainS achieves state-of-the-art average precision performance for pixel-level predictions on the Fishyscapes L&F and RoadAnomaly datasets. While anomaly segmentation on existing datasets seems to slowly saturate, we find that the more challenging task of anomaly instance segmentation is far from this point. Our method provides anomaly instance masks that can be used for model introspection and collection of rare instances and results can further be improved both through better anomaly point proposals and better instance segmentation.

Acknowledgements. This project was partially funded by the Ford University Alliance Program (project FA0347). Compute resources were granted by RWTH Aachen under project 'supp0003'. We thank Ali Athar, George Lydakis, Idil Esen Zulfikar, Fabian Rempfer and the reviewers for helpful feedback.

References

1. Besnier, V., Bursuc, A., Picard, D., Briot, A.: Triggering failures: out-of-distribution detection by learning from local adversarial attacks in semantic segmentation. In: International Conference on Computer Vision (ICCV) (2021)
2. Bevandić, P., Krešo, I., Oršić, M., Šegvić, S.: Simultaneous semantic segmentation and outlier detection in presence of domain shift. In: German Conference on Pattern Recognition (GCPR) (2019)
3. Blum, H., Sarlin, P.E., Nieto, J., Siegwart, R., Cadena, C.: The fishyscapes benchmark: measuring blind spots in semantic segmentation. Int. J. Comput. Vis. **129**(11), 3119–3135 (2021)
4. Cao, Y., et al.: Segment any anomaly without training via hybrid prompt regularization. arXiv preprint arXiv:2305.10724 (2023)
5. Chan, R., et al.: SegmentMeIfYouCan: a benchmark for anomaly segmentation. In: Proceedings of the Neural Information Processing Systems Track on Datasets and Benchmarks (2021)
6. Chan, R., Rottmann, M., Gottschalk, H.: Entropy maximization and meta classification for out-of-distribution detection in semantic segmentation. In: International Conference on Computer Vision (ICCV) (2021)
7. Chen, L.C., Zhu, Y., Papandreou, G., Schroff, F., Adam, H.: Encoder-decoder with atrous separable convolution for semantic image segmentation. In: Ferrari, V., Hebert, M., Sminchisescu, C., Weiss, Y. (eds.) ECCV 2018. LNCS, vol. 11211, pp. 833–851. Springer, Cham (2018). https://doi.org/10.1007/978-3-030-01234-2_49
8. Cheng, B., Misra, I., Schwing, A.G., Kirillov, A., Girdhar, R.: Masked-attention mask transformer for universal image segmentation. In: Conference on Computer Vision and Pattern Recognition (CVPR) (2022)
9. Cordts, M., et al.: The cityscapes dataset for semantic urban scene understanding. In: Conference on Computer Vision and Pattern Recognition (CVPR) (2016)
10. Di Biase, G., Blum, H., Siegwart, R., Cadena, C.: Pixel-wise anomaly detection in complex driving scenes. In: Conference on Computer Vision and Pattern Recognition (CVPR) (2021)
11. Ding, Z., Wang, J., Tu, Z.: Open-vocabulary universal image segmentation with MaskCLIP. In: International Conference on Machine Learning (ICML) (2023)
12. Dosovitskiy, A., et al.: An image is worth 16×16 words: transformers for image recognition at scale. In: International Conference on Learning Representations (ICLR) (2021)
13. Gasperini, S., Marcos-Ramiro, A., Schmidt, M., Navab, N., Busam, B., Tombari, F.: Holistic segmentation. arXiv preprint arXiv:2209.05407 (2022)

14. Grcić, M., Bevandić, P., Kalafatić, Z., Šegvić, S.: Dense anomaly detection by robust learning on synthetic negative data. arXiv preprint arXiv:2112.12833 (2021)

15. Grcić, M., Bevandić, P., Šegvić, S.: DenseHybrid: hybrid anomaly detection for dense open-set recognition. In: Avidan, S., Brostow, G., Cissé, M., Farinella, G.M., Hassner, T. (eds.) ECCV 2022. LNCS, vol. 13685, pp. 500–517. Springer, Cham (2022). https://doi.org/10.1007/978-3-031-19806-9_29

16. Guo, C., Pleiss, G., Sun, Y., Weinberger, K.Q.: On calibration of modern neural networks. In: International Conference on Machine Learning (ICML) (2017)

17. Gupta, K., Javed, S.A., Gandhi, V., Krishna, K.M.: MergeNet: a deep net architecture for small obstacle discovery. In: International Conference on Robotics and Automation (ICRA) (2018)

18. Hendrycks, D., Gimpel, K.: A baseline for detecting misclassified and out-of-distribution examples in neural networks. In: International Conference on Learning Representations (ICLR) (2018)

19. Hendrycks, D., Mazeika, M., Dietterich, T.: Deep anomaly detection with outlier exposure. In: International Conference on Learning Representations (ICLR) (2019)

20. Hwang, J., Oh, S.W., Lee, J.Y., Han, B.: Exemplar-based open-set panoptic segmentation network. In: Conference on Computer Vision and Pattern Recognition (CVPR) (2021)

21. Ji, W., Li, J., Bi, Q., Liu, T., Li, W., Cheng, L.: Segment anything is not always perfect: an investigation of sam on different real-world applications. In: Conference on Computer Vision and Pattern Recognition Workshop (CVPR'W) (2023)

22. Jia, C., et al.: Scaling up visual and vision-language representation learning with noisy text supervision. In: International Conference on Machine Learning (ICML) (2021)

23. Jiang, C.M., Najibi, M., Qi, C.R., Zhou, Y., Anguelov, D.: Improving the intra-class long-tail in 3D detection via rare example mining. In: Avidan, S., Brostow, G., Cissé, M., Farinella, G.M., Hassner, T. (eds.) ECCV 2022. LNCS, vol. 13670, pp. 158–175. Springer, Cham (2022). https://doi.org/10.1007/978-3-031-20080-9_10

24. Jung, S., Lee, J., Gwak, D., Choi, S., Choo, J.: Standardized max logits: a simple yet effective approach for identifying unexpected road obstacles in urban-scene segmentation. In: International Conference on Computer Vision (ICCV) (2021)

25. Kendall, A., Gal, Y.: What uncertainties do we need in Bayesian deep learning for computer vision? In: Neural Information Processing Systems (NIPS) (2017)

26. Kirillov, A., et al.: Segment anything. In: International Conference on Computer Vision (ICCV) (2023)

27. Lakshminarayanan, B., Pritzel, A., Blundell, C.: Simple and scalable predictive uncertainty estimation using deep ensembles. In: Neural Information Processing Systems (NIPS) (2017)

28. Lee, K., Lee, K., Lee, H., Shin, J.: A simple unified framework for detecting out-of-distribution samples and adversarial attacks. In: Neural Information Processing Systems (NIPS) (2018)

29. Li, K., et al.: CODA: a real-world road corner case dataset for object detection in autonomous driving. In: Avidan, S., Brostow, G., Cissé, M., Farinella, G.M., Hassner, T. (eds.) ECCV 2022. LNCS, vol. 13698, pp. 406–423. Springer, Cham (2022). https://doi.org/10.1007/978-3-031-19839-7_24

30. Liang, C., Wang, W., Miao, J., Yang, Y.: GMMSeg: Gaussian mixture based generative semantic segmentation models. In: Neural Information Processing Systems (NIPS) (2022)

31. Liang, S., Li, Y., Srikant, R.: Enhancing the reliability of out-of-distribution image detection in neural networks. In: International Conference on Learning Representations (ICLR) (2018)

32. Lin, T.Y., et al.: Microsoft COCO: common objects in context. In: Fleet, D., Pajdla, T., Schiele, B., Tuytelaars, T. (eds.) ECCV 2014. LNCS, vol. 8693, pp. 740–755. Springer, Cham (2014). https://doi.org/10.1007/978-3-319-10602-1_48

33. Lis, K., Honari, S., Fua, P., Salzmann, M.: Detecting road obstacles by erasing them. arXiv preprint arXiv:2012.13633 (2021)
34. Lis, K., Nakka, K., Fua, P., Salzmann, M.: Detecting the unexpected via image resynthesis. In: International Conference on Computer Vision (ICCV) (2019)
35. Liu, Y., et al.: Opening up open-world tracking. In: Conference on Computer Vision and Pattern Recognition (CVPR) (2022)
36. Liu, Z., et al.: Swin transformer: hierarchical vision transformer using shifted windows. In: Conference on Computer Vision and Pattern Recognition (CVPR) (2021)
37. Ma, J., He, Y., Li, F., Han, L., You, C., Wang, B.: Segment anything in medical images. arXiv preprint arXiv:2304.12306 (2023)
38. Mukhoti, J., Gal, Y.: Evaluating Bayesian deep learning methods for semantic segmentation. arXiv preprint arXiv:1811.12709 (2019)
39. Nayal, N., Yavuz, M., Henriques, J.F., Güney, F.: RbA: segmenting unknown regions rejected by all. In: International Conference on Computer Vision (ICCV) (2023)
40. Ohgushi, T., Horiguchi, K., Yamanaka, M.: Road obstacle detection method based on an autoencoder with semantic segmentation. In: Ishikawa, H., Liu, C.L., Pajdla, T., Shi, J. (eds.) ACCV 2020. LNCS, vol. 12627, pp. 223–238. Springer, Cham (2021). https://doi.org/10.1007/978-3-030-69544-6_14
41. Pinggera, P., Ramos, S., Gehrig, S., Franke, U., Rother, C., Mester, R.: Lost and found: detecting small road hazards for self-driving vehicles. In: International Conference on Intelligent Robots and Systems (IROS) (2016)
42. Radford, A., et al.: Learning transferable visual models from natural language supervision. In: International Conference on Machine Learning (ICML) (2021)
43. Rao, Y., et al.: DenseCLIP: language-guided dense prediction with context-aware prompting. In: Conference on Computer Vision and Pattern Recognition (CVPR) (2022)
44. Singh, A., Kamireddypalli, A., Gandhi, V., Krishna, K.M.: LiDAR guided Small obstacle Segmentation. In: International Conference on Intelligent Robots and Systems (IROS) (2020)
45. Tang, L., Xiao, H., Li, B.: Can SAM segment anything? When SAM meets camouflaged object detection. arXiv preprint arXiv:2304.04709 (2023)
46. Tian, Y., Liu, Y., Pang, G., Liu, F., Chen, Y., Carneiro, G.: Pixel-wise energy-biased abstention learning for anomaly segmentation on complex urban driving scenes. In: Avidan, S., Brostow, G., Cissé, M., Farinella, G.M., Hassner, T. (eds.) ECCV 2022. LNCS, vol. 13699, pp. 246–263. Springer, Cham (2022). https://doi.org/10.1007/978-3-031-19842-7_15
47. Valdenegro-Toro, M.: I find your lack of uncertainty in computer vision disturbing. In: Conference on Computer Vision and Pattern Recognition Workshop (CVPR'W) (2021)
48. Wong, K., Wang, S., Ren, M., Liang, M., Urtasun, R.: Identifying unknown instances for autonomous driving. In: Conference on Robot Learning (CoRL) (2019)
49. Wu, J., et al.: Medical SAM adapter: adapting segment anything model for medical image segmentation. arXiv preprint arXiv:2304.12620 (2023)
50. Xia, Y., Zhang, Y., Liu, F., Shen, W., Yuille, A.L.: Synthesize then compare: detecting failures and anomalies for semantic segmentation. In: Vedaldi, A., Bischof, H., Brox, T., Frahm, J.M. (eds.) ECCV 2020. LNCS, vol. 12346, pp. 145–161. Springer, Cham (2020). https://doi.org/10.1007/978-3-030-58452-8_9
51. Xie, E., Wang, W., Yu, Z., Anandkumar, A., Alvarez, J.M., Luo, P.: SegFormer: simple and efficient design for semantic segmentation with transformers. In: Neural Information Processing Systems (NIPS) (2021)
52. Xu, J., et al.: GroupViT: semantic segmentation emerges from text supervision. In: Conference on Computer Vision and Pattern Recognition (CVPR) (2022)
53. Xue, F., Ming, A., Zhou, Y.: Tiny obstacle discovery by occlusion-aware multilayer regression. IEEE Trans. Image Process. (TIP) **29**, 9373–9386 (2020)

54. Yu, T., et al.: Inpaint anything: segment anything meets image inpainting. arXiv preprint arXiv:2304.06790 (2023)
55. Zou, X., et al.: Generalized decoding for pixel, image, and language. In: Conference on Computer Vision and Pattern Recognition (CVPR) (2022)
56. Zou, X., et al.: Segment everything everywhere all at once. arXiv preprint arXiv:2304.06718 (2023)

Local Spherical Harmonics Improve Skeleton-Based Hand Action Recognition

Katharina Prasse[1]([✉])(ID), Steffen Jung[1,2](ID), Yuxuan Zhou[3](ID), and Margret Keuper[1,2](ID)

[1] University of Siegen, 57076 Siegen, Germany
katharina.prasse@uni-mannheim.de
[2] Max Planck Institute for Informatics, Saarland Informatics Campus, 66123 Saarbrücken, Germany
[3] University of Mannheim, 68131 Mannheim, Germany

Abstract. Hand action recognition is essential. Communication, human-robot interactions, and gesture control are dependent on it. Skeleton-based action recognition traditionally includes hands, which belong to the classes which remain challenging to correctly recognize to date. We propose a method specifically designed for hand action recognition which uses relative angular embeddings and local Spherical Harmonics to create novel hand representations. The use of Spherical Harmonics creates rotation-invariant representations which make hand action recognition even more robust against inter-subject differences and viewpoint changes. We conduct extensive experiments on the hand joints in the First-Person Hand Action Benchmark with RGB-D Videos and 3D Hand Pose Annotations, and on the NTU RGB+D 120 dataset, demonstrating the benefit of using Local Spherical Harmonics Representations. Our code is available at https://github.com/KathPra/LSHR_LSHT.

Keywords: Hand Action Recognition · Spherical Harmonics · Rotation Invariance · Relative Angular Embeddings

1 Introduction

Hand actions are everywhere. They can be observed during conversations, and provide valuable information about the atmosphere, hierarchy, backgrounds, and emotions. Furthermore, their fine-grained differences make hand actions a challenging recognition task. Skeleton-based action recognition naturally contains hand actions, which remain challenging to distinguish between. Especially human-computer interactions require the accurate recognition of hand actions in order to understand e.g. air quotes or the thumbs-up gesture. When hand action recognition is further optimized, a vast field of applications stands to benefit from

Supplementary Information The online version contains supplementary material available at https://doi.org/10.1007/978-3-031-54605-1_5.

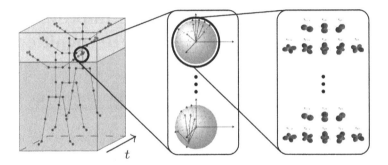

Fig. 1. Hands should receive particular emphasis as they contain the highest joint density and their mutual interaction is key to recognising hand actions. Hand joints (left) are first depicted as local spherical coordinates (middle) before being represented in terms of their Local Spherical Harmonics (right). The hand joint representation is then fed into the model as additional input.

it; hand motion understanding in the medical field, gesture control, and robotics are mere examples. Moreover, the increasing number of online interactions creates many scenarios when only a subset of the body joints is available for action recognition. Out of all body joints, hand joints are most likely to be included in digital recordings and have an expressive nature. We thus focus on hand actions explicitly and our proposed method allows to better distinguish between them. Since hands are very flexible, their embedding can benefit majorly from a local, relative description.

Action recognition is an active field of research since the late 1990s [26]. First advances into the field employed Recurrent Neural Networks [RNNs], among others Long Short-Term Memory Networks [LSTM], to capture the action over time [6,47,51]. Later, CNNs were fed action as a 2D map including semantic information as features e.g., joint type, time stamp, and position [19,24,42,48]. In recent years, Graph Convolutional Networks [GCN] are frequently employed and show a strong performance [3,31,32,44]. In contrast to CNNs, GCNs can use the inherent structure of the skeleton data. The joints are represented as nodes in the graph and the edges indicate their physical connections [31] or correlations [3]. Action recognition uses various forms of input data, ranging from RGB+Depth video data to skeleton joint Cartesian coordinates extracted from videos. Using skeleton data increases model efficiency and enhances robustness against variations in viewpoint and appearance [3,31,49]. In general, action recognition greatly benefits from understanding hand motion [11,36], which motivates us to focus particularly on hand joints. We describe each hand joint relative to the remaining hand joints. This way, the inter-joint relationships are explicitly included in the data and do not have to be inferred by the model.

We propose to represent fine-grained motion through angular embeddings and local Spherical Harmonics, as visualized in Fig. 1. We hypothesize that local spherical representations are better suited than Cartesian coordinates for several reasons: (1) Hand joints are very close in absolute position. When depicting them in terms of their relative position, small changes become more apparent. (2) The mutual interaction between fingers within each hand is one of the most important cues for action recognition. (3) Hands are very flexible. Considering their relative joint positions in terms of spherical projections facilitates robustness to slight motion variations. In previous works, cylindrical [41] coordinates have been shown to improve detection accuracy. We propose an angular embedding based on local Spherical Harmonics representations [12] as we find it suitable for describing the relative positions of the hand joints, i.e. modelling inter-joint relationships. Further, the data transformation makes the representation more robust against inter-subject differences and viewpoint changes, as it is partially rotation-invariant. We further propose hand joints' Local Spherical Harmonic Transforms [12], a fully rotation-invariant representation. To our knowledge, we are the first to employ Spherical Harmonics in the field of hand action recognition.

This study's main contributions can be summarized as follows:

1. We depict each hand joint in terms of its local neighbourhood to enable better hand-action recognition.
2. We combine angular embeddings with the standard input as an explicit motion description to better represent the hand's inter-joint relationships.
3. We combine Spherical Harmonic Transforms with the standard input as a rotation-invariant motion description to increase the robustness of hand action recognition against viewpoint or orientation changes.
4. We show that angular representations, explicitly representing inter-joint relations, can improve the egocentric hand action recognition on FPHA [11] by a significant margin.
5. We further show that angular spherical embeddings can also be leveraged by classical human skeleton-based action recognition models such as CTR-GCN [3], improving hand-based action recognition accuracy.

2   Related Work

2.1   Skeleton-Based Action Recognition

Skeleton-based action recognition initially employed Recurrent Neural Networks (RNN) to learn features over time [6,47,51]. Long Short-Term Memory Networks (LSTMs) were popular as they were able to regulate learning over time. Furthermore, Temporal State-Space Models (TF) [10], Gram Matrices [50], and Temporal Recurrent Models (HBRNN) [6] were popular choices. Prior to using learned features, hand-crafted features were employed and achieved competitive levels of accuracy compared to modern methods [11,37]. Lastly, Key-pose models such as Moving Pose made use of a modified kNN clustering to detect actions [46], whereas Hu et al. proposed a joint heterogeneous feature learning framework [16]. Graph Convolution Networks (GCNs) for skeleton-based action recognition have been proposed e.g., in [25,30,34,44,45] and are defined directly on the graph, in contrast to Convolutional Neural Networks (CNNs). GCNs can be divided into two categories, i.e. spectral [1,5,14,21] and spatial [3,44] methods. While the research is mainly pushed in the direction of GCNs, CNNs and transformers remain part of the scientific discourse on action recognition [7,15,43].

While different methods have been proposed over time, one main tendency can be distilled from previous research: It is beneficial in terms of model accuracy to incorporate additional information [3,16,28,31,46,49]. Qin et al. [28] have included angles between several body joints into their model. Recently, multi-modal ensembles have been shown to increase the overall accuracy [3,4,28]. While skeleton-based action recognition mainly focuses on the whole body, e.g., the popular NTU RGB-D 120 benchmark dataset [NTU 120] [23], several researchers have seen the merit in focusing on hand actions [11,36], and among them, Garcia et al. published the First-Person Hand Action Benchmark [FPHA] [11]. This dataset consists of egocentric recordings of daily hand actions in three categories, i.e. *social, kitchen* and *office actions*. Both datasets are included in this research. It is our goal to advance skeleton-based hand action recognition. We thus limit the review of skeleton-based action literature to the most relevant works.

2.2   Frequency Domain Representations for Action Recognition

Representing the skeleton information in the frequency instead of the spatial domain has two main advantages. Firstly, noise can be removed more easily and secondly, rotation invariance can be introduced. When transferring data from the spatial to the frequency domain, the data is represented as a sum of frequencies. When the input's data format is Cartesian coordinates, a Fourier Transformation is commonly used; when the input is spherical coordinates, Spherical Harmonics can be employed. Besides the different input formats, these methods are equivalent. They take a function and map it from the spatial domain to the frequency domain by approximating it as sums of sinusoids [2]. Many previous works on action recognition have employed Fourier Transformation [29,39,41].

Removing noise from human recording is always beneficial, e.g. when a waving hand is shaking, excluding the shaking, a high-frequency motion, makes it easier to correctly identify the action. Since the frequency domain data is complex, it has to be transformed in order to be fed into standard neural networks. Using the magnitude, a representation invariant to rotations, renders data normalization superfluous [35] and can improve recognition accuracies in use cases with varying viewpoints.

2.3   Spherical Harmonics in 3D Point Clouds

We are the first to employ Spherical Harmonics in skeleton-based action recognition to our knowledge. In 3D Point Clouds however, Spherical Harmonics are explored to make data representations robust or equivariant to rotations [8,27,33]. Esteves et al. [8] map 3D point clouds to spherical functions and propose spherical convolutions, which are robust against random rotations. Similarly, Spezialetti et al. propose a self-supervised learning framework for using spherical CNNs to learn objects' canonical surface orientation in order to detect them independent of SO(3) rotations [33]. Poulard et al. [27] propose spherical kernels for convolution which directly operate in the point clouds. Li et al. [22] compare several aforementioned methods [8,27,33] in settings where the data points are either rotated around one or all three axes during training. They highlight the strong performance of SPH-Net [27] whose accuracy remains on the same level independent of the number of axis rotated around during training. Fang et al. [9] points out the superiority of common CNNs over Spherical CNNs. Hence, we employ Spherical Harmonics as embeddings to which standard CNNs or GCNs can be applied.

3   Method

We propose multi-modal hand joint representations from which our model learns feature representations. Skeleton-based action recognition generally uses the five-dimensional Cartesian coordinates $X \in \mathbb{R}^{N \times M \times C \times T \times V}$, where N describes the batch size, M the number of persons in the action recording, C the channel dimension, T the number of frames, and V the number of joints. We combine the Cartesian coordinates with a local embedding, created using Spherical Harmonics basis functions.

3.1   Local Spherical Coordinates

We first incorporate the hand joints' local neighbourhood by using each joint as the center of the coordinate system once while depicting the other joints' position relative to the center joint, as shown in Fig. 2. We combine the local representations of all hand joints to capture fine-grained motion e.g., the differences between "making ok sign" and "making peace sign", even though the absolute positions of the thumb and index finger are very similar between both actions.

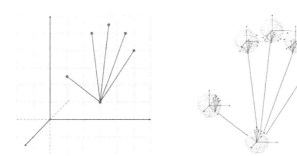

Fig. 2. Conversion between Cartesian global coordinates (left) and local spherical coordinates (right), where all coordinates are computed relative to each other joint. The global coordinates are Cartesian, while the local coordinates are spherical.

This transforms $X \in \mathbb{R}^{N \times M \times C \times T \times V}$ into $X_{loc} \in \mathbb{R}^{N \times M \times C \times T \times V \times V}$ where the last dimension contains the joint's local neighbourhood relative to its center joint's position. We compute the local neighbourhood for all hand joints, as we expect to gain the biggest advantage from investigating their local neighbourhood.

Moreover, we convert the local coordinates from Cartesian to Spherical coordinates as their angles are more suitable for describing hand motion than positions. Spherical coordinates consist of three values (r, θ, ϕ) and are used to describe point positions in 3D space, as visualized in Fig. 3(a). They can be computed using Cartesian coordinates as inputs. The radius $r \in [0, \infty)$ is defined as the length of the vector from the origin to the coordinate point, i.e. $r = \sqrt{x^2 + y^2 + z^2}$. The polar angle $\theta = \arctan \frac{\sqrt{x^2+y^2}}{z}$ describes the point's latitude and is defined for $\theta \in [0, \pi]$. The azimuthal angle $\phi = \arctan \frac{y}{x}$ describes the point's longitude and is defined for $\phi \in [0, 2\pi]$. The azimuth describes the point's location in the xy-plane relative to the positive x-axis.

3.2 Spherical Harmonics Based Hand Joint Representations

We propose angular embeddings and Spherical Harmonics as novel representations for hand action recognition, which we realize through local spherical coordinates. All Spherical Harmonics-based representations naturally offer a coarse to fine representation while being interpretable in terms of frequency bands developed on a sphere. This includes representations using the Spherical Harmonics basis functions and the full Spherical Harmonic Transform. Moreover, the magnitude of Spherical Harmonic Transforms is rotation-invariant which is a helpful property for hand action recognition [12].

Figure 3 visualizes how we first transform the hand coordinates from Cartesian to spherical coordinates (a) before representing them in terms of their Spherical Harmonic basis functions (b).

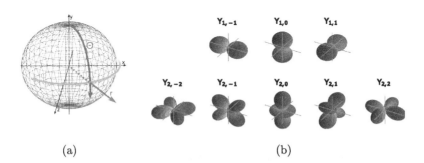

(a)   (b)

Fig. 3. (a) Conversion between Cartesian coordinates (x, y, z) and spherical coordinates (r, θ, ϕ). Spherical coordinates consist of the radius r, the polar angle θ and the azimuthal angle ϕ; (b) Visualization of the real part of Spherical Harmonics, where red indicates positive values while blue indicates negative values. The distance from the origin visualizes the magnitude of the Spherical Harmonics in the respective angular direction.

A function on the sphere can be represented in Spherical Harmonics as

$$f(\theta, \phi) = \sum_{\ell=0}^{\infty} \sum_{m=-\ell}^{m=\ell} a_m^\ell Y_m^\ell(\theta, \phi) \qquad (1)$$

with

$$Y_{\ell,m}(\theta, \phi) = \sqrt{\frac{(\ell - m)!(2\ell + 1)}{(\ell + m)!4\pi}} e^{im\phi} P_\ell^m \cos\theta \qquad (2)$$

where $Y_m^\ell(\theta, \phi)$ are the Spherical Harmonics basis functions and the $!$ indicates a factorial operation. Spherical Harmonics take two spherical coordinates as input, the azimuth θ and the polar angle ϕ. They further include the associated Legendre polynomial P_ℓ^m and have the parameter degree ℓ, in accordance to which the order m is set, i.e. $m \in [-\ell, \ell]$; both ℓ and m are real numbers. The magnitude of the Local Spherical Harmonics basis function Representation [LSHR] is invariant against rotations around the y-axis, since the magnitude of the complex exponential function is 1. The magnitude of the Local Spherical Harmonic Transforms [LSHT] is SO(3) rotation invariant. We argue that such representations are beneficial when learning to recognize hand actions across different views. We further expect these representations to support recognition in spite of hand orientation differences between subjects.

The Spherical Harmonics for $\ell \in \{1, 2\}$ are employed for skeleton-based hand action recognition, as visualized in Fig. 3(b). The inclusion of $\ell = 0$ does not contain action-specific information, and we assume that all relevant information is contained within the first two bands, i.e. $\ell \le 2$. The parameter ℓ is defined as the number of nodal lines, or bands, thus with larger ℓ, higher frequencies are represented; the removal of high frequencies reduces the noise in the data.

The chosen Spherical Harmonics representation is stacked along the channel dimension and concatenated to the original input. Since Spherical Harmonics are complex numbers, i.e. $x = a + bi$, they cannot directly be fed into standard neural networks. They need to either be represented by their real and imaginary parts, or by their magnitude and phase. When using a single part, the representation is no longer complete and the input cannot be recovered entirely. The real and imaginary parts are a complete representation of the complex number. When only the real or only the imaginary part is used, the representation is no longer complete, mathematically speaking. The magnitude has the property of being rotation-invariant [12].

3.3   Models

We include angular embeddings, a local Spherical Harmonics representation (LSHR), and Spherical Harmonic Transforms (LSHT) both in a simple baseline model (GCN-BL) and an advanced model (CTR-GCN), both proposed by Chen et al. [3]. The Channel-wise Topology Refinement Graph Convolution Model (CTR-GCN), proposed by Chen et al., achieves state-of-the-art results with a clean model architecture and a small number of epochs [3]. Both models are described in the subsequent paragraph, closely following Chen et al.'s description. They each consist of 10 layers, where each layer contains both a spatial graph convolutional network (GCN) module and a temporal convolutional network (TCN) module. While the CTR-GCN model learns a non-shared topology for the channels and dynamically infers joint relations during inference, the GCN-BL model learns a static topology shared between all channels. Further implementation details can be found in the supplementary material.

3.4   Evaluation

The angular embeddings and Spherical Harmonics are evaluated in terms of their accuracy improvement both on all body joints [Imp.] and with a focus on hand joints [Hand Imp.]. During training, we randomly rotate the input data.

The local Spherical Harmonics representations are concatenated to the standard model input, the Cartesian coordinates, before the first layer. This causes a negligible increase in the number of parameters since only the input dimensionality is modified but not the layer outputs. When evaluating the effect of hand joints' angular embeddings or Spherical Harmonics, the model is compared to the original implementation. In order to maintain the data structure of $X \in \mathbb{R}^{N \times M \times C \times T \times V}$, zeros are inserted for all non-hand joints. Our ablation studies contain a model trained exclusively on angular embeddings evaluated on FPHA [11]. Furthermore, the NTU120 [23] ablations include a baseline model of identical dimensionality, where random numbers replace the angular embeddings.

4   Experiments

4.1   Datasets

The benefits of Local Spherical Harmonics representations (LSHR) and Local Spherical Harmonic Transforms (LSHT) of hand joints are shown on two datasets: Mainly, the First-Person Hand Action Benchmark is assessed. It is created by Garcia-Hernando et al. [11] and consists of shoulder-mounted camera recordings of six subjects each performing 45 action classes four to six times. The dataset contains 1175 skeleton recordings over time, including the wrist and four joints for each finger as shown in

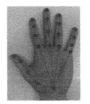

Fig. 4. Visualization of hand joints in First-Person Hand Action Benchmark [11] (own visualization).

Fig. 4. This dataset is split 1:1 into train and test sets. The viewpoints differ between recordings, which makes the recognition simultaneously Cross-Subject and Cross-Setup tasks.

Secondly, the benchmark dataset NTU RGB+D 120 [23] is employed. It contains 120 action classes, which can be split into daily, medical, and criminal actions [23]. The dataset contains 114,480 videos featuring 106 distinct subjects in 32 scenarios (camera height and distance to subject). The dataset can be evaluated in two settings, i.e. Cross-Subject and Cross-Setup. In the Cross-Subject evaluation, the 106 subjects are split into the train and test set. In the Cross-Setup setting, some recording angles and backgrounds are exclusively used for training, while others are used for testing. Both cases have the same train-test split, i.e. 1:1. The computation of local Spherical Harmonics was exclusively done for the eight hand joints, i.e. both left and right wrist, hand, thumb, and finger.

4.2   Implementation Details

Experiments are conducted on NVIDIA Tesla V100 GPUs with the PyTorch learning framework. The models proposed by Chen et al. [3], GCN-BL and CTR-GCN, have the same hyperparameter settings, i.e. SGD with a momentum of 0.9, weight decay of 0.0004, and training for 65 epochs including 5 warm-up epochs. The learning rate is initialized with 0.1 and decays by a factor of 0.1 at epochs 35 and 55. The batch size is 64 and all action recordings are resized to 64 frames. For the FPHA dataset, a batch size of 25 was chosen, due to the smaller size of this dataset. Experiments are run on AMD Ryzen 9 5900x.

4.3   Experimental Results

Experiments on the First-Person Hand Action Benchmark (FPHA) demonstrate the strength of angular embeddings, a local Spherical Harmonics representation [LSHR], as shown in Table 1. The model accuracy increases for both the GCN-BL [3] and the CTR-GCN [3] model. We ablate our method by selecting angular

Table 1. Evaluation of the GCN-BL [3] and CTR-GCN [3] Model with Local Spherical Harmonics Representations [LSHR] and Local Spherical Harmonic Transforms [LSHT] evaluated on FPHA [11] using the real and imaginary parts (R& I) or the rotation-invariant magnitude (M), compared against the original model, and LSHR exclusively (*). Our Method significantly increases accuracy.

Method	Param.	Rotation Invariance	Acc (%)
GCN BL	2.1 M	✗	80.52
+ LSHR (R&I)	2.1 M	✗	88.35
+ LSHR (M)	2.1 M	✓	**89.04**
+ LSHT (M)	2.1 M	✓	87.30
excl. LSHR (M)	2.1 M	✓	83.83*
CTR-GCN	1.4 M	✗	74.26
+ LSHR (R&I)	1.5 M	✗	90.26
+ LSHR (M)	1.5 M	✓	**92.52**
+ LSHT (M)	1.4 M	✓	89.04
excl. LSHR (M)	1.5 M	✓	85.57*

embeddings as the sole model input; they outperform the original model by a large margin. The original CTR-GCN model suffers from severe overfitting causing their test accuracy to remain below the GCN-BL model's test accuracy. The original GCN-BL model overfits less and thus has a higher accuracy.

As Table 1 shows, the largest increase over the original model is achieved with the CTR-GCN model, using the rotation-invariant magnitude of the angular embedding, a local Spherical Harmonics representation [LSHR] (+18%). Local Spherical Harmonic Transforms [LSHT] also outperform the original model by a large margin (+15%). The results indicate that learning a local relative hand representation directly from the basis functions is favourable over employing their Spherical Harmonics. The performance of the GCN-BL model differs from the CTR-GCN model, possibly due to the design of the model. While GCN-BL has a shared topology, the CTR-GCN model uses a channel-wise topology. Further angular embedding formats are reported in the supplementary material.

When comparing our method to others evaluated on the first-person hand action benchmark, we clearly outperform previous models by a large margin, as shown in Table 2. Our accuracy is 7% higher than the best previously reported model using the Gram Matrix [50].

Our method is clearly superior when evaluated on a hands-only dataset such as FHPH [11]. Furthermore, when evaluating it on a body dataset, it remains superior to the original model's performance. We evaluate angular embeddings, a local Spherical Harmonics representation [LSHR], on the NTU120 dataset. For both the Cross-Subject and Cross-Setup benchmarks, we assess various input formats. These benchmarks give further insights into the performance of rotation-invariant features. Within the Cross-Subject benchmark, we can evaluate the robustness of angular embeddings and Spherical Harmonics against inter-subject differences. The Cross-Setup benchmark allows us to evaluate the rotation-invariance of our method explicitly. The results using the GCN-BL model confirm the findings from the FPHA dataset, that angular embeddings, a local Spherical Harmonics representation [LSHR], increase the overall model accuracy (see Table 3). This improvement is even larger when exclusively

Table 2. Model Evaluation on First-Person Hand Action Benchmark [11]. Our model using the magnitude of the angular embeddings outperforms all other models.

Method	Acc (%)
1-layer LSTM [11]	78.73
2-layer LSTM [11]	80.14
Moving Pose [46]	56.34
Lie Group [38]	82.69
HBRNN [6]	77.40
Gram Matrix [50]	85.39
TF [10]	80.69
JOULE-pose [16]	74.60
TCN [20]	78.57
LEML [18]	79.48
SPDML-AIM [13]	78.40
SPDNet [17]	83.79
SymNet-v1 [40]	81.04
SymNet-v2 [40]	82.96
GCN-BL [3]	80.52
CTR-GCN [3]	74.26
Ours	**92.52**

assessing hand-related action classes [Hand Imp.]. The full list of hand vs. non-hand-related action classes can be found in the supplementary material. In the Cross-Subject setting, the full spectrum, i.e. real and imaginary parts of angular embeddings, induces the largest accuracy increase, as expected. In this case, the use of a rotation-invariant representation is not as advantageous for cross-subject action recognition. In the Cross-Setup setting, the largest accuracy increase was achieved when using the magnitude of the angular embedding, in line with our expectations, that the rotation invariant representation is well suited for this setting. The phase information reduces model accuracy, as it contains rotation information and thus hinders recognition when different viewpoints are compared. When investigating the differences between local angular embeddings, a local Spherical Harmonics representation [LSHR], and Spherical Harmonic Transforms [LSHT] on the NTU120 dataset, it becomes apparent, that the GCN-BL model benefits from the inclusion of Local angular Spherical Harmonics Representations [LSHR]. The CTR-GCN model, however, achieves higher levels of accuracy when the local Spherical Harmonic Transforms [LSHT] are employed (Table 4).

Table 3. Format Comparison of the joint modality using GCN-BL with angular embeddings on NTU120. Our method increases overall accuracy (Imp.) and hand-related action accuracy (Hand Imp.) compared to a random baseline (Rand. BL).

Dataset	Format	Rand. BL Acc. (%)	Ours Acc. (%)	Imp	Hand Imp
X-Sub	Real	83.89	84.38	↑ +0.5	↑ +0.9
	Imaginary	83.89	84.39	↑ +0.5	**↑ +1.0**
	Magnitude	83.89	84.20	↑ +0.3	↑ +0.3
	Real & Imag	83.18	84.01	**↑ +0.8**	**↑ +1.0**
	Mag. & Phase	83.18	83.72	↑ +0.5	↑ +0.7
X-Set	Real	85.62	85.93	↑ +0.3	↑ +0.5
	Imaginary	85.62	85.98	↑ +0.4	↑ +0.7
	Magnitude	85.62	86.21	**↑ +0.6**	**↑ +1.0**
	Real & Imag	85.49	85.91	↑ +0.4	↑ +0.7
	Mag. & Phase	85.49	85.39	↓ −0.1	↓ −0.5

The ensemble performance is increased by the inclusion of angular embeddings, local Spherical Harmonics representations [LSHR], or Spherical Harmonic Transforms [LSHT] as reported in Table 5. The model using the full Local Spherical Harmonic Transforms [LSHT] outperforms the other models by a small margin. As our method only includes joints, the bone modalities are always taken from the original model and do not contain any angular embeddings or Spherical Harmonic Transforms.

We conduct further experiments on the NTU120 benchmarks comparing rotation-invariant and complete angular embeddings, a local Spherical Harmonics representation [LSHR], for which we report both the hand accuracy and the overall accuracy in the supplementary material. As our method focuses on hand

Table 4. Single modality evaluation using local Spherical Harmonics representations [LSHR], and rotation-invariant Local Spherical Harmonic Transforms [LSHT] on both NTU120 benchmarks [23]. Rotation-invariant hand joint representations increase the model's accuracy.

Dataset	Model	Joint	Original Acc. (%)	LSHR (Ours) Acc. (%)	LSHT (Ours) Acc. (%)
X-Sub	GCN-BL	Loc	83.75	84.20 (↑ **0.5**)	84.03 (↑ 0.3
		Vel.	80.30	80.53 (↑ **0.2**)	80.32 (±0)
	CTR-GCN	Loc	85.08	85.31 (↑ **0.2**)	85.27 (↑ **0.2**)
		Vel	81.12	81.45 (↑ 0.3)	81.53 (↑ **0.4**)
X-Set	GCN-BL	Loc	85.64	86.21 (↑ **0.6**)	85.75 (↑ 0.1)
		Vel	82.25	82.41 (↑ **0.2**)	82.25 (±0)
	CTR-GCN	Loc	86.76	86.63 (↓ 0.1)	87.01 (↑ **0.3**)
		Vel	83.12	83.32 (↑ 0.2)	83.42 (↑ **0.3**)

Table 5. Ensemble Evaluation of the CTR-GCN model in its original version compared with two local Spherical Harmonics representations [LSHR], full-spectrum (real and imaginary part) and rotation invariance (magnitude), and the full Spherical Harmonic Transforms [LSHT]. LSHT outperforms all other models by a small margin.

Modality	Method	NTU RGB+D 120	
		X-Sub (%)	X-Set(%)
Loc.	CTR-GCN	**88.8**	90.0
	LSHR (full spectrum)	88.6	90.1
	LSHR (rotation invariant)	**88.8**	90.0
	LSHT (rotation invariant)	**88.8**	**90.2**
Loc. & Vel.	CTR-GCN	89.1	90.6
	LSHR (full spectrum)	88.9	90.5
	LSHR (rotation invariant)	89.1	90.6
	LSHT (rotation invariant)	**89.2**	**90.7**

joints, the hand accuracy increases are larger than the overall accuracy increases, when compared to the original model.

5   Discussion and Conclusion

Our rotation-invariant joint representations on the basis of local Spherical Harmonics improve skeleton-based hand action recognition. Their inclusion allows us to better distinguish between fine-grained hand actions. Both the theoretical framework and the experimental results affirm that hand joints' local Spherical Harmonics improve skeleton-based hand action recognition. We clearly outperform other methods the hands-only First-Person-Hand-Action-Benchmark [11].

The evaluations on the NTU120 Cross-Subject and Cross-Setup benchmarks further confirm our findings. Our experiments have shown that rotation-invariant hand representations increase robustness against inter-subject orientation differences and viewpoint changes, thus resulting in higher accuracy levels. On the NTU120 dataset, the overall best model performance is achieved in the Cross-Setup setting using the joint location modality, as expected due to the rotation invariance of the features. The Cross-Subject setting benefited more from the rotation invariance than expected, hinting that inter-subject differences can be reduced using angular embeddings. Thinking of the action "making a peace sign" exemplifies this, as different subjects have slightly different orientations of their hands. We aim to open the door for future research in the adaptation of angular embedding to this and other data modalities. Furthermore, the number of hand joints included in the NTU120 is four per hand, which appears to make the sampling of additional data points a meaningful investigation.

Acknowledgements. This work is partially supported by the BMBF project 16DKWN027b Climate Visions and DFG research unit 5336 Learning2Sense. All experiments were run on the computational resources of the University of Siegen and the Max Planck Institute for Informatics. We would like to thank Julia Grabinski for her guidance.

References

1. Bruna, J., Zaremba, W., Szlam, A., LeCun, Y.: Spectral networks and locally connected networks on graphs. arXiv preprint arXiv:1312.6203 (2013)
2. Brunton, S.L., Kutz, J.N.: Fourier and Wavelet Transforms, pp. 47–83. Cambridge University Press (2019). https://doi.org/10.1017/9781108380690.003
3. Chen, Y., Zhang, Z., Yuan, C., Li, B., Deng, Y., Hu, W.: Channel-wise topology refinement graph convolution for skeleton-based action recognition. In: Proceedings of the IEEE/CVF International Conference on Computer Vision, pp. 13359–13368 (2021)
4. Chi, H., Ha, M.H., Chi, S., Lee, S.W., Huang, Q., Ramani, K.: InfoGCN: representation learning for human skeleton-based action recognition. In: Proceedings of the IEEE/CVF Conference on Computer Vision and Pattern Recognition, pp. 20186–20196 (2022)
5. Defferrard, M., Bresson, X., Vandergheynst, P.: Convolutional neural networks on graphs with fast localized spectral filtering. In: Advances in Neural Information Processing Systems, vol. 29 (2016)
6. Du, Y., Wang, W., Wang, L.: Hierarchical recurrent neural network for skeleton based action recognition. In: Proceedings of the IEEE Conference on Computer Vision and Pattern Recognition, pp. 1110–1118 (2015)
7. Duan, H., Zhao, Y., Chen, K., Lin, D., Dai, B.: Revisiting skeleton-based action recognition. In: Proceedings of the IEEE/CVF Conference on Computer Vision and Pattern Recognition, pp. 2969–2978 (2022)
8. Esteves, C., Allen-Blanchette, C., Makadia, A., Daniilidis, K.: Learning so (3) equivariant representations with spherical CNNs. In: Proceedings of the European Conference on Computer Vision (ECCV), pp. 52–68 (2018)

9. Fang, J., Zhou, D., Song, X., Jin, S., Yang, R., Zhang, L.: RotPredictor: unsupervised canonical viewpoint learning for point cloud classification. In: 2020 International Conference on 3D Vision (3DV), pp. 987–996. IEEE (2020)

10. Garcia-Hernando, G., Kim, T.K.: Transition forests: learning discriminative temporal transitions for action recognition and detection. In: Proceedings of the IEEE Conference on Computer Vision and Pattern Recognition, pp. 432–440 (2017)

11. Garcia-Hernando, G., Yuan, S., Baek, S., Kim, T.K.: First-person hand action benchmark with RGB-D videos and 3D hand pose annotations. In: Proceedings of Computer Vision and Pattern Recognition (CVPR) (2018)

12. Green, R.: Spherical harmonic lighting: the gritty details. In: Archives of the Game Developers Conference, vol. 56, p. 4 (2003)

13. Harandi, M., Salzmann, M., Hartley, R.: Dimensionality reduction on SPD manifolds: the emergence of geometry-aware methods. IEEE Trans. Pattern Anal. Mach. Intell. 40(1), 48–62 (2017)

14. Henaff, M., Bruna, J., LeCun, Y.: Deep convolutional networks on graph-structured data. arXiv preprint arXiv:1506.05163 (2015)

15. Hu, H., Dong, S., Zhao, Y., Lian, D., Li, Z., Gao, S.: TransRAC: encoding multiscale temporal correlation with transformers for repetitive action counting. arXiv preprint arXiv:2204.01018 (2022)

16. Hu, J.F., Zheng, W.S., Lai, J., Zhang, J.: Jointly learning heterogeneous features for RGB-D activity recognition. In: Proceedings of the IEEE Conference on Computer Vision and Pattern Recognition, pp. 5344–5352 (2015)

17. Huang, Z., Van Gool, L.: A Riemannian network for SPD matrix learning. In: Proceedings of the AAAI Conference on Artificial Intelligence, vol. 31 (2017)

18. Huang, Z., Wang, R., Shan, S., Li, X., Chen, X.: Log-Euclidean metric learning on symmetric positive definite manifold with application to image set classification. In: International Conference on Machine Learning, pp. 720–729. PMLR (2015)

19. Ke, Q., Bennamoun, M., An, S., Sohel, F., Boussaid, F.: A new representation of skeleton sequences for 3D action recognition. In: Proceedings of the IEEE Conference on Computer Vision and Pattern Recognition, pp. 3288–3297 (2017)

20. Kim, T.S., Reiter, A.: Interpretable 3D human action analysis with temporal convolutional networks. In: 2017 IEEE Conference on Computer Vision and Pattern Recognition Workshops (CVPRW), pp. 1623–1631. IEEE (2017)

21. Kipf, T.N., Welling, M.: Semi-supervised classification with graph convolutional networks. arXiv preprint arXiv:1609.02907 (2016)

22. Li, F., Fujiwara, K., Okura, F., Matsushita, Y.: A closer look at rotation-invariant deep point cloud analysis. In: Proceedings of the IEEE/CVF International Conference on Computer Vision, pp. 16218–16227 (2021)

23. Liu, J., Shahroudy, A., Perez, M., Wang, G., Duan, L.Y., Kot, A.C.: NTU RGB+ D 120: a large-scale benchmark for 3D human activity understanding. IEEE Trans. Pattern Anal. Mach. Intell. 42(10), 2684–2701 (2019)

24. Liu, M., Liu, H., Chen, C.: Enhanced skeleton visualization for view invariant human action recognition. Pattern Recogn. 68, 346–362 (2017)

25. Liu, Z., Zhang, H., Chen, Z., Wang, Z., Ouyang, W.: Disentangling and unifying graph convolutions for skeleton-based action recognition. In: Proceedings of the IEEE/CVF Conference on Computer Vision and Pattern Recognition, pp. 143–152 (2020)

26. Minami, K., Nakajima, H., Toyoshima, T.: Real-time discrimination of ventricular tachyarrhythmia with Fourier-transform neural network. IEEE Trans. Biomed. Eng. 46(2), 179–185 (1999)

27. Poulenard, A., Rakotosaona, M.J., Ponty, Y., Ovsjanikov, M.: Effective rotation-invariant point CNN with spherical harmonics kernels. In: 2019 International Conference on 3D Vision (3DV), pp. 47–56. IEEE (2019)
28. Qin, Z., et al.: Fusing higher-order features in graph neural networks for skeleton-based action recognition. IEEE Trans. Neural Netw. Learn. Syst. (2022)
29. Rodriguez, M.D., Ahmed, J., Shah, M.: Action MACH a spatio-temporal maximum average correlation height filter for action recognition. In: 2008 IEEE Conference on Computer Vision and Pattern Recognition, pp. 1–8. IEEE (2008)
30. Shi, L., Zhang, Y., Cheng, J., Lu, H.: Two-stream adaptive graph convolutional networks for skeleton-based action recognition. In: CVPR (2019)
31. Shi, L., Zhang, Y., Cheng, J., Lu, H.: AdaSGN: adapting joint number and model size for efficient skeleton-based action recognition. In: ICCV (2021)
32. Si, C., Jing, Y., Wang, W., Wang, L., Tan, T.: Skeleton-based action recognition with spatial reasoning and temporal stack learning. In: Proceedings of the European conference on computer vision (ECCV), pp. 103–118 (2018)
33. Spezialetti, R., Stella, F., Marcon, M., Silva, L., Salti, S., Di Stefano, L.: Learning to orient surfaces by self-supervised spherical CNNs. In: Advances in Neural Information Processing Systems, vol. 33, pp. 5381–5392 (2020)
34. Tang, Y., Tian, Y., Lu, J., Li, P., Zhou, J.: Deep progressive reinforcement learning for skeleton-based action recognition. In: Proceedings of the IEEE Conference on Computer Vision and Pattern Recognition, pp. 5323–5332 (2018)
35. Temerinac, M., Reisert, M., Burkhardt, H.: Invariant features for searching in protein fold databases. Int. J. Comput. Math. **84**(5), 635–651 (2007)
36. Trivedi, N., Thatipelli, A., Sarvadevabhatla, R.K.: NTU-X: an enhanced large-scale dataset for improving pose-based recognition of subtle human actions. In: Proceedings of the Twelfth Indian Conference on Computer Vision, Graphics and Image Processing, pp. 1–9 (2021)
37. Veličković, P., Cucurull, G., Casanova, A., Romero, A., Lio, P., Bengio, Y.: Graph attention networks. arXiv preprint arXiv:1710.10903 (2017)
38. Vemulapalli, R., Arrate, F., Chellappa, R.: Human action recognition by representing 3D skeletons as points in a lie group. In: Proceedings of the IEEE Conference on Computer Vision and Pattern Recognition, pp. 588–595 (2014)
39. Wang, J., Liu, Z., Wu, Y., Yuan, J.: Mining actionlet ensemble for action recognition with depth cameras. In: 2012 IEEE Conference on Computer Vision and Pattern Recognition, pp. 1290–1297. IEEE (2012)
40. Wang, R., Wu, X.J., Kittler, J.: SymNet: a simple symmetric positive definite manifold deep learning method for image set classification. IEEE Trans. Neural Netw. Learn. Syst. **33**(5), 2208–2222 (2021)
41. Weinland, D., Ronfard, R., Boyer, E.: Free viewpoint action recognition using motion history volumes. Comput. Vis. Image Underst. **104**(2–3), 249–257 (2006)
42. Weng, J., Liu, M., Jiang, X., Yuan, J.: Deformable pose traversal convolution for 3D action and gesture recognition. In: Proceedings of the European Conference on Computer Vision (ECCV), pp. 136–152 (2018)
43. Xu, K., Ye, F., Zhong, Q., Xie, D.: Topology-aware convolutional neural network for efficient skeleton-based action recognition. In: Proceedings of the AAAI Conference on Artificial Intelligence, vol. 36, pp. 2866–2874 (2022)
44. Yan, S., Xiong, Y., Lin, D.: Spatial temporal graph convolutional networks for skeleton-based action recognition. In: Thirty-Second AAAI Conference on Artificial Intelligence (2018)

45. Ye, F., Pu, S., Zhong, Q., Li, C., Xie, D., Tang, H.: Dynamic GCN: context-enriched topology learning for skeleton-based action recognition. In: Proceedings of the 28th ACM International Conference on Multimedia, pp. 55–63 (2020)
46. Zanfir, M., Leordeanu, M., Sminchisescu, C.: The moving pose: an efficient 3D kinematics descriptor for low-latency action recognition and detection. In: Proceedings of the IEEE International Conference on Computer Vision, pp. 2752–2759 (2013)
47. Zhang, P., Lan, C., Xing, J., Zeng, W., Xue, J., Zheng, N.: View adaptive recurrent neural networks for high performance human action recognition from skeleton data. In: Proceedings of the IEEE International Conference on Computer Vision, pp. 2117–2126 (2017)
48. Zhang, P., Lan, C., Xing, J., Zeng, W., Xue, J., Zheng, N.: View adaptive neural networks for high performance skeleton-based human action recognition. IEEE Trans. Pattern Anal. Mach. Intell. **41**(8), 1963–1978 (2019)
49. Zhang, P., Lan, C., Zeng, W., Xing, J., Xue, J., Zheng, N.: Semantics-guided neural networks for efficient skeleton-based human action recognition. In: Proceedings of the IEEE/CVF Conference on Computer Vision and Pattern Recognition, pp. 1112–1121 (2020)
50. Zhang, X., Wang, Y., Gou, M., Sznaier, M., Camps, O.: Efficient temporal sequence comparison and classification using gram matrix embeddings on a Riemannian manifold. In: Proceedings of the IEEE Conference on Computer Vision and Pattern Recognition, pp. 4498–4507 (2016)
51. Zhu, W., et al.: Co-occurrence feature learning for skeleton based action recognition using regularized deep LSTM networks. In: Proceedings of the AAAI Conference on Artificial Intelligence, vol. 30 (2016)

3D Reconstruction and Neural Rendering

LMD: Light-Weight Prediction Quality Estimation for Object Detection in Lidar Point Clouds

Tobias Riedlinger[1]([✉])[iD], Marius Schubert[1][iD], Sarina Penquitt[1][iD],
Jan-Marcel Kezmann[1], Pascal Colling[2][iD], Karsten Kahl[1][iD],
Lutz Roese-Koerner[2], Michael Arnold[2], Urs Zimmermann[2],
and Matthias Rottmann[1][iD]

[1] School of Mathematics and Natural Sciences, IZMD, University of Wuppertal,
Wuppertal, Germany
{riedlinger,schubert,kkahl,rottmann}@math.uni-wuppertal.de,
jankezmann@t-online.de
[2] Aptiv Services Deutschland GmbH, Wuppertal, Germany
{pascal.colling,lutz.roese-koerner,michael.arnold,
urs.zimmermann}@aptiv.com

Abstract. Object detection on Lidar point cloud data is a promising technology for autonomous driving and robotics which has seen a significant rise in performance and accuracy during recent years. Particularly uncertainty estimation is a crucial component for down-stream tasks and deep neural networks remain error-prone even for predictions with high confidence. Previously proposed methods for quantifying prediction uncertainty tend to alter the training scheme of the detector or rely on prediction sampling which results in vastly increased inference time. In order to address these two issues, we propose LidarMetaDetect (LMD), a light-weight post-processing scheme for prediction quality estimation. Our method can easily be added to any pre-trained Lidar object detector without altering anything about the base model and is purely based on post-processing, therefore, only leading to a negligible computational overhead. Our experiments show a significant increase of statistical reliability in separating true from false predictions. We propose and evaluate an additional application of our method leading to the detection of annotation errors. Explicit samples and a conservative count of annotation error proposals indicates the viability of our method for large-scale datasets like KITTI and nuScenes. On the widely-used nuScenes test dataset, 43 out of the top 100 proposals of our method indicate, in fact, erroneous annotations.

Keywords: Lidar point cloud · object detection · uncertainty estimation · annotation quality

T. Riedlinger, M. Schubert, S. Penquitt and J.-M. Kezmann—Equal contribution.

Supplementary Information The online version contains supplementary material available at https://doi.org/10.1007/978-3-031-54605-1_6.

U. Köthe and C. Rother (Eds.): DAGM GCPR 2023, LNCS 14264, pp. 85–99, 2024.
https://doi.org/10.1007/978-3-031-54605-1_6

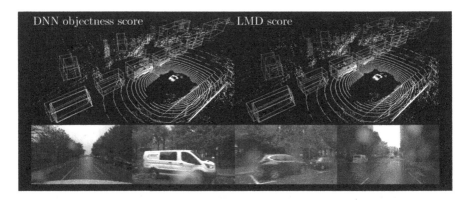

Fig. 1. Prediction of a Lidar point cloud object detector with the native objectness score (*left*) and LMD meta classifier scores (*right*) and corresponding camera images below. Ground truth annotations are depicted in pink while predictions are color-coded from red (low confidence) to green (high confidence). Detections based on the objectness score are highly threshold-dependent and may lead to false positive detections. Detections based on LMD scores are more reliable and separate true from false predictions more sharply.

1   Introduction

In recent years, deep learning has achieved great advances in the field of 3D object detection on Lidar data [9,21,22,24]. Deep neural network (DNN) architectures for this task are well-developed, however, there is little work in the area of uncertainty quantification (UQ) for such models [2,11,12,15,23]. UQ is crucial for deployment of DNN-based object detection in the real world, since DNNs as statistical models statistically make erroneous predictions. Down-stream algorithms are supposed to further process the predictions of perception algorithms and rely on statistically accurate and meaningful UQ. Aleatoric uncertainty is usually estimated by adding variance parameters to the network prediction and fitting them to data under a specific assumption for the distribution of residuals [2,4,5,11,12]. Such approaches usually alter the training objective of the detector by appealing to the negative log-likelihood loss for normally distributed residuals. Epistemic uncertainty is oftentimes estimated via Monte-Carlo (MC) dropout [2] or deep ensembles [23]. In such approaches, model sampling leads to a significant increase in inference time. Inspired by lines of research [16,19] in the field of 2D object detection on camera images, we develop a framework for UQ in 3D object detection for Lidar point clouds. This approach does not alter the training objective and can be applied to any pre-trained object detector and does not require prediction sampling. Our framework, called LidarMetaDetect (short LMD), performs two UQ tasks: (1) meta classification, which aims at estimating the probability of a given prediction being a true positive vs. being a false positive; (2) meta regression, which estimates the localization quality of a prediction compared with the ground truth. Note that, outside the context of

UQ for DNNs, the terms meta classification and meta regression refer to different concepts, see [10] and [20], respectively. LMD operates as a post-processing
module and can be combined with any DNN without modifying it. Our methods
learn on a small sample of data to assess the DNN's reliability in a frequentist
sense at runtime, i.e., in the absence of ground truth. In essence, we handcraft a
number of uncertainty scores on bounding box level, by which we convert both
UQ tasks into structured machine learning tasks. To the best of our knowledge,
our method is the first purely post-processing-based UQ method for 3D object
detection based on Lidar point clouds. We conduct in-depth numerical studies on
the KITTI [6], nuScenes [1] as well as a propriety dataset. We include comparisons of our methods with baseline methods on common uncertainty quantification benchmarks, ablation studies of relevant parameters and the relevance of our
uncertainty features. This is complemented with down stream tasks where (1) we
demonstrate that our UQ increases the separation of true and false predictions
and leads to well-calibrated confidence estimates and (2) we show that our UQ
can be utilized for the detection of erroneous annotations in Lidar object detection datasets. We evaluate our method's annotations error detection capabilities
by reviewing its proposals on moderate samples from KITTI and nuScenes. Our
contributions can be summarized as follows:

- We develop the first purely post-processing based UQ framework for 3D object
  detection in Lidar point clouds.
- We compare our UQ methods to baselines and show that they clearly outperform the DNN's built-in estimates of reliability.
- We find annotation errors in the most commonly used publicly available Lidar
  object detection datasets, i.e., KITTI and nuScenes.

We make our code publicly available at https://github.com/JanMarcel
Kezmann/MetaDetect3D.

2   Related Work

In recent years, technologically sophisticated methods such as perception in Lidar
point clouds have received attention in the UQ branch due to their potential
industrial relevance in the autonomous driving sector. Methods for 3D object
detection roughly fall into the categories of aleatoric and epistemic UQ. Aleatoric
UQ methods usually build on estimating distributional noise by adding a variance output for each regression variable while epistemic UQ methods utilize
some kind of model sampling either appealing to MC dropout or deep ensembles.
Meyer et al. [11] estimate aleatoric uncertainty by a two-dimensional discretization scheme over the Lidar range and introducing a variance-weighted regression loss for a multi-modal distributional prediction in order to improve detection performance. Meyer and Thakurdesai [12] estimate aleatoric uncertainty
by adding scale regression variables to the network output, modeling Laplace-
distributed residuals under a label noise assumption via a Kullback-Leibler divergence loss. Feng et al. [5] estimate heteroscedastic aleatoric uncertainty for the

region proposal and the detection head of an object detector separately by modeling diagonal-covariance normally distributed bounding box regression. Feng et al. [4] achieve joint estimation of aleatoric and epistemic UQ by adding regression variables that model the covariance diagonal of a multi-variate normal distribution of the four bounding box parameters alongside MC dropout total variance for the epistemic component. Chen et al. [2] extract aleatoric uncertainty information from a self-supervised projection-reconstruction mechanism propagated to 3D object detection on camera images. Further, epistemic uncertainty of object localization is quantified via MC dropout. Yang et al. [23] perform UQ for 3D object detection on Lidar and extend the multi-input multi-output model MIMO [8] which modifies the network to be supplied simultaneously with n inputs and providing n outputs. This simulates a deep ensemble at inference time at the cost of increased memory consumption for input and output layers.

In the field of 2D object detection in camera images by DNNs, methods for UQ have been developed in a series of works [16,19] related with research on UQ in semantic segmentation [17,18]. Schubert et al. [19] utilize the pre-NMS anchor statistics in a post-processing approach to obtain box-wise confidence and IoU-estimates. Riedlinger et al. [16] use instance-wise gradient scores in a post-processing scheme to obtain calibrated uncertainty estimates improving detection performance. Inspired by these lines of research, we develop a framework for UQ in 3D object detection for Lidar point clouds. We use lightweight post-processing models on top of a pre-trained Lidar point cloud object detector in order to obtain improved uncertainty and IoU-estimates. In contrast to previous work, our approach has the advantage that it may be applied to any pretrained object detector without alteration of training or architecture and does not carry the computational and memory cost of sampling weights in a Bayesian manner like MC dropout or deep ensembles. We show that this approach leads to more reliable object detection predictions and that it can be applied in an intuitive way in order to detect annotation errors in object detection datasets.

3   Proposed Method

In this section we describe our post-processing mechanism and how it can be applied to improve detection performance and to detect annotation errors. Our method assumes an object detector $f(\cdot)$ which maps point clouds $\boldsymbol{X}$ to a list of N bounding boxes

$$f(\boldsymbol{X}) = \left\{ \widehat{b}^1, \ldots, \widehat{b}^N \right\}. \tag{1}$$

Point clouds $\boldsymbol{X} = (\boldsymbol{p}_1, \ldots, \boldsymbol{p}_{N_{\mathrm{pt}}})$ consist of Lidar points $\boldsymbol{p} = (x, y, z, r) \in \mathbb{R}^4$ represented by three coordinates (x, y, z) and a reflectance value r each. Bounding boxes are represented by features $\widehat{b}^j(\boldsymbol{X}) = (\widehat{x}^j, \widehat{y}^j, \widehat{z}^j, \widehat{\ell}^j, \widehat{w}^j, \widehat{h}^j, \widehat{\theta}^j, \widehat{s}^j, \widehat{\pi}_1^j, \ldots, \widehat{\pi}_C^j)$. Here, $\widehat{x}^j, \widehat{y}^j, \widehat{z}^j, \widehat{\ell}^j, \widehat{w}^j, \widehat{h}^j, \widehat{\theta}^j$ define the bounding box geometry, $\widehat{s}^j$ is the objectness score and $(\widehat{\pi}_1^j, \ldots, \widehat{\pi}_C^j)$ is the predicted categorical probability distribution. The latter defines the predicted class

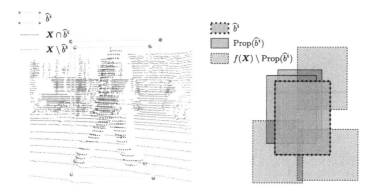

Fig. 2. Left: Illustration of the P^i and Φ^i features counting Lidar points falling into a given predicted box. From the points $\boldsymbol{X} \cap \widehat{b}^i$, reflection statistics are generated. Right: Schematic illustration of the proposal set $\mathrm{Prop}(\widehat{b}^i)$ for a given predicted box $\widehat{b}^i$ (here, in two dimensions for simplicity). From the proposal boxes, further pre-NMS statistics are derived.

$\widehat{\kappa}^j = \mathrm{argmax}_{c=1,\ldots,C}\, \widehat{\pi}_c^j$ while the objectness score $\widehat{s}^j$ is the model's native confidence estimate for each prediction. Out of the N bounding boxes, only a small amount N_{NMS} will be left after non-maximum suppression (NMS) filtering and contribute to the final prediction of the detector

$$\mathrm{NMS}[f(\boldsymbol{X})] = \left\{ \widehat{b}^i : i \in I_{\mathrm{NMS}} \right\}, \tag{2}$$

where we let $I_{\mathrm{NMS}} \subset \{1, \ldots, N\}$ denote the post-NMS index set indicating survivor boxes.

LMD Features. From this information we generate geometrical and statistical features for each $\widehat{b}^i \in \mathrm{NMS}[f(\boldsymbol{X})]$ for the purpose of UQ. In addition to the bounding box features

$$\widehat{\phi}^i := \{\widehat{x}^i, \widehat{y}^i, \widehat{z}^i, \widehat{\ell}^i, \widehat{w}^i, \widehat{h}^i, \widehat{\theta}^i, \widehat{s}^i, \widehat{\kappa}^i\} \tag{3}$$

of $\widehat{b}^i$ we compute the geometric features *volume* $V^i = \widehat{\ell}^i \widehat{w}^i \widehat{h}^i$, *surface area* $A^i = 2(\widehat{\ell}^i \widehat{w}^i + \widehat{\ell}^i \widehat{h}^i + \widehat{w}^i \widehat{h}^i)$, *relative size* $F^i = V^i/A^i$, *number of Lidar points* $P^i = |\boldsymbol{X} \cap \widehat{b}^i|$ within $\widehat{b}^i$ and *fraction of Lidar points* $\Phi^i = P^i/|\boldsymbol{X}|$ in $\widehat{b}^i$, see Fig. 2 on the left for an illustration. Moreover, each Lidar point that falls into $\widehat{b}^i$ (i.e., in $\boldsymbol{X} \cap \widehat{b}^i$) has a reflectance value r. We add the maximal ($\rho^i_{\max}$), mean (ρ^i_{mean}) and standard deviation (ρ^i_{std}) over all reflectance values of points in $\widehat{b}^i$. Lastly, for each $\widehat{b}^i$, we take the pre-NMS statistics into consideration which involves all proposal boxes in $f(\boldsymbol{X})$ that are NMS-filtered by $\widehat{b}^i$, i.e., the pre-image

$$\mathrm{Prop}(\widehat{b}^i) := \mathrm{NMS}^{-1}[\{\widehat{b}^i\}]. \tag{4}$$

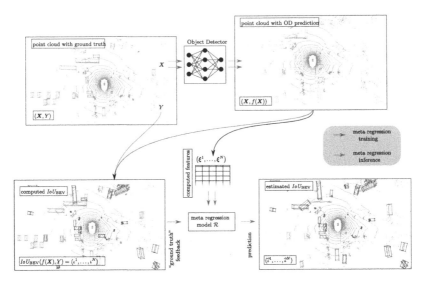

Fig. 3. Schematic illustration of the LMD meta regression pipeline. Training of the model is based on the output $f(\boldsymbol{X})$ of a fixed (frozen) object detector and the bounding box ground truth Y. Meta classification follows the same scheme with binary training targets $\tau^i = 1_{\{\iota^i > 0.5\}}$.

These are characterized by having a significant three-dimensional IoU_{3D} with $\widehat{b}^i$, see Fig. 2 on the right. The number of proposal boxes $N^i := |\mathrm{Prop}(\widehat{b}^i)|$ is an important statistics since regions with more proposals are more likely to contain a true prediction. We further derive minimum, maximum, mean and standard deviation statistics over proposal boxes $\widehat{b} \in \mathrm{Prop}(\widehat{b}^i)$ for all

$$m^i \in \widehat{\phi}^i \cup \{V^i, A^i, F^i, P^i, \Phi^i, \rho^i_{\max}, \rho^i_{\mathrm{mean}}, \rho^i_{\mathrm{std}}\}, \tag{5}$$

as well, as the IoU_{3D} and bird-eye intersection over union IoU_{BEV} values between $\widehat{b}^i$ and all proposals $\mathrm{Prop}(\widehat{b}^i)$. Overall, this amounts to a vector $\boldsymbol{\xi}^i(\boldsymbol{X})$ of length $n = 90$ consisting of co-variables (features) on which post-processing models are fit in order to predict the IoU_{BEV} between $\widehat{b}^i$ and the ground truth or classify samples as true (TP) or false positives (FP). We call a box a TP if $IoU_{BEV} \geq 0.5$, otherwise we declare it FP.

Post-processing. On an annotated hold-out dataset $\mathcal{D}_{\mathrm{val}}$ (consisting of point cloud-annotation tuples $(\boldsymbol{X}, Y)$), we compute a structured dataset denoted $\mathsf{X} = (\boldsymbol{\xi}^1, \ldots, \boldsymbol{\xi}^{N_{\mathrm{val}}}) \in \mathbb{R}^{n \times N_{\mathrm{val}}}$ consisting of feature vectors for each of the N_{val} predicted boxes over all of $\mathcal{D}_{\mathrm{val}}$. The illustration of our method in Fig. 3 shows this scheme for one particular Lidar frame $(\boldsymbol{X}, Y)$ and the respective prediction on it. Further, we compute $\iota^i := IoU_{BEV}(\widehat{b}^i(\boldsymbol{X}), Y)$ between prediction and ground truth form $\mathcal{D}_{\mathrm{val}}$ as target variables $\mathsf{Y} = (\iota^1, \ldots, \iota^{N_{\mathrm{val}}}) \in \mathbb{R}^{N_{\mathrm{val}}}$. We then fit a light-weight *(meta-) regression model* $\mathcal{R} : \boldsymbol{\xi}^i \mapsto \mathsf{Y}_i$ on (X, Y) which acts as post-processing module of the detector in order to produce IoU_{BEV}-estimates $\widehat{\iota}^i := \mathcal{R}(\boldsymbol{\xi}^i)$ for each detection $\widehat{b}^i$. Similarly, we fit a binary *(meta-) classification model* $\mathcal{C}$ obtaining the binary targets $1_{\{Y>0.5\}}$ which allows us to generate alternative confidence estimates $\widehat{\tau}^i := \mathcal{C}(\boldsymbol{\xi}^i) \in [0,1]$ for each prediction $\widehat{b}^i$ in post-processing. Note that $\mathcal{C}$ is a potentially non-monotonous function of the features $\boldsymbol{\xi}^i$ and, therefore, can change the obtained confidence ranking per frame and influence detection performance as opposed to re-calibration methods [7,14].

Meta classification empirically turns out to produce confidence estimates which are both, sharper (in the sense of separating TPs from FPs) and better calibrated that those produced natively by the detector, i.e., the objectness score. However, when regarding the cases of disagreement between the computed IoU_{BEV} and $\mathcal{C}$, we frequently find that $\mathcal{C}$ is to be trusted more than the computed IoU_{BEV} due to missing annotations. We use this observation in order to generate proposals (in descending estimation $\widehat{\tau}^i$) based on the object detector in comparison with the given ground truth (FP according to the ground truth, i.e., $\iota^i < 0.5$) that serve as suggestions of annotation errors.

4   Numerical Results

In this section we study meta classification and meta regression performance for two benchmark datasets as well as a proprietary dataset by Aptiv. The meta classification results are presented in terms of accuracy and area under receiver operator characteristics curve ($AUROC$ [3]) and the meta regression results are presented in terms of R^2. We compare our uncertainty quantification method LidarMetaDetect (LMD) with two baseline methods (score, box features). Moreover, we detect annotation errors on both benchmark datasets using LMD.

Implementation Details. We implemented our method in the open source MMDetection3D toolbox [13]. For our experiments, we consider the Point-Pillars [9] and CenterPoint [24] architectures. The mean average precision ($mAP@IoU_{0.5}$) for KITTI based on IoU_{BEV} is 69.0 for CenterPoint and 68.8 for PointPillars. On KITTI, the $mAP@IoU_{0.5}$ based on IoU_{3D} is 64.2 for CenterPoint and 68.8 for PointPillars and for Aptiv, the $mAP@IoU_{0.5}$ based on IoU_{3D} is 39.5 for CenterPoint and 43.7 for PointPillars. NuScenes performance is given as a weighted sum of mAP as well as the nuScenes detection score (NDS). For CenterPoint, the mAP is 57.4 and the NDS is 65.2 and for Point-Pillars the mAP is 40.0 and the NDS is 53.3. For KITTI and Aptiv, the models were trained individually while available public model weights from MMDetection3D are used for nuScenes. The performance results obtained have all been evaluated on respective test datasets. For KITTI, the images and associated point clouds are split scene-wise, such that the training set consists of 3,712, the validation set of 1,997, and the test set of 1,772 frames. For nuScenes, the validation set is split scene-wise into 3,083 validation and 2,936 test frames. The Aptiv dataset consists of 50 sequences, split into $27, 14, 9$ sequences with about

145K, 75K, 65K cuboid annotations for training, validation and testing, respectively. Every sequence is about two minutes long while every fifth point cloud is annotated. The covered locations are countryside, highway and urban from and around (anonymous). The dataset includes four classes: 1. smaller vehicles likes cars and vans, 2. larger vehicles like busses and trucks, 3. pedestrians and 4. motorbikes and bicycles.

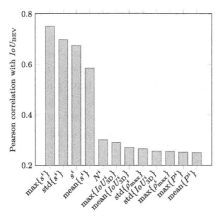
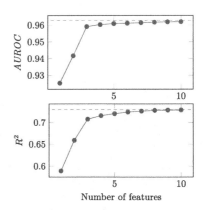

Fig. 4. Strongest correlation coefficients for constructed box-wise features and IoU_{BEV} for the CenterPoint architecture on the nuScenes test dataset and a score threshold $\tau = 0.1$.

Fig. 5. Feature selection via greedy heuristic for CenterPoint, nuScenes and score threshold 0.1. *Top*: meta classification $AUROC$. *Bottom*: meta regression R^2. The dashed line shows the performance when incorporating all features (LMD).

Correlation of Box-Wise Features with the IoU_{BEV}. Figure 4 shows the Pearson correlation coefficients of the constructed box-wise dispersion measures with the IoU_{BEV} of prediction and ground truth for CenterPoint on the nuScenes test dataset. The score features have strong correlations (>0.5) with the IoU_{BEV}. Note that, although the four score-related features show the highest individual correlation, these features may be partially redundant. The number of candidate boxes N^i is also reasonably correlated with the IoU_{BEV} (0.3007), whereas the remaining features only show a minor correlation (<0.3). However, they may still contribute to higher combined explanatory information in meta classification.

Comparison of Different Meta Classifiers and Regressors. Different models can serve as post-processing modules for meta classification ($\mathcal{C}$) and meta regression ($\mathcal{R}$, see Sect. 3). For meta classification, the meta models under consideration are logistic regression (LogReg), random forest (RF), gradient boosting (GB) and a multilayer perceptron (MLP) with two hidden layers. For meta regression, analogous regression models are used, only the logistic regression is replaced with a ridge regression (RR).

Table 1. Comparison of meta classification accuracy and $AUROC$ as well as meta regression R^2 values for the score baseline, bounding box features and LMD for CenterPoint and nuScenes test dataset with score threshold 0.1; higher values are better. Bold numbers indicate the highest performance and underlined numbers represent the second highest (row-wise). Models used are Logistic Regression (LogReg), Ridge Regression (RR), Random Forest (RF), Gradient Boosting (GB) and a Multi Layer Perceptron (MLP).

Method	Meta Classification								Meta Regression			
	Accuracies				$AUROC$s				R^2			
	LogReg	RF	GB	MLP	LogReg	RF	GB	MLP	RR	RF	GB	MLP
Score	**0.8777**	0.8524	0.8772	<u>0.8773</u>	**0.8644**	0.8617	0.8623	<u>0.8640</u>	0.4641	0.4675	<u>0.4733</u>	**0.4751**
Box Features	0.8877	<u>0.9049</u>	**0.9203**	0.8975	0.9056	<u>0.9454</u>	**0.9529**	0.9293	0.5292	<u>0.6681</u>	**0.6792**	0.6249
LMD	0.9118	0.9166	**0.9297**	<u>0.9200</u>	0.9450	<u>0.9581</u>	**0.9628**	0.9530	0.6451	<u>0.7242</u>	**0.7296**	0.7122

The respective meta models are trained on the box-wise features ξ^i of the validation sets $\mathcal{D}_{\text{val}}$ and evaluated on the features of the test sets which are disjoint from $\mathcal{D}_{\text{val}}$. LMD uses all available features to train the meta models, whereas in the score baseline only the score of the prediction $\widehat{s}^i$ is used to fit the meta model. For the bounding box features baseline, the box features of the prediction $\widehat{\phi}^i$ are used, in which the score $\widehat{s}^i$ is also included. Table 1 presents meta classification accuracy and $AUROC$ as well as meta regression R^2 for the CenterPoint architecture on the nuScenes dataset. For the score baseline, all meta models perform similarly well. For the meta classification accuracy there are differences of up to 2.53 percent points (pp), for the $AUROC$ of at most 0.27 pp and for meta regression R^2 of up to 1.10 pp. For the box features the maximum differences increase to 3.26 pp in terms of accuracy, to 4.73 pp for $AUROC$ and to 15.00 pp for R^2. In particular, for the box features and LMD, the non-linear models (RF, GB, MLP) outperform the linear model in both learning tasks. LMD outperforms the baselines box features/score by 0.94/5.20 pp in terms of accuracy, by 0.99/9.84 pp in terms of $AUROC$ and by 5.04/25.45 pp in terms of R^2. If overfitting of the meta model is made unlikely by choosing appropriate hyperparameters, the performance of the meta model typically benefits from adding more features, since the available information and number of parameters for fitting are increased. Overall, GB outperforms all other meta models, especially when multiple features are used to train and evaluate the respective learning task. Therefore, only results based on GB are shown in the following experiments. This finding may be attributed to the efficient fitting procedure and discontinuous nature of GB models.

Comparison for Different Datasets and Networks. Table 2 shows meta classification accuracy and $AUROC$ as well as meta regression R^2 for all network-dataset combinations based on GB models. In all cases LMD outperforms both base-

Table 2. Comparison of meta classification accuracy and $AUROC$ as well as meta regression R^2 for the score baseline, bounding box features and LMD for all available network-dataset combinations with IoU_{BEV} threshold 0.5, score threshold 0.1 and GB as meta model. Bold numbers indicate the highest performance and underlined numbers represent the second highest (row-wise).

Dataset	Network	Meta Classification						Meta Regression		
		Accuracies			$AUROC$s			R^2		
		Score	Box	LMD	Score	Box	LMD	Score	Box	LMD
KITTI	PointPillars	0.8921	0.8931	**0.9004**	0.9530	0.9537	**0.9592**	0.7108	0.7131	**0.7287**
	CenterPoint	0.8688	0.8691	**0.8806**	0.9274	0.9343	**0.9466**	0.6235	0.6472	**0.6840**
nuScenes	PointPillars	0.8398	0.8708	**0.8915**	0.8129	0.9002	**0.9280**	0.4055	0.5593	**0.6413**
	CenterPoint	0.8772	0.9203	**0.9297**	0.8623	0.9529	**0.9628**	0.4732	0.6792	**0.7296**
Aptiv	PointPillars	0.7939	0.8489	**0.8615**	0.8558	0.9274	**0.9396**	0.5096	0.6568	**0.6924**
	CenterPoint	0.8265	0.8440	**0.8548**	0.8914	0.9134	**0.9275**	0.5456	0.6286	**0.6591**

lines and the bounding box features outperform the score baseline. This is to be expected, since the score is contained in the box features and the box features are contained in the set of features of LMD. The improvement from the score baseline to LMD ranges from 0.83 to 6.76 pp in terms of meta classification accuracy, from 0.62 to 10.51 pp in terms of $AUROC$ and from 1.79 to 25.64 pp in terms of meta regression R^2. The improvement from the bounding box features to LMD ranges from 0.73 to 2.07 pp in terms of meta classification accuracy, from 0.55 to 2.78 pp in terms of $AUROC$ and from 1.56 to 8.20 pp in terms of meta regression R^2. This illustrates that the addition of features, other than just the bounding box features themselves, has a significant impact on meta classification and meta regression performances and, therefore, separation of TP and FP predictions.

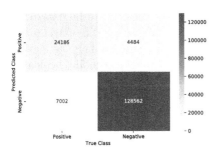

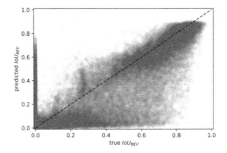

Fig. 6. Confusion matrix of a GB classifier for LMD on CenterPoint, nuScenes and score threshold 0.1.

Fig. 7. Box-wise scatter plot of true IoU_{BEV} and predicted IoU_{BEV} values for LMD on CenterPoint, nuScenes and score threshold 0.1. The predictions are based on a GB regressor.

For CenterPoint and nuScenes, the confusion matrix Fig. 6 shows that the GB classifier based on LMD identifies most TPs and true negatives. Therefore, predictions that are in fact FPs are also predicted as FPs. Note, that here we regard "meta" true negatives conditional on the detectors prediction (each example is a detection TP or FP that is binarily classified). The values on the off-diagonals indicate the errors of the meta classifier. 7,002 predictions are predicted as FPs even though they are TPs. In contrast, 4,484 predictions are predicted as TPs, even though they are actually FPs. Figure 7 shows a scatter plot of the true IoU_{BEV} of prediction and ground truth and the IoU_{BEV} estimated by LMD meta regression based on a GB model, where each point represents one prediction. Well-concentrated points around the identity (dashed line) indicate well-calibrated IoU_{BEV}-estimates and, therefore, object-wise quality estimates. We observe a cluster of under-estimations for small IoU_{BEV} below the diagonal (bottom left) and false positives, vertically above true $IoU_{\mathrm{BEV}} = 0$ on the left.

Feature Selection for Meta Classification and Meta Regression. Overall, LMD is based on 90 features, which partly describe very similar properties. In order to get a subset of features which contains as few redundancies as possible but is still powerful, we apply a greedy heuristic. Starting with an empty set, a single feature that improves the meta prediction performance maximally is added iteratively. Figure 5 shows results in terms of *AUROC* for meta classification and in terms of R^2 for meta regression for CenterPoint on nuScenes. The tests for the meta classification and the meta regression are independent of each other, i.e., the selected features of the two saturation plots do not have to match. When using five selected features, the associated meta models perform already roughly as well as when using all features (LMD), i.e., 0.19 pp worse in terms of meta classification *AUROC* and 0.92 pp worse in terms of meta regression R^2. With ten features used, the respective differences with the results obtained by LMD are < 0.1 pp and thus negligible. The tests for the greedy selection heuristic for all network-dataset-combinations are shown in the appendix.

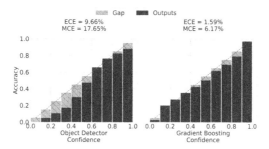

Fig. 8. Reliability plots of the score (left) and GB classifier for LMD (right) with calibration errors (ECE, MCE) for CenterPoint, nuScenes test dataset, score threshold 0.1 and IoU_{BEV} threshold 0.5.

Confidence Calibration. The score and the meta classifier confidences are divided into 10 confidence bins to evaluate their calibration errors. Figure 8 shows exemplary reliability plots for the object detector score and LMD based on a GB classifier with corresponding expected (ECE [14]) and maximum calibration error (MCE [14]). The score is over-confident in the lower confidence ranges and well-calibrated in the upper confidence ranges, whereas the GB classifier for LMD is well-calibrated overall. This observation is also reflected in numerical calibration errors, as the GB classifier for LMD outperforms the score by 8.07 pp in terms of ECE and by 11.48 pp in terms of MCE. This indicates that LMD improves the statistical reliability of the confidence assignment.

Fig. 9. Proposed annotation errors in nuScenes (top two) and KITTI (bottom two). Top images show point clouds with annotations in purple and the proposal in red. Camera images aid the evaluation. (Color figure online)

Annotation Error Detection as an Application of Meta Classification. The task of annotations error detection with LMD is inspired by Fig. 7. There are a number of predictions with $IoU_{\mathrm{BEV}} = 0$ but with high predicted IoU_{BEV}. After looking at these FPs it has been noticed that the prediction itself is, in fact, correct and the corresponding ground truth is not. More precisely, incorrect ground truth corresponds to missing labels, labels with a wrong assigned class or the location of the annotation is inaccurate, i.e., the 3D bounding box is not correctly aligned with the point cloud. Annotation error detection with LMD works as follows: all FP predictions, i.e., predictions that have $IoU_{\mathrm{BEV}} < 0.5$ with the ground truth, are sorted by the predicted IoU_{BEV} in descending order across all images. Then, the first 100 predictions, i.e., the top 100 FPs with highest predicted IoU_{BEV}, are manually reviewed, see Fig. 9 for examples of proposals by this method. In this case, a GB classifier is used to predict the box-wise IoU_{BEV}. We compare LMD against a score baseline which works in the same way, except that the FPs are sorted by the objectness score. As a random baseline, 100 randomly drawn FPs are considered for review which provides an insight into how well the respective test dataset is labeled. In general, if it was unclear whether an annotation error was present or not, this case was not marked as annotation error, i.e., the following numbers are a conservative (under-)estimation. LMD finds 43 annotation errors from 100 proposals and, in contrast, the score only 6 out of 100. Even the random baseline still finds 3 annotation errors, which indicates that there is a significant number of annotation errors in the nuScenes test dataset and that these can be found at far smaller effort with LMD than with the score. Annotation error detection counts for nuScenes and KITTI test datasets are shown in the appendix.

5   Conclusion

In this work we have introduced a purely post-processing-based uncertainty quantification method (LMD). A post-processing module, which is simple to fit and can be plugged onto any pre-trained Lidar object detector, allows for swift estimation of confidence (meta classification) and localization precision (meta regression) in terms of IoU_{BEV} at inference time. Our experiments show that separation of true and false predictions obtained from LMD is sharper than that of the base detector. Statistical reliability is significantly improved in terms of calibration of the obtained confidence scores and IoU_{BEV} is estimated to considerable precision at inference time, i.e., without knowledge of the ground truth. In addition to statistical improvement in decision making, we introduce a method for detecting annotation errors in real-world datasets based on our uncertainty estimation method. Error counts of hand-reviewed proposals which are shown for broadly used public benchmark datasets suggest a highly beneficial industrial use case of our method beyond improving prediction reliability. We also hope that our investigations will spark future research in the domains of light-weight uncertainty estimation and annotation error detection for large-scale datasets.

Acknowledgement. We gratefully acknowledge financial support by the state Ministry of Economy, Innovation and Energy of Northrhine Westphalia (MWIDE) and the European Fund for Regional Development via the FIS.NRW project BIT, grant no. EFRE-0400216, as well as "Projekt UnrEAL", grant no. 01IS22069, funded by the German Federal Ministry of Education and Research.

References

1. Caesar, H., et al.: nuScenes: a multimodal dataset for autonomous driving. In: 2020 IEEE/CVF Conference on Computer Vision and Pattern Recognition (CVPR), Seattle, WA, USA, pp. 11618–11628. IEEE (2020). https://doi.org/10.1109/CVPR42600.2020.01164. https://ieeexplore.ieee.org/document/9156412/

2. Chen, H., Huang, Y., Tian, W., Gao, Z., Xiong, L.: MonoRUn: monocular 3D object detection by reconstruction and uncertainty propagation. In: 2021 IEEE/CVF Conference on Computer Vision and Pattern Recognition (CVPR), Nashville, TN, USA, pp. 10374–10383. IEEE (2021). https://doi.org/10.1109/CVPR46437.2021.01024. https://ieeexplore.ieee.org/document/9578186/

3. Davis, J., Goadrich, M.: The relationship between precision-recall and ROC curves. Technical report, Department of Computer Sciences and Department of Biostatistics and Medical Informatics, University of Wisconsin-Madison (2006). https://minds.wisconsin.edu/bitstream/handle/1793/60482/TR1551.pdf

4. Feng, D., Rosenbaum, L., Dietmayer, K.: Towards safe autonomous driving: capture uncertainty in the deep neural network for lidar 3D vehicle detection. In: 2018 21st International Conference on Intelligent Transportation Systems (ITSC), pp. 3266–3273 (2018). https://doi.org/10.1109/ITSC.2018.8569814. ISSN 2153-0017

5. Feng, D., Rosenbaum, L., Timm, F., Dietmayer, K.: Leveraging heteroscedastic aleatoric uncertainties for robust real-time LiDAR 3D object detection. In: 2019 IEEE Intelligent Vehicles Symposium (IV), pp. 1280–1287 (2019). https://doi.org/10.1109/IVS.2019.8814046. ISSN 2642-7214

6. Geiger, A., Lenz, P., Urtasun, R.: Are we ready for autonomous driving? The KITTI vision benchmark suite. In: 2012 IEEE Conference on Computer Vision and Pattern Recognition, pp. 3354–3361 (2012). https://doi.org/10.1109/CVPR.2012.6248074. ISSN 1063-6919

7. Guo, C., Pleiss, G., Sun, Y., Weinberger, K.Q.: On calibration of modern neural networks (2017)

8. Havasi, M., et al.: Training independent subnetworks for robust prediction (2021). http://arxiv.org/abs/2010.06610 [cs, stat]

9. Lang, A.H., Vora, S., Caesar, H., Zhou, L., Yang, J., Beijbom, O.: PointPillars: fast encoders for object detection from point clouds. In: 2019 IEEE/CVF Conference on Computer Vision and Pattern Recognition (CVPR), Long Beach, CA, USA, pp. 12689–12697. IEEE (2019). https://doi.org/10.1109/CVPR.2019.01298. https://ieeexplore.ieee.org/document/8954311/

10. Lin, W.H., Hauptmann, A.: Meta-classification: combining multimodal classifiers. In: Zaïane, O.R., Simoff, S.J., Djeraba, C. (eds.) PAKDD 2002. LNCS, vol. 2797, pp. 217–231. Springer, Heidelberg (2003). https://doi.org/10.1007/978-3-540-39666-6-14

11. Meyer, G.P., Laddha, A., Kee, E., Vallespi-Gonzalez, C., Wellington, C.K.: LaserNet: an efficient probabilistic 3D object detector for autonomous driving. In: 2019 IEEE/CVF Conference on Computer Vision and Pattern Recognition (CVPR), Long Beach, CA, USA, pp. 12669–12678. IEEE (2019). https://doi.org/10.1109/CVPR.2019.01296. https://ieeexplore.ieee.org/document/8953739/

12. Meyer, G.P., Thakurdesai, N.: Learning an uncertainty-aware object detector for autonomous driving. In: 2020 IEEE/RSJ International Conference on Intelligent Robots and Systems (IROS), pp. 10521–10527 (2020). https://doi.org/10.1109/IROS45743.2020.9341623. ISSN 2153-0866

13. MMDetection3D Contributors: OpenMMLab's Next-generation Platform for General 3D Object Detection (2020). https://github.com/open-mmlab/mmdetection3d, original-date: 2020-07-08T03:39:45Z

14. Naeini, M.P., Cooper, G.F., Hauskrecht, M.: Obtaining well calibrated probabilities using Bayesian binning. In: Proceedings of the Twenty-Ninth AAAI Conference on Artificial Intelligence (2015)

15. Pitropov, M., Huang, C., Abdelzad, V., Czarnecki, K., Waslander, S.: LiDAR-MIMO: efficient uncertainty estimation for LiDAR-based 3D object detection. In: 2022 IEEE Intelligent Vehicles Symposium (IV), pp. 813–820 (2022). https://doi.org/10.1109/IV51971.2022.9827244

16. Riedlinger, T., Rottmann, M., Schubert, M., Gottschalk, H.: Gradient-based quantification of epistemic uncertainty for deep object detectors. In: 2023 IEEE/CVF Winter Conference on Applications of Computer Vision (WACV), Waikoloa, HI, USA, pp. 3910–3920. IEEE (2023). https://doi.org/10.1109/WACV56688.2023.00391. https://ieeexplore.ieee.org/document/10030773/

17. Rottmann, M., et al.: Prediction error meta classification in semantic segmentation: detection via aggregated dispersion measures of softmax probabilities. In: 2020 International Joint Conference on Neural Networks (IJCNN), pp. 1–9 (2020). https://doi.org/10.1109/IJCNN48605.2020.9206659. ISSN 2161-4407

18. Rottmann, M., Maag, K., Chan, R., Hüger, F., Schlicht, P., Gottschalk, H.: Detection of false positive and false negative samples in semantic segmentation. In: 2020 Design, Automation & Test in Europe Conference & Exhibition (DATE), pp. 1351–1356 (2020). https://doi.org/10.23919/DATE48585.2020.9116288. ISSN 1558-1101

19. Schubert, M., Kahl, K., Rottmann, M.: MetaDetect: uncertainty quantification and prediction quality estimates for object detection. In: 2021 International Joint Conference on Neural Networks (IJCNN), pp. 1–10 (2021). https://doi.org/10.1109/IJCNN52387.2021.9534289. ISSN 2161-4407

20. Stanley, T.D., Jarrell, S.B.: Meta-regression analysis: a quantitative method of literature surveys. J. Econ. Surv. **19**(3), 299–308 (2005). https://doi.org/10.1111/j.0950-0804.2005.00249.x. https://onlinelibrary.wiley.com/doi/abs/10.1111/j.0950-0804.2005.00249.x

21. Yan, Y., Mao, Y., Li, B.: Second: sparsely embedded convolutional detection. Sensors **18**(10), 3337 (2018)

22. Yang, B., Luo, W., Urtasun, R.: PIXOR: real-time 3D object detection from point clouds. In: 2018 IEEE/CVF Conference on Computer Vision and Pattern Recognition, Salt Lake City, UT, USA, pp. 7652–7660. IEEE (2018). https://doi.org/10.1109/CVPR.2018.00798. https://ieeexplore.ieee.org/document/8578896/

23. Yang, Q., Chen, H., Chen, Z., Su, J.: Uncertainty estimation for monocular 3D object detectors in autonomous driving. In: 2021 6th International Conference on Robotics and Automation Engineering (ICRAE), pp. 55–59 (2021). https://doi.org/10.1109/ICRAE53653.2021.9657820

24. Yin, T., Zhou, X., Krahenbuhl, P.: Center-based 3D object detection and tracking. In: 2021 IEEE/CVF Conference on Computer Vision and Pattern Recognition (CVPR), Nashville, TN, USA, pp. 11779–11788. IEEE (2021). https://doi.org/10.1109/CVPR46437.2021.01161. https://ieeexplore.ieee.org/document/9578166/

A Network Analysis for Correspondence Learning via Linearly-Embedded Functions

Sharik Siddiqi[1,2] and Zorah Lähner[1(✉)]

[1] University of Siegen, Hölderlinstr. 3, 57076 Siegen, Germany
s.siddiqi@iab-weimar.de, zorah.laehner@uni-siegen.de
[2] IAB – Institut für Angewandte Bauforschung,
Über der Nonnenwiese 1, 99428 Weimar, Germany

Abstract. Calculating correspondences between non-rigidly deformed shapes is the backbone of many applications in 3D computer vision and graphics. The functional map approach offers an efficient solution to this problem and has been very popular in learning frameworks due to its low-dimensional and continuous nature. However, most methods rely on the eigenfunctions of the Laplace-Beltrami operator as a basis for the underlying function spaces. While these have many advantages, they are also sensitive to non-isometric deformations and noise. Recently a method to learn the basis functions along with suitable descriptors has been proposed by Marin et al.. We do an in-depth analysis of the architecture proposed, including a new training scheme to increase robustness against sampling inconsistencies and an extension to unsupervised training which still obtains results on-par with the supervised approach.

Keywords: Non-Rigid Correspondence · Unsupervised Learning · Functional Maps · 3D Descriptors · Basis Learning

1 Introduction

The problem of shape correspondence between 3D shapes acts as the foundation in many applications, for example texture and motion transfer, statistical shape modelling or 3D medical applications. The goal is to find a meaningful map between the surfaces of shapes which can vary in shape or pose but with a semantic relation. In contrast to the 3-dimensional rigid case, where only six parameters are necessary to describe the deformation (rotation and translation), the non-rigid scenario involves degrees of freedom for every vertex on the source shape, thus, the search space becomes computationally infeasible to deal with.

To overcome this issue, the concept of functional maps was introduced in [21]. Instead of computing a correspondence between vertices, functional maps compute a correspondence between function spaces on the surface of the shapes.

Supplementary Information The online version contains supplementary material available at https://doi.org/10.1007/978-3-031-54605-1_7.

U. Köthe and C. Rother (Eds.): DAGM GCPR 2023, LNCS 14264, pp. 100–114, 2024.
https://doi.org/10.1007/978-3-031-54605-1_7

Using the Laplace-Beltrami eigenbasis to define these function spaces reduces the correspondence problem to a low-dimensional, continuous optimisation. Due to this, functional maps have been widely popular [8,19,22], especially in learning applications [11,14,27] (see also Sect. 2.2). However, the Laplace-Beltrami eigenfunctions are sensitive to non-isometric deformations and noise associated with the surface. The most common solution is to learn the *descriptor* functions which are robust against the target deformations [11,14,27] while keeping the basis unchanged. To make the *basis* functions robust, the approach of [17] proposed to learn both the basis functions as well as the descriptors used to calculate the functional maps in a data-driven way. However, the method is supervised and relies on a large training dataset with labelled point-to-point correspondences. There is a deficit of such datasets because their generation is very expensive or relies on artificial data which is often too regular to learn robustness against noise. In this paper, we analyse the framework of [17], show points of improvement and propose strategies to overcome the problems of labelled data and sampling irregularity.

Contributions. We provide an analysis of several aspects of the framework in [17] to overcome performance bottlenecks. This includes hyper parameters and base network choice, as well as two extensions to make the training unsupervised and robust against sampling inconsistencies. In order to make the shape matching pipeline [17] sampling invariant and more general, we perform a random sampling scheme during training which provides a trade-off between high computational demand and dependence on the sampling of the input shapes. Additionally, we propose an unsupervised version for the same setup which tackles the shape correspondence task by leveraging prior geometric information associated with the compared shapes as regularisers in order to overcome the need for labelled data which is expensive to produce for the correspondence problem.

2   Related Work

We provide an introduction to learning and non-learning-based non-rigid shape correspondence approaches that are directly related to our method. For a in-depth survey of the topic the interested reader may refer to [28] and [20].

2.1   Non-rigid Correspondence Methods

The problem of finding correspondences between two non-rigidly deformed shapes is often posed as an quadratic assignment problem (QAP) where the solution is a permutation that matches vertices in a way such that the geodesic distances between all pairs of points are as similar as possible [13]. However, this formulation is NP-hard [4] and assumes that the optimal solution can be described by a permutation which is often not the case in reality. Many non-optimal algorithms to solve the QAP problem have been proposed, for example convex relaxations [13], and heuristics for non-convex formulations [12]. To work around the permutation constraint, soft-correspondences are a popular choice [5,26], or the usage of elastic matching formulations [10,34]. Nevertheless, many of these approaches struggle with high resolution meshes. A possible work-around is to add regularization in the extrinsic embedding space, for example by restricting the motion between the input shapes to be volume-preserving [7]. One very widely-used solution is to move from the space of vertex correspondences to functional correspondences. In [21], Ovsjanikov et al. proposed the so-called functional maps that represent correspondences as a transformation matrix between two fixed function basis spaces. Using the frequency ordering of the Laplace-Beltrami eigenspace, this means the correspondence can be approximated by a small matrix with no constraints on the entries. This is also the representation we choose in this paper.

2.2   Functional Map-Based Learning Approaches

Since functional maps provide a continuous and memory-efficient way to represent correspondence, they have been a popular choice in learning-based correspondence approaches. The first attempt to incorporate functional maps into a learning framework was done in DeepFMs [14] by learning the optimal combination of descriptors before optimizing the functional map matrix. This lead to a variety of follow-up work in which this strategy is refined [29], the functional map matrix itself is predicted [15], the framework is made unsupervised [2,11], and the properties of the functional map matrix [27] or of the deformation between the shapes are imposed [9].

However, most of these methods like original work [21], still rely on the usage of the eigenfunctions of the Laplace-Beltrami operator as basis functions. While this selection has many advantages in the setting of non-rigid shape matching, it is also sensitive to non-isometric deformations and noise which deters the performance in these settings. Alternative basis sets have been proposed in the literature, for example in [6,18,23], but most of them work best for fixed settings. Instead of using a predetermined basis set, the approach of [17] suggests to learn the optimal function basis in combination with the descriptor functions from a training set. This works very well, even in the presence of noise, but the approach requires large amounts of labelled data for a supervised training. In this work, we propose a novel way to train this kind of framework in a completely unsupervised way, inspired by the unsupervised descriptor-learning methods of [2,11], thus eliminating the need for accumulation and labelling of huge volumes of data.

3   Background

3.1   Functional Maps

Functional maps frame the correspondence problem in terms of function spaces instead of points on the surface. Let $\mathcal{F}(\mathcal{X})$, $\mathcal{F}(\mathcal{Y})$ be two comparable function spaces on the shapes $\mathcal{X}, \mathcal{Y}$ discretised with n vertices with basis sets $\{\phi_j\}_{j\geq 1} \subset \mathcal{F}(\mathcal{X})$ and $\{\psi_i\}_{i\geq 1} \subset \mathcal{F}(\mathcal{Y})$ respectively. Then, a *functional map* is a linear mapping $C_{\mathcal{X}\mathcal{Y}} : \mathcal{F}(\mathcal{X}) \rightarrow \mathcal{F}(\mathcal{Y})$ between the function spaces. In the case of finite basis sets with cardinality k, the linear mapping can be written simply as a matrix and computed either by construction through a given point-to-point correspondence P or optimised to preserve certain descriptor functions. For a given $P \in \{0,1\}^{n\times n}$ representing the correspondence between the vertices of input shapes $(\mathcal{X}, \mathcal{Y})$ and the basis functions stacked into $\Phi \in \mathbb{R}^{n\times k}$ and $\Psi \in \mathbb{R}^{n\times k}$.

The functional map matrix C can be computed using

$$C = \Psi^{\dagger} \cdot P \cdot \Phi. \tag{1}$$

where † refers to the Pseudo-inverse which is either the transpose or mass-corrected transpose depending on how the eigenfunctions were computed. In the case where no point-wise correspondence is given, the functional map can be approximated from a set of comparable vertex descriptor functions. Consider a set of q corresponding functions $G_{\mathcal{X}} = (f_1, \ldots, f_q) \in \mathbb{R}^{n\times q}$ and $G_{\mathcal{Y}} = (g_1, \ldots, g_q) \in \mathbb{R}^{n\times q}$ (such that $G_{\mathcal{X}} \approx T_F G_{\mathcal{Y}}$, where T_F can be thought of as some sort of functional correspondence), C is computed by solving this least-square problem with k^2 variables

$$\min_{C \in \mathbb{R}^{k\times k}} \left\| G_{\mathcal{X}}^{\top} \Phi - G_{\mathcal{Y}}^{\top} \Psi C \right\|_F^2 \tag{2}$$

which has a closed form solution given by:

$$C = (G_{\mathcal{Y}}^{\top} \Psi)^{-1} (G_{\mathcal{X}}^{\top} \Phi) \tag{3}$$

$\|.\|_F$ denotes the calculation of the Frobenius norm. The most common choice for Φ, Ψ are the first k-eigenfunctions of the Laplace-Beltrami operator, as it was proposed in [21], which provide a basis for square integrable functions L^2 on the surface.

3.2   Linearly-Invariant Embedding

Our method is based on the general network architecture proposed in Marin et al. [17] which proposes to learn both the function basis and the optimal descriptors, associated with the learned basis set, in a joint training regime. The framework uses two PointNet [24] networks, one for the basis functions called *linearly invariant embedding network*, and other for the descriptors, called *probe function network*, which are trained sequentially. An overview of the pipeline is shown in Fig. 1.

Linearly Invariant Embedding. The first step is to train a Siamese network which outputs the embedding functions for each input shape $\mathcal{X}, \mathcal{Y}$. Given a fixed function set $\Phi_{\mathcal{X}}, \Phi_{\mathcal{Y}}$ and a ground-truth correspondence $\Pi_{\mathcal{X}\mathcal{Y}}^{gt}$, The generation of $\Phi_{\mathcal{X}}, \Phi_{\mathcal{Y}}$ is learned through the loss function

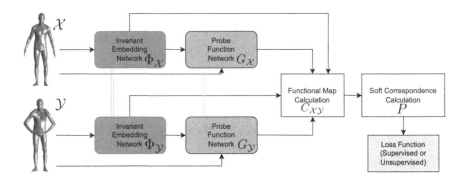

Fig. 1. Overview of the framework. The invariant embedding network generates a basis set Φ. which is then used to generate descriptor functions G. for this basis. Both are used to compute a functional map $C_{\mathcal{X}\mathcal{Y}}$ and soft correspondence P for either the loss function or solution. Networks in the same colour share weights.

$$L(\Phi_{\mathcal{X}}, \Phi_{\mathcal{Y}}) = \frac{1}{n_\beta} \sum \|S_{\mathcal{X}\mathcal{Y}} P_{\mathcal{X}} - \Pi_{\mathcal{X}\mathcal{Y}}^{gt} P_{\mathcal{X}}\|_2^2 \tag{4}$$

where n_β represents the total correspondence cases and $S_{\mathcal{X}\mathcal{Y}}$ denotes a soft permutation matrix which provides an approximate point to point mapping between the defined shapes in a matrix format given by:

$$(S_{\mathcal{X}\mathcal{Y}})_{ij} = \frac{e^{-\|\widehat{\Phi}_{\mathcal{X}}^i - \Phi_{\mathcal{Y}}^j\|_2}}{\sum_{k=1}^{n_y} e^{-\|\widehat{\Phi}_{\mathcal{X}}^i - \Phi_{\mathcal{Y}}^k\|_2}} \tag{5}$$

Equation 4 aims to preserve the coordinate function $P_{\mathcal{X}}$ of $\mathcal{X}$ through the soft correspondence induced by $\Phi_{\mathcal{X}}, \Phi_{\mathcal{Y}}$.

Probe Functions. After completely training the embedding network, the next step is to generate the probe functions based on which the functional map between $\Phi_{\mathcal{X}}$ and $\Phi_{\mathcal{Y}}$ can be predicted with the ground-truth knowledge. The probe functions are also generated by a Siamese network which is trained using the ground-truth functional maps $C_{\mathcal{Y}\mathcal{X}}^{gt} = \Phi_{\mathcal{X}}^{\dagger} \Pi_{\mathcal{Y}\mathcal{X}}^{gt} \Phi_{\mathcal{Y}}$ and $C_{\mathcal{Y}\mathcal{X}} = (\Phi_{\mathcal{X}}^{\dagger} G_{\mathcal{X}})(\Phi_{\mathcal{Y}}^{\dagger} G_{\mathcal{Y}})^{-1}$. The loss function simply compares $C_{\mathcal{Y}\mathcal{X}}^{gt}$ and $C_{\mathcal{Y}\mathcal{X}}$:

$$L(G_{\mathcal{X}}, G_{\mathcal{Y}}) = \|C_{\mathcal{Y}\mathcal{X}}^{gt} - C_{\mathcal{Y}\mathcal{X}}\|_2 \tag{6}$$

4   Method

In this section we describe two major changes we made to the training procedure in order to make it robust to sampling (Sect. 4.2) and shift to unsupervised domain (Sect. 4.1). Additional experiments on single aspects of the architecture are described in Sect. 5.

For two shapes $\mathcal{X}, \mathcal{Y}$, we denote the basis which is the output of the embedding network as $\Phi_{\mathcal{X}}, \Phi_{\mathcal{Y}} \in \mathbb{R}^{n \times k}$, where n and k are the number of vertices and the number of basis functions, respectively. The descriptor functions generated by the probe network are $G_{\mathcal{X}}, G_{\mathcal{Y}} \in \mathbb{R}^{n \times m}$ where m is the descriptor dimension which is a hyperparameter. Finally, $C_{\mathcal{X}\mathcal{Y}}$ indicates the functional map from the function space on $\mathcal{X}$ to $\mathcal{Y}$. The function space is spanned by $\Phi_{\mathcal{X}}, \Phi_{\mathcal{Y}}$ unless indicated otherwise. Notice that with given $\Phi_{\mathcal{X}}, \Phi_{\mathcal{Y}}$ and $G_{\mathcal{X}}, G_{\mathcal{Y}}$, a functional map can always be computed using Eq. (3).

4.1 Unsupervised Training

We adapt the training strategy of [17] to work without the need for labelled ground-truth correspondences. As described in Sect. 3.2 and Fig. 1, the pipeline has two networks that are trained sequentially and both use the ground-truth as part of the loss function. In Eq. (4) the true correspondence is directly included as $\Pi_{\mathcal{X}\mathcal{Y}}^{gt}$ and in Eq. (6) it is used to generate $C_{\mathcal{Y}\mathcal{X}}^{gt}$ using the computed embedding functions. Both networks have to be made unsupervised separately.

Invariant Embedding Network. To make the embedding network unsupervised, we need to remove the need for the ground-truth permutation from the calculation of the functional map $C_{\mathcal{Y}\mathcal{X}}$ in Eq. (4). To achieve this, we utilise handcrafted descriptors for the computation of $C_{\mathcal{Y}\mathcal{X}}$ as is done in the original functional maps framework and explained in Eq. (3). This is only done during training when the learned probe functions are not available yet. To make up for the robustness of the ground-truth, we can impose different meaningful properties of the optimal solution, like orthonormality, to guide the optimisation [27].

In the end, our solution involves aligning pairwise features instead of comparing to the ground-truth and imposing orthonormality both on the resulting functional map as well on the basis functions. Then, the loss function has the following structure:

$$L_{\text{embed}}(\mathcal{X}, \mathcal{Y}) = \ell_{\text{dist}}(\mathcal{X}, \mathcal{Y}) + \alpha \ell_{\text{orth-func}}(\mathcal{X}, \mathcal{Y}) + \beta \ell_{\text{orth-basis}}(\mathcal{X}, \mathcal{Y}) \quad (7)$$

where α and β weight the significance of the orthonormality conditions w.r.t the overall optimisation landscape. We obtained good results with $\alpha = \beta = 0.1$. The terms are defined below.

Distortion Minimisation Term $\ell_{\text{dist}}(\mathcal{X}, \mathcal{Y})$. Instead of comparing whether the soft-correspondence induced by $\Phi_{\mathcal{X}}, \Phi_{\mathcal{Y}}$ imposes the same transformation on $P_{\mathcal{X}}$ as the ground-truth, we will compare whether the soft-correspondence aligns pair-wise properties of $\mathcal{X}$ and $\mathcal{Y}$. Given two matrices $\mathbf{D}_{\mathcal{X}}, \mathbf{D}_{\mathcal{Y}} \in \mathbb{R}^{n \times n}$ that define comparable pair-wise properties on $\mathcal{X}, \mathcal{Y}$, the loss reads as

$$\ell_{\text{dist}}(\mathcal{X}, \mathcal{Y}) = \frac{1}{|\mathcal{Y}|^2} \left\| \mathbf{D}_{\mathcal{Y}} - \mathbf{Q}^{\top} \mathbf{D}_{\mathcal{X}} \mathbf{Q} \right\|_{\text{F}}^2 \quad (8)$$

where $\mathbf{Q} = \mathbf{P} \circ \mathbf{P}$ is the Hadamard product of $\mathbf{P} = \left| \boldsymbol{\Phi}_{\mathcal{Y}} \mathbf{C}_{\mathcal{X}\mathcal{Y}} \boldsymbol{\Phi}_{\mathcal{X}}^{\top} \mathbf{A}_{\mathcal{X}} \right|^{\wedge}$ which is the column normalised $(|\cdot|^{\wedge})$ reversal of Eq. (1) to get a soft correspondence from a given functional map. $\mathbf{A}_{\mathcal{X}}$ is the mass matrix of $\mathcal{X}$. The Hadamard product means that the loss function is derived from the expected deviation from the optimal solution when the columns of Q are interpreted as probabilities of the correspondence of one point. In this step, the $G_{\mathcal{X}}, G_{\mathcal{Y}}$ in the computation of $\mathbf{C}_{\mathcal{X}\mathcal{Y}}$ are manually chosen. We show experiments on this choice in Sect. 5.5. As has been proposed previously in the literature, we try the geodesic distances [11] and heat kernel [2] for $D.$. The results can be found in Sect. 5.5. This term ensures that the geometric structure of the shapes is preserved through the functional map imposed by the embedding functions, which is a property of any good solution.

Orthonormality of the Basis Functions $\ell_{\text{orth-basis}}(\mathcal{X}, \mathcal{Y})$. Orthonormality of the basis functions is desirable as it allows for the efficient calculation and regularisation of the functional map. We impose orthonormality by penalising deviation from the identity in the following form:

$$\ell_{\text{orth-basis}}(\mathcal{X}, \mathcal{Y}) = \left\| \boldsymbol{\Phi}_{\mathcal{X}}^{\top} A_{\mathcal{X}} \boldsymbol{\Phi}_{\mathcal{X}} - \mathbb{I} \right\|_{\text{F}}^{2} + \left\| \boldsymbol{\Phi}_{\mathcal{Y}}^{\top} A_{\mathcal{Y}} \boldsymbol{\Phi}_{\mathcal{Y}} - \mathbb{I} \right\|_{\text{F}}^{2} \qquad (9)$$

where $\mathbb{I}$ is the identity matrix and $A.$ again is the mass matrix of the respective shape which is used to weight the inner product on the surface.

Orthonormality of the Functional Map $\ell_{\text{orth-func}}(\mathcal{X}, \mathcal{Y})$. Orthonormality of the functional map matrix C is associated to area preservation [21] and has been shown to work well as a regularisation term when learning of functional maps [27]. If $\mathbf{C}_{\mathcal{X}\mathcal{Y}}$ is the functional map obtained through Eq. (3), the orthonormality can be enforced as follows:

$$\ell_{\text{orth-func}}(\mathcal{X}, \mathcal{Y}) = \left\| \mathbf{C}_{\mathcal{X}\mathcal{Y}}^{\top} \mathbf{C}_{\mathcal{X}\mathcal{Y}} - \mathbb{I} \right\|_{\text{F}}^{2} \qquad (10)$$

where $\mathbb{I}$ represents the identity matrix.

Probe Function Network. Once the embedding network has been trained, the next step is to train the probe network to generate optimal descriptors that work with new embedding functions. Again, we only need to replace the loss function with an unsupervised counterpart. We adjust the loss function from the embedding network (Eq. (7)) to make it suitable for the new task by dropping the orthonormality of the basis functions which is not needed in this case. The final loss function is then defined as

$$L_{\text{probe}}(\mathcal{X}, \mathcal{Y}) = \ell_{\text{dist}}(\mathcal{X}, \mathcal{Y}) + \alpha \ell_{\text{orth-func}}(\mathcal{X}, \mathcal{Y}) \qquad (11)$$

where $\ell_{\text{dist}}(\mathcal{X}, \mathcal{Y})$ and $\ell_{\text{orth-func}}(\mathcal{X}, \mathcal{Y})$ can be obtained from Eqs. (8) and (10) respectively. Here, instead of fixing $G_{\mathcal{X}}, G_{\mathcal{Y}}$, we fix $\boldsymbol{\Phi}_{\mathcal{X}}, \boldsymbol{\Phi}_{\mathcal{Y}}$ within the loss functions. We use $\alpha = 0.1$.

4.2   Subsampling Scheme

In the proposed approach of [17] all shapes are subsampled to a fixed amount of vertices to make the training feasible. The sampled vertices are the same for all shapes to preserve the ground-truth information from the full shape to make the supervised training possible. However, this leads to incentives for the network to rely on the fixed vertex sampling instead of learning robustness against different vertex distributions which will be present in realistic datasets.

We propose to use a flexible training scheme that simulates varying and non-uniform vertex sampling on the surface. To that end, our training uses a different subset of vertices of a full shape in each training epoch. To achieve a full coverage of the surface we choose a subset $F \subset \mathcal{X}$ with farthest point sampling that stays the same in all epochs – similar to how the training set is chosen in [17]. Further, we add a certain percentage of randomly chosen vertices to the training set. This set changes in each epoch and forces the network to generalise to a wide variety of vertex positions. Unfortunately, this cannot be simply combined with the unsupervised scheme from Sect. 4.1 because it requires either storing a huge geodesic distance matrix with n^2 entries, or computing geodesics on-the-fly which is very slow. However, we show that this strategy vastly improves the performance of the original pipeline when evaluating on full resolution shapes.

5   Experiments

In the following section we describe the experiments done for this paper. Section 5.3 gives a comparison of the supervised approach of [17] with our unsupervised training scheme. In Sect. 5.4 we describe how the random sampling training improves the results of the supervised approach. And finally, in Sect. 5.5 we do an ablation study of several aspects of the original architecture. The mean geodesic error results and hyper parameters of all experiments can be found in the supplementary material.

5.1   Datasets

We use two datasets: the SURREAL [32] dataset consisting of 1000 human shapes with varying pose and body shape. We use this dataset as the training and validation set during the training phase in a ratio of 49:1. For testing we use the registration of the FAUST [3] dataset which contains 100 human shapes of 10 individuals in 10 poses each. We call the setting with two shapes from the same individual *isometric* and from two different individuals *non-isometric*. In order to keep the problem size tractable, all shapes are downsampled to 1000 and 2100 vertices (as indicated in the experiment description).

Both datasets originally use the SMPL [16] mesh connectivity and, thus, have a compatible sampling which makes the task easier. However, we introduce different downsampling strategies in the experiments in Sect. 5.4 to generate inconsistent samplings with increased complexity.

For pre-processing, we zero-mean the coordinate functions of all shapes and add random rotations in the range of $(-\pi/2, \pi/2)$ around the y-axis for augmenting the training data.

5.2   Evaluation

We evaluate using the mean geodesic error and cumulative geodesic error plots. For a pair of shapes $(\mathcal{A}, \mathcal{B})$, let $a \in \mathcal{A}$ be the source point, $b \in \mathcal{B}$ the calculated match for a, and $b^* \in \mathcal{B}$ the ground-truth match of a. We measure the relative geodesic error of the correspondence (a, b) as:

$$\epsilon(a, b) = \frac{\text{dist}_{\text{geo}}(b, b^*)}{\text{diam}(\mathcal{B})} \tag{12}$$

where $\text{dist}_{\text{geo}}(b, b^*)$ represents the geodesic distance between points b and b^* on surface $\mathcal{B}$ and $\text{diam}(\mathcal{B})$ is the geodesic diameter associated with $\mathcal{B}$. The mean geodesic error is the average of $\epsilon(a, b)$ for all calculated matches (a, b).

The cumulative geodesic error curve plots the percentage of correspondences that are below the threshold given on the x-axis in percentage of the geodesic diameter of $\mathcal{B}$. The performance comparison is done on pairs of isometric and non-isometric shapes.

Qualitative Results. We visualise the results by colour transfer. For a correspondence between shapes $\mathcal{X}$ and $\mathcal{Y}$, we plot a fixed, smooth colour function based on the 3D coordinates of $\mathcal{X}$ and then use the computed correspondence to transfer the colourmap to shape $\mathcal{Y}$. Wrong correspondences are visible through wrong colours and non-smooth areas. See Fig. 2.

5.3   Correspondence Accuracy

We evaluate the performance of our unsupervised setup against the original implementation of [17] on both isometric (from the same class in FAUST) and non-isometric (from different classes) pairs. We report the results and some qualitative examples in Fig. 2. Even though we do not use any ground-truth information, we were able to achieve results on-par with the supervised approach. Interestingly, there is nearly no difference in results between the isometric and non-isometric cases, especially for the unsupervised training, which is an indicator that the usage of learned basis functions instead of isometry-invariant Laplace-Beltrami eigenfunctions is indeed more robust against deviations from the isometry assumption.

5.4   Different Sampling

The SURREAL and FAUST template datasets have the same mesh topology due to the usage of the same SMPL model. This is not a realistic assumption in many settings since a registration to a joint mesh already assumes a correspondence

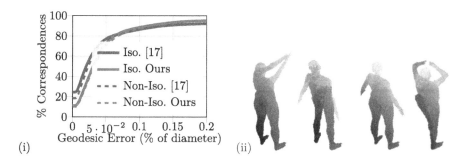

Fig. 2. (Left) Comparison of results on the FAUST test dataset. (Right) Qualitative examples of the results on the FAUST dataset with 1000 vertices. The results are overall accurate except some small noise, see for example the right hand in (ii).

was computed through the registration process. Instead real-world scans have varying connectivity and different sampling density on different mesh parts due to the acquisition process. We simulate this effect by downsampling our shapes with farthest point sampling (FPS) plus a certain percentage of random points instead of a fixed, consistent subset for all shapes as explained in Sect. 4.2.

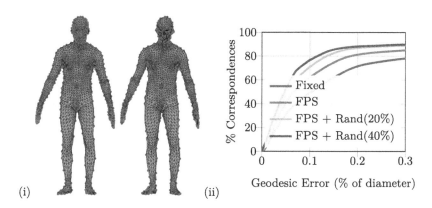

Fig. 3. (i) Examples of the same shape with different sampling. (Left) 1000 of 6980 vertices sampled via FPS. (Right) 600 vertices sampled with FPS and 400 randomly. (ii) Effect of different sampling methods on the results. Using FPS and adding randomly sampled points prevents the network from overfitting on the point distribution and makes the results more robust.

We report the results and an example of the sampling in Fig. 3. Our results show that introducing randomness in the sampling process during training significantly improves the results due to the network being less dependent on the fixed point distribution. However, there needs to be a trade-off between computational load due to addition of more points and improvement in performance.

5.5   Ablation Study

We tested the influence of the different design choices made and justify our decisions with the following ablation study. The mean geodesic errors of all experiments are reported in the supplementary material.

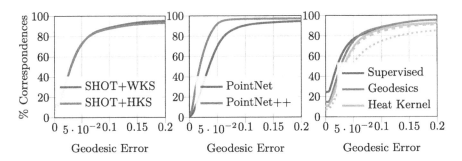

Fig. 4. Cumulative error curves of different settings and architectures. (Left) We test the influence of the different descriptor selection in training of the basis network. The performance difference is minimal. (Middle) Using PointNet++ [25] instead of PointNet [24] as the base architecture significantly improves the performance. (Right) Comparison of the supervised approach in [17], our unsupervised approach with geodesics, and our unsupervised approach with heat kernels. For heat kernel we try a fixed time ($t = 0.01$, dotted), one time reduction ($t = 0.01 \rightarrow 0.007$, dashed), and two time reductions ($t = 0.01 \rightarrow 0.007 \rightarrow 0.005$, solid).

Network Type. The embedding and probe networks from [17] are realised through a PointNet architecture [24]. However, PointNet is known to be well-suited for global feature learning but less to learn distinctive local features due to the global max-pooling. PointNet++ [25] is an extension of PointNet which overcomes these shortcomings and should be able to learn point-wise descriptors better. The replacement of PointNet with PointNet++ results in performance improvement shown in Fig. 4.

Interestingly, the usage of PointNet++ also solves the problem of front-back symmetry flips in the solution. The human shape has very few features that can distinguish the front from the back side (e.g. the face and feet facing forward) and none of them are present on global scale. Due to focus being only on the global scale features in the case of a simple PointNet, the solution often mixes up front and back sides of the shape-pairs but with the usage of PointNet++ this problem is solved. See Fig. 5 for an example.

Learning of Probe Functions. In the unsupervised scenario, the absence of the ground-truth prompts the utilisation of handcrafted descriptors in Eq. 3 to simplify the functional map generation as explained in Sect. 4.1. We propose the use of well-tried HKS [30], WKS [1], and SHOT [31] as $G_\mathcal{X}, G_\mathcal{Y}$ for training the basis network. The HKS and WKS are purely intrinsic while SHOT includes extrinsic information. A combination of intrinsic and extrinsic descriptors often leads to the best results and, eventually, we decided to choose WKS and SHOT based on the results in Fig. 4.

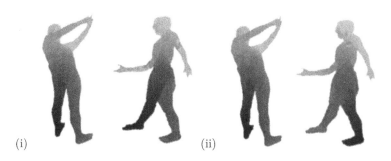

(i)   (ii)

Fig. 5. (i) Front-back symmetry swap when using PointNet due to its global properties. (ii) Correct solution on the same pair when using PointNet++ instead.

Pair-Wise Descriptors. Two pair-wise descriptors are popular choices in the context of non-rigid shape correspondence, namely, the geodesic distances and heat kernel which have for example been used in [11] and [2]. While the geodesics are more expensive to compute, the heat kernel has a time parameter t that has to be chosen. The lower t the more local the heat kernel which leads to more accurate correspondences but a less convex energy landscape [33]. Therefore, reducing the time parameter after a certain amount of epochs can improve the results by applying a sort of coarse-to-fine scheme [2]. We show the results of all choices including the supervised method of [17] in Fig. 4. While the time reduction helps the heat kernel approach, the geodesic distances still perform better.

Network Dimensions. Both the output dimensions of the embedding and the probe network are variables to be chosen. A larger basis and descriptor size allows for more information about the shapes to be processed but at the same time increases the network size and, thus, the complexity of training. The effect on the result is minimal as compared to the associated computational load. Our choice is $d_{out} = 20$ for the embedding network and $d_{out} = 40$ for the probe network due to better trade-off between the complexity and performance (Table 1).

Table 1. Effects of the network output sizes on the embedding and probe networks. We test the effect after the training of the embedding and probe network separately. E stands for embedding and P for probe.

	40-d probe		20-d embedd			final
	20-d E	30-d E	40-d P	50-d P	60-d P	30-d E, 50-d P
after basis train.	0.0204	0.0157	0.0204	0.0204	0.0204	0.0157
after probe train. (full)	**0.1099**	0.1126	**0.1099**	0.1119	0.1152	**0.1051**

6 Conclusion

In this paper, we analysed several aspects of the linear embedding framework of [17] for functional maps in the context of non-rigid shape correspondence. In addition to network hyper parameters, we proposed an extension to make the whole pipeline unsupervised and show that the same performance can be achieved without the use of labelled training data. Additionally, we devised a training strategy based on random sampling during training that improves the robustness of the fixed sampling training in [17] against sampling related artefacts. Overall, we achieved several improvements over the original pipeline which can be used to boost the performance in many applications.

Acknowledgements. Zorah Lähner is supported by a KI-Starter grant of the Ministry of Culture and Science of the State of North Rhine-Westphalia.

References

1. Aubry, M., Schlickewei, U., Cremers, D.: The wave kernel signature: a quantum mechanical approach to shape analysis. In: International Conference on Computer Vision (ICCV) (2011)
2. Aygün, M., Lähner, Z., Cremers, D.: Unsupervised dense shape correspondence using heat kernels. In: Conference on 3D Vision (3DV) (2020)
3. Bogo, F., Romero, J., Loper, M., Black, M.J.: FAUST: dataset and evaluation for 3D mesh registration. In: IEEE Conference on Computer Vision and Pattern Recognition (CVPR) (2014)
4. Burghard, O., Klein, R.: Efficient lifted relaxations of the quadratic assignment problem. In: Vision, Modeling & Visualization (VMV) (2017)
5. Cao, D., Roetzer, P., Bernard, F.: Unsupervised learning of robust spectral shape matching. In: Transactions on Graphics (Proceedings of SIGGRAPH) (2023)
6. Colombo, M., Boracchi, G., Melzi, S.: PC-GAU: PCA basis of scattered gaussians for shape matching via functional maps. In: Smart Tools and Applications in Graphics (STAG) (2022)
7. Eisenberger, M., Lähner, Z., Cremers, D.: Divergence-free shape correspondence by deformation. Comput. Graph. Forum (CGF) **38**(5) (2019)
8. Eisenberger, M., Lähner, Z., Cremers, D.: Smooth shells: multi-scale shape registration with functional maps. In: IEEE Conference on Computer Vision and Pattern Recognition (CVPR) (2020)

9. Eisenberger, M., Toker, A., Leal-Taixé, L., Cremers, D.: Deep shells: unsupervised shape correspondence with optimal transport. In: 34th Conference on Neural Information Processing Systems (NeurIPS) (2020)
10. Ezuz, D., Heeren, B., Azencot, O., Rumpf, M., Ben-Chen, M.: Elastic correspondence between triangle meshes. Comput. Graph. Forum (CGF) (2019)
11. Halimi, O., Litany, O., Rodolà, E., Bronstein, A.M., Kimmel, R.: Unsupervised learning of dense shape correspondence. In: IEEE Conference on Computer Vision and Pattern Recognition (CVPR) (2019)
12. Holzschuh, B., Lähner, Z., Cremers, D.: Simulated annealing for 3D shape correspondence. In: Conference on 3D Vision (3DV) (2020)
13. Kezurer, I., Kovalsky, S.Z., Basri, R., Lipman, Y.: Tight relaxation of quadratic matching. In: Computer Graphics Forum (CGF), vol. 34 (2015)
14. Litany, O., Remez, T., Rodolà, E., Bronstein, A., Bronstein, M.: Deep functional maps: Structured prediction for dense shape correspondence. In: International Conference on Computer Vision (ICCV) (2017)
15. Liu, S., Xu, H., Yan, D.M., Hu, L., Liu, X., Li, Q.: WTFM layer: an effective map extractor for unsupervised shape correspondence. Comput. Graph. Forum **41**(7), 51–61 (2022)
16. Loper, M., Mahmood, N., Romero, J., Pons-Moll, G., Black, M.J.: SMPL: a skinned multi-person linear model. ACM Trans. Graph. (Proc. SIGGRAPH Asia) **34**(6), 248:1–248:16 (2015)
17. Marin, R., Rakotosaona, M.J., Melzi, S., Ovsjanikov, M.: Correspondence learning via linearly-invariant embedding. In: Conference on Neural Information Processing Systems (NeurIPS) (2020)
18. Melzi, S., Rodolà, E., Castellani, U., Bronstein, M.M.: Localized manifold harmonics for spectral shape analysis. Comput. Graph. Forum (CGF) **37**(6) (2018)
19. Melzi, S., Ren, J., Rodolà, E., Sharma, A., Wonka, P., Ovsjanikov, M.: Zoomout: spectral upsampling for efficient shape correspondence. Comput. Graph. Forum (CGF) (2019)
20. Monji-Azad, S., Hesser, J., Löw, N.: A review of non-rigid transformations and learning-based 3D point cloud registration methods. ISPRS J. Photogrammetry Remote Sens. (2023)
21. Ovsjanikov, M., Ben-Chen, M., Solomon, J., Butscher, A., Guibas, L.: Functional maps: a flexible representation of maps between shapes. ACM Trans. Graph. (ToG) (Proc. SIGGRAPH) (2012)
22. Pai, G., Ren, J., Melzi, S., Wonka, P., Ovsjanikov, M.: Fast sinkhorn filters: using matrix scaling for non-rigid shape correspondence with funcitonal maps. In: IEEE Conference on Computer Vision and Pattern Recognition (CVPR) (2021)
23. Panine, M., Kirgo, M., Ovsjanikov, M.: Non-isometric shape matching via functional maps on landmark-adapted bases. Comput. Graph. Forum (CGF) (2022)
24. Qi, C.R., Su, H., Mo, K., Guibas, L.J.: Pointnet: deep learning on point sets for 3D classification and segmentation. IEEE Conference on Computer Vision and Pattern Recognition (CVPR) (2017)
25. Qi, C.R., Yi, L., Su, H., Guibas, L.J.: PointNet++: deep hierarchical feature learning on point sets in a metric space. In: Neural Information Processing Systems (NeurIPS) (2017)
26. Rodolà, E., Bronstein, A., Albarelli, A., Bergamasco, F., Torsello, A.: A game-theoretic approach to deformable shape matching. In: IEEE Conference on Computer Vision and Pattern Recognition (CVPR) (2012)

27. Roufosse, J.M., Sharma, A., Ovsjanikov, M.: Unsupervised deep learning for structured shape matching. In: International Conference on Computer Vision (ICCV) (2019)
28. Sahillioğlu, Y.: Recent advances in shape correspondence. Vis. Comput. (2020)
29. Sharp, N., Attaiki, S., Crane, K., Ovsjanikov, M.: DiffusionNet: discretization agnostic learning on surfaces. Trans. Graph. (ToG) (2022)
30. Sun, J., Ovsjanikov, M., Guibas, L.: A concise and provably informative multi-scale signature based on heat diffusion. In: Symposium on Geometry Processing (SGP) (2009)
31. Tombari, F., Salti, S., Di Stefano, L.: Unique signatures of histograms for local surface description. In: Daniilidis, K., Maragos, P., Paragios, N. (eds.) ECCV 2010. LNCS, vol. 6313, pp. 356–369. Springer, Heidelberg (2010). https://doi.org/10.1007/978-3-642-15558-1_26
32. Varol, G., et al.: Learning from synthetic humans. In: CVPR (2017)
33. Vestner, M., et al.: Efficient deformable shape correspondence via kernel matching. In: International Conference on 3D Vision (3DV) (2017)
34. Windheuser, T., Schlickewei, U., Schmidt, F.R., Cremers, D.: Large-scale integer linear programming for orientation-preserving 3D shape matching. Comput. Graph. Forum (CGF) **30**(5) (2011)

HiFiHR: Enhancing 3D Hand Reconstruction from a Single Image via High-Fidelity Texture

Jiayin Zhu[✉], Zhuoran Zhao, Linlin Yang, and Angela Yao

National University of Singapore, Singapore, Singapore
{zhujiayin,zhuoran.zhao}@u.nus.edu, {yangll,ayao}@comp.nus.edu.sg

Abstract. We present HiFiHR, a high-fidelity hand reconstruction approach that utilizes render-and-compare in the learning-based framework from a single image, capable of generating visually plausible and accurate 3D hand meshes while recovering realistic textures. Our method achieves superior texture reconstruction by employing a parametric hand model with predefined texture assets, and by establishing a texture reconstruction consistency between the rendered and input images during training. Moreover, based on pretraining the network on an annotated dataset, we apply varying degrees of supervision using our pipeline, *i.e.*, self-supervision, weak supervision, and full supervision, and discuss the various levels of contributions of the learned high-fidelity textures in enhancing hand pose and shape estimation. Experimental results on public benchmarks including FreiHAND and HO-3D demonstrate that our method outperforms the state-of-the-art hand reconstruction methods in texture reconstruction quality while maintaining comparable accuracy in pose and shape estimation. Our code is available at https://github.com/viridityzhu/HiFiHR.

Keywords: 3D Hand Reconstruction · 3D from Single Images

1 Introduction

With the development of VR/AR, photo-realistic 3D reconstruction has gained raising attention, and significant progress has been made in the human body and face [12,13,31,35,36]. Hands, as the main medium through which people interact with the world, are also essential to be accurately reconstructed.

Existing works [1,5,14,20,24] leverage differentiable rendering [3] and a parametric hand model, such as MANO [27], to reconstruct 3D hand meshes from images. These methods excel in achieving precise pose estimation while also demonstrating high efficiency during inference. Another recent line of work

---

Supplementary Information The online version contains supplementary material available at https://doi.org/10.1007/978-3-031-54605-1_8.

adapts NeRF-based [31] 3D reconstruction by modeling geometry and texture properties together from ray queries, resulting in high-quality textures [4,6,21]. However, these methods have limitations: (1) Render-based approaches often neglect texture reconstruction or achieve limited accuracy using simplistic representations. (2) NeRF-based methods require videos or multi-view images as input, and suffer from high computational complexity and limited generalization.

In practical applications, obtaining multi-view images can be time-consuming or unfeasible, leaving us with scenarios where only a single image is available. In such cases, render-based methods remain the most viable option. However, monocular images of hands commonly suffer from severe occlusion and depth ambiguity, posing challenges for reconstructing plausible hand structures. This motivates the need for high-fidelity texture reconstruction, as it has the potential to facilitate accurate estimation of hand pose and shape. In contrast, NIMBLE [18], an anatomy-based hand model, embeds numerous texture assets and leverages physical-based rendering [23] for a high-fidelity texture representation. Moreover, it physically constrains the texture by the relative motion between muscles, bones, and skins, which leads to reliable estimation results. Leveraging this novel texture representation holds great potential for enhancing hand reconstruction quality.

Building upon these challenges, our work focuses on achieving high-fidelity texture reconstruction in single-image scenarios. Leveraging the advantage of NIMBLE [18] in a rendering pipeline, we build a HiFiHR (High-fidelity hand reconstruction) model which is able to predict 3D hand pose, shape, texture, and lighting from single input images (Fig. 1).

Furthermore, previous works have attempted to enhance pose estimation through texture reconstruction. However, these efforts have primarily concentrated on single supervision settings, such as self-supervision by S^2HAND [5] and weak supervision by SMHR [26]. Additionally, the limited quality of the reconstructed textures in these approaches hinders their performance. As a result, no significant conclusions have been drawn, leaving room for further exploration. In our work, we comprehensively investigate this question across various levels of supervision, aiming to ascertain the extent to which high-fidelity texture reconstruction consistency can aid the learning of pose and shape.

The main contributions of this work can be concluded as follows.

1. By leveraging the advantages of model-based methods, our approach produces high-fidelity and consistent hand textures from a single input image, resulting in a more realistic representation of the reconstructed 3D hands.
2. We investigate the impact of hand texture reconstruction on pose and shape estimation under varying levels of supervision. Our findings reveal that high-fidelity texture consistency aids pose and shape learning in self-supervision, but introduces noise in weak supervision. And the effect is minimal in full supervision with stronger constraints from 3D labels.
3. Quantitative and qualitative experiments on two single-hand reconstruction benchmarks, i.e., FreiHAND and HO-3D, verify the effectiveness of our approach in both pose and shape accuracy and texture reconstruction quality.

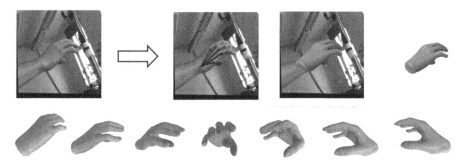

Fig. 1. Our method reconstructs a realistic 3D hand from a monocular image leveraging the NIMBLE [18] hand model and the proposed texture reconstruction consistency. It synthesizes lifelike hands from just a single view, delivering plausible representations from every perspective.

2 Related Work

2.1 Parametric Hand Models

Given parameters on hand pose and shape, parametric hand models infer a hand mesh with vertices and faces. MANO [27] is a widely used hand model, which follows SMPL [19] to adopt linear blend skinning to deform a mesh based on a kinematic skeleton. However, MANO does not capture a texture space. One follow-up work, HTML [24], captures hand texture from two image sequences and fits a MANO template to extract the texture from the scanned mesh. Furthermore, an anatomy-based hand model, NIMBLE [18], creates a better hand texture model via PCA and pre-defined texture assets. The photorealistic texture is represented with diffuse, normal, and specular maps, and a more reliable hand pose can be achieved by enforcing inner bones and muscles to match anatomic and kinematic rules.

2.2 Hand Texture Reconstruction

Boukhayma *et al.* [1] introduce the first end-to-end deep learning-based method that predicts both 3D hand shape and pose from RGB images in the wild. It leverages MANO as a pre-computed hand model and a re-projection module. Similarly, S^2HAND [5] and SMHR [26] achieve 3D hand reconstruction with texture, also adopting MANO as a pre-computed hand model. However, these works achieve limited texture reconstruction because of the simple texture representation, *i.e.*, RGB values of each vertex in the mesh. DeepHandMesh [20] mainly focuses on shape reconstruction, while also providing a method to unwrap multiview RGB images to a high-quality 1024×1024 texture map. Moreover, LiveHand [21] and HandAvatar [4] are two recent NeRF-based works that also achieve photo-realistic texture, but they are not suitable in scenarios when there is only one image available.

Differently, this work aims to achieve high-fidelity 3D hand texture reconstruction from a single image. Based on NIMBLE, a 3D hand mesh with high-resolution texture UV maps can be estimated from the 2D image. By employing a differentiable renderer, weak supervision on hand texture is achieved through consistency between the rendered 2D image and the input image. Additionally, the pipeline incorporates pre-computed texture assets in NIMBLE, enabling the generation of plausible texture estimations for unseen or occluded parts of the hand, even when the input is derived from a monocular view. The iterative render-and-compare loop further ensures accurate alignment of the reconstructed 3D hand with the 2D image.

3   Methods

3.1   Overview

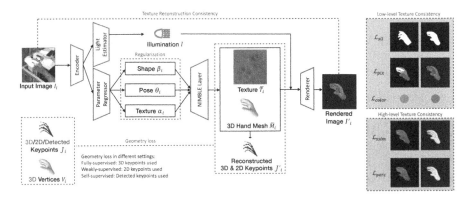

Fig. 2. Overview of our 3D hand reconstruction pipeline. Given one single-view image, our method generates a plausible and high-fidelity 3D textured hand mesh. The method is supervised by geometry loss, texture reconstruction consistency loss, and regularization. Geometry loss adopts different settings under different kinds of supervision. On the right are details of the texture reconstruction consistency, which consists of a low-level consistency and a high-level consistency.

Our end-to-end pipeline is able to reconstruct 3D hand given a single RGB image, as demonstrated in Fig. 2. Given the input image I_i, where $i \in [1, N]$ and N is the number of samples in the dataset, we adopt an encoder $\mathcal{E}$, a NIMBLE [18] hand layer $\mathcal{N}$, and a differentiable renderer $\mathcal{R}$, to obtain a textured 3D hand mesh M_i and a rendered image I'_i.

3.2   Model Structure

Parameter Encoder. An encoder $\mathcal{E}$ is trained to estimate the parameters including shape β_i, pose θ_i, texture α_i, and illumination l_i:

$$\{\beta_i, \theta_i, \alpha_i, l_i\} = \mathcal{E}(I_i). \tag{1}$$

The encoder consists of a visual feature extractor, *e.g.*, Efficientnet [32], and independent MLP layers for each parameter. β_i, θ_i, and α_i are NIMBLE parameters controlling hand shape, pose, and appearance. They are vectors of length 20, 30, and 10, respectively, following the default setting of NIMBLE.

Disentangling lighting from texture is a crucial factor for obtaining plausible hand texture. This is because the feasible texture space of NIMBLE is limited to natural skin tones, while images in the wild often have more complex lighting conditions such as colorful lights that NIMBLE cannot fit. Therefore, we also estimate illumination l_i from the input image, which is a vector of length 6, defining directional lighting from a direction (x_i, y_i, z_i) with color (r_i, g_i, b_i):

$$l_i = (x_i, y_i, z_i, r_i, g_i, b_i). \tag{2}$$

NIMBLE Layer. NIMBLE takes the parameters estimated by the encoder $\mathcal{E}$ as input and generates a realistic 3D hand with bone, muscle, and skin geometry, as well as a photo-realistic appearance:

$$\{\bar{M}_i, \bar{T}_i\} = \mathcal{N}(\beta_i, \theta_i, \alpha_i), \tag{3}$$

where $\bar{M}_i = \{M_i^{skin}, M_i^{bone}, M_i^{muscle}\}$, which consists of a skin mesh, a bone mesh, and a muscle mesh. And $\bar{T}_i = \{T_i^{diff}, T_i^{spec}, T_i^{norm}\}$, which consists of a diffuse map, a specular map, and a normal map.

The skin mesh is physically conditioned by the bone mesh and muscle mesh to obtain plausible hand skin, which contains 5990 vertices and 9984 faces. 25 joints are obtained using a regressor from the skin mesh. However, commonly used datasets only provide annotations for the 778 vertices and 21 joints defined by MANO, and the 25 NIMBLE joints are not compatible. Thus, an additional linear layer is utilized to regress the 778 MANO vertices from the skin mesh, denoted as M_i. Additionally, we adopt the MANO regressor to obtain 21 MANO joints, denoted as J_i^{3D}, from M_i.

Differentiable Render. The generated textured mesh is then rendered back into the image domain as I_i' by a differentiable neural renderer PyTorch3D [25] utilizing the illumination l_i [3]:

$$I_i' = \mathcal{R}(M_i, T_i^{diff}, l_i, k_i), \tag{4}$$

where k_i is the ground truth camera intrinsic parameters. The 2D keypoints J_i' are also re-projected from 3D joints J_i^{3D} given k_i. Note that because the PyTorch3D renderer [25] does not support physical-based rendering yet, we only use T_i^{diff} as the texture UV mapping.

3.3   Training Objective

We train the pipeline using single-view hand images. The optimization objective is to minimize the difference between the input and the rendered hand images, with different levels of supervision on joints and vertices. The overall training loss $\mathcal{L}$ consists of three parts including geometry loss $\mathcal{L}_{geo}$, texture reconstruction consistency loss $\mathcal{L}_{tex}$, and regularization $\mathcal{L}_{regu}$:

$$\mathcal{L} = w_{geo}\mathcal{L}_{geo} + w_{tex}\mathcal{L}_{tex} + w_{regu}\mathcal{L}_{regu}, \tag{5}$$

where w_{geo}, w_{tex}, and w_{regu} are weighting factors for each loss term.

Geometry Loss. The geometry of the mesh is constrained with the following terms:

$$\mathcal{L}_{geo}^{3D} = w_{jnt}\mathcal{L}_{jnt} + w_{vert}\mathcal{L}_{vert} + w_{direc}\mathcal{L}_{direc} + w_{len}\mathcal{L}_{len}, \tag{6}$$

$$\mathcal{L}_{geo}^{2D} = w_{jnt}\mathcal{L}_{jnt}^{2D} + w_{direc}\mathcal{L}_{direc}^{2D}. \tag{7}$$

w_{jnt}, w_{vert}, w_{direc}, and w_{len} are weighting factors for each loss term. In the full 3D supervision scheme, we train the pipeline using $\mathcal{L}_{geo}^{3D}$ where all the loss terms are in 3D space, e.g., the 3D joint loss L_{jnt}. While in the weak 2D supervision scheme, we only employ $\mathcal{L}_{geo}^{2D}$ where all the loss terms are in 2D space after projection. $\mathcal{L}_{jnt}$ and $\mathcal{L}_{vert}$ penalize the l_1-distance between the predicted and ground-truth joint and vertex positions, respectively. $\mathcal{L}_{direc}$ is the loss on bone directions, where a bone is defined as the vector between two adjacent joints. $\mathcal{L}_{len}$ penalizes the difference in edge lengths of all faces. Furthermore, in the self-supervision scheme, we only utilize $\mathcal{L}_{jnt}^{2D}$ and $\mathcal{L}_{direc}^{2D}$ with detected 2D joints obtained through OpenPose [2] at an offline stage, along with corresponding bone directions. The confidence score provided by OpenPose is integrated into $\mathcal{L}_{jnt}^{2D}$ and $\mathcal{L}_{direc}^{2D}$, which shows the probability of joints being detected correctly. Please refer to the supplementary for more information on the losses.

Texture Reconstruction Consistency. The texture reconstruction consistency is designed to ensure the consistency between the input and rendered images, and is formulated as:

$$\mathcal{L}_{tex} = \underbrace{w_{pix}\mathcal{L}_{pix} + w_{color}\mathcal{L}_{color} + w_{sil}\mathcal{L}_{sil}}_{\mathcal{L}_{low\text{-}level}} + \underbrace{w_{ssim}\mathcal{L}_{ssim} + w_{perc}\mathcal{L}_{perc}}_{\mathcal{L}_{high\text{-}level}} \tag{8}$$

$\mathcal{L}_{pix}$ is a per-pixel l_1 loss between the input and rendered images, $\mathcal{L}_{color}$ encourages the mean RGB colors to be close, $\mathcal{L}_{sil}$ penalizes the difference between silhouettes, $\mathcal{L}_{ssim}$ measures the structural similarity between the two images [33], and $\mathcal{L}_{perc}$ is the LPIPS loss [17,37] that captures the perceptual difference between the two images by comparing the features extracted using the AlexNet model [16]. We use a hand mask to extract the foreground hand of the input image to make a comparison with the rendered hand. In the full supervision and weak supervision schemes, we use the ground-truth hand mask. In the self-supervision scheme, we use the predicted hand mask. w_{pix}, w_{color}, w_{sil}, w_{ssim}, and w_{perc} are weighting factors for each loss term.

Among these texture reconstruction consistency terms, the low-level texture consistency $\mathcal{L}_{low-level}$ consists of $\mathcal{L}_{pix}$, $\mathcal{L}_{color}$, and $\mathcal{L}_{sil}$, which operates at the low level of pixel values and results in sensitivity to geometry misalignment. To mitigate this issue, we also include the high-level texture consistency $\mathcal{L}_{high-level}$, consisting of $\mathcal{L}_{ssim}$ and $\mathcal{L}_{perc}$, to enable abstract comparisons of the textures and align more closely with human perceptual results.

Regularization. We also add l_2-regularizers on the magnitude of the shape, pose, and texture parameters to ensure the results are plausible, where w_β, w_θ, and w_α are weighting factors for each loss term:

$$\mathcal{L}_{regu} = w_\beta\|\beta\|_2 + w_\theta\|\theta\|_2 + w_\alpha\|\alpha\|_2. \tag{9}$$

4 Experiment

4.1 Implementation Details

The proposed method is implemented with PyTorch [22]. We use EfficientNet [32] pretrained on the ImageNet dataset as our feature extractor. The input to our model is a 224×224 RGB image. In our training process, the batch size is set to 50. The initial learning rate is 10^{-3} and is decreased by 2 at the epoch of 50, 80, 110, and 160. We use Adam [15] for optimization. We train our model on one NVIDIA QUADRO RTX 8000 GPU. In the full supervision setting, we mainly refer to existing works [5,26] to set $w_{geo} = 100, w_{tex} = 0.01, w_{regu} = 0.01, w_{jnt} = 2, w_{vert} = 1.5, w_{direc} = 0.06, w_{len} = 1, w_{pix} = 2, w_{color} = 0.2, w_{sil} = 0.08, w_{ssim} = 1, w_{perc} = 10^{-6}$. More discussion of weight ablation studies can be seen in the supplementary materials.

4.2 Datasets and Evaluation Metrics

Our pipeline is initially pretrained on a synthetic dataset, either RHD or DART-set, and then train and evaluate on two real-world datasets, including FreiHAND and HO-3Dv2.

RHD [39]. RHD is a considerable synthetic dataset that includes 3D annotations for both singular and interacting hand postures. The dataset synthesizes hand positions from an array of 20 unique characters engaged in a diverse set of 39 actions. It offers a substantial supply of images for empirical study, with $41,258$ training instances and $2,728$ instances for evaluation, thereby providing a slight perturbation in the data distribution.

DARTset [7]. DARTset is a large-scale hand dataset with diverse poses, textures, and accessories, comprising 800K samples split into a training set (758,378) and a test set (28,877). Among these hands, 25% are assigned an accessory. In our experiment, we used 100,000 samples from the training set and 288,77 samples from the test set to pretrain our pipeline.

FreiHAND [40]. FreiHAND is a commonly used dataset that contains single-hand images in the wild. There are 32, 560 images for training and 3, 960 images for testing. For each sample, one RGB image and annotations for 3D joints and vertices labels are provided.

HO-3Dv2 [8]. HO-3D is 3D pose annotations for hands and objects under severe occlusions from each other. It contains annotations for 77,558 images which are split into 66,034 training images (from 55 sequences) and 11,524 evaluation images (from 13 sequences). Evaluations are conducted by submitting our estimated results to their online system.

Evaluation Metrics. As with existing works [1,5], we use the mean per joint position error (MPJPE) and mean per vertex position error (MPVPE) in cm between the prediction and ground truth after Procrustes alignment to evaluate the 3D reconstruction accuracy of the joints and mesh vertices. To evaluate the texture reconstruction accuracy, we use metrics that focus on the rendered image quality. The L1 distance of two images is used for a low-level representation of the reconstruction quality. SSIM [33] and PSNR are used to reflect image similarity as the rendering quality. Besides, consistent with some recent works [4,34], we also adopt LPIPS [37] as high-level metrics representing the human perception of the texture quality.

Table 1. Comparison on FreiHAND [40]. The column "Supv." indicates whether the supervision level is 2D or 3D. The column "Tex." indicates whether the method is able to reconstruct hand texture.

Methods	Supv	MPJPE↓	MPVPE↓	Tex	L1↓	PSNR↑	SSIM↑	LPIPS↓
Biomechanical [30]	2D	1.13	–	No	–	–	–	–
S^{2}HAND [5]	2D	1.18	1.19	Yes	0.12	16.61	0.79	0.43
SMHR [26]	2D	1.07	1.10	Yes	–	16.64	–	–
Ours$_{weak}$	2D	1.23	1.24	Yes	0.02	20.00	0.93	**0.09**
Ours$_{self}$	2D	1.31	1.33	Yes	**0.02**	**20.04**	**0.94**	0.10
Ours$_{self*}$	2D	1.66	1.65	Yes	0.03	17.88	0.92	0.13
Boukhayma et $al.$ [1]	3D	3.50	1.32	No	–	–	–	–
ObMan [10]	3D	1.33	1.33	No	–	–	–	–
ManoCNN [40]	3D	1.10	1.09	No	–	–	–	–
ManoFit [40]	3D	1.37	1.37	No	–	–	–	–
HTML [24][†]	3D	1.11	1.10	Yes	–	–	–	–
HIU [38]	3D	0.71	0.86	No	–	–	–	–
SMHR [26]	3D	0.80	0.81	Yes	–	16.64	–	–
Ours$_{full}$	3D	1.21	1.23	Yes	0.03	**19.55**	0.94	0.10

[†]: Due to the unavailability of HTML's 3D reconstruction implementation codes, which were not published alongside their hand layer codes, we cannot reproduce their results or provide texture reconstruction metrics for comparison.

4.3   Comparison to State-of-the-Art Methods

In this section, we evaluate the reconstruction performance of our approach and compare it with the state-of-the-art methods on two widely used single-hand datasets, FreiHAND [40] and HO-3Dv2 [8]. Following SMHR [26], we mainly focus on the model-based methods for a fair comparison.

Comparison on Geometry Reconstruction Quality. We first report the comparison results on the geometry reconstruction using MPJPE and MPVPE with state-of-the-art methods [1,5,10,24,26,30,38,40]. Note that most existing works focus on the 3D geometry reconstruction and ignore textures, while our work is able to reconstruct the geometry as well as the high-quality texture.

Table 1 shows the results on FreiHAND [40], and Table 2 shows the results on HO-3Dv2 [8]. Ours$_\text{full}$ is our method under full 3D supervision, *i.e.*, supervised with ground truth 3D joints and vertices. Ours$_\text{weak}$ is weakly supervised by only 2D ground truth joints, *i.e.*, $\mathcal{L}_{jnt}^{2D}$. While the definition of self-supervision is controversial, we implement two versions for discussion. Ours$_\text{self}$ follows S^{2}HAND [5] to detect noisy 2D joints via OpenPose [28] and utilize the confidence-aware 2D joint loss, and another version, Ours$_{\text{self}*}$, does not adopt any form of 2D annotation and is only supervised by input images using texture reconstruction consistency losses.

Table 2. Comparison on HO-3Dv2 [8]. The column "Supv." indicates whether the supervision level is 2D or 3D. The column "Tex." indicates whether the method is able to reconstruct hand texture.

Methods	Supv	MPJPE↓	MPVPE↓	Tex	L1↓	PSNR↑	SSIM↑	LPIPS↓
PeCLR [29]	2.5D	1.09	–	No	–	–	–	–
S^{2}HAND [5]	2D	1.14	1.12	Yes	–	13.92	–	–
SMHR [26]	2D	1.03	1.01	Yes	–	16.78	–	–
Ours$_\text{weak}$	2D	1.16	1.23	Yes	0.01	23.66	0.95	0.12
Ours$_\text{self}$	2D	1.23	1.26	Yes	**0.01**	**26.50**	**0.96**	**0.10**
Ours$_{\text{self}*}$	2D	1.48	1.51	Yes	–	–	–	–
HO3D [8]	3D	1.07	1.06	No	–	–	–	–
ObMan [10]	3D	–	1.10	No	–	–	–	–
Photometric [9]	3D	1.11	1.14	No	–	–	–	–
SMHR [26]	3D	1.01	0.97	Yes	–	16.78	–	–
Ours$_\text{full}$	3D	1.16	1.22	Yes	0.01	**23.97**	0.95	0.12

Our method achieves comparable pose and shape accuracy with state-of-the-art methods under all kinds of supervision. Note that previous works like S^{2}HAND [5] and SMHR [26] use additional branches to perform keypoint estimation or hand localization while our pipeline does not rely on an extra branch. Our focus lies in studying the impact of texture reconstruction on pose and shape learning across different levels of supervision, rather than solely aiming for the best results in pose and shape reconstruction. Consequently, we employ a simplified structure and training settings. Therefore, our experimental results remain competitive, demonstrating the robustness and effectiveness of our approach.

Comparison on Texture Reconstruction Quality. Secondly, we compare our texture reconstruction quality with several existing methods that are able to generate hand textures [5, 26]. (See the texture metrics in Table 1 and Table 2).

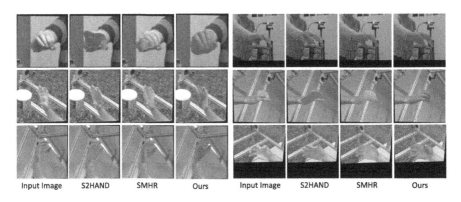

Input Image   S2HAND   SMHR   Ours   Input Image   S2HAND   SMHR   Ours

Fig. 3. Visualization comparison of texture quality with the state-of-the-art methods on FreiHAND and HO-3Dv2. The results clearly demonstrate the superior accuracy, high fidelity, and overall plausibility of our reconstructed hand texture compared to other methods.

It can be clearly seen that our texture reconstruction quality outperforms all the methods. It achieves a 20.2% increase on FreiHAND and a 57.9% increase on HO-3Dv2 in PSNR compared to the previous state-of-the-art method, SMHR [26]. This is mainly because of our high-fidelity texture representation, *i.e.*, physical-based rendering [23], which represents texture using multiple high-resolution UV maps. Instead, S^{2}HAND [5] and SMHR [26] simply represent textures as per-vertex RGB values, which are crude and lack realism. Moreover, we achieve high LPIPS values, showing that our method produces high-fidelity hands in human perception. Here we exclude the texture quality results of Self* from the HO-3Dv2 evaluation because of the significant influence of inaccurate pose and shape estimation on these results.

Figure 4 showcases the visualization results of our reconstructed hands, highlighting the generation of high-fidelity hands with detailed skin features such as palm prints, nails, and bone bumps. Even in challenging scenarios with extreme poses and severe occlusions, our method produces plausible hand reconstructions despite limited information about the hand texture. Besides, Fig. 3 visually compares our method with state-of-the-art approaches, demonstrating the superior accuracy, high fidelity, and plausibility of our reconstructed hand texture.

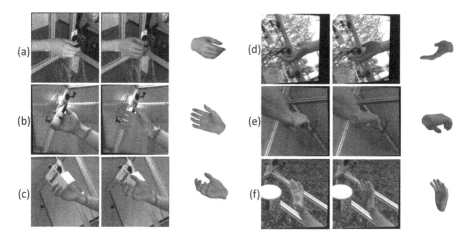

Fig. 4. Qualitative hand reconstruction results on FreiHAND and HO-3Dv2. (a)(b) High-fidelity details such as skin bumps and palm prints. (c)(d)(e) Plausible hands even severely occluded, in extreme poses or viewpoints. (f) Plausible hand even when the input image is in motion blur.

4.4 Evaluation on Texture Reconstruction Consistency with Different Supervision Settings

In this section, we evaluate the effectiveness of our proposed texture reconstruction consistency under different levels of supervision. The experiments in Table 3 align with the settings of $Ours_{full}$, $Ours_{weak}$, $Ours_{self}$, and $Ours_{self*}$, respectively. In experiments without texture reconstruction, we do not implement texture reconstruction consistency losses. Since $Ours_{self*}$ solely employs texture reconstruction losses, there is no corresponding experiment without texture.

Under full 3D supervision, the reconstruction of textures does not significantly affect the pose and shape results. This is attributed to the stronger influence of full 3D supervision compared to textures, causing the texture reconstruction less effective. However, when we reduce the level of supervision to weak 2D supervision, reconstructing textures does not attribute to the pose and shape accuracy. In fact, it introduces noise, resulting in a marginal increase of 0.05 in MPJPE and 0.07 in MPVPE. Nevertheless, as we further decrease the level of supervision to self-supervision using detected noisy keypoints, the texture reconstruction consistency becomes instrumental in learning accurate pose and shape, which improves results in a reduction of MPJPE by 0.02 and MPVPE by 0.03. This indicates that texture consistency loss improves hand reconstruction in the absence of reliable annotations, reducing the reliance on labeled data. In the last experiment, Self*, we adopt a more rigorous form of self-supervision with solely the self-consistency of textures, without any explicitly defined keypoints as auxiliaries for the training. However, this approach yields unsatisfactory results, with an MPJPE of only 1.66. We believe this is because hand has complex pose configurations and depth ambiguities. Only using texture consistency loss can not learn this information well, which focuses more on pixel-level and perceptual-level features. This also indicates that using only the proposed texture consistency loss terms is insufficient to extract adequate information about hand pose and shape from the images.

Table 3. Effect of texture reconstruction consistency with different supervision settings on FreiHAND [40]. The first column indicates the supervision setting, and the second column indicates whether texture reconstruction is included.

Supervision	Texture	MPJPE↓	MPVPE↓	L1↓	PSNR↑	SSIM↑	LPIPS↓
Full	Yes	1.21	1.23	0.03	19.40	0.94	0.11
Full	No	1.21	1.24	–	–	–	–
Weak	Yes	1.28	1.31	0.02	20.00	0.94	0.10
Weak	No	1.23	1.24	–	–	–	–
Self	Yes	1.31	1.33	0.02	20.04	0.94	0.10
Self	No	1.33	1.35	–	–	–	–
Self*	Yes	1.66	1.65	0.03	17.88	0.92	0.13

4.5   Ablation Study

Effect of Our Components. We evaluate the effect of our components in Table 4, using the baseline model with full 3D supervision. The proposed light estimator plays a crucial role in estimating directional lighting and disentangling it from texture, contributing to an increase in PSNR. Besides, replacing the EfficientNet-b3 backbone with ResNet50 [11] leads to a significant decrease in pose and shape performance. Furthermore, we explore pretraining the pose and shape estimator on DART [7] instead of RHD [39], which leads to a slight increase in performance. DART offers a significantly larger dataset, with more diverse pose and shape distribution than RHD. Here we only use 1/7 of its training dataset for pretraining, so the result highlights its potential for enhancing accuracy. Note that we chose RHD as the pretraining dataset for our baseline to ensure a fair comparison, as it is the most widely utilized pretraining dataset. We also assess the effectiveness of our losses. Removing $\mathcal{L}_{vert}$ in full supervision results in a slight decrease in MPVPE. Removing $\mathcal{L}_{perc}$ leads to a noticeable decrease in the quality of the reconstructed texture. Additional ablation studies on losses can be found in the supplementary materials.

Limitations. Some limitations and weaknesses remain. First, using directional light to represent illumination is limited in some complex scenarios. Furthermore, our method does not consider hand-object interaction scenarios. Figure 5 shows some failure cases, including object occlusion, extreme pose and texture, and personal features. To address these limitations, we suggest exploring an enhanced pipeline and considering hand-object interaction scenarios.

Table 4. Ablation study on FreiHAND test set [40]. We study the impact by changing one specific component in each experiment.

Methods	MPJPE↓	MPVPE↓	PSNR↑
Ours	1.21	1.23	19.547
w/o light estimator	1.22	1.25	18.983
ResNet50 as backbone	1.30	1.32	19.582
pretrain on DART	1.20	1.22	19.755
w/o $\mathcal{L}_{vert}$	1.21	1.25	–
w/o $\mathcal{L}_{perc}$	1.21	1.23	19.512

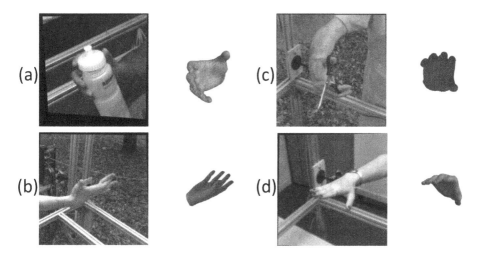

Fig. 5. Failure cases. (a) Incorrect texture color due to occlusion. (b) Incorrect pose due to extreme pose. (c) Incorrect pose due to severe hand-object interaction. (d) Unable to reconstruct the black nail.

5   Conclusions

We present a 3D hand reconstruction method that is able to generate hands with high-fidelity textures from single input images. Our approach surpasses current state-of-the-art methods in texture quality while maintaining competitive pose and shape accuracy. Through extensive experiments across various levels of supervision, we provide valuable insights into the influence of high-fidelity hand texture reconstruction on pose and shape estimation: in scenarios with noisy and relatively weak supervision, textures effectively contribute to pose and shape learning, whereas their impact becomes less significant under stronger supervision. In future work, we aim to extend our research to more complex scenarios that involve hand-object interaction and explore advanced loss terms for texture reconstruction consistency.

References

1. Boukhayma, A., de Bem, R., Torr, P.H.: 3D hand shape and pose from images in the wild. In: Computer Vision and Pattern Recognition, pp. 10843–10852 (2019)
2. Cao, Z., Simon, T., Wei, S.E., Sheikh, Y.: Realtime multi-person 2D pose estimation using part affinity fields. In: Computer Vision and Pattern Recognition, pp. 7291–7299 (2017)
3. Chen, W., et al.: Learning to predict 3D objects with an interpolation-based differentiable renderer. In: Advances in Neural Information Processing Systems (2019)
4. Chen, X., Wang, B., Shum, H.Y.: Hand avatar: free-pose hand animation and rendering from monocular video. arXiv preprint arXiv:2211.12782 (2022)
5. Chen, Y., et al.: Model-based 3D hand reconstruction via self-supervised learning. In: Computer Vision and Pattern Recognition (2021)
6. Corona, E., et al.: Lisa: learning implicit shape and appearance of hands. In: Computer Vision and Pattern Recognition, pp. 20533–20543 (2022)
7. Gao, D., et al.: Dart: articulated hand model with diverse accessories and rich textures. arXiv preprint arXiv:2210.07650 (2022)
8. Hampali, S., Rad, M., Oberweger, M., Lepetit, V.: Honnotate: a method for 3D annotation of hand and object poses. In: Computer Vision and Pattern Recognition (2020)
9. Hasson, Y., Tekin, B., Bogo, F., Laptev, I., Pollefeys, M., Schmid, C.: Leveraging photometric consistency over time for sparsely supervised hand-object reconstruction. In: Computer Vision and Pattern Recognition, pp. 571–580 (2020)
10. Hasson, Y., et al.: Learning joint reconstruction of hands and manipulated objects. In: Computer Vision and Pattern Recognition, pp. 11807–11816 (2019)
11. He, K., Zhang, X., Ren, S., Sun, J.: Deep residual learning for image recognition. arXiv preprint arXiv:1512.03385 (2015)
12. Hong, Y., Peng, B., Xiao, H., Liu, L., Zhang, J.: HeadNeRF: a real-time nerf-based parametric head model. In: Computer Vision and Pattern Recognition (2022)
13. Jiang, W., Yi, K.M., Samei, G., Tuzel, O., Ranjan, A.: NeuMan: neural human radiance field from a single video. In: Avidan, S., Brostow, G., Cissé, M., Farinella, G.M., Hassner, T. (eds.) ECCV 2022. LNCS, vol. 13692, pp. 402–418. Springer, Cham (2022). https://doi.org/10.1007/978-3-031-19824-3_24
14. Karunratanakul, K., Prokudin, S., Hilliges, O., Tang, S.: Harp: personalized hand reconstruction from a monocular RGB video. arXiv preprint arXiv:2212.09530 (2022)
15. Kingma, D.P., Ba, J.: Adam: a method for stochastic optimization. arXiv preprint arXiv:1412.6980 (2014)
16. Krizhevsky, A., Sutskever, I., Hinton, G.E.: ImageNet classification with deep convolutional neural networks. Commun. ACM 60(6), 84–90 (2017)
17. Ledig, C., et al.: Photo-realistic single image super-resolution using a generative adversarial network. In: Computer Vision and Pattern Recognition, pp. 4681–4690 (2017)
18. Li, Y., et al.: Nimble: a non-rigid hand model with bones and muscles. ACM Trans. Graph. 41(4) (2022)
19. Loper, M., Mahmood, N., Romero, J., Pons-Moll, G., Black, M.J.: SMPL: a skinned multi-person linear model. ACM Trans. Graph. 34(6), 248:1–248:16 (2015)
20. Moon, G., Shiratori, T., Lee, K.M.: DeepHandMesh: a weakly-supervised deep encoder-decoder framework for high-fidelity hand mesh modeling. In: Vedaldi, A., Bischof, H., Brox, T., Frahm, J.-M. (eds.) ECCV 2020. LNCS, vol. 12347, pp. 440–455. Springer, Cham (2020). https://doi.org/10.1007/978-3-030-58536-5_26

21. Mundra, A., Wang, J., Habermann, M., Theobalt, C., Elgharib, M., et al.: LiveHand: real-time and photorealistic neural hand rendering. arXiv preprint arXiv:2302.07672 (2023)
22. Paszke, A., et al.: Automatic differentiation in PyTorch. In: NeurIPS Autodiff Workshop (2017)
23. Pharr, M., Jakob, W., Humphreys, G.: 01 - introduction. In: Pharr, M., Jakob, W., Humphreys, G. (eds.) Physically Based Rendering, 3rd edn., pp. 1–55. Morgan Kaufmann, Boston (2017)
24. Qian, N., Wang, J., Mueller, F., Bernard, F., Golyanik, V., Theobalt, C.: HTML: a parametric hand texture model for 3D hand reconstruction and personalization. In: Vedaldi, A., Bischof, H., Brox, T., Frahm, J.-M. (eds.) ECCV 2020. LNCS, vol. 12356, pp. 54–71. Springer, Cham (2020). https://doi.org/10.1007/978-3-030-58621-8_4
25. Ravi, N., et al.: Accelerating 3D deep learning with PyTorch3D. arXiv:2007.08501 (2020)
26. Ren, J., Zhu, J., Zhang, J.: End-to-end weakly-supervised single-stage multiple 3D hand mesh reconstruction from a single RGB image. Comput. Vis. Image Underst. **232**, 103706 (2023)
27. Romero, J., Tzionas, D., Black, M.J.: Embodied hands: modeling and capturing hands and bodies together. ACM Trans. Graph. **36**(6) (2017)
28. Simon, T., Joo, H., Matthews, I., Sheikh, Y.: Hand keypoint detection in single images using multiview bootstrapping. In: Computer Vision and Pattern Recognition (2017)
29. Spurr, A., Dahiya, A., Wang, X., Zhang, X., Hilliges, O.: Self-supervised 3D hand pose estimation from monocular RGB via contrastive learning. In: International Conference on Computer Vision, pp. 11230–11239 (2021)
30. Spurr, A., Iqbal, U., Molchanov, P., Hilliges, O., Kautz, J.: Weakly supervised 3D hand pose estimation via biomechanical constraints. In: Vedaldi, A., Bischof, H., Brox, T., Frahm, J.-M. (eds.) ECCV 2020. LNCS, vol. 12362, pp. 211–228. Springer, Cham (2020). https://doi.org/10.1007/978-3-030-58520-4_13
31. Su, S.Y., Yu, F., Zollhöfer, M., Rhodin, H.: A-NeRF: articulated neural radiance fields for learning human shape, appearance, and pose. In: Advances in Neural Information Processing Systems (2021)
32. Tan, M., Le, Q.: EfficientNet: rethinking model scaling for convolutional neural networks. In: International Conference on Machine Learning, pp. 6105–6114. PMLR (2019)
33. Wang, Z., Bovik, A., Sheikh, H., Simoncelli, E.: Image quality assessment: from error visibility to structural similarity. IEEE Trans. Image Process. **13**(4), 600–612 (2004)
34. Weng, C.Y., Curless, B., Srinivasan, P.P., Barron, J.T., Kemelmacher-Shlizerman, I.: HumanNeRF: free-viewpoint rendering of moving people from monocular video. In: Computer Vision and Pattern Recognition, pp. 16210–16220 (2022)
35. Xu, H., Alldieck, T., Sminchisescu, C.: H-NeRF: neural radiance fields for rendering and temporal reconstruction of humans in motion. In: Advances in Neural Information Processing Systems, vol. 34, pp. 14955–14966 (2021)
36. Xu, T., Fujita, Y., Matsumoto, E.: Surface-aligned neural radiance fields for controllable 3D human synthesis. In: Computer Vision and Pattern Recognition, pp. 15883–15892 (2022)
37. Zhang, R., Isola, P., Efros, A.A., Shechtman, E., Wang, O.: The unreasonable effectiveness of deep features as a perceptual metric. In: Computer Vision and Pattern Recognition, pp. 586–595 (2018)

38. Zhang, X., et al.: Hand image understanding via deep multi-task learning. In: International Conference on Computer Vision, pp. 11281–11292 (2021)
39. Zimmermann, C., Brox, T.: Learning to estimate 3D hand pose from single RGB images. Technical report, arXiv:1705.01389 (2017)
40. Zimmermann, C., Ceylan, D., Yang, J., Russell, B., Argus, M., Brox, T.: Frei-HAND: a dataset for markerless capture of hand pose and shape from single RGB images. In: International Conference on Computer Vision, pp. 813–822 (2019)

Point2Vec for Self-supervised Representation Learning on Point Clouds

Karim Abou Zeid$^{(\boxtimes)}$, Jonas Schult, Alexander Hermans, and Bastian Leibe

RWTH Aachen University, Aachen, Germany
{abouzeid,schult,hermans,leibe}@vision.rwth-aachen.de
https://vision.rwth-aachen.de/point2vec

Abstract. Recently, the self-supervised learning framework data2vec has shown inspiring performance for various modalities using a masked student–teacher approach. However, it remains open whether such a framework generalizes to the unique challenges of 3D point clouds. To answer this question, we extend data2vec to the point cloud domain and report encouraging results on several downstream tasks. In an in-depth analysis, we discover that the leakage of positional information reveals the overall object shape to the student even under heavy masking and thus hampers data2vec to learn strong representations for point clouds. We address this 3D-specific shortcoming by proposing point2vec, which unleashes the full potential of data2vec-like pre-training on point clouds. Our experiments show that point2vec outperforms other self-supervised methods on shape classification and few-shot learning on ModelNet40 and ScanObjectNN, while achieving competitive results on part segmentation on ShapeNetParts. These results suggest that the learned representations are strong, highlighting point2vec as a promising direction for self-supervised learning of point cloud representations.

1 Introduction

In this work, we address the task of self-supervised representation learning on 3D point clouds. With the ever increasing availability of affordable consumer-grade 3D sensors, point clouds are becoming a widely adopted data representation for capturing real-world objects and environments [1,6–8,15]. They provide accurate 3D geometry information, making them a valuable input for many applications in the field of robotics, autonomous driving [7,8], and AR/VR applications. The 3D computer vision community has made impressive progress by developing 3D-centric approaches which directly process 3D point clouds to semantically understand 3D objects and environments [14,35,36,39]. However, these approaches typically rely on fully-supervised training *from scratch* [46], requiring time-consuming and labor-intensive human annotations. For example, semantically annotating a single room-scale scene of the ScanNet dataset takes about 22

K. A. Zeid and J. Schult—Equal contribution.

Supplementary Information The online version contains supplementary material available at https://doi.org/10.1007/978-3-031-54605-1_9.

minutes [15]. This results in a lack of large-scale annotated point cloud datasets, making it challenging to learn strong representations from limited data.

At the same time, self-supervised training has shown impressive results in natural language processing [16,47], speech [3,26], and 2D vision [2,9,12,22,23], enabling learning of meaningful representations from massive unlabeled datasets without any human annotations. Only recently, we have seen self-supervised methods being successfully applied to Transformer architectures for 2D vision [2,9,23] and 3D point clouds [34,49,51]. Baevski *et al.* propose data2vec [2], a modality-agnostic self-supervised learning framework showing competitive performance in speech recognition, image classification, and natural language understanding. Data2vec uses a joint-embedding architecture [2,9,22] with a *student* Transformer encoder and a *teacher* network parameterized as the exponential moving average of the student weights. Specifically, the teacher first predicts latent representations using an uncorrupted view of the input, which the student network then predicts from a masked view of the same input.

In this paper, our aim is to apply data2vec-like pre-training to point clouds. The key difference to top-performing approaches for point cloud representation learning such as Point-MAE [34], Point-M2AE [51] and Point-BERT [49] is the target representation. The self-attention in the student Transformer encoder of data2vec generates *contextualized* feature targets that contain *global* information of the entire input. In contrast, Point-MAE [34] and Point-M2AE [51] explicitly reconstruct only *local* point cloud patches, and Point-BERT [49] is restricted to a fixed-sized vocabulary of token representations. To apply data2vec [2] on point clouds, we use the same underlying 3D-specific Transformer model as Point-BERT [49] and Point-MAE [34]. In experiments, we show that these modality-specific adaptations to data2vec already enable competitive performance compared to highly 3D-specific self-supervised approaches [29,34,44,49,51]. Encouraged by these

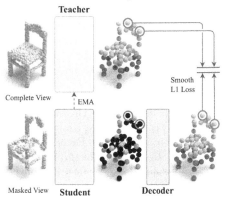

Fig. 1. Overview of point2vec. During training, a teacher network □ predicts latent representations using a complete view of the point cloud. The student network □ predicts the same representations, but from a partial view. A shallow decoder □ then reconstructs the latent representations of masked regions ●, which we can use to train the student and the decoder, whereas the teacher uses an exponential moving average of the student weights. (Color figure online)

promising results, we perform a subsequent analysis that reveals a crucial and point cloud specific shortcoming that restricts data2vec's representation learning capabilities: data2vec uses masked embeddings in the student network which carry positional information. Unlike images, text, and speech, the positional information in point clouds contains semantic meaning, namely 3D point locations (Fig. 4). Feeding masked embeddings with positional information into the student network therefore reveals the overall object shape to the student which makes the masking operation far less effective, as also reported by Pang *et al.* [34] in the context of masked autoencoders for point clouds. Based on this analysis, we propose point2vec that effectively addresses the leakage of positional information to the student and thus unleashes the full potential of data2vec-like pre-training for point clouds. To this end, we exclude masked embeddings from the student network. This prevents the overall object shape from being revealed, while also decreasing the computational cost. Instead, we introduce a shallow decoder which processes masked embeddings together with the student's outputs and which is trained to regress the representations of the teacher (Fig. 1).

Evaluating the quality of the learned representations on downstream tasks is a crucial step for analyzing self-supervised methods. After pre-training on the ShapeNet dataset [10], our experiments demonstrate that point2vec outperforms other self-super-vised methods on both the ModelNet40 [45] and ScanObjectNN [43] shape classification benchmarks. Additionally, point2vec achieves state-of-the-art performance on few-shot classification on ModelNet40 and competitive results on Part Segmentation on ShapeNetPart [48]. These findings suggest that the learned representations are strong and transferable, indicating that point2vec is a promising approach for self-supervised point cloud representation learning.

To summarize, our contributions are: **(1)** We extend the seminal work data2vec [2] to the point cloud domain. **(2)** In our experiments, we discover a crucial shortcoming of data2vec that hampers its representation learning capabilities for point clouds: Masked embeddings leak positional information to the student, revealing the overall object shapes even under heavy masking. **(3)** We propose point2vec which unleashes the full potential of data2vec-like pre-training for self-supervised representation learning by addressing the aforementioned shortcomings. Point2vec learns strong and transferable features in a self-supervised manner, outperforming self-supervised approaches on several downstream tasks.

2   Related Work

Self-supervised Learning. Recently, self-supervised learning gained much attention due to its promise to learn meaningful data representations without any human annotations. At the heart of self-supervised learning is the *pretext* task, offering a vast range of diverse options. One such line of work investigates contrastive learning objectives [12,24,33,41,42], *i.e.* maximizing feature similarity across multiple views of the same training sample while simultaneously minimizing the similarity to other training samples. Contrastive learning approaches typically rely on a careful choice of data augmentations, negative sample mining, or large batch sizes [22]. Addressing these limitations, student–teacher approaches [2,5,9,13,22] follow a *joint-embedding* architecture, *i.e.* two copies of the same network are trained to produce similar latent representations for two views of the identical input. Among them and most important to our work is data2vec [2], which relies on a teacher first generating targets by predicting latent representations using the complete view of the input and a student which predicts these targets using only a *masked* view of the same input. Inspired by data2vec's flexibility across a wide range of modalities, in this paper, we seek to unlock the full potential of data2vec-like pre-training for point clouds by specifically taking the unique characteristics of point clouds into account.

Self-supervised Learning on Point Clouds. The success of self-supervised learning in 2D vision [2,4,5,9,12,22,23,33], natural language processing [2,16], and speech [2,3] has inspired a number of recent works proposing self-supervised learning frameworks for point cloud understanding tasks. Among them, contrastive self-supervised frameworks are typically deployed for room-scale pre-training. The pioneering work of Xie *et al.* [46] contrasts corresponding 3D points from multiple partial views of a reconstructed static scene, showing impressive improvements when fine-tuned on several scene-level downstream tasks. Extending upon this, Hou *et al.* [25] propose to leverage both point-level correspondences and spatial contexts of 3D scenes. In contrast to room-scale pre-training, we see a line of work developing self-supervised methods tailored towards single object understanding tasks [19,21,27,29,34,37,40,44,49,51]. They typically use the inherent structure and geometry of 3D point clouds to learn meaningful representations, *e.g.* by explicitly reconstructing point cloud patches using the Chamfer distance [34,51], discriminating masked points from noise [29], or performing point cloud completion for occluded regions [44]. Another line of work additionally leverages multi-modal information to improve the latent representation of 3D point clouds, *i.e.* incorporating knowledge from models on 2D images [17,21,52,53] or text descriptions [21,52]. The advances of above methods are orthogonal to our approach point2vec as it operates on point clouds only. Most relevant to our work are Transformer-based self-supervised learning approaches on point clouds. Due to the sucess of pre-trained Transformer architectures in various domains [2,9,16,23], we recently see a shift towards pre-training Transformer-based approaches for point clouds [29,32,49,51]. Among them, Point-BERT [49] introduces a standard ViT-like [18] backbone to point clouds and extends BERT pre-training to point clouds [16]. Point-MAE [34] and Point-M2AE [51] follow the masked autoencoder approach proposed by He *et al.* [23]. In contrast to these methods, we do not explicitly reconstruct masked point cloud patches but predict contextualized targets in the latent feature space, circumventing the need to define sophisticated distance metrics to compare point cloud patches.

3   Method

The aim of this work is to unlock the full potential of data2vec-like [2] pre-training on point clouds by addressing point cloud specific challenges. To achieve this, we first summarize the technical concepts of data2vec (Sect. 3.1) and show how to learn rich representations on point clouds using data2vec pre-training (Sect. 3.2). Finally, we propose point2vec, which accounts for the point cloud specific limitations of data2vec (Sect. 3.3).

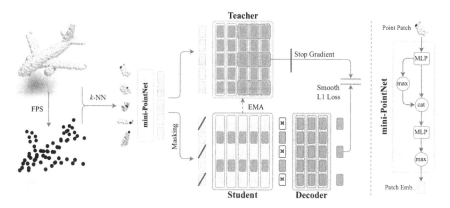

Fig. 2. Point2Vec pre-training. Our model divides the input point cloud into point patches using farthest point sampling (FPS) and k-NN aggregation. We obtain patch embeddings by applying a mini-PointNet □ to each point patch (*right*). The teacher Transformer encoder □ infers a contextualized representation for all patch embeddings which, after normalization and averaging over the last K Transformer layers, serve as training targets. The student's input is a masked view on the input data, *i.e.* we randomly mask out a ratio of patch embeddings and only pass the remaining embeddings into the student Transformer encoder □. After applying a shallow decoder □ on the outputs of the student, padded with learned mask embeddings Ⓜ, we train the student and decoder to predict the latent teacher representation of the patch embeddings. (Color figure online)

3.1 Data2vec

Data2vec [2] is designed to pre-train Transformer-based models, which involve a feature encoder that maps the input data to a sequence of embeddings. These embeddings are subsequently passed to a standard Transformer encoder to generate the final latent representations. During pre-training, two versions of the Transformer encoder are kept: a *student* and a *teacher*. The teacher is a momentum encoder, *i.e.* its parameters Δ track the student's parameters θ by being updated after each training step according to an exponential moving average (EMA) rule [2,9,22,24]: $\Delta \leftarrow \tau\Delta + (1 - \tau)\theta$, where $\tau \in [0, 1]$ is the EMA decay rate. The teacher provides the training targets, which the student predicts given a corrupted version of the same input. In a first step, the teacher encodes the uncorrupted input sequence. The training targets are then constructed by averaging the outputs of the last K blocks of the teacher, which are normalized to prevent a single block from dominating the sum. Due to the self-attention layers, these targets are *contextualized*, *i.e.* they incorporate global information from the whole input sequence. This is an important difference to other masked-prediction methods such as BERT [16] and MAE [23], where the targets only comprise local information, *e.g.* a word or an image patch. The student is given a masked version of the same input, where some of the embeddings in the input sequence are substituted by a special learned *mask embedding*. The student's task is to predict the targets corresponding to the masked parts of the input. The model is trained by optimizing a Smooth L1 loss on the regressed targets.

3.2 Data2vec for Point Clouds

To apply data2vec to point clouds, we utilize the same underlying model as Point-BERT [49] and Point-MAE [34]. This model is well suited for data2vec pre-training: it extracts a sequence of patch embeddings from the input point cloud and feeds it to a standard Transformer encoder. For downstream tasks, we append a task-specific head to the Transformer encoder (Sect. 4). Next, we describe the point cloud embedding and the Transformer in detail and conclude with a summary of data2vec for point clouds.

Point Cloud Embedding. First, we sample n center points from the input point cloud using farthest point sampling (FPS) [36]. Grouping the center points' k-nearest neighbors (k-NN) in the point cloud yields n contiguous *point patches*, *i.e.* sub-clouds of k elements. Next, we normalize the point patches by subtracting the corresponding center point from the patch's points. This untangles the positional and the structural information. As point clouds are permutation-invariant, we use a mini-PointNet [35] (Fig. 2, *right*) that maps each normalized point patch to a *patch embedding*.

The mini-PointNet involves the following steps: First, we map each point of a patch to a feature vector using a shared MLP. Then, we concatenate max-pooled features to each feature vector. The resulting feature vectors are then passed through a second shared MLP and a final max-pooling layer to obtain the patch embedding.

Transformer Encoder. The central component of the model is a standard Transformer encoder. The patch embeddings form the input sequence to the Transformer encoder. Since the point patches are normalized, the patch embeddings carry no positional information; therefore, a two-layer MLP maps each center point to a position embedding, which is then added to the corresponding patch embedding. Due to the special importance of positional information in point clouds, the position embeddings are added again before each subsequent Transformer block to ensure that the positional information is incorporated at every step of the encoding process.

Data2vec–pc. To establish a baseline, we apply the unmodified data2vec approach to the previously described underlying model of Point-BERT and Point-MAE. Going forward, we will refer to this approach as data2vec–pc.

3.3 Point2vec

In Fig. 2, we present the complete pipeline of our point2vec model. Directly applying data2vec to point cloud data without modifications is not optimal, as the position embeddings are also added to the mask embeddings, revealing the overall shape of the point cloud to the student. As positions are the only features, this makes the masking far less effective, as noted by Pang *et al.* [34] in the context of masked autoencoders.

To solve this issue, we adopt an approach inspired by MAE [23], where we only feed the non-masked embeddings to the student □. A separate decoder □, implemented as a shallow Transformer encoder, takes the output of the student and the previously held-back masked embeddings Ⓜ as input and predicts the training targets. In contrast to data2vec–pc, this approach does not suffer from leaking positional information from the masked-out point patches to the student. Moreover, utilizing an MAE-inspired setup provides additional benefits: First, the student is more computationally efficient, as it only needs to process the non-masked embeddings. Second, the model's inputs during fine-tuning are more similar to those during pre-training because they are no longer dominated by masked embeddings which are absent during fine-tuning. This likely makes the learned representations more transferable to downstream tasks.

4 Experiments

In this section, we describe the self-supervised pre-training of point2vec on ShapeNet [10] (Sect. 4.1). Next, we compare point2vec with top-performing self-supervised approaches and our baseline method data2vec–pc on three well-established datasets and four downstream tasks (Sect. 4.2). Finally, we put the spotlight on the architectural changes from our data2vec adaptation for point clouds to our proposed model point2vec which address the unique challenges of 3D point clouds (Sect. 4.3). In the supplementary material, we provide detailed hyperparameters of our model. Code and checkpoints will be made available.

4.1 Self-supervised Pre-training

Following the pre-training protocol propagated by Point-BERT [49], Point-MAE [34] and Point-M2AE [51], we pre-train point2vec on the training split of ShapeNet [10] consisting of 41 952 synthetic 3D meshes of 55 categories, *e.g.* '*chair*', '*guitar*', '*airplane*'. We set the number of Transformer blocks to 12 with an internal dimension of 384. To pre-train our point-based approach, we uniformly sample 8192 points from the surfaces of the objects and then resample 1024 points using farthest point sampling [36]. During the point cloud embedding step we sample $n=64$ center points and $k=32$ nearest neighbors. We train point2vec with a batch size of 512 for 800 epochs using the AdamW [31] optimizer and a cosine learning rate decay [30] with a maximal learning rate of 10^{-3} after 80 epochs of linear warm-up. For data2vec–pc, we increase the batch size and learning rate to 2048 and 2×10^{-3}, respectively, as this empirically led to better results. Following data2vec [2], we set $\beta=2$ for the Smooth L1 loss and average the last $K=6$ blocks of the teacher. We use minimal data augmentations during pre-training: we randomly scale the input with a factor between $[0.8, 1.2]$ and rotate around the gravity axis. Pre-training takes roughly 18 hours on a single V100 GPU.

4.2 Main Results on Downstream Tasks

In order to evaluate the effectiveness of point2vec's self-supervised learning capabilities, we test point2vec against top-performing self-supervised methods on four

Table 1. Part Segmentation on ShapeNetPart [48]. We report mean IoU across all part categories mIoU_C and all instance mIoU_I.

Method	mIoU_C	mIoU_I
Transf.-OcCo [49]	83.4	85.1
Point-BERT [49]	84.1	85.6
MaskPoint [29]	84.4	86.0
Point-MAE [34]	84.1	86.1
Point-M2AE [51]	**84.9**	**86.5**
from scratch	84.1	85.7
data2vec–pc	84.1	85.9
point2vec (Ours)	84.6	86.3

Table 2. Shape Classification on ScanObjNN [43]. We report the overall accuracy over the three subsets OBJ-BG, OBJ-ONLY and the most challenging variant PB-T50-RS.

Method	Overall Accuracy		
	OBJ-BG	OBJ-ONLY	PB-T50-RS
Transf.-OcCo [49]	84.9	85.5	78.8
Point-BERT [49]	87.4	88.1	83.1
MaskPoint [29]	89.3	89.7	84.6
Point-MAE [34]	90.0	88.3	85.2
Point-M2AE [51]	**91.2**	88.8	86.4
from scratch	88.1	88.8	84.3
data2vec–pc	89.7	88.1	85.5
point2vec (Ours)	**91.2**	**90.4**	**87.5**

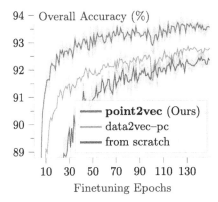

Overall Accuracy (%)

— **point2vec** (Ours)
— data2vec–pc
— from scratch

Finetuning Epochs

Fig. 3. Learning Curves for ModelNet40 [45]. We show the mean (solid line) and the standard deviation (shaded background) over 6 independent runs of point2vec, data2vec–pc as well as the model trained *from scratch* on ModelNet40. Point2vec consistently outperforms the baselines by a large margin.

Table 3. Shape Classification on ModelNet40 [45]. We report the overall accuracy with and without voting.

Method	Overall Accuracy	
	+Voting	−Voting
Transf.-OcCo [49]	92.1	–
ParAE [19]	–	92.9
STRL [27]	93.1	–
Point-BERT [49]	93.2	92.7
PointGLR [37]	–	93.0
OcCo [44]	93.0	–
MaskPoint [29]	93.8	–
Point-MAE [34]	93.8	93.2
Point-M2AE [51]	94.0	93.4
from scratch	93.3	93.0
data2vec–pc	93.6	93.3
point2vec (Ours)	**94.8**	**94.7**

different downstream tasks on well-established benchmarks. To that end, we discard the teacher network as well as the decoder and append a task-specific head to the student network. We then fine-tune the full network end-to-end for the specific task. We provide detailed hyperparameters for all downstream tasks in the supplementary material.

Synthetic Shape Classification. After pre-training on ShapeNet, we fine-tune our model for shape classification on ModelNet40 [45] consisting of 12 311 *synthetic* 3D models of 40 semantic categories. We obtain the semantic class label by passing the concatenated mean- and max-pooled output of the Transformer encoder into a 3-layer MLP and finetune the whole network end-to-end. We use minimal data augmentations consisting only of resampling 1024 points with farthest point sampling, applying random anisotropic scaling of up to 40%, centering at the origin, and rescaling to the unit sphere. Other commonly used augmentations did not improve performance, *e.g.* random rotations around the axis of gravity and random translations are detrimental as ModelNet40 instances are canonically oriented. During the point cloud embedding step we sample n=64 center points and k=32 nearest neighbors. In Table 3, we report a new state-of-the-art for shape classification on ModelNet40 [45] among self-supervised methods by a large margin of +1.3% without voting [34,49,51]. Interestingly, pre-training with data2vec–pc results only in marginal improvements (+0.3% without voting) over the same model trained *from scratch* on ModelNet40. Unlike data2vec–pc, we observe that point2vec unleashes the full potential of data2vec-like pre-training on ModelNet40 by achieving substantial performance gains of +1.7% over the baseline trained from scratch. In Fig. 3, we plot the accuracy per training epoch of point2vec, data2vec–pc, as well as our baseline trained *from scratch* on ModelNet40. We observe that point2vec outperforms our strong baselines by a consistent margin throughout the entire training. Point2vec effectively learns strong feature representations on ShapeNet, resulting in a significantly accelerated adaptation to the fine-tuning task (Fig. 3).

Real-World Shape Classification. Next, we fine-tune point2vec on ScanObjectNN [43] containing 2902 *real-world* object scans of 15 semantic classes. In contrast to shape classification on ModelNet40, we do not resample points but use all 2048 points and sample n=128 center points for the point cloud embedding step. We found more aggressive scaling to be detrimental and use random anisotropic scaling of up to 10%. Although pre-trained on synthetic data, Table 2 shows that point2vec generalizes well to cluttered real-world data and achieves state-of-the-art performance among self-super-vised methods by a significant margin of +1.1% on PB-T50-RS, the most difficult variant of the dataset. We observe that pre-training point2vec on ShapeNet plays a crucial role to its strong performance. Compared to the baseline trained from scratch on ScanObjectNN, pre-training with point2vec achieves an performance gain of +3.2%. We again report improvements of point2vec over data2vec–pc of up to +2.3%.

Few-Shot Classification. Following the standard evaluation protocol proposed by Sharma *et al.* [40], we test the few-shot capabilities of point2vec in a m-way, n-shot setting. To this end, we randomly sample m classes and select n instances for training at random for each of these classes. For testing, we randomly pick 20 unseen instances from each of the m support classes. We provide the standard deviation over 10 independent runs. In Table 4, we report a new state-of-the-art by improvements up to +1.3% in the most difficult 10-way 10-shot setting. Point2vec clearly outperforms the data2vec–pc baseline in all settings. We con-

Table 4. Few-Shot Classification on ModelNet40 [45]. Mean and standard deviation over 10 runs.

Method	5-way		10-way	
	10-shot	20-shot	10-shot	20-shot
OcCo [44]	91.9±3.6	93.9±3.1	86.4±5.4	91.3±4.6
Transf.-OcCo [49]	94.0±3.6	95.9±2.3	89.4±5.1	92.4±4.6
Point-BERT [49]	94.6±3.1	96.3±2.7	91.0±5.4	92.7±5.1
MaskPoint [29]	95.0±3.7	97.2±1.7	91.4±4.0	93.4±3.5
Point-MAE [34]	96.3±2.5	97.8±1.8	92.6±4.1	95.0±3.0
Point-M2AE [51]	96.8±1.8	98.3±1.4	92.3±4.5	95.0±3.0
from scratch	93.8±3.2	97.1±1.9	90.1±4.6	93.6±3.9
data2vec–pc	96.2±2.6	97.8±2.2	92.6±4.9	95.0±3.2
point2vec (Ours)	**97.0**±2.8	**98.7**±1.2	**93.9**±4.1	**95.8**±3.1

clude that point2vec learns rich feature representations which are also well suited for transfer learning in a low-data regime.

Part Segmentation. Finally, we address the task of part segmentation, which assigns a semantic part label to each point in a 3D point cloud of a single object. For this purpose, we employ a simple segmentation head that is similar to the segmentation head in Point-MAE [34]. First, we average the outputs of the 4th, 8th, and 12th Transformer blocks to incorporate features from multiple levels of abstraction. We then concatenate the mean- and max-pooling of the n averaged token outputs, along with the one-hot encoded class label of the object, to obtain a global feature vector. At the same time, we up-sample the n averaged outputs from the corresponding center points to all points using a PointNet++ [36] *feature propagation layer*, which uses inverse distance weighting and a shared MLP to produce a local feature vector for each point. Finally, we concatenate the global feature vector with each local feature vector and a shared MLP predicts a part label for each point. In Table 1, we report competitive results on ShapeNetPart [48] which consists of 16 881 3D models of 16 semantic categories. Apart from Point-M2AE [51], point2vec outperforms all other self-supervised methods. We hypothesize that Point-M2AE's multi-scale U-Net like architecture [38] enables to learn more expressive spatially localized features which results in slightly better scores ($+0.2\,\mathrm{mIoU}_I$). Since point2vec relies on a standard single-scale Transformer backbone, we see multi-scale Transformers for 3D point clouds as an interesting orthogonal improvement, similar to the advances in 2D vision [11,20,28,50] extending vision Transformers [18] with multi-scale capabilities.

4.3   Analysis

Leakage of Positional Information. The main limitation of data2vec–pc is that it directly feeds masked embeddings, along with their positional informa-

Table 5. Ablation. We find that a deferred shallow decoder (**D**) (Fig. 2 ▢) predicting the teacher's representations for masked patches shows consistent improvements but we identify that concealing positional information (**no** Ⓜ) from the student is key.

	no Ⓜ	D	+Voting	−Voting	PB-T50-RS
			ModelNet40		**ScanObjNN**
data2vec–pc	✗	✗	93.6	93.3	85.5
	✗	✓	94.0	93.6	86.8
point2vec	✓	✓	**94.8**	**94.7**	**87.5**

(a) Disclosed Positions (**data2vec–pc**)   (b) Concealed Positions (**point2vec**)

Fig. 4. Leakage Of Positional Information. The center points ● of masked point patches are associated with the masked embeddings (Fig. 2, Ⓜ). (a) data2vec–pc discloses the positions of masked patches to the student, revealing the chair's overall shape. (b) point2vec excludes masked embeddings from the student and therefore conceals the positions of the masked patches.

tion, to the student network, which undermines the effectiveness of masking. To visualize this problem, we show a representative example in Fig. 4(a). Revealing the positions of masked patches of the chair inadvertently weakens the learning objective because it allows the student to rely on the positional information instead of truly learning to predict the teacher's representations of the corresponding masked-out patches. To mitigate this issue, point2vec excludes masked embeddings from the student and only subsequently feeds them to the decoder. As a result, several sections of the chair in Fig. 4(b) are effectively concealed from the student network, leading to a more resilient learning framework. In Table 5, we report that point2vec outperforms our baseline data2vec–pc by a significant margin of up to +2.0%. In particular, we observe that the decoder itself provides consistent improvements, but the key contribution of point2vec is to conceal positional information from the student, *i.e.*, shifting mask tokens from the encoder's input to the decoder (**no** Ⓜ). Complementary to our findings, He *et al.* [23] show that moving masked embeddings to a deferred shallow decoder reduces memory requirements and training time significantly. Our find-

Table 6. Masking Strategy. We explore two variants for masking the input of the student. For **(a)** random masking, we uniformly mask out a given ratio of all embeddings. For **(b)** block masking, we mask out a random embedding and its nearest neighbors. We report the overall accuracy on ModelNet40 and ScanObjectNN.

(a) 65% *random* masking

(b) 65% *block* masking

| | | Overall Accuracy | | |
| | | ModelNet40 | | ScanObjNN |
Strategy	Masking Ratio	+Voting	−Voting	PB-T50-RS
random	45%	94.5	94.3	86.8
random	65%	**94.8**	**94.7**	**87.5**
random	85%	94.5	93.8	86.7
block	25%	93.9	93.7	86.3
block	45%	94.5	93.8	87.4
block	65%	94.0	93.9	86.1

ings align with those of Pang *et al.* [34], who found similar benefits for masked autoencoders on point clouds.

Masking Strategy. The masking strategy defines which of the student's input embeddings are masked (Fig. 2, ⬚). In this study, we investigate two variants of masking strategies with different masking ratios: *random* masking and *block* masking. For random masking, we mask out a specified ratio of embeddings for the student. In contrast, block masking masks out a random embedding and its nearest neighbors such that the specified masking ratio is achieved. This strategy puts focus on masking out spatially contiguous regions of the point cloud whereas random masking is independent of position. Our findings, summarized in Table 6, reveal that random masking with a 65% masking ratio performs best for both ModelNet40 and ScanObjectNN, while block masking lags behind. We attribute this to the high level of ambiguity that arises when masking a spatially contiguous region, resulting in several potential point clouds that could have given rise to the masked input. While we seek a challenging pretext task to learn rich representations, ambiguity should not be the primary source of difficulty.

We recap that our masking strategy is applied to patch embeddings rather than individual points. Consequently, points may belong to *both* masked and unmasked patches. While certain masked patches may be easy to predict, our masking ratio of 65% ensures that there are still plenty of regions entirely masked (Fig. 4, Table 6). As a result, we conclude that the masking ratio is a sensitive

Fig. 5. Visualization of Learned Representations. We use PCA to project the learned representations into RGB space. Both a random initialization and data2vec–pc pre-training show a fairly strong positional bias, whereas point2vec exhibits a stronger semantic grouping without being trained on downstream dense prediction tasks.

hyperparameter that requires some careful tuning to strike the right balance of difficulty for the pretext task.

Visualization of representations learned by point2vec. In Fig. 5, we show qualitative examples of representations of ModelNet40 instances after pre-training on ShapeNet. Both a random initialization and data2vec–pc pre-training show a strong positional bias, whereas point2vec exhibits a stronger semantic grouping without being trained on downstream dense prediction tasks. Unlike data2vec–pc, point2vec conceals positional information from the student, forcing it to learn more about the semantics of the data, resulting in more semantically meaningful representations.

5   Conclusion

In this work, we have extended data2vec to the point cloud domain. Through an in-depth analysis, we have discovered that the disclosure of positional information to the student network hampers data2vec's ability to learn strong representations on point clouds. To overcome this limitation, we have introduced point2vec, a self-supervised representation learning approach which unleashes the full potential of data2vec-like pre-training on point clouds. Point2vec achieves remarkable results on various downstream tasks, surpassing other self-supervised learning approaches in few-shot learning as well as shape classification on well-established benchmarks. Future work might include extending point2vec for scene-level representation learning.

Acknowledgments. This work has been funded, in parts, by the ERC CoG grant DeeViSe (ERC-2017-CoG-773161) and by the BMBF project 6GEM (16KISK036K). We gratefully acknowledge computing resources granted by RWTH Aachen University (thes1313, supp0003) and thank Idil Esen Zulfikar and István Sárándi for helpful discussions and feedback.

References

1. Armeni, I., et al.: 3D semantic parsing of large-scale indoor spaces. In: IEEE Conference on Computer Vision and Pattern Recognition (2016)
2. Baevski, A., Hsu, W.N., Xu, Q., Babu, A., Gu, J., Auli, M.: Data2vec: a general framework for self-supervised learning in speech, vision and language. In: International Conference on Machine Learning (2022)
3. Baevski, A., Zhou, Y., Mohamed, A., Auli, M.: wav2vec 2.0: a framework for self-supervised learning of speech representations. In: Neural Information Processing Systems (2020)
4. Bao, H., Dong, L., Piao, S., Wei, F.: BEiT: BERT pre-training of image transformers. In: International Conference on Learning Representations (2022)
5. Bardes, A., Ponce, J., LeCun, Y.: Vicreg: variance-invariance-covariance regularization for self-supervised learning. In: International Conference on Learning Representations (2022)
6. Baruch, G., et al.: ARKitscenes - a diverse real-world dataset for 3D indoor scene understanding using mobile RGB-D data. In: Neural Information Processing Systems (2021)
7. Behley, J., et al.: SemanticKITTI: a dataset for semantic scene understanding of LiDAR sequences. In: International Conference on Computer Vision (2019)
8. Caesar, H., et al.: nuScenes: a multimodal dataset for autonomous driving. In: IEEE Conference on Computer Vision and Pattern Recognition (2020)
9. Caron, M., et al.: Emerging properties in self-supervised vision transformers. In: International Conference on Computer Vision (2021)
10. Chang, A.X., et al.: Shapenet: an information-rich 3D model repository. arXiv preprint arXiv:1512.03012 (2015)
11. Chen, C.F.R., Fan, Q., Panda, R.: CrossViT: cross-attention multi-scale vision transformer for image classification. In: International Conference on Computer Vision (2021)
12. Chen, T., Kornblith, S., Norouzi, M., Hinton, G.: A simple framework for contrastive learning of visual representations. In: International Conference on Machine Learning (2020)
13. Chen, X., He, K.: Exploring simple siamese representation learning. In: IEEE Conference on Computer Vision and Pattern Recognition (2021)
14. Choy, C., Gwak, J., Savarese, S.: 4D spatio-temporal convnets: minkowski convolutional neural networks. In: IEEE Conference on Computer Vision and Pattern Recognition (2019)
15. Dai, A., Chang, A.X., Savva, M., Halber, M., Funkhouser, T., Nießner, M.: Scannet: richly-annotated 3D reconstructions of indoor scenes. In: Proceedings of the IEEE Conference on Computer Vision and Pattern Recognition (2017)
16. Devlin, J., Chang, M.W., Lee, K., Toutanova, K.: Bert: pre-training of deep bidirectional transformers for language understanding. In: Proceedings of the 2019 Conference of the North American Chapter of the Association for Computational Linguistics (2018)
17. Dong, R., et al.: Autoencoders as cross-modal teachers: can pretrained 2D image transformers help 3D representation learning? In: International Conference on Learning Representations (2023)
18. Dosovitskiy, A., et al.: An image is worth 16x16 words: transformers for image recognition at scale. In: International Conference on Learning Representations (2020)

19. Eckart, B., Yuan, W., Liu, C., Kautz, J.: Self-supervised learning on 3D point clouds by learning discrete generative models. In: IEEE Conference on Computer Vision and Pattern Recognition (2021)
20. Fan, H., et al.: Multiscale vision transformers. In: International Conference on Computer Vision (2021)
21. Gao, M., et al.: ULIP: learning a unified representation of language, images, and point clouds for 3D understanding. In: IEEE Conference on Computer Vision and Pattern Recognition (2023)
22. Grill, J.B., et al.: Bootstrap your own latent-a new approach to self-supervised learning. In: Neural Information Processing Systems (2020)
23. He, K., Chen, X., Xie, S., Li, Y., Dollár, P., Girshick, R.: Masked autoencoders are scalable vision learners. In: IEEE Conference on Computer Vision and Pattern Recognition (2022)
24. He, K., Fan, H., Wu, Y., Xie, S., Girshick, R.: Momentum contrast for unsupervised visual representation learning. In: IEEE Conference on Computer Vision and Pattern Recognition (2020)
25. Hou, J., Graham, B., Nießner, M., Xie, S.: Exploring data-efficient 3D scene understanding with contrastive scene contexts. In: IEEE Conference on Computer Vision and Pattern Recognition (2021)
26. Hsu, W.N., Tsai, Y.H.H., Bolte, B., Salakhutdinov, R., Mohamed, A.: Hubert: how much can a bad teacher benefit ASR pre-training? In: IEEE Conference on Acoustics, Speech and Signal Processing (2021)
27. Huang, S., Xie, Y., Zhu, S.C., Zhu, Y.: Spatio-temporal self-supervised representation learning for 3D point clouds. In: International Conference on Computer Vision (2021)
28. Li, Y., et al.: MViTv2: improved multiscale vision transformers for classification and detection. In: IEEE Conference on Computer Vision and Pattern Recognition (2022)
29. Liu, H., Cai, M., Lee, Y.J.: Masked discrimination for self-supervised learning on point clouds. In: European Conference on Computer Vision (2022)
30. Loshchilov, I., Hutter, F.: SGDR: stochastic gradient descent with warm restarts. In: International Conference on Learning Representations (2017)
31. Loshchilov, I., Hutter, F.: Decoupled weight decay regularization. In: International Conference on Learning Representations (2019)
32. Ma, X., Qin, C., You, H., Ran, H., Fu, Y.: Rethinking network design and local geometry in point cloud: a simple residual MLP framework. In: International Conference on Learning Representations (2022)
33. van den Oord, A., Li, Y., Vinyals, O.: Representation Learning with Contrastive Predictive Coding. arXiv preprint arXiv:1807.03748 (2018)
34. Pang, Y., Wang, W., Tay, F.E., Liu, W., Tian, Y., Yuan, L.: Masked autoencoders for point cloud self-supervised learning. In: European Conference on Computer Vision (2022)
35. Qi, C.R., Su, H., Mo, K., Guibas, L.J.: Pointnet: deep learning on point sets for 3D classification and segmentation. In: IEEE Conference on Computer Vision and Pattern Recognition (2017)
36. Qi, C.R., Yi, L., Su, H., Guibas, L.J.: PointNet++: deep hierarchical feature learning on point sets in a metric space. In: Advances in Neural Information Processing Systems (2017)
37. Rao, Y., Lu, J., Zhou, J.: Global-local bidirectional reasoning for unsupervised representation learning of 3D point clouds. In: IEEE Conference on Computer Vision and Pattern Recognition (2020)

38. Ronneberger, O., Fischer, P., Brox, T.: U-net: convolutional networks for biomedical image segmentation. In: International Conference on Medical Image Computing and Computer-Assisted Intervention (2015)

39. Schult, J., Engelmann, F., Hermans, A., Litany, O., Tang, S., Leibe, B.: Mask3D for 3D semantic instance segmentation. In: IEEE International Conference on Robotics and Automation (2023)

40. Sharma, C., Kaul, M.: Self-supervised few-shot learning on point clouds. In: Neural Information Processing Systems (2020)

41. Tian, Y., Krishnan, D., Isola, P.: Contrastive multiview coding. In: European Conference on Computer Vision (2020)

42. Tian, Y., Sun, C., Poole, B., Krishnan, D., Schmid, C., Isola, P.: What makes for good views for contrastive learning? In: Neural Information Processing Systems (2020)

43. Uy, M.A., Pham, Q.H., Hua, B.S., Nguyen, D.T., Yeung, S.K.: Revisiting point cloud classification: a new benchmark dataset and classification model on real-world data. In: International Conference on Computer Vision (2019)

44. Wang, H., Liu, Q., Yue, X., Lasenby, J., Kusner, M.J.: Unsupervised point cloud pre-training via occlusion completion. In: International Conference on Computer Vision (2021)

45. Wu, Z., et al.: 3D ShapeNets: a deep representation for volumetric shapes. In: International Conference on Computer Vision (2015)

46. Xie, S., Gu, J., Guo, D., Qi, C.R., Guibas, L., Litany, O.: PointContrast: unsupervised pre-training for 3D point cloud understanding. In: European Conference on Computer Vision (2020)

47. Yang, Z., Dai, Z., Yang, Y., Carbonell, J., Salakhutdinov, R.R., Le, Q.V.: XLNet: generalized autoregressive pretraining for language understanding. In: Neural Information Processing Systems (2019)

48. Yi, L., et al.: A scalable active framework for region annotation in 3D shape collections. In: SIGGRAPH Asia (2016)

49. Yu, X., Tang, L., Rao, Y., Huang, T., Zhou, J., Lu, J.: Point-BERT: pre-training 3D point cloud transformers with masked point modeling. In: IEEE Conference on Computer Vision and Pattern Recognition (2022)

50. Zhang, P., et al.: Multi-scale vision longformer: a new vision transformer for high-resolution image encoding. In: International Conference on Computer Vision (2021)

51. Zhang, R., et al.: Point-M2AE: multi-scale masked autoencoders for hierarchical point cloud pre-training. In: Advances in Neural Information Processing Systems (2022)

52. Zhang, R., et al.: Pointclip: point cloud understanding by clip. In: IEEE Conference on Computer Vision and Pattern Recognition (2022)

53. Zhang, R., Wang, L., Qiao, Y., Gao, P., Li, H.: Learning 3D representations from 2D pre-trained models via image-to-point masked autoencoders. In: IEEE Conference on Computer Vision and Pattern Recognition (2023)

FullFormer: Generating Shapes Inside Shapes

Tejaswini Medi[1]([⊠]), Jawad Tayyub[2], Muhammad Sarmad[3], Frank Lindseth[3], and Margret Keuper[1,4]

[1] University of Siegen, Siegen, Germany
tejaswini.medi@uni-siegen.de
[2] Endress + Hauser, Maulburg, Germany
jawad.tayyub@endress.com
[3] Norwegian University of Science and Technology, Trondheim, Norway
muhammad.sarmad@ntnu.no
[4] Max Planck Institute for Informatics, Saarbrücken, Germany
keuper@mpi-inf.mpg.de

Abstract. Implicit generative models have gained significant popularity in the realm of 3D data modeling and have recently demonstrated their efficacy in both encoding and producing high-quality 3D shapes. However, prevailing research predominantly focuses on generating outer shells of 3D shapes, ignoring internal geometric details. In this work, we alleviate this limitation by presenting an implicit generative model that facilitates the generation of complex 3D shapes with rich internal structures. Our proposed model utilizes unsigned distance fields, enabling the representation of nested 3D shapes by learning from watertight and non-watertight data. Furthermore, We employ a transformer-based auto-regressive model for shape generation that leverages context-rich tokens from vector quantized shape embeddings. The generated tokens are decoded into unsigned distance field values which further render into novel 3D shapes exhibiting intrinsic details. We demonstrate that our model achieves state-of-the-art point cloud generation results on the popular ShapeNet classes 'Cars', 'Planes', and 'Chairs'. Further, we curate a dataset that exclusively comprises of shapes with realistic internal details from the 'Cars' category of ShapeNet, denoted *Full-Cars*. This dataset allows us to demonstrate our method's efficacy in generating shapes with rich internal geometry. The code is available at FullFormer.

Keywords: Implicit Generative Models · Unsigned Distance Field

1 Introduction

Continuous representations of data as implicit functions are revolutionizing many research areas of computer vision and graphics. The idea of having a continuously learned implicit function to represent 3D data is efficient since these functions can

---

T. Medi, J. Tayyub and M. Sarmad—These authors contributed equally to this work.

Supplementary Information The online version contains supplementary material available at https://doi.org/10.1007/978-3-031-54605-1_10.

U. Köthe and C. Rother (Eds.): DAGM GCPR 2023, LNCS 14264, pp. 147–162, 2024.
https://doi.org/10.1007/978-3-031-54605-1_10

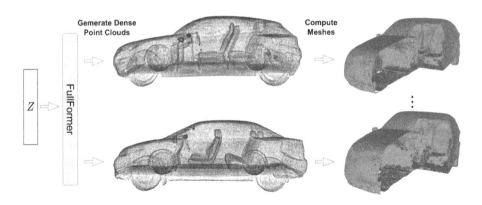

Fig. 1. This paper addresses generating 3D objects with rich internal geometric details.

represent diverse topologies while being agnostic to resolution [12]. Recently, neural networks have been successfully utilized to parameterize such implicit functions, leading to a wide range of applications such as geometry representation [1,29,36], image super-resolution [10] or generative modeling [33,47,58].

Implicit representations for 3D shapes fall into two main categories: one captures the outer surface using occupancy grids, while the other employs distance fields that are able to encode both the surface and internal structure. Occupancy networks [29] define the surface as a continuous decision boundary of a deep neural network classifier whereas DeepSDF [36] represents a 3D surface using a signed distance field (SDF). A significant benefit of using SDF is its easy extraction of surface enabled by the marching cubes algorithm [26]. However, many implicit neural networks based on SDF or Occupancy grids require 3D shapes to be watertight which are often not readily available. Atzmon et al. [1] propose a sign agnostic loss function to learn an SDF from non-watertight data; however, their model requires careful initialization of the neural network parameters and often misses thin structures. Another drawback of SDFs stems from their inherent nature, i.e., 3D shapes are modeled as inside and outside. Recent works, namely 3PSDF [8] and NeAT [28], introduce a 'null' sign in addition to the conventional 'in' and 'out' labels of SDF. This enables the representation of surfaces that can be both watertight and open. However, this approach requires denser sampling in order to insert a null separator layer between multiple surfaces to prevent artifacts.

An alternative implicit representation for complex, non-watertight shapes utilizes unsigned distance fields (UDFs). In UDFs, a 3D shape is delineated through a regressive function that predicts the unsigned distance of a given point in space to the nearest surface of the 3D shape. This representation is capable of encoding multiple-layered internal 3D geometries since distance values are not limited to binary inside or outside flags. However, standard marching cubes algorithm [26] cannot be used for extracting the surface from a UDF since finding a zero-level set by is not possible with UDFs. Chibane et al. [13] proposed algorithms that circumvent this problem and extract point clouds comprising of internal geometries from UDFs. Additionally, several studies have showcased the application of UDFs for shape reconstruction [12,57]. Nonetheless, shape completion/synthesis or novel shape generation with UDFs remains unexplored. In this paper, we present an approach that leverages UDF's capability to represent nested 3D shapes to learn and generate rich internal details of 3D shapes, while ensuring the high quality and diversity of the generated samples.

Facilitating the learning of complex shapes requires a suitable encoding of distant shape contexts. This is especially true when shapes with internal structures are considered, local shape context is not sufficient to model long-range relationships for example between the overall height of a car and the shape or tilting of its seats (the shape of seats in a sports car are quite genre specific). To facilitate the encoding of relationships at varying spatial distances, transformer-based models that leverage self-attention are the method of choice [14,53]. Transformers are proven to be effective in modeling data distributions and generating realistic samples in image generation [16], 3D shape completion [55] and 3D generation tasks [11,31,59]. Unfortunately, transformers can not directly learn from UDF representations since they rely on discrete token representations. Leveraging the advantages of transformers for shape generation with internal structure is therefore non-trivial. In this paper, we contribute the following:

- Our paper presents a generative framework based on implicit neural networks that generate 3D shapes with internal details while modeling long-range shape dependencies as a sequence. With this type of shape-dependent sequencing, transformer-based shape learning can be effectively integrated with UDFs.
- The generative model can be trained using both watertight and non-watertight 3D data. Moreover, it has the capability of generating a variety of topologies, while placing equal emphasis on external and internal aspects.
- We demonstrate that our method outperforms previous point cloud generation approaches in terms of qualitative and quantitative results on different ShapeNet categories as well as on the *FullCars* dataset, a dataset curated from ShapeNet 'Cars' with internal geometric details and non-watertight surfaces.

2 Related Work

Generative Adversarial Networks. A standard generative model used in computer vision applications is the generative adversarial network (GAN) [17]. Recent works [10,24] have shown 3D shape generation combining implicit neural networks and generative adversarial networks. However, the quality of output suffers due to mode collapse and catastrophic forgetting stemming from the instability of GAN training [25,50].

Score-Based Models. Another form of generative models is denoising diffusion probabilistic models, also known as score matching models [20,22,49]. These models learn to model the gradient of the log probability density function with respect to the real sample. Diffusion models have achieved state-of-the-art results in many downstream tasks such as super-resolution, and data generation [3,6,45,58].

Likelihood-Based Models. Variational autoencoders (VAEs) and auto-regressive models (ARs) are two commonly used likelihood-based models. Both aim to learn a probability distribution over the input data. While VAEs are fast at inference time, the quality of generated samples is often inferior compared to that of GANs [23,44]. Conversely, auto-regressive models (ARs) are able to represent data distribution with high fidelity but generate samples slowly [5,35,38,43]. To overcome these limitations, hybrid models have been proposed which combine auto-regressive transformer models and vector quantized VAEs [11,16,31,55,59]. Our proposed method builds upon this hybrid model setup and focuses on generating 3D shapes with internal structures. Our generation approach is related to previous works like ShapeFormer [55] and Pointcloud VQVAE [11]. ShapeFormer [55] utilizes a latent transformer architecture to learn from compact and discretely encoded sequences that approximate 3D shapes, specifically for 3D shape completion utilizing occupancy fields. However, ShapeFormer does not address the task of unconditional shape generation and works on only watertight data. Moreover, they also employ a local pooled PointNet model [42] for feature extraction, which can limit the expressiveness of the feature embeddings. Conversely, Pointcloud VQVAE [11] uses a learned canonical space to align semantically similar point cloud categories into sequences and employs a latent transformer model similar to ShapeFormer to learn these point cloud sequences. However, this method is restricted to point-cloud generation with a fixed number of points. It lacks an implicit representation of 3D shapes, limiting its ability to generate arbitrary resolution shapes or shapes with internal structures. In contrast, our method utilizes implicit representation of 3D shapes along with incorporating locality inductive biases, as in CNNs, in extracted features that allow for tractable feature embeddings. Therefore, we opt for using an IF-Net-based [7] encoder. Moreover, since our method utilises UDFs, it is capable of generating novel shapes with internal structures and isn't constrained by watertight-only models.

Implicit Neural Generative Models. In recent years, neural implicit networks have gained significant attention for their efficacy in 3D representational learning by reconstructing complex 3D shapes [1,8,19,21,30,37,41,46,48,57,61]. While several models have explored implicit representation for 3D surface reconstruction, only a few have used it for 3D model generation [19,31,58,59]. In general, these works rely on a type of neural representation that encapsulates a 3D surface by taking a spatial coordinate value as input and outputs a parameter: ones or zeros for points inside or outside the surface [30] or a signed distance from the surface [37]. However, as mentioned before, these representations do not preserve the multi-layer geometry of 3D shapes. Recently, NDF [13] and GIFS [57] have demonstrated that UDFs are capable of representing inner details within 3D models. Despite its advantages in representation power, learning a UDF is more challenging than an SDF. UDF prediction is a regression problem while SDF and occupancy field are usually classification problems. This makes the problem of training a UDF non-trivial, requiring sophisticated regression algorithms. Direct replacement of SDF with a UDF is not expected to produce viable results immediately. Additionally, due to the lack of a sign in the UDF representation, the model requires a sign-agnostic loss function which has to be carefully initialized and therefore introduces further difficulty than learning an SDF [1,8]. In this paper, we propose a deep implicit generative framework that utilizes UDFs to generate high-quality 3D

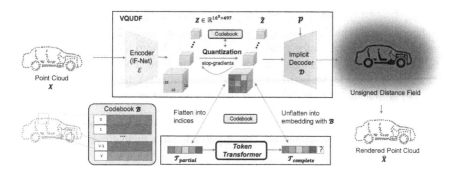

Fig. 2. Approach: Key ingredients of our pipeline are vector quantized autoencoder (VQUDF), unsigned distance field (UDF), and latent transformer. The first stage is learning a VQUDF that takes voxelized point clouds as input to a CNN-based encoder and utilizes an implicit decoder to output a UDF of the 3D shape. UDF ensures rich internal details are retained in a continuous data representation. Latent codes from the learned VQUDF are used to train an autoregressive transformer. This transformer learns to generate novel latent codes at test time. An implicit decoder then decodes generated latent codes to output a UDF. A 3D shape is then rendered from the UDF as a more tractable data format such as a point cloud.

models with internal geometric structures. Our work highlights the potential of UDFs in generating rich 3D models. This has significant implications for various applications, such as product design, robotics, CAD designs, and medical imaging, whereby internal geometries are crucial for accurate modeling and simulation.

3   Method

The objective of this work is to leverage the representational power of unsigned distance fields (UDF) in order to implicitly model 3D shapes while retaining their internal geometric details. To achieve this goal, we utilize the learning capabilities of transformers and incorporate UDF-based implicit function learning to develop an autoregressive generative model capable of generating 3D shapes with internal structures. However, the complexity of the autoregressive generation model increases considerably with the input sequence length [53]. This problem is exasperated when the data representation is a dense 3D model. Therefore, instead of representing a 3D model as voxels, point clouds, or discrete patches directly, we learn a compact and discrete representation whereby a shape is encoded using a codebook of context-rich parts. This allows an autoregressive transformer model to capture long-range interactions between these contextual parts and effectively model the distributions over the full shapes.

Figure 2 details the complete framework of our approach. Our method can be sectioned into two parts. First, we describe a form of an autoencoder, namely Vector Quantized Unsigned Distance Field (VQUDF), which learns a context-rich codebook, as detailed in Sect. 3.1. Then we present the latent transformer architecture as a generative model capable of producing novel shapes, as outlined in Sect. 3.2.

3.1 Sequential Encoding with VQUDF

A 3D shape is represented as a point cloud input denoted by $\mathbf{X} \in \mathbb{R}^{N \times 3}$. To harness the power of transformers in the generation, we encode $\mathbf{X}$ into a discrete *sequence* of tokens. This discrete *sequence* must encapsulate the complete geometric information of the 3D shape. Inspired by ideas from [31,52,55], we formalize the encoder, codebook, and decoder architecture for generating 3D shapes with internal geometry using UDFs.

Encoder: To generate 3D shapes with internal structures using transformers, we require a compact and discrete representation of the input shape that maintains high geometric resolution. The input to our encoder is a sparse voxelized point cloud defining a 3D shape. When dealing with voxel data representations, capturing local spatial context is essential since the correlation between neighboring voxels significantly impacts the overall shape of the object. CNNs are well-suited for capturing prior inductive bias of strong spatial locality within the images [15]. By incorporating local priors from CNNs, we can effectively capture the spatial context of the input data and encode it into a compact feature grid utilizing ideas from neural discrete representation learning [52]. To achieve this, the first step is to employ a CNN-based feature extractor $\mathcal{E}$ called IF-Net [13]. IF-Net takes a sparse voxelized point cloud $\mathbf{X}$ and maps it to a set of *multi-scale* grid of deep features $\mathbf{F}_1, ..., \mathbf{F}_m$ s.t. $\mathbf{F}_k \in \mathcal{F}_k^{K^3}$ and $\mathcal{F}_k \in \mathbb{R}^c$. Note that the resolution K reduces, and the number of channels c increases as k increases. For tractability, we interpolate feature grids $\mathbf{F}_1, ..., \mathbf{F}_{m-1}$ to the scale of final feature grid $\mathbf{F}_m$ using trilinear interpolation. This provides us with a good trade-off between model complexity and shape details. A concatenation of $\mathbf{F}_1, ..., \mathbf{F}_m$ along the channel dimension results in a compact feature grid $\mathbf{Z} \in \mathbb{R}^{K^3 \times C}$, i.e. $\mathbf{Z}$ is a continuous latent feature representation.

Quantization: A discrete description of the world can aid learning by compressing information in many domains, such as language or images [9,32,52]. We posit that 3D models are no exception and can greatly benefit from discrete representations. In addition, to utilize the generative transformer model, the input shape is preferably a discrete *sequence*. Therefore, we employ vector quantization to transform the continuous latent feature representation $\mathbf{Z}$ into a sequence of tokens $\mathcal{T}$ using a learned codebook $\mathcal{B}$ of context-rich codes $\mathcal{B} = \{\mathbf{b}_i\}_{i=1}^V \subset \mathbb{R}^{n_z}$ where n_z is the length $K \times C$ of a code. Following a row-major ordering [16], each feature slice $\mathbf{z}_i \in \mathbf{Z}$ is clamped to the nearest code in the codebook $\mathcal{B}$ using Eq. 1, Fig. 2, which results in a quantized feature grid $\hat{\mathbf{Z}}$. A sequence of tokens $\mathcal{T}$ is then defined as the ordered set of indices $(t_i) \forall i \in \{1, .., |\mathcal{T}|\}$.

$$t_i = \mathrm{argmin}_{j \in \{1, .., V\}} \|\mathbf{z}_i - \mathbf{b}_j\| \tag{1}$$

Decoder: As stated earlier, we aspire to learn an implicit representation of shapes to benefit from properties of such models, for example, no watertight shape restrictions, arbitrary resolution, and encoding internal structures. To achieve this, we train a decoder to output an unsigned distance field $\mathrm{UDF}(\mathbf{p}, \mathcal{S}) = \min_{\mathbf{q} \in \mathcal{S}} \|\mathbf{p} - \mathbf{q}\|$ which is a function that approximates the unsigned distances between the sample points $\mathbf{p}$ and the surface of the shape $\mathcal{S}$. Formally, the decoder is defined as a neural function $\mathcal{D}(\hat{\mathbf{Z}}, \mathbf{p}) : \mathbb{R}^{K^3 \times C} \times \mathbb{R}^3 \mapsto \mathbb{R}^+$ that regresses the UDF from a set of point $\mathbf{p}$ conditioned on the latent discrete feature grid $\hat{\mathbf{Z}}$. The dense point cloud algorithm provided by Chibane et al. [12] is used further to convert UDF to a final point cloud denoted by $\hat{\mathbf{X}}$.

Training VQUDF: The training process involves learning the encoder $\mathcal{E}$, codebook $\mathcal{B}$, and the decoder $\mathcal{D}$ simultaneously. The overall loss function is denoted in Eq. (2).

$$\mathcal{L}_{\text{VQUDF}}(\mathcal{E}, \mathcal{B}, \mathcal{D}) = \| \text{ UDF}(\mathbf{p}, \mathcal{S}) - \text{UDF}_{gt}(\mathbf{p}, \mathcal{S}) \|_2^2 + \mathcal{L}_c \qquad (2)$$

The first term denotes the reconstruction loss, which is computed as the difference between predicted and ground truth UDFs. This method is different from the commonly utilized approach of computing loss between predicted and true point clouds. The second term $\mathcal{L}_c$ denotes the commitment loss in Eq. (3).

$$\mathcal{L}_c = \| \text{ sg}[\mathcal{E}(\mathbf{X})] - \hat{\mathbf{Z}} \|_2^2 + \| \text{ sg}[\hat{\mathbf{Z}}] - \mathcal{E}(\mathbf{X}) \|_2^2 \qquad (3)$$

Different from vanilla NDF training, our pipeline has a non-differentiable quantization operation. Following previous works [2,52], we utilize a straight-through gradient estimator to circumvent this problem. Under this approach, gradients are simply copied over from the decoder to the encoder. This method ensures joint training of the codebook, the encoder, and the decoder.

3.2   Generating a Sequence of Latent Vectors

Latent Transformer: Transformers have shown tremendous performance in generating images by modeling them as a sequence of tokens and learning to generate such sequences [34,39]. Transformers are unconstrained by the locality bias of CNNs allowing them to capture long-range dependencies in images. 3D models with internal structures also exhibit long-range dependencies, for example, the number and shape of seats in a car depend on the body being either a sedan or a sports car. Previous works [11,18,31,54,55,60] have successfully demonstrated capturing these dependencies using transformers for 3D models. We represent 3D shapes as a sequence of tokens $\mathcal{T} = (t_1, ..., t_{|\mathcal{T}|})$ resulting from our trained VQUDF framework. Recall that each token t_i is an index of the closest codebook latent embedding to the continuous latent feature grid. The generation of shapes is modeled as an autoregressive prediction of these indices. A transformer learns to predict the distribution of the next indices given prior ones. The likelihood of the complete sequence $\mathcal{T}$ is described as $p(\mathcal{T}) = \prod_{i=1}^{|\mathcal{T}|} p(t_i | t_{1...i-1})$.

Transformer Training: The generation of latent codes as a sequence of tokens using transformers is highlighted in Fig. 2. The learned weights of the trained VQUDF autoencoder are frozen before the training of the transformer. VQUDF is first used to create a training dataset of 3D shape latent embeddings. These latent embeddings are used in the training of the transformer. The training objective for generation is maximizing the log-likelihood of tokens in a randomly sampled sequence to represent the 3D shape $p(\mathcal{T})$:

$$\mathcal{L}_{\text{Transformer}} = \mathbb{E}_{x \sim p(x)}[-\log p(\mathcal{T})] \qquad (4)$$

After training, this model starts with the [START] token and predicts the next indices forming a complete sequence $\mathcal{T}$ until a [END] token is predicted. By mapping indices in the sequence $\mathcal{T}$ back to the corresponding codebook entries, a discrete latent feature grid $\hat{\mathbf{Z}}$ is recovered. The 3D shape is then reconstructed using the implicit decoder $\mathcal{D}$, which results in a UDF from which point cloud $\hat{\mathbf{X}}$ is extracted as in [13].

4   Experiments

This section thoroughly evaluates our proposed approach on the standard object categories of *Cars*, *Planes*, and *Chairs* from ShapeNetCore [4] dataset. Additionally, we curate a new dataset named 'Full Cars', which constitutes a subset of the *Cars* category of the ShapeNetCore v2 dataset, on which we evaluate our proposed approach and competing methods on their ability to generate shapes with internal structures. Our experiments demonstrate our method's effectiveness in generating high-quality shapes with internal structures. We compare our point cloud generation results against multiple SOTA baselines and show superior qualitative and quantitative results on the task of shape generation. More qualitative results along with an ablation study evaluating the use of UDF over SDF are provided in the supplementary material.

4.1   Implementation Details

We train our models in two stages. First, we train the VQUDF module, followed by a latent transformer module. For training, we utilize stock hardware comprising one Nvidia RTX Quadro GPU with 48GB of VRAM. All code is written in PyTorch [40] whereby a portion is acquired from open repositories of [13, 16]. For training both modules, we use a batch size of 1 and the Adam optimizer. For VQUDF training, we employ a learning rate of 1e-6 and ReLU activation, whereas the transformer's training uses a learning rate of 4.5e-6. Furthermore, the transformer has 12 layers and 8 attention heads. The length of the input sequence to the transformer model is set as 7952; the codebook size is 8192, with each codebook having a dimensionality of 512.

Datasets. We conduct experiments on the standard object categories of *Cars*, *Planes*, and *Chairs* from ShapeNetCore [4] dataset. Additionally, we curate a new dataset named 'Full Cars', which constitutes a subset of the *Cars* category of the ShapeNetCore v2 dataset. The 'Full Cars' dataset includes cars with diverse and realistic internal geometry such as seats, steering wheels, shift sticks, and other internal structures. The primary objective of this dataset is to demonstrate the capability of our model in generating novel and realistic shape interiors. Note that there is a strong interdependency between internal structures and outer car shapes. Further descriptions of datasets and additional training details, including the architecture of our model, are presented in the supplementary material.

4.2   VQUDF Reconstruction Performance

The input point cloud is sampled and voxelized before feeding into the VQUDF encoder. Table 1 summarises the number of sampled points and voxel resolution across different datasets. Recall that the input 3D shape is encoded into a feature grid $\hat{Z}$ where each channel comprises a feature block of resolution K^3. The quality of encoded information and generation capability depends on the dimensionality and resolution K of the 3D latent feature grid $\hat{Z}$. Figure 3 shows reconstruction results of the VQUDF module on the Full Cars dataset with different values of K such that resolution of the 3D latent feature becomes $\hat{\mathbf{Z}} \in \mathbb{R}^{64^3 \times C}$, $\hat{\mathbf{Z}} \in \mathbb{R}^{16^3 \times C}$ and $\hat{\mathbf{Z}} \in \mathbb{R}^{8^3 \times C}$ respectively, where C is the number of channels. Note that the fidelity of internal geometries increases progressively with the dimensionality K of $\hat{\mathbf{Z}}$. However, increased K results in a large quantized sequence length $\mathcal{T}$ making transformer training difficult. Hence, a good trade-off between geometrical fidelity and memory footprint is achieved by selecting $\hat{\mathbf{Z}} \in \mathbb{R}^{16^3 \times C}$ which is then processed into a tractable sequence of tokens to generate shapes with internal details.

Fig. 3. Reconstruction Results: Our model reconstruction results with different latent space resolutions 64^3, 16^3 and 8^3 respectively (left to right).

Table 1. Number of sampled points and voxel resolution during training VQUDF across different datasets. The *Full Cars* dataset used for evaluating the ability of models to generate shapes with internal structures is curated by us from ShapeNet Cars

Dataset	Points Sampled	Voxel resolution
ShapeNet *Cars*	10000	256^3
ShapeNet *Planes*	5000	32^3
ShapeNet *Chairs*	4000	32^3
Full Cars	10000	256^3

4.3   Baselines

We evaluate our approach against well-established baselines as well as current SOTA methods for 3D point cloud generation. The first method we compare against is Graph Convolution GAN [51], which relies on GAN-based generation and employs localized operations in the form of graph convolutions to generate point clouds. Another method of comparison is denoising diffusion probabilistic models [27] for point cloud generation. Lastly, we compare against PointFlow [56], which utilizes normalizing flows for point cloud generation. These models naturally carry the ability to learn inside details of 3D models, provided that they have been trained on datasets with internal structures. However, they do not utilize an implicit continuous representation to capture internal details. Hence, these methods are constrained not only by a fixed number of points in generated shapes but also by their capacity to accurately represent the interiors of predicted 3D shapes.

4.4   Metrics

For quantitative evaluation, we use three different metrics following previous works.

MMD: Minimum matching distance (MMD) indicates the faithfulness of generated samples with real data. A lower MMD indicates that generated samples are realistic towards ground truth samples.

COV: Diversity is an important aspect of generative models. A high coverage score (COV) indicates that the model does not suffer from mode collapse and has high sample diversity.

JSD: Jenson-Shannon divergence (JSD) computes the symmetric similarity between distributions of generated samples and reference samples. A lower value of JSD is desirable. However, this metric is dependent on the selection of the reference set.

4.5 Qualitative Results

In this section, we show the qualitative performance of our generative model on the considered datasets.

ShapeNet: SOme samples of generated point clouds with 2048 points from our model and comaparative approaches for classes *chairs* and *airplanes* are presented in Fig. 4. We highlight that our model does not rely on any priors in the form of preset tokens in the input sequence, thus ensuring the complete unconditioned generation of 3D shapes. The performance of our method is apparent in terms of higher fidelity and realistic shapes generated. We further note that immense diversity is present in the generated shapes, whereby all samples in Fig. 4 are of distinct visual design. More results of generated mesh samples of *Planes* and *Chairs* are provided in the supplementary material.

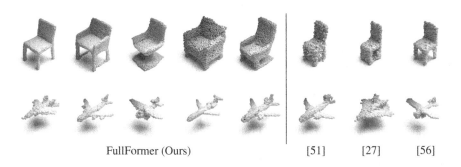

FullFormer (Ours)   [51]   [27]   [56]

Fig. 4. Outer Hull Generation: Our results show high-quality point cloud generation when trained on object categories of chairs and aeroplanes of the ShapeNet dataset. We highlight clear visual improvement over previous methods, namely GraphCNN-GAN [51], Diffusion [27] and PointFlow [56].

Full Cars: We experiment on the Full Cars dataset to showcase the veracity of our approach's key feature to generate high-fidelity outer shells with intricate internal geometric details. The qualitative results of randomly generated cars are presented in Fig. 5 demonstrating the efficacy of our model in generating samples with rich internal geometric structures. Additionally, generated cars in Fig. 5 demonstrate a remarkable level of diversity, for example, varied genres of cars with different numbers of seats. We also present in Fig. 6 comparative generation results having uniformly sampled 2048 points from Diffusion [27], PointFlow [56], and our FullFormer model. We retrain comparative methods on the 'Full Cars' dataset by preprocessing input data as required for those methods. Our approach achieves a clear visual superiority over comparative methods, which fail to generate any discernible internal structures. It is also important to note that shapes in the training data lack dense internal geometries. Despite this limitation, our method is able to learn a general model which is capable of generating shapes with internal structures given noisy real-world raw data.

Fig. 5. Generation: Diverse generation results from our Fullformer model trained on the Full Cars dataset exhibiting internal structures. A high degree of detail is clearly visible in the generated dense point clouds. Note that, not only seats conditioned on car genre, but also minute details such as steering wheels are generated. High point clouds quality further allows for surface meshes (bottom) to be computed of the non-watertight shapes with internal structures.

4.6   Quantitative Results

In this section, we present a quantitative evaluation of our model's performance in point cloud generation. The metrics discussed in Sect. 4.4 are tabulated in Table 2. Our method achieves state-of-the-art performance on all the metrics for the 'Full Cars' dataset, validating the capability of FullFormer in generating complete shapes with rich insides. High coverage and low JSD further demonstrate that generated models exhibit high diversity which we also observe visually. Moreover, we achieve the best performance in MMD and coverage across all classes of cars, chairs, and planes of the ShapeNet dataset compared with other baselines. While it is true that FullFormer appears to achieve higher JSD values than PointFlow [56] and Diffusion [27] for the ShapeNet dataset, however qualitative results continue to show diversity in all the considered datasets. Therefore the lower score of JSD for the ShapeNet dataset is hypothesized to be a cause of reference set selection.

[27]   [56]   [51]   FullFormer (Ours)

Fig. 6. Generation Comparison: From left to right (Diffusion [27], Point Flow [56], Graph-CNN GAN [51], FullFormer (Ours)). Our model (with 16^3 latent space resolution) shows high-quality internal structure generation results compared to the other mentioned models. It is apparent that other comparative models do not achieve discernable internal structures in generation results. All point clouds in this figure are sampled to 2048 points.

4.7 Limitations

Unlike the high-fidelity achieved on outer shells, generated internal details exhibit lower quality. A sampling of the feature space limits the details of the shape's geometry. Our model evaluation is also constrained by the scarcity of available shape datasets with rich internal structures. Furthermore, we used off-the-shelf methods to mesh our dense point clouds which degraded the quality of our final results. Particularly fine details and thin structures are of generated shapes hard to assess from generated point clouds. This is due to a lack of direct algorithms to extract the surface of 3D shapes from an unsigned distance field.

Table 2. We quantitatively compare the point cloud generation results of our method with GraphCNN-GAN [51], Diffusion [27] and PointFlow [56]. We report minimum matching distance (MMD), coverage score (COV), and Jenson and Shannon divergence (JSD) for comparison. We use Chamfer distance (CD) for MMD and COV calculations. MMD scores are multiplied by 10^3 and JSD are multiplied by 10^{-1}. Our proposed FullFormer improves consistently over all previous methods in terms of MMD and COV. It also improves over previous methods in terms of JSD on the Full Cars dataset.

Dataset	GraphCNN-GAN [51]			Diffusion [27]			PointFLow [56]			**Ours (FullFormer)**		
	MMD↓	COV↑	JSD↓	MMD↓	COV↑	JSD↓	MMD↓	COV↑	JSD↓	MMD↓	COV↑	JSD↓
ShapeNet *Cars*	3.18	16	4.67	1.4	17.7	**2.21**	1.28	29.67	3.16	**1.13**	**29.72**	2.29
ShapeNet *Planes*	1.1	31.09	1.75	0.98	36.73	**0.65**	1.41	35.87	1.06	**0.92**	**37.37**	0.83
ShapeNet *Chairs*	4.213	33.5	1.24	**3.79**	36.2	**0.42**	4.19	33.23	0.82	**3.79**	**37**	1.06
Full Cars	2.32	20	3.81	1.24	21.23	2.83	1.18	24.85	3.39	**0.93**	**25.07**	**2.72**

5   Conclusion

In this work, we present FullFormer, a novel two-stage generative model designed to generate 3D objects with intricate internal structures. Our approach employs a vector quantized autoencoder (VQUDF) to learn 3D shape geometry in the first stage and employ a latent transformer model in the second stage for shape generation. This latent transformer is trained autoregressively on indices of quantized shape embeddings learned by the VQUDF, making it computationally efficient. Consequently, the trained transformer can generate latent codes unconditionally. Generated codes are fed into a learned decoder (VQUDF) to output UDF representation from which 3D shapes are retrieved ensuring that generated shapes have details of internal structure and high-fidelity outer surface at arbitrary resolution. We further demonstrate superior qualitative and quantitative point cloud results compared to previous state-of-the-art methods. The ability to generate high-quality 3D shapes has implications across various domains, from computer graphics and virtual reality to manufacturing and design, paving the way for exciting future research in the field.

References

1. Atzmon, M., Lipman, Y.: SAL: sign agnostic learning of shapes from raw data. In: Proceedings of the IEEE/CVF Conference on Computer Vision and Pattern Recognition, pp. 2565–2574 (2020)
2. Bengio, Y., Léonard, N., Courville, A.: Estimating or propagating gradients through stochastic neurons for conditional computation (2013). https://doi.org/10.48550/ARXIV.1308.3432
3. Cai, R., et al.: Learning gradient fields for shape generation. In: Vedaldi, A., Bischof, H., Brox, T., Frahm, J.M. (eds.) ECCV 2020. LNCS, vol. 12348, pp. 364–381. Springer, Cham (2020). https://doi.org/10.1007/978-3-030-58580-8_22
4. Chang, A.X., et al.: ShapeNet: an information-rich 3D model repository (2015). https://doi.org/10.48550/ARXIV.1512.03012
5. Chen, M., et al.: Generative pretraining from pixels. In: International Conference on Machine Learning, pp. 1691–1703. PMLR (2020)
6. Chen, N., Zhang, Y., Zen, H., Weiss, R.J., Norouzi, M., Chan, W.: WaveGrad: estimating gradients for waveform generation. arXiv preprint arXiv:2009.00713 (2020)
7. Chen, P.H., Luo, Z.X., Huang, Z.K., Yang, C., Chen, K.W.: If-net: an illumination-invariant feature network (2020). https://doi.org/10.48550/ARXIV.2008.03897
8. Chen, W., Lin, C., Li, W., Yang, B.: 3PSDF: three-pole signed distance function for learning surfaces with arbitrary topologies. In: Proceedings of the IEEE/CVF Conference on Computer Vision and Pattern Recognition (2022)
9. Chen, X., et al.: Variational lossy autoencoder. arXiv preprint arXiv:1611.02731 (2016)
10. Chen, Z., Zhang, H.: Learning implicit fields for generative shape modeling. In: Proceedings of the IEEE/CVF Conference on Computer Vision and Pattern Recognition, pp. 5939–5948 (2019)
11. Cheng, A.C., Li, X., Liu, S., Sun, M., Yang, M.H.: Autoregressive 3D shape generation via canonical mapping. In: Avidan, S., Brostow, G., Cissé, M., Farinella, G.M., Hassner, T. (eds.) ECCV 2022. LNCS, vol. 13663, pp. 89–104. Springer, Cham (2022). https://doi.org/10.1007/978-3-031-20062-5_6
12. Chibane, J., Pons-Moll, G.: Implicit feature networks for texture completion from partial 3D data. In: Bartoli, A., Fusiello, A. (eds.) ECCV 2020. LNCS, vol. 12536, pp. 717–725. Springer, Cham (2020). https://doi.org/10.1007/978-3-030-66096-3_48
13. Chibane, J., Pons-Moll, G., et al.: Neural unsigned distance fields for implicit function learning. In: Advances in Neural Information Processing Systems, vol. 33, pp. 21638–21652 (2020)
14. Dosovitskiy, A., et al.: An image is worth 16×16 words: transformers for image recognition at scale. arXiv preprint arXiv:2010.11929 (2020)

15. d'Ascoli, S., Touvron, H., Leavitt, M.L., Morcos, A.S., Biroli, G., Sagun, L.: ConViT: improving vision transformers with soft convolutional inductive biases. In: International Conference on Machine Learning, pp. 2286–2296. PMLR (2021)
16. Esser, P., Rombach, R., Ommer, B.: Taming transformers for high-resolution image synthesis. In: Proceedings of the IEEE/CVF Conference on Computer Vision and Pattern Recognition, pp. 12873–12883 (2021)
17. Goodfellow, I., et al.: Generative adversarial nets. In: Advances in Neural Information Processing Systems, vol. 27 (2014)
18. Guo, M.H., Cai, J.X., Liu, Z.N., Mu, T.J., Martin, R.R., Hu, S.M.: PCT: point cloud transformer. Comput. Vis. Media **7**, 187–199 (2021)
19. Hertz, A., Perel, O., Giryes, R., Sorkine-Hornung, O., Cohen-Or, D.: SPAGHETTI: editing implicit shapes through part aware generation. ACM Trans. Graph. **41**(4) (2022). https://doi.org/10.1145/3528223.3530084
20. Ho, J., Jain, A., Abbeel, P.: Denoising diffusion probabilistic models. In: Advances in Neural Information Processing Systems, vol. 33, pp. 6840–6851 (2020)
21. Hui, K.H., Li, R., Hu, J., Fu, C.W.: Neural wavelet-domain diffusion for 3D shape generation. In: SIGGRAPH Asia 2022 Conference Papers, pp. 1–9 (2022)
22. Hyvärinen, A., Dayan, P.: Estimation of non-normalized statistical models by score matching. J. Mach. Learn. Res. **6**(4) (2005)
23. Kingma, D.P., Welling, M.: Auto-encoding variational bayes. arXiv preprint arXiv:1312.6114 (2013)
24. Kleineberg, M., Fey, M., Weichert, F.: Adversarial generation of continuous implicit shape representations. arXiv preprint arXiv:2002.00349 (2020)
25. Ledig, C., et al.: Photo-realistic single image super-resolution using a generative adversarial network. In: Proceedings of the IEEE Conference on Computer Vision and Pattern Recognition, pp. 4681–4690 (2017)
26. Lorensen, W.E., Cline, H.E.: Marching cubes: a high resolution 3D surface construction algorithm. ACM SIGGRAPH Comput. Graph. **21**(4), 163–169 (1987)
27. Luo, S., Hu, W.: Diffusion probabilistic models for 3D point cloud generation. In: Proceedings of the IEEE/CVF Conference on Computer Vision and Pattern Recognition, pp. 2837–2845 (2021)
28. Meng, X., Chen, W., Yang, B.: Neat: learning neural implicit surfaces with arbitrary topologies from multi-view images. In: Proceedings of the IEEE/CVF Conference on Computer Vision and Pattern Recognition (CVPR), pp. 248–258 (2023)
29. Mescheder, L., Oechsle, M., Niemeyer, M., Nowozin, S., Geiger, A.: Occupancy networks: learning 3D reconstruction in function space (2018). https://doi.org/10.48550/ARXIV.1812.03828
30. Mescheder, L., Oechsle, M., Niemeyer, M., Nowozin, S., Geiger, A.: Occupancy networks: learning 3D reconstruction in function space. In: Proceedings of the IEEE/CVF Conference on Computer Vision and Pattern Recognition, pp. 4460–4470 (2019)
31. Mittal, P., Cheng, Y.C., Singh, M., Tulsiani, S.: AutoSDF: shape priors for 3D completion, reconstruction and generation. In: CVPR (2022)
32. Mnih, A., Gregor, K.: Neural variational inference and learning in belief networks. In: International Conference on Machine Learning, pp. 1791–1799. PMLR (2014)
33. Niemeyer, M., Geiger, A.: Giraffe: representing scenes as compositional generative neural feature fields. In: Proceedings of the IEEE/CVF Conference on Computer Vision and Pattern Recognition, pp. 11453–11464 (2021)
34. van den Oord, A., Kalchbrenner, N., Kavukcuoglu, K.: Pixel recurrent neural networks (2016). https://doi.org/10.48550/ARXIV.1601.06759

35. van den Oord, A., Kalchbrenner, N., Vinyals, O., Espeholt, L., Graves, A., Kavukcuoglu, K.: Conditional image generation with PixelCNN decoders. arXiv preprint arXiv:1606.05328 (2016)
36. Park, J.J., Florence, P., Straub, J., Newcombe, R., Lovegrove, S.: DeepSDF: learning continuous signed distance functions for shape representation (2019). https://doi.org/10.48550/ARXIV.1901.05103
37. Park, J.J., Florence, P., Straub, J., Newcombe, R., Lovegrove, S.: DeepSDF: learning continuous signed distance functions for shape representation. In: Proceedings of the IEEE/CVF Conference on Computer Vision and Pattern Recognition, pp. 165–174 (2019)
38. Parmar, N., et al.: Image transformer. In: International Conference on Machine Learning, pp. 4055–4064 (2018)
39. Parmar, N., et al.: Image transformer (2018). https://doi.org/10.48550/ARXIV.1802.05751
40. Paszke, A., et al.: PyTorch: an imperative style, high-performance deep learning library. In: Advances in Neural Information Processing Systems, vol. 32, pp. 8024–8035. Curran Associates, Inc. (2019). http://papers.neurips.cc/paper/9015-pytorch-an-imperative-style-high-performance-deep-learning-library.pdf
41. Peng, S., Niemeyer, M., Mescheder, L., Pollefeys, M., Geiger, A.: Convolutional occupancy networks. In: Vedaldi, A., Bischof, H., Brox, T., Frahm, J.M. (eds.) ECCV 2020. LNCS, vol. 12348, pp. 523–540. Springer, Cham (2020). https://doi.org/10.1007/978-3-030-58580-8_31
42. Qi, C.R., Su, H., Mo, K., Guibas, L.J.: PointNet: deep learning on point sets for 3D classification and segmentation (2016). https://doi.org/10.48550/ARXIV.1612.00593
43. Razavi, A., van den Oord, A., Vinyals, O.: Generating diverse high-fidelity images with VQ-VAE-2. In: Advances in Neural Information Processing Systems, pp. 14866–14876 (2019)
44. Rezende, D.J., Mohamed, S., Wierstra, D.: Stochastic backpropagation and approximate inference in deep generative models. In: Xing, E.P., Jebara, T. (eds.) Proceedings of the 31st International Conference on Machine Learning, pp. 1278–1286. No. 2 in Proceedings of Machine Learning Research, PMLR, Beijing, China (2014). https://proceedings.mlr.press/v32/rezende14.html
45. Saharia, C., Ho, J., Chan, W., Salimans, T., Fleet, D.J., Norouzi, M.: Image super-resolution via iterative refinement. arXiv preprint arXiv:2104.07636 (2021)
46. Sarmad, M., Ruspini, L., Lindseth, F.: Photo-realistic continuous image super-resolution with implicit neural networks and generative adversarial networks. In: Proceedings of the Northern Lights Deep Learning Workshop, vol. 3 (2022)
47. Schwarz, K., Liao, Y., Niemeyer, M., Geiger, A.: Graf: generative radiance fields for 3D-aware image synthesis. In: Advances in Neural Information Processing Systems, vol. 33, pp. 20154–20166 (2020)
48. Sitzmann, V., Martel, J., Bergman, A., Lindell, D., Wetzstein, G.: Implicit neural representations with periodic activation functions. In: Advances in Neural Information Processing Systems, vol. 33, pp. 7462–7473 (2020)
49. Song, Y., Ermon, S.: Generative modeling by estimating gradients of the data distribution. In: Advances in Neural Information Processing Systems, vol. 32 (2019)
50. Thanh-Tung, H., Tran, T.: Catastrophic forgetting and mode collapse in GANs. In: 2020 International Joint Conference on Neural Networks (IJCNN), pp. 1–10. IEEE (2020)
51. Valsesia, D., Fracastoro, G., Magli, E.: Learning localized generative models for 3D point clouds via graph convolution. In: International Conference on Learning Representations (2019)
52. Van Den Oord, A., Vinyals, O., et al.: Neural discrete representation learning. In: Advances in Neural Information Processing Systems, vol. 30 (2017)
53. Vaswani, A., et al.: Attention is all you need. In: Advances in Neural Information Processing Systems, vol. 30 (2017)

54. Xiang, P., et al.: SnowflakeNet: point cloud completion by snowflake point deconvolution with skip-transformer. In: Proceedings of the IEEE/CVF International Conference on Computer Vision, pp. 5499–5509 (2021)
55. Yan, X., Lin, L., Mitra, N.J., Lischinski, D., Cohen-Or, D., Huang, H.: ShapeFormer: transformer-based shape completion via sparse representation. In: Proceedings of the IEEE/CVF Conference on Computer Vision and Pattern Recognition, pp. 6239–6249 (2022)
56. Yang, G., Huang, X., Hao, Z., Liu, M.Y., Belongie, S., Hariharan, B.: PointFlow: 3D point cloud generation with continuous normalizing flows. In: Proceedings of the IEEE/CVF International Conference on Computer Vision, pp. 4541–4550 (2019)
57. Ye, J., Chen, Y., Wang, N., Wang, X.: GIFS: neural implicit function for general shape representation. In: Proceedings of the IEEE/CVF Conference on Computer Vision and Pattern Recognition (CVPR), pp. 12829–12839 (2022)
58. Zeng, X., et al.: Lion: latent point diffusion models for 3D shape generation. In: Advances in Neural Information Processing Systems (NeurIPS) (2022)
59. Zhang, B., Nießner, M., Wonka, P.: 3DILG: irregular latent grids for 3D generative modeling. In: Oh, A.H., Agarwal, A., Belgrave, D., Cho, K. (eds.) Advances in Neural Information Processing Systems (2022). https://openreview.net/forum?id=RO0wSr3R7y-
60. Zhao, H., Jiang, L., Jia, J., Torr, P.H., Koltun, V.: Point transformer. In: Proceedings of the IEEE/CVF International Conference on Computer Vision, pp. 16259–16268 (2021)
61. Zheng, X., Liu, Y., Wang, P., Tong, X.: SDF-StyleGAN: Implicit SDF-based StyleGAN for 3D shape generation. In: Computer Graphics Forum, vol. 41, pp. 52–63. Wiley Online Library (2022)

GenLayNeRF: Generalizable Layered Representations with 3D Model Alignment for Human View Synthesis

Youssef Abdelkareem[1(✉)], Shady Shehata[2], and Fakhri Karray[1,2]

[1] University of Waterloo, 200 University Ave W, Waterloo, ON N2L 3G1, Canada
{yafathi,karray}@uwaterloo.ca
[2] Mohamed bin Zayed University of Artificial Intelligence,
Masdar City, Abu Dhabi, United Arab Emirates
{shady.shehata,fakhri.karray}@mbzuai.ac.ae

Abstract. Novel view synthesis (NVS) of multi-human scenes imposes challenges due to the complex inter-human occlusions. Layered representations handle the complexities by dividing the scene into multi-layered radiance fields, however, they are mainly constrained to per-scene optimization making them inefficient. Generalizable human view synthesis methods combine the pre-fitted 3D human meshes with image features to reach generalization, yet they are mainly designed to operate on single-human scenes. Another drawback is the reliance on multi-step optimization techniques for parametric pre-fitting of the 3D body models that suffer from misalignment with the images in sparse view settings causing hallucinations in synthesized views. In this work, we propose, GenLayNeRF, a generalizable layered scene representation for free-viewpoint rendering of multiple human subjects which requires no per-scene optimization and very sparse views as input. We divide the scene into multi-human layers anchored by the 3D body meshes. We then ensure pixel-level alignment of the body models with the input views through a novel end-to-end trainable module that carries out iterative parametric correction coupled with multi-view feature fusion to produce aligned 3D models. For NVS, we extract point-wise image-aligned and human-anchored features which are correlated and fused using self-attention and cross-attention modules. We augment low-level RGB values into the features with an attention-based RGB fusion module. To evaluate our approach, we construct two multi-human view synthesis datasets; DeepMultiSyn and ZJU-MultiHuman. The results indicate that our proposed approach outperforms generalizable and non-human per-scene NeRF methods while performing at par with layered per-scene methods without test time optimization.

Keywords: Novel View Synthesis · NeRF · Multi-Human · Mesh Alignment

1 Introduction

Novel view synthesis (NVS) of scenes with human subjects has numerous applications in telepresence, virtual reality, etc. The extensions [6, 15, 26, 37] of the well-known

---

Supplementary Information The online version contains supplementary material available at
https://doi.org/10.1007/978-3-031-54605-1_11.

U. Köthe and C. Rother (Eds.): DAGM GCPR 2023, LNCS 14264, pp. 163–177, 2024.
https://doi.org/10.1007/978-3-031-54605-1_11

NeRF [21] architecture achieved competitive synthesis results using sparse views, yet suffered with human subjects due to their complex motions. NeuralBody [25] anchored NeRF with pre-fitted 3D human models to regularize the training producing more photo-realistic output. A main constraint was the inefficient per-scene optimization requirement. Recently, state-of-the-art human-based synthesis methods [3,12,20,44] merged the concepts of the human model anchors and the image features to generalize to unseen poses and human identities. However, they were only designed to operate on scenes with single human subjects. Multi-human scenes introduce additional challenges due to how humans occlude each other and the complexity of their close interactions. Layered scene representations [42] are a possible solution to operate in the complex multi-person setting. Shuai et al. [30] utilized a layered architecture by representing the human entities using NeuralBody [25] and weakly supervising the human instance segmentation. Nevertheless, the method suffers from the per-scene optimization problem which hinders its applicability to wider real-world domains. Another issue with existing Human NVS methods [12,30,44] is the reliance on multi-step optimization methods [2,29,43] for the estimation of pre-fitted 3D body models. Such methods hinder the ability of end-to-end learning and suffer from error accumulation throughout the fitting steps which lead to inaccurate parameter fitting and misaligned body models and consequently hurts the synthesis quality of the novel views.

In this paper, we propose generalizable layered neural radiance fields to achieve free-viewpoint rendering of multi-human subjects, while requiring no test-time optimization for novel subjects or poses. We fuse the concepts of implicit feature aggregation and layered scene representations to synthesize novel views of complex human interactions from very sparse input streams. Specifically, we divide the scene into a set of human layers anchored by the 3D human body meshes. We then introduce a novel end-to-end trainable human-image alignment module that utilizes an iterative feedback loop [41] to correct parametric errors in the pre-fitted human models and produces pixel-aligned human layers for better synthesis quality. For view synthesis, we extract a set of point-wise image-aligned and human-anchored features for all views and effectively aggregate them using self-attention and cross-attention modules. We also include an RGB fusion module that embeds the fused features with low-level pixel information from the images for retaining high-frequency details.

Our main contributions are summarized as follows:

– We propose a generalizable layered representation with a novel combination of three attention-based feature fusion modules for free-viewpoint rendering of multi-human scenes from sparse input views while operating on novel human subjects and poses.
– We present a novel human-image alignment module that corrects misalignment errors in the pre-fitted human models through an end-to-end trainable iterative feedback loop coupled with multi-view self-attention feature fusion.
– We surpass state-of-the-art generalizable and non-human per-scene NeRF methods while performing at par with the multi-human per-scene methods without requiring long per-scene training procedures.

2 Related Work

2.1 Neural View Synthesis

Recent progress has been made in utilizing neural networks along with differentiable rendering for novel view synthesis [1,5,13,32,33,36,38]. NeRF [21] encapsulated the full continuous 5D radiance field of scenes inside a Multi-Layer Perceptron (MLP). They achieved photo-realistic results but failed to work on highly deformable scenes with non-static subjects. Deformable NeRF methods [23,26] modeled the dynamic subjects by training a deformation network that transforms 3D points to a canonical space before querying the MLP. Yet, they show poor synthesis quality for human subjects with complex deformations. NeuralBody [25] anchored NeRF with a deformable human model [18] to provide a prior over the human body shape and correctly render self-occluded regions. However, they lacked generalization capabilities for novel scenes. Per-scene optimization NeRF methods [21,25,26,30] need to be trained from scratch on each scene which is often impractical due to the large time and computational costs. Generalizable NeRF methods [34,35,39] offer a solution by conditioning NeRF on pixel-aligned features generated from the input images which enhanced the results for unseen scenes with sparse input views. Recently, NHP [12] combined the 3D human mesh with image features to accurately represent complex body dynamics and generalize to novel human subjects and poses. HumanNeRF [44] enhanced the quality through efficient fine-tuning procedures and neural appearance blending techniques. However, the blending module operates on pre-scanned synthetic data with accurate depth maps and cannot be extended to real-world data. One limitation of state-of-the-art generalizable human methods [3,12,44] lies in the inability to be extended to multi-human scenes which are challenging due to the inter-human occlusions and interactions.

Layered scene representations [19] were proposed to handle complex scenes with multiple human subjects. ST-NeRF [42] modeled each human layer using a deformable model similar to D-NeRF [26] to achieve editable free-viewpoint rendering. Recently, Shuai et al. [30] extended ST-NeRF by modeling the human subjects using Neural-Body [25] and predicted human segmentation masks as part of the network training. The restriction of both methods is requiring per-scene training procedures for learning, yielding them inefficient to use. We tackle the existing research gap by proposing a generalizable layered scene representation for synthesizing novel views of multi-human subjects through a combination of image features and layered neural radiance fields. We achieve free-viewpoint rendering for scenes with an arbitrary number of humans from very sparse input views, while generalizing to novel subjects and poses at test time without extra optimization.

2.2 Human Mesh Recovery

Mesh Recovery of human subjects has grabbed significant research attention due to its adoption in 3D geometry reconstruction and novel view synthesis. One direction of approaches solves the task through a multi-step optimization process which fits the parametric human models (i.e. SMPL [18]) based on 2D observations such as keypoints or silhouettes [8,31]. Bogo et al. [2] utilized 2D joint predictions from monocular input to guide the SMPL fitting process for single-human scenes. Zhang et al. [43] tackled a more challenging multi-person setting by leveraging triangulated 3D keypoints and a two-step parametric fitting process for enhanced results. The main issues with multi-step methods are breaking the end-to-end learning and the error accumulation throughout the steps, especially in sparse-view datasets. Specifically, 2D keypoints predictions could suffer from inaccurate joints in certain views which hurts the triangulation process leading to low-quality 3D keypoint predictions. The parametric model fitting is subject to errors due to the abundance of hyperparameters [43] that require meticulous finetuning and the accumulated errors from the previous steps. On the other hand, regression-based approaches aim for better human-image alignment by directly regressing the body models from input images [10,11,16,17,40,41]. PyMAF [41] introduced a feedback loop with multi-scale contexts to correct parametric deviations for producing highly aligned meshes from monocular input images for single-humans.

Existing Human NVS approaches [3,12,20,25,44] utilize pre-fitted 3D observations computed using multi-step optimization approaches [29,43]. However, in sparse-view settings, the pre-fitted predictions suffer from misalignment errors that consequently hurt the quality of the synthesized views. Mihajlovi et al. [20] utilized 3D keypoints instead of body models to avoid parametric fitting errors. L-NeRF [30] introduced a time-synchronization step that accounts for the multi-view image de-synchronization by producing a per-view body model using predicted time offsets. However, they do not account for parametric errors occurring in the multi-step fitting process. In this work, we propose a novel regression-based human-image alignment module that ensures the correction of parametric errors leading to aligned body models with multi-view input.

3   Methodology

3.1   Problem Definition

Given a synchronized set Ω of frames I taken from B sparse input viewpoints of a scene with N arbitrary number of humans, such that $\Omega = \{I_1, .., I_B\}$, our target is to synthesize a novel view frame $\{I_q\}$ of the scene from a query viewing direction q. Each input viewpoint b is represented by the corresponding camera intrinsics K, and camera rotation R and translation t, where $b = \{K_b, [R_b|t_b]\}$. The N pre-fitted 3D human body meshes are given for each input frame. Each human h is represented using the SMPL [18] model which is a deformable skinned model defined in terms of pose and shape parameters Θ_h^0 while also being vertex-based where each model s_h consists of 6,480 vertices, such that $s_h \in \mathbf{R}^{6,480 \times 3}$. For an input view image $I_b \in \mathbf{R}^{H \times W \times 3}$ with height H and width W, we extract a multi-scale feature pyramid $I'_{b,\{0:T-1\}}$ with T levels using a ResNet34 [9] backbone network f, pre-trained on ImageNet, such that $I'_{b,\{0:T-1\}} = f(I_b)$. The operation is carried out for all input views b in $\{1, .., B\}$. A full overview of the proposed architecture is shown in Fig. 1.

3.2   Human-Image Alignment Module

Pre-fitted human body models can suffer from misalignment with the input images due to error accumulation throughout the multi-step fitting process [43], especially in sparse

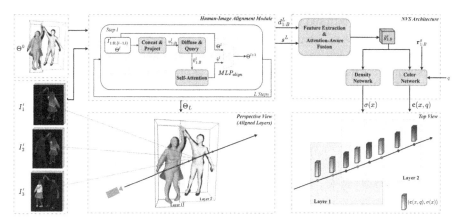

Fig. 1. Overview of the GenLayNeRF approach. We consolidate a layered scene representation where each human subject is modeled using the SMPL model. Regarding our alignment module, at a step l, low and high-resolution feature planes $I'_{1:B,\{l-1,l\}}$ are concatenated and the SMPL vertices are projected on them to produce feature-embedded vertices $v^l_{1:B}$ (Concat & Project). We then diffuse the vertices to continuous spaces and query them at downsampled vertex locations to generate multi-view human features $\tilde{v}^l_{1:B}$ (Diffuse & Query), which are fused using self-attention and passed along with parameters Θ^l to predict the adjusted parameters Θ^{l+1}. In our NVS architecture, we project rays through the aligned scene layers and sample per-layer 3D points within the intersections areas with the layers (shown in the top view). Point-wise features are extracted and fused to output the final fused features $\tilde{g}^x_{1:B}$, which are passed to the density network to predict the volume density $\sigma(x)$, whereas the color network uses the raw RGB values $\mathbf{r}^x_{1:B}$ and q to predict the color $\mathbf{c}(x, q)$.

view settings, which causes hallucinations in synthesized views. We propose an alignment module that is end-to-end trainable with our NVS architecture and carries out iterative parametric correction with closed feedback [41] to ensure a better alignment of the SMPL models with the multi-view input images. The module takes the prefitted SMPL parameters Θ^0_h as input and returns the aligned and adjusted parameters Θ^L_h. Specifically, we employ an iterative process with L steps, such that, for a step $l > 0$, low-resolution features $I'_{b,l-1}$ from level $l - 1$ for view b are upsampled using deconvolution [22] and concatenated with high-resolution feature plane $I'_{b,l}$ at level l resulting in a contextualized and localized feature plane $I''_{b,l}$. Human vertices s^l_h are embedded with image features by projection on the multi-view feature map, such that, $v^l_{h,b} = I''_{b,l}[K_b((R_b s^l_h) + t_b)]$. $v^l_{h,b} \in \mathbf{R}^{6,480 \times C_1}$ represents the features of the vertices projected on feature map $I''_{b,l}$ for human h. The preceding part corresponds to "Concat & Project" in Fig. 1.

Our target is to retrieve a compact and continuous per-human feature representation to be used for parameter adjustment. For that reason, the sparse human vertices $v^l_{h,b}$ need to be diffused into a continuous space that can be queried at any location. We incorporate the SparseConvNet [7,25] architecture which utilizes 3D sparse convolution to diffuse the vertex features into different nearby continuous spaces for every human and view. The diffused vertices are denoted as $d_{h,b}^l$. To obtain the per-human features, we downsample the vertices s_h^l, such that $\tilde{s}_h^l \in \mathbf{R}^{431 \times 3}$, and query the diffused vertex spaces at the downsampled locations to obtain the multi-view per-human vertex features which are then processed and flattened to obtain a compact version denoted as $\tilde{v}_{h,b}^l \in \mathbf{R}^{1 \times C_2}$. The preceding part corresponds to "Diffuse & Query" in Fig. 1. Afterward, we effectively correlate the multi-view human features using a self-attention module, such that,

$$
\begin{aligned}
mv_h^l &= soft(\frac{1}{\sqrt{d_{k_1}}} query(\tilde{v}_{h,1:B}^l) \cdot key(\tilde{v}_{h,1:B}^l)^T), \\
\hat{v}_{h,1:B}^l &= mv_h^l \cdot val_1(\tilde{v}_{h,1:B}^l) + val_2(\tilde{v}_{h,1:B}^l), \\
mv_h^l &\in \mathbf{R}^{B \times B}, \quad \tilde{v}_{h,1:B}^l \in \mathbf{R}^{B \times C_2},
\end{aligned}
\tag{1}
$$

where key, $query$, and (val_1, val_2) represent the key, query, and value embeddings of the corresponding argument features respectively, and d_{k_1} denotes the dimensionality of the key embedding. $soft$ denotes the softmax operation. We carry out view-wise averaging for multi-view fusion on the view-aware human features such that, $\hat{v}_h^l = \frac{1}{B} \sum_b \hat{v}_{h,b}^l$. Lastly, the fused per-human features are concatenated ($\oplus$) with the current SMPL parameters and passed to a correction MLP that predicts parameter alignment offsets $\Delta\Theta_h^l$ which are added to the current parameters, such that,

$$
\begin{aligned}
\Delta\Theta_h^l &= MLP_{align}([\hat{v}_h^l \oplus \Theta_h^l]), \\
\Theta_h^{l+1} &= \Theta_h^l + \Delta\Theta_h^l,
\end{aligned}
\tag{2}
$$

The updated parameters Θ_h^{l+1} are used to retrieve the adjusted SMPL vertices s_h^{l+1} and are passed to the next step $l + 1$. After L steps, the aligned SMPL parameters Θ_h^L, vertices s_h^L, and diffused spaces $d_{h,1:B}^L$ are passed to our layered NVS architecture.

3.3 Layered Scene Representation

Scenes with multiple humans suffer from inter-human occlusions that become evident when subjects closely interact together. A practical solution to handle complex multi-human scenarios is dividing the scene into distinct layers where each layer models an entity using a neural radiance field [19,42]. Entities can be humans, objects, or background. Our proposed approach focuses mainly on human layers represented using the SMPL [18] model which is responsible for preserving the local geometry and appearance of humans making it possible to model their complex deformations and occluded areas.

Our aim is to render the full novel view image I_q from a query viewpoint q. To achieve that, we first use the camera-to-world projection matrix, defined as $\mathbf{P}^{-1} = [R_q|t_q]^{-1} K_q^{-1}$, to march 3D rays across the multi-layered scene. In practice, we have a ray for each pixel p in the final image, where the ray origin $r_0 \in \mathbf{R}^3$ is the camera center and the ray direction is given as $i = \frac{\mathbf{P}^{-1}p - r_0}{||\mathbf{P}^{-1}p - r_0||}$. 3D points x are sampled across the rays at specific depth values z, where $x = r(z) = r_0 + zi$. Since we have several human layers in the scene, we determine the intersection areas of the rays with the humans using the 3D bounding box around each layer defined by the minimum and maximum vertex points of the aligned SMPL meshes $s_{1:N}^L$. We then sample depth values within the n_p intersecting areas only such that $z \in [[z_{near_1}, z_{far_1}], .., [z_{near_{n_p}}, z_{far_{n_p}}]]$. This guarantees that the sampled points lie within the areas of the relevant human subjects as clear in the top view shown in Fig. 1.

3.4   Feature Extraction and Attention-Aware Fusion

In our proposed approach, we extract multi-view image features for each query point x and effectively merge them using attention-based fusion modules to derive the needed spatially-aligned feature vectors. This enables us to extrapolate to novel human subjects and poses by learning implicit correlations between the independent human layers.

Image-Aligned and Human-Anchored Features. Image-aligned point-wise features are extracted by projecting the point x on all the feature maps $I_{b,L}''$ to collect the corresponding image-aligned features for each view b denoted as p_b^x. In addition, human-anchored features are beneficial for maintaining the complex geometric structure of the human body by anchoring the network on the available SMPL body priors. Existing layered scene representations [30] follow the approach of NeuralBody [25] by encoding the vertices of human layers using learnable embeddings that are unique to each layer in each training scene. In our approach, we utilize the vertices $v_{1:N,1:B}^L$ embedded with image features from the alignment module to enable a generalizable approach conditioned on the input images. The radiance field predictor is queried using continuous 3D sampled points. For that reason, we utilize the diffused vertex spaces $d_{h,1:B}^L$ for each human h and transform x to the SMPL coordinate space of its corresponding human layer. Trilinear interpolation is then utilized to retrieve the corresponding human-anchored features g_b^x from the diffused spaces of each view b.

Attention-Aware Feature Fusion. To fuse the point-wise feature representations $g_{1:B}^x$, $p_{1:B}^x$ for point x, one strategy is a basic averaging approach [27,28]. This leads to smoother output and ineffective utilization of the information seen from distinct views. To learn effective cross-view correlations, we employ a self-attention module that attends between all the multi-view human-anchored features $g_{1:B}^x$ where each feature in one view is augmented with the extra features seen from the other views. Each view feature is first concatenated with its corresponding viewing direction d_b'. The formulation is the same as the one shown in Eq. (1). The produced view-aware human-anchored features are denoted as $\hat{g}_{1:B}^x$.

We additionally make use of the rich spatial information in the image-aligned features by carrying out cross-attention from the view-aware human-anchored features to the image-aligned features. The similarity between the multi-view image features and the per-view vertex features is used to re-weigh the image features and embed them with the vertex features. The fused features $\tilde{g}_{1:B}^x$ are calculated with a formulation similar to Eq. (1). The detailed formulation of our cross-attention and self-attention modules is shown in the supplementary material. Afterward, we carry out view-wise averaging, such that $\tilde{g}^x = \frac{1}{B}\sum_b \tilde{g}_b^x$, to generate the final fused feature representation for x.

3.5 Radiance Field Predictor

Color Network. To predict the color $\mathbf{c}$ of point x, we use the query viewing direction q to model the view-dependent effects [21]. In addition, we explicitly augment the high-level features with low-level pixel-wise information to leverage the high-frequency details in the images. This has been achieved with an RGB fusion module which concatenates the high-level features with the encoded raw RGB values $\mathbf{r}_b^x$ for each view b. RGB values from closer input views are assigned higher weights by cross-attending q with the input viewing directions $d'_{1:B}$ such that,

$$
\tilde{c}^x = MLP_{c_1}(\tilde{g}^x_{1:B}; \gamma(q); p^x_{1:B}),
$$
$$
\hat{c}^x_{1:B} = \{[\tilde{c}^x \oplus \gamma(\mathbf{r}^x_1)], ..., [\tilde{c}^x \oplus \gamma(\mathbf{r}^x_B)]\},
$$
$$
rgb^x_{att} = soft(\frac{1}{\sqrt{d_{k_2}}}query(q) \cdot key(d'_{1:B})^T), \tag{3}
$$
$$
\mathbf{c}(x, q) = MLP_{c_2}(rgb^x_{att} \cdot val_1(\hat{c}^x_{1:B})),
$$
$$
rgb^x_{att} \in \mathbf{R}^{1 \times B},
$$

Density Network. We predict volume density $\sigma(x)$ for point x using the fused feature $\tilde{g}^x$, such that, $\sigma(x) = MLP_\sigma(\tilde{g}^x)$.

MLP_σ, MLP_{c_1}, and MLP_{c_2} consist of fully connected layers described in the supplementary material. $\gamma : \mathbf{R}^3 \to \mathbf{R}^{(6 \times l)+3}$ denotes a positional encoding [21] with $2 \times l$ basis functions and d_{k_2} is set to 16.

3.6 Layered Volumteric Rendering and Loss Functions

Layered volumetric rendering is used to accumulate the predicted RGB and density for all points across human layers. The points in intersecting areas n_p the layers are sorted based on their depth value z before accumulation. The detailed formulation is shown in the supplementary material. Given a ground truth novel view image I_q^{gt}, all network weights are supervised using the L2 Norm ($||.||$) photo-metric loss. In addition, we include two losses to explicitly supervise the training of our alignment module weights. Given a set of pseudo ground truth 2D keypoints J^{gt}, we derive the predicted 2D keypoints $\tilde{J}$ from the adjusted vertices s^L following PyMAF [41] and minimize the keypoint difference weighted by the ground truth confidence of each body joint. We also include a regularization term on the SMPL parameters to avoid large parametric deviations. The final loss function for our network is written as,

$$
\mathbf{L} = \lambda_{ph}||I_q^{gt} - I_q|| + \lambda_{kpts}||J^{gt} - \tilde{J}|| + \lambda_{reg}||\Theta^L||, \tag{4}
$$

4 Experiments

In this section, we introduce the datasets, baselines, experimental results, and ablation studies. Details about our training procedure are in the supplementary material.

Table 1. Comparison with generalizable and per-scene NeRF methods on the DeepMultiSyn and ZJU-MultiHuman Datasets. "G" and "S" denote generalizable and per-scene methods, respectively. "*" refers to human-based methods. PSNR and SSIM metric values are the greater the better. "ft" refers to finetuning.

	Method	DeepMultiSyn		ZJUMultiHuman	
		PSNR	SSIM	PSNR	SSIM
	(a) Seen Models, Seen Poses				
	NeRF	15.49	0.497	16.42	0.525
S	D-NeRF	17.08	0.702	18.53	0.748
	L-NeRF*	24.04	0.858	25.10	0.903
	Ours$_{ft}$	**25.05**	**0.889**	**25.21**	**0.916**
	PixelNeRF	14.81	0.534	19.74	0.629
	SRF	20.39	0.724	17.87	0.657
G	IBRNet	19.45	0.741	20.03	0.766
	NHP*	20.91	0.698	21.75	0.813
	Ours	**24.01**	**0.859**	**25.02**	**0.901**

	Method	DeepMultiSyn		ZJUMultiHuman	
		PSNR	SSIM	PSNR	SSIM
	(b) Seen Models, Unseen Poses				
S	L-NeRF*	22.12	0.825	23.02	0.871
	PixelNeRF	14.14	0.520	16.88	0.560
	SRF	18.07	0.663	17.93	0.680
G	IBRNet	18.01	0.710	19.84	0.772
	NHP*	20.26	0.677	20.64	0.791
	Ours	**23.45**	**0.862**	**23.76**	**0.882**
	(c) Unseen Models, Unseen Poses				
	PixelNeRF	13.12	0.457		
	SRF	13.95	0.548		
G	IBRNet	18.80	0.672	Not Applicable	
	NHP*	19.51	0.678		
	Ours	**21.03**	**0.802**		

4.1 Datasets

The existence of readily-available open-source multi-human view synthesis datasets is limited. To solve this challenge, we construct two new datasets, ZJU-MultiHuman and DeepMultiSyn. Both datasets will be published to be used by multi-human view synthesis methods. We also include a subset of the single-human ZJU-MoCap dataset for diversity. Extra details on the datasets are included in the supplementary material.

DeepMultiSyn. The DeepMultiSyn dataset is an adaptation of the 3D reconstruction dataset published by DeepMultiCap [45]. We take the raw real-world multi-view sequences and process them for novel view synthesis. There exist 3 video sequences of scenes containing 2 to 3 human subjects captured from 6 synchronized cameras. Following NeuralBody [25], we use EasyMoCap [29] to fit the SMPL human models for all the subjects in the available frames. Additionally, we predict the human segmentation masks following [14] to separate the humans from the background. This dataset is considered challenging due to the existence of close interactions and complex human actions such as boxing, and dancing activities.

ZJU-MultiHuman. The ZJU-MultiHuman dataset consists of one video sequence with 600 frames taken from 8 uniformly distributed synchronized cameras. The video sequence was published online [29] with the calibration files. The captured scene contains 4 different human subjects. Similar to DeepMultiSyn, we predict the SMPL models and segmentation masks utilizing [14,29].

4.2 Baselines

We compare our proposed approach with generalizable and per-scene NeRF methods.

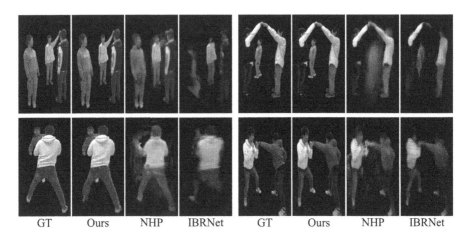

Fig. 2. Comparison with generalizable methods on **seen models/unseen poses** [top row] and **unseen models/unseen poses** [bottom row] for the DeepMultiSyn Dataset.

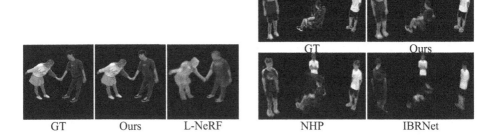

Fig. 3. Comparison with a per-scene multi-human method [30] on **seen models/unseen poses** on the DeepMultiSyn Dataset.

Fig. 4. Comparison with generalizable methods on **seen models/unseen poses** for the ZJU-MultiHuman Dataset.

Comparison with Generalizable NeRF Methods. Generalizable human-based NeRF methods [3,12,20,44] operate only on scenes with single humans. We choose to compare against NHP [12] after adjusting it to work on multi-human scenes by using the segmentation masks to render a separate image for each individual in the scene. We then superimpose the human images based on their depth to render the novel view image. Regarding non-human methods, PixelNeRF [39] is the first to condition NeRF

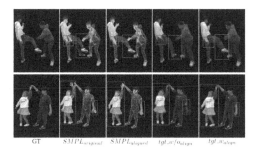

GT $SMPL_{original}$ $SMPL_{aligned}$ tgt_w/o_{align} tgt_w_{align}

Fig. 5. Visualization of the output of our human-image alignment module ($SMPL_{aligned}$) given the misaligned pre-fitted model ($SMPL_{original}$). "tgt_w_{align}" and "tgt_w/o_{align}" denote the rendered image with/without our alignment module.

Table 2. Ablation study results on **seen models** and **unseen poses** for the DeepMultiSyn dataset. "# V." denotes the number of views.

crs	slf	rgb	align	V.	PSNR ↑	SSIM ↑
				3	20.92	0.7860
✓				3	21.45	0.8005
✓	✓			3	21.98	0.8093
✓	✓	✓		3	22.19	0.8260
✓	✓	✓	✓	3	**23.45**	**0.8620**
✓	✓	✓	✓	1	21.98	0.8091
✓	✓	✓	✓	2	22.32	0.8379
✓	✓	✓	✓	4	23.72	0.8711

on pixel-aligned features for generalization. IBRNet [35] and SRF [4] additionally utilize image-based rendering and stereo correspondences, respectively, to achieve generalizable properties. All methods were trained on all human scenes simultaneously.

Comparison with Per-Scene Methods. We evaluate our performance compared to the multi-human layered scene representation approach [30], denoted as L-NeRF. We also compare against D-NeRF [26] and the original NeRF [21] method. All of the mentioned approaches are trained on each scene separately with the same train-test splits.

4.3   Experimental Results

Our evaluation spans three generalization settings as follows:

Seen Models, Seen Poses. In this setting, we test on the same human subjects and poses that the model is trained on. Table 1a indicates the results in terms of the per-scene and generalizable baselines. Regarding the generalizable approaches, our method exhibits the best overall performance on both datasets on all metrics. For the per-scene approaches, our proposed method performs at par with the state-of-the-art per-scene baseline (L-NeRF), while effectively saving computational and time resources by taking 50 h to converge on all the scenes simultaneously compared to 144 h for per-scene training. After per-scene finetuning, our method surpasses L-NeRF on both datasets. Qualitative comparisons for the per-scene methods are included in the supplementary material.

Pose Generalization. We additionally test all approaches on the same human subjects seen during training, but with novel poses. On both datasets, Table 1b shows that our approach outperforms all the generalizable NeRF methods on all metrics. L-NeRF lags behind our method on the DeepMultiSyn dataset due to the complex novel poses which validates the pose generalization ability of our method on challenging motions. In Fig. 2 and Fig. 4, IBRNet fails to model the full body of the human subjects properly, while NHP fails to represent areas of occlusions where subjects highly overlap. However, our method successfully models the body shapes and can handle overlapping areas which validates the effectiveness of the layered scene representation in the generalizable multi-human setting. Figure 3 shows how L-NeRF fails to properly render the appearance of subjects when presented with complex unseen poses.

Human Generalization. A challenging setting would be testing on human subjects and poses not seen during training. This was done on the DeepMultiSyn dataset by leaving out two different scenes for testing. Table 1c validates that our method has the best generalization capability as it outperforms all other methods by a large margin. The bottom row of Fig. 2 shows that our method better represents the main body features of the novel human subjects. IBRNet fails to render some body parts like the legs, while NHP suffers from more blur artifacts, especially in overlapping areas. In the supplementary material, we show that our method surpasses NHP by a large margin even on single humans in the ZJU-MoCap dataset for both pose and human generalization settings.

4.4   Ablation Studies

Effect of Human-Image Alignment. We evaluate the impact of the proposed human-image alignment module on the synthesis quality. Quantitatively, Table 2 shows the superior enhancement offered by the alignment module (align) on both metrics. In Fig. 5, we demonstrate the large misalignment between the pre-fitted SMPL model and the image which caused severe hallucinations in the synthesized image (areas with red boxes). Our module successfully aligns the SMPL model with the images leading to higher-quality synthesis results. We include additional results of our module in the supplementary material.

Effect of Fusion modules. We assess the effect of different fusion modules on the synthesis results. From Table 2, the second row uses the cross-attention module (crs) in Sec. 3.4 and it shows a noticeable improvement over doing basic average pooling in the first row. This indicates the effectiveness of the correlation learned between the vertex and image features. The addition of the self-attention module (slf) in Sec. 3.4 in the third row led to the incorporation of multi-view aware features and achieved a slight enhancement on both metrics. The last row adds the raw RGB fusion module (rgb) in the Color Network presented in Sec. 3.5. It enhances the performance, especially on the SSIM metric, validating the importance of utilizing low-level information.

Effect of Number of Views. We evaluate the performance of our proposed approach when given a different number of input views at test time. Table 2 indicates that using 4 views leads to an enhancement in both metrics due to the extra information available. Decreasing the number of views gradually degrades the performance. However, using only one input view, our method outperforms all the generalizable NeRF methods in Table 1 that use 3 input views.

5   Limitations and Future Work

Several enhancements to our proposed method could be investigated further. As our two proposed datasets were sufficient to show the generalization capability of our method, there is room for improvement by elevating the diversity in terms of the number of scenes, camera views, distinct humans, and complex actions. This would lead to better generalization capabilities on broader challenging scenarios. Furthermore, our method suffers from blur artifacts representing human clothing details such as skirts as seen in Fig. 3. One could experiment with integrating a deformation model [26] to represent small deformations such as textured clothing. In addition, adjustments could be made to allow for human-image alignment for more complex body models such as SMPL-X [24]. Lastly, a research direction could explore the optimization of the body model parameters from scratch with multi-view time synchronization taken into consideration.

6 Conclusion

We introduce a generalizable layered scene representation for free-viewpoint rendering of multi-human scenes using very sparse input views while operating on unseen poses and subjects without test time optimization. We additionally present a novel end-to-end human-image alignment module that corrects parametric errors in the pre-fitted body models leading to pixel-level alignment of human layers with the input images. Regarding view synthesis, we divide the scene into a set of multi-human layers. We then generate point-wise image features and human-anchored features and utilize a combination of cross-attention and self-attention modules that effectively fuse the information seen from different viewpoints. In addition, we introduce an RGB fusion module to embed low-level pixel values into the color prediction for higher-quality results. We assess the efficacy of our approach on two newly proposed multi-human datasets. Experimental results show that our method outperforms state-of-the-art generalizable NeRF methods in different generalization settings and performs at par with layered per-scene methods without long per-scene optimization runs. We also validate the effectiveness of our alignment module by showing its significant enhancement on the synthesis quality. Our module could be integrated with existing SMPL-based synthesis methods to elevate the performance by improving the human-image alignment.

References

1. Aliev, K.A., Ulyanov, D., Lempitsky, V.S.: Neural point-based graphics. ArXiv abs/1906.08240 (2020)
2. Bogo, F., Kanazawa, A., Lassner, C., Gehler, P., Romero, J., Black, M.J.: Keep it SMPL: automatic estimation of 3d human pose and shape from a single image. ArXiv abs/1607.08128 (2016)
3. Cheng, W., et al.: Generalizable neural performer: learning robust radiance fields for human novel view synthesis. ArXiv abs/2204.11798 (2022)
4. Chibane, J., Bansal, A., Lazova, V., Pons-Moll, G.: Stereo radiance fields (SRF): learning view synthesis from sparse views of novel scenes. In: IEEE Conference on Computer Vision and Pattern Recognition (CVPR). IEEE (2021)
5. Flynn, J., et al.: DeepView: view synthesis with learned gradient descent. In: 2019 IEEE/CVF Conference on Computer Vision and Pattern Recognition (CVPR), pp. 2362–2371 (2019)
6. Gao, C., Shih, Y., Lai, W.S., Liang, C.K., Huang, J.B.: Portrait neural radiance fields from a single image. ArXiv abs/2012.05903 (2020)

7. Graham, B., Engelcke, M., van der Maaten, L.: 3D semantic segmentation with submanifold sparse convolutional networks. In: 2018 IEEE/CVF Conference on Computer Vision and Pattern Recognition, pp. 9224–9232 (2018)

8. Guan, P., Weiss, A., Balan, A.O., Black, M.J.: Estimating human shape and pose from a single image. In: 2009 IEEE 12th International Conference on Computer Vision, pp. 1381–1388 (2009)

9. He, K., Zhang, X., Ren, S., Sun, J.: Deep residual learning for image recognition. In: 2016 IEEE Conference on Computer Vision and Pattern Recognition (CVPR), pp. 770–778 (2016)

10. Kocabas, M., Huang, C.H.P., Hilliges, O., Black, M.J.: PARE: part attention regressor for 3D human body estimation. In: 2021 IEEE/CVF International Conference on Computer Vision (ICCV), pp. 11107–11117 (2021)

11. Kundu, J.N., Rakesh, M., Jampani, V., Venkatesh, R.M., Babu, R.V.: Appearance consensus driven self-supervised human mesh recovery. ArXiv abs/2008.01341 (2020)

12. Kwon, Y., Kim, D., Ceylan, D., Fuchs, H.: Neural human performer: learning generalizable radiance fields for human performance rendering. In: NeurIPS (2021)

13. Li, J., Feng, Z., She, Q., Ding, H., Wang, C., Lee, G.H.: MINE: towards continuous depth MPI with nerf for novel view synthesis. In: 2021 IEEE/CVF International Conference on Computer Vision (ICCV), pp. 12558–12568 (2021)

14. Li, P., Xu, Y., Wei, Y., Yang, Y.: Self-correction for human parsing. IEEE Trans. Pattern Anal. Mach. Intell. (2020). https://doi.org/10.1109/TPAMI.2020.3048039

15. Li, T., et al.: Neural 3D video synthesis. ArXiv abs/2103.02597 (2021)

16. Lin, K., Wang, L., Liu, Z.: End-to-end human pose and mesh reconstruction with transformers. In: 2021 IEEE/CVF Conference on Computer Vision and Pattern Recognition (CVPR), pp. 1954–1963 (2020)

17. Lin, K., Wang, L., Liu, Z.: Mesh graphormer. In: 2021 IEEE/CVF International Conference on Computer Vision (ICCV), pp. 12919–12928 (2021)

18. Loper, M., Mahmood, N., Romero, J., Pons-Moll, G., Black, M.J.: SMPL: a skinned multi-person linear model. ACM Trans. Graphics (Proc. SIGGRAPH Asia) **34**(6), 248:1–248:16 (2015)

19. Lu, E., Cole, F., Dekel, T., Xie, W., Zisserman, A., Salesin, D., Freeman, W.T., Rubinstein, M.: Layered neural rendering for retiming people in video. ACM Trans. Graphics (TOG) **39**, 1–14 (2020)

20. Mihajlović, M., Bansal, A., Zollhoefer, M., Tang, S., Saito, S.: KeypointNeRF: generalizing image-based volumetric avatars using relative spatial encoding of keypoints. In: Avidan, S., Brostow, G., Cissé, M., Farinella, G.M., Hassner, T. (eds.) ECCV 2022. LNCS, vol. 13675, pp. 179–197. Springer, Cham (2022). https://doi.org/10.1007/978-3-031-19784-0_11

21. Mildenhall, B., Srinivasan, P.P., Tancik, M., Barron, J.T., Ramamoorthi, R., Ng, R.: NeRF: representing scenes as neural radiance fields for view synthesis. In: Vedaldi, A., Bischof, H., Brox, T., Frahm, J.-M. (eds.) ECCV 2020. LNCS, vol. 12346, pp. 405–421. Springer, Cham (2020). https://doi.org/10.1007/978-3-030-58452-8_24

22. Noh, H., Hong, S., Han, B.: Learning deconvolution network for semantic segmentation. In: 2015 IEEE International Conference on Computer Vision (ICCV), pp. 1520–1528 (2015)

23. Park, K., et al.: Deformable neural radiance fields (2020). https://arxiv.org/abs/2011.12948

24. Pavlakos, G., et al.: Expressive body capture: 3D hands, face, and body from a single image. In: Proceedings IEEE Conference on Computer Vision and Pattern Recognition (CVPR), pp. 10975–10985 (2019)

25. Peng, S., et al.: Neural body: implicit neural representations with structured latent codes for novel view synthesis of dynamic humans. In: 2021 IEEE/CVF Conference on Computer Vision and Pattern Recognition (CVPR), pp. 9050–9059 (2021)

26. Pumarola, A., Corona, E., Pons-Moll, G., Moreno-Noguer, F.: D-NeRF: neural radiance fields for dynamic scenes (2020). https://arxiv.org/abs/2011.13961

27. Saito, S., Huang, Z., Natsume, R., Morishima, S., Kanazawa, A., Li, H.: PIFu: pixel-aligned implicit function for high-resolution clothed human digitization. In: 2019 IEEE/CVF International Conference on Computer Vision (ICCV), pp. 2304–2314 (2019)
28. Saito, S., Simon, T., Saragih, J.M., Joo, H.: PIFuHD: multi-level pixel-aligned implicit function for high-resolution 3D human digitization. In: 2020 IEEE/CVF Conference on Computer Vision and Pattern Recognition (CVPR), pp. 81–90 (2020)
29. Shuai, Q., Geng, C., Fang, Q., Peng, S., Shen, W., Zhou, X., Bao, H.: EasyMocap - make human motion capture easier. Github (2021). https://github.com/zju3dv/EasyMocap
30. Shuai, Q., et al.: Novel view synthesis of human interactions from sparse multi-view videos. In: ACM SIGGRAPH (2022)
31. Sigal, L., Balan, A.O., Black, M.J.: Combined discriminative and generative articulated pose and non-rigid shape estimation. In: NIPS (2007)
32. Sitzmann, V., Thies, J., Heide, F., Nießner, M., Wetzstein, G., Zollhöfer, M.: DeepVoxels: learning persistent 3D feature embeddings. 2019 IEEE/CVF Conference on Computer Vision and Pattern Recognition (CVPR), pp. 2432–2441 (2019)
33. Thies, J., Zollhöfer, M., Nießner, M.: Deferred neural rendering: image synthesis using neural textures. arXiv Computer Vision and Pattern Recognition (2019)
34. Trevithick, A., Yang, B.: GRF: learning a general radiance field for 3D scene representation and rendering. ArXiv abs/2010.04595 (2020)
35. Wang, Q., et al.: IBRNet: learning multi-view image-based rendering. In: 2021 IEEE/CVF Conference on Computer Vision and Pattern Recognition (CVPR), pp. 4688–4697 (2021)
36. Wu, M., Wang, Y., Hu, Q., Yu, J.: Multi-view neural human rendering. In: 2020 IEEE/CVF Conference on Computer Vision and Pattern Recognition (CVPR), pp. 1679–1688 (2020)
37. Xian, W., Huang, J.B., Kopf, J., Kim, C.: Space-time neural irradiance fields for free-viewpoint video. In: 2021 IEEE/CVF Conference on Computer Vision and Pattern Recognition (CVPR), pp. 9416–9426 (2021)
38. Yan, X., Yang, J., Yumer, E., Guo, Y., Lee, H.: Perspective transformer nets: learning single-view 3D object reconstruction without 3D supervision. ArXiv abs/1612.00814 (2016)
39. Yu, A., Ye, V., Tancik, M., Kanazawa, A.: pixelNeRF: neural radiance fields from one or few images. In: 2021 IEEE/CVF Conference on Computer Vision and Pattern Recognition (CVPR), pp. 4576–4585 (2021)
40. Zanfir, A., Bazavan, E.G., Xu, H., Freeman, B., Sukthankar, R., Sminchisescu, C.: Weakly supervised 3D human pose and shape reconstruction with normalizing flows. ArXiv abs/2003.10350 (2020)
41. Zhang, H., et al.: PyMAF: 3D human pose and shape regression with pyramidal mesh alignment feedback loop. In: 2021 IEEE/CVF International Conference on Computer Vision (ICCV), pp. 11426–11436 (2021)
42. Zhang, J., et al.: Editable free-viewpoint video using a layered neural representation. ACM Trans. Graphics **40**, 1–18 (2021)
43. Zhang, Y., Li, Z., An, L., Li, M., Yu, T., Liu, Y.: Lightweight multi-person total motion capture using sparse multi-view cameras. In: 2021 IEEE/CVF International Conference on Computer Vision (ICCV), pp. 5540–5549 (2021)
44. Zhao, F., et al.: HumanNeRF: generalizable neural human radiance field from sparse inputs. ArXiv abs/2112.02789 (2021)
45. Zheng, Y., et al.: DeepMultiCap: performance capture of multiple characters using sparse multiview cameras. In: International Conference on Computer Vision (ICCV), pp. 6219–6229 (2021)

RC-BEVFusion: A Plug-In Module for Radar-Camera Bird's Eye View Feature Fusion

Lukas Stäcker[1,2]([✉]) [iD], Shashank Mishra[2,3] [iD], Philipp Heidenreich[1] [iD],
Jason Rambach[3] [iD], and Didier Stricker[2,3] [iD]

[1] Stellantis, Opel Automobile GmbH, Rüsselsheim am Main, Germany
lukas.staecker@external.stellantis.com
[2] Rheinland-Pfälzische Technische Universität Kaiserslautern-Landau,
Kaiserslautern, Germany
[3] German Research Center for Artificial Intelligence, Kaiserslautern, Germany

Abstract. Radars and cameras belong to the most frequently used
sensors for advanced driver assistance systems and automated driving
research. However, there has been surprisingly little research on radar-
camera fusion with neural networks. One of the reasons is a lack of
large-scale automotive datasets with radar and unmasked camera data,
with the exception of the nuScenes dataset. Another reason is the difficulty of effectively fusing the sparse radar point cloud on the bird's eye
view (BEV) plane with the dense images on the perspective plane. The
recent trend of camera-based 3D object detection using BEV features has
enabled a new type of fusion, which is better suited for radars. In this
work, we present RC-BEVFusion, a modular radar-camera fusion network on the BEV plane. We propose two novel radar encoder branches,
and show that they can be incorporated into several state-of-the-art
camera-based architectures. We show significant performance gains of
up to 28% increase in the nuScenes detection score, which is an important step in radar-camera fusion research. Without tuning our model for
the nuScenes benchmark, we achieve the best result among all published
methods in the radar-camera fusion category.

1 Introduction

The development of advanced driver assistance systems (ADAS) and automated
driving functions has made remarkable progress in recent years, resulting in
increased safety and convenience for drivers. A robust environment perception
is the key requirement for these systems, which rely on sensors such as radar,
camera, or LiDAR to detect surrounding objects. Each sensor has its own advantages and disadvantages that must be considered when designing a perception
system. An extensive review on multi-modular automotive object detection is
presented in [4].

Supplementary Information The online version contains supplementary material
available at https://doi.org/10.1007/978-3-031-54605-1_12.

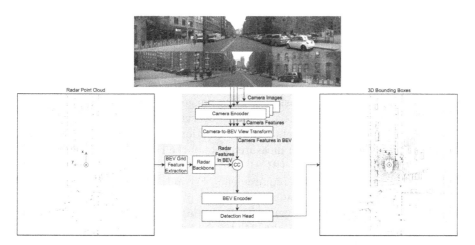

Fig. 1. Overview of RC-BEVFusion network architecture. The block marked in grey is inherited from an exchangeable camera-only baseline, while the block marked in blue shows our proposed radar-camera fusion plug-in module. (Color figure online)

Radar sensors are advantageous in that they are less affected by adverse environmental conditions such as rain, fog, or darkness, and they have a longer detection range when compared to cameras and LiDARs. However, they are limited in their ability to provide detailed information about the shape and texture of objects [58]. Cameras, on the other hand, provide rich visual information and can recognize objects based on their appearance, but their performance can be affected by changes in lighting conditions and inaccurate depth estimation [11,24]. LiDARs provide detailed 3D information and are less affected by lighting conditions, but they can be expensive and have limited range [58].

Sensor fusion has the potential to overcome these limitations of individual sensors. In particular, the combination of radar and camera sensors arguably offers the most complementary features. The main challenge is how to associate radar and camera features given that conventional radars provide data on the bird's eye view (BEV) plane, whereas cameras provide data on the image plane. Projecting radar points to the image discards too much geometric information, whereas projecting camera features to the sparse radar points discards too much semantic information [22].

Recent advancements in camera-only networks using view transformers [10, 36] have enabled a new type of fusion on the BEV plane, which is well suited for radar data. In this paper, we propose RC-BEVFusion, a novel radar-camera fusion architecture on the BEV plane inspired by [22] and illustrated in Fig. 1. In contrast to previous radar-camera fusion techniques [14,31,35], our architecture allows radar and camera features to equally contribute to the final detections, enabling the network to detect obstacles that may be missed by one of the modalities. It is a flexible architecture that inherits several elements from an exchangable camera-only baseline: a camera encoder, a camera-to-BEV view transformer, a BEV encoder and a detection head. On top of these modules, we propose two radar encoder branches: RadarGridMap and BEVFeatureNet. Our results show that they can be used as a plug-in module in various camera-based architectures and significantly enhance their performance.

To train and evaluate our network, we need a large-scale automotive dataset with radar point clouds, unmasked camera images with a lot of variety in the scenes and 3D object annotations. A recent overview on radar datasets is given in [58]. First, there are datasets with conventional 2+1D radar sensors that provide a list of detections with measurements of the range, range rate, azimuth angle, and radar cross section (RCS). Out of these, the nuScenes dataset [1] is the only one that fulfils our requirements. Second, there are recent datasets with high-performance 3+1D radar sensors that provide denser point clouds and additionally measure the elevation angle. From this group, the Astyx [27] dataset is too small, while the View-of-Delft [34] dataset is medium-sized but has limited visual variety in the images due to the high annotation frequency. The recently presented TJ4DRadSet [55] may be a future option but the data is not fully released yet. In this work, we therefore choose to conduct our experiments with the nuScenes dataset [1].

The remaining paper is organized as follows. Section 2 provides an overview of related work on automotive object detection with camera-only, radar-only and radar-camera fusion. Section 3 describes the proposed radar-camera fusion architecture on the BEV plane. Section 4 presents extensive experimental results on the nuScenes dataset and demonstrates the effectiveness of the proposed architecture. Finally, Sect. 5 concludes the paper and outlines future work.

2   Related Work

The task of 3D object detection is mostly conducted with the help of cameras, LiDARs and, less frequently, radars. In the following, we give an overview of recent advances on image-only and radar-only object detection, as well as LiDAR-camera and radar-camera sensor fusion.

2.1   Image-Only Object Detection

Image-based 3D object detection is a difficult task in the field of computer vision because it involves identifying and localizing objects in 3D space using only a single camera as a sensor. This is in contrast to LiDAR and radar systems, which provide depth measurements and can more accurately determine the 3D location of objects.

Early approaches to image-based 3D object detection focused on using known geometric information to estimate 3D bounding boxes from 2D detections [28]. More recent techniques have extended existing 2D object detection models with additional detection heads specifically designed for 3D object detection [43,48, 57]. Some approaches have also used predicted depth maps as auxiliary features [26] or to create a pseudo-LiDAR point cloud, which is then processed using LiDAR-based object detectors [49].

The most recent research in this area has mainly followed two directions. The first is the use of transformer-based techniques, which leverage the ability of transformer models to process sequences of data and perform self-attention to learn more complex relationships between features [20, 50]. The second direction is the development of BEV-based object detectors. To this end, the features need to be transformed from the image plane to the BEV plane. A pioneering work uses orthographic feature transform [39], where a voxel grid is projected to the image to extract features. To reduce memory consumption, the voxel grid is then collapsed along the vertical axis to create BEV features. More recent methods are based on the Lift-Splat-Shoot (LSS) view transformer [36], which lifts image features into a 3D pseudo point cloud via dense depth prediction, before again collapsing the vertical dimension to create BEV features. The idea is first incorporated into a 3D object detection network in [10], and later refined with LiDAR-based depth supervision [18] and temporal stereo [17]. In [56], a more efficient view transformer in terms of memory and computations is introduced by formulating LSS into matrix operations with decomposed ring and ray matrices, and compressing image features and the estimated depth map along the vertical dimension. In this work, we build upon these BEV-based object detectors and integrate our radar-camera fusion as a plug-in module.

2.2   Radar-Only Object Detection

Automotive radars are a common sensor used in autonomous vehicles for detecting objects in the environment. These radars typically provide a preprocessed list of detections, but the sparsity and lack of semantic information make it difficult to use the data for stand-alone 3D object detection. As a result, much of the research in this area has focused on either semantic segmentation of radar point clouds [42] or experimental setups using the raw radar cube [25, 33].

Recently, there have been some point cloud-based techniques for object detection as well. These can be broadly divided into convolutional and graph-based approaches. Some convolutional approaches assign each point in the point cloud to a cell in a BEV grid and include feature layers such as the maximum RCS and Doppler values [5, 40]. Since the BEV grid is similar in structure to an image, traditional convolutional networks can be applied for object detection. Other convolutional approaches use variants of PointPillars [15] to create a pillar grid automatically from the point cloud [34, 40]. In contrast, graph neural network based approaches perform object detection directly on the radar point cloud [3, 41]. Recent work combines both approaches by first extracting features with a graph neural network and then mapping the features to a BEV grid for further processing [45]. In this work, we examine radar feature encoders inspired by these ideas.

2.3   Sensor Fusion Object Detection

Sensor fusion aims at leveraging the strengths of a diverse sensor combination. Most sensor fusion research focuses on LiDAR-camera fusion, as LiDAR provides accurate 3D information and cameras provide high semantic value, while sharing the same optical propagation principles. There are several techniques for fusing LiDAR and camera data. Some approaches are based on projecting 2D detections from the camera into a frustum and matching them with LiDAR points to refine the 3D detections [37,51]. Other techniques augment the LiDAR points with semantics from the image and use LiDAR-based object detectors to perform detection [7,46,47]. The most recent approaches to LiDAR-camera fusion involve extracting BEV features from both the LiDAR and camera data and fusing them on the BEV plane before applying a joint BEV encoder to perform object detection [6,19,22].

When compared to LiDAR, automotive radar uses a different wavelength and measurement principle. As a consequence, radar typically shows strong RCS fluctuations and reduced resolution in range and angle, resulting in less dense point clouds. Moreover, whereas modern radars also measure elevation, many conventional radars only provide detections on the BEV plane. These differences make the fusion especially challenging and prevent the simple replacement of LiDAR with radar processing. Early research commonly projected the radar detections onto the image plane to associate the data. This approach can be used to find regions of interest in the image [29,30] or to create additional image channels with radar data that can be used with image-based networks [2,32,44].

More recent methods have moved away from this 2D approach and instead focus on fusing based on 3D information. One approach is to refine image-based 3D detections with associated radar data [31]. This can be sub-optimal because it discards the possibility of radar-only detections. Another approach is to project 3D regions of interest (ROIs) to the image and BEV plane to extract features from each sensor [13]. Finally, cross-attention has been used to align and fuse the features in 3D [12,35]. In this work, we propose a novel architecture to fuse radar and camera data on the BEV plane.

3   RC-BEVFusion

In this section, we describe our proposed model architectures. We start by giving an overview of the general fusion architecture, before providing more detail on the proposed radar encoders, the camera-only networks we use as baselines and the loss function.

3.1   Overview

In this work, we introduce a novel radar branch and use it as a plug-in module on different camera-based 3D object detection networks to improve their performance. The prerequisite for our proposed radar-camera fusion is that the camera-only network uses BEV features as an intermediate representation. The general architecture is shown in Fig. 1. The block marked in grey is inherited from an exchangeable camera-only baseline, while the block marked in blue shows our proposed radar plug-in module.

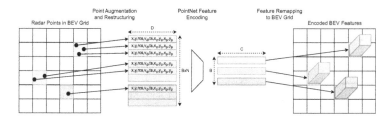

Fig. 2. BEVFeatureNet radar encoder. The radar detections are mapped to BEV grid cells for augmentation and restructuring into a dense tensor. After applying a simplified PointNet, the encoded features are remapped to the BEV grid.

First, BEV features are extracted from the images and the radar point cloud separately. To this end, a backbone network is used to extract features from each image before they are transformed into joint BEV features with a view transformer. We set up our radar encoder so that it creates BEV features in the same shape and geometric orientation as the camera BEV features. The features are then fused by concatenation followed by a 1×1 convolutional layer that reduces the embedding dimension to the original dimension of the camera BEV features. We can then use the same BEV encoder and 3D detection heads that are used in the respective camera-only network, introducing little overhead with our fusion.

3.2 Radar Encoders

We propose two radar encoders, RadarGridMap and BEVFeatureNet, which we explain in the following. They each consist of two stages: First, we create a regular, structured BEV grid from the sparse radar point cloud. Then, we apply a convolutional backbone that further encodes the BEV features.

RadarGridMap. Inspired by [5], we design a hand-crafted radar BEV grid. We map each detection to a cell on the grid and fill the cell with four channels: the number of detections per cell, the maximum RCS value, and the minimum and maximum signed compensated Doppler values.

After the grid mapping, we use a small generalized ResNet [8] as our radar backbone. We use 16 layers grouped into residual blocks with BatchNorm and ReLU. We use two downsampling stages that double the channels but reduce the resolution of the BEV grid. We design the size of the BEV grid so that the output of the radar backbone has the same shape as the camera BEV features.

BEVFeatureNet. The BEVFeatureNet illustrated in Fig. 2 is inspired by the pillar feature encoding of PointPillars [15], but adapted for radar data. First, we map each point of the radar point cloud to a cell in a predefined BEV grid. In the original pillar feature encoding, each point in the LiDAR point cloud has

Table 1. Camera-only network configurations. For FPN-LSS, SECOND-FPN and Generalized ResNet, we indicate the number of output channels of the module. For LSS and MatrixVT, we indicate the number of channels and the resolution of the output BEV feature in meters. MF denotes multi-frame temporal fusion.

Model	Camera Encoder	View Transf	BEV Encoder	Head	Input Res	MF
BEVDet [10]	Swin-Tiny	LSS	Gen. ResNet-512	CenterPoint	704 × 256	
	FPN-LSS-256	80-0.4-0.4	FPN-LSS-256			
BEVDepth [18]	ResNet-50	LSS	ResNet-18	CenterPoint	704 × 256	✓
	SECOND-FPN-128	80-0.8-0.8	SECOND-FPN-64			
BEVStereo [17]	ResNet-50	LSS	ResNet-18	CenterPoint	704 × 256	✓
	SECOND-FPN-128	80-0.8-0.8	SECOND-FPN-64			
MatrixVT [56]	ResNet-50	MatrixVT	ResNet-18	CenterPoint	704 × 256	
	SECOND-FPN-128	80-0.8-0.8	SECOND-FPN-64			

coordinates x, y, and z, and reflectivity r. Further, the point is augmented with the distances to the arithmetic mean of all points in its pillar, x_c, y_c, and z_c and the offsets to the pillar center x_p and y_p. The 2+1D radar point cloud in nuScenes [1] does not have a z-coordinate or a reflectivity r, but instead it has a radial velocity v_d, measured via the Doppler effect, and an RCS. We therefore discard the z-axis and its augmented feature, replace the reflectivity with the RCS, and include the radial velocity values. We further aggregate multiple radar sweeps and append the timestamp difference to the latest sweep t_s to each point. Thus, we obtain the 9-dimensional feature set:

$$\vec{F} = [x, y, \text{RCS}, v_d, t_s, x_c, y_c, x_p, y_p] \tag{1}$$

As in [15], we then use a set of non-empty BEV grid cells B with a fixed number of points per cell N_p to create a dense tensor of size (F, B, N_p). If the number of non-empty BEV grid cells or the number of points per cell is lower or higher than the fixed number, we apply zero-padding or random sampling, respectively. For each point, we then apply a simplified PointNet [38] with a 1×1 convolutional layer followed by BatchNorm and ReLU resulting in a tensor of shape (C, B, N_p), before a max operation over the points per cell reduces the dimension to (C, B). We then map the C-dimensional features back to their position on the BEV grid. Finally, the same convolutional backbone as for RadarGridMap is applied.

3.3   Camera-Only Baselines

We selected various camera-only baselines to showcase the plug-in character of our radar fusion module. In this section, we list details for the camera baselines we examined. A compact overview of the modules is given in Table 1.

BEVDet. BEVDet [10] is the first network that uses BEV-based features for object detection on the nuScenes dataset. First, high-level features from each of the N_i input images of shape (H_i, W_i) are extracted separately. To this end, a SwinTransformer-Tiny [21] backbone network outputs multi-scale feature maps, which are then processed using the feature pyramid network from [36], FPN-LSS, which upsamples the low resolution feature maps to match the high resolution map, concatenates them and runs them through a ResNet [8] block. This leads to a feature map of shape $(N_i, H_i/8, W_i/8, C)$ with C feature channels. Then, a 1×1 convolution followed by a Softmax is used to predict a depth classification into D pre-defined depth bins. An outer product across the feature and depth classification channels creates a very large tensor of shape $(N_i, H_i/8, W_i/8, D, C)$. Using the intrinsic and extrinsic calibration matrices of each camera, this tensor can be unprojected into a pseudo-pointcloud. The vertical dimension of this pseudo-pointcloud is then collapsed by summing up the features from all points that fall into the same cell of a pre-defined BEV grid with shape (H_{bev}, W_{bev}). We follow the implementation of [22], which provides computationally efficient BEV pooling and uses a heavier view transformer to enable more accurate depth estimation, which is important to associate the features from radar and camera. To further encode the BEV features, the generalized ResNet [8] structure from [36] followed again by FPN-LSS is used.

BEVDepth. BEVDepth [18] uses a similar structure to BEVDet [10] but aims to achieve a more accurate depth estimation. To this end, the single convolutional layer for depth estimation in BEVDet [10] is replaced with a camera-aware DepthNet module, that concatenates and flattens the camera's intrinsic and extrinsic calibration parameters and uses an MLP to rescale them to match the dimension of the image features C. This calibration vector is used to re-weight the image features using a Squeeze-and-Excitation module [9]. During training, BEVDepth [18] further uses the depth value from projected LiDAR points on the image to directly supervise the depth estimation via binary cross-entropy loss. We use the released configuration, which encodes the images with a ResNet-50 [8] backbone followed by the feature pyramid net from [52], SECOND-FPN, which concatenates upsampled multi-scale feature maps. The BEV encoder uses a ResNet-18 again followed by SECOND-FPN. The view transformer has a lower resolution than the one we use for BEVDet [10]. It also uses a multi-frame fusion with one previous keyframe, thus two images from each camera taken 500 ms apart are used to create the BEV features, resulting in more accurate velocity estimation.

BEVStereo. BEVStereo [17] builds upon BEVDepth [18] and uses the same configuration for most modules. In addition to the monocular depth estimation with DepthNet, it introduces a temporal stereo depth estimation module, which is based on multi-view-stereo [53]. To this end, for each pixel in the current image feature map, several depth candidates are predicted and used to retrieve corresponding features from the previous image features using a homography warping. The confidence of each candidate is evaluated based on the current and previous feature's similarity and used to iteratively optimize the depth candidates. After three iterations, the depth candidates are used to construct the stereo depth. Since the stereo depth is not viable for pixels that do not have corresponding pixels in the previous image, a convolutional WeightNet module is used to combine the monocular depth estimations from the current and previous image with the stereo depth estimation to produce the final depth estimates.

MatrixVT. In MatrixVT [56], an alternative view transformer is proposed. The view transformation step of LSS [36] is first generalized into matrix operations, which leads to a very large and sparse feature transportation tensor of shape $(H_{bev}, W_{bev}, N_i, H_i/8, W_i/8, D)$, which transforms the image feature tensor with depth estimates to the BEV features. To combat this, the image feature and the dense depth prediction are compressed along the vertical dimension, resulting in prime feature and prime depth matrices. This is feasible due to the low response variance in the height dimension of the image. To further reduce its sparsity, the feature transportation tensor is orthogonally decomposed into a ring tensor, which encodes distance information, and a ray tensor, which encodes directional information. Using efficient mathematical operations, the resulting view transformer achieves lower computational cost and memory requirements. We use a configuration based on BEVDepth [18], which only replaces the view transformer with MatrixVT [56] and does not use multi-frame fusion.

3.4   Detection Head and Loss

All examined camera baselines use the CenterPoint [54] detection head, so we can apply the same loss in all architectures. For each class k, CenterPoint [54] predicts a BEV heatmap with peaks at object center locations. The heatmap is trained using a ground-truth heatmap y filled with Gaussian distributions around ground truth object centers. Given the heatmap score p_{kij} at position i, j in the BEV grid and the ground truth y_{kij}, we can compute the Gaussian focal loss [16] as:

$$
L_{hm} = -\frac{1}{N_o} \sum_{k=1}^{K} \sum_{i=1}^{H_{bev}} \sum_{j=1}^{W_{bev}} \begin{cases} (1 - p_{kij})^\alpha \log(p_{kij}) & y_{kij} = 1 \\ (1 - y_{kij})^\beta (p_{kij})^\alpha \log(1 - p_{kij}) & \text{otherwise} \end{cases} \tag{2}
$$

where N_o is the number of objects per image, K is the number of classes, H_{bev} and W_{bev} are the height and width of the BEV grid, and α and β are hyperparameters. In addition, CenterPoint [54] has regression heads that output all parameters needed to decode 3D bounding boxes: a sub-pixel location refinement, a height above ground, the dimensions, the velocity, and the sine and cosine of the yaw rotation angle. The regression heads are trained with L1 loss.

4   Experimental Results

In this section, we present our experimental results. We first give some more information on the dataset, evaluation metrics and training settings. We then list quantitative results on the nuScenes validation set to ensure a fair comparison between our proposed fusion networks with their camera-only baselines. We also show results for the nuScenes [1] test benchmark and provide an inference example for a qualitative comparison. Ablative studies, detailed class-wise results, rain and night scene evaluation and more qualitative examples are provided in the supplementary material.

4.1   Data and Metrics

For our experiments, we need a large-scale, real-world dataset with unmasked camera images, series-production automotive radars and 3D bounding box annotations. To the best of our knowledge, the nuScenes dataset [1] is currently the only dataset that fulfils these requirements. It covers data from six cameras at 12 Hz, five conventional 2+1D radar sensors at 13 Hz and one LiDAR at 20 Hz, as well as 1.4 million 3D bounding boxes annotated at 2 Hz. We follow the official splits into 700 training, 150 validation and 150 test scenes and reduce the 27 annotated classes to the 10 classes evaluated on the benchmark. We also use the official metrics: the mean average precision (mAP), the true positive metrics covering mean errors for translation (mATE), scale (mASE), orientation (mAOE), velocity (mAVE) and nuScenes attribute (mAAE), as well as the condensed nuScenes detection score (NDS).

4.2   Quantitative Evaluation

Training Details. For our radar-camera fusion networks, we adopt the configurations from the camera-only baselines listed in Table 1 to allow for a fair comparison. In addition, we design our radar encoder branch so that the BEV features have the same shape and orientation as the camera BEV features. To increase the point cloud density while limiting the use of outdated data, we choose to aggregate five radar sweeps, which corresponds to 300 ms of past data. The aggregated radar point cloud is still sparse when compared with LiDAR data, so that we can reduce the number of non-empty grid cells and points per grid cell of the BEVFeatureNet drastically with respect to the pillar feature encoding in [15]. We empirically find that setting $B = 2000$, $N_p = 10$, and $C = 32$ is sufficient, which allows for little computational overhead. For the Gaussian focal loss, we follow [16] and set $\alpha = 2$ and $\beta = 4$. We train for 20 epochs with an AdamW [23] optimizer, a base learning rate of 2e−4 and weight decay of 1e−2.

NuScenes Validation Results. We show the results for our radar-camera fusion networks w.r.t. their camera-only baselines on the nuScenes validation split in Table 2. First, we compare the two radar encoders with our model based on BEVDet. In both cases, the proposed fusion offers significant performance increases, with the mAP increasing up to 24% and the NDS 28%. The up to 23% reduced translation error shows how the direct depth measurements provided by the radar can lead to more precise location predictions. The most significant improvement of 55% is achieved for the velocity error, which is enabled by

Table 2. Experimental results for our radar-camera fusion used in different architectures on the nuScenes val split. The inference latency T is measured on a Nvidia RTX 2080 Ti. *We use the implementation of BEVDet-Tiny with a heavier view transformer from [22]. †We list the results as reported by the authors.

	Cam. model	Radar model		mAP↑	NDS↑	mATE↓	mASE↓	mAOE↓	mAVE↓	mAAE↓	T[ms]
[10]	BEVDet*	None		0.350	0.411	0.660	0.275	0.532	0.918	0.260	122
Ours	BEVDet*	RadarGridMap		0.429	0.525	0.523	0.272	0.507	0.412	0.183	132
			Δ_r	23%	28%	−21%	−1%	−5%	−55%	−30%	
Ours	BEVDet*	BEVFeatureNet		0.434	0.525	0.511	0.270	0.527	0.421	0.182	139
			Δ_r	24%	28%	−23%	−2%	−1%	−54%	−30%	
[18]†	BEVDepth	None		0.359	0.480	0.612	0.269	0.507	0.409	0.201	132
Ours	BEVDepth	BEVFeatureNet		0.405	0.521	0.542	0.274	0.512	0.309	0.181	146
			Δ_r	13%	9%	−11%	2%	1%	−24%	−10%	
[17]†	BEVStereo	None		0.372	0.500	0.598	0.270	0.438	0.367	0.190	308
Ours	BEVStereo	BEVFeatureNet		0.423	0.545	0.504	0.268	0.453	0.270	0.174	322
			Δ_r	14%	9%	−16%	−1%	3%	−26%	−8%	
[56]	MatrixVT	None		0.319	0.400	0.669	0.281	0.494	0.912	0.238	54
Ours	MatrixVT	BEVFeatureNet		0.386	0.495	0.549	0.275	0.539	0.423	0.193	64
			Δ_r	21%	24%	−18%	−2%	9%	−54%	−19%	

Table 3. Experimental results for published radar-camera fusion models on the nuScenes test benchmark.

Model	mAP↑	NDS↑	mATE↓	mASE↓	mAOE↓	mAVE↓	mAAE↓
CenterFusion [31]	0.326	0.449	0.631	0.261	0.516	0.614	0.115
CRAFT [14]	0.411	0.523	0.467	0.268	0.456	0.519	**0.114**
TransCAR [35]	0.422	0.522	0.630	0.260	**0.383**	0.495	0.121
Ours (BEVDet)	**0.476**	**0.567**	**0.444**	**0.244**	0.461	**0.439**	0.128

the direct velocity measurement of the radar. This effect also helps determining whether an object is currently moving or stopped, thus reducing the attribute error. The two metrics that remain relatively unaffected by the fusion are scale and orientation error. This is as expected since the sparse radar detections do not help to determine an object's size or orientation. Overall, we observe similar results for the RadarGridMap and the BEVFeatureNet encoder. This demonstrates the effectiveness and modularity of the proposed BEV-based feature fusion. In general, we recommend using the BEVFeatureNet because it requires less hand-crafted input, is more scalable, and achieves slightly better results.

In the second part of Table 2, we use the BEVFeatureNet encoder as a plug-in branch in different camera-only baselines. We observe significant performance increase for all examined architectures, again confirming the modularity of the proposed architecture. There are two potential reasons for the difference in relative performance increase between the camera-only baselines. First, BEVDepth and BEVStereo use temporal fusion and therefore achieve better velocity prediction and overall scores, leading to smaller margins for the radar-camera fusion.

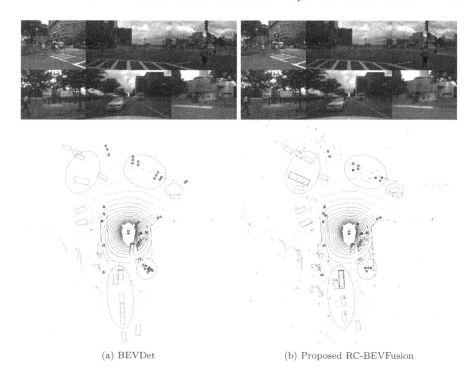

(a) BEVDet   (b) Proposed RC-BEVFusion

Fig. 3. Inference example at daytime. Predicted 3D bounding boxes projected to all six cameras (top) and BEV plane (bottom) with LiDAR points (black) and radar points (red) for reference. Our proposed fusion network more accurately detects pedestrians and vehicles (s. dashed red ellipses). (Color figure online)

Second, we use a BEVDet variant with a heavier view transformer especially designed for fusion on the BEV space. This modification may explain the relatively high performance gains.

Finally, we also measure the inference latency on an Nvidia RTX 2080 Ti GPU to demonstrate that our fusion approach introduces only small computational overhead due to the efficient radar encoder design.

NuScenes Test Results. For the nuScenes test benchmark, we show our results compared to other published radar-camera fusion models in Table 3. We note that many methods tune their models for the benchmark submission by enlarging their network and the input image resolution and by using test time augmentation. All of these techniques trade off smaller performance gains for large computational cost and are therefore not helpful in an automotive application in which fast decisions are required. For instance, the authors of BEVDet achieve 15.6 frames per second with the tiny configuration similar to ours, while the base configuration used for the benchmark achieves only 1.9 frames per second [10]. We therefore combat this trend and only retrain our model with scenes from the training and validation set for the test submission. As shown in Table 3, our proposed RC-BEVFusion with BEVFeatureNet and BEVDet significantly outperforms previously published radar-camera fusion networks in all metrics except the orientation error, even without tuning for the benchmark, while achieving 7.2 frames per second. A key advantage of our architecture compared to existing methods [14,31,35], is that radar and camera features can equally contribute to the final detections, allowing the model to detect objects that might be missed by each single modality.

4.3   Qualitative Evaluation

To get a better impression of the difference in object detection performance, we present an inference example for BEVDet [10] and RC-BEVFusion based on BEVFeatureNet and BEVDet in Fig. 3. We show the camera-only inference results and radar-camera fusion results in the left and right subfigure, respectively. We show the full surround view with all six cameras, the top row shows the front left, center and right camera, while the bottom row shows the back right, center and left camera. On the bottom, we show a BEV perspective with LiDAR points in black for reference and radar points in red for the fusion network only. In each perspective, we show the projected 3D bounding boxes predicted by the networks, where the color indicates the class: pedestrians are blue, cars are yellow and trucks are orange.

In the scene, we see a crowded intersection with lots of cars and pedestrians. At first, the visual impression when looking at the camera images is that most objects are well detected. However, comparing the dashed red ellipses in the BEV perspective on the right, we can see that the radar-camera fusion enables much more accurate detection of the pedestrians in the front and back right area, as well as the cars in the front left, front right and back area.

5   Conclusion

In this work, we have presented a novel radar-camera fusion architecture on the BEV plane. We propose two radar encoders and show that they can be integrated into several camera-based architectures that use BEV features. In our experiments, the proposed radar-camera fusion outperforms the camera-only baselines by a large margin, demonstrating its effectiveness. Without tuning the model for the test submission to avoid unrealistic computational cost, we outperform previously published radar-camera fusion networks. Our qualitative evaluation shows improved localization accuracy at daytime and higher recall at nighttime. In future work, we want to study the potential of BEV-based radar-camera fusion with the high-resolution, 3+1D radar sensors appearing in recently introduced datasets.

Acknowledgment. This work is partly funded by the German Federal Ministry for Economic Affairs and Climate Action (BMWK) and partly financed by the European

Union in the frame of NextGenerationEU within the project "Solutions and Technologies for Automated Driving in Town" (FKZ 19A22006P) and partly funded by the Federal Ministry of Education and Research Germany in the funding program Photonics Research Germany under the project FUMOS (FKZ 13N16302). The authors would like to thank the consortia for the successful cooperation.

References

1. Caesar, H., et al.: nuScenes: a multimodal dataset for autonomous driving. arXiv preprint arXiv:1903.11027 (2019)
2. Chadwick, S., Maddern, W., Newman, P.: Distant vehicle detection using radar and vision. In: 2019 International Conference on Robotics and Automation (ICRA), pp. 8311–8317. IEEE (2019)
3. Danzer, A., Griebel, T., Bach, M., Dietmayer, K.: 2D car detection in radar data with pointnets. In: IEEE Intelligent Transportation Systems Conference (ITSC), pp. 61–66. IEEE (2019)
4. Di, F., et al.: Deep multi-modal object detection and semantic segmentation for autonomous driving: datasets, methods, and challenges. IEEE Trans. Intell. Transp. Syst. **22**, 1341–1360 (2020)
5. Dreher, M., Erçelik, E., Bänziger, T., Knoll, A.: Radar-based 2D car detection using deep neural networks. In: IEEE 23rd International Conference on Intelligent Transportation Systems (ITSC), pp. 1–8. IEEE (2020)
6. Drews, F., Di, F., Faion, F., Rosenbaum, L., Ulrich, M., Gläser, C.: DeepFusion: a robust and modular 3D object detector for lidars, cameras and radars. In: IEEE/RSJ International Conference on Intelligent Robots and Systems (IROS), pp. 560–567. IEEE (2022)
7. Fei, J., Chen, W., Heidenreich, P., Wirges, S., Stiller, C.: SemanticVoxels: sequential fusion for 3D pedestrian detection using lidar point cloud and semantic segmentation. In: IEEE International Conference on Multisensor Fusion and Integration for Intelligent Systems (MFI), pp. 185–190. IEEE (2020)
8. He, K., Zhang, X., Ren, S., Sun, J.: Deep residual learning for image recognition. In: Proceedings of the IEEE/CVF Conference on Computer Vision and Pattern Recognition, pp. 770–778 (2016)
9. Hu, J., Shen, L., Sun, G.: Squeeze-and-excitation networks. In: Proceedings of the IEEE Conference on Computer Vision and Pattern Recognition, pp. 7132–7141 (2018)
10. Huang, J., Huang, G., Zhu, Z., Du, D.: BEVDet: high-performance multi-camera 3D object detection in bird-eye-view. arXiv preprint arXiv:2112.11790 (2021)
11. Hung, W.C., Kretzschmar, H., Casser, V., Hwang, J.J., Anguelov, D.: LET-3D-AP: longitudinal error tolerant 3D average precision for camera-only 3D detection. arXiv preprint arXiv:2206.07705 (2022)
12. Hwang, J.J., et al.: CramNet: camera-radar fusion with ray-constrained cross-attention for robust 3D object detection. In: Avidan, S., Brostow, G., Cissé, M., Farinella, G.M., Hassner, T. (eds.) ECCV 2022. LNCS, vol. 13698, pp. 388–405. Springer, Cham (2022). https://doi.org/10.1007/978-3-031-19839-7_23
13. Kim, Y., Choi, J.W., Kum, D.: GRIF net: gated region of interest fusion network for robust 3D object detection from radar point cloud and monocular image. In: IEEE/RSJ International Conference on Intelligent Robots and Systems (IROS), pp. 10857–10864. IEEE (2020)

14. Kim, Y., Kim, S., Choi, J.W., Kum, D.: CRAFT: camera-radar 3D object detection with spatio-contextual fusion transformer. arXiv preprint arXiv:2209.06535 (2022)
15. Lang, A.H., Vora, S., Caesar, H., Zhou, L., Yang, J., Beijbom, O.: PointPillars: fast encoders for object detection from point clouds. In: Proceedings of the IEEE/CVF Conference on Computer Vision and Pattern Recognition, pp. 12697–12705 (2019)
16. Law, H., Deng, J.: CornerNet: detecting objects as paired keypoints. In: Proceedings of the European Conference on Computer Vision (ECCV), pp. 734–750 (2018)
17. Li, Y., Bao, H., Ge, Z., Yang, J., Sun, J., Li, Z.: BEVStereo: enhancing depth estimation in multi-view 3D object detection with dynamic temporal stereo. arXiv preprint arXiv:2209.10248 (2022)
18. Li, Y., et al.: BEVDepth: acquisition of reliable depth for multi-view 3D object detection. arXiv preprint arXiv:2206.10092 (2022)
19. Liang, T., et al.: BEVFusion: a simple and robust lidar-camera fusion framework. arXiv preprint arXiv:2205.13790 (2022)
20. Liu, Y., Wang, T., Zhang, X., Sun, J.: PETR: position embedding transformation for multi-view 3D object detection. arXiv preprint arXiv:2203.05625 (2022)
21. Liu, Z., Lin, Y., Cao, Y., Hu, H., Wei, Y., Zhang, Z., Lin, S., Guo, B.: Swin transformer: hierarchical vision transformer using shifted windows. In: Proceedings of the IEEE/CVF International Conference on Computer Vision, pp. 10012–10022 (2021)
22. Liu, Z., et al.: BEVFusion: multi-task multi-sensor fusion with unified bird's-eye view representation. arXiv preprint arXiv:2205.13542 (2022)
23. Loshchilov, I., Hutter, F.: Decoupled weight decay regularization. arXiv preprint arXiv:1711.05101 (2017)
24. Ma, X., et al.: Delving into localization errors for monocular 3D object detection. In: Proceedings of the IEEE/CVF Conference on Computer Vision and Pattern Recognition, pp. 4721–4730 (2021)
25. Major, B., et al.: Vehicle detection with automotive radar using deep learning on range-azimuth-doppler tensors. In: Proceedings of the IEEE/CVF International Conference on Computer Vision Workshops (2019)
26. Manhardt, F., Kehl, W., Gaidon, A.: ROI-10D: monocular lifting of 2D detection to 6D pose and metric shape. In: Proceedings of the IEEE/CVF Conference on Computer Vision and Pattern Recognition, pp. 2069–2078 (2019)
27. Meyer, M., Kuschk, G.: Automotive radar dataset for deep learning based 3D object detection. In: 2019 16th European Radar Conference (EuRAD), pp. 129–132. IEEE (2019)
28. Mousavian, A., Anguelov, D., Flynn, J., Kosecka, J.: 3D bounding box estimation using deep learning and geometry. In: Proceedings of the IEEE/CVF Conference on Computer Vision and Pattern Recognition, pp. 7074–7082 (2017)
29. Nabati, R., Qi, H.: RRPN: radar region proposal network for object detection in autonomous vehicles. In: 2019 IEEE International Conference on Image Processing (ICIP), pp. 3093–3097. IEEE (2019)
30. Nabati, R., Qi, H.: Radar-camera sensor fusion for joint object detection and distance estimation in autonomous vehicles. arXiv preprint arXiv:2009.08428 (2020)
31. Nabati, R., Qi, H.: CenterFusion: center-based radar and camera fusion for 3D object detection. In: Proceedings of the IEEE/CVF Winter Conference on Applications of Computer Vision, pp. 1527–1536 (2021)
32. Nobis, F., Geisslinger, M., Weber, M., Betz, J., Lienkamp, M.: A deep learning-based radar and camera sensor fusion architecture for object detection. In: 2019 Sensor Data Fusion: Trends, Solutions, Applications (SDF), pp. 1–7. IEEE (2019)

33. Palffy, A., Dong, J., Kooij, J.F.P., Gavrila, D.M.: CNN based road user detection using the 3D radar cube. IEEE Robot. Autom. Lett. **5**(2), 1263–1270 (2020)
34. Palffy, A., Pool, E., Baratam, S., Kooij, J.F.P., Gavrila, D.M.: Multi-class road user detection with 3+ 1D radar in the view-of-delft dataset. IEEE Robot. Autom. Lett. **7**(2), 4961–4968 (2022)
35. Pang, S., Morris, D., Radha, H.: TransCAR: transformer-based camera-and-radar fusion for 3D object detection. arXiv preprint arXiv:2305.00397 (2023)
36. Philion, J., Fidler, S.: Lift, splat, shoot: encoding images from arbitrary camera rigs by implicitly unprojecting to 3D. In: Vedaldi, A., Bischof, H., Brox, T., Frahm, J.-M. (eds.) ECCV 2020. LNCS, vol. 12359, pp. 194–210. Springer, Cham (2020). https://doi.org/10.1007/978-3-030-58568-6_12
37. Qi, C.R., Liu, W., Wu, C., Su, H., Guibas, L.J.: Frustum pointnets for 3D object detection from RGB-D data. In: Proceedings of the IEEE/CVF Conference on Computer Vision and Pattern Recognition, pp. 918–927 (2018)
38. Qi, C.R., Su, H., Mo, K., Guibas, L.J.: PointNet: deep learning on point sets for 3D classification and segmentation. In: Proceedings of the IEEE/CVF Conference on Computer Vision and Pattern Recognition, pp. 652–660 (2017)
39. Roddick, T., Kendall, A., Cipolla, R.: Orthographic feature transform for monocular 3D object detection. arXiv preprint arXiv:1811.08188 (2018)
40. Scheiner, N., Kraus, F., Appenrodt, N., Dickmann, J., Sick, B.: Object detection for automotive radar point clouds-a comparison. AI Perspect. **3**(1), 1–23 (2021)
41. Scheiner, N., Schumann, O., Kraus, F., Appenrodt, N., Dickmann, J., Sick, B.: Off-the-shelf sensor vs. experimental radar-how much resolution is necessary in automotive radar classification? arXiv preprint arXiv:2006.05485 (2020)
42. Schumann, O., Hahn, M., Dickmann, J., Wöhler, C.: Semantic segmentation on radar point clouds. In: 2018 21st International Conference on Information Fusion (FUSION), pp. 2179–2186. IEEE (2018)
43. Simonelli, A., Bulo, S.R., Porzi, L., López-Antequera, M., Kontschieder, P.: Disentangling monocular 3D object detection. In: Proceedings of the IEEE/CVF International Conference on Computer Vision, pp. 1991–1999 (2019)
44. Stäcker, L., Heidenreich, P., Rambach, J., Stricker, D.: Fusion point pruning for optimized 2D object detection with radar-camera fusion. In: Proceedings of the IEEE/CVF Winter Conference on Applications of Computer Vision, pp. 3087–3094 (2022)
45. Ulrich, M., et al.: Improved orientation estimation and detection with hybrid object detection networks for automotive radar. arXiv preprint arXiv:2205.02111 (2022)
46. Vora, S., Lang, A.H., Helou, B., Beijbom, O.: PointPainting: sequential fusion for 3D object detection. In: Proceedings of the IEEE/CVF Conference on Computer Vision and Pattern Recognition, pp. 4604–4612 (2020)
47. Wang, C., Ma, C., Zhu, M., Yang, X.: PointAugmenting: cross-modal augmentation for 3D object detection. In: Proceedings of the IEEE/CVF Conference on Computer Vision and Pattern Recognition, pp. 11794–11803 (2021)
48. Wang, T., Zhu, X., Pang, J., Lin, D.: FCOS3D: fully convolutional one-stage monocular 3D object detection. In: Proceedings of the IEEE/CVF International Conference on Computer Vision, pp. 913–922 (2021)
49. Wang, Y., Chao, W.L., Garg, D., Hariharan, B., Campbell, M., Weinberger, K.Q.: Pseudo-lidar from visual depth estimation: bridging the gap in 3D object detection for autonomous driving. In: Proceedings of the IEEE/CVF Conference on Computer Vision and Pattern Recognition, pp. 8445–8453 (2019)

50. Wang, Y., Guizilini, V.C., Zhang, T., Wang, Y., Zhao, H., Solomon, J.: DETR3D: 3D object detection from multi-view images via 3D-to-2D queries. In: Conference on Robot Learning, pp. 180–191. PMLR (2022)

51. Wang, Z., Jia, K.: Frustum convnet: sliding frustums to aggregate local point-wise features for amodal 3D object detection. In: IEEE/RSJ International Conference on Intelligent Robots and Systems (IROS), pp. 1742–1749. IEEE (2019)

52. Yan, Y., Mao, Y., Li, B.: Second: sparsely embedded convolutional detection. Sensors **18**(10), 3337 (2018)

53. Yao, Y., Luo, Z., Li, S., Fang, T., Quan, L.: MVSNet: depth inference for unstructured multi-view stereo. In: Proceedings of the European Conference on Computer Vision (ECCV), pp. 767–783 (2018)

54. Yin, T., Zhou, X., Krahenbuhl, P.: Center-based 3D object detection and tracking. In: Proceedings of the IEEE/CVF Conference on Computer Vision and Pattern Recognition, pp. 11784–11793 (2021)

55. Zheng, L., et al.: TJ4DRadSet: a 4D radar dataset for autonomous driving. arXiv preprint arXiv:2204.13483 (2022)

56. Zhou, H., Ge, Z., Li, Z., Zhang, X.: MatrixVT: efficient multi-camera to BEV transformation for 3D perception. arXiv preprint arXiv:2211.10593 (2022)

57. Zhou, X., Wang, D., Krähenbühl, P.: Objects as points. arXiv preprint arXiv:1904.07850 (2019)

58. Zhou, Y., Liu, L., Zhao, H., López-Benítez, M., Yu, L., Yue, Y.: Towards deep radar perception for autonomous driving: datasets, methods, and challenges. Sensors **22**(11), 4208 (2022)

Parallax-Aware Image Stitching Based on Homographic Decomposition

Simon Seibt[1($\boxtimes$)], Michael Arold[1], Bartosz von Rymon Lipinski[1], Uwe Wienkopf[2], and Marc Erich Latoschik[3]

[1] Game Tech Lab, Faculty of Computer Science, Nuremberg Institute of Technology,
Nuremberg, Germany
simon.seibt@th-nuernberg.de

[2] Institute for Applied Computer Science, Nuremberg Institute of Technology,
Nuremberg, Germany

[3] Human-Computer Interaction Group, Institute of Computer Science,
University of Wuerzburg, Wuerzburg, Germany

Abstract. Image stitching plays a crucial role for various computer vision applications, like panoramic photography, video production, medical imaging and satellite imagery. It makes it possible to align two images captured at different views onto a single image with a wider field of view. However, for 3D scenes with high depth complexity and images captured from two different positions, the resulting image pair may exhibit significant parallaxes. Stitching images with multiple or large apparent motion shifts remains a challenging task, and existing methods often fail in such cases. In this paper, a novel image stitching pipeline is introduced, addressing the aforementioned challenge: First, iterative dense feature matching is performed, which results in a multi-homography decomposition. Then, this output is used to compute a per-pixel multidimensional weight map of the estimated homographies for image alignment via weighted warping. Additionally, the homographic image space decomposition is exploited using combinatorial analysis to identify parallaxes, resulting in a parallax-aware overlapping region: Parallax-free overlapping areas only require weighted warping and blending. For parallax areas, these operations are omitted to avoid ghosting artifacts. Instead, histogram- and mask-based color mapping is performed to ensure visual color consistency. The presented experiments demonstrate that the proposed method provides superior results regarding precision and handling of parallaxes.

Keywords: Image Stitching · Parallaxes · Feature Matching

1 Introduction

Image stitching is an important technique in computer vision that combines two or more images with overlapping areas into a single high-resolution, wide-field image. It is used in various media applications, including generation of panoramic images for virtual tours, computation of high-resolution photo mosaics from multiple satellite images, and in medical imaging procedures [18, 19, 27, 33].

© The Author(s), under exclusive license to Springer Nature Switzerland AG 2024
U. Köthe and C. Rother (Eds.): DAGM GCPR 2023, LNCS 14264, pp. 195–208, 2024.
https://doi.org/10.1007/978-3-031-54605-1_13

Typically, conventional image stitching methods are executed in three stages [25]: (1) Extraction and matching of features between an image pair, (2) Estimation of a global homography based on the feature matches, and (3) Perspective transformation and blending of the target image onto the reference image. One of the most challenging steps here is image warping using one global estimated homography. A homographic relation can be used to describe feature correspondences for points, which lie on the same plane in 3D space [7]. However, if the captured 3D scene is not planar, i.e. including foreground objects at different scene depths, and the camera baseline between an image pair is large, then parallaxes can be observed [11]. In such cases, stitching results based on planar transformation models, such as the aforementioned global homography approach, often exhibit visual artifacts, like distortions and ghosting.

To address the issue of parallax artifacts in stitching of a single image pair, various warping methods were developed previously. For example, some approaches divide an image into regular pixel cells, which are then warped using different geometric models, such as [5, 11, 12, 29]. In order to additionally optimize warping, energy minimization frameworks were utilized [12, 31]. Also, local alignment techniques were introduced to register specific regions of the image while hiding artifacts in misaligned regions through seam-cutting methods, such as [6, 16, 28, 30]. However, images with high depth complexity and large parallaxes still represent a challenge as neighboring pixels in the reference image may not have corresponding adjacent pixels in the target image.

In this paper, a new image stitching pipeline is introduced that addresses the aforementioned problem. The main contribution of this work comprises an accurate and robust stitching method for image pairs, which exhibit complex structures and multiple depth layers, while avoiding visual artifacts caused by parallaxes: The presented solution utilizes results from the work of Seibt et al. [24], *dense feature matching* (DFM), for detection of robust and accurate feature correspondences between image pairs. DFM targets at images of real scenes with significant depth complexities, offering high precision and recall values.

The corresponding pipeline is based on a *homographic decomposition* of the image space, providing the following advantages for image stitching in terms of alignment accuracy and parallax handling: (a) Conventional feature matching is extended to an iterative rematching process. The search for correct feature matches is thus re-executed per iteration with an individually estimated homographic transformation. By utilizing the resulting homographic decomposition, DFM positionally refines matching feature points in the target image and extrapolates additional points that could not be matched using standard "one-shot matching" methods. The result of the rematching process is a precise set of dense feature matches, each associated with a homography matrix, recovering multiple tangent planes in a 3D scene. (b) Additionally, Delaunay triangulation of the dense feature point set is used to determine the overlapping region of an image pair. (c) Through combinatorial analysis of the underlying per-vertex homography configurations in the overlapping region, "parallax awareness" is handled and "critical image areas" (i.e. containing occlusions) are identified by so-called *inhomogeneous* triangles. The overlapping sub-region without visible parallaxes is classified as *homogeneous*.

Subsequently, these differently classified regions are processed in the proposed stitching pipeline as follows: (1) For both, the homogeneous (overlapping) region and non-overlapping region of the target image, a multidimensional weight map is computed. It is used to control the contributions of the multi-homography decomposition results in order to achieve an accurate and robust perspective transformation for warping. The concept of utilizing a stitching weight map was inspired by Gao at el. [5]: In their approach, two-dimensional weights were used for dual homography warping. (2) For the inhomogeneous (overlapping) region, weight-based transformations and blending would result in ghosting artifacts due to parallaxes. Instead, a histogram- and mask-based color mapping is executed. (3) After perspective transformation, non-overlapping sub-areas in the target image may result in undesirable intersections with overlapping sub-areas in the reference image. These intersecting sub-areas are cut out in order to prevent additional visual artifacts. (4) In the last step, the perspective transformation on the cropped target image is performed utilizing the weight map. Additionally, the overlapping homogeneous region is blended to obtain smooth visual transitions.

2 Related Work

Over the years, various stitching methods were proposed, which can be broadly categorized into three types: Adaptive warping methods, shape-preserving warping methods and seam-based methods. For the adaptive warping methods, Gao et al. [5] introduced a dual homography method that can only handle scenes with a distant and a ground plane. The method adaptively blends the homographies estimated for the two planes according to positions of clustered feature points. Zaragoza et al. [29] estimated optimal homographies for each regular grid cell using moving direct linear transformations (MDLT). They assigned higher weight to feature points closer to the target cell based on alignment error. Liu and Chin [17] introduced an extension of [29] by inserting appropriate point correspondences in automatically identified misaligned regions to improve the underlying warp. Zhang et al. [31] minimized distortions in warped images by incorporating a scale-preserving term and a line-preserving term. Li et al. [12] proposed an analytical warping function based on thinplate splines with radial basis functions to approximate the projection bias. Lee and Sim [10] described an epipolar geometry-based video stitching method. It is suitable for handling large parallaxes, requiring temporal motion information of foreground objects. Lee and Sim [11] also proposed a solution that uses warping of residual vectors to distinguish matching features from different depth planes, resulting in more naturally stitched images. Liao and Li [14] introduced a method that simultaneously emphasizes different features under single-perspective warps, including alignment, distortion, and saliency. Chen et al. [4] proposed a method for complex image pairs with moving pedestrians. It includes a structure preservation module based on grid constraints and a composite ghost removal module using YOLOv4, ensuring unique preservation of each pedestrian after stitching. Jia et al. [9] introduced the characteristic number to match co-planar local sub-regions, and additionally considered global co-linear structures using a separate objective function. While [5] is only capable of handling scenes with two planar regions, methods such as [12, 29, 31] can warp backgrounds containing multiple planar regions. However, these methods often rely on the assumption of continuous scene depths with minimal parallaxes. That poses a challenge for aligning foreground objects with large parallaxes, which have abrupt depth changes relative to the background.

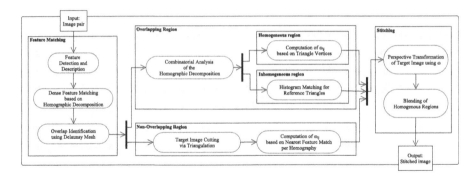

Fig. 1. UML-based activity diagram of the presented image stitching pipeline: main stages in grey, sub-activities in white color. (Color figure online)

Shape-preserving warping-based methods are commonly introduced to mitigate perspective distortions in non-overlapping regions of an image pair. Chang et al. [2] presented a warping method that combines a projective and a similarity transformation. It smoothly extrapolates the projective transformation of overlapping regions to non-overlapping regions, gradually transitioning from projection to similarity across the image. Chen et al. [3] estimated the scale and rotation for each image and designed an objective function for warping based on a global similarity prior. Lin et al. [15] proposed a homography linearization method that also smoothly extrapolates warps from overlapping to non-overlapping regions. Li et al. [13] described a quasi-homography warp to solve the line bending problem by linear scaling of the horizontal homography component.

Seam-based methods produce visually appealing image stitching results, but typically lack geometric precision due to local alignment: Gao et al. [6] introduced a seam-cutting loss to measure the discontinuity between warped target and reference images. They estimated multiple homographies using RANSAC and selected the optimal one with the minimum seam-cutting loss. Lin et al. [16] improved stitching performance using iterative warp and seam estimation. Zhang et al. [30] used local homographies to align specific image regions and applied content preserving warping for further refinement. Misalignment artifacts were hidden via seam cutting. Xue et al. [28] introduced a method that integrates point-line features as alignment primitives. They used a pixel difference evaluation model to iteratively compute and update their smoothing term to find the most suitable seam.

Previous deep-learning-based stitching methods [20,21,32] face significant challenges, like limitation to mostly synthetic training datasets, unsatisfactory performance for real-world images and issues with preservation of the original image resolutions.

3   Parallax-Aware Image Stitching Pipeline

In the following sub-sections the four main stages of the presented stitching pipeline are described, including all corresponding processing steps (overview in Fig. 1).

3.1   Dense Feature Matching

In the first pipeline stage, DFM is executed to generate a precise and dense set of feature matches between an image pair. This makes it possible to identify the overlapping pixel region and to obtain a homographic decomposition of the image space: DFM performs *iterative rematching* to give mismatched feature points a further chance to be considered in subsequent processing steps, resulting in potentially larger matching sets and increased recall values. During rematching an individual homography is estimated per iteration, searching for feature matches that correspond to the same plane in 3D space. In practice, a single homography can span multiple surfaces. So, feature points are clustered per iteration to improve the homography estimation by recalculating it for each cluster. The result of rematching is the *homographic decomposition*, i.e. a set of feature point pair clusters, each associated with a distinct homography matrix (illustration in Fig. 2(c)).

Additionally, rematching involves incremental Delaunay triangulation of the reference feature set and a mapping of the resulting mesh to the target image. As described in [24] further DFM processing steps utilize this mesh as follows: *Delaunay outlier detection* removes false positive matches by detecting reference-to-target triangle edge intersections, which are often caused by repeated patterns. *Focused matching* simulates "visual focusing" by executing local rematching per Delaunay triangle, resulting in the detection of additional detailed feature points. Additionally, matching accuracy is increased using positional *feature refinement* by taking advantage of neighboring homography candidates per feature point. Finally, *feature extrapolation* is used to detect additional feature points by utilizing multiple local homography candidates per Delaunay triangle.

The overall DFM result is a *refined homographic decomposition* (see Fig. 2(d)). The triangulation results are illustrated in Fig. 2(e–h). Figure 2(e) and 2(f) depict the outcome of the initial iterative rematching. Figure 2(g) and 2(h) show densified meshes resulting from execution of further DFM processing steps, mentioned previously. As can be seen, the meshes have undergone substantial refinement, resulting in a better approximation of geometric structures in the scene.

3.2   Overlapping Region

The next step of the stitching pipeline builds on the final DFM Delaunay triangulation of the reference image feature set and the corresponding mapping to the target image. Pixels, which are located within the triangle mesh and its mapping, respectively, define the overlapping region for stitching. Further processing of this region requires segmentation of the corresponding Delaunay mesh into *homogeneous* and *inhomogeneous* triangles: Homogeneity – in context of a feature point mesh – is defined for a triangle t with vertices $v_i \in V_t$ as follows [24]: Let H be the set of homography matrices resulting from homographic decomposition, $h_i \in H$ the (initially) associated homography with feature point vertex v_i. Then, t is homogeneous, if:

$$\exists h_{hom} \in H, \forall i \in \{1, 2, 3\} : h_{hom} * v_i \approx h_i * v_i. \tag{1}$$

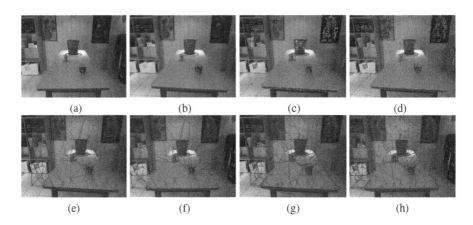

(a)   (b)   (c)   (d)

(e)   (f)   (g)   (h)

Fig. 2. (a, b) Input image pair; (c) Clustered features in the reference image after DFM's iterative rematching. Each color represents one cluster with an individual homography; (d) Matched features after further DFM processing, incl. focused matching, refinement and extrapolation: initially matched source features in blue (cf. image c), further features in green; (e) Triangulation of matched features after initial iterative rematching; (f) Mapping of the mesh in image e to target image; (g, h) Densified triangulations using the final feature matching set after further DFM processing. (Color figure online)

Homographic decompositions commonly have high variances in homography-to-vertex associations with initially one homography per vertex. The *homogenization* process is executed in order to relax the detection of inhomogeneous triangles for feature detection. In this work, it is used to improve segmentation of the overlapping region for stitching: The homogenization uses the connectivity information of the Delaunay feature set mesh to search for local equivalently transforming homography matrices. Each feature point is successively transformed from the reference image to the target image using homographies of neighboring features. Each time, the reprojection error is calculated and compared against the threshold parameter of the RANSAC algorithm (used during rematching). If the reprojection error of a neighboring homography is smaller, then it is (additionally) assigned to the current feature point. Notice that in the resulting (homogenized) *multi-homographic decomposition* a feature point can be associated with multiple locally equivalent transforming matrices. Consequently, an ablation of the homogenization process would prevent robust detection of inhomogeneous triangles (parallax areas). This would inevitably result in ghosting artifacts after final blending. The homogenization process is shown in Algorithm 1 and illustrated in Fig. 3(a).

The next pipeline step aims at a seamless overlapping region for stitching. Hence, the multi-homographic decomposition is used to compute a multidimensional warping weight map ω for the homogeneous sub-region: For each pixel in the reference image, a point-triangle intersection test is executed based on the Delaunay mesh. On a hit, the three vertices of the corresponding enclosing triangle are selected and the Euclidean distance d_i to each vertex is calculated. Then, each initially per-vertex associated homography H_i for a pixel position (x, y) is weighted using the following equation:

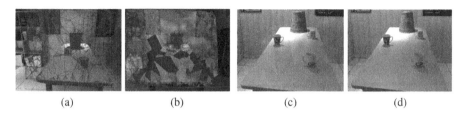

(a)   (b)   (c)   (d)

Fig. 3. (a) Segmented overlapping region of a reference image with homogeneous (blue) and inhomogeneous triangles (red); (b) Visualization of a multidimensional per-pixel weight map for an overlapping homogeneous region of a target image. Each homography is represented by a unique color. The pixel color in the overlapping homogeneous region is a combination of colors according to the weighted homographies; (c) Stitching result of an overlapping region. The homogeneous region was transformed and blended. The inhomogeneous region was unprocessed; (d) The same stitching result with color mapping applied to the inhomogeneous region. (Color figure online)

$$\omega(x, y, i) = \frac{1/d_i^2}{\sum_{k=1}^{n} 1/d_k^2} \tag{2}$$

where $n = 3$, corresponding to the simplex dimension of a triangle. Using reciprocal squared distances results in a smoother transition between the homography clusters during weighted warping [5]. An example visualization of the multidimensional weight map for an overlapping homogeneous region is shown in Fig. 3(b).

As introduced, inhomogeneous regions represent "critical image areas", typically exhibiting parallaxes. These cannot be aligned properly. To avoid ghosting artifacts, computation of the weight matrix, weighted transformation and blending are omitted for this region. In order to prevent visual color discrepancies between the blended overlapping region and the non-blended parallax region, color histograms are precomputed for both, the inhomogeneous area of the reference image and the separately blended homogeneous area. Subsequently, histogram-matching-based color mapping is performed

---

Algorithm 1. Homogenization (of overlapping region)

Input: Source feature point set P, corresponding
           target feature point set P', global homography set H,
           threshold parameter ϵ of RANSAC
Output: P and P' associated with multiple $h \in H$
1: **for each** $p \in P$ and corresponding $p' \in P'$ **do**
2:    **for each** $h \in H$ | neighbor of p has homography h **do**
3:        Transform p into the target image: $p_T := h * p$
4:        **if** $d(p', p_T) < \epsilon$ **then**
5:           Assign h to local homography set of p
6:        **end if**
7:    **end for**
8: **end for**

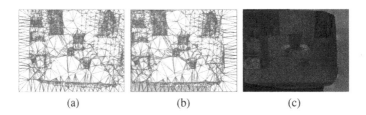

(a)   (b)   (c)

Fig. 4. (a) Triangulation of a reference feature set (blue triangles) with additional border points (black triangles) considered for cutting. (b) Triangulation mesh mapped to the target feature set including border points. Orange target triangles are cropped. (c) Visualization of a multidimensional per-pixel weight map for a non-overlapping region in a target image (border pixel area). Each estimated homography is associated with an individual color. The final visualization color of a pixel results from the weighted mixture of all associated homography colors. Black pixels illustrate the cut out border areas of the target image. (Color figure online)

per color channel: Pixels of the inhomogeneous region are modulated using histogram equalization w.r.t. the histogram of the homogeneous region [1]. Figure 3(c–d) shows an example color mapping result in an inhomogeneous region.

3.3   Non-overlapping Region

In this stage, the non-overlapping region is processed, preparing it for later perspective transformation regarding correct alignment and prevention of blending artifacts.

First, triangular sub-regions in the non-overlapping target image area, which would intersect with the overlapping region of the reference image after perspective transformation, are identified: Auxiliary points are placed at the image border rectangle (per image) using an equidistant distribution with a density corresponding to the number of edge vertices of the Delaunay mesh. These border vertices are triangulated incrementally with the existing mesh of the overlapping region in the reference image. The resulting mesh is then mapped to the target image, and corresponding triangles in the reference and target images are compared: If a triangle area in the target image is smaller than the corresponding triangle area in the reference image, then it conveys less visual information for stitching. In this case, this target triangle's pixel area is cut out. The target image cutting process is illustrated in Fig. 4(a–b).

The second step is the extension of the multidimensional per-pixel weight map ω to the non-overlapping region for later perspective transformation: For each feature point cluster resulting from DFM's iterative rematching (cf. Subsect. 3.1) and each pixel position (x', y') in the cropped target image, the closest feature point is determined. Then, for every cluster homography H_j – based on the pixel distance d_j between (x', y') and the closest feature point – its weight $\omega(x', y', j)$ is calculated according to Eq. 2. Here, number n refers the total number of estimated homographies (representing n many weight matrices). The closer a selected pixel is to a feature cluster, the higher is the weight assigned to its respective homography. Incorporating all homographies with their corresponding weights results in robust perspective transformation for the non-overlapping region. An example visualization of the extended multidimensional weight map is shown in Fig. 4(c).

3.4   Stitching

The last pipeline stage comprises final stitching computations, including perspective transformation of the cropped target image. For each target pixel, the final homography is computed using the multidimensional per-pixel weight map ω as follows:

$$H(x,y) = \sum_{k=1}^{n} \omega(x,y,k)H_k \mid \sum_{k=1}^{n} \omega(x,y,k) = 1 \tag{3}$$

Perspective transformation warping using multiple weighted homographies may result in small pixel gaps in the resulting image due to scaling and projective distortions, respectively. This gap-filling problem is solved using backward warping in combination with inverse bilinear interpolation. Finally, pixels in the homogeneous region of the reference image, which overlap with the transformed pixels from the target image, are uniformly blended to achieve a visually smooth transition in the stitching result.

4   Experiments and Discussion

The underlying software prototype was developed in C++ using the OpenCV 4 library. The implemented stitching pipeline was tested with ten image pairs, each with challenging varying parallax dimensions. The evaluation set includes three image pairs of the newly captured "Cellar Room" dataset, including different camera baselines and viewing directions. Additionally, image pairs "Propeller", "Building", "Seattle", "Backyard", "Adobe" and "Garden" were picked from the "Parallax-tolerant Image Stitching" dataset [30]. And lastly, image pair "Dwarves" is from the "Middlebury Stereo" datasets [8, 23].

4.1   Evaluation

The first evaluation part includes the comparison of visual results w.r.t. other three well-known stitching methods: Global homography (GH), APAP [29] and ELA [12]. GH represents a "basic stitching algorithm", aligning image pairs using a single dominant homography. Our implementation of GH additionally incorporates USAC [22] for a more reliable outlier removal during feature matching. APAP and ELA are adaptive image alignment methods (Source codes were provided by the respective authors). APAP uses moving direct linear transformation (MLDT) to compute homographies for grid cells using a spatial distance-based weighting scheme. ELA aligns grid cells by approximating the warping error analytically. In Fig. 5 all image stitching results are presented. Comparisons to approaches with a different methodological focus were avoided, like shape-preserving warping [2, 3, 13, 15] and seam-cutting [6, 16, 28, 30], respectively.

(a) I (b) J (c) GH   (d) APAP   (e) ELA   (f) Proposed

Fig. 5. Image stitching results of the proposed pipeline, including comparisons to other three methods: GH (described in text), APAP [29] and ELA [12]. The scenes are arranged from top to bottom in the following order: Three different scenes of "Cellar Room", one scene of "Propeller", "Building", "Seattle", "Dwarves", "Backyard", "Adobe" and "Garden".

The second part of the evaluation focuses on a quantitative analysis: The methods and test image pairs used in this part are the same as those shown in Fig. 5. Firstly, the image alignment performance of the overlapping region was evaluated using the structural similarity index measure (SSIM) [26]. The overlapping region was extracted using DFM's Delaunay triangulation (cf. Subsects. 3.1 and 3.2). The computed SSIM scores for the overlapping region are presented in Fig. 6. Secondly, the non-overlapping region, which is susceptible to perspective distortion, was also evaluated as follows (Overall results, incl. time measurements, are in the next sub-section): To simulate ground truth for the used image pairs, their overlapping regions were cropped in the image pairs. Subsequently, each cropped area was uniformly subdivided into one simulated overlapping and two (left and right) non-overlapping regions. The new simulated image pairs were again stitched using the presented methods, and the perspective-transformed non-overlapping regions were evaluated against ground truth using SSIM.

4.2 Results

In comparison to the other evaluated methods, the proposed pipeline achieves significantly improved stitching quality for all scenes regarding the handling of parallaxes: In the first image pair of "Cellar Room" only small parallaxes are noticeable (mainly due to the table in the foreground). So, no significant parallax artifacts are visible in any of the methods' stitching results. However, the propsed method is the only one that exhibits precise alignment of foreground and background objects, including accurately overlapping joints of the floor flows. The second and third image pairs of "Cellar Room" contain larger parallaxes. In contract to the proposed method, GH, APAP and ELA produce significant misalignment artifacts in the overlapping region. The image pair of "Propeller" exhibits noticeable parallaxes, particularly around the rotor blades. Again, stitching results of GH, APAP and ELA contain clearly recognizable visual defects in the parallax regions. Additionally, they fail to compute a proper perspective transformation for the non-overlapping region of the target image, as the right tree is slightly skewed. For the image pair of "Building", ELA and the proposed method provide the most plausible perspective transformation for the non-overlapping region. However, all other methods produce parallax artifacts at the trees, including corresponding misalignments of the overlapping region. The image pair of "Seattle" has the largest parallaxes in the presented evaluation. Only the proposed method handles the inhomogeneous region appropriately. The image pairs of "Dwarves" and "Backyard" have a high depth complexity and various minor parallaxes. Due to the variety of objects with different scene depths, GH, APAP and ELA fail to align both, foreground and background objects simultaneously. However, for the image pair of "Backyard", GH, APAP and ELA provide a better perspective transformation than the proposed method (Notice the slightly sheared cottage on the left). The perspective transformation of the image pair of "Adobe" is plausible for all methods except GH. But, APAP and ELA fail to prevent ghosting artifacts at the palm trees, caused by larger parallaxes. For the image pair of "Garden", all perspective transformation of the non-overlapping region provide similar visual qualities. Nevertheless, GH, APAP, or ELA result again in ghosting artifacts, particularly at the foreground garden pavilion. Additionally, most of the trees in the background appear blurred compared to the proposed method.

The results of the quantitative evaluation can be summarized as follows: The presented method significantly improves image alignment of the overlapping region in all scenes compared to the other evaluated methods. GH, APAP, and ELA have average SSIM scores of 0.44, 0.54, and 0.61 and harmonic SSIM scores of 0.40, 0.48, and 0.56, respectively. The proposed method achieves the best results, i.e. an average SSIM score

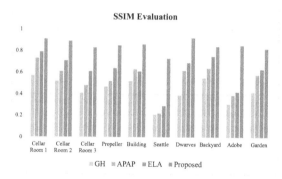

Fig. 6. Image alignment evaluations using SSIM metric.

of 0.85 (ca. 39% to 93% increase) and a harmonic SSIM score of also 0.85 (ca. 52% to 113% increase). Moreover, the proposed solution also shows improvement in the SSIM score for the non-overlapping region: Here, GH, APAP, and ELA have average SSIM scores of 0.33, 0.47, and 0.57, with harmonic SSIM scores of 0.29, 0.46, and 0.55, respectively. The presented solution achieves an average SSIM score of 0.63 (ca. 11% to 91% increase) and a harmonic SSIM score of 0.61 (ca. 11% to 110% increase). Regarding runtime measurements, the described processing pipeline takes on average 27 s for feature matching, 14 s for the overlapping region, 11 s for the non-overlapping region and 15 s for stitching, resulting in a total time of 67 s. The other evaluated methods are on average faster: GH takes 23 s, APAP 21 s and ELA 29 s for the total processing time. However, their visual quality is significantly worse compared to the proposed method.

The presented solution has some limitations: The robustness of the stitching process is primarily determined by the quality of the DFM results, particularly the homographic decomposition. In this evaluation, the given default settings of DFM were used, as this directly led to satisfactory results. But generally, incorrect parameter settings may cause errors, like undetected parallax regions, typically leading to ghosting artifacts. In such cases, manual re-parameterization of DFM would be necessary for improving quality.

5   Conclusions

In this paper, a novel image stitching method for image pairs with high depth complexity and larger parallaxes is presented. The first stage of the proposed stitching pipeline utilizes dense feature matching to generate a homographic decomposition of the image space, including precise and dense feature correspondences between image pairs. Using Delaunay triangulation of the matching set makes it possible to identify the overlapping region for stitching. In the second stage, the homogenization algorithm is used to compute a "parallax-tolerant" overlapping region. This is realized by detection and segmentation of "inhomogeneous" sub-regions, which are typically caused by parallax effects. Inhomogeneous image parts are not considered for perspective transformation, nor for blending, during stitching. For perspective transformation of the parallax-free overlapping region, a multidimensional per-pixel weight map of the target image is computed. Additionally, color mapping assures uniform blending results for the inhomogeneous image region. In the third pipeline stage, the non-overlapping region is partially cropped to exclude border areas that would produce visual artifacts after perspective warping. Finally, the multidimensional weight map is extended to provide robust weighting for perspective transformation even in the non-overlapping image region. The presented results on challenging real-world stitching datasets demonstrate that the proposed method achieves accurate and robust image alignments, minimizing ghosting artifacts. It outperforms the other evaluated methods in term of visual quality and structural similarity. Future work includes multi-stitching of several images and performance optimizations.

References

1. Acharya, T., Ray, A.K.: Image Processing - Principles and Applications (2005)
2. Chang, C.H., Sato, Y., Chuang, Y.Y.: Shape-preserving half-projective warps for image stitching. In: IEEE Conference on Computer Vision and Pattern Recognition, pp. 3254–3261 (2014)
3. Chen, Y.-S., Chuang, Y.-Y.: Natural image stitching with the global similarity prior. In: Leibe, B., Matas, J., Sebe, N., Welling, M. (eds.) ECCV 2016. LNCS, vol. 9909, pp. 186–201. Springer, Cham (2016). https://doi.org/10.1007/978-3-319-46454-1_12
4. Chen, Y., Xue, W., Chen, S.: Large parallax image stitching via structure preservation and multi-matching. In: Zhang, H., et al. (eds.) NCAA 2022. CCIS, vol. 1638, pp. 177–191. Springer, Singapore (2022). https://doi.org/10.1007/978-981-19-6135-9_14
5. Gao, J., Kim, S.J., Brown, M.S.: Constructing image panoramas using dual-homography warping. In: IEEE Conference on Computer Vision and Pattern Recognition, pp. 49–56 (2011)
6. Gao, J., Li, Y., Chin, T.J., Brown, M.S.: Seam-driven image stitching. In: Eurographics (2013)
7. Hartley, R., Zisserman, A.: Multiple View Geometry in Computer Vision (2003)
8. Hirschmuller, H., Scharstein, D.: Evaluation of cost functions for stereo matching. In: IEEE Conference on Computer Vision and Pattern Recognition, pp. 1–8 (2007)
9. Jia, Q., Li, Z., Fan, X., Zhao, H., Teng, S., Ye, X., Latecki, L.J.: Leveraging line-point consistence to preserve structures for wide parallax image stitching. In: IEEE Conference on Computer Vision and Pattern Recognition, pp. 12181–12190 (2021)
10. Lee, K.Y., Sim, J.Y.: Stitching for multi-view videos with large parallax based on adaptive pixel warping. IEEE Access **6**, 26904–26917 (2018)
11. Lee, K.Y., Sim, J.Y.: Warping residual based image stitching for large parallax. In: IEEE Conference on Computer Vision and Pattern Recognition, pp. 8195–8203 (2020)
12. Li, J., Wang, Z., Lai, S., Zhai, Y., Zhang, M.: Parallax-tolerant image stitching based on robust elastic warping. IEEE Trans. Multimed. **20**, 1672–1687 (2018)
13. Li, N., Xu, Y., Wang, C.: Quasi-homography warps in image stitching. IEEE Trans. Multimed. **20**, 1365–1375 (2017)
14. Liao, T., Li, N.: Single-perspective warps in natural image stitching. IEEE Trans. Image Process. **29**, 724–735 (2020)
15. Lin, C.C., Pankanti, S.U., Ramamurthy, K.N., Aravkin, A.Y.: Adaptive as-natural-as-possible image stitching. In: IEEE Conference on Computer Vision and Pattern Recognition, pp. 1155–1163 (2015)

16. Lin, K., Jiang, N., Cheong, L.-F., Do, M., Lu, J.: SEAGULL: seam-guided local alignment for parallax-tolerant image stitching. In: Leibe, B., Matas, J., Sebe, N., Welling, M. (eds.) ECCV 2016. LNCS, vol. 9907, pp. 370–385. Springer, Cham (2016). https://doi.org/10.1007/978-3-319-46487-9_23

17. Liu, W.X., Chin, T.J.: Correspondence insertion for as-projective-as-possible image stitching. ArXiv (2016)

18. Lyu, W., Zhou, Z., Chen, L., Zhou, Y.: A survey on image and video stitching. Virtual Reality Intell. Hardw. **1**, 55–83 (2019)

19. Megha, V., Rajkumar, K.K.: Automatic satellite image stitching based on speeded up robust feature. In: International Conference on Artificial Intelligence and Machine Vision, pp. 1–6 (2021)

20. Nie, L., Lin, C., Liao, K., Liu, M., Zhao, Y.: A view-free image stitching network based on global homography. J. Vis. Commun. Image Representation **73**, 102950 (2020)

21. Nie, L., Lin, C., Liao, K., Liu, S., Zhao, Y.: Unsupervised deep image stitching: reconstructing stitched features to images. IEEE Trans. Image Process. **30**, 6184–6197 (2021)

22. Raguram, R., Chum, O., Pollefeys, M., Matas, J., Frahm, J.M.: USAC: a universal framework for random sample consensus. IEEE Trans. Pattern Anal. Mach. Intell. **35**, 2022–2038 (2013)

23. Scharstein, D., Pal, C.: Learning conditional random fields for stereo. In: IEEE Conference on Computer Vision and Pattern Recognition, pp. 1–8 (2007)

24. Seibt, S., Von Rymon Lipinski, B., Latoschik, M.E.: Dense feature matching based on homographic decomposition. IEEE Access **10**, 21236–21249 (2022)

25. Szeliski, R.: Image alignment and stitching: a tutorial. Found. Trends Comput. Graph. Vision **2**, 1–104 (2006)

26. Wang, Z., Bovik, A., Sheikh, H., Simoncelli, E.: Image quality assessment: from error visibility to structural similarity. IEEE Trans. Image Process. **13**, 600–612 (2004)

27. Win, K.P., Kitjaidure, Y., Hamamoto, K.: Automatic stitching of medical images using feature based approach. Adv. Sci. Technol. Eng. Syst. J. **4**, 127–133 (2019)

28. Xue, W., Xie, W., Zhang, Y., Chen, S.: Stable linear structures and seam measurements for parallax image stitching. IEEE Trans. Circuits Syst. Video Technol. **32**, 253–261 (2022)

29. Zaragoza, J., Chin, T.J., Brown, M.S., Suter, D.: As-projective-as-possible image stitching with moving DLT. In: IEEE Conference on Computer Vision and Pattern Recognition, pp. 2339–2346 (2013)

30. Zhang, F., Liu, F.: Parallax-tolerant image stitching. In: IEEE Conference on Computer Vision and Pattern Recognition, pp. 3262–3269 (2014)

31. Zhang, G., He, Y., Chen, W., Jia, J., Bao, H.: Multi-viewpoint panorama construction with wide-baseline images. IEEE Trans. Image Process. **25**, 3099–3111 (2016)

32. Zhao, Q., Ma, Y., Zhu, C., Yao, C., Feng, B., Dai, F.: Image stitching via deep homography estimation. Neurocomputing **450**, 219–229 (2021)

33. Zhao, Q., Wan, L., Feng, W., Zhang, J., Wong, T.T.: Cube2video: navigate between cubic panoramas in real-time. IEEE Trans. Multimed. **15**, 1745–1754 (2013)

Photogrammetry and Remote Sensing

DustNet: Attention to Dust

Andreas Michel[1,2(✉)] , Martin Weinmann[2] , Fabian Schenkel[1,2],
Tomas Gomez[3], Mark Falvey[3], Rainer Schmitz[3], Wolfgang Middelmann[1],
and Stefan Hinz[2]

[1] Fraunhofer Institute of Optronics, System Technologies and Image Exploitation
IOSB, Karlsruhe, Germany
andreas.michel@iosb.fraunhofer.de
[2] Institute of Photogrammetry and Remote Sensing, Karlsruhe Institute
of Technology, Karlsruhe, Germany
[3] Meteodata, Santiago, Chile

Abstract. Detecting airborne dust in common RGB images is hard. Nevertheless, monitoring airborne dust can greatly contribute to climate protection, environmentally friendly construction, research, and numerous other domains. In order to develop an efficient and robust airborne dust monitoring algorithm, various challenges have to be overcome. Airborne dust may be opaque as well translucent, can vary heavily in density, and its boundaries are fuzzy. Also, dust may be hard to distinguish from other atmospheric phenomena such as fog or clouds. To cover the demand for a performant and reliable approach for monitoring airborne dust, we propose DustNet, a dust density estimation neural network. DustNet exploits attention and convolutional-based feature pyramid structures to combine features from multiple resolution and semantic levels. Furthermore, DustNet utilizes highly aggregated global information features as an adaptive kernel to enrich high-resolution features. In addition to the fusion of local and global features, we also present multiple approaches for the fusion of temporal features from consecutive images. In order to validate our approach, we compare results achieved by our DustNet with those results achieved by methods originating from the crowd-counting and the monocular depth estimation domains on an airborne dust density dataset. Our DustNet outperforms the other approaches and achieves a 2.5% higher accuracy in localizing dust and a 14.4% lower mean absolute error than the second-best approach.

Keywords: Dust Monitoring · Visual Regression · Deep Learning

1 Introduction

Monitoring airborne dust emissions is a valuable and important task since airborne dust significantly affects climate, human health, infrastructure, buildings, and various socio-economic sectors. The emergence of airborne dust particles can occur due to natural phenomena such as strong winds, wildfires, and seismic activities but may also be caused by human activity. Typical anthropogenic

U. Köthe and C. Rother (Eds.): DAGM GCPR 2023, LNCS 14264, pp. 211–226, 2024.
https://doi.org/10.1007/978-3-031-54605-1_14

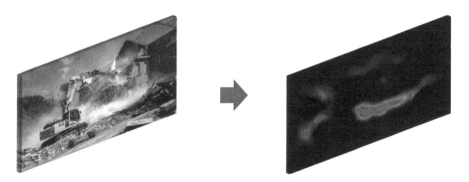

Fig. 1. DustNet objective. The objective of our method consists in estimating the dust level in a given RGB image or sequence. The left part shows a scene of a construction site [12], while the right part shows a dust density map of the scene.

pollution sources are construction, traffic, or mining sites. Although completely mitigating dust emissions is not feasible, suppressing emissions with focused measures is possible. This e.g. includes watering untreated roads, speeding down vehicles, or reducing mining activities. However, optimizing dust mitigation strategies would require practical and economic dust emission monitoring. Most conventional instrument-based *in-situ* monitoring equipment focuses on identifying the impact of dust emissions but is limited in attributing responsibilities. On the other hand, remote sensing 3D dust scanning technologies, such as lidar, are not economically feasible on a large scale and may produce noisy and hard-to-interpret data in complex terrains. Hence, visual monitoring via camera-based systems would be preferable for identifying airborne dust emissions. However, visual dust density estimation is still underexplored. One of the possible reasons for the scarcity of research in this domain is that detecting dust in an image is a highly ill-posed problem. There is a multitude of issues why detecting dust is so hard: dust may vary significantly in terms of density, and it can be opaque as well as translucent. Furthermore, dust density variation can be very imbalanced. For example, in dry regions, the dense dust of dust storms will emerge less frequently than transparent dust due to low winds and only sporadically occur during particular meteorological configurations. Also, dust can be emitted at a wide range of locations and for various reasons. The transparency of dust implies that the appearance of dust is easily affected by environments, and its boundaries are usually fuzzy. As a result, images with dust appear partially blurry and usually have low spatial contrast. Classical algorithms usually cannot exploit these partial blur effects because other atmospheric effects like fog or clouds can cause similar effects. Also, for humans, detecting dust in an image sequence is much easier than in a single image, but exploiting temporal data by an algorithm is challenging. For example, moving clouds, vehicles, or shadows can easily distort results of optical flow-based methods. In addition, there is no clear color scheme for dust. Opaque dust can show a brownish color like in a dust storm, but it can also have a black shade in a mining explosion. Overall, the aforementioned properties of dust indicate the need for a more sophisticated approach.

In the last decade, deep learning has had huge success in various tasks like classification [15], object detection [30], neural linguistic processing [35], and remote sensing [41]. However, airborne dust monitoring, obstructed by the aforementioned challenges, is not well researched, and most scientific papers focus on satellite images [16], or related tasks like smoke binary segmentation [37]. Recently, De Silva et al. published a binary dust segmentation dataset called URDE [7]. While this can be seen as a first important step towards dust monitoring, we believe that a regression approach could be more beneficial. In contrast to semantic segmentation, which predicts a label on a per-pixel basis, the continuous range of dust densities rather suits a regression strategy. Furthermore, the vague boundaries of dust make it challenging to create discrete hard labels.

Accordingly, this work focuses on density estimation (see Fig. 1) and thus is most related to DeepDust [27]. DeepDust estimates density maps on single images. In order to detect dust, it exploits multiscale feature maps by utilizing feature pyramid network [20] (FPN) structures. In contrast to that work, we also address the fusion of temporal information. Furthermore, we also exploit attention strategies and rely not only on a strictly convolutional method.

In order to validate the effectiveness of our approach, we compare achieved results to those of visual density estimation techniques originating from other domains, including monocular depth estimation (MDE) and crowd counting. MDE is the task of estimating the scene depth on a per-pixel basis, whereas crowd counting is the task of approximating the number of people in a given image. Though both tasks differ strongly from dust density estimation, our method is heavily influenced by ideas of both domains. In summary, the main contributions of this work are the following: (1) We research the underexplored field of airborne dust density estimation and propose various neural network architectures. (2) Our proposed neural networks combine attention-based and convolutional-based FPN structures to merge local and global features. (3) Our work addresses the fusion of temporal features in the field of dust density estimation. (4) In order to demonstrate the effectiveness of the proposed neural network architectures, we compare the achievements by our novel techniques with those of methods originating from the crowd counting and MDE domains on the Meteodata dust dataset.

2 Related Work

In this section, we briefly summarize related work with a focus on vision transformers, crowd counting and MDE.

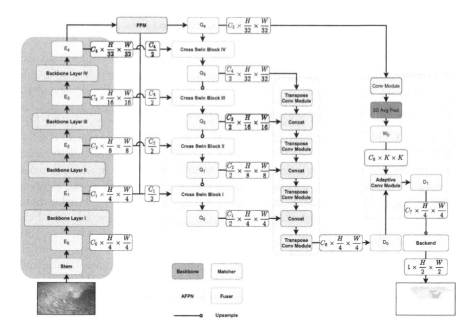

Fig. 2. Overview of our proposed DustNet. The basic blocks are a backbone, the AFPN, the matcher, the PPM, the fuser, and the backend.

2.1 Vision Transformer

Vaswani et al. [35] introduced the transformer architecture in 2017 in the field of natural language processing (NLP). The centerpiece of the transformer architecture is the multi-head attention module. Inspired by the success of the transformer architecture in NLP, the vision transformer (VIT) [8] introduced the transformer encoder successfully in the vision domain. In order to improve the performance of vision transformer especially in high-resolution settings, Liu et al. [23] introduced a hierarchical architecture, the swin transformer (Swin), which utilizes shifted windows to achieve a linear computational complexity. The attention is calculated only between patches, which are part of a specific window. The windows are shifted to create connections between features of the previous windows. The second version of the swin transformer [22] improves this approach further by an alternative positional encoding scheme and replacing the scaled dot attention with cosine attention, which performs better in higher resolutions.

2.2 Crowd Counting

Density estimation methods [19,21,26,31,39] have been used successfully in crowd counting. The objective of crowd counting is to predict a coarse density map of the relevant target objects, e.g. usually people. The ground truth is generated by smoothing center points with a multi-dimensional Gaussian distribution. Recent approaches are focused on increasing the spatial invariance [26]

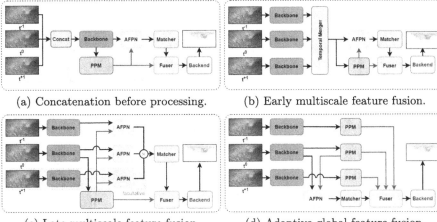

(a) Concatenation before processing.   (b) Early multiscale feature fusion.

(c) Late multiscale feature fusion.   (d) Adaptive global feature fusion.

Fig. 3. Different fusion approaches of DustNet. The fusion strategy spans from early (a) to late (d) feature merging of each consecutive image.

or dealing with noise in the density maps [6]. Most works are designed for individual images, but Avvenuti et al. [2] take advantage of the temporal correlation between consecutive frames in order to lower localization and count error.

2.3 Monocular Depth Estimation

The first CNN-based method for monocular depth estimation was presented by Eigen et al. [9]. They utilized global and local information in order to predict a depth image from a single image. Further improvements of the pure CNN approaches focus on Laplacian pyramids [32], multi-scale convolutional fusion [36], structural information [17], the exploitation of coplanar pixels [28] to improve the predicted depth, reformulation of the depth prediction task as a classification-regression problem [11] and hybrids between CNN and vision transformer-based architectures [8]. Recently, the PixelFormer architecture [1] combines transformer architectures with an adaptive bin center approach inspired by [3] and adds skip connection modules to improve the feature flow between different encoder feature levels.

3 Method

In the following, we introduce our proposed DustNet architecture illustrated in Fig. 2. After presenting the submodules, we focus on the different temporal fusion approaches illustrated in Fig. 3.

3.1 Network Structure

Overview. DustNet processes input image sequences X of the dimensions $T \times H \times W \times 3$ to a continuous dust density map $\frac{H}{2} \times \frac{W}{2} \times 1$. T may consist of a maximum of three consecutive images, where the target y is assigned to

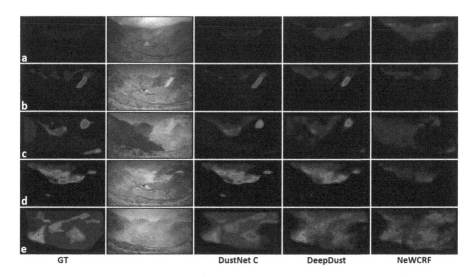

GT   DustNet C   DeepDust   NeWCRF

Fig. 4. An opencast mine scene with varying dust densities from the Meteo-data dust dataset. Overall, the dust densities increase from **a** to **e**. Our proposed model DustNet C can well distinguish between clouds and dust, regress different dust levels, and has a low false positive rate. Overall, DustNet outperforms the other methods.

the image x_{t^0}. The images are fed into the backbone, which produces multiple feature maps with decreasing resolution and ascending information aggregation. The backbone features are passed to a pyramid pooling module (PPM) [40] and the attention feature pyramid network (AFPN). Hereby, in order to reduce the computational complexity, only half of the channels of feature maps are transferred to the AFPN. The PPM head aggregates global information fed into the AFPN and the Fuser module. The AFPN mixes the feature maps of different resolutions and information aggregation levels. The processed feature maps are transferred to the matcher module, accumulating the features maps into one high-resolution map. Then, the high-resolution features are merged with the global information features aggregated from the PPM head in the fuser module. Eventually, the combined features are processed by the backend, which consists of multiple sequences of CNNs, into a dust map.

Backbone. The backbone consists of a stem module and four blocks. We use this common backbone scheme in order to leverage pre-trained neural networks. We prefer a convolutional backbone like ResNet [13] instead of a transformer backbone due to the requirement to process high-resolution images. The backbone produces multiple feature maps with the resolution scales $\{\frac{1}{4}, \frac{1}{8}, \frac{1}{16}, \frac{1}{32}\}$ of the original images with the number of channels C of $\{256, 512, 1024, 2048\}$.

Pyramid Pooling Module. We utilized a PPM head [40] like in [1,38] to aggregate global information of the whole image. We use global average pooling of scales $\{1, 2, 3, 6\}$ to extract the information. After extracting the features, we concatenate them and process them by a convolutional layer to the feature map Q_4 with the dimension of $512 \times \frac{H}{32} \times \frac{W}{32}$.

Attention Feature Pyramid Network. The AFPN mixes high-resolution features with low semantics with low-resolution high semantic features. But instead of a traditional FPN like [20] utilizing CNNs, we are inspired by [1] and use four Swin blocks with cross window attention to improve the feature flow between the feature map layers. However, instead of applying scaled dot attention, we utilize cosine attention similar to [22]. This lead to increased performance in higher resolutions. The key and value matrix inputs are derived from the backbone feature maps, but to reduce computational complexity, we transfer only half of the channels. The query matrix is filled by the output of the upsampled stage before. The query matrix with the coarsest resolution originates from the global aggregated features of the PPM head.

Matcher. The matcher module also has an FPN-like architecture [20]. We upsample feature maps from the AFPN via a transpose convolution module (TCM). It consists of a 2D TCM with a stride and kernel size of two, followed by batch normalization [14] and a SiLU [10] activation function. Like [18] suggests, we apply only batch normalization without dropout [33]. The coarsest resolution feature map derived from the AFPN is fed to the first TCM block. The following AFPN feature maps are respectively concatenated to the output of the TCM block and processed via the next TCM block. The output of the matcher module has the dimension of $C_6 \times \frac{H}{4} \times \frac{W}{4}$. We choose a channel number C_6 of 256.

Fuser. The fuser module processes the high-resolution features D_0 by leveraging the aggregated features Q_4 of the PPM head. Q_4 is fed into a 2D pointwise convolutional kernel, followed by a SiLU activation function, and pooled by global average pooling to a feature map W_0 of the dimension $C_6 \times K \times K$. W_0 serves as an adaptive kernel for the adaptive convolutional layer [34], which enriches the feature map D_0 from the matcher with global information.

Backend. The backend consists of N blocks of a sequence of a 2D convolution layer, batch normalization, and SiLU activation functions that predict the dust map. We branch the features into two parallel blocks for each stage and accumulate the outputs. Hereby, we choose a dilation of three for one branch to increase the receptive field. After four stages, a pointwise convolutional layer predicts the dust maps.

3.2 Temporal Fusion

In order to leverage the temporal information between consecutive images, we developed and studied different approaches. Figure 3 illustrates the different fusion strategies. Hereby the fusion strategy spans from early to late fusion.

Concatenate Images. An obvious way to concatenate the images to $D \times H \times W$ is where the product of the number of images T and the number of channels C is

Fig. 5. Display of the generalization ability of DustNet. The shown results of DustNet are produced on the URDE validation RandomDataset897 [7]. Hereby, DustNet S is trained on the Meteodata dust dataset and applied on the URDE dataset without finetuning.

the new channel dimension D. This approach is illustrated in Fig. 3a. Examples of this approach can be found in [5] or [24]. Hereby the backbones are usually specially adapted to 3D input (Fig. 5).

Early Multiscale Feature Fusion. Figure 3b shows the methodology behind this fusion aspect. Features from three backbones, which share weights, are fed into the temporal merger (TM) neural network. TM subtracts the feature maps of image x_{t-1} and x_{t+1} respectively from x_{t^0} and multiplies the difference. We pass the new feature maps through a 2D pointwise convolutional layer and add skip connections from the feature maps of the image x_{t^0} to the output.

Late Multiscale Feature Fusion. This approach represents a simple fusion of AFPN features (see Fig. 3c). Backbone and AFPN weights are shared between the instances. The PPM head is only fed with the backbone features from image x_{t^0}. In order to reduce the computational complexity and avoid convergence problems, only two consecutive images may be used.

Adaptive Global Information Feature Fusion. The goal hereby is to calculate the global aggregated features from a PPM head for each image. Backbone and PPM weights are shared. The local feature branch is only fed with the multiscale backbone features from image x_{t^0}. The fusion of the temporal information occurs in the fuser module. For each PPM head, an adaptive convolutional layer is added.

Table 1. Comparison of the best-performing density estimation methods on the Meteo-data dust dataset.

	Params	MeM	Time	MAE	MSE	Acc	Pre	Rec
CanNet	**18 M**	**4.8 GB**	**7.1 ms**	20.21	855.40	0.79	0.80	0.79
DeepDust	101 M	32.8 GB	20.3 ms	19.60	749.36	0.78	0.80	0.79
PixelFormer	140 M	15.2 GB	43.3 ms	21.53	825.50	0.78	0.81	0.79
NeWCRF	140 M	16.8 GB	36.7 ms	20.00	822.68	0.78	0.80	0.78
DustNet S	64 M	8.8 GB	21.6 ms	19.27	705.47	0.80	0.81	0.80
DustNet A	65 M	8.8 GB	23.5 ms	18.77	701.73	0.79	0.81	0.80
DustNet B	67 M	9.6 GB	46.4 ms	26.60	1528.08	0.67	0.75	0.68
DustNet C	68 M	12.8 GB	37.8 ms	**16.77**	**601.49**	**0.81**	**0.83**	**0.82**
DustNet D	86 M	10.4 GB	45.0 ms	17.44	639.10	**0.81**	**0.83**	0.81

4   Experimental Results

In this section, we explain our experiment's implementation details, present and discuss our achieved results, and finally detail our ablation study and the limitations of our approach.

4.1   Dataset

We conduct experiments on the extended Meteodata dust dataset [27]. The extended dataset includes a variety of scenes from opencast mines with a wide range of dust levels, lighting conditions, and cloud conditions. The ground truth is aimed at mimicking the human perception of dust in a given image regarding opaqueness and estimated dust density levels. The dataset comprises 2298 consecutive RGB image triplets with a 1000 × 1920 pixels resolution. An image triplet consists of three consecutive images with a ground truth dust density map for the enclosed image. The average time between two consecutive images amounts to ten seconds. The pixels of the ground truth span are mapped to an 8-bit unsigned integer datatype, where the pixel values are proportional to the dust density. We split the dataset into a training dataset with 1906, a validation dataset with 144, and a test dataset with 248 image triplets. The challenges of this dataset are manifold. The high resolution of the images is a high computational burden.

Furthermore, the strong variance in dust levels, in combination with the highly imbalanced frequency of the different dust levels, complicates the estimation of the different dust levels. In order to display the generalization ability of our approach and the dust dataset, we also conduct a qualitative analysis on the URDE dataset [7]. It consists of images with a size of 1024×1024 pixels and contains scenes on dusty roads.

Table 2. Binned regression results of density estimation methods on the Meteodata dust dataset: The values of the pixels are binned into zero dust (ZB), low dust (LB), medium dust (MB), and high dust (HB) density. Overall, our proposed DustNet C outperforms the other methods.

	MAE					MSE				
	ØB	ZB	LB	MB	HB	ØB	ZB	LB	MB	HB
CanNet	38.08	12.04	23.61	42.65	74.01	2917.5	376.6	856.4	2540.3	7896.8
DeepDust	30.11	12.18	23.93	37.04	47.28	1640.2	367.5	873.3	1979.9	3340.2
PixelFormer	40.68	14.19	25.00	36.05	87.48	2864.6	377.1	892.5	1863.6	8325.3
NeWCRF	34.19	10.88	25.24	40.82	59.81	2255.0	324.9	954.5	2371.2	5369.3
DustNet S	31.35	12.41	22.35	39.45	51.20	1756.6	340.8	754.7	2152.6	3778.1
DustNet A	32.21	10.36	23.17	40.61	54.68	1837.3	281.8	795.0	2195.5	4076.9
Dustnet B	64.05	**7.95**	34.85	77.80	135.61	6948.3	**151.1**	1553.7	6698.8	19389.4
DustNet C	**27.29**	8.70	**21.97**	**33.29**	**45.19**	**1361.7**	257.4	**738.9**	**1579.2**	**2871.3**
DustNet D	31.13	8.24	22.36	41.59	52.33	1767.1	189.4	742.9	2295.1	3841.0

Table 3. Results of the ablation study on the Meteodata dust dataset: The base model is DustNet C with two consecutive images as inputs. The modules following a ✗ are replaced.

	Params	MeM	Time	MAE	MSE	Acc	Pre	Rec
1x Img Input	64 M	8.8 GB	**21.6 ms**	19.27	705.47	0.80	0.81	0.80
2x Img Input	68 M	12.8 GB	37.8 ms	**16.77**	**601.49**	0.81	**0.83**	0.82
3x Img Input	68 M	16.0 GB	64.6 ms	17.83	675.34	0.81	0.82	0.82
✗ AFPN	**32 M**	**7.2 GB**	27.3 ms	19.85	805.74	0.79	0.80	0.79
✗ Fuser	68 M	12.8 GB	38.0 ms	19.63	754.25	0.80	0.81	0.80
✗ Matcher	64 M	12.0 GB	29.5 ms	17.08	651.39	**0.83**	**0.83**	**0.83**

4.2   Benchmark Selection

Temporal dust density estimation is not well-researched. To our best knowledge, only DeepDust [27] focuses on a directly related task. Methods like temporal density estimation methods from other domains, like crowd counting [2], are not designed for a large time lag between two consecutive images and high-resolution scenes and therefore have convergence problems. From the methods available, we selected, in addition to DeepDust, CanNet [21], a lightweight fully convolutional crowd-counting approach and two state-of-the-art MDE models represented by NeWCRF [38] and PixelFormer [1]. For both MDE methods, we select as a backbone the base swin transformer [23] model with a window size of twelve.

4.3   Implementation Details

All experiments are conducted on four Nvidia A100 GPUs with 80 GB memory. We use l2 loss and the AdamW [25] optimizer ($\beta_1 = 0.9, \beta_2 = 0.999$) with a

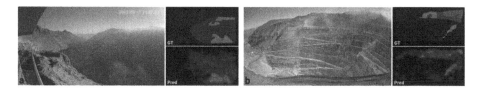

Fig. 6. Opencast mines. Results of DustNet C on mine sites that are not included in the training or validation dataset.

weight decay of 10^{-5}. During training, we start with a learning rate of $\alpha = 3 \cdot 10^{-4}$ and train for 50 epochs with a frozen backbone. After 50 epochs, we unfreeze the backbone and train for further 20 epochs.

Our proposed networks are trained with a ResNet101 [13] backbone. We deploy the following proposed architectures: **DustNet S** is the version of Dust-Net as shown in Fig. 2. It processes only a single image. **DustNet A** is equivalent to Fig. 3a. Compared to DustNet S, the capacity for input channels is increased to nine channels. **DustNet B** consists of three backbones with shared weights and a temporal merger module (Fig. 3b). **DustNet C** takes only two consecutive images as input (Fig. 3c). It merges the multiscale AFPN features. **DustNet D** consists of multiple backbones and PPM heads with shared weights (Fig. 3d). Each aggregated global information feature map from the PPM head is an adaptive weight.

4.4 Evaluation Metrics

We are interested in the localization and regression ability of our proposed models. We map all pixel values under 30 to zero and the remaining pixels to one to validate the localization aspect. This threshold was derived from the labeling process of the Meteodata dust dataset, which maps all values under 30 to zero. As a result, we can now apply standard classification metrics like accuracy (Acc), precision (Pre), and recall (Rec). In order to validate the quality of the predicted regression, we use standard metrics represented by mean absolute error (MAE) and mean squared error (MSE). Furthermore, to fairly assess the performance on tail values of imbalanced datasets, we consider the idea of balanced metrics [4]. Therefore, we bin our data into four bins: zero dust density bin (ZB), low dust density bin (LB), medium dust density bin (MB), and high dust density bin (HB). For each bin, we calculate the MAE and MSE. Following [4,29], we compute the mean across all bins and obtain the average binned mean absolute error ØB-MAE and the average binned mean squared error ØB-MSE.

4.5 Quantitative Results

Table 1 compares the best-performing density estimation methods on the Meteodata dust dataset. The best-performing model on a single image is our proposed

DustNet S, and the best-performing model for consecutive images is our Dust-Net C. In particular, in the case of the binned regression metrics (see Table 2), DustNet C outperforms the other methods vastly. Due to the imbalance of the dataset, a small difference in the metrics can lead to a big qualitative difference. CanNet is the most computationally efficient method tested on the Meteodata dust dataset and can classify dust decently but cannot regress well in the higher dust levels. PixelFormer performs worse regarding regression. Possible reasons include the inability of the Swin transformer backbone to process high-resolution images well and the adaptive bin center prediction module. The Swin transformer backbone and the conditional random field modules could also influence NeWCRF's performance. DustNet's performance gain over DeepDust could be caused by the improved feature flow, particularly between high- and low-level features.

4.6   Qualitative Results

Figure 4 illustrates an opencast mining scene with varying dust densities from the Meteodata dust dataset. The overall airborne dust in the scene increases from **a** to **e**. Figure 4a demonstrates the ability of DustNet to distinguish between dust, shadows, and clouds. The other methods lack the ability to differentiate in comparison to DustNet. From Fig. 4c, our method shows its performance on more specific singular dust plumes. Finally, in Fig. 4d and **e**, our method performs well in more dense dust scenes. Nearly in all cases, our model surpasses the other approaches.

Figure 6 shows the result of DustNet C on further mining sites displayed. Here again, DustNet is able to produce good results. In order to demonstrate the generalization ability of our approach, we applied a DustNet S without retraining on the URDE dataset. Also, as seen in the images, our DustNet S displays a good performance. Due to the hard segmentation boundaries and the neglect of low dust density on the URDE dataset, a quantitative evaluation would, in our opinion, not be appropriate.

4.7   Ablation Study

In order to show the efficacy of our proposed method, we choose the best-performing proposed architecture DustNet C, change the number of input images and replace several modules (see Table 3). We replace the AFPN, the matcher, and the fuser module, respectively.

Inputs. We compare the performance change of our proposed method in varying the number of consecutive images. Backbone and AFPN weights are shared in our experiment. The use of two consecutive images outperforms the other options.

AFPN. In the AFPN ablation experiment, the AFPN is removed, and the features from the backbone are passed directly to the matcher. Removing the AFPN halves nearly the number of parameters, but it causes a big increase in MAE and MSE.

Matcher. In the matcher ablation experiment, we replace the matcher with a simple convolutional layer followed by an activation function for channel adaption. The feature map with the highest resolution from the AFPN is processed by the added convolutional layer and fed into the fuser module. The accuracy increases slightly for the tradeoff of a decreased regression ability. But the main reason for keeping the matcher is the increased differentiation ability between dust and similar visual effects like clouds. Removing the matcher leads to a significant drop.

Fuser. In the last ablation experiment, a traditional convolutional layer replaces the adaptive convolutional layer. Hence, the aggregated global information features cannot enrich the matcher's features. This leads to a significant increase in MAE and MSE.

4.8 Limitations and Future Work

Figure 4c illustrates one of the shortcomings of our model. Our model can easily ignore small plumes of dust. We assume that neglecting small dust areas for the tradeoff of fewer false positives leads to a lower loss and therefore is a negative side effect of the training process. Also, we suppose that the l2 loss function leads to a worse MSE in bins with scarcer values (see Table 2). Furthermore, the ground truth of the Meteodata dust dataset has a high uncertainty compared to a classification or object detection dataset. For example, in Fig. 4g, we assume that our model represents the real dust conditions than the ground truth. The ground truth does not cover the small dust plume behind the truck, and overall undervalues the dust density in the dense dust plumes. Therefore a better metrical result causes not automatically a higher performance in a real-world scenario. An extensive comparison between density estimation and semantic segmentation of dust could be a valuable extension of this work. Furthermore, future work should address handling long-tailed visual regression data and increase the sensitivity for smaller dust plumes.

5 Conclusion

In this paper, we have presented DustNet, a dust density estimation neural network. DustNet computes for every pixel in a given image a dust density. Hereby DustNet exploits and fuses local, global, and temporal information. DustNet cannot only regress different dust levels but also distinguish between dust and similar visual effects like clouds. Our proposed approach outperforms a range of other approaches on the Meteodata dust dataset.

Acknowledgment. The images in the presented figures and those used for creating the Meteodata dust dataset are from the pit of Minera Los Pelambres, which collaborates with Meteodata in the advanced use of cameras for emission control strategies. The permission to use the images in this publication is kindly appreciated.

References

1. Agarwal, A., Arora, C.: Attention attention everywhere: monocular depth prediction with skip attention. In: Proceedings of the IEEE/CVF Winter Conference on Applications of Computer Vision, pp. 5861–5870 (2023)
2. Avvenuti, M., Bongiovanni, M., Ciampi, L., Falchi, F., Gennaro, C., Messina, N.: A spatio-temporal attentive network for video-based crowd counting. In: Proceedings of the 2022 IEEE Symposium on Computers and Communications, pp. 1–6. IEEE (2022)
3. Bhat, S.F., Alhashim, I., Wonka, P.: AdaBins: depth estimation using adaptive bins. In: Proceedings of the IEEE/CVF Conference on Computer Vision and Pattern Recognition, pp. 4009–4018 (2021)
4. Brodersen, K.H., Ong, C.S., Stephan, K.E., Buhmann, J.M.: The balanced accuracy and its posterior distribution. In: Proceedings of the 2010 20th International Conference on Pattern Recognition, pp. 3121–3124. IEEE (2010)
5. Cheng, B., Choudhuri, A., Misra, I., Kirillov, A., Girdhar, R., Schwing, A.G.: Mask2former for video instance segmentation. arXiv preprint arXiv:2112.10764 (2021)
6. Cheng, Z.Q., Dai, Q., Li, H., Song, J., Wu, X., Hauptmann, A.G.: Rethinking spatial invariance of convolutional networks for object counting. In: Proceedings of the IEEE/CVF Conference on Computer Vision and Pattern Recognition, pp. 19638–19648 (2022)
7. De Silva, A., Ranasinghe, R., Sounthararajah, A., Haghighi, H., Kodikara, J.: A benchmark dataset for binary segmentation and quantification of dust emissions from unsealed roads. Sci. Data **10**(1), 14 (2023)
8. Dosovitskiy, A., et al.: An image is worth 16×16 words: transattentions for image recognition at scale. arXiv preprint arXiv:2010.11929 (2020)
9. Eigen, D., Puhrsch, C., Fergus, R.: Depth map prediction from a single image using a multi-scale deep network. In: Advances in Neural Information Processing Systems, vol. 27 (2014)
10. Elfwing, S., Uchibe, E., Doya, K.: Sigmoid-weighted linear units for neural network function approximation in reinforcement learning. Neural Netw. **107**, 3–11 (2018)
11. Fu, H., Gong, M., Wang, C., Batmanghelich, K., Tao, D.: Deep ordinal regression network for monocular depth estimation. In: Proceedings of the IEEE Conference on Computer Vision and Pattern Recognition, pp. 2002–2011 (2018)
12. gabort@AdobeStock: (2023). https://www.stock.adobe.com
13. He, K., Zhang, X., Ren, S., Sun, J.: Deep residual learning for image recognition. In: Proceedings of the IEEE Conference on Computer Vision and Pattern Recognition, pp. 770–778 (2016)
14. Ioffe, S., Szegedy, C.: Batch normalization: accelerating deep network training by reducing internal covariate shift. In: Proceedings of the International Conference on Machine Learning, pp. 448–456 (2015)
15. Krizhevsky, A., Sutskever, I., Hinton, G.E.: ImageNet classification with deep convolutional neural networks. Commun. ACM **60**(6), 84–90 (2017)
16. Lee, J., et al.: Machine learning based algorithms for global dust aerosol detection from satellite images: inter-comparisons and evaluation. Remote Sens. **13**(3) (2021)
17. Lee, M., Hwang, S., Park, C., Lee, S.: EdgeConv with attention module for monocular depth estimation. In: Proceedings of the IEEE/CVF Winter Conference on Applications of Computer Vision, pp. 2858–2867 (2022)

18. Li, X., Chen, S., Hu, X., Yang, J.: Understanding the disharmony between dropout and batch normalization by variance shift. In: Proceedings of the IEEE/CVF Conference on Computer Vision and Pattern Recognition, pp. 2682–2690 (2019)
19. Li, Y., Zhang, X., Chen, D.: CSRNet: dilated convolutional neural networks for understanding the highly congested scenes. In: Proceedings of the IEEE Conference on Computer Vision and Pattern Recognition, pp. 1091–1100 (2018)
20. Lin, T.Y., Dollár, P., Girshick, R., He, K., Hariharan, B., Belongie, S.: Feature pyramid networks for object detection. In: Proceedings of the IEEE Conference on Computer Vision and Pattern Recognition, pp. 2117–2125 (2017)
21. Liu, W., Salzmann, M., Fua, P.: Context-aware crowd counting. In: Proceedings of the IEEE Conference on Computer Vision and Pattern Recognition, pp. 5099–5108 (2019)
22. Liu, Z., et al.: Swin transattention attention v2: scaling up capacity and resolution. In: Proceedings of the IEEE/CVF Conference on Computer Vision and Pattern Recognition, pp. 12009–12019 (2022)
23. Liu, Z., Lin, Y., Cao, Y., Hu, H., Wei, Y., Zhang, Z., Lin, S., Guo, B.: Swin transattention attention: hierarchical vision transattention attention using shifted windows. In: Proceedings of the IEEE/CVF International Conference on Computer Vision, pp. 10012–10022 (2021)
24. Liu, Z., et al.: Video swin transattention attention. In: Proceedings of the IEEE/CVF Conference on Computer Vision and Pattern Recognition, pp. 3202–3211 (2022)
25. Loshchilov, I., Hutter, F.: Decoupled weight decay regularization. arXiv preprint arXiv:1711.05101 (2017)
26. Luo, A., et al.: Hybrid graph neural networks for crowd counting. In: Proceedings of the AAAI Conference on Artificial Intelligence, vol. 34, pp. 11693–11700 (2020)
27. Michel, A., Weinmann, M., et al.: Terrestrial visual dust density estimation based on deep learning. In: Proceedings of the 2023 IEEE International Geoscience and Remote Sensing Symposium (2023)
28. Patil, V., Sakaridis, C., Liniger, A., Van Gool, L.: P3Depth: monocular depth estimation with a piecewise planarity prior. In: Proceedings of the IEEE/CVF Conference on Computer Vision and Pattern Recognition, pp. 1610–1621 (2022)
29. Ren, J., Zhang, M., Yu, C., Liu, Z.: Balanced MSE for imbalanced visual regression. In: Proceedings of the IEEE/CVF Conference on Computer Vision and Pattern Recognition, pp. 7926–7935 (2022)
30. Ren, S., He, K., Girshick, R., Sun, J.: Faster R-CNN: towards real-time object detection with region proposal networks. In: Advances in Neural Information Processing Systems, vol. 28 (2015)
31. Sam, D.B., Surya, S., Babu, R.V.: Switching convolutional neural network for crowd counting. In: Proceedings of the 2017 IEEE Conference on Computer Vision and Pattern Recognition, pp. 4031–4039. IEEE (2017)
32. Song, M., Lim, S., Kim, W.: Monocular depth estimation using laplacian pyramid-based depth residuals. IEEE Trans. Circuits Syst. Video Technol. **31**(11), 4381–4393 (2021)
33. Srivastava, N., Hinton, G., Krizhevsky, A., Sutskever, I., Salakhutdinov, R.: Dropout: a simple way to prevent neural networks from overfitting. J. Mach. Learn. Res. **15**(1), 1929–1958 (2014)
34. Su, H., Jampani, V., Sun, D., Gallo, O., Learned-Miller, E., Kautz, J.: Pixel-adaptive convolutional neural networks. In: Proceedings of the IEEE/CVF Conference on Computer Vision and Pattern Recognition, pp. 11166–11175 (2019)

35. Vaswani, A., et al.: Attention is all you need. In: Advances in Neural Information Processing Systems, vol. 30 (2017)
36. Wang, L., Zhang, J., Wang, Y., Lu, H., Ruan, X.: CLIFFNet for monocular depth estimation with hierarchical embedding loss. In: Vedaldi, A., Bischof, H., Brox, T., Frahm, J.-M. (eds.) ECCV 2020, Part V. LNCS, vol. 12350, pp. 316–331. Springer, Cham (2020). https://doi.org/10.1007/978-3-030-58558-7_19
37. Yuan, F., Zhang, L., Xia, X., Huang, Q., Li, X.: A wave-shaped deep neural network for smoke density estimation. IEEE Trans. Image Process. **29**, 2301–2313 (2020)
38. Yuan, W., Gu, X., Dai, Z., Zhu, S., Tan, P.: Neural window fully-connected CRFs for monocular depth estimation. In: Proceedings of the IEEE/CVF Conference on Computer Vision and Pattern Recognition, pp. 3916–3925 (2022)
39. Zhang, Y., Zhou, D., Chen, S., Gao, S., Ma, Y.: Single-image crowd counting via multi-column convolutional neural network. In: Proceedings of the IEEE Conference on Computer Vision and Pattern Recognition, pp. 589–597 (2016)
40. Zhao, H., Shi, J., Qi, X., Wang, X., Jia, J.: Pyramid scene parsing network. In: Proceedings of the IEEE Conference on Computer Vision and Pattern Recognition, pp. 2881–2890 (2017)
41. Zhu, X.X., et al.: Deep learning in remote sensing: a comprehensive review and list of resources. IEEE Geosci. Remote Sens. Mag. **5**(4), 8–36 (2017)

Leveraging Bioclimatic Context for Supervised and Self-supervised Land Cover Classification

Johannes Leonhardt[1](✉) ⓘ, Lukas Drees[1] ⓘ, Jürgen Gall[1,2] ⓘ,
and Ribana Roscher[1,3] ⓘ

[1] University of Bonn, Bonn, Germany
{jleonhardt,ldrees,jgall,ribana.roscher}@uni-bonn.de
[2] Lamarr Institute for Machine Learning and Artificial Intelligence,
Dortmund, Germany
[3] Forschungszentrum Jülich GmbH, Jülich, Germany

Abstract. Modern neural networks achieve state-of-the-art results on land cover classification from satellite imagery, as is the case for almost all vision tasks. One of the main challenges in this context is dealing with geographic variability in both image and label distributions. To tackle this problem, we study the effectiveness of incorporating bioclimatic information into neural network training and prediction. Such auxiliary data can easily be extracted from freely available rasters at satellite images' georeferenced locations. We compare two methods of incorporation, learned embeddings and conditional batch normalization, to a bioclimate-agnostic baseline ResNet18. In our experiments on the EuroSAT and BigEarthNet datasets, we find that especially the use of conditional batch normalization improves the network's overall accuracy, generalizability, as well as training efficiency, in both a supervised and a self-supervised learning setup. Code and data are publicly available at https://t.ly/NDQFF.

Keywords: Remote Sensing · Land Cover Classification · Multi-Modal Learning · Data Shift · Conditional Batch Normalization

1 Introduction

Land cover data has diverse applications, including the study of climate change, resource and disaster management, as well as spatial planning, stressing its importance for both science and practice [41, 48]. Therefore, the extraction of land cover data from satellite imagery is one of the most extensively studied tasks in remote sensing and Earth observation. Recent developments in satellite

This work was partly funded by the Deutsche Forschungsgemeinschaft (DFG, German Research Foundation) - SFB 1502/1-2022 - Projektnummer: 450058266 and partly funded by the Deutsche Forschungsgemeinschaft (DFG, German Research Foundation) under Germany's Excellence Strategy – EXC 2070 – 390732324.

U. Köthe and C. Rother (Eds.): DAGM GCPR 2023, LNCS 14264, pp. 227–242, 2024.
https://doi.org/10.1007/978-3-031-54605-1_15

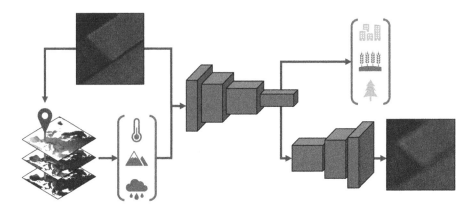

Fig. 1. Schematic summary of the presented approach: Satellite images' georeferencing are used to extract bioclimatic information like temperature, elevation, and percipitation (blue) from geographical rasters for each image. This is provided to the neural networks as an additional input modality. In the supervised setting (top), an encoder and a classification head directly predict the land cover class label (red). In the self-supervised setting (bottom), the encoder is pre-trained using a symmetric decoder for image reconstruction. (Color figure online)

technology and deep learning methods have further amplified this area of study, boosting the accuracy, as well as the spatial and temporal resolution of current land cover products.

One of the main challenges of land cover mapping remains the great geographic variability in both the distributions of images X and class labels Y. This raises questions about both the accuracy and generalizability of the resulting models [16,26,44]. To tackle this issue, we draw a connection between land cover and bioclimatology – the study of the physical environment's effects on life on Earth [43] – and leverage bioclimatic auxiliary information in a multi-modal learning approach to support land cover classification models. We argue that by explicitly incorporating bioclimatic context, models learn representations, which are more invariant to bioclimatic context, and thus more discriminative with regard to the land cover-relevant image content.

In particular, we point out two connected, yet distinct interactions between the two: First, some land cover classes are more prevalent in some bioclimatic regimes: In Boreal climates, for instance, one is much more likely to observe the class *Coniferous Forest* than in Atlantic climates, where the class *Pastures* may be much more prevalent, instead. We call this effect bioclimatic prior shift $P(Y|A = a_1) \neq P(Y|A = a_2)$, as it can be described by an inequality of prior class probabilities depending on the regional bioclimatic conditions A.

Second, we observe that land cover classes can appear differently depending on the bioclimatic circumstances: As an example, the kinds of crops cultivated in different bioclimates have a big effect on the appearance of classes like *Annual Crop* and *Perennial Crop*. As this effect describes a change in the distribution of the inputs with respect to A, we call this effect bioclimatic covariate shift $P(X|A = a_1) \neq P(X|A = a_2)$.

To evaluate bioclimate-aware neural networks' abilities to counteract these effects, we first conduct extensive experiments on EuroSAT, a Europe-wide benchmark for land cover classification [15]. We find that models which leverage bioclimatic data by means of conditional batch normalization [6] reliably outperform both the model with added learned embeddings and the bioclimate-agnostic model with respect to overall accuracy, generalizability, and training efficiency.

Besides the supervised case, we also consider a self-supervised learning setup, where the encoder is trained on the pretext task of image reconstruction [21]. We find that the resulting representations are better separable with respect to land cover, if bioclimatic data are incorporated into the training through conditional batch normalization. Furthermore, we achieve additional improvements for the supervised setting by initializing the model with the pre-trained weights.

At the same time, we show that the bioclimate-aware models do not suffer from the recently described pitfall of shortcut learning [34], which we examine using the Grad-CAM tool for model interpretability [33].

We finally provide a brief outlook regarding the approach's applicability in more large-scale and complex settings. To this end, we show that classification accuracy is also improved for supervised training on the much larger, multi-label BigEarthNet [37,38] dataset.

A graphical outline of our approach is presented in Fig. 1.

2   Related Work

Improving neural networks by learning from multiple data modalities at once is an intensely studied topic in the field of deep learning [31]. While many pioneering works of the field have focused on image or video understanding tasks based on additional text or audio [6,28,30,35], the framework has since been applied to many other applications and modalities like medicine [4,25] or robotics [19,22].

A popular method specifically designed for fusing complex structured data with context data from other modalities is conditional batch normalization [6]. The method has since proven its effectiveness for many tasks such as style transfer [8,17], super-resolution [45], domain adaptation [24], and image synthesis [29,50].

Although most land cover classification approaches rely on images as the only input modality [7,15,37], multi-modal learning approaches are of great interest to the domain of remote sensing. Most importantly, RGB- or multispectral data have been combined with other types of imagery like SAR [1,38], Lidar data [2], or street-level imagery [36]. Our work differs from such approaches as we do not fuse satellite imagery with another image sensor modality, but with bioclimatic auxiliary information, which is easily obtainable and universally applicable to a wide range of remote sensing data and applications.

More recently, co-georeferenced, multi-modal datasets have been used explicitly for self-supervised neural network pretraining [14,32]. In analogy to our approach, the additional modality can sometimes be derived either directly or indirectly from the images' georeferencing. For instance, latitude and longitude information have been used to not only improve classification accuracy of geo-tagged images [40], but also to design a geography-aware self-supervised contrastive training objective, which was also applied to remote sensing images [3]. Similarly, satellite images have been enriched with land cover statistics derived from existing products to aid general representation learning [23]. The difference between these works and our approach, however, is that we do not use the bioclimatic context information for deriving an entirely new objective, but explicitly provide it to the network as an additional input modality, while relying on standard, non-geographic loss functions in both the supervised and self-supervised setting. This makes our approach less specific to certain realizations of self-supervised learning and thus, more universally applicable to a wide range of training schemes. In addition, it is safe to assume that georeferencing information is available for most satellite remote sensing, but not natural image datasets.

Closely related to our work, conditional regularization approaches have been adapted for some applications in Earth observation: For predicting wildfires from various static and dynamic geographical variables, for example, location-aware denormalization layers are used in conjunction with a multi-branch neural network [9]. It is also used to extract geometric information from auxiliary GIS data for individual building segmentation in SAR images [39] and for generating high-resolution satellite images from a set of semantic descriptors [27].

3   Methodology

3.1   Data Preparation

We conduct the majority of our experiments on the EuroSAT benchmark for satellite image land cover classification [15]. In this dataset, there are 27000 geo-referenced images x from the Sentinel-2 mission, which are distributed across the European continent. The images have a size of 64×64 pixels and 13 spectral bands in the visible and infrared domains. The bands are originally at different spatial resolutions between 10 m and 60 m, but have been sampled to a common 10 m grid using bicubic interpolation. Each of the images is associated with one land cover label y, distinguishing between the 10 classes *Annual Crop, Forest, Herbaceous Vegetation, Highway, Industrial, Pasture, Perennial Crop, Residential, River,* and *Sea & Lake.*

In addition, we use BigEarthNet [37,38] as an example of a larger-scale and more complex dataset. Like EuroSAT, it contains pairs of Sentinel-2 images and land cover class labels across Europe. BigEarthNet is, however, much larger at 519341 120×120 pixel images. Furthermore, it is a multi-label dataset with 19 land cover classes with the possibility of an image being assigned to multiple labels. For a list of classes, we refer to Fig. 2.

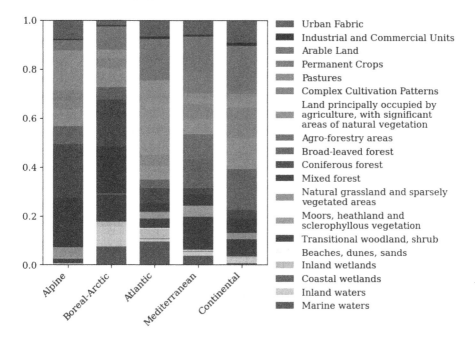

Urban Fabric
Industrial and Commercial Units
Arable Land
Permanent Crops
Pastures
Complex Cultivation Patterns
Land principally occupied by agriculture, with significant areas of natural vegetation
Agro-forestry areas
Broad-leaved forest
Coniferous forest
Mixed forest
Natural grassland and sparsely vegetated areas
Moors, heathland and sclerophyllous vegetation
Transitional woodland, shrub
Beaches, dunes, sands
Inland wetlands
Coastal wetlands
Inland waters
Marine waters

Fig. 2. The variability of land cover class label distributions across the different bio-geographic regions in BigEarthNet provides an indication of prior shift.

For both EuroSAT and BigEarthNet, bioclimatic auxiliary vectors a are derived from the WorldClim-BIO dataset [12]. It contains worldwide rasters of a total of 19 bioclimatic variables and one additional elevation raster from the shuttle radar topography mission [11] at a resolution of 10 arcmin, which roughly equates to 18.5 km in north-south direction, and between 8 km and 15 km in west-east direction for our region of interest. Among the bioclimatic variables are e.g. the mean annual temperature, temperature seasonality, and annual precipitation. For a full list, we refer to the link in the corresponding reference [12]. To assign a set of values to a specific image, the rasters are sampled at the center location of the image using nearest neighbor interpolation. As the images are much higher-resolved than the auxiliary rasters, variability of climatic variables across the footprint area of single images is negligible.

Similarly, we also provide each image with a biogeographic label b, which is derived in a similar fashion from maps by the European Environmental Agency [10]. We differentiate between the five regions *Alpine, Boreal-Arctic, Atlantic, Mediterranean* (including *Macaronesia, Steppic* and *Black Sea*), and *Continental* (including *Pannonian*) as a proxy for bioclimatic variability. These data, however, will not be used during the training of the neural network, but only serve data split and evaluation purposes. It must be stressed, that the extraction of both a and b is straightforward, as satellite images' locations are contained in their georeferencing metadata in the majority of cases. The approach is thereby generally transferable to any georeferenced dataset.

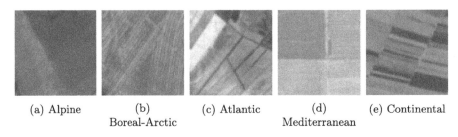

(a) Alpine   (b)   (c) Atlantic   (d)   (e) Continental
Boreal-Arctic   Mediterranean

Fig. 3. The variability of example EuroSAT images for the class *Annual Crop* from different biogeographical regions provide indication of covariate shift.

For training, validating, and testing the neural network models, both datasets are split into fixed subsets of 60%, 20%, and 20%, respectively. We perform the split with respect to the biogeographic label b, instead of the labels y as is originally the case for EuroSAT [15]. This deviation is to ensure even bioclimatic diversity throughout the data splits, so that the models can be reliably evaluated regarding their geographic generalizability later on. The satellite images' pixel values, as well as the bioclimatic auxiliary vectors are normalized to the range $[0, 1]$ and we apply random horizontal and vertical flips to the images during training and validation for data augmentation purposes.

To illustrate the presence of the previously discussed bioclimatic data shift effects in the considered datasets, we provide some visual examples: First, the BigEarthNet class distributions for the different biogeographic regions are shown in Fig. 2, providing an indication for bioclimatic prior shift. Second, we show one EuroSAT image of the class *Annual Crop* for each of the biogeographic regions in Fig. 3 to highlight the presence of bioclimatic covariate shift. We note that there may also be other reasons for data shift, such as sampling bias or other unconsidered environmental variables, which are out of the scope of this work.

3.2 Neural Network Architectures and Training

Given the data quadruples $\{x, y, a, b\}$ as described above, a neural network shall predict a land cover label from the image, i.e. approximate the conditional distribution $P(Y|X)$. The most important component of prediction is a fully convolutional image encoder $\mathcal{E}$, which yields an intermediate representation $z = \mathcal{E}(x)$. We use the ResNet18 architecture [13], where the original input and pooling layer is replaced by a single layer of strided convolutions with subsequent batch normalization in order to adapt the architecture to the respective dataset's image size.

In the supervised setting, the network is completed by a one-layer classification head $\mathcal{C}$ to output land cover class label predictions $\widehat{y} = \mathcal{C}(z)$. The two model components are trained in an end-to-end fashion to minimize the Cross Entropy Loss between $\widehat{y}$ and y using the Adam optimizer [20]. As for the hyperparameters, we use a learning rate of 1×10^{-5} for both datasets and a batch size of 64 and 512 for EuroSAT and BigEarthNet, respectively. To determine the optimal number of epochs needed for training, early stopping with a patience of 5 epochs for EuroSAT and 10 for BigEarthNet based on the validation accuracy is utilized.

For the self-supervised case, which is only employed on EuroSAT, the encoder is trained on the pretext task of image reconstruction [21]. To this end, the encoder is complemented by a ResNet18 Decoder $\mathcal{D}$, which mirrors the encoder's structure using transpose convolutions in place of convolution and pooling layers [47]. For the reconstruction loss, we use a weighted average of a base L1 loss (l_1), which only considers pixel-wise differences and the negative structural similarity index measure (l_{SSIM}), which also reflects structural differences between the images [46,49]:

$$l_{\text{rec.}}(x, \widehat{x}) = (1 - \lambda)l_1(x, \widehat{x}) + \lambda(1 - l_{\text{SSIM}}(x, \widehat{x})). \tag{1}$$

The parameters of the model are also optimized end-to-end with Adam, but the number of epochs is constantly set to 200. For the learning rate and the batch size, we use the same specifications as described above and the additional weighting hyperparameter is set to $\lambda = 0.1$ for our experiments.

After training, the bottleneck representation z must preserve as much visual information about the image as possible in order for the decoder to be able to reconstruct the image. As a result, the trained encoder serves as a reasonable initialization for the subsequent supervised downstream task of land cover class prediction, for which training is otherwise performed as in the supervised setting described above.

3.3 Leveraging Bioclimatic Data

In order to alleviate the issues regarding data shift in the neural networks, the models are not only given the images x, but also the bioclimatic auxiliary vector a. Thereby, the resulting models explicitly approximate $P(Y|X, A)$. We explore two methods for incorporating the bioclimatic context into the neural networks:

In the first case, we apply a fully connected linear layer $\mathcal{M}$ with learnable parameters to a. This embedding of the bioclimatic context is then simply added to the encoder output to yield the intermediate representation $z = \mathcal{E}(x) + \mathcal{M}(a)$.

As the second method for leveraging the bioclimatic context, we replace all batch normalization layers in both the encoder and the decoder with conditional batch normalization layers. Batch normalization in itself is one of the most popular regularization techniques in deep neural networks [18]. Its aim is to reduce the internal covariate shift of a layer's hidden representations h_{ij}, where the index i refers to the batch dimension, and j refers to the feature or channel dimension. First, they are standardized using the features' means μ_j and variances σ_j^2, for which running estimates are stored:

$$h_{ij} \leftarrow \frac{h_{ij} - \mu_j}{\sqrt{\sigma_j^2 + \epsilon}}. \tag{2}$$

Afterward, they are rescaled by learnable scale and offset parameters γ_j and β_j:

$$h_{ij} \leftarrow \gamma_j h_{ij} + \beta_j. \tag{3}$$

As an extension to regular batch normalization, conditional batch normalization [6] makes these layers' parameters dependent on some auxiliary data which in our application is the images' bioclimatic context a_i. Thus, the learnable parameters are not optimized for directly, but as the result of a fully connected linear layer $\mathcal{T}$, which is individually applied to each a_i:

$$\gamma_{ij}, \beta_{ij} = \mathcal{T}(a_i). \tag{4}$$

Note that in conditional batch normalization, the learned scale and bias parameters are different for the samples within a batch, which is not the case in standard batch normalization. The statistics μ_j and σ_j^2, on the other hand, are still computed and applied independently of a_i.

The resulting bioclimate-aware neural networks, abbreviated as ResNet18-Emb and ResNet18-CBN, can be trained in the exact same fashion as the bioclimate-agnostic ResNet18, allowing for a direct comparison between the three different methods in both the supervised and the self-supervised setting.

4   Experiments and Evaluation

4.1   Accuracy

First, we train and test the different neural networks on EuroSAT. We compare the overall accuracy, $\mathrm{Acc}(y, \widehat{y}) = \frac{1}{N} \sum_{i=0}^{N} 1(y_i = \widehat{y}_i)$ with N denoting the number of samples, of the bioclimate-aware and bioclimate-agnostic models in Table 1. All models are trained from both random initializations and initializations from self-supervised pre-training, which we simply refer to as the supervised and self-supervised settings, respectively.

Table 1. Averages and standard deviations of test overall accuracy across 10 train runs on EuroSAT.

Model	Acc, Supervised in %	Acc, Self-Supervised in %
ResNet18	95.68 ± 0.41	96.04 ± 0.36
ResNet18-Emb	95.90 ± 0.34	96.13 ± 0.28
ResNet18-CBN	**96.93** ± 0.61	**97.10** ± 0.23

The results show that ResNet18-CBN significantly outperforms both ResNet18-Emb and the bioclimate-agnostic model. Unexpectedly, a learned embedding did not lead to significant improvements, which indicates that it matters how the bioclimatic context is incorporated into the neural network. Secondly, small improvements can be seen for all models if the encoder is initially trained on the self-supervised reconstruction objective. It is notable, that the randomly initialized ResNet18-CBN still outperforms the pretrained, bioclimate-agnostic model.

4.2   Generalizability

Besides their accuracy, we also quantify the models' generalizability as an additional assessment metric in Table 2. In fact, we consider two different notions of generalizability: in a classical machine learning sense and in a geographic sense.

In the classical machine learning sense, generalization describes the difference in accuracy between training and test data. This difference, which we denote by Gen-ML, should be as small as possible, as a large gap indicates that the model overfits to the distribution of the training data and is not sufficiently regularized.

In the geographic sense, we define generalizability as a model's ability to perform equally well across different biogeographical regions b. For quantification, we compute the accuracies over each regional subset of the test data and calculate their standard deviation with respect to the overall accuracy, as described in Sect. 4.1:

$$\text{Gen-Geo}(y, \widehat{y}) = \sqrt{\frac{1}{B} \sum_b (\text{Acc}(y_b, \widehat{y}_b) - \text{Acc}(y, \widehat{y}))^2}, \tag{5}$$

where B is the number of biogeographical regions considered. We acknowledge that by equally dividing the samples from all biogeographic regions in our train-test-split, we only consider the geographic generalizability within the domain of the training data. This is different from domain adaptation-related works which evaluate and improve models regarding their geographic generalizability outside the domain of the training data, e.g. different continents or cities [42].

Table 2. Averages and standard deviations of test generalizability metrics Gen-ML and Gen-Geo across 10 training runs on EuroSAT.

Model	Gen-ML in %		Gen-Geo in %	
	Supervised	Self-Supervised	Supervised	Self-Supervised
ResNet18	3.36 ± 0.55	2.64 ± 0.40	1.21 ± 0.34	$\mathbf{1.01 \pm 0.19}$
ResNet18-Emb	3.32 ± 0.53	2.60 ± 0.60	1.21 ± 0.27	1.18 ± 0.18
ResNet18-CBN	$\mathbf{1.85 \pm 1.09}$	$\mathbf{1.80 \pm 0.26}$	$\mathbf{1.02 \pm 0.23}$	$\mathbf{1.01 \pm 0.16}$

Both metrics of generalizability are best for ResNet18-CBN, while ResNet18-Emb again only slightly outperforms the bioclimate-agnostic baseline. Improvements with self-supervised pretraining are most significant for the bioclimate-agnostic model, but also improve both metrics of the bioclimate-aware models. Based on the results on Gen-ML, we conclude that leveraging bioclimatic context through conditional batch normalization effectively regularizes neural network training for land cover classification. As for Gen-Geo, we can also see that ResNet18-CBN models generally achieve more geographically consistent classification results, which implies that bioclimatic data shift effects are successfully counteracted, especially in the supervised setting.

4.3   Training Efficiency

Here, we report the number of training epochs the model needs to pass certain accuracy thresholds p on the validation data, which we denote by Eff-p.

To account for variability regarding floating point operations, and thereby the time it takes to train a single epoch, we also need to determine relative walltime multiplicators α for each model. To this end, 10 epochs of training are run independently of training on the same physical GPU. The walltimes of each epoch are recorded and averaged. We define the supervised, bioclimate-agnostic ResNet18 as our baseline and set its $\alpha = 1$, accordingly. We track the validation accuracy throughout training with respect to the relative number of epochs, i.e. the number of epochs multiplied by α. The curves are averaged across the ten different runs (Table 3).

Table 3. Efficiency characteristics and metrics Eff-0.95 of the implemented models as derived from the averaged training curves across 10 training runs on EuroSAT.

Model	α	#Param.s	Eff-0.95, Supervised	Eff-0.95, Self-Supervised
ResNet18	1.000	12.556M	13.208	12.000
ResNet18-Emb	1.080	12.567M	13.651	15.379
ResNet18-CBN	1.242	12.749M	**12.993**	**9.954**

The results largely confirm the findings from Secs. 4.1 and 4.2. Training times of ResNet18-CBN are reduced compared to the bioclimate-agnostic baseline in both the supervised setting and the self-supervised setting, although the difference is more significant with respect to the latter, where training is about 23% faster on average. Meanwhile, no improvements can be detected for ResNet18-Emb, where we even observe a surprising decline in efficiency when pre-training the model in a self-supervised manner.

4.4   Autoencoder Reconstructions and Representations

Below, we show an example image, as well as the corresponding reconstructions by the different autoencoders during the pre-training step in the self-supervised setting. The results for l_1 and l_{SSIM} on the test set are reported in Table 4.

Once again, ResNet18-CBN quantitatively outperforms the other two approaches in terms of reconstruction loss. The poor reconstruction quality is to be expected due to the very large drop in dimensionality from the original image to the latent representations: The images originally contain $64 \times 64 \times 13 = 53248$ values and are compressed into just 512. Despite this subjectively poor performance on the pretext task, the quantitative results from the previous sections suggest that the self-supervised pretraining benefits subsequent land cover classification and thus, that the encoder has learned useful land cover-relevant features (Fig. 4).

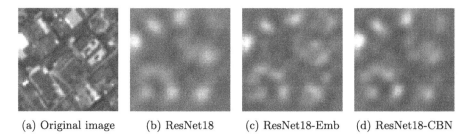

   (a) Original image   (b) ResNet18   (c) ResNet18-Emb   (d) ResNet18-CBN

Fig. 4. RGB visualization of the original EuroSAT image and autoencoder reconstructions of the different models.

To quantitatively evaluate the quality of the representations, we fit a simple Support Vector Machine (SVM) classifier with a Gaussian radial basis function kernel [5] to predict y from z with frozen encoder weights. The resulting overall accuracies are reported in Table 4. Again, ResNet18-CBN outperforms both the bioclimate-agnostic baseline and ResNet18-Emb. We also investigate the effect of applying CBN to only $\mathcal{E}$ and only $\mathcal{D}$. We notice that reconstructing quality suffers when only applying CBN to $\mathcal{E}$, whereas performance on the downstream task is similar. On the other hand, accuracy of the SVM declines significantly when applying CBN only to $\mathcal{D}$, while reconstruction quality even slightly improves with respect to both l_1 and l_{SSIM}.

Table 4. Averages and standard deviations of evaluation metrics of autoencoder reconstructions and representations across 10 training runs.

Model	l_1	l_{SSIM}	SVM-Acc in %
ResNet18	0.0110 ± 0.0005	0.9232 ± 0.0052	76.45 ± 5.34
ResNet18-Emb	0.0104 ± 0.0004	0.9300 ± 0.0035	79.52 ± 2.30
ResNet18-CBN	0.0095 ± 0.0002	0.9344 ± 0.0024	$\mathbf{83.73 \pm 1.01}$
ResNet18-CBN ($\mathcal{E}$ only)	0.0114 ± 0.0006	0.9247 ± 0.0038	83.05 ± 2.35
ResNet18-CBN ($\mathcal{D}$ only)	$\mathbf{0.0091 \pm 0.0002}$	$\mathbf{0.9384 \pm 0.0021}$	75.25 ± 3.05

4.5 Sanity Checks for Conditional Batch Normalization

To confirm the integrity of ResNet18-CBN, we perform two basic sanity checks: First, we study if our observed improvements are actually due to the incorporation of bioclimatic context, and not due to differences between standard batch normalization and conditional batch normalization with respect to the overall optimization scheme as described in Sect. 3.3. To this end, we shuffle the auxiliary vectors a within each data split so that images are associated with 'fake' bioclimatic data which were originally derived for a different image.

If the bioclimatic context in itself were irrelevant, this would have only little effect on the results. However, we find that models perform worse under this manipulation with an average overall accuracy of 0.9496 across 10 runs, which is worse than ResNet18-CBN with unshuffled bioclimatic auxiliary vectors and the bioclimate-agnostic baseline, as reported in Sect. 4.1. This strengthens our hypothesis that bioclimatic context is useful auxiliary information in the context of land cover classification by ruling out the possibility that improvements are merely to changes in the optimization scheme.

Another recently raised concern about multi-modal learning using conditional batch normalization is that depending on the dataset, particularly the type and quality of the auxiliary data, shortcut learning may be encouraged [34]. Shortcut learning describes the phenomenon where models counterintuitively focus too strongly on the auxiliary information and thus do not learn meaningful features from the primary data source, i.e. the images.

We want to test if this effect is prevalent for our application and thus compute attribution maps, which indicate the relevant locations of an image with respect to specific class outputs. In particular, we apply Grad-CAM [33] to the last layer of the trained ResNet18 models from the supervised setting. Because the attribution maps are originally given in the respective layer's spatial dimension, they are upsampled to the original image size using bicubic interpolation.

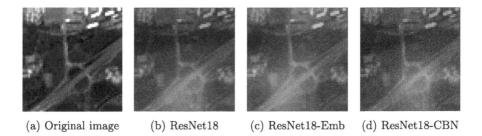

(a) Original image   (b) ResNet18   (c) ResNet18-Emb   (d) ResNet18-CBN

Fig. 5. RGB visualization of the original image and overlayed Grad-CAM attribution maps from the different models for a data sample of the class *Highway*.

We visually compare the attribution maps from the models, which are once again averaged over the ten different runs, for a test data sample in Fig. 5. The classes *Highway* and *River* are particularly useful in this context, as they contain localizable objects in the image, which the Grad-CAM attributions should ideally highlight. We find that the attribution maps derived from both bioclimate-aware and -agnostic models are well aligned in this context, indicating that sensible visual features are learned despite the use of auxiliary information. There is thus no indication that the bioclimate-aware models suffer from the pitfall of shortcut learning. The most likely explanation is that bioclimatic context is not in itself informative enough to solve the prediction task, but still represents useful information to regularize neural network training.

4.6 Towards Large-Scale Application

While the simplicity of the EuroSAT dataset makes it suitable for the kinds of extensive experiments described above, it also causes the baseline ResNet18 to perform rather well, leaving only little room for improvement. We therefore provide additional accuracy metrics for supervised training on BigEarthNet, which is more challenging due to its about 200 times larger size and the presence of multiple labels for each image, as described in Sect. 3.1. In addition, unlike in EuroSAT, the label distribution is highly unbalanced, as shown in Fig. 2, which is why we report the micro- and macro-averaged F1-scores besides overall accuracy in Table 5.

Table 5. Test accuracy metrics on BigEarthNet.

Model	Acc in %	F1 (micro) in %	F1 (macro) in %
ResNet18	93.79	78.68	72.95
ResNet18-Emb	93.83	78.73	72.47
ResNet18-CBN	**94.30**	**79.57**	**75.68**

The results confirm our conclusions from the experiments on EuroSAT as ResNet18-CBN stands out as the best performer across all metrics and ResNet18-Emb does not offer significant improvements over the baseline. This is an indication that the approach is generally transferable to more data-intensive and complex scenarios. We are therefore optimistic, that it will also be a suitable building block within other types of neural networks, e.g. for semantic segmentation, which we plan to investigate in future work.

5 Conclusion

We showed that leveraging bioclimatic auxiliary data in a multi-modal setup benefits the training of neural networks for both supervised and self-supervised land cover classification regarding all considered quantitative and qualitative aspects. The incorporation by means of conditional batch normalization lead to particularly good results, whereas improvements were surprisingly marginal when using added embeddings. Because of the universal applicability to a wide range of other datasets and architectures, these insights can have a great impact on the growing interdisciplinary field of machine learning for Earth observation.

References

1. Alemohammad, H., Booth, K.: LandCoverNet: a global benchmark land cover classification training dataset. In: AI for Earth Sciences Workshop at NeurIPS (2020)
2. Audebert, N., Le Saux, B., Lefèvre, S.: Beyond RGB: very high resolution urban remote sensing with multimodal deep networks. ISPRS J. Photogramm. Remote. Sens. **140**, 20–32 (2018)

3. Ayush, K., et al.: Geography-aware self-supervised learning. In: Proceedings of the IEEE/CVF International Conference on Computer Vision, pp. 10181–10190 (2021)

4. Cao, Y., Steffey, S., He, J., Xiao, D., Tao, C., Chen, P., Müller, H.: Medical image retrieval: a multimodal approach. Cancer Inform. **13**, CIN–S14053 (2014)

5. Cortes, C., Vapnik, V.: Support-vector networks. Mach. Learn. **20**, 273–297 (1995)

6. De Vries, H., Strub, F., Mary, J., Larochelle, H., Pietquin, O., Courville, A.C.: Modulating early visual processing by language. In: Advances in Neural Information Processing Systems, vol. 30 (2017)

7. Demir, I., et al.: DeepGlobe 2018: a challenge to parse the earth through satellite images. In: Proceedings of the IEEE/CVF Conference on Computer Vision and Pattern Recognition Workshops, pp. 172–181 (2018)

8. Dumoulin, V., Shlens, J., Kudlur, M.: A learned representation for artistic style. In: International Conference on Learning Representations (2016)

9. Eddin, M.H.S., Roscher, R., Gall, J.: Location-aware adaptive normalization: a deep learning approach for wildfire danger forecasting. IEEE Trans. Geosci. Remote Sens. **61**, 1–18 (2023)

10. EEA: Biogeographical regions Europe 2016 (2016). https://www.eea.europa.eu/ds_resolveuid/9b7911cc33ad4a9c940847a7ff653a40

11. Farr, T.G., et al.: The shuttle radar topography mission. Rev. Geophys. **45**(2) (2007)

12. Fick, S.E., Hijmans, R.J.: WorldClim 2: new 1-km spatial resolution climate surfaces for global land areas. Int. J. Climatol. **37**(12), 4302–4315 (2017). https://worldclim.org/data/worldclim21.html

13. He, K., Zhang, X., Ren, S., Sun, J.: Deep residual learning for image recognition. In: Proceedings of the IEEE/CVF Conference on Computer Vision and Pattern Recognition, pp. 770–778 (2016)

14. Heidler, K., et al.: Self-supervised audiovisual representation learning for remote sensing data. Int. J. Appl. Earth Obs. Geoinf. **116**, 103130 (2023)

15. Helber, P., Bischke, B., Dengel, A., Borth, D.: EuroSAT: a novel dataset and deep learning benchmark for land use and land cover classification. IEEE J. Sel. Top. Appl. Earth Obs. Remote Sens. **12**(7), 2217–2226 (2019)

16. Hu, L., Robinson, C., Dilkina, B.: Model generalization in deep learning applications for land cover mapping. arXiv preprint arXiv:2008.10351 (2020)

17. Huang, X., Belongie, S.: Arbitrary style transfer in real-time with adaptive instance normalization. In: Proceedings of the IEEE/CVF International Conference on Computer Vision, pp. 1501–1510 (2017)

18. Ioffe, S., Szegedy, C.: Batch normalization: accelerating deep network training by reducing internal covariate shift. In: International Conference on Machine Learning, pp. 448–456 (2015)

19. Jain, A., Singh, A., Koppula, H.S., Soh, S., Saxena, A.: Recurrent neural networks for driver activity anticipation via sensory-fusion architecture. In: IEEE International Conference on Robotics and Automation, pp. 3118–3125 (2016)

20. Kingma, D.P., Ba, J.: Adam: a method for stochastic optimization. In: International Conference for Learning Representations (2014)

21. Kramer, M.A.: Nonlinear principal component analysis using autoassociative neural networks. AIChE J. **37**(2), 233–243 (1991)

22. Lenz, I., Lee, H., Saxena, A.: Deep learning for detecting robotic grasps. Int. J. Robot. Res. **34**(4–5), 705–724 (2015)

23. Li, W., Chen, K., Chen, H., Shi, Z.: Geographical knowledge-driven representation learning for remote sensing images. IEEE Trans. Geosci. Remote Sens. **60**, 1–16 (2021)

24. Li, Y., Wang, N., Shi, J., Hou, X., Liu, J.: Adaptive batch normalization for practical domain adaptation. Pattern Recogn. **80**, 109–117 (2018)

25. Liang, M., Li, Z., Chen, T., Zeng, J.: Integrative data analysis of multi-platform cancer data with a multimodal deep learning approach. IEEE/ACM Trans. Comput. Biol. Bioinf. **12**(4), 928–937 (2014)

26. Lu, X., Gong, T., Zheng, X.: Multisource compensation network for remote sensing cross-domain scene classification. IEEE Trans. Geosci. Remote Sens. **58**(4), 2504–2515 (2019)

27. Marín, J., Escalera, S.: SSSGAN: satellite style and structure generative adversarial networks. Remote Sens. **13**(19), 3984 (2021)

28. Ngiam, J., Khosla, A., Kim, M., Nam, J., Lee, H., Ng, A.Y.: Multimodal deep learning. In: Proceedings of the 28th International Conference on Machine Learning, pp. 689–696 (2011)

29. Park, T., Liu, M.Y., Wang, T.C., Zhu, J.Y.: Semantic image synthesis with spatially-adaptive normalization. In: Proceedings of the IEEE/CVF Conference on Computer Vision and Pattern Recognition, pp. 2337–2346 (2019)

30. Perez, E., Strub, F., De Vries, H., Dumoulin, V., Courville, A.: FiLM: visual reasoning with a general conditioning layer. In: Proceedings of the AAAI Conference on Artificial Intelligence, vol. 32 (2018)

31. Ramachandram, D., Taylor, G.W.: Deep multimodal learning: a survey on recent advances and trends. IEEE Signal Process. Mag. **34**(6), 96–108 (2017)

32. Scheibenreif, L., Hanna, J., Mommert, M., Borth, D.: Self-supervised vision transformers for land-cover segmentation and classification. In: Proceedings of the IEEE/CVF Conference on Computer Vision and Pattern Recognition, pp. 1422–1431 (2022)

33. Selvaraju, R.R., Cogswell, M., Das, A., Vedantam, R., Parikh, D., Batra, D.: Grad-CAM: visual explanations from deep networks via gradient-based localization. In: Proceedings of the IEEE International Conference on Computer Vision, pp. 618–626 (2017)

34. Sheth, I., Rahman, A.A., Havaei, M., Kahou, S.E.: Pitfalls of conditional batch normalization for contextual multi-modal learning. In: I Can't Believe It's Not Better Workshop at NeurIPS (2022)

35. Srivastava, N., Salakhutdinov, R.R.: Multimodal learning with deep Boltzmann machines. In: Advances in Neural Information Processing Systems, vol. 25 (2012)

36. Suel, E., Bhatt, S., Brauer, M., Flaxman, S., Ezzati, M.: Multimodal deep learning from satellite and street-level imagery for measuring income, overcrowding, and environmental deprivation in urban areas. Remote Sens. Environ. **257**, 112339 (2021)

37. Sumbul, G., Charfuelan, M., Demir, B., Markl, V.: BigEarthNet: a large-scale benchmark archive for remote sensing image understanding. In: IEEE International Geoscience and Remote Sensing Symposium, pp. 5901–5904. IEEE (2019)

38. Sumbul, G., et al.: BigEarthNet-MM: a large-scale, multimodal, multilabel benchmark archive for remote sensing image classification and retrieval [software and data sets]. IEEE Geosci. Remote Sens. Mag. **9**(3), 174–180 (2021)

39. Sun, Y., Hua, Y., Mou, L., Zhu, X.X.: CG-Net: conditional GIS-aware network for individual building segmentation in VHR SAR images. IEEE Trans. Geosci. Remote Sens. **60**, 1–15 (2021)

40. Tang, K., Paluri, M., Fei-Fei, L., Fergus, R., Bourdev, L.: Improving image classification with location context. In: Proceedings of the IEEE/CVF International Conference on Computer Vision, pp. 1008–1016 (2015)

41. Townshend, J.G.: Land cover. Int. J. Remote Sens. **13**(6–7), 1319–1328 (1992)
42. Tuia, D., Persello, C., Bruzzone, L.: Domain adaptation for the classification of remote sensing data: an overview of recent advances. IEEE Geosci. Remote Sens. Mag. **4**(2), 41–57 (2016)
43. Turner, M.G., Gardner, R.H.: Landscape Ecology in Theory and Practice. Springer, New York (2015). https://doi.org/10.1007/978-1-4939-2794-4
44. Wang, J., Zheng, Z., Ma, A., Lu, X., Zhong, Y.: LoveDA: a remote sensing land-cover dataset for domain adaptive semantic segmentation. In: NeurIPS Datasets and Benchmarks Track (2021)
45. Wang, X., Yu, K., Dong, C., Loy, C.C.: Recovering realistic texture in image super-resolution by deep spatial feature transform. In: Proceedings of the IEEE/CVF Conference on Computer Vision and Pattern Recognition, pp. 606–615 (2018)
46. Wang, Z., Bovik, A.C., Sheikh, H.R., Simoncelli, E.P.: Image quality assessment: from error visibility to structural similarity. IEEE Trans. Image Process. **13**(4), 600–612 (2004)
47. Wickramasinghe, C.S., Marino, D.L., Manic, M.: ResNet autoencoders for unsupervised feature learning from high-dimensional data: deep models resistant to performance degradation. IEEE Access **9**, 40511–40520 (2021)
48. Wulder, M.A., Coops, N.C., Roy, D.P., White, J.C., Hermosilla, T.: Land cover 2.0. Int. J. Remote Sens. **39**(12), 4254–4284 (2018)
49. Zhao, H., Gallo, O., Frosio, I., Kautz, J.: Loss functions for image restoration with neural networks. IEEE Trans. Comput. Imaging **3**(1), 47–57 (2016)
50. Zhu, P., Abdal, R., Qin, Y., Wonka, P.: SEAN: image synthesis with semantic region-adaptive normalization. In: Proceedings of the IEEE/CVF Conference on Computer Vision and Pattern Recognition, pp. 5104–5113 (2020)

Automatic Reverse Engineering: Creating Computer-Aided Design (CAD) Models from Multi-view Images

Henrik Jobczyk and Hanno Homann[(⊠)]

Hannover University of Applied Sciences, Hanover, Germany
`henrik.jobczyk@stud.hs-hannover.de`, `hanno.homann@hs-hannover.de`

Abstract. Generation of computer-aided design (CAD) models from multi-view images may be useful in many practical applications. To date this problem is usually solved with an intermediate point-cloud reconstruction and involves manual work to create the final CAD models. In this contribution, we present a novel network for an automated reverse engineering task. Our network architecture combines three distinct stages: A convolutional neural network as the encoder stage, a multi-view pooling stage and a transformer-based CAD sequence generator.

The model is trained and evaluated on a large number of simulated input images and extensive optimization of model architectures and hyper-parameters is performed. A proof-of-concept is demonstrated by successfully reconstructing a number of valid CAD models from simulated test image data. Various accuracy metrics are calculated and compared to a state-of-the-art point-based network.

Finally, a real world test is conducted supplying the network with actual photographs of two three-dimensional test objects. It is shown that some of the capabilities of our network can be transferred to this domain, even though the training exclusively incorporates purely synthetic training data. However to date, the feasible model complexity is still limited to basic shapes.

Keywords: computer-aided design (CAD) · multi-view reconstruction · encoder-decoder network

1 Introduction

Ever since the invention of 3D-printing in the middle of the 20th century, it stimulates the imagination of laypersons and engineers alike. Nowadays this technology is an integral part of the product development cycle in many industries and its application often goes beyond the production of mere prototypes.

Even though online 3D printing services increase availability at affordable prices, their use in everyday life is not straightforward. This work is focuses on the central problem of 3D-printing: The generation of digital 3D objects is a

U. Köthe and C. Rother (Eds.): DAGM GCPR 2023, LNCS 14264, pp. 243–259, 2024.
https://doi.org/10.1007/978-3-031-54605-1_16

skill requiring specialized technical expertise and training, posing a significant barrier for consumer adoption.

To give a practical example, a simple mechanical part within a bigger and more expensive appliance such as a washing machine or dryer fails and renders the device unusable. The point of failure is identified but the manufacturer can not offer a spare part. If the user could simply take a few photos using a smartphone camera and have a computer-aided design (CAD) model created automatically by software, the problem could be solved in a short time at minimal financial and environmental cost.

This work proposes an end-to-end solution for this reverse engineering problem, which is to our knowledge the first of its kind. Our network architecture is illustrated in Fig. 1 and will be described in detail further below after revisiting the state-of-the-art. For proof-of-concept, our model was trained on a large number of renderings from simulated CAD objects. Our results indicate that the image-based approach may outperform a current point-based method. Finally, two real world objects were photographed and reconstructed.

Our main contributions are: (1) We present the first end-to-end model to generate CAD sequences from multi-view images, (2) comparison of two different multi-view fusion strategies, and (3) initial results on real-world photos.

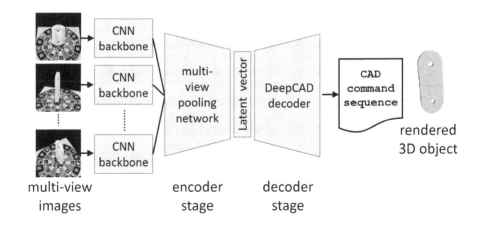

Fig. 1. ARE-Net architecture: Input images taken from multiple view angles are fed into an encoder-decoder network to generate CAD sequence file. Multi-view fusion is facilitated (a) using a fully-connected network (FCN) or (b) using a gated recurrent unit (GRU) to allow varying numbers of input images. The decoder part of the DeepCAD auto-encoder is employed as the generative decoder.

2   Related Work

2.1   Traditional Photogrammetry Approaches to Reconstructing CAD Models

Photogrammetry is frequently deployed as an image-based technique to measure three-dimensional shapes using inexpensive cameras. The most common monocular approaches are based on the Structure from Motion (SfM) method first described in [35]. Here, the software is provided with several images from different perspectives and then computes a point-cloud of the object of interest.

Automatically extracting a CAD model from a point-cloud is however not straight-forward. For example, the professional AutoCAD software can import but not post-process point clouds as of today [3]. Thus far, CAD model creation mostly remains a manual task.

Kim et al. [15] proposed 3D registration of given CAD model using the iterative closest point (ICP) method. Budroni et al. [5] have demonstrated the fitting of planar surfaces to point clouds for reconstructing of 3D models of interior rooms. More recently, Lui [19] proposed automatic reverse-engineering of CAD models from points clouds by iteratively fitting primitive models based on the RANSAC algorithm. In conclusion, there are few existing approaches which are however domain-specific. Instead, a neural-network based approach might generalize better in the long term.

2.2   Learning-Based Object Reconstruction

Detection of 3D objects from multiple view perspectives has been addressed by Rukhovich et al. [33]. Similar to [39], they used a fully convolutional network. Notably the number of monocular images in their multi-view input can vary from inference to inference, offering high versatility. This is achieved by extracting features with conventional a Convolutional Neural Network (CNN), followed by pooling and back-projecting into a 3D volumetric space. In this space, bounding boxes are predicted by three-dimensional convolutions.

For 3D surface reconstruction, deep learning models have been suggested for different kinds of object representations, including point clouds [1,6,8,12,21, 48,49], triangle meshes [10,23,26,38], voxel grids [18,42,47], cubic blocks [46], parametric surfaces [13,16,17,34,40,45], and signed distance fields (SDFs) [14, 28]. The majority of the studies above (e.g. [1,14,26,28]) use auto-encoders, with a feature bottleneck between an encoder and a decoder stage. This network architecture also allows to simplify training by separating the two stages. To date, discrete CAD models have not been investigated for 3D surface representation.

2.3   Multi-view Convolutional Networks

A 3D multi-view CNN (MVCNN) for object classification was introduced by Su et al. [36]. They provide a certain number of images taken of the object as input to a common CNN and pool the extracted features using an element-wise maximum operation. The pooled information is then processed by a second CNN and a final prediction is made. Notably they conclude that inputting 12 evenly spaced perspectives offers the best trade-off between prediction accuracy and memory as well as time resources.

Their concept as been studied for classifying 3D shapes from point clouds [22,31]. In general, working with MVCNNs seems to be a viable approach for extracting information from 3D scenes. Leal et al. [37] compared different 3D shape classifiers, identifying MVCNNs as superior to other methods due to better generalizability and outperforming several point-based and voxel-based approaches. Consequently, this approach will be followed in this work.

2.4   Recurrent Convolutional Networks

While MVCNNs showed good results for classification tasks, the simple pooling methods (e.g. element-wise max-pooling [36]) might allow a single view to over-rule all other views. Geometric information not visible in some images might be lost for a 3D reconstruction task. Hence, we alternatively consider Recurrent CNNs as a more preservative information extractor.

Zreik et al. [50] used a Recurrent Neural Network (RNN) for spacial aggregation of extracted information from 3D angiography images after pre-processing by a 3D-CNN. Liu et al. [20] combined a traditional 2D CNN backbone and an RNN to synthesize multi-view features for a prediction of plant classes and conditions. After extensive experiments, they conclude that a combination of MobileNet as a backbone and a Gated Recurrent Unit (GRU) delivers the best trade-off of classification accuracy and computational overhead. Hence, GRUs will be evaluated in this study for multi-view pooling.

2.5   Generation of CAD Representations

Even though most methods described above generate three-dimensional data, none of them directly attempts CAD file generation by means of generating a construction sequence comparable to manual CAD design. Thus their resulting models cannot easily be modified by an average user. However, recent research has started to address the direct generation of parametric 2D CAD models:

Willis et al. [41] first proposed generative models for CAD sketches, producing curve primitives and explicitly considering topology. SketchGen [27] generates CAD sketches in a graph representation, with nodes representing shape primitives and edges embodying the constraints. Similarly, Ganin et al. [9] utilized off-the-shelf data serialization protocols to embed construction sequences parsed from the online CAD editor Onshape [24].

DeepCAD by Wu et al. [44] was the first approach going beyond the 2D domain of CAD sketch generation. They formulated CAD modeling as a generation of command sequences, specifically tailored as an input to a transformer-based auto-encoder. The publicly available Onshape API was used to build a large dataset of 3D object models for training.

Each object is represented by a CAD sequence, consisting of three common types of commands: (1) Creation of a closed curve profile ("sketch") on a 2D plane, (2) 3D extrusions of such sketches and (3) boolean operations between the resulting 3D objects. Each of the CAD commands supports a number of parameters, which may be a mixture of continuous and discrete values. To conform with their neural network, Wu et al. sort each command's parameters into a generalized parameter vector and all continuous parameters are quantized to 8-bits. The maximum number of commands in a given CAD construction sequence was limited to 60, corresponding to the longest sequence length in the dataset.

These CAD sequences are processed by an auto-encoder, trained to compress a given CAD model into a latent vector (dimension of 256) and then to reconstruct the original model from that embedding. This means, a random but valid CAD object can be constructed using a given 256-dimensional latent vector. In this work, chose the decoder part of DeepCAD as the generative stage of our new model as introduced next.

3 Methods

3.1 Network Architecture

We introduce a novel network architecture for end-to-end generation of CAD models from multiple input images. The network is composed of three stages: (1) a CNN encoder backbone to extract information from each input image individually, (2) a pooling network that aggregates this information into a common latent vector, and (3) a generative decoder network constructing the output CAD sequences. This network structure is illustrated in Fig. 1.

Considering its successful track record in object detection and classification as well as its small size, we chose the residual network architecture (ResNet) [11] as our encoder backbone. As the visual complexity of our input images is relatively low, we assumed that a smaller, more shallow variant of the network should suffice. Thus only its smallest two variants were evaluated, namely ResNet-18 and ResNet-34. The input image size is adjustable by means of ResNet's adaptive average pooling layer. In this work, we used 128×128 monochrome as well as 224×224 RGB input images. The output of the last fully connected layer, a vector of fixed length 512, is fed into the pooling network. All input views are processed by the backbone network individually but share the same parameters.

The task of the multi-view pooling stage is to combine the information from multiple views. We evaluated two different network architectures during the experiments: (a) a simple feed-forward fully connected network (FCN) as a baseline model and (b) a gated recurrent unit (GRU). Following [7] and [20], we assume that a recurrent pooling approach should perform favorable, even though its training is inherently more challenging [29] because of the possible vanishing and exploding gradient problems.

The FCN pooling network concatenates the outputs of all backbone CNNs and propagates them through a numbers of layers (1 to 6 layers were evaluated) of linearly decreasing size with a final layer size of 256. This forms the latent vector compatible to the subsequent DeepCAD decoder network.

Unlike the FCN pooling which processes all input views simultaneously, the alternative GRU pooling receives the input views from the backbone CNN sequentially one after the other. This makes it more suitable for varying numbers of images. For evaluation of the GRU pooling stage, we tested different numbers of layers (1 to 8) of identical dimension, different temporal pooling strategies (mean, max, last) and different layer dimensions (64, 128, 256, 512, 1024, 2048). A single fully connected layer is used to achieve the latent vector size of 256.

Both pooling network variants use rectified linear units (ReLU) as their non-linear activation function in all layers except the last. The final layer generates the latent vector. Here the hyperbolic tanget function ($tanh$) is utilized as it provides output in the range $[-1, 1]$ as required for the DeepCAD decoder network.

The final stage of the ARE-Net is formed by the decoder from the Deep-CAD library [43] which generates CAD construction sequences from the 256-dimensional latent vector.

3.2 Two-Stage Training

Training was performed in two stages: First, the full DeepCAD auto-encoder was pre-trained as described in [44]. After this training, the final latent vector of each CAD object from the training set was saved. Second, simulated image views were rendered from the ground truth CAD sequences and used to train our backbone and multi-view pooling networks. As the loss function, we used the mean-squared error between the predicted latent vectors of the simulated images and the ground-truth latent vectors from the first training stage. We employed the ADAM-optimizer, using 10 epochs during hyper-parameter optimization and 140 epochs for the final model.

4   Experimental Setup

4.1 Training Data

Training images were generated from the DeepCAD dataset consisting of 178,238 CAD models. From each CAD sequence, a 3D mesh object and two different projection datasets were generated: (1) A simple dataset of 128×128 grayscale images from 10 fixed and evenly spaced view angles as shown in Fig. 2. (2) A complex dataset of 256×256 RGB images with random but uniform object color from 24 randomly spaced viewing angles. In the second dataset the photogrammetry ground-plane from [4] was used as a base on which each model rests. It is composed of non-repeating patterns and is used as a turntable for real objects during the final real world test. The intention is to provide the model with additional information on orientation and scale of the objects, otherwise lost due to the random viewing angles.

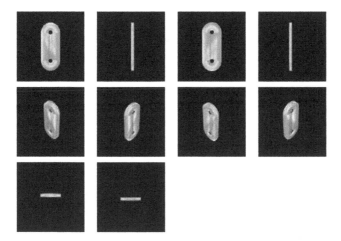

Fig. 2. Example of training images from one CAD model: (top row) central view from four sides, (middle row) elevated view, (bottom row) top and bottom views.

For training on the simple dataset, all 10 images were used. When training on the complex dataset, a random selection of 5 to 20 images was chosen. To allow an unbiased comparison of our network to former work by the DeepCAD researchers, the same training-, validation- and testing-split (90%-5%-5%) used in [44] was applied.

4.2   Hyper-parameter Optimization

Our model contains several hyper-parameters requiring optimization. General parameters are the learning rate, drop out ratio, weight decay and the number of ResNet backbone layers. The parameters of the two pooling networks are the number and dimensions of layers. For the GRU network, the temporal pooling strategy (mean, max, last) also needed investigation. In order to identify suitable hyper-parameters such as network attributes and training parameters which remain constant during any given training run an incremental experimentation procedure is followed. For hyper-parameter optimization, the Optuna library [25] was used. It allows for efficient search through the high dimensional search space and automatically records results and useful statistics.

4.3   Accuracy Metrics

To compare the accuracy of the predicted CAD models, three different metrics were employed: The command accuracy ACC_{cmd} measures the agreement of the predicted CAD command type $\hat{t}_i$ with the ground truth command type t_i for a CAD construction sequence of N_c steps:

$$ACC_{cmd} = \frac{1}{N_c} \sum_{i=1}^{N_c} \left(t_i == \hat{t}_i \right) \qquad (1)$$

While ACC_{cmd} measures that fraction of correct commands, the correctness of the continuous parameters of each command shall also be evaluated. The parameter accuracy ACC_{param} quantifies the agreement of a predicted 8-bit CAD parameter $\hat{p}_{i,j}$ to its ground-truth counterpart $p_{i,j}$. Only correctly predicted commands $N_{c2} \leq N_c$ were evaluated and a threshold of $\eta = 3$ was used, as suggested in [44]:

$$ACC_{param} = \frac{1}{N_{c2}} \sum_{i=1}^{N_{c2}} \sum_{j=1}^{|\hat{p}_i|} \left(|p_{i,j} - \hat{p}_{i,j}| \leq \eta \right) \qquad (2)$$

For geometric evaluation of the 3D model, the so-called Chamfer Distance CD was used [2,30]. It computes the shortest distance of one point x on the surface S_1 of the predicted object to the closest point y on the surface S_2 of the ground-truth object. This is carried out in both directions. In this work, 2000 surface points were evaluated per model.

$$CD = \frac{1}{S_1} \sum_{x \in S_1} \min_{y \in S_2} ||x - y||_2^2 + \frac{1}{S_2} \sum_{x \in S_2} \min_{y \in S_1} ||y - x||_2^2 \qquad (3)$$

4.4   Benchmark Comparison

As no other method generating CAD models is known to us, comparison is performed using the following two methods: (1) The original DeepCAD auto-encoder is fed with ground-truth CAD-sequences to encode a latent vector and decoded again. The predicted CAD sequence is then evaluated by the accuracy metrics described above. By using loss-less input CAD sequences, this approach represents the ideally achievable results in our comparison and will be referred to as the "baseline".

(2) For a more realistic comparison, the PointNet++ encoder [32] was evaluated as a state-of-the-art method. Point-clouds were sampled from the ground-truth 3D objects. The PointNet++ encoder was used to map the point-clouds into a latent vector and then processed by the Deep-CAD decoder as proposed by [44].

4.5   Reconstruction from Photographic Images

For an initial assessment of the performance of our method on real world images, two test objects were chosen: a cardboard box representing a very simple case and a camera mount as a more complex example. Both are intentionally of uniform color to match the simulated objects seen during training. The objects were placed on a paper version of the photogrammetry ground plane. Then 20 pictures from varying perspectives were taken by a smartphone camera while changing the inclination angle relative to the ground plane and rotating a turntable underneath the object. The image background behind the objects was then cropped away manually. All pictures were sized down to 224×224 pixels and passed into the Automatic Reverse Engineering Network (ARE-Net) with GRU pooling as trained on the simulated complex dataset.

5   Results

The best performing hyper-parameters are summarized in Table 1. On the simple dataset the GRU with a shallow ResNet18 backbone had sufficient distinguishing power, whereas ResNet34 performed better for the simpler FCN network as well as for the GRU for the complex dataset. Three FC layers were optimal for FCN pooling, but more than one layer didn't increase performance of the GRU pooling stages. As for the GRU-specific parameters, sightly larger networks proved favorable for the complex dataset.

Table 1. Best hyper-parameters found by our optimization.

Pooling network	FCN	GRU	GRU
Dataset	simple	simple	complex
Learning rate	$1.3 \cdot 10^{-4}$	$4.8 \cdot 10^{-4}$	$1.5 \cdot 10^{-4}$
Drop out	4.8%	16.1%	17.2%
Weight decay	$5.45 \cdot 10^{-5}$	$3.18 \cdot 10^{-6}$	$4.38 \cdot 10^{-6}$
Backbone	ResNet34	ResNet18	ResNet34
FC layers	3	1	1
GRU pooling	–	*max*	*last*
GRU layers	–	1	2
GRU dimension	–	1024	2048

Table 2 compares the accuracy metrics of our models using the optimized hyper-parameters. It stands out that the GRU pooling network trained on the simple dataset achieved the best overall performance. It reaches an ACC_{cmd} of 92.8%, an ACC_{param} of 78.8% and a median CD of $1.75 \cdot 10^3$. However, the fraction of 18.4% of CAD models that could not be constructed is notably worse than for the point cloud encoder. The percentage of invalid CAD topologies is reported as "CAD model invalid". valid. An invalid sequence may occur, for example, if a curve sketch command is not followed by a 3D extrusion. This tends to occur more often for longer command sequences.

The ARE-Net models trained on the simple datasets surpass the one trained on the complex data. The random variation of perspectives and number of input images during training represent a harder problem which did not provide an advantage in this comparison.

Table 2. Quantitative results of CAD reconstruction of the presented ARE-Net, Deep-CAD with point cloud network and the DeepCAD auto-encoder.

Method	ACC_{cmd} ↑	ACC_{param} ↑	median CD ↓	CAD model invalid ↓
ARE-Net FC (simple data)	92.14%	74.2%	$4.21 \cdot 10^3$	18.1%
ARE-Net GRU (simple data)	**92.83%**	**78.8%**	**$1.75 \cdot 10^3$**	18.4%
ARE-Net GRU (complex data)	92.78%	74.6%	$4.07 \cdot 10^3$	18.8%
DeepCAD PointNet++	84.95%	74.2%	$10.3 \cdot 10^3$	**12.1%**
Baseline:				
DeepCAD auto-encoder	99.50%	98.0%	$0.75 \cdot 10^3$	2.7%

The accuracy on the test set of the ARE-Net with GRU pooling is plotted in Fig. 3 as a function of the number of input images. Above 13 images the accuracy barely increases, which is in line with [36] describing 12 images as a useful lower bound, beyond which the accuracy of their network levels.

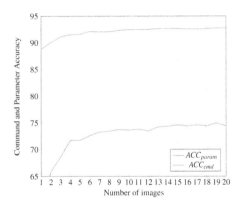

Fig. 3. Accuracy results for different numbers of input images passed into the ARE-Net using the complete object test set.

Figure 4 compares the reconstructed geometries. The following observations can be made: A variety of reconstructions is quite successful. Often times the network seems to "comprehend" the basic form of the shape present, but lacks the ability to exactly reproduce it quantitatively. For example, regarding the yellow object in the bottom right corner of Fig. 4, it is clear that the model has recognized the basic shape of the plate and manages to reproduce it quite well. It also extracts the correct number of holes but still fails to reproduce their size and exact position.

Conversely, a fraction of about 18% of more complex ground-truth models could not be successfully reconstructed, some examples are show in Fig. 5. Visual comparison shows that these models are generally more complex than their valid counterparts, e.g. containing holes of different diameters or extrusion into different spatial directions.

Fig. 4. Random selection from the test set of representative good (green) and poor (yellow) reconstruction results. The model predictions are shown on the left, next to their corresponding ground-truth models. (Color figure online)

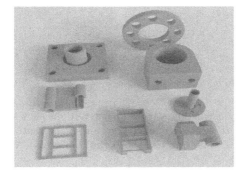

Fig. 5. Random selection from the test set of ground-truth models that could not be successfully reconstructed.

Two representative photos of our real world objects and their reconstructions are shown in Fig. 6. The reconstructed CAD sequence of the cardbox is a perfect cube with equal side lengths, up to the 8-bit precision. As for the more complicated camera mount, a valid CAD model could be created from the photos. However, only the basic L-shape is represented by the model. The relative dimensions are inaccurate and details like the screw holes are completely missing. Moreover, the reconstruction exhibits a prominent elongated bar at the bottom which is not at all present in the original model. This second real-world reconstruction was hence only partially successful.

6   Discussion and Conclusions

We developed a novel method for end-to-end generation of CAD sequences directly from photographic images using an encoder-decoder network architecture. Models were trained in a two-stage approach on 2D renderings of simulated

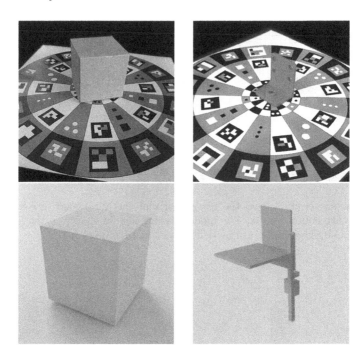

Fig. 6. Real object reconstruction attempts: The top row show selected photos of the two objects placed on the photogrammetry ground-plane (left: cardboard box, right: camera mount angle). The bottom row shows the respective CAD reconstructions.

CAD objects and positively evaluated. A first proof-of-concept of the method on real photos was realized.

Two different multi-view pooling stages were compared: a feed-forward fully-connected network (FCN) and a gated recurrent unit (GRU). A number of hyper-parameters were extensively optimized. Our results show that the additional complexity introduced by the GRU pays off by producing a significant improvement in all three accuracy metrics. Moreover, the GRU takes in the individual images one after the other such that the number of input images can be handled more flexibly. Our experiments confirm the earlier finding [36] that around 12 different views of an object can be considered a practical lower bound, with little improvement above that number.

Comparing our CAD models reconstructed from rendered images of the test set to reconstructions from 3D point-clouds by the state-of-the art PointNet++ encoder, our encoders successfully created valid CAD sequences in more than 80% of the cases which is lower than the success rate of the point-cloud encoder. Regarding the accuracy measures, our encoders outperformed the point-cloud encoder by a large margin.

Most importantly, our work establishes the basic feasibility of image-based reverse engineering of 3D CAD models by neural networks. In future applications this might reduce the amount of time-consuming work of highly trained engineers or enable untrained laymen to work with CAD technologies for 3D printing previously inaccessible without specialized training.

Current limitations of the approach include that the length of CAD sequences is still limited to 60 commands, hence only supporting relatively simple objects. Also our representation is limited to planar and cylindrical surfaces, while many real-world objects may include more flexible triangle meshes or spline representations.

Furthermore, the exact position and size of object details - especially small holes - must be improved for practical applications. The loss function used to train the DeepCAD decoder network penalizes deviations of the CAD parameters but does not contain a distance metric [44]. We believe that an end-to-end training of the complete model may improve these results, allowing for more specialized loss functions to get a more direct handle on the quantitative sequence parameters.

Future work should also focus on improving the image rendering of the training data. This may include physics-based rendering techniques such as ray-tracing to better simulate real-world cases and the incorporation of reflections, image blur and noise to better mimic an actual picture taken by the end-user. Data augmentation by different backgrounds and model textures should also be considered. Just like the camera view angles, the distance and translation of the object should also be varied. A fine-tuning of the model parameters training with a (limited) set of real-world photos of 3D-printed objects from given CAD models could also be pursued. Finally different backbone and/or pooling architectures, such as attention based techniques could be explored going forward.

Generally the direction proposed in this work seems promising. It will be interesting to see what this or similar approaches will lead to down the line. One may predict that experts and consumers might soon be using parametric, CAD generating 3D-scanning-applications, just as naturally as optical character recognition (OCR) is used today, saving countless hours of repetitive work and providing unpreceded possibilities of interaction and creation in this three-dimensional world.

Acknowledgements. We would like to thank Rundi Wu and his co-workers for openly sharing their ground-braking DeepCAD work and providing extensive support materials such as their dataset, the generative CAD decoder, the point-cloud encoder and evaluation metrics.

References

1. Achlioptas, P., Diamanti, O., Mitliagkas, I., Guibas, L.: Learning representations and generative models for 3D point clouds. In: International Conference on Machine Learning, pp. 40–49. PMLR (2018)
2. Agarwal, N., Yoon, S.E., Gopi, M.: Learning Embedding of 3D models with Quadric Loss, July 2019. http://arxiv.org/abs/1907.10250, arXiv:1907.10250arXiv:1907.10250 [cs]

3. Autodesk-Support: Which point cloud file formats can autocad import? (2022). https://www.autodesk.com/support/technical/article/caas/sfdcarticles/sfdcarticles/Which-point-cloud-file-formats-can-AutoCAD-import.html. Accessed 18 July 2023

4. Boessenecker, R.: The Coastal Paleontologist, Atlantic edition: photogrammetry turntable backgrounds - free to use, June 2020. https://coastalpaleo.blogspot.com/2020/06/photogrammetry-turntable-backgrounds.html. Accessed 25 Apr 2022

5. Budroni, A., Boehm, J.: Automated 3d reconstruction of interiors from point clouds. Int. J. Archit. Comput. **8**(1), 55–73 (2010)

6. Cai, R., et al.: Learning gradient fields for shape generation. In: Vedaldi, A., Bischof, H., Brox, T., Frahm, J.M. (eds.) Computer Vision – ECCV 2020. ECCV 2020. LNCS, vol. 12348, pp. 364–381. Springer, Cham (2020). https://doi.org/10.1007/978-3-030-58580-8_22

7. Cho, K., et al.: Learning phrase representations using RNN encoder-decoder for statistical machine translation. In: Proceedings of the 2014 Conference on Empirical Methods in Natural Language Processing (EMNLP), pp. 1724–1734. Association for Computational Linguistics, Doha, Qatar (2014). https://doi.org/10.3115/v1/D14-1179, http://aclweb.org/anthology/D14-1179

8. Fan, H., Su, H., Guibas, L.: A point set generation network for 3D object reconstruction from a single image. In: 2017 IEEE Conference on Computer Vision and Pattern Recognition (CVPR), pp. 2463–2471. IEEE, Honolulu, HI, July 2017. https://doi.org/10.1109/CVPR.2017.264, http://ieeexplore.ieee.org/document/8099747/

9. Ganin, Y., Bartunov, S., Li, Y., Keller, E., Saliceti, S.: Computer-aided design as language. In: Ranzato, M., Beygelzimer, A., Dauphin, Y., Liang, P.S., Vaughan, J.W. (eds.) Advances in Neural Information Processing Systems, vol. 34, pp. 5885–5897. Curran Associates, Inc. (2021). https://proceedings.neurips.cc/paper/2021/file/2e92962c0b6996add9517e4242ea9bdc-Paper.pdf

10. Groueix, T., Fisher, M., Kim, V.G., Russell, B.C., Aubry, M.: A papier-mache approach to learning 3D surface generation. In: 2018 IEEE/CVF Conference on Computer Vision and Pattern Recognition, pp. 216–224. IEEE, Salt Lake City, UT, USA, June 2018. https://doi.org/10.1109/CVPR.2018.00030, https://ieeexplore.ieee.org/document/8578128/

11. He, K., Zhang, X., Ren, S., Sun, J.: Deep residual learning for image recognition. In: 2016 IEEE Conference on Computer Vision and Pattern Recognition (CVPR), pp. 770–778. IEEE, Las Vegas, NV, USA, June 2016. https://doi.org/10.1109/CVPR.2016.90, http://ieeexplore.ieee.org/document/7780459/

12. Insafutdinov, E., Dosovitskiy, A.: Unsupervised learning of shape and pose with differentiable point clouds. Adv. Neural Inf. Process. Syst. **31** (2018)

13. Jayaraman, P.K., et al.: UV-Net: learning from boundary representations, April 2021. http://arxiv.org/abs/2006.10211, arXiv:2006.10211 [cs]

14. Jiang, Y., Ji, D., Han, Z., Zwicker, M.: Sdfdiff: differentiable rendering of signed distance fields for 3D shape optimization. In: Proceedings of the IEEE/CVF Conference on Computer Vision and Pattern Recognition, pp. 1251–1261 (2020)

15. Kim, C., Lee, J., Cho, M.: Fully automated registration of 3D cad model with point cloud from construction site. In: Proceedings of the 28th International Symposium on Automation and Robotics in Construction, ISARC 2011, pp. 917–922 (2011)

16. Lambourne, J.G., et al.: BRepNet: a topological message passing system for solid models. In: 2021 IEEE/CVF Conference on Computer Vision and Pattern Recognition (CVPR), pp. 12768–12777. IEEE, Nashville, TN, USA,

June 2021. https://doi.org/10.1109/CVPR46437.2021.01258, https://ieeexplore. ieee.org/document/9578870/

17. Li, C., Pan, H., Bousseau, A., Mitra, N.J.: Sketch2CAD: sequential CAD modeling by sketching in context. ACM Trans. Graph. **39**(6), 1–14 (2020). https://doi.org/ 10.1145/3414685.3417807, https://dl.acm.org/doi/10.1145/3414685.3417807

18. Liao, Y., Donne, S., Geiger, A.: Deep marching cubes: learning explicit surface representations. In: 2018 IEEE/CVF Conference on Computer Vision and Pattern Recognition, pp. 2916–2925. IEEE, Salt Lake City, UT, June 2018. https://doi. org/10.1109/CVPR.2018.00308, https://ieeexplore.ieee.org/document/8578406/

19. Liu, J.: An adaptive process of reverse engineering from point clouds to cad models. Int. J. Comput. Integr. Manuf. **33**(9), 840–858 (2020)

20. Liu, X., Xu, F., Sun, Y., Zhang, H., Chen, Z.: Convolutional recurrent neural networks for observation-centered plant identification. J. Electr. Comput. Eng. **2018**, 1–7 (2018). https://doi.org/10.1155/2018/9373210, https://www.hindawi. com/journals/jece/2018/9373210/

21. Mo, K., et al.: StructureNet: hierarchical graph networks for 3D shape generation. ACM Trans. Graph. **38**(6), 1–19 (2019). https://doi.org/10.1145/3355089.3356527, https://dl.acm.org/doi/10.1145/3355089.3356527

22. Mohammadi, S.S., Wang, Y., Bue, A.D.: Pointview-GCN: 3D shape classification with multi-view point clouds. In: 2021 IEEE International Conference on Image Processing (ICIP), pp. 3103–3107. IEEE, Anchorage, AK, USA, September 2021. https://doi.org/10.1109/ICIP42928.2021.9506426, https://ieeexplore. ieee.org/document/9506426/

23. Nash, C., Ganin, Y., Eslami, S.M.A., Battaglia, P.W.: PolyGen: An Autoregressive Generative Model of 3D Meshes, February 2020. http://arxiv.org/abs/2002.10880, number: arXiv:2002.10880 [cs, stat]

24. Onshape, P.I.: Onshape | Product Development Platform. https://www.onshape. com/en/, https://www.onshape.com/. Accessed 12 Apr 2022

25. Optuna, P.N.I.: Optuna - A hyperparameter optimization framework. https:// optuna.org/, https://optuna.org/. Accessed 24 July 2022

26. Pan, J., Han, X., Chen, W., Tang, J., Jia, K.: Deep mesh reconstruction from single RGB images via topology modification networks. In: Proceedings of the IEEE/CVF International Conference on Computer Vision, pp. 9964–9973 (2019)

27. Para, W., et al.: SketchGen: generating constrained CAD aketches. In: Ranzato, M., Beygelzimer, A., Dauphin, Y., Liang, P.S., Vaughan, J.W. (eds.) Advances in Neural Information Processing Systems, vol. 34, pp. 5077–5088. Curran Associates, Inc. (2021). https://proceedings.neurips.cc/paper/2021/file/ 28891cb4ab421830acc36b1f5fd6c91e-Paper.pdf

28. Park, J.J., Florence, P., Straub, J., Newcombe, R., Lovegrove, S.: Deepsdf: learning continuous signed distance functions for shape representation. In: Proceedings of the IEEE/CVF Conference on Computer Vision and Pattern Recognition, pp. 165–174 (2019)

29. Pascanu, R., Mikolov, T., Bengio, Y.: On the difficulty of training Recurrent Neural Networks, February 2013. http://arxiv.org/abs/1211.5063, arXiv:1211.5063 [cs]

30. programmersought.com: Chamfer Distance - Programmer Sought. https://programmersought.com/article/11413715914/#3D_16, https:// programmersought.com/article/11413715914/#3D_16. Accessed 10 May 2022

31. Qi, C.R., Su, H., NieBner, M., Dai, A., Yan, M., Guibas, L.J.: Volumetric and multiview CNNs for object classification on 3D data. In: 2016 IEEE Conference on Computer Vision and Pattern Recognition (CVPR), pp. 5648–5656. IEEE, Las Vegas,

NV, USA, June 2016. https://doi.org/10.1109/CVPR.2016.609, http://ieeexplore. ieee.org/document/7780978/

32. Qi, C.R., Yi, L., Su, H., Guibas, L.J.: Pointnet++: deep hierarchical feature learning on point sets in a metric space. Adv. Neural Inf. Process. Syst. **30** (2017)

33. Rukhovich, D., Vorontsova, A., Konushin, A.: ImVoxelNet: Image to Voxels Projection for Monocular and Multi-View General-Purpose 3D Object Detection, October 2021. http://arxiv.org/abs/2106.01178, arXiv:2106.01178 [cs]

34. Sharma, G., Liu, D., Maji, S., Kalogerakis, E., Chaudhuri, S., Měch, R.: ParSeNet: a parametric surface fitting network for 3D point clouds, September 2020. http://arxiv.org/abs/2003.12181, arXiv:2003.12181 [cs]

35. Shimon, U.: The interpretation of structure from motion. Proc. R. Soc. Lond. Ser. B. Biol. Sci. **203**(1153), 405–426 (1979). https://doi.org/10.1098/rspb.1979.0006, https://royalsocietypublishing.org/doi/10.1098/rspb.1979.0006

36. Su, H., Maji, S., Kalogerakis, E., Learned-Miller, E.: Multi-view convolutional neural networks for 3D shape recognition. In: 2015 IEEE International Conference on Computer Vision (ICCV), pp. 945–953. IEEE, Santiago, Chile, December 2015. https://doi.org/10.1109/ICCV.2015.114, http://ieeexplore.ieee.org/document/7410471/

37. Su, J.C., Gadelha, M., Wang, R., Maji, S.: A deeper look at 3D shape classifiers. In: Leal-Taixé, L., Roth, S. (eds.) Computer Vision – ECCV 2018 Workshops, LNCS, vol. 11131, pp. 645–661. Springer, Cham (2019). https://doi.org/10.1007/978-3-030-11015-4_49

38. Wang, N., Zhang, Y., Li, Z., Fu, Y., Liu, W., Jiang, Y.G.: Pixel2Mesh: generating 3D mesh models from single RGB images. In: Ferrari, V., Hebert, M., Sminchisescu, C., Weiss, Y. (eds.) Computer Vision – ECCV 2018, LNCS, vol. 11215, pp. 55–71. Springer, Cham (2018). https://doi.org/10.1007/978-3-030-01252-6_4

39. Wang, T., Zhu, X., Pang, J., Lin, D.: FCOS3D: Fully Convolutional One-Stage Monocular 3D Object Detection, September 2021. http://arxiv.org/abs/2104.10956, arXiv:2104.10956 [cs]

40. Wang, X., et al.: PIE-NET: Parametric Inference of Point Cloud Edges, October 2020. http://arxiv.org/abs/2007.04883, arXiv:2007.04883 [cs]

41. Willis, K.D.D., Jayaraman, P.K., Lambourne, J.G., Chu, H., Pu, Y.: Engineering sketch generation for computer-aided design. In: 2021 IEEE/CVF Conference on Computer Vision and Pattern Recognition Workshops (CVPRW), pp. 2105–2114. IEEE, Nashville, TN, USA, June 2021. https://doi.org/10.1109/CVPRW53098.2021.00239, https://ieeexplore.ieee.org/document/9523001/

42. Wu, J., Zhang, C., Xue, T., Freeman, W.T., Tenenbaum, J.B.: Learning a Probabilistic Latent Space of Object Shapes via 3D Generative-Adversarial Modeling, January 2017. http://arxiv.org/abs/1610.07584, arXiv:1610.07584 [cs]

43. Wu, R.: DeepCAD - code for our ICCV 2021 paper DeepCAD: A Deep Generative Network for Computer-Aided Design Models, June 2022. https://github.com/ChrisWu1997/DeepCAD. Accessed 24 June 2022

44. Wu, R., Xiao, C., Zheng, C.: DeepCAD: a deep generative network for computer-aided design models. In: 2021 IEEE/CVF International Conference on Computer Vision (ICCV), pp. 6752–6762. IEEE, Montreal, QC, Canada, October 2021. https://doi.org/10.1109/ICCV48922.2021.00670, https://ieeexplore.ieee.org/document/9710909/

45. Xu, X., Peng, W., Cheng, C.Y., Willis, K.D., Ritchie, D.: Inferring CAD modeling sequences using zone graphs. In: 2021 IEEE/CVF Conference on Computer Vision and Pattern Recognition (CVPR), pp. 6058–6066. IEEE, Nashville,

TN, USA, June 2021. https://doi.org/10.1109/CVPR46437.2021.00600, https://ieeexplore.ieee.org/document/9577867/

46. Yagubbayli, F., Tonioni, A., Tombari, F.: LegoFormer: Transformers for Block-by-Block Multi-view 3D Reconstruction, June 2021. http://arxiv.org/abs/2106.12102, arXiv:2106.12102 [cs]

47. Yan, X., Yang, J., Yumer, E., Guo, Y., Lee, H.: Perspective transformer nets: learning single-view 3D object reconstruction without 3D supervision. Adv. Neural Inf. Process. Syst. **29** (2016)

48. Yang, G., Huang, X., Hao, Z., Liu, M.Y., Belongie, S., Hariharan, B.: Point-Flow: 3D point cloud generation with continuous normalizing flows. In: 2019 IEEE/CVF International Conference on Computer Vision (ICCV), pp. 4540–4549. IEEE, Seoul, Korea (South), October 2019. https://doi.org/10.1109/ICCV.2019.00464, https://ieeexplore.ieee.org/document/9010395/

49. Yang, Y., Feng, C., Shen, Y., Tian, D.: FoldingNet: point cloud auto-encoder via deep grid deformation. In: 2018 IEEE/CVF Conference on Computer Vision and Pattern Recognition, pp. 206–215. IEEE, Salt Lake City, UT, June 2018. https://doi.org/10.1109/CVPR.2018.00029, https://ieeexplore.ieee.org/document/8578127/

50. Zreik, M., van Hamersvelt, R.W., Wolterink, J.M., Leiner, T., Viergever, M.A., Isgum, I.: A recurrent CNN for automatic detection and classification of coronary artery plaque and stenosis in coronary CT angiography. IEEE Trans. Med. Imaging **38**(7), 1588–1598 (2019). https://doi.org/10.1109/TMI.2018.2883807, https://ieeexplore.ieee.org/document/8550784/

Characterization of Out-of-distribution Samples from Uncertainty Maps Using Supervised Machine Learning

Lina E. Budde[1]([✉])[ID], Dimitri Bulatov[2][ID], Eva Strauss[2][ID], Kevin Qiu[2][ID], and Dorota Iwaszczuk[1][ID]

[1] Technical University of Darmstadt, Department of Civil and Environmental Engineering, Remote Sensing and Image Analysis, 64287 Darmstadt, Germany
{lina.budde,dorota.iwaszczuk}@tu-darmstadt.de

[2] Scene Analysis Division, Fraunhofer Institute of Optronics, System Technologies and Image Exploitation, 76275 Ettlingen, Germany
{dimitri.bulatov,eva.strauss,kevin.qiu}@iosb.fraunhofer.de

Abstract. The quality of land use maps often refers to the data quality, but distributional uncertainty between training and test data must also be considered. In order to address this uncertainty, we follow the strategy to detect out-of-distribution samples using uncertainty maps. Then, we use supervised machine learning to identify those samples. For the investigations, we use an uncertainty metric adapted from depth maps fusion and Monte-Carlo dropout based predicted probabilities. The results show a correlation between out-of-distribution samples, misclassifications and uncertainty. Thus, on the one hand, out-of-distribution samples are identifiable through uncertainty, on the other hand it is difficult to distinguish between misclassification, anomalies and out-of-distribution.

Keywords: Potsdam dataset · error detection · semantic segmentation

1 Introduction

1.1 Motivation

A major use case of semantic segmentation in remote sensing is the generation of land cover maps. Since these maps serve as a basis for derived products and also political decisions, they must be up-to-date, complete, and trustworthy. While up-to-dateness of the map can be satisfied by the temporal availability of the image data, completeness and trustworthiness mean that the object-related classes correspond to the actual object types in the real world. Hereby, both data and model quality influence the completeness and trustworthiness.

Moreover, completeness in the use of semantic segmentation requires that the world of classes is closed. However, especially while working with high-resolution

Supplementary Information The online version contains supplementary material available at https://doi.org/10.1007/978-3-031-54605-1_17.

data from urban scenes, there are out-of-distribution (OOD) samples and anomalies. These samples are usually unified into a particular class, which is called "clutter", "void", "urban asset", or similar [21,23]. Due to limited reference data, which also may include mislabelings, OOD samples may occur in the test data, but do not belong to any object-specific class in the training samples. Anomalous pixels, in contrast, are present in both, training and test data, but the appearance of anomalous pixels differs from class representing training samples, e.g. image defects.

1.2   Problem Statement

Due to the mixing of OOD and anomalies in a joint heterogeneous "clutter" class, this class is often misclassified. However, anomalies and OOD samples are not the only cause of misclassifications. Thus, reasons for misclassifications are among others: (i) incorrect ground truth labels, (ii) anomalies in the images, (iii) OOD samples or (iv) model overfitting. This mix of different sources of misclassifications makes detection and understanding of OOD samples more complex and without specific labeling, the separation of OOD samples is difficult.

Recently, a publication establishing correlation of OOD, anomalous samples and misclassifications based on uncertainty came out [19]. The next logical step would be establishing a workflow allowing for prediction on whether an uncertainty corresponds to an OOD sample, to a misclassification, or to a false alarm.

To do this, it is crucial to understand the two different types of errors. First, not all uncertain predictions are incorrect nor anomalous (false positives, error type 1) and second, not all misclassifications are necessarily uncertain (false negatives, error type 2). To address both types of errors, error detection strategies depend on the task [19]. When undetected misclassification is costly (as in the case of credit card fraud), one must choose a threshold for the false-positive error generously and put more effort into interactive detection of the false-negative errors. Contrarily, if addressing possible misclassifications is more costly, as in surveillance tasks, then too high false alarm rates are undesirable [25]. In addition to uncertainty, other attributes can be helpful in characterizing OOD samples and supporting their identification.

1.3   Our Solution in a Nutshell

The aim of this work is to characterize OOD samples for identification with different machine learning methods. In addition, two semantic segmentation models are compared in terms of their ability to identify OOD samples. We assume, the OOD samples are part of a "clutter" class in the data. After inference with Monte-Carlo dropout [8], a uncertainty map is computed and thresholded. The threshold value is derived automatically to segment the pixels exhibiting higher uncertainties into connected components. These components have radiometric and geometric features, which, in turn, represent an input for conventional classifiers such as Random Forest [3] or Import Vector Machines [30]. The classifier outputs binary labels for regions to belong to the possible OOD samples and anomalies or to be misclassified.

The remainder of the paper begins with the related work in Sect. 2, followed by the methodology description in Sect. 3. Section 4 describes the experimental setup that provides the basis for the results in Sect. 5. Finally, Sect. 6 contains conclusions and future work.

2   Related Work

The deep learning methods are very powerful, but they have the dubious reputation to be black boxes taking rather non-transparent decisions. Therefore, in recent years, deep learning models have been increasingly evaluated regarding uncertain predictions. This trend can also be observed in the remote sensing domain [4,6,15]. To identify errors and especially find their sources, observing uncertainty is not enough. According to the current literature, this leads to anomaly detection and detection of OOD samples.

Anomaly detection is more of an unsupervised task because we do not know a-priori what the anomaly is [25]. Therefore, architectures specialized in the anomaly detection task are frequently applied [29]. Examples of unsupervised strategies for retrieving anomalies include mixture-model-based [11], density-based and reconstruction-based approaches [29]. However, semi-supervised or even fully supervised methods are not completely uncommon. For example, [24] investigate a component based on so-called meta-classification in the autonomous driving domain and [27] use Random Forest (RF) to classify thermal anomalies versus shortcomings of a thermal simulator.

The survey of [10] points out that in addition to model and data uncertainties, there is also a distributional uncertainty. This distributional uncertainty is related to OOD samples. To solve the difficulty of distinguishing between in-domain and OOD samples, several authors cited in [10] identify these samples by perturbing the input data [16], or analyzing the softmax probabilities [13], possibly with relaxations of the neural network model, for example using dropouts [4]. To overcome the issues the limited amount of ground truth information and the closed world assumption, the OOD detection becomes important [9,26].

Information about errors and causes, such as OOD samples, are important to improve the quality of land cover maps. However, the results of the semantic segmentation are desired as well [1]. To our knowledge, there is no approach that provides semantic segmentation and at the same time methods to identify the OOD samples in remote sensing. Thus, our contribution contains:

1. dual task pipeline with semantic segmentation and uncertainty mapping,
2. quantitative analysis of the correlation between uncertainty and possible errors and
3. characterization and identification of OOD samples using machine learning.

3   Methodology

By using Monte Carlo dropout, the average softmax outputs of an input image over multiple inferences can be interpreted as probabilities [8]. The resulting

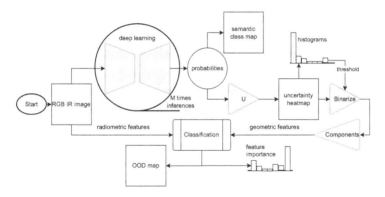

Fig. 1. The flowchart visualizes the processing steps. Based on the probabilities from the deep learning models, the semantic map, and the uncertainty heatmap are generated. By analyzing the histogram distribution, the heatmap is binarized, and the connected components are selected and assigned to a class OOD.

varying inferences can be evaluated in two ways: the variance between the inferences and, from the mean of the inferences, the ambiguities of the class probabilities. For the identification of the OOD regions, we use such ambiguities. Ideally, the maximum probability is near one while all other classes' probabilities are near zero. The class with the maximum probability is selected for the semantic segmentation task. In contrast, if the class probabilities are uniformly distributed, the class decision is subject to the greatest uncertainty. According to Fig. 1, we determine the deviations from the ideal case by calculating the related uncertainty (Sect. 3.1). To characterize and identify the OOD samples, a meta-classification on the component level is performed using Random Forest with geometric and radiometric features (Sect. 3.3). To use such components for classification, the uncertainties are binarized by the histogram-based threshold (Sect. 3.2). For evaluation, the labeling described in Sect. 3.4 allows to detect the errors of the uncertainty and OOD maps.

3.1 Uncertainty Determination

In contrast to using common uncertainty metrics such as entropy [4,6] propose a confidence metric which was originally developed in the context of depth maps fusion [18] and adapted by us to measure uncertainty [19]. The confidence has a value range from zero to $\frac{1}{C}$ where C denotes the number of classes. By subtracting the confidence values from one, the confidence is interpreted as uncertainty

$$U = 1 - \left(\sum_{c=1}^{C} \exp \left[\frac{-(s - \min_{c \in C}(s))^2}{Q_{0.75} \left[0.5 \cdot (s - \min_{c \in C}(s)) \right]^2} \right] \right)^{-1}, \tag{1}$$

where $Q_{0.75}$ is the 75%-quantile and adjusts the uncertainty values. Further,

$$s = s_{c,h,w} = \min(-\log_2(\overline{P}_{c,h,w}), 2048) \tag{2}$$

is used in (1) using the truncated negative logarithm of the averaged predicted probabilities for each class c, pixel position h and w. The upper bound 2048 avoids numerical problems when using 16-bit values.

3.2   Histogram Analysis

For analyzing the correlation between the uncertainty values from (1) with OOD samples and misclassifications, the corresponding distribution is determined. To calculate the distribution, we represent the uncertainty values as a discrete set $X = \{x_0, x_1, \ldots, x_N\}$, whereby $x_0 = \min(U)$ and $x_N = \max(U)$ with U from 1. For $n \in \{1, \ldots, N\}$, we have $x_n = x_0 + nh$ with bin width h and the number of bins $N + 1$. Let $f, g : x_n \in X \mapsto \mathbb{R}$ be two functions describing a histogram with bin width h, chosen in the way that $x_N = \max(U)$, and the number of bins $N + 1$. Hereby, f represents the distribution of mask pixels which are related to OOD samples or misclassifications and g the complement mask pixels. The bin height is defined from the frequency m as density

$$f(x_n) = \frac{m_n}{\sum_i m_n \cdot h} \tag{3}$$

and for g analogously. We call x_k an intersection of f and g, and it is defined by the change of the sign

$$\Leftrightarrow$$
$$\exists k : \; f(x_{k-1}) \geq g(x_{k-1}) \wedge f(x_k) < g(x_k)$$
$$\vee \tag{4}$$
$$\exists k : \; f(x_{k-1}) \leq g(x_{k-1}) \wedge f(x_k) > g(x_k).$$

Based on [19], the first intersection x_{k^*} is used as a threshold for binarization of the uncertainty.

3.3   Connected Component Analysis

Based on the binary classification with the threshold from (4), median filter and morphological opening is applied to avoid isolated pixels. The resulting uncertainty map is segmented based on connected components. For each component, features are computed and used to characterize the different error sources in a machine-learning framework.

The problem is non-linear and the features correlate strongly. In order to cope with the non-linearity, the RF classifier [3] is known to be quite suitable; it can also cope with correlated features to a certain extent. For example, if one uses a few features for one decision tree and increases the number of decision trees, then the trees are supposed to be less correlated and the overall accuracy

Table 1. If the reference mask and the uncertainty map is unequal this correspond with error type 1 and 2.

	$\neg M$	M
$\neg B$	background	error type 2 (false negative)
B	error type 1 (false positive)	identified

increases. This strategy, theoretically well-founded in [14] and applied, among others, in [27], has been adopted in our work as well. The classification of the components leads to a feature importance, used to characterize the OOD map, which shows the overlap between uncertainty and "clutter" class.

We are motivated to compare RF with a classifier that is able to cope with correlated features. To this end, the Import Vector Machines classifier (IVM) was applied. This classifier was developed by [30] and represents an alternative to Support Vector Machines in the sense that the output is probabilistic and is therefore comparable with that of RF. We used the implementation of [22] with radial-bases functions for kernel trick. The results are shown in Supplementaries.

3.4 Evaluation

For evaluating the distributions similarity, the Kullback-Leibler (KL) divergence is used at the maximum density of the mask class $x_{\max}$ from the histograms in (3) [2]

$$\mathrm{KL} = g(x_{\max}) \cdot \log\left(\frac{g(x_{\max})}{f(x_{\max})}\right) - g(x_{\max}) + f(x_{\max}) \tag{5}$$

$$x_{\max} = \arg\max_{x \in X} f(x). \tag{6}$$

Furthermore, for the evaluation of the resulting maps, that means the semantic segmentation, the uncertainty, and the OOD maps, we use the confusion matrix. This confusion matrix leads to F1-scores and overall accuracy, but also to the amount of occurrences of error type 1 and 2. Let B be a binary uncertainty map based on the threshold from (4) and M a mask used as reference. The results of the confusion matrix are labeled accordingly with Table 1. Furthermore, the Cohen's kappa coefficient is used to measure the correlation between detected OOD samples and clutter.

4 Experimental Setup

The presented methodology is tested on the ISPRS Potsdam dataset [23]. Before using this data for deep learning, the sample images are prepared as in [19].

4.1   Dataset Preparation

First, the dataset is split into training, validation, and test data. The multi-spectral images with channels red, green, blue, and near-infrared are used. However, to process images of size 6000 × 6000 pixels, they are divided into small patches of 512 × 512 pixels. The test data are tiled by an overlap of 50 pixels. In the reference, six classes are defined: impervious surface, building, low vegetation, tree, car, and clutter. In this contribution we are mainly interested in the latter class which contains the OOD samples. In total, 818 training and 243 validation patches are randomly selected. For testing, a total number of 1350 patches is used.

4.2   Deep Learning Models

For the experiments, we use a U-Net [20] and DeepLab V3+ [5] model, which is referred to as DeepLab in this work. For both models, a ResNet 101 encoder [12] with ImageNet [7] initialization is used. To be able to use multi-spectral images with more than three channels, the first convolution layer is changed accordingly. For training, the AdamW optimizer [17] and the cross entropy loss function are used. The hyperparameter settings are a learning rate of 0.001, a weight decay of 0.01, a batch size of 9, a dropout rate of 0.5, and 300 epochs. The SMP Toolbox [28] is used for the model construction. Data augmentation is applied with 90°, 180° and 270° rotations. During testing, we evaluate the models with 100 Monte-Carlo inferences.

4.3   Evaluation Strategy

For each model, two different masks are used to generate the histogram distributions: the clutter pixels extracted from the ground truth and the model predictions compared with the ground truth, representing misclassifications. In addition, we select 75% of our connected components as training data and the rest as test data. For feature extraction, we use the multi-spectral image channels and entropy features with four different kernel sizes as radiometric features. The mean value and variance over all pixels lying in this component are calculated. To these radiometric features, we add two geometric properties of the connected component, namely area and eccentricity, yielding 18 features in total. Training data is further balanced in order for the learner not to overfit towards the most frequent class. The ratio between the number of training examples of the most and least frequent class was set to 1, 1.5, 2.5, and 4. The components are evaluated with RF using 10, 25, and 50 trees.

5   Results and Discussion

5.1   Semantic Segmentation

For the semantic segmentation task, both models provide similar quantitative results (Table 2). Looking closely at the differences between U-Net and DeepLab

Table 2. The quality of the semantic segmentation is evaluated by the overall accuracy and the F1 values of the test dataset using the U-Net and DeepLab model. In addition, the class frequency from the ground truth is presented. The results are given as a percentage value.

model	overall accuracy	impervious surfaces	building	low vegetation	tree	car	clutter
ground truth frequency		38.4	24.9	16.5	12.3	2.2	5.6
U-Net	86.2	90.4	**92.9**	80.6	**81.1**	**89.8**	48.8
DeepLab	**86.5**	**90.5**	92.8	**81.5**	80.9	88.2	**53.1**

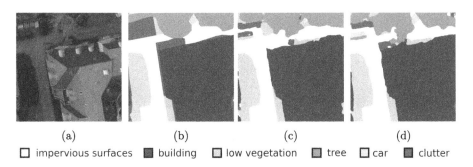

(a)   (b)   (c)   (d)

☐ impervious surfaces ■ building ☐ low vegetation ■ tree ☐ car ■ clutter

Fig. 2. Visualization of the semantic segmentation: (a) RGB input, (b) ground truth, (c) prediction from U-Net, and (d) prediction from DeepLab.

for the different classes, U-Net performs better (+1.6%) for the car class, which is the least frequent class and can be considered as a small object class with high-contrast and high in-class variation. In contrast, in the clutter class (red pixels), DeepLab outperforms U-Net by 4%. The differences in the other classes are below 1%. Looking at the clutter class in the example displayed in Fig. 2, anomalies at the building edges represented by facade pixels could not well predicted (Fig. 2c, 2d) compared to the ground truth (Fig. 2b). Although the F1 score for clutter is better for DeepLab, U-Net predicts the garbage cans better in this example. This shows the difficulty of prediction of OOD samples and anomalies. For this reason, the following analyses focus on this clutter class which contains the OOD samples.

5.2 Uncertainty Analysis

As mentioned in Sect. 3, the mean value can be calculated from the standard deviations per class from several inferences. In our results, this mean is 0.011 for DeepLab and 0.005 for U-Net. Therefore, the predicted probabilities can be considered reliable.

The class prediction, in contrast, has ambiguities represented by the uncertainties from (1). The relationship between uncertainty and clutter is displayed by the density distributions in Fig. 3. The highest uncertainty values correlate

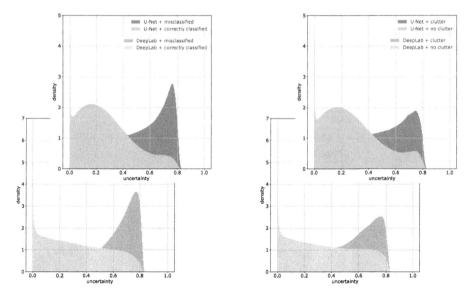

Fig. 3. The distributions of the U-Net and DeepLab uncertainties with the misclassification mask are presented on the left and with the clutter mask as in [19] on the right. The imbalance of the data is considered by calculating density.

Table 3. The KL divergence measures the similarity of the uncertainty distributions for U-Net and DeepLab. The intersection point at the misclassification mask is used as a threshold for the connected component formation.

model	KL clutter mask	KL misclassification mask	threshold
U-Net	0.95	3.19	0.434
DeepLab	1.01	3.62	0.508

with clutter. However, the same correlation occurs between uncertainty and misclassifications. Thus, clutter and misclassification are also correlated. Even if the peak density of uncertainty for misclassified pixels is higher compared with the clutter. For both, clutter and misclassification masks, the maximum density increases when using DeepLab. The KL divergences between the distributions are given in Table 3. Although the density increases, the lower divergence indicates a more similar distribution of clutter versus no-clutter and correctly versus misclassified pixels for U-Net. Independent of the model, data related misclassifications are often characterized by high uncertainty. However, the source of the misclassification, i.e. wrong ground truth label, OOD sample, or anomaly, can hardly be distinguished based on the distribution.

However, in the example in Fig. 4a and 4c the highest uncertainties occur in the predicted clutter area and the object borders. By the threshold values from Table 3 and the labeling principle from Table 1 the uncertainty maps are evaluated. Thus, Fig. 4b and 4d visualizes the errors by using only the uncertainty

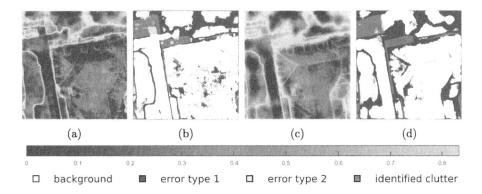

Fig. 4. The uncertainty values for U-Net (a) and DeepLab (c) are evaluated with clutter mask (b) and (d), respectively. Type 1 (blue) and type 2 (yellow) errors occur in both models. The green regions represent the area where clutter appears together with high uncertainty. (Color figure online)

Table 4. Proportion of errors represented as percentage of the uncertainty maps. Differences to the sum of 100 is caused by rounding.

mask	model	background	error type 1	error type 2	identified
misclassification	U-Net	71	19	4	7
misclassification	DeepLab	66	24	3	8
clutter	U-Net	72	22	3	3
clutter	DeepLab	66	28	2	3

values for the OOD identification. Applying the clutter mask, all other classes are assigned to the background. Due to high uncertainty, areas with misleading clutter regions (error type 1, blue) exist. In contrast, low uncertainties leads to missing clutter identification (error type 2, yellow). The correctly identified clutter regions (green) have higher completeness in DeepLab in this example. However, with DeepLab, larger contiguous error type 1 regions form.

Evaluated quantitatively, 3% of the clutter pixels cannot be identified via their uncertainty with U-Net (error type 2 in Table 4). With DeepLab, the proportion of error type 2 pixels decreases at the expense of the amount of error type 1 and correct background class. In contrast to error type 2, error type 1 is very high with a proportion of up to 28 %. Thus, to reduce the type 1 error and analyze the characteristics of the misclassified and clutter pixels in more detail, the connected component analysis is used.

5.3 Connected Component Analysis

The results from the component-based classification in Table 5 show that U-Net and DeepLab models correlate moderately with the reference masks in the assessment of clutter pixels and quite low in the assessment of the incorrect pixels. The

Table 5. Selection of results from the meta-classification. We specify the number of trees in Random Forest classifier. By OA and κ, we denote Overall Accuracy and Cohen's kappa coefficient, respectively. All numbers are given in percentages. For the results of all configurations, including import vector machines, see Supplementary Material (Table S1).

mask	model	metric	balancing factor 1			balancing 1.5			balancing 2.5		
			10 Trees	25 T	50 T	10 T	25 T	50 T	10 T	25 T	50 T
clutter	DeepLab	OA	66.4	66.1	66.1	73.6	74.3	74.8	81.8	83.1	83.8
		κ	14.9	16.0	16.7	17.9	20.8	**21.2**	16.8	18.9	20.4
clutter	U-Net	OA	67.1	66.8	67.1	74.9	75.5	75.9	82.4	82.8	83.3
		κ	18.5	20.6	21.2	19.7	22.0	22.8	22.1	23.2	**23.8**
misclassification	DeepLab	OA	59.3	60.5	62.0	65.5	66.3	67.6	67.8	69.5	70.0
		κ	8.5	**11.3**	13.4	8.9	8.6	9.2	5.5	6.4	5.3
misclassification	U-Net	OA	62.7	63.9	64.5	68.1	69.9	70.5	69.2	70.5	71.1
		κ	12.6	16.6	**17.0**	11.3	14.4	14.3	8.8	9.3	9.0

results of U-Net are always slightly higher than that of DeepLab. One problem of lower performance of DeepLab is related to the connected components. Due to the larger size of the components, they include both clutter and no-clutter pixels, which makes a clear assignment difficult.

In addition, we are dealing with extremely unbalanced data: the highest overall accuracies can be achieved by simply assigning all connected components to the "normal" class, which sets κ to zero. Not mentioned in Table 5 is the dependency on the minimum leaf size parameter of RF. Smaller minimum leaf size tends to overfit for the small number of trees while a larger value makes RF more independent of the tree number.

The features used are strongly correlated, which not only exacerbates the overfitting, but also makes it more difficult to assess their importance. Nevertheless, the feature importance values of RF in Fig. 5 show more detailed characteristics of the uncertain regions compared to deep learning results. The variance inside each component is less important than the mean values. The top three features using 50 Trees and the U-Net results are the mean blue, red and near infrared compared to area, mean red and the first mean entropy feature using DeepLab. However, the importance values for all features except eccentricity vary in a range of 0.9 to 2.0 and are thus similar in importance.

Our example (Fig. 6) shows our final predicted clutter map, which contains OOD samples and anomalies. Comparing this predicted map with the RGB input and the corresponding ground truth, this map detected more anomalies correctly as labeled in the ground truth as clutter, for example the distorted tree pixels. However, with the used features the separation between OOD samples and anomalies could not reached.

There are some errors of type 2 that we leave unchecked in this work, but mostly they are close to the correctly identified components. Overall, DeepLab

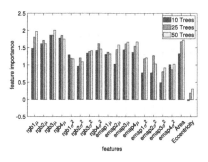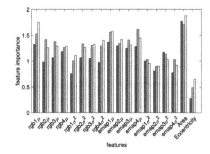

Fig. 5. Feature importance of the 18 different component-based features using RF for U-Net (left) and DeepLab (right) for identification of clutter.

Fig. 6. The RGB, the ground truth, and the predicted clutter map are presented from left to right. The clutter map contains the desired OOD samples as well as anomalies. The green color represents the correctly identified components, the blue components shows the errors of the RF classifier. The true negative and all not used image parts are white background. (Color figure online)

results tend to produce quite large components, which are not of much help while the results of U-Net seem more concordant with the anomalous regions.

6   Conclusion and Future Work

We presented a contribution on detection and analysis of OOD samples. Two goals pursued here were to establish a correlation between the uncertain and OOD samples within a workflow for semantic segmentation as well as their identification using connected component analysis and shallow learning. The first goal could be achieved with the applied deep learning models and the generated uncertainty maps. Significant values for KL divergence in the distributions confirm the correlation between the classification uncertainty and OOD samples and anomalies, represented by clutter pixels. For the second goal, we analyzed the uncertain regions with methods of machine learning. We considered low-level image-based features and Random Forest as conventional classifier. At the current stage of our research, moderate correlations could be established since the values of Cohen's kappa have not exceeded 0.25 for clutter pixels and 0.2 for misclassifications.

To improve the OOD detection in future work, the dependency on very big and inhomogeneously filled with clutter or misclassified pixels should addressed. Thus, applying clustering methods such as super-pixel could generate more categorical components. Further, evaluation of multi-modal data is becoming increasingly popular in remote sensing; thus extending the classifier with additional features derived from 3D data may increase the accuracy. In this paper, we concentrated on the type 1 errors. However, the type 2 errors, that is, possible misclassification despite allegedly certain regions, are equally important and should be tackled in the future. Finally, evaluation on further dataset would provide some clues on the generalizability of the proposed methods.

Acknowledgment. We would like to thank Timo Kullmann for his help during the implementations of the neural networks.

References

1. Bevandić, P., Krešo, I., Oršić, M., Šegvić, S.: Simultaneous semantic segmentation and outlier detection in presence of domain shift. In: Fink, G., Frintrop, S., Jiang, X. (eds.) Pattern Recognition. DAGM GCPR 2019. LNCS, vol. 11824, pp. 33–47. Springer, Cham (2019). https://doi.org/10.1007/978-3-030-33676-9_3

2. Boyd, S., Vandenberghe, L.: Convex Optimization. Cambridge University Press, Cambridge (2004). https://doi.org/10.1017/CBO9780511804441

3. Breiman, L.: Random forests. Mach. Learn. **45**(1), 5–32 (2001)

4. Budde, L.E., Bulatov, D., Iwaszczuk, D.: Identification of misclassified pixels in semantic segmentation with uncertainty evaluation. Int. Arch. Photogramm. Remote Sens. Spat. Inf. Sci. **XLIII-B2-2021**, 441–448 (2021). https://doi.org/10.5194/isprs-archives-XLIII-B2-2021-441-2021, https://isprs-archives.copernicus.org/articles/XLIII-B2-2021/441/2021/

5. Chen, L., Zhu, Y., Papandreou, G., Schroff, F., Adam, H.: Encoder-decoder with atrous separable convolution for semantic image segmentation. CoRR abs/1802.02611 (2018). https://arxiv.org/abs/1802.02611

6. Dechesne, C., Lassalle, P., Lefèvre, S.: Bayesian deep learning with Monte Carlo dropout for qualification of semantic segmentation. In: 2021 IEEE International Geoscience and Remote Sensing Symposium IGARSS, pp. 2536–2539 (2021). https://doi.org/10.1109/IGARSS47720.2021.9555043

7. Deng, J., Dong, W., Socher, R., Li, L.J., Li, K., Fei-Fei, L.: Imagenet: a large-scale hierarchical image database. In: IEEE Conference on Computer vision and Pattern Recognition, pp. 248–255. IEEE (2009)

8. Gal, Y., Ghahramani, Z.: Dropout as a Bayesian approximation: representing model uncertainty in deep learning. ArXiv abs/1506.02142 (2015)

9. Gawlikowski, J., Saha, S., Kruspe, A., Zhu, X.X.: Towards out-of-distribution detection for remote sensing. In: 2021 IEEE International Geoscience and Remote Sensing Symposium IGARSS, pp. 8676–8679 (2021). https://doi.org/10.1109/IGARSS47720.2021.9553266

10. Gawlikowski, J., et al.: A survey of uncertainty in deep neural networks. CoRR abs/2107.03342 (2021). https://arxiv.org/abs/2107.03342

11. Hazel, G.G.: Multivariate gaussian MRF for multispectral scene segmentation and anomaly detection. IEEE Trans. Geosci. Remote Sens. **38**(3), 1199–1211 (2000)

12. He, K., Zhang, X., Ren, S., Sun, J.: Deep residual learning for image recognition. In: 2016 IEEE Conference on Computer Vision and Pattern Recognition (CVPR), pp. 770–778 (2016). https://doi.org/10.1109/CVPR.2016.90

13. Hendrycks, D., Gimpel, K.: A baseline for detecting misclassified and out-of-distribution examples in neural networks. arXiv preprint arXiv:1610.02136 (2016)

14. James, G., Witten, D., Hastie, T., Tibshirani, R.: An Introduction to Statistical Learning, vol. 112. Springer, Berlin, Heidelberg (2013). https://doi.org/10.1007/978-1-0716-1418-1

15. Kampffmeyer, M., Salberg, A.B., Jenssen, R.: Semantic segmentation of small objects and modeling of uncertainty in urban remote sensing images using deep convolutional neural networks. In: 2016 IEEE Conference on Computer Vision and Pattern Recognition Workshops (CVPRW), pp. 680–688 (2016). https://doi.org/10.1109/CVPRW.2016.90

16. Liang, S., Li, Y., Srikant, R.: Enhancing the reliability of out-of-distribution image detection in neural networks. arXiv preprint arXiv:1706.02690 (2017)

17. Loshchilov, I., Hutter, F.: Fixing weight decay regularization in adam. CoRR abs/1711.05101 (2017). https://arxiv.org/abs/1711.05101

18. Pollefeys, M., et al..: Detailed real-time urban 3D reconstruction from video. Int. J. Comput. Vis. **78**(2–3), 143–167 (2008). https://doi.org/10.1007/s11263-007-0086-4, https://dx.doi.org/10.1007/s11263-007-0086-4

19. Qiu, K., Bulatov, D., Budde, L.E., Kullmann, T., Iwaszczuk, D.: Influence of out-of-distribution examples on the quality of semantic segmentation in remote sensing. In: IGARSS 2023–2023 IEEE International Geoscience and Remote Sensing Symposium. Pasadena, July 2023

20. Ronneberger, O., Fischer, P., Brox, T.: U-Net: convolutional networks for biomedical image segmentation. In: Navab, N., Hornegger, J., Wells, W., Frangi, A. (eds.) Medical Image Computing and Computer-Assisted Intervention – MICCAI 2015. MICCAI 2015. LNCS, vol. 9351, pp. 234–241. Springer, Cham (2015). https://doi.org/10.1007/978-3-319-24574-4_28, https://arxiv.org/abs/1505.04597v1

21. Roscher, R., Volpi, M., Mallet, C., Drees, L., Wegner, J.D.: Semcity toulouse: a benchmark for building instance segmentation in satellite images. ISPRS Ann. Photogramm. Remote Sens. Spat. Inf. Sci. **V-5-2020**, 109–116 (2020)

22. Roscher, R., Waske, B., Forstner, W.: Incremental import vector machines for classifying hyperspectral data. IEEE Trans. Geosci. Remote Sens. **50**(9), 3463–3473 (2012)

23. Rottensteiner, F., Sohn, G., Gerke, M., Wegner, J., Breitkopf, U., Jung, J.: Results of the ISPRS benchmark on urban object detection and 3D building reconstruction. ISPRS J. Photogramm. Remote Sens. **93**, 256–271 (2014). https://doi.org/10.1016/j.isprsjprs.2013.10.004

24. Rottmann, M., Maag, K., Chan, R., Hüger, F., Schlicht, P., Gottschalk, H.: Detection of false positive and false negative samples in semantic segmentation, 08 December 2019. https://arxiv.org/pdf/1912.03673v1

25. Ruff, L., et al.: A unifying review of deep and shallow anomaly detection. Proc. IEEE **109**(5), 756–795 (2021)

26. da Silva, C.C.V., Nogueira, K., Oliveira, H.N., dos Santos, J.A.: Towards open-set semantic segmentation of aerial images. CoRR abs/2001.10063 (2020). https://arxiv.org/abs/2001.10063

27. Strauß, E., Bulatov, D.: A region-based machine learning approach for self-diagnosis of a 4D digital thermal twin. ISPRS Ann. Photogramm. Remote Sens. Spat. Inf. Sci. **10** (2022)
28. Yakubovskiy, P.: Segmentation models pytorch (2020). https://github.com/qubvel/segmentation_models.pytorch
29. Yuan, S., Wu, X.: Trustworthy anomaly detection: a survey, 16 February 2022. https://arxiv.org/pdf/2202.07787v1
30. Zhu, J., Hastie, T.: Kernel logistic regression and the import vector machine. J. Comput. Graph. Stat. **14**(1), 185–205 (2005)

Underwater Multiview Stereo Using Axial Camera Models

Felix Seegräber[1,2]($\boxtimes$) ID, Patricia Schöntag[1] ID, Felix Woelk[2] ID,
and Kevin Köser[1] ID

[1] GEOMAR Helmholz Centre for Ocean Research Kiel, Kiel, Germany
`felix_seegraeber@gmx.de`
[2] Kiel University of Applied Sciences, Kiel, Germany

Abstract. 3D models, generated from underwater imagery, are a valuable asset for many applications. When acquiring images underwater, light is refracted as it passes the boundary layers between water, housing and the air inside the housing due to the different refractive indices of the materials. Thus the geometry of the light rays changes in this scenario and the standard pinhole camera model is not applicable. As a result, pinhole 3D reconstruction methods can not easily be applied in this environment. For the dense reconstruction of scene surfaces the added complexity is especially challenging, as these types of algorithms have to match vast amounts of image content. This work proposes the refractive adaptation of a PatchMatch Multi-View Stereo algorithm. The refraction encountered at flat port underwater housings is explicitly modeled to avoid systematic errors in the reconstruction. Concepts derived from the axial camera model are employed to handle the high demands of Multi-View Stereo regarding accuracy and computational complexity. Numerical simulations and reconstruction results on synthetically generated but realistic images with ground truth validate the effectiveness of the approach.

Keywords: axial camera · multiview stereo · refractive projection · underwater imagery · 3d reconstruction

1 Introduction and Previous Work

Motivation. In the underwater environment, 3D reconstruction is employed for various use cases in research and industry such as 3D maps of underwater habitats and geological structures, identifying and monitoring discarded munition and explosives in the Baltic and North Sea or visual support of autonomous underwater navigation. However, there are unique challenges for image acquisition and 3D reconstruction in the underwater environment one of which is the refractive distortion of light. It travels through multiple interfaces between water, glass and air because cameras are usually placed in dedicated housings with a *flat port* glass interface to protect them from water and pressure. As a result,

© The Author(s), under exclusive license to Springer Nature Switzerland AG 2024
U. Köthe and C. Rother (Eds.): DAGM GCPR 2023, LNCS 14264, pp. 275–288, 2024.
https://doi.org/10.1007/978-3-031-54605-1_18

the pinhole camera model, on which key parts of classical 3D reconstruction algorithms are based, is invalid.

Refractive Distortion in Underwater Environment. For some controlled environments it is possible to mitigate a large portion of the refractive effects by calibrating the whole camera setup underwater. This allows the lens distortion parameters to absorb large parts of the refraction for fixed viewing distances [16]. But since the refractive distortion is dependent on the distance of the scene to the camera this approach introduces systematic errors [13,27]. Therefore, a more robust and flexible solution requires explicit modeling of refraction. One approach for compensating flat port refraction is to construct a more extensive compensation model, realized by calculating the distortion per pixel for a fixed distance and storing it in a lookup [19]. Undistorting refractive image data using this lookup allows to return to the pinhole camera model with little error. A major drawback of this method is that it requires very small distances between the center of projection and the housing interface in the order of a few millimeters. Otherwise, the reprojection error for objects not at the calibration distance becomes significant. More generic solutions model the physical path of light rays. It has been shown that with refraction at a flat interface, light rays intersect at a common axis, forming an axial camera model [1]. This holds for a single layer of refraction ("thin glass") and interface-camera alignment [27] also with a more complex system of two layers of refraction ("thick glass") with potential interface tilt [24] and even at a spherical interface, when the camera is not centered inside [25].

Consequently, in this work a refractive Multi-View Stereo algorithm is developed based on insights from the axial camera model. We chose to base our proposed method on the common flat port scenario, two interfaces with potential interface tilt. Agrawal et al. [1] derived the respective analytical projection under refraction. While all models allow dealing with refraction very precisely, they are not easily compatible with in-air reconstruction algorithms, that heavily rely on the characteristics of the pinhole camera model. So it is necessary to make explicit adaptions or design completely new approaches.

The proposed method follows a state-of-the-art PatchMatch approach while replacing key components with newly developed refractive counterparts. Since dense reconstruction requires large-scale matching between a very large number of pixels, computational efficiency is a major concern. Tradeoffs between accuracy and runtime have to be taken into consideration to make the method feasible.

Refractive Multi-View Stereo Reconstruction. Multi-View Stereo (MVS) methods usually recover the camera poses and a sparse set of 2D-3D correspondences from image features in a Structure-from-Motion (SfM) step. This data is then used in conjunction with the input images to initialize the MVS algorithm which generates a dense point cloud or even a mesh [7]. While this work does not focus on SfM, the challenges regarding refraction are similar. Chari and Sturm [5] provide a theory for relative pose estimation with single layer refraction. Kang et al. [15] derive specific refractive constraints for single layer refractive SfM and utilize an adapted version [4] of the Patch-Based Multi-View Stereo (PMVS) algorithm [8] for dense reconstruction. Refractive SfM enabled by refractive bundle adjustment is presented in [14]. The virtual cameras, first introduced for a bundle adjustment error during calibration in [24], inspired the virtual camera homography proposed in this work.

Less attention has been given to dense MVS incorporating refraction. [4,15] adapt PMVS for refraction, but focus on the SfM part and are not very detailed regarding dense reconstruction. Jordt et al. [11,12] developed a refractive plane sweep algorithm for dense reconstruction. They avoid computationally expensive refractive forward projections by back projecting and calculating the matching cost for a plane in 3D space. A more recent work [3] tackles Multi-View Stereo for arbitrarily shaped interfaces, targeted on reconstructing e.g. insects trapped in ember. Image pixels are exhaustively matched while replacing projections with solving the 4th degree polynomial for single layer refracive projection. Their proposed solution is not fully operational in its current state, the main inhibitor being its extreme computational complexity. This is a general challenge for Multi-View Stereo with refraction, where the extensive pixel matching over multiple images, in combination with the more computationally expensive projections, result in infeasible runtimes.

Contributions. In summary the following contributions are made: A. We introduce local virtual camera homographies between axial cameras and B. an efficient forward projection that is based on discrete line search rather than expensive solving of high-order polynomials. C. Both is used in our suggested extension of state-of-the-art patch-match multi view stereo for refractive scenarios. The effectiveness of the approach is proven by extensive evaluations on ground-truth models with real-world textures using physically-based raytracing.

2   Axial Model with Virtual Camera Approximation

The core concept of PatchMatch Multi-View Stereo is to approximate the scene surface with a collection of planes. Correctness of the planes is scored by warping pixel patches into neighboring views utilizing the homography induced by these planes [23,26,29]. Homographies being invalid under refraction as well as the high computational complexity of refractive projection are the main challenges for refractive PatchMatch.

Virtual Camera Homography. Because it is not possible to formulate a general homography for two refractive cameras and a plane, we substitute a pinhole camera for single rays of a refractive camera. These virtual cameras, first introduced in [24] for calibration, are located at the intersection of the ray with the camera axis and aligned with the interface normal. When evaluating the photometric consistency between pixels x_i and x_j in two neighboring views, the homography of their respective virtual cameras is utilized. Since the homography is used for a whole pixel patch, an assumption made here is that the virtual camera of the central pixel is a good pinhole approximation for all patch pixels.

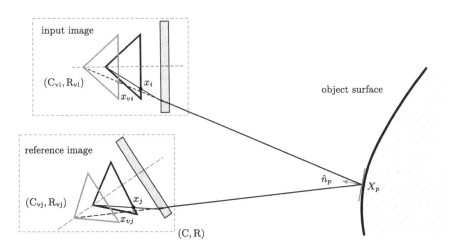

Fig. 1. Refractive PatchMatch, introducing virtual cameras to enable homography warping. The poses of the virtual cameras are given relative to their parent camera.

This is plausible since the refractive distortion is minimal between neighboring pixels.

Let the poses of input and reference virtual camera be C_{vi}, R_{vi} and C_{vj}, R_{vj} respectively. They are both known relative to their parent camera coordinate system. The input camera coincides with the world coordinate system and the reference camera pose is R, C, compare Fig. 1. The pose of the reference virtual camera relative to the input virtual camera is:

$$C_{vij} = R_{vi}(C + R^T C_{vj} - C_{vi}), \quad R_{vij} = R_{vj} R R_{vi}{}^T. \tag{1}$$

Using these poses, the virtual camera homography is:

$$H_{vij} = K_{vj} \left(R_{vij} - \frac{R_{vij} C_{vij} \hat{n}_{vp}^T}{\hat{n}_{vp}^T X_{vp}} \right) K_{vi}{}^{-1}. \tag{2}$$

K_{vj}, K_{vi} are the camera matrices of the respective virtual cameras and $X_{vp} = R_{vi} X_p - R_{vi} C_{vi}$, $\hat{n}_{vp} = R_{vi} \hat{n}_p$ are the plain point and normal in input virtual camera coordinates.

The role of the homography in the PatchMatch cost function is to map pixel coordinates between the two images. To match the pixel coordinates of x and x_v we move the virtual principal point, shifting the virtual image plane, until $x_v = x$. With this requirement, c_{vx}, c_{vy} can be calculated from the ray in water X_w:

$$c_{vx} = x - f_{vx} x'_{vwx}, \quad c_{vy} = x - f_{vy} x'_{vwy}. \tag{3}$$

Here x'_{vw} is X_w transformed into the virtual camera coordinate system and normalized. The virtual focal length is set to $f_v = f$.

function *AlgorithmicRefractiveForwardProjection(X, K, $\hat{n}$, L, width, height)*
  $x_p, x_n := \texttt{Project}(K, X), \texttt{Project}(K, \hat{n})$
  $S_{start}, S_{end} := \texttt{ClipLine}(x_p, x_p - x_n, width, height)$
  $t := 0.5(S_{end} - S_{start})$
  $x := S_{start} + t$
  while $|t| \geq \sqrt{2}/4$ **do**
      $q := \texttt{Round}(x)$
      $C_v, \hat{X}_v := L(q)$
      $\alpha := ((X - C_v) \cdot \hat{n})/|(X - C_v)|$
      $\beta := \hat{X}_v \cdot \hat{n}$
      $forward := \alpha < \beta$
      if *forward* **then**
        | $S_{start} := x$
      end
      $t := 0.5t$
      $x := S_{start} + t$
  end
  if *forward* **and** $|x - S_{end}| < 0.5$ **then**
    | **return** *false*
  else
    | **return** x
  end

Algorithm 1: Algorithmic Refractive Forward Projection

Virtual Camera Lookup. An advantage of the virtual camera model is that it can be precalculated from the camera and interface parameters, independently of the scene. The parameters per virtual camera consist of its camera center C_v and the ray vector $\hat{X}_v = \hat{X}_w$, each in the parent camera coordinates, as well as the virtual principal point c_v. Since dimensions of the image and the lookup match, an integer pixel location x can be directly used to get the corresponding virtual camera, i.e. $L(x) = \left\{ C_v(x), \hat{X}_v(x), c_v(x) \right\}$. This representation resembles a general camera model, storing a point and direction for each pixel, as proposed by [10].

Algorithmic Refractive Forward Projection. Determining the reference virtual camera for the virtual camera homography, requires to find x_j by projecting X_p (c.f. Fig. 1). The analytical refractive forward projection involves solving a 12th degree polynomial [1], which is computationally expensive. Additionally, the virtual camera lookup is only calculated to pixel precision, giving the opportunity to trade off accuracy for speed with an algorithmic approach.

The algorithmic refractive forward projection 1 exploits that the location of a refractive projection x of 3D point X can be constraint to a 2D ray $R = \{x_p + t(x_p - x_n)|t \geq 0\}$. R lies on the intersection of the plane of refraction [1] with the image plane. x_p is the "naive" pinhole projection of X and x_n the intersection of camera axis and image plane. Under real world conditions the light is refracted towards the camera axis and x_p is always closer to x_n than x.

This can be shown from Snell's law, if the refractive indices of glass, water and air adhere to the inequality $\mu_g > \mu_w > \mu_a$. R is limited to the image boundaries using the Liang-Barsky line clipping algorithm [18] yielding search line S. A point x on S can be tested by comparing $\overrightarrow{C_v(x)X}$ to $\hat{X}_v(x)$. If they are equal, x is the refractive projection of X. If they are not equal, the angles $\alpha(x)$, between $\overrightarrow{C_v(x)X}$ and $\hat{n}$ and $\beta(x)$ between $\hat{X}_v(x)$ and $\hat{n}$ can be used to limit S to one side of the currently tested point. Because the angles between $\hat{X}_v(x)$ and $\hat{n}$ steadily increase on R, if $\alpha(q) > \beta(q)$ the correct refractive projection lies on the upper line segment and vice versa. The search terminates if the search line reaches a length below $\frac{\sqrt{2}}{4}$. This is necessary, since the virtual camera lookup is only calculated to pixel precision, which means that α and β are calculated from a rounded value, resulting in a small error. To determine if a point X projects inside the image boundaries, x is compared to the end of the search line S_{end}. If the last iteration of the loop indicated that the target location is further in the direction of t and the current location hypothesis is close to the endpoint, i.e. $|x - S_{end}| < 0.5$, the projection is considered outside of the image.

3   Refractive PatchMatch

The proposed method extends PatchMatch Multi-View Stereo for refractive images, by integrating the virtual camera homography and algorithmic refractive forward projection into the procedure. As a proof of concept the complete algorithm was integrated into OpenMVS [21] which is largely based on the Patch-Match variant described in [26] but includes several modifications. The following sections present the integration based on this implementation.

Refractive Depth Map. For the application in the refractive patch match algorithm it is useful to change the interpretation of values in the depth map. The depth λ_p for a pinhole camera describes the distance between the camera center C and the scene point X along the viewing ray, related by projection: $X = \lambda_p K^{-1} x'$. To retain the alignment of depth vector and viewing ray under refraction, the interpretation of depth changes to:

$$X = C_v + \lambda \hat{X}_v, \tag{4}$$

the distance between the virtual camera center C_v and X. Both C_v and viewing ray $\hat{X}_v$ are contained in lookup L, which makes this calculation efficient. Both representations can be easily converted into each other. If λ_r is the refractive depth and λ_p the pinhole depth, the λ_p can be calculated from λ_r as:

$$\lambda_p = |C_v + \lambda_r \hat{X}_v|. \tag{5}$$

View Selection. View selection is based on [9]. It is generally compatible with refraction, but considers crowd sourced images. As this scenario is not typical underwater, view selection scaling was disabled for refractive images, to avoid having to rescale and recalculate the virtual camera lookups.

Patch Similarity. The photometric similarity between two pixel patches in input and reference image is quantified using a Normalized Cross Correlation score, as defined in for example [17]. The patch coordinates of the input image are warped onto the reference image using the current plane hypothesis of the scored pixel. This cost function is adapted by replacing the homography with the virtual camera homography H_v (2). The resulting error is combined with the following measures to a single confidence score for each pixel.

Neighborhood Smoothness. To encourage a smooth surface between neighboring pixels, dedicated point and angular smoothness terms are employed. While mostly compatible, the point smoothness Δ_p has to be modified to respect the varying depth interpretation with (4) and (5):

$$\Delta_{vp}(n) = \frac{d_v(n)}{|C_v + \lambda \hat{X}_v|}, \tag{6}$$

with $d_v(n) = \hat{n}_p \cdot X_{vp}(n) + |C_v + \lambda \hat{X}_v|$ and $X_{vp}(n) = C_v(n) + \lambda(n)\hat{X}_v(n)$. $d_v(n)$ is the distance of the current plane hypothesis to the plane point $X_{vp}(n)$ of neighboring pixel n.

Depth Map Consistency. Consistency between neighboring views is evaluated using a *forward-backward reprojection error* $|x_i - x_{ij}|$ [23,28]. x_i, x_j are the current input pixel location and the corresponding reference image location respectively. x_{ij} is determined by back projecting x_j using depth λ_j and forward projecting the resulting 3D point into the input image. To adapt this score for refraction, the pixel distance is calculated in the input virtual camera image:

$$x_{vij} = K_{vi}R_v(R^T \lambda_j K_j^{-1} x_j' + C - C_v). \tag{7}$$

While this introduces some additional error, due to the virtual camera only being an approximation, the distance is expected to be in the range of a few pixels, where the approximation is still good.

Plane Propagation. As proposed for example in [23], depth values are propagated by intersecting the viewing ray of the current pixel with the neighboring plane. With the refractive depth map, propagated depth λ_{new} must be the distance between C_v and the neighboring plane $X_{vp}(n), \hat{n}(n)$ in direction of $\hat{X}_v$:

$$\lambda_{new} = \frac{(X_{vp}(n) - C_v) \cdot \hat{n}(n)}{\hat{X}_v \cdot \hat{n}(n)}, \tag{8}$$

with $X_{vp}(n) = C_v(n) + \lambda(n)\hat{X}_v(n)$. This way λ_{new} aligns with the refractive depth interpretation of the current pixel, i.e. $X_p = C_v + \lambda_{new}\hat{X}_v$.

Merging Depth Maps. Depth Maps are merged and converted to point clouds by interpolating between the plane points and normals, using the respective confidence score of each point as a weight. 3D points are calculated utilizing the refractive depth interpretation (4). To find corresponding pixel positions in neighboring views, the algorithmic refractive forward projection is used.

4   Evaluation

In this section the algorithmic refractive forward projection and the virtual camera homography are evaluated regarding accuracy and sensitivity to potential error sources. If not noted otherwise, the camera and interface parameters used in the following subsections are: 80° field of view (FOV), centered principal point, distance to interface $d_a = 2$ cm, interface thickness $d_g = 1.4$ cm with no interface tilt.

Algorithmic Refractive Forward Projection. To evaluate the accuracy, a pixel position x is refractively back projected into 3D point X, which is then reprojected into image point x_r, using the algorithmic refractive forward projection. The Euclidean distance $e = |x - x_r|$ between the two image points forms a reprojection error. Figure 2 shows the distribution of e, calculated over a 1000 × 1000 image, subpixel positions reprojected in 0.1 pixel steps. Three parameters were varied: A higher FOV results in increased incident angles, amplifying the refractive distortion. The distance of the camera to the interface d_a has a strong effect on the distribution of virtual camera locations along the camera axis. Increasing d_a moves the intersections of the rays with the camera axis, i.e. the virtual camera centers, further away from the real camera center, increasing the overall spread along the axis. This effect is also noted in [19], which they call an increase of the "focus section". Finally, tilting the interface normal strongly influences the overall geometry of the system, making it a good candidate as a potential error source. Even with strong variation in these parameters the overall distribution of the error stays similar with a mean of roughly a quarter pixel.

The runtime of the algorithmic projection is dependent on the search line length and therefore on the image size. Nevertheless, tests show that it is still faster than a reference implementation of the analytical version [19] by factors of about 18 to 34 for image sizes of 2 MP to 10 MP.

Virtual Camera Homography. The assumption for the virtual camera homography is that a virtual camera is a good approximation even for neighboring rays. To test this, two stereo camera setups are simulated: A generic stereo setup with 1m baseline and 4m plane distance and a setup with a translated ($x = 0.5$ m, $z = -1$ m) reference camera to limit potential symmetries in the transformation. Figure 3 shows schematics of the arrangement.

Patches were calculated as: 9 × 9 window size, skipping every second pixel, resulting in 5 × 5 patches. All image sizes in this section were enlarged by a 4 pixel border to compensate for the patch size. To calculate the error for a pixel q in patch B, centered on pixel x, q is warped to the reference image using the virtual camera homography of x, yielding $H_v(q)$. The true value for q is determined by backprojecting it into space, intersecting with the plane and projecting refractively into the reference image to get the true reference position q_r. The distance $e_H = |H_v(q) - q_r|$ is the error for a single pixel in a patch, while $e_{BH} = \frac{1}{n}\sum_{q \in B} |H_v(q) - q_r|$, with n being the number of pixels in B, is the mean error of the whole patch. Note that to determine the reference position q_r in exact

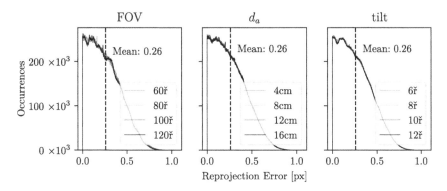

Fig. 2. Reprojection error distributions for different camera setups. For a 1000×1000 image FOV (*left*), interface distance d_a (*middle*) and interface tilt(*right*) are varied.

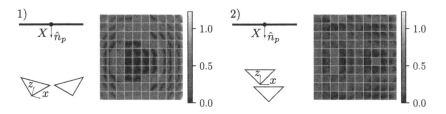

Fig. 3. Setups 1 and 2 for the virtual homography evaluation. The images show the patch pixel error e_H for a 10×10 image in the respective setup. Each cell represents the patch at the specific pixel position, concatenated to form the whole image. The cell contents are the errors of each patch pixel location forming the 5×5 patch.

values the analytic refractive projection derived in [1], with the implementation from [19] is used.

Figure 3 shows e_H, the error for each patch pixel "exploded" for a 10×10 image: The 5×5 error values for each patch are concatenated forming a cell in the image grid. Each grid cell represents the patch of the respective pixel, the cell contents the error value of the specific patch pixel. The central value in each patch corresponds to the approximated and then rounded refractive projection which was used to look up the reference virtual camera for H_v. In most cases, this rounding error seems to dominate the overall patch error. The average patch error, i.e. the average patch color in Fig. 3, is mostly close to the central pixels color. Interestingly, for some patches the central pixel does not hold the lowest value in the patch, indicating that the rounding error cancels out the virtual camera error for some patch pixels.

The resulting mean patch errors, for 100×100 images in setup 1 and 2, are shown in Fig. 4. The same values were used for both cameras in the setup, assuming a Multi-View Stereo scenario with a single camera device. In addition to the parameters varied before, the homography plane normal is rotated around

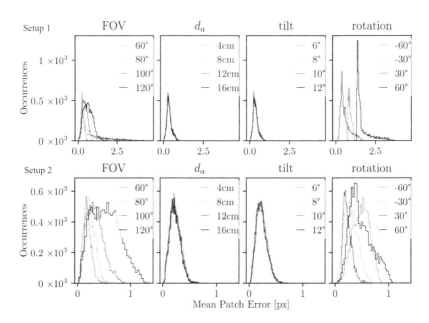

Fig. 4. Mean patch error e_{BH} for setup 1 (*top*) and 2 (*bottom*), 100 × 100 images. The overall mean of each series from left to right, top to bottom is for the top row.

the y-axis for an additional series. For most of the variations, the projection error is a significant contributor to the mean patch error, visible as the distinct patterns in the images. For high field of views or strong plane angles, the error caused by the virtual camera approximation becomes the dominant factor. The more the refractive rays deviate from pinhole rays, the stronger the error seems to be.

Refractive Dense Reconstruction. The complete dense reconstruction algorithm, described in Sect. 3, was tested on synthetic images. The images were rendered using the Blender toolbox published in [20]. The 3D model [2] was chosen to depict a geological scene which could potentially be found underwater. Only the geometric effects of refraction were considered. Other water related effects, such as scattering and attenuation, were not modeled. The prerequisite sparse point cloud and camera pose information were generated by the SfM pipeline in COLMAP [22]. Because there is currently no readily available SfM solution which supports refraction, each image was rendered once with and without an refractive flatport interface. Sparse point cloud and pose information were generated from in-air SfM using the unrefracted images. They were then combined with the refracted versions of the images to form the input for the refractive dense reconstruction. A subset of the rendered images, recovered

Fig. 5. Excerpt from the synthetic test images (left): Images were rendered from the same poses, with (*bottom row*) and without (*top row*) refraction. Right: Poses and sparse point cloud.

poses and sparse point cloud is shown in Fig. 5. Images were rendered in 3.1 MP resolution, 2048 × 1536 pixels. The 10 poses were manually chosen such that most of the image is filled by the rendered model. Since the FOV is effectively reduced by the refraction, the unrefracted images cover more area and contain some background at the borders.

Two reconstructions were run using the images and sparse point cloud as inputs. One with the refracted images and the adapted refractive dense reconstruction procedure and one using the unmodified OpenMVS CPU implementation as a reference. The usual method of comparing the generated depth maps with the ground truth depth maps was not possible. Generating depth maps under refraction is currently not supported with the used renderer. Instead, the reconstruction quality was quantified by comparing the generated point clouds with the original model mesh. As the poses were extracted from the rendered images, the relation to the original model was lost. To compare the point clouds, they were aligned and registered with the model mesh using CloudCompare [6]. The tool also offers the functionality to calculate the distance between the cloud points and the model mesh, which is shown in Fig. 6. The model units are unknown, but from measures taken of its content it is plausible that they are meters. The variance of the unrefracted and refracted points is 2.58×10^{-6} and 3.72×10^{-6} respectively. The absolute mean distance is 0.88×10^{-3} for the unrefracted and 1.28×10^{-3} for the refracted points.

The reconstruction results for this set of images is very promising. The density and accuracy is comparable to its in-air counter part. Experiments on real underwater images, incorporating all noise and calibration errors existent in real world data, should be conducted to properly validate the algorithm.

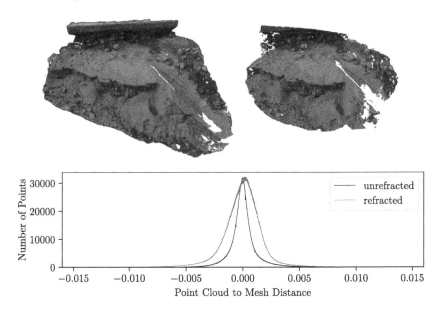

Fig. 6. Reconstructed point clouds (*top*) and point cloud model mesh distance (*bottom*). The refracted point cloud (*top right*) is cut off compared to the unrefracted one (*top left*) because the refraction effectively narrows the FOV. The clouds contain 4,200,659 (unrefracted) and 4,635,708 (refracted) 3D points.

5   Conclusion

We presented a novel approach to refractive Multi-View Stereo. It allows 3D reconstruction of underwater images which suffer from complex refractive distortion due to flat port housings. The proposed method extends a state-of-the-art PatchMatch algorithm with concepts derived from the refractive axial camera model. The refractive matching of pixel patches is enabled by pixel precise pinhole camera approximations stored in a lookup. Utilizing this lookup allows the application of a newly developed efficient algorithmic refractive forward projection. This retains feasible runtimes while maintaining sufficient accuracy to reconstruct high quality dense point clouds. Numerical simulations and a complete refractive dense reconstruction with our method show that the algorithmic refractive projection is accurate to subpixel precision. Density and quality of the generated point cloud is comparable between the refractive and in-air algorithm. Further speed ups can be assumed if an optimized implementation, e.g. using GPUs, is considered in the future. Other potential for future work is in improvement of the virtual camera approximation. Investigating e.g. focal length modification or interpolation between virtual cameras could increase accuracy.

References

1. Agrawal, A., Ramalingam, S., Taguchi, Y., Chari, V.: A theory of multi-layer flat refractive geometry. In: 2012 IEEE Conference on Computer Vision and Pattern Recognition. IEEE, June 2012. https://doi.org/10.1109/cvpr.2012.6248073
2. Carena, S.: Foreset beds, Spain (3d model) (2022). https://skfb.ly/otPRA
3. Cassidy, M., Melou, J., Queau, Y., Lauze, F., Durou, J.D.: Refractive multi-view stereo. In: 2020 International Conference on 3D Vision (3DV). IEEE, November 2020. https://doi.org/10.1109/3dv50981.2020.00048
4. Chang, Y.J., Chen, T.: Multi-view 3D reconstruction for scenes under the refractive plane with known vertical direction. In: 2011 International Conference on Computer Vision. IEEE, November 2011. https://doi.org/10.1109/iccv.2011.6126262
5. Chari, V., Sturm, P.: Multiple-view geometry of the refractive plane. In: Proceedings of the British Machine Vision Conference 2009. British Machine Vision Association (2009). https://doi.org/10.5244/c.23.56
6. Cloud Compare Developers: Cloudcompare (2023). https://www.cloudcompare.org/
7. Furukawa, Y., Hernández, C.: Multi-view stereo: a tutorial. Found. Trends® Comput. Graph. Vis. **9**(1–2), 1–148 (2015). https://doi.org/10.1561/0600000052
8. Furukawa, Y., Ponce, J.: Accurate, dense, and robust multiview stereopsis. IEEE Trans. Pattern Anal. Mach. Intell. **32**(8), 1362–1376 (2010). https://doi.org/10.1109/tpami.2009.161
9. Goesele, M., Snavely, N., Curless, B., Hoppe, H., Seitz, S.M.: Multi-view stereo for community photo collections. In: 2007 IEEE 11th International Conference on Computer Vision. IEEE (2007). https://doi.org/10.1109/iccv.2007.4408933
10. Grossberg, M., Nayar, S.: A general imaging model and a method for finding its parameters. In: Proceedings Eighth IEEE International Conference on Computer Vision. ICCV 2001. IEEE Comput. Soc (2001). https://doi.org/10.1109/iccv.2001.937611
11. Jordt, A., Köser, K., Koch, R.: Refractive 3D reconstruction on underwater images. Methods Oceanogr. **15–16**, 90–113 (2016). https://doi.org/10.1016/j.mio.2016.03.001
12. Jordt-Sedlazeck, A., Jung, D., Koch, R.: Refractive plane sweep for underwater images. In: Weickert, J., Hein, M., Schiele, B. (eds.) Pattern Recognition. GCPR 2013. LNCS, pp. 333–342. Springer, Berlin, Heidelberg (2013). https://doi.org/10.1007/978-3-642-40602-7_36
13. Jordt-Sedlazeck, A., Koch, R.: Refractive calibration of underwater cameras. In: Fitzgibbon, A., Lazebnik, S., Perona, P., Sato, Y., Schmid, C. (eds.) Computer Vision – ECCV 2012. ECCV 2012. LNCS, vol. 7576, pp. 846–859. Springer, Berlin, Heidelberg (2012). https://doi.org/10.1007/978-3-642-33715-4_61
14. Jordt-Sedlazeck, A., Koch, R.: Refractive structure-from-motion on underwater images. In: 2013 IEEE International Conference on Computer Vision. IEEE, December 2013. https://doi.org/10.1109/iccv.2013.14
15. Kang, L., Wu, L., Yang, Y.H.: Two-view underwater structure and motion for cameras under flat refractive interfaces. In: Fitzgibbon, A., Lazebnik, S., Perona, P., Sato, Y., Schmid, C. (eds.) Computer Vision – ECCV 2012. ECCV 2012. LNCS, vol. 7575, pp. 303–316. Springer, Berlin, Heidelberg (2012). https://doi.org/10.1007/978-3-642-33765-9_22
16. Lavest, J.M., Rives, G., Lapresté, J.T.: Underwater camera calibration. In: Vernon, D. (eds.) Computer Vision – ECCV 2000. ECCV 2000. LNCS, vol. 1843,

pp. 654–668. Springer, Berlin, Heidelberg (2000). https://doi.org/10.1007/3-540-45053-x_42

17. Lewis, J.: Fast normalized cross-correlation. Ind. Light Magic 10 (2001)
18. Liang, Y.D., Barsky, B.A.: A new concept and method for line clipping. ACM Trans. Graph. **3**(1), 1–22 (1984). https://doi.org/10.1145/357332.357333
19. Łuczyński, T., Pfingsthorn, M., Birk, A.: The pinax-model for accurate and efficient refraction correction of underwater cameras in flat-pane housings. Ocean Eng. **133**, 9–22 (2017). https://doi.org/10.1016/j.oceaneng.2017.01.029
20. Nakath, D., She, M., Song, Y., Köser, K.: An optical digital twin for underwater photogrammetry. PFG - J. Photogramm. Remote Sens. Geoinf. Sci. (2022). https://doi.org/10.1007/s41064-021-00190-9
21. OpenMVS authors: OpenMVS (2022). https://github.com/cdcseacave/openMVS
22. Schönberger, J.: COLMAP (2022). https://colmap.github.io/
23. Schönberger, J.L., Zheng, E., Frahm, J.M., Pollefeys, M.: Pixelwise view selection for unstructured multi-view stereo. In: Leibe, B., Matas, J., Sebe, N., Welling, M. (eds.) Computer Vision – ECCV 2016. ECCV 2016. LNCS, vol. 9907, pp. 501–518. Springer, Cham (2016). https://doi.org/10.1007/978-3-319-46487-9_31
24. Sedlazeck, A., Koch, R.: Calibration of housing parameters for underwater stereo-camera rigs. In: Proceedings of the British Machine Vision Conference 2011. British Machine Vision Association (2011). https://doi.org/10.5244/c.25.118
25. She, M., Nakath, D., Song, Y., Köser, K.: Refractive geometry for underwater domes. ISPRS J. Photogramm. Remote Sens. **183**, 525–540 (2022). https://doi.org/10.1016/j.isprsjprs.2021.11.006, https://www.sciencedirect.com/science/article/pii/S092427162100304X
26. Shen, S.: Accurate multiple view 3d reconstruction using patch-based stereo for large-scale scenes. IEEE Trans. Image Process. **22**(5), 1901–1914 (2013). https://doi.org/10.1109/tip.2013.2237921
27. Treibitz, T., Schechner, Y., Kunz, C., Singh, H.: Flat refractive geometry. IEEE Trans. Pattern Anal. Mach. Intell. **34**(1), 51–65 (2012). https://doi.org/10.1109/tpami.2011.105
28. Zhang, G., Jia, J., Wong, T.T., Bao, H.: Recovering consistent video depth maps via bundle optimization. In: 2008 IEEE Conference on Computer Vision and Pattern Recognition. IEEE, June 2008. https://doi.org/10.1109/cvpr.2008.4587496
29. Zheng, E., Dunn, E., Jojic, V., Frahm, J.M.: PatchMatch based joint view selection and depthmap estimation. In: 2014 IEEE Conference on Computer Vision and Pattern Recognition. IEEE, June 2014. https://doi.org/10.1109/cvpr.2014.196

Pattern Recognition in the Life Sciences

3D Retinal Vessel Segmentation in OCTA Volumes: Annotated Dataset MORE3D and Hybrid U-Net with Flattening Transformation

Julian Kuhlmann[1], Kai Rothaus[2], Xiaoyi Jiang[1(✉)], Henrik Faatz[2], Daniel Pauleikhoff[2], and Matthias Gutfleisch[2]

[1] Faculty of Mathematics and Computer Science, University of Münster, Münster, Germany
xjiang@uni-muenster.de

[2] Department of Ophthalmology, St. Franziskus-Hospital, Münster, Germany

Abstract. Optical Coherence Tomography Angiography (OCTA) extends the 3D structural representation of the retina from conventional OCT with an additional representation of "flow" and is used as non-invasive angiography technique in ophthalmology today. While there are several works for the segmentation of vascular network in OCTA images, most of them are tested on 2D enface images (top view projection) only. Such 2D enface images have the drawback that they depend on a good 3D segmentation of retinal layers, the so-called slabs. Especially in case of retinal diseases (e.g. exudations of the retina) this segmentation is not always clear, even for medical experts. In contrast, we consider the problem of full 3D segmentation of retinal vessels in OCTA images. We present the dataset MORE3D (Münster Octa REtina 3D dataset) that is the first one with 3D annotation. We introduce a general flattening transformation that simplifies and accelerates the 3D data labeling and processing, and also enables a specialized data augmentation. Moreover, we realize a hybrid U-net to achieve a first reference segmentation performance on our dataset. In addition to the common performance metrics we also apply skeleton-based metrics for a more comprehensive structural performance evaluation. With this work we contribute to the advancement of 3D retinal vessel segmentation in OCTA volumes.

Keywords: Optical Coherence Tomography Angiography · 3D annotated dataset · flattening transformation · vascular network segmentation

1 Introduction

The OCT technology enables deep scanning of the retinal layers and provides a 3D structural representation of the retinal layers. The OCT angiography introduced in 2014 [39] extends the structural OCT by the "flow". For each voxel the variation in time of the reflected laser spectrum is measured [16]. This variation

U. Köthe and C. Rother (Eds.): DAGM GCPR 2023, LNCS 14264, pp. 291–306, 2024.
https://doi.org/10.1007/978-3-031-54605-1_19

Fig. 1. Visualization of a volume with vessels crossing in different depths. From left to right: single 2D slice, rendered 3D volume, 2D projection (enface image).

is mainly caused by the travel of erythrocytes in the blood. The resulting OCTA volume represents the "flow". Besides motion artifacts during the image capture, there are projection artifacts and a rather large proportion of white noise. The morphology of the vascular network is a suitable biomarker for various pathological changes of the retina [10]. This has been demonstrated especially in quantitative morphological analysis of choroidal neovascularisations (CNV) in neovascular age-related macular degeneration (nAMD), which is the most common cause for legal blindness in the western world.

Currently, most algorithms realize vessel segmentation by a depth-limited 2D projection within anatomical retinal layers. A 2D OCTA enface image is generated pixel-wise by aggregating (e.g. averaging, maximum, or minimum) the flow information of the corresponding voxel stack in the specific retinal layer (slab). Depending on the manufacturer of the OCTA device there are different segmentation layers. In this paper we have used the Avanti™ from OptoVue, which segments the retinal vascular layers into a) the superficial vascular plexus, limited by the inner limiting membrane (ILM) and inner plexiform layer (IPL) –9 µm, and b) the deep vascular plexus, limited by IPL –9 µm and outer plexiform layer (OPL) +9 µm. Furthermore, c) the outer retina and d) the choriocapillaris are defined. For each of these so-called slabs a 2D enface OCTA image is generated by the Avanti™ software. Other OCTA manufactors have slightly different slab definitions but the approach to reduce the data to 2D enface images is the same. This 2D-projection procedure has the drawback that it depends on a good segmentation of morphological retinal layers (slabs). Especially in case of retinal diseases (e.g. exudations of the retina, disordering of retinal layers) the slab segmentation is not always clear, even for medical experts.

In this work we consider full 3D segmentation in OCTA images. Such a segmentation helps distinguish vessels that are merged in 2D images due to projection. For example, vessels in different depths of the retina may be crossing in the enface image (see Fig. 1). A full segmentation in 3D OCTA is challenging due to the different sources of noise. Additionally, segmentation inaccuracy affects differently on popular performance metrics for 2D and 3D cases, see the discussion in Sect. 2.

Related Work. There exist a few publicly available datasets with OCTA enface images: ROSE [30], OCTA-500 [21], FAROS [43], see more details in Sect. 2. However, there is no publicly available OCTA dataset with 3D manual vessel annotations yet.

Table 1. Comparison of datasets of OCTA images.

OCTA dataset	Data	Ground Truth
OCTA-500 [21]	3D volumes	2D pixel level (enface image)
ROSE [30]	3D volumes	2D pixel level (enface image) or centerlines only
FAROS [43]	3D volumes	2D pixel level (enface image)
Our dataset MORE3D	3D volumes	**3D voxel level**

A survey on segmentation and classification methods for OCTA images can be found in [32]. Numerous works exist for vesselness computation [19] and vesselness segmentation in 2D retinal fundus images [18,41]. Recent works have addressed several problems using OCTA, e.g. enhancement [27], quantification of choroidal neovascularization [42], detection of diabetic retinopathy [7], 3D shape modeling of retinal microvasculature [46], and 3D retinal vessel density mapping [35]. Relatively few work deals with the segmentation of vascular network in OCTA images. They verify on 2D enface images only [3,6,8,13,14,22,24,26,28, 31] or segment 3D vessels without related ground truth [33,46].

Contributions. Our key contributions are: 1) A flattening transformation dedicated to 3D OCTA images to simplify and accelerate the 3D data labeling and processing. It also enables a specialized data augmentation. 2) A novel 3D OCTA dataset with 3D labeled vessel network. To our knowledge it is the first one of this kind in the literature. 3) A hybrid U-net that achieves a first reference segmentation performance on our dataset based on an integration of vesselness measures and different data sources. 4) In addition to the popular voxel-based performance metrics we also apply skeleton-based evaluation metrics to study structural quality of segmentation. Generally, with our work we also resolve the problem of the dependence on an appropriate pre-segmentation for 2D enface images.

2   2D vs. 3D Vessel Detection

Here we briefly discuss differences between 2D and 3D vessel detection.

Datasets. In this paper we present the first 3D OCTA dataset MORE3D with *3D labeled vessel network*. As shown in Fig. 2, the 3D ground truth provides a much more detailed view of the structure of the vessels: The overall curvation, the different diameters in depth or even small crossings from one vessel above another (compare Fig. 1). To our best knowledge, there are three datasets containing 3D OCTA volumes [21,30,43]. But they only include 2D labeled ground truth (see Table 1 for a comparison).

Segmenting and analyzing the retinal vascular structure in 3D offers many advantages in comparison to processing 2D enface images. The retinal vasculature is morphologically differentiated by their (increasing) distance to the ILM in a superficial, intermediate, and deep plexus [20]. Many pathologies affect the

Fig. 2. 3D ground truth.

Fig. 3. Profile of a perfectly round vessel (white) in 2D (left) and 3D (right), where the orange visualizes the area when 1/6 higher diameter than the real vessel is segmented. (Color figure online)

plexus differently [1,38]. In practice, medical experts still use individual enface images. With our presented method, the 3D structure of the vessels is made directly available, which simplifies the working of medical experts.

Complexity of Vessel Detection. Before we introduce the performance metrics in Sect. 6 we want to emphasize that the absolute values of derived metrics have different significance in 2D (e.g. enface image based processing) and 3D (e.g. our work based on 3D annotation). If we overestimate the diameter r of the vessel by p percent (see Fig. 3), then we can determine the True Positive Rate and similarly the Positive Predictive Value if we underestimate the vessel diameter by p percent (see Appendix for the formulas). For example, with $p = 0.2$ we have $TPR_{2D} = 0.8333$ but only $TPR_{3D} = 0.6944$ and $PPV_{2D} = 0.8$ but only $PPV_{3D} = 0.64$ for a vessel like in Fig. 3. So if we compare the values of 2D and 3D metrics where TPR or PPV are involved we should take into account that the 3D values are always lower for similar performing algorithm compared to a 2D case. For the False Positive rate (FPR) the influence is much lower, since in retinal vessel segmentation tasks the amount of negatives in the ground truth is much greater than the amount of positives and therefore usually $TN \gg FP$.

3   Flattening Transformation for 3D OCTA Images

We want to take advantage of the physiology of the eye. The retinal vascular network evolves parallel to the Internal Limiting Membrane (ILM) of the surface of the retina. Thus, we can transform the OCTA image so that the vascular network subsequently evolves in the x/y plane. We call this the "flattening transformation".

Let $I(x, y, z)$ be a 3D OCTA image. We define the 3D vascular network $V(x, y, z)$ and function $f_I(x, y)$ by:

$$V(x,y,z) = \begin{cases} 1, & \text{if vascular network} \\ 0, & \text{otherwise} \end{cases} \quad , \quad f_I(x,y) = \{z, \text{ where } (x,y,z) \in \text{ILM}\}$$

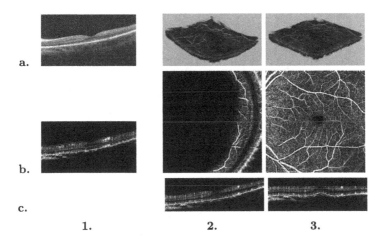

Fig. 4. Flattening transformation. x/z slice of OCT (**a.1.**) and OCTA (**b.1.**) with the detected ILM (blue) and ONL (Outer Nuclear Layer, green). 3D OCTA: original (**a.2.**) and flattened (**a.3.**). Row **b.2./3.**: x/y slice corresponding to the red line in row **c.2./3.**. Row **c.2./3.**: x/z slice corresponding the red line in the row **b.2./3.**.

where the latter represents the distance between the top of the OCTA image and the detected ILM, see Fig. 4. Then the flattened image I' is defined by:

$$I'(x, y, z) = I(x, y, z - f_I(x, y) + b) \tag{1}$$

where $b > 0$ is an offset. The offset leads to a shift so that we still have a part of the vitreous body above the retina new image, see Fig. 4. This transformation implies that the ILM in the flattened image is a plane $f_{I'}(x, y) = b = const$. After the transformation, the vascular network in I' evolves parallel to the x/y plane, see Fig. 4. The related inverse transformation of (1) is given by:

$$V(x, y, z) = V'(x, y, z - b + f(x, y))$$

In addition, the flattening transformation considerably simplifies and accelerates the data labeling by a big margin. Without this, the annotator has to label on slices similar to the one in Fig. 4.b.2, where the vessels dip in and out of the slices and often the decision if a voxel belongs to the vascular network depends on the slices above or below. With the flattening transformation, instead, the annotator can work on images similar to the one in Fig. 4.b.3, which allows much faster decisions and labeling of bigger areas at once.

4 OCTA Dataset MORE3D with 3D Labeled Vessel Network

Our dataset consists of 21 OCT and OCTA 3D volumes that were provided by the Department of Ophthalmology, St. Franziskus Hospital, Münster. It will be made available at: https://www.uni-muenster.de/PRIA/forschung/more3d. html. All the OCTA scans were captured with the Avanti™ from Optovue and

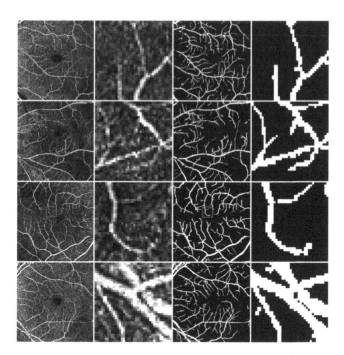

Fig. 5. Illustration of OCTA images (in x/y plane with 1 voxel thickness in z-direction) and their annotations. From left to right: OCTA, enlarged section of the OCTA, Ground Truth, enlarged section of the Ground Truth.

have a resolution of nearly isotropic 304×304 voxels in the x/y axis and 640 for OCT respectively 160 for OCTA in the z-axis. Hence 4 voxels in the z-axis in OCT correspond to 1 voxel in OCTA. Since the OCTA images are derived from the OCT image, they are naturally aligned. We found that the vessels are stretched in the z-direction (see [17] for further information). With the definition of the Signal-to-Noise Ratio as $SNR = 10 \cdot \log_{10}(\frac{\mu}{\sigma})$, where μ is the average signal value and σ is the standard deviation, our dataset after normalization to $[0, 1]$ has an $SNR_{\text{OCTA}} = -1.12$. This is substantially lower than the popular 2D DRIVE fundus retinal image data set [40] with $SNR_{\text{Drive}} = 8.07$, thus indicating the much higher complexity of the OCTA segmentation task at hand.

We segmented the ILM and the ONL, whereby the ONL was refined by hand afterwards due to higher difficulty. The Region of Interest (ROI) was set as all voxels in between the detected ILM and ONL. The resulting ROIs contain between about 1.2 – 1.6 millions voxels depending on the physiology of the eye. This corresponds to an average ROI thickness of 13–17 voxels or ~ 0.16–0.22mm. Each dataset has a labeled vascular network of 42,000–125,000 voxels (average 76,000 voxels), which amounts to 3–10% of the ROI. The average cross-section area for the vessels is $13.86px \pm 8.73px$, which equals around $4px \pm 2px$ as average vessel diameter.

The superficial and deep vascular network was first hand labeled by the first author (9 datasets) or a student assistant (12 datasets). Afterwards it was corrected by a medical expert. These double graded segmentations are taken as ground truth (GT). The time needed to label one dataset was about 8–12 h plus 1–3 h for the corrections by the medical expert. As one can see in Fig. 5, the dataset provides various challenges, very bright vessels, bright background noise to very low intensity and small vessels next to noisy background. The hand labeling was performed on the flattened OCTA images in the x/y plane. The proposed flattening transformation considerably increased the labeling speed and reduced the difficulty to recognize the vessels. The average gradient/slope of the ILM is $5.9\% \pm 3.9\%$ with a median of 5.1%. Thus, the flattening transformation will not disrupt the original structure.

The only needed parameter for the flattening transformation is the ILM. Since this transformation is a voxel-wise shift by the position of the ILM, small mistakes in the ILM result in small errors in the transformation, as long as the segmented ILM stays smooth. Furthermore, the ILM is easily detectable in the OCT image so that a smooth ILM for the OCTA image is given due to the lower resolution in the z-axis.

5   3D Vascular Network Segmentation

5.1   Vesselness Measures

A common approach to segmenting vessels is the use of vesselness measures. We consider 12 vesselness measures, which can be divided into three groups: Multiscale filter based (Ricci [34], Chaudhuri [4], Läthèn [29], Azzopardi [2]), morphological operation (Zana [45], Sazak [37]), and multiscale eigenvalue based (Jerman [15], Frangi [11], Sato [36], Li [23], Erdt [9], Zhou [47]). A selection of such measures will be integrated into the segmentation network.

5.2   Hybrid U-Net Architecture

The decision if a voxel belongs to the background or to a vessel is of local nature. Thus, we choose a patch-based CNN approach to reduce the computational cost and increase the speed. We choose an input patch size as $28 \times 28 \times 5$ and our output patch size $16 \times 16 \times 1$ in $x/y/z$ due to the following reasons. We added 6 voxels in both x and y direction for the input patch so that for each voxel in the output patch we know at least the 13×13 local surrounding in the x/y plane. During labeling it was observed that most voxels could be labeled by viewing the current slice in the x/y plane and for the challenging voxels it was enough to scroll through 1–2 extra slices in the z-direction to decide between vessel and background. Thus, we chose the z-size of the input patch as 5 so that we include 2 slices above and 2 below the output patch location. To reduce imbalance between foreground and background voxels we only learn with patches whose $16 \times 16 \times 1$ GT contains at least 1 foreground voxel.

In this work we focus on integrating vesselness measures and different data sources for boosting segmentation performance. We will study which vesselness

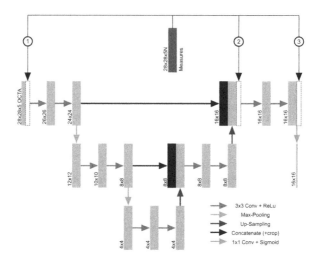

Fig. 6. Hybrid U-net with 3 options to insert vesselness measures: At the front (1), in the middle (2), and at the end (3). The input is 3D of size $28 \times 28 \times (5 \cdot (N+1))$, where N is the number of vesselness measures used as input. After the first 3D convolution we continue with a 2D U-net, starting with 64 channels, double the channels with every max pooling layer, and then reduce to half of the number of channels with every up-sampling. The voxel-wise weighted loss is not shown here.

measures are the best to be used (see Sect. 6) and at which position of the hybrid U-net we should insert vesselness measures to perform best. Neural networks like U-net certainly have some capacity of learning the vesselness. But providing such information explicitly may simplify the network learning. Note that there are other ways of utilizing vesselness measures. For instance, the Frangi-net [12] reformulates the 2D Frangi vesselness measure into a pre-weighted neural network, which leads to a network that is equivalent to the multi-scale Frangi filter.

Insertion Position of Vesselness Measures. There are potentially 3 positions to insert N vesselness measures into the U-net (see Fig. 6; we do not consider multiple insertion positions necessary): a) Front: We concatenate the vesselness measures directly to the OCTA, resulting in an increased input patch size $28 \times 28 \times (5 \cdot (N+1))$. b) Middle: We insert the vesselness measures directly after the upwards path of the U-net, but before the next convolutional layer. The size of the enhanced image patches will be cropped to $16 \times 16 \times (5 \cdot N)$. c) End: We insert the vesselness measures after the last 3×3 convolution layer but before the final 1×1 convolutional layer with the Sigmoid layer. The size of the enhanced image patches will be cropped to $16 \times 16 \times (5 \cdot N)$. We empirically study which one is most beneficial.

Voxel-wise Weighted Loss using GT Labels. To cope with the imbalance between foreground and background and the fact that smaller vessel are significantly harder to segment we will adjust the voxel-wise weight in the loss function. Two approaches will be studied.

The first approach is vessel diameter based. From the labeled GT we can calculate a vessel diameter for each foreground voxel. We propose a weighting function f for a given voxel x and a diameter function $d(x)$ as:

$$w_{\text{diam}}(x, \alpha, n) = \begin{cases} 1, & \text{if } x \text{ is in background} \\ \alpha \left(\frac{d_{\max}}{d(x)} \right)^n, & \text{otherwise} \end{cases}$$

where $d_{\max}$ is the maximum expected vessel diameter and α is a tuneable parameter to increase or decrease the influence of the weights. For $\alpha = 1$ and $n = 0$ we will receive a uniform response. A higher α increases the focus on the foreground to cope with the imbalance. The higher we choose $n > 0$, the more we will emphasize the difficult smaller vessels in comparison to the wider vessels.

The second approach is edge-based. We use the GT to find all foreground voxels F whose 26-neighborhood contains at least one background voxel and all background voxels B whose 26-neighborhood contains at least one foreground voxel. Then

$$w_{\text{edge}}(x, \alpha) = \begin{cases} \alpha, & x \in F \text{ or } x \in B \\ 1, & \text{otherwise} \end{cases}$$

We will compare the proposed voxel-wise weighted losses with three other losses that address the imbalance problem: (1) The Dice loss, (2) the weighted loss, where each class is weighted by $\frac{1}{classsize}$, and (3) the focal loss [25].

5.3 Flattening-Based Data Augmentation

3D pixel-to-pixel labels are labor-intensive and difficult to obtain [24]. Thus, we use data augmentation to make maximum use of our 21 hand labeled 3D volumes. We flip the volume along x/z plane and rotate it around the z axis in $90°$ steps, increasing the amount of volumes by the factor 8. All other rotations or flips are not used since they might create vascular networks that are not feasible in the human eye. To generate sufficient feasible augmented date, we proceed as follows: a) Flatten the OCTA volume with the flattening transformation (1); b) Tilt the OCTA volume by adding a gradient in the x and y axis. By using the flattening transformation and restricting the norm of the gradient in the second step we make sure that we do not tear up the vascular network and still have a feasible representation of the retina. With this technique we are able to further increase amount of augmentation by the factor 25.

6   Experimental Results

6.1   Evaluation Metrics

Voxel-based Evaluation Metrics. We use the following popular methods derived from TP, FP, TN, FN, TPR, TNR, FPR and PPV of the confusion matrix:

- F1-score (same as Dice): $F1 = 2(PPV \times TPR)/(PPV + TPR)$
- Area Under ROC Curve (AUC)
- Accuracy: $Acc = (TP + TN)/(TP + TN + FP + FN)$
- Kappa score: $(Acc - p_e)/(1 - p_e)$ with $p_e = \frac{(TP+FN)(TP+FP)+(TN+FP)(TN+FN)}{(TP+TN+FP+FN)^2}$
- False Discovery Rate: $FDR = FP/(FP + TP)$
- G-mean score: $\sqrt{Sensitivity \times Specificity}$

Due to the imbalance between foreground and background some evaluation metrics deliver very high values, e.g. AUC and Accuracy [5].

Skeleton-Based Evaluation Metrics. We also use the skeleton similarity metrics [44] to compare the skeleton of the vessel network. For each segment i, a curve similarity cs_i and a thickness similarity ts_i are computed segment-wise between the GT and the segmentation. The skeleton similarity for one segment is then given by: $ss_i = \alpha \cdot cs_i + (1 - \alpha) \cdot ts_i$ where $\alpha \in [0, 1]$ is tuneable parameter to weight cs_i and ts_i. The overall skeleton similarity SS is computed by summing up the individual ss_i weighted with the corresponding segment length. Based on SS, weighted TP and FN are computed, while FP and TN are defined as usual. Finally, the skeleton-based sensitivity (rSe), specificity (rSp), and accuracy (rAcc) are derived (see [44] for more details).

6.2 Vesselness Measures on OCTA Images

We normalized the voxel values to $[0, 1]$ and due to the high noise level in 3D OCTA images we applied a mean filter smoothing. We tested different sizes and found that a filter of size $3 \times 3 \times 3$ is well suited. The results of vesselness measures are presented in Table 2. We calculated the result for 4 different combinations: 2D methods on original image, 2D methods on flattened images, 3D methods on original image, and 3D methods on flattened images. We present the average F1-scores on 21 volumes of our OCTA dataset with 3D labeled vessel network for 12 vesselness measures. Other performance measures provided similar results.

The best performing methods are the morphological operations proposed by Zana [45]. In 2D with our flattening technique it outperforms methods and combinations which are not based on morphological operation by 3.9% points with an F1-score of 0.7721. Furthermore, the AUC values for the measure by Zana are the best for every tested combinations. Overall, we selected one best performing method from each category for further use: Ricci [34], Zana [45], Frangi [11], all 2D flattened.

6.3 3D Vessel Segmentation in OCTA Images

We performed a 3-fold cross validation. The optimal threshold to binarize the neural network output is determined on the training data based on F1-score and then applied to the validation data. With data augmentation as described above we have a total amount of $14 \times 8 \times 25 = 2800$ training volumes for each

Table 2. Study of vesselness measures: F1-scores on 21 images for vesselness measures. Method category: 1) multiscale filter based, 2) morphological operation, 3) multiscale eigenvalue based. *3D implementation not available.

Category	Method	2D	flattened 2D	3D	flattened 3D
1)	Ricci	0.7390	0.7438	0.5643	0.5601
	Chaudhuri	0.6909	0.6942	0.6455	0.6514
	Läthèn	0.6840	0.6709	0.6788	0.6902
	Azzopardi	0.6686	0.6309	*	*
2)	Zana	**0.7594**	**0.7721**	**0.7184**	**0.7134**
	Sazak	0.7371	0.7131	0.7000	0.7018
3)	Jerman	0.6626	0.6557	0.6932	0.6886
	Frangi	0.7042	0.7123	0.6931	0.6939
	Sato	0.6864	0.6673	0.5778	0.5809
	Li	0.6173	0.5995	0.6462	0.6483
	Erdt	0.6864	0.6673	0.6963	0.6972
	Zhou	0.6849	0.6705	0.6602	0.6643

Table 3. Insertion position of vesselness measures in hybrid U-net with all inputs.

measure position	F1-score	AUC	Acc	G-mean	Kappa	FDR	rSe	rSp	rAcc
front	**0.8547**	**0.9933**	**0.9836**	**0.9149**	**0.8460**	**0.1315**	0.8152	**0.9833**	0.9185
middle	0.8389	0.9906	0.9822	0.9001	0.8292	0.1352	**0.8361**	0.9788	**0.9258**
end	0.8444	0.9917	0.9823	0.9104	0.8350	0.1453	0.7960	0.9818	0.9115

cross validation step. Each volume contains ~2500–3000 patches with at least one foreground voxel. We used the Adam optimizer for training.

Insertion Position of Vesselness Measures. Table 3 indicates that an insertion at the front performs best in terms of all voxel-based metrics. The middle position even reduced the performance in most vovel-based metrics compared to the vanilla U-net without added vesselness measures (compare Table 4). In contrast, rSe and rAcc increase. At first glance this is counter-intuitive. However, a look at the results reveals an over-segmentation (i.e. extracting more vessel segments), thus affecting negatively the voxel-based metrics but positively the skeleton-based metrics. We will use the front insertion option in the following.

Segmentation Performance by Combination of Input Sources. Table 4 shows the results. The use of vesselness measures consistently increases all metrics. Adding one measure, e.g. Ricci [34], increases the performance for all voxel-based measures. The skeleton-based rSe and rAcc receive best values when adding Zana [45] whereas rSp is best using Ricci [34]. Using all input sources (OCTA, OCT and all three vesselness measures) tops all voxel-based metrics and is close to the best performance in the skeleton-based metrics. Thus, we will only consider this all-input combination for the following experiments.

Table 4. Segmentation performance by combination of input sources.

CNN input	F1-score	AUC	Acc	G-mean	Kappa	FDR	rSe	rSp	rAcc
OCTA	0.8428	0.9923	0.9824	0.9064	0.8335	0.1400	0.8160	0.9799	0.9172
OCTA+OCT	0.8434	0.9920	0.9823	0.9079	0.8340	0.1410	0.8156	0.9806	0.9167
OCTA+Ricci [34]	0.8502	0.9928	0.9832	0.9111	0.8413	0.1334	0.8051	**0.9839**	0.9159
OCTA+Zana [45]	0.8476	0.9928	0.9829	0.9078	0.8385	0.1326	**0.8252**	0.9801	**0.9206**
OCTA+Frangi [11]	0.8436	0.9923	0.9826	0.9056	0.8343	0.1368	0.8082	0.9805	0.9146
all combined	**0.8547**	**0.9933**	**0.9836**	**0.9149**	**0.8460**	0.1315	0.8152	0.9833	0.9185

Table 5. Voxel-wise weighted loss using all inputs. [†] The result was close to binarized, leading to a low sampling rate for the AUC, which causes a low AUC.

loss weighting	F1-score	AUC	Acc	G-mean	Kappa	FDR	rSe	rSp	rAcc
uniform	0.8547	0.9933	0.9836	0.9149	0.8460	**0.1315**	0.8152	0.9833	0.9185
$w_{\mathrm{diam}}(x, 2, 2)$	0.8436	0.9930	0.9822	0.9133	0.8342	0.1530	**0.8667**	0.9701	**0.9306**
$w_{\mathrm{edge}}(x, 10)$	**0.8574**	**0.9938**	**0.9838**	0.9175	**0.8488**	0.1316	0.8144	**0.9844**	0.9203
$w_{\mathrm{edge}}(x, 20)$	0.8514	0.9933	0.9827	**0.9263**	0.8422	0.1616	0.8461	0.9767	0.9268
Weighted classes	0.8327	0.9912	0.9812	0.8985	0.8228	0.1445	0.8163	0.9746	0.9153
Dice loss	0.8559	$(0.9456)^{†}$	0.9836	0.9191	0.8472	0.1375	0.8045	0.9819	0.9169
Focal loss [25]	0.8485	0.9931	0.9828	0.9104	0.8394	0.1357	0.8296	0.9821	0.9245

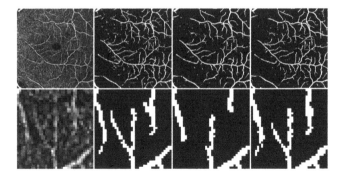

Fig. 7. Illustration of results on a flattened slice. From left to right: OCTA, GT, U-net with OCTA as input, hybrid U-net with all-input combination and voxel-wise weighted loss $w_{\mathrm{diam}}(x, 2, 2)$.

Voxel-wise Weighted Loss. After analyzing the labeled data we set the maximum expected diameter to $d_{\max} = 7$. A pixel-wise weighted loss with $w_{\mathrm{edge}}(x, 10)$ (compare Table 5) increased the performance in every voxel-based metric except G-mean. It achieved the overall best skeleton-based rSp = 0.9844.

Figure 7 shows an example using the weighted loss $w_{\mathrm{diam}}(x, 2, 2)$. It outperforms all other presented methods and combinations in skeleton-based rSe and rAcc, but has one of the highest false detection rates. Visually, this setup tends to overestimate the vessel diameter in the z-axis and underestimates the diameter in the x/y plane. This is also indicated by the higher amount of small voxel groups in Fig. 7 (upper row, right image). These groups belong to vessels whose diameter in the z-axis was overestimated. This explains the lower values in the voxel-based metrics. The use of the proposed voxel-wise weighted losses was able to outperform the three compared losses addressing the imbalance problem.

7 Conclusion

In this work we presented several contributions to 3D retinal vessel segmentation in OCTA volumes. The proposed flattening transformation considerably accelerates the 3D data labeling and enables a specialized data augmentation. As another advantage it may simplify the training of neural networks that are not rotation-invariant, thus potentially making them more difficult to work on the raw curved images. On the other hand, the influence of the flattening transformation on the subsequent analysis is not consistent. Figure 2 reveals that dependent of the operator, the unflattened version may be favorable. We have presented the first OCTA dataset MORE3D with 3D labeled vessel network. It will foster the research in the community. A hybrid U-net was realized to achieve a first reference segmentation performance on our dataset. The presented work helps resolve the problem of the dependence on an appropriate pre-segmentation for 2D enface images that are the dominating source of data in the literature.

In future we will examine adapting alternate backbone network architectures to full 3D vessel segmentation. Moreover, we will explore transfer learning to efficiently and effectively process OCTA volumes from other manufacturers using the outcome of this work. A fundamental issue is the fact that the absolute values of metrics have different significance for 2D and 3D images (see Sect. 2). It is thus helpful to find a way that enables to compare the results of 2D and 3D vessel detection problem instances.

Acknowledgments. This work was supported by the Dr. Werner Jackstädt-Stiftung.

Appendix

If we overestimate the diameter r of the vessel by p percent (see Fig. 3), then the True Positive Rate will become:

$$TPR_{2D}(p) = \frac{2r}{2r + 2pr} = \frac{1}{1 + p}$$

$$TPR_{3D}(p) = \frac{\pi r^2}{\pi r^2 + (\pi(r + pr)^2 - \pi r^2)} = \frac{1}{(1 + p)^2}$$

Similarly if we underestimate the vessel diameter by p percent we have Positive Predictive Value:

$$PPV_{2D}(p) = \frac{2(r - pr)}{2(r - pr) + 2pr} = 1 - p$$

$$PPV_{3D}(p) = \frac{\pi(r - pr)^2}{\pi(r - pr)^2 + (\pi r^2 - \pi(r - pr)^2)} = (1 - p)^2$$

These results can be used to compare the inherent complexity of vessel detection in 2D vs. 3D (see Sect. 2).

References

1. Ashraf, M., et al.: Vascular density of deep, intermediate and superficial vascular plexuses are differentially affected by diabetic retinopathy severity. Investig. Ophthalmol. Vis. Sci. **61**(10), 53 (2020)
2. Azzopardi, G., et al.: Trainable COSFIRE filters for vessel delineation with application to retinal images. Med. Image Anal. **19**(1), 46–57 (2015)
3. Breger, A., et al.: Blood vessel segmentation in en-face OCTA images: a frequency based method. CoRR abs/2109.06116 (2021)
4. Chaudhuri, S., et al.: Detection of blood vessels in retinal images using two-dimensional matched filters. IEEE Trans. Med. Imaging **8**(3), 263–269 (1989)
5. Davis, J., Goadrich, M.: The relationship between precision-recall and roc curves. In: 23rd International Conference on Machine Learning (ICML), pp. 233–240 (2006)
6. Eladawi, N., et al.: Automatic blood vessels segmentation based on different retinal maps from OCTA scans. Comput. Biol. Med. **89**, 150–161 (2017)
7. Eladawi, N., et al.: Early signs detection of diabetic retinopathy using optical coherence tomography angiography scans based on 3D multi-path convolutional neural network. In: IEEE International Conference on Image Processing (ICIP), pp. 1390–1394 (2019)
8. Engberg, A.M.E., et al.: Automated quantification of retinal microvasculature from OCT angiography using dictionary-based vessel segmentation. In: 23rd Conference on Medical Image Understanding and Analysis (MIUA), pp. 257–269 (2019)
9. Erdt, M., Raspe, M., Suehling, M.: Automatic hepatic vessel segmentation using graphics hardware. In: Dohi, T., Sakuma, I., Liao, H. (eds.) Medical Imaging and Augmented Reality. MIAR 2008. LNCS, vol. 5128, pp. 403–412 . Springer, Berlin, Heidelberg (2008). https://doi.org/10.1007/978-3-540-79982-5_44
10. Faatz, H., et al.: Optical coherence tomography angiography of types 1 and 2 choroidal neovascularization in age-related macular degeneration during anti-vegf therapy: evaluation of a new quantitative method. Eye **33**(9), 1466–1471 (2019)
11. Frangi, A.F., et al.: Multiscale vessel enhancement filtering. In: Wells, W.M., Colchester, A., Delp, S. (eds.) Medical Image Computing and Computer-Assisted Intervention – MICCAI'98. MICCAI 1998. LNCS, vol. 1496, pp. 130–137. Springer, Berlin, Heidelberg (1998). https://doi.org/10.1007/BFb0056195
12. Fu, W., et al.: Frangi-net. In: Maier, A., Deserno, T., Handels, H., Maier-Hein, K., Palm, C., Tolxdorff, T. (eds.) Bildverarbeitung fur die Medizin 2018. Informatik aktuell, pp. 341–346. Springer Vieweg, Berlin, Heidelberg (2018). https://doi.org/10.1007/978-3-662-56537-7_87
13. Hao, J., et al.: Retinal structure detection in OCTA image via voting-based multitask learning. IEEE Trans. Med. Imaging **41**(12), 3969–3980 (2022)
14. Hu, K., et al.: Joint-seg: treat foveal avascular zone and retinal vessel segmentation in OCTA images as a joint task. IEEE Trans. Instrum. Meas. **71**, 1–13 (2022)
15. Jerman, T., et al.: Enhancement of vascular structures in 3D and 2D angiographic images. IEEE Trans. Med. Imaging **35**(9), 2107–2118 (2016)
16. Jia, Y., et al.: Split-spectrum amplitude-decorrelation angiography with optical coherence tomography. Opt. Express **20**(4), 4710–4725 (2012)
17. Kuhlmann, J., et al.: Axial stretching of vessels in the retinal vascular plexus with 3D OCT-angiography. Transl. Vis. Sci. Technol. **11**, 21 (2022)
18. Kumar, K.S., Singh, N.P.: Analysis of retinal blood vessel segmentation techniques: a systematic survey. Multimed. Tools Appl. **82**(5), 7679–7733 (2023)

19. Lamy, J. et al.: Vesselness filters: a survey with benchmarks applied to liver imaging. In: 25th International Conference on Pattern Recognition (ICPR), pp. 3528–3535 (2020)
20. Lavia, C., Bonnin, S., Maule, M., Erginay, A., Tadayoni, R., Gaudric, A.: Vessel density of superficial intermediate and deep capillary plexus using optical coherence tomography angiography. Retina **39**(2), 247–258 (2019)
21. Li, M., et al.: OCTA-500: a retinal dataset for optical coherence tomography angiography study. CoRR abs/2012.07261 (2020)
22. Li, M., Zhang, W., Chen, Q.: Image magnification network for vessel segmentation in OCTA images. In: Yu, S., et al. (eds.) Pattern Recognition and Computer Vision. PRCV 2022. LNCS, vol. 13537, pp. 426–435. Springer, Cham (2022). https://doi.org/10.1007/978-3-031-18916-6_35
23. Li, Q., Sone, S., Doi, K.: Selective enhancement filters for nodules, vessels, and airway walls in two- and three-dimensional CT scans. Med. Phys. **30**(8), 2040–2051 (2003)
24. Li, M., et al.: Image projection network: 3D to 2D image segmentation in OCTA images. IEEE Trans. Med. Imaging **39**(11), 3343–3354 (2020)
25. Lin, T., et al.: Focal loss for dense object detection. IEEE Trans. Pattern Anal. Mach. Intell. **42**(2), 318–327 (2020)
26. Liu, X., et al.: OCTA retinal vessel segmentation based on vessel thickness inconsistency loss. In: IEEE International Conference on Image Processing (ICIP), pp. 2676–2680 (2022)
27. Liu, Y., et al.: Projection artifact suppression for inner retina in OCT angiography. In: IEEE 16th International Symposium on Biomedical Imaging (ISBI), pp. 592–596 (2019)
28. Liu, Y., et al.: Disentangled representation learning for OCTA vessel segmentation with limited training data. IEEE Trans. Med. Imaging **41**(12), 3686–3698 (2022)
29. Läthén, G., Jonasson, J., Borga, M.: Blood vessel segmentation using multi-scale quadrature filtering. Pattern Recognit. Lett. **31**, 762–767 (2010)
30. Ma, Y., et al.: ROSE: a retinal OCT-Angiography vessel segmentation dataset and new model. IEEE Trans. Med. Imaging **40**(3), 928–939 (2021)
31. Ma, Z., et al.: Retinal OCTA image segmentation based on global contrastive learning. Sensors **22**(24), 9847 (2022)
32. Meiburger, K.M., et al.: Automatic segmentation and classification methods using Optical Coherence Tomography Angiography (OCTA): a review and handbook. Appl. Sci. **11**, 9734 (2021)
33. Pissas, T., et al.: Deep iterative vessel segmentation in OCT Angiography. Biomed. Opt. Express **11**(5), 2490 (2020)
34. Ricci, E., Perfetti, R.: Retinal blood vessel segmentation using line operators and support vector classification. IEEE Trans. Med. Imaging **26**(10), 1357–1365 (2007)
35. Sarabi, M.S., et al.: 3D retinal vessel density mapping with OCT-Angiography. IEEE J. Biomed. Health Inform. **24**(12), 3466–3479 (2020)
36. Sato, Y., et al.: Tissue classification based on 3D local intensity structures for volume rendering. IEEE Trans. Med. Imaging **6**(2), 160–180 (2000)
37. Sazak, C., Nelson, C.J., Obara, B.: The multiscale bowler-hat transform for blood vessel enhancement in retinal images. Pattern Recognit. **88**, 739–750 (2019)
38. Spaide, R.F., Klancnik, J.M., Cooney, M.J.: Retinal vascular layers in macular telangiectasia type 2 imaged by optical coherence tomographic angiography. JAMA Ophthalmol. **133**(1), 66–73 (2015)
39. Spaide, R.F., et al.: Optical coherence tomography angiography. Prog. Retin. Eye Res. **64**, 1–55 (2018)

40. Staal, J., Abràmoff, M.D., Niemeijer, M., Viergever, M.A., van Ginneken, B.: Ridge-based vessel segmentation in color images of the retina. IEEE Trans. Med. Imaging **23**(4), 501–509 (2004)
41. Sule, O.O.: A survey of deep learning for retinal blood vessel segmentation methods: taxonomy, trends, challenges and future directions. IEEE Access **10**, 38202–38236 (2022)
42. Taibouni, K., et al.: Automated quantification of choroidal neovascularization on optical coherence tomography angiography images. Comput. Biol. Med. **114**, 103450 (2019)
43. Xiao, P., et al.: OMSN and FAROS: OCTA microstructure segmentation network and fully annotated retinal OCTA segmentation dataset. CoRR abs/2212.13059 (2022)
44. Yan, Z., Yang, X., Cheng, K.: A skeletal similarity metric for quality evaluation of retinal vessel segmentation. IEEE Trans. Med. Imaging **37**(4), 1045–1057 (2018)
45. Zana, F., Klein, J.: Segmentation of vessel-like patterns using mathematical morphology and curvature evaluation. IEEE Trans. Image Process. **10**(7), 1010–1019 (2001)
46. Zhang, J., et al.: 3D shape modeling and analysis of retinal microvasculature in OCT-Angiography images. IEEE Trans. Med. Imaging **39**(5), 1335–1346 (2020)
47. Zhou, C., et al.: Automatic multiscale enhancement and segmentation of pulmonary vessels in CT pulmonary angiography images for cad applications. Med. Phys. **34**(12), 4567–4577 (2007)

M(otion)-Mode Based Prediction of Ejection Fraction Using Echocardiograms

Ece Ozkan[1]([✉])[iD], Thomas M. Sutter[2]([✉])[iD], Yurong Hu[3][iD], Sebastian Balzer[4],
and Julia E. Vogt[2][iD]

[1] Department of Brain and Cognitive Sciences, MIT, Cambridge, USA
`eoezkan@mit.edu`
[2] Department of Computer Science, ETH Zurich, Zurich, Switzerland
`suttetho@inf.ethz.ch, julia.vogt@inf.ethz.ch`
[3] Department of Information Technology and Electrical Engineering, ETH Zurich,
Zurich, Switzerland
[4] Department of Biosystems Science and Engineering, ETH Zurich, Zurich,
Switzerland

Abstract. Early detection of cardiac dysfunction through routine screening is vital for diagnosing cardiovascular diseases. An important metric of cardiac function is the left ventricular ejection fraction (EF), where lower EF is associated with cardiomyopathy. Echocardiography is a popular diagnostic tool in cardiology, with ultrasound being a low-cost, real-time, and non-ionizing technology. However, human assessment of echocardiograms for calculating EF is time-consuming and expertise-demanding, raising the need for an automated approach. In this work, we propose using the M(otion)-mode of echocardiograms for estimating the EF and classifying cardiomyopathy. We generate multiple artificial M-mode images from a single echocardiogram and combine them using off-the-shelf model architectures. Additionally, we extend contrastive learning (CL) to cardiac imaging to learn meaningful representations from exploiting structures in unlabeled data allowing the model to achieve high accuracy, even with limited annotations. Our experiments show that the supervised setting converges with only ten modes and is comparable to the baseline method while bypassing its cumbersome training process and being computationally much more efficient. Furthermore, CL using M-mode images is helpful for limited data scenarios, such as having labels for only 200 patients, which is common in medical applications.

Keywords: Echocardiography · M-mode Ultrasound · Ejection Fraction · Computer Assisted Diagnosis (CAD)

1 Introduction

Cardiovascular diseases (CVD) are the leading cause of death worldwide, responsible for nearly one-third of global deaths [29]. Early assessment of cardiac

---

E. Ozkan and T. M. Sutter—Shared first authorship.

© The Author(s), under exclusive license to Springer Nature Switzerland AG 2024
U. Köthe and C. Rother (Eds.): DAGM GCPR 2023, LNCS 14264, pp. 307–320, 2024.
https://doi.org/10.1007/978-3-031-54605-1_20

dysfunction through routine screening is essential, as clinical management and behavioral changes can prevent hospitalizations and premature deaths. An important metric for assessing cardiac (dys)function is the left ventricular (LV) ejection fraction (EF), which evaluates the ratio between LV end-systolic and end-diastolic volumes [3,21].

Echocardiography is the most common and readily available diagnostic tool to assess cardiac function, ultrasound (US) imaging being a low-cost, non-ionizing, and rapid technology. However, the manual evaluation of echocardio-grams is time-consuming, operator-dependent, and expertise-demanding. Thus, there is a clear need for an automated method to assist clinicians in estimating EF.

M(otion)-mode is a form of US, in which a single scan line is emitted and received at a high frame rate through time to evaluate the dynamics to assess different diseases [23]. M-mode is often utilized in clinical practice e. g. in lung ultrasonography [1,25] or echocardiography [6,7,10,26]. Since cardiac function assessment relies on heart dynamics, M-mode images can be an excellent alternative to B(rightness)-mode image- or video-based methods. However, little effort is directed toward exploiting M-mode images in an automated manner.

Data collection and annotation are expensive for most applications. Therefore, learning from limited labeled data is critical in data-limited problems, such as in healthcare. To overcome this data bottleneck, self-supervised learning (SSL) methods have been recently proposed to learn meaningful high-level representations from unlabeled data [16,24].

Related Work. A few existing works [14,18] reconstruct M-mode images from B-mode videos to detect pneumothorax using CNNs. Furthermore, authors in [27] propose an automatic landmark localization method in M-mode images. A more related method using M-mode images in an automated manner to estimate EF is [22], which uses single M-mode images in parasternal long-axis view to measure chamber dimensions for calculating EF.

For automated EF prediction, some previous works exploit either still-images [8,17,31] or spatio-temporal convolutions on B(rightness)-mode echocardiography videos [21]. However, still-image-based methods have a high variability [20], and video-based methods rely on a complex pipeline with larger models. Furthermore, [19] uses vision transformers and CNNs to tackle the problem of estimating the LV EF, and [15] uses geometric features of the LV derived from ECG video frames to estimate EF. The authors in [28] evaluate ML-based methods in a multi-cohort setting using different imaging modalities. In the SSL setting, [5] propose a contrastive learning framework for deep image regression, which consists of a feature learning branch via a novel adaptive-margin contrastive loss and a regression prediction branch using echocardiography frames as input.

Our Contribution. We propose to extract images from readily available B-mode echocardiogram videos, each mimicking an M-mode image from a different scan line of the heart. We combine the different artificial M-mode images using off-the-shelf model architectures and estimate their EF to diagnose cardiomyopathy in a supervised regime. Using M-mode images allows the model to naturally observe the motion and sample the heart from different angles while bypassing cumbersome 3D models. Secondly, we propose an alternative scheme for predicting EF using generated M-mode images in a self-supervised fashion while extending contrastive learning. We design a problem-specific contrastive loss for M-mode images to learn representations with structure and patient awareness. We evaluate both regimes on the publicly available EchoNet-Dynamic dataset ([20]) and demonstrate both models' effectiveness.

To the best of our knowledge, this is the first work on image-based and temporal information incorporating cardiac function prediction methods to estimate EF. Furthermore, our method can easily be applied to other problems where cardiac dynamics play an essential role in the diagnosis. To ensure reproducibility, we made the code available: https://github.com/thomassutter/mmodeecho.

2   Methods

This work aims to create a pipeline with as little intervention as possible; thus, our method consists of two parts, as shown in Fig. 1. The first part is extracting M-mode images from readily available B-mode videos. The second part includes representation learning, which are lower-level information that preserves more information of the input image and are used to predict EF from M-mode images, including two schemes: supervised and self-supervised learning.

2.1   From B-Mode Videos to M-Mode Images

Assume our dataset contains N patients. For each patient $i = \{1, 2, \cdots, N\}$, the label y_i indicates its EF. Furthermore, the B-mode echocardiogram video of each patient i is given of size $h \times w \times t$ with h being height, w width, and t number of frames of the video. The m-th M-mode image of patient i is given as x_i^m with $m = \{1, 2, \cdots, M\}$. It is a single line of pixels through the center of the image with an angle θ_m over frames, assuming LV is around the center throughout the video, as in Fig. 1(a). This image, corresponding to θ_m, is then of size $s_m \times t$, with s_m as the length of the scan line. For simplicity, we set $s_m = h \ \forall \ m$ independent of its angle θ_m. For generating multiple M-mode images, a set of M angles $\boldsymbol{\theta} = [\theta_1, \ldots, \theta_M]$ is used to generate M M-mode images, where the angles $\boldsymbol{\theta}$ are equally spaced between $0°$ and $180°$.

While the proposed approach for generating M-mode images is intuitive and works well (see Sect. 3.3), other approaches are also feasible. For instance, the center of rotation in the middle of the image in our M-mode generation process could be changed. Like that, we could mimic the behavior of the data collection process as every generated M-mode image would resemble a scan line of the US probe. However, the main goal of this work is to highlight the potential of M-mode images for the analysis of US videos. Given our convincing results, we leave the exploration of different M-mode generation mechanisms for future work.

2.2   Learning Representations from M-Mode Images

Supervised Learning for EF Prediction. We aim to learn supervised representations using off-the-shelf model architectures to estimate EF. Instead of

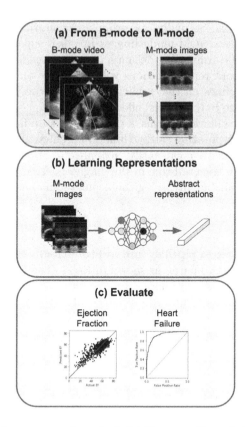

Fig. 1. Overview of our proposed method. (a) Generate M-mode images from B-mode echocardiography videos at different scan lines. (b) Learn representations from the generated M-mode images using supervised and self-supervised learning schemes. (c) Evaluate EF prediction to diagnose cardiomyopathy.

using a single M-mode, one can aggregate the information of M-mode images from the same patient to increase robustness. We evaluate two fusion methods for aggregating information among the M M-mode images: early-fusion and late-fusion [2]. With early fusion, we construct a $M \times s \times t$ image with the M M-mode images being the M channels of the newly created image. In late-fusion, we exploit three different methods. For all of the late-fusion schemes, we first infer an abstract representation z_i^m for every M-mode image x_i^m. The representations z_i^m are then aggregated to a joint representation $\tilde{z}_i$ using an LSTM cell [11], averaging, or concatenating.

We utilize a standard ResNet architecture [9] with 2D-convolutional layers independent of the fusion principle. With 2D-convolutions, we assume a single M-mode image as a 2D gray-scale image with two spatial dimensions, s and t.

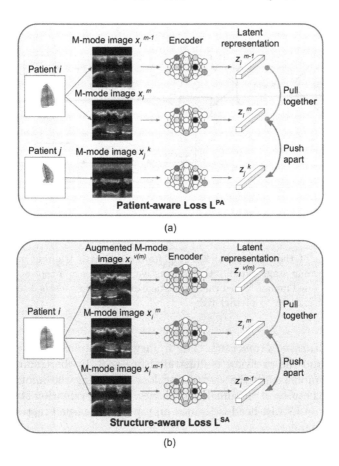

Fig. 2. Overview of our proposed SSL method. The contrastive loss includes (a) patient awareness to attract similarity between data from the same patient while discouraging it between different patients and (b) structure awareness to take the (possible) dissimilarity from the same patient into account.

Self-supervised Learning for EF Prediction. This part aims to learn meaningful representations from unlabeled data to estimate EF using echocardiograms. To this end, we propose an SSL scheme for M-mode images based on contrastive learning, where M-mode images from the same patient can naturally serve as positive pairs since they share labels for many downstream tasks. As discussed by [30], bio-signal data is inherently highly heterogeneous; thus, when applying learning-based methods to patient data, we need to consider both the similarity and the difference between samples originating from the same patient. Thus, we propose a problem-specific contrastive loss with patient and structure awareness, as shown in Fig. 2.

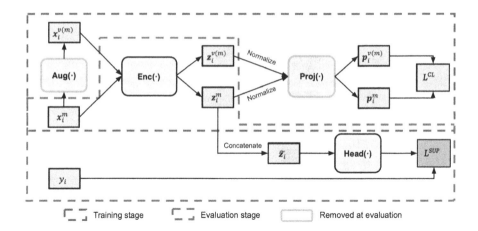

Fig. 3. Schema of the contrastive learning framework with training and evaluation stages. The training stage exploits the contrastive loss to learn a representation leveraging the unlabelled images. The evaluation stage exploits these learned representations in a supervised manner to predict EF.

Contrastive Learning Framework. The framework contains training and evaluation stages and the overview is illustrated in Fig. 3. In the training stage, we optimize the model with the contrastive loss leveraging the information from underlying structures of the unlabeled images. In the evaluation stage, a multilayer perceptron (MLP) head is trained on top of the learned representations in a supervised manner.

For each generated M-mode image x_i^m, we generate its augmented view $x_i^{v(m)}$ using the $Aug(\cdot)$ module. So the augmented dataset is represented as $\{(x_i^m, x_i^{v(m)}, y_i)\}$. The encoder network $Enc(\cdot)$ maps each image x_i^m to a feature vector z_i^m. We utilize a standard ResNet architecture [9].

In the training stage, z_i^m is normalized to the unit hyper-sphere before being passed to the projection network. Following the work [4], we introduce a learnable non-linear projection network between the representation and the contrastive loss. The projection network $Proj(\cdot)$ takes the normalized lower-level representation z_i^m as input and outputs the higher-level representation p_i^m. We use a two-layer MLP with ReLU activation as $Proj(\cdot)$ in this work.

In the evaluation stage, we initialize the parameters of the encoder network $Enc(\cdot)$ with the model obtained from contrastive learning and add an MLP head $Head(\cdot)$ to the top. For each patient i, we have M feature vectors $z_i^m \in \mathbb{R}^K$. The M vectors are then fused to get the joint representation $\tilde{z}_i \in \mathbb{R}^{K \times M}$ and passed to $Head(\cdot)$. One can have different fusion methods for aggregating information among the M vectors, e. g. using an LSTM cell [11], averaging, or concatenating.

Contrastive Loss for M-mode Images. To account for (dis)similarities, we design two loss functions for learning both patient- and structure-awareness.

(a) Patient-aware loss: The goal is to attract the representations from the same patient to be similar while pushing apart representations from different patients (see Fig. 2 (a)). This enforces two M-mode images to be considered similar if they are from the same patient and dissimilar if they are from different patients. The patient-aware loss is given as:

$$L^{PA} = -\frac{1}{M-1} \sum_{i=1}^{N} \sum_{m=1}^{M} \sum_{l \neq m} \log \frac{\exp(\boldsymbol{p}_i^m \cdot \boldsymbol{p}_i^l/\tau)}{\sum_{j,k} \exp(\boldsymbol{p}_i^m \cdot \boldsymbol{p}_j^k/\tau) - \exp(\boldsymbol{p}_i^m \cdot \boldsymbol{p}_i^m/\tau)} \quad (1)$$

where N is the number of patients in one batch, M is the number of original M-mode images used for each patient, and τ is the temperature scaling parameter. The term $\boldsymbol{p}_i^m$ represents the output of $Proj(\cdot)$.

Inspired by [30], we tried defining a neighborhood function to limit the similarity of M-mode images from the same patient. However, incorporating neighbourhood to patient-awareness did not further improve the results; thus, we used all M-mode images per patient to define the patient-aware loss.

(b) Structure-aware loss: If we only use patient-aware loss L^{PA}, there exists a risk that all images from the same patient collapse to a single point [30]. So we propose the structure-aware loss to introduce some diversity (see Fig. 2 (b)). To incorporate this into the learned representations, we construct positive pairs from each M-mode image with its augmentation and consider other combinations as negative pairs. It is then defined as:

$$L^{SA} = -\sum_{i=1}^{N} \sum_{m=1}^{2M} \log \frac{\exp(\boldsymbol{p}_i^m \cdot \boldsymbol{p}_i^{v(m)}/\tau)}{\sum_{l \neq m} \exp(\boldsymbol{p}_i^m \cdot \boldsymbol{p}_i^l/\tau)} \quad (2)$$

If image m is an original image, then $v(m)$ represents its augmented view; if image m is an augmented image, then $v(m)$ represents the original image. Minimizing L^{SA} drives the representation pairs from the augmented images in the numerator close while pushing the representations in the denominator far away, where the denominator contains M-mode images from the same patient.

Finally, we combine the two losses to get structure-aware and patient-aware contrastive loss for M-mode images using the hyperparameter α to control the trade-off between the awareness terms:

$$L^{CL} = \alpha L^{PA} + (1-\alpha)L^{SA}. \quad (3)$$

3   Experiments and Results

3.1   Dataset

We use the publicly available EchoNet-Dynamic dataset [20]. It contains 10'030 apical-4-chamber echocardiography videos from individuals who underwent imaging between 2016–2018 as part of routine clinical care at Stanford University

Hospital. Each B-mode video was cropped and masked to remove information outside the scanning sector and downsampled into standardized 112×112 pixel videos. For simplicity, we used videos with at least 112 frames. We use the official splits with 7465 training, 1289 validation, and 1282 test set samples.

3.2 Experimental Setup

We evaluate the models' performance using classification accuracy for five random seeds and report the mean performance and standard deviation. During training, all supervised models optimize the estimation of EF as a regression task. For testing, we use a constant threshold τ for classifying cardiomyopathy. In all experiments, we set $\tau = 0.5$. Hence, an estimation of $\hat{\tau} < 0.5$ results in classifying a sample as cardiomyopathic.

We evaluate all models using the area under the receiver operating characteristic (AUROC) and the area under the precision-recall curve (AUPRC) with respect to whether a patient is correctly classified as healthy or cardiomyopathic. Additionally, we report the mean absolute error (MAE) and the root mean squared error (RMSE) of the predicted EF with respect to the true EF in the Supplementary Material. We report the mean performance, including standard deviations over five random seeds for all results.

We use the training set from EchoNet for pre-training (SSL), and apply a linear learning rate scheduler during the first 30 epochs as warm-up. For the supervised fine-tuning, we select different proportions of the training set in the limited labeled data scenario. All M-mode models are trained for 100 epochs using Adam optimizer [12] with an initial learning rate of 0.001 and a batch size of 64. For image augmentation, we apply random horizontal flip and Gaussian noise. For the fusion method of the M-mode representations we used concatenation. For the EchoNet model, we use the same model and parameters as in [21]. The model is trained for 45 epochs with a learning rate of 0.0001 and a batch size of 20. We do not use test-time augmentation for any of the models. We report the full set of hyperparameters used in our experiments in Table 1.

3.3 Results and Discussion

Evaluating M-Mode Images in Supervised Setting. We train and evaluate models with different numbers of M-modes for $M \in \{1, 2, 5, 10, 20, 50\}$. We use the complete training set, including labels, as we are interested in the performance of the models depending on the number of available M-modes. Figure 4 shows the results for different numbers of M-modes. We see that late fusion models benefit from an increasing number of modes, whereas the early fusion method overfits quickly and never achieves a comparable performance.

Evaluating Limited Data Regime. We evaluate the accuracy of the different models introduced in Sect. 2 for different amount of labeled training samples. As

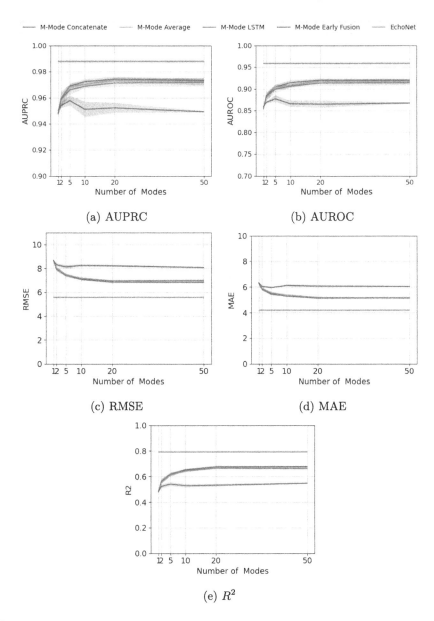

Fig. 4. Performance for different numbers of M-mode images using early and late-fusion methods. In (a), we evaluate the classification performance with respect to AUPRC and AUROC in (b), the regression performance with respect to RMSE in (c), MAE in (d), and R^2-score in (e).

most medical datasets do not have the size of EchoNet-Dynamic [13], methods for medical machine learning should perform best in the limited labeled data regime. We use *E2E* for the supervised and *CL* for the self-supervised setting.

Table 1. List the hyperparameters used in our experiments. We use the same hyperparameters for E2E setup and the fine-tuning stage of SSL setup (denoted as "_sup" in Table 1). "_cl" denotes the hyper-parameters used in the SSL pre-training stage.

Parameter	Value	Description
lr_sup	0.001	learning rate for supervised training
lr_cl	1.0	learning rate for SSL training
opt	Adam	optimizer for SSL and supervised training
bsz_sup	64	batch size for supervised training
bsz_cl	256	batch size for SSL training
epoch_sup	100	epochs for supervised training
epoch_cl	300	epochs for SSL training
epoch_warm	30	warm-up epochs for SSL training
α	0.8	loss trade-off
τ	0.01	temperature scaling
Dim_e	512	$Enc(\cdot)$ output dimension
Dim_ph	2048	$Proj(\cdot)$ hidden layer dimension
Dim_po	128	$Proj(\cdot)$ output dimension
Dim_lstm	256	LSTM output dimension

Additionally, we introduce $E2E+$ and $CL+$, which, inspired by EchoNet [21], uses random short clips for each training epoch. Both models use M-mode images of 32 frames with a sampling period of 2. We train and evaluate models using $p\%$ of the full training set for $p \in \{1, 2, 3, 5, 10, 20, 30, 50, 75, 100\}$. All M-mode methods are trained with $M = 10$.

Figure 5 shows the limited labeled data experiment results. Although we are not able to reach the performance of the EchoNet model for any number of modes (see Fig. 4b) if the number of labeled training samples is high (see Fig. 5a), both supervised and self-supervised learning methods using M-mode instead of B-mode can outperform the EchoNet model in the low labeled data regime ($p < 5\%$, Fig. 5b). Also, we observe that using shorter clips is useful for the self-supervised learning methods, with $CL+$ being able to achieve an AUROC over 0.85 with only around 200 labeled samples.

Computational Cost. Furthermore, we compare the number of parameters and computational costs for different models in Table 2, where we used a multi-GPU setup with four NVIDIA GeForce RTX 2080 Ti GPUs. We report the computation time in seconds per batch (sec/B) and milliseconds per sample (msec/sample), and the memory requirements in gigabytes per batch (GB/B).

Our proposed M-mode image based models require around six times less time and ten times less memory to train and run inference per sample. Given the used memory per batch, we could increase the batch size for the M-mode methods,

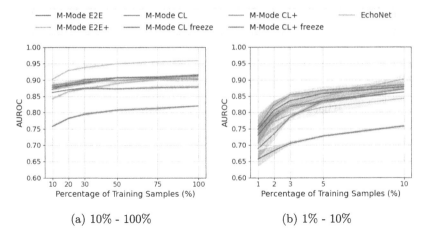

Fig. 5. Results for different training set sizes using the proposed end-to-end supervised (E2E) and contrastive learning (CL) approaches. In (a), we train and evaluate the models on 10%–100% labeled training samples, in (b) only on 1%-10% of the samples. E2E and CL models are trained using a fixed long clip with length 112; E2E+ and CL+ are trained using random short clips with length 32. CL freeze and CL+ freeze are fine-tuned with the encoder parameters frozen.

lowering the computation time per sample even further, whereas the baseline model is already at the limit due to its architecture.

4   Discussion and Conclusion

In this work, we propose to generate M-mode images from readily available B-mode echocardiography videos and fuse these to estimate EF and, thus, cardiac dysfunction. Our results show that M-mode-based prediction methods are comparable to the baseline method while avoiding its complex training routine and reducing the computational cost and the need for expensive expert input.

Conventional M-mode images have a very high sampling rate, which results in a high temporal resolution so that even very rapid motion can be recorded. The

Table 2. Computational costs. We evaluate the EchoNet and the proposed M-mode methods with respect to the number of parameters, the computation time, and the memory requirements. All M-mode models are evaluated using $M = 10$. E2E defines the end-to-end supervised and CL the contrastive learning approach.

Model	BS	#Params (Mio.)	Time (sec/B)		Time (msec/sample)		Memory (GB/B)	
			Train	Test	Train	Test	Train	Test
EchoNet	20	31.5	2.898	2.474	144.9	123.7	5.294	1.187
E2E & CL	64	11.7	1.568	1.330	24.5	21.1	1.013	0.120

generated M-mode images have significantly less temporal resolution than the conventional M-mode images from US machines. However, our results indicate that exploiting generated M-mode images does not limit the performance for EF estimation. As we do not use the M-mode images collected directly from the US machines, there is no need for an additional data collection step.

Additionally, we show the potential of pre-trained methods. In scenarios where expensive expert labels are not readily available, pre-training using unlabeled M-mode images outperforms more complicated pipelines highlighting the potential of M-Mode based pipelines for clinical use cases. In our future work, we want to investigate the use cases for M-mode on different diseases and further improve the performance of the proposed pre-training pipeline.

Acknowledgements. EO was supported by the SNSF grant P500PT-206746 and TS by the grant 2021-911 of the Strategic Focal Area "Personalized Health and Related Technologies (PHRT)" of the ETH Domain (Swiss Federal Institutes of Technology).

References

1. Avila, J., et al.: Does the addition of M-Mode to B-mode ultrasound increase the accuracy of identification of lung sliding in traumatic pneumothoraces? J. Ultrasound Med. **37**(11), 2681–2687 (2018)
2. Baltrušaitis, T., Ahuja, C., Morency, L.P.: Multimodal machine learning: a survey and taxonomy. IEEE Trans. Pattern Anal. Mach. Intell. **41**(2), 423–443 (2018)
3. Bamira, D., Picard, M.H.: Imaging: echocardiology-assessment of cardiac structure and function. In: Encyclopedia of Cardiovascular Research and Medicine, pp. 35–54. Elsevier (2018)
4. Chen, T., Kornblith, S., Norouzi, M., Hinton, G.: A simple framework for contrastive learning of visual representations. In: International Conference on Machine Learning, pp. 1597–1607 (2020)
5. Dai, W., Li, X., Chiu, W.H.K., Kuo, M.D., Cheng, K.T.: Adaptive contrast for image regression in computer-aided disease assessment. IEEE Trans. Med. Imaging **41**(5), 1255–1268 (2022)
6. Devereux, R.B., Lutas, E.M., Casale, P.N., Kligfield, P., Eisenberg, R.R., et al.: Standardization of M-mode echocardiographic left ventricular anatomic measurements. J. Am. Coll. Cardiol. **4**(6), 1222–1230 (1984)
7. Gaspar, H.A., Morhy, S.S., Lianza, A.C., de Carvalho, W.B., Andrade, J.L., et al.: Focused cardiac ultrasound: a training course for pediatric intensivists and emergency physicians. BMC Med. Educ. **14**(1) (2014)
8. Ghorbani, A., Ouyang, D., Abid, A., He, B., Chen, J.H., Harrington, R.A., et al.: Deep learning interpretation of echocardiograms. NPJ Digit. Med. (2020)
9. He, K., Zhang, X., Ren, S., Sun, J.: Deep residual learning for image recognition. In: Proceedings of the IEEE Conference on Computer Vision and Pattern Recognition, pp. 770–778 (2016)
10. Hensel, K.O., Roskopf, M., Wilke, L., Heusch, A.: Intraobserver and interobserver reproducibility of M-mode and B-mode acquired mitral annular plane systolic excursion (MAPSE) and its dependency on echocardiographic image quality in children. PLoS ONE **13**(5), e0196614 (2018)

11. Hochreiter, S., Schmidhuber, J.: Long short-term memory. Neural Comput. **9**(8), 1735–1780 (1997)
12. Kingma, D.P., Ba, J.: Adam: a method for stochastic optimization. arXiv preprint arXiv:1412.6980 (2014)
13. Kiryati, N., Landau, Y.: Dataset growth in medical image analysis research. J. Imaging **7**(8), 155 (2021)
14. Kulhare, S., Zheng, X., Mehanian, C., Gregory, C., Zhu, M., Gregory, K., et al.: Ultrasound-based detection of lung abnormalities using single shot detection convolutional neural networks. In: Simulation, Image Processing, and Ultrasound Systems for Assisted Diagnosis and Navigation (2018)
15. Lagopoulos, A., Hristu-Varsakelis, D.: Measuring the left ventricular ejection fraction using geometric features. In: IEEE International Symposium on Computer-Based Medical Systems, pp. 1–6. IEEE, July 2022
16. LeCun, Y., Misra, I.: Self-supervised learning: the dark matter of intelligence. Meta AI **23** (2021)
17. Madani, A., Ong, J.R., Tibrewal, A., Mofrad, M.R.K.: Deep echocardiography: data-efficient supervised and semi-supervised deep learning towards automated diagnosis of cardiac disease. NPJ Digit. Med. **1**(1) (2018)
18. Mehanian, C., Kulhare, S., Millin, R., Zheng, X., Gregory, C., Zhu, M., et al.: Deep learning-based pneumothorax detection in ultrasound videos, pp. 74–82 (2019)
19. Muhtaseb, R., Yaqub, M.: EchoCoTr: Estimation of the LV ejection fraction from spatiotemporal echocardiography, pp. 370–379 (2022)
20. Ouyang, D., He, B., Ghorbani, A., Lungren, M.P., Ashley, E.A., et al.: Echonet-Dynamic: a large new cardiac motion video data resource for medical machine learning. In: NeurIPS ML4H Workshop (2019)
21. Ouyang, D., He, B., Ghorbani, A., Yuan, N., Ebinger, J., Langlotz, C.P., et al.: Video-based AI for beat-to-beat assessment of cardiac function. Nature **580**(7802), 252–256 (2020)
22. Sarkar, P.G., Chandra, V.: A novel approach for detecting abnormality in ejection fraction using transthoracic echocardiography with deep learning. Int. J. Online Biomed. Eng. **16**(13), 99 (2020)
23. Saul, T., Siadecki, S.D., Berkowitz, R., Rose, G., Matilsky, D., Sauler, A.: M-mode ultrasound applications for the emergency medicine physician. J. Emerg. Med. **49**(5), 686–692 (2015)
24. Shurrab, S., Duwairi, R.: Self-supervised learning methods and applications in medical imaging analysis: a survey. PeerJ Comput. Sci. **8**, e1045 (2022)
25. Singh, A.K., Mayo, P.H., Koenig, S., Talwar, A., Narasimhan, M.: The use of M-mode ultrasonography to differentiate the causes of B lines. Chest **153**(3), 689–696 (2018)
26. Skinner, H., Kamaruddin, H., Mathew, T.: Tricuspid annular plane systolic excursion: comparing transthoracic to transesophageal echocardiography. J. Cardiothorac. Vasc. Anesth. **31**(2), 590–594 (2017)
27. Tian, Y., Xu, S., Guo, L., Cong, F.: A periodic frame learning approach for accurate landmark localization in M-mode echocardiography. In: IEEE International Conference on Acoustics, Speech and Signal Processing (2021)
28. Tromp, J., Seekings, P.J., Hung, C.L., Iversen, M.B., Frost, M.J., et al.: Automated interpretation of systolic and diastolic function on the echocardiogram: a multicohort study. Lancet Digit. Health **4**(1) (2022)
29. WHO: Cardiovascular diseases (CVDs) (2022). https://www.who.int/news-room/fact-sheets/detail/cardiovascular-diseases-(cvds)

30. Yèche, H., Dresdner, G., Locatello, F., Hüser, M., Rätsch, G.: Neighborhood contrastive learning applied to online patient monitoring. In: International Conference on Machine Learning, pp. 11964–11974 (2021)
31. Zhang, J., Gajjala, S., Agrawal, P., Tison, G.H., Hallock, L.A., et al.: Fully automated echocardiogram interpretation in clinical practice. Circulation **138**(16), 1623–1635 (2018)

Improving Data Efficiency for Plant Cover Prediction with Label Interpolation and Monte-Carlo Cropping

Matthias Körschens[1,2]([✉])(iD), Solveig Franziska Bucher[1,2,3](iD),
Christine Römermann[1,2,3](iD), and Joachim Denzler[1,2,3](iD)

[1] Friedrich Schiller University, 07743 Jena, Germany
{matthias.koerschens,solveig.franziska.bucher,christine.roemermann,
joachim.denzler}@uni-jena.de
[2] German Centre for Integrative Biodiversity Research (iDiv) Halle-Jena-Leipzig,
04103 Leipzig, Germany
[3] Michael Stifel Center Jena, 07743 Jena, Germany

Abstract. The plant community composition is an essential indicator of environmental changes and is, for this reason, usually analyzed in ecological field studies in terms of the so-called plant cover. The manual acquisition of this kind of data is time-consuming, laborious, and prone to human error. Automated camera systems can collect high-resolution images of the surveyed vegetation plots at a high frequency. In combination with subsequent algorithmic analysis, it is possible to objectively extract information on plant community composition quickly and with little human effort. An automated camera system can easily collect the large amounts of image data necessary to train a Deep Learning system for automatic analysis. However, due to the amount of work required to annotate vegetation images with plant cover data, only few labeled samples are available. As automated camera systems can collect many pictures without labels, we introduce an approach to interpolate the sparse labels in the collected vegetation plot time series down to the intermediate dense and unlabeled images to artificially increase our training dataset to seven times its original size. Moreover, we introduce a new method we call Monte-Carlo Cropping. This approach trains on a collection of cropped parts of the training images to deal with high-resolution images efficiently, implicitly augment the training images, and speed up training. We evaluate both approaches on a plant cover dataset containing images of herbaceous plant communities and find that our methods lead to improvements in the species, community, and segmentation metrics investigated.

Keywords: Convolutional Neural Networks · Plant Cover Prediction · Ecology · Biodiversity Monitoring · Small Data · Monte-Carlo · Time Series

Supplementary Information The online version contains supplementary material available at https://doi.org/10.1007/978-3-031-54605-1_21.

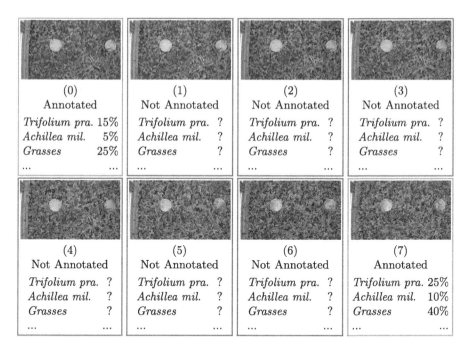

Fig. 1. From the entire dataset, since there are weekly annotations, but daily images, only about one in seven images is annotated. While the images do not significantly differ from one day to the next, the small differences between the images can still help the model learn intermediate growth stages of the plants.

1   Introduction

The plant community composition is an essential indicator for environmental changes such as changes in climate change [18–20], insect abundance [23,24], and land-use [7,9]. Hence, this kind of data is usually collected by plant ecologists [3,7,18,23], for example, in the form of measuring the plant cover, in regular, but rather long, time intervals. The plant cover is defined as the percentage of area of ground covered by each plant species disregarding any occlusion. Usually, many different plant species are contained in a single plot, which often overgrow and occlude each other, making the estimation of the plant cover a very complex task.

Automated plant cover prediction can be a vital asset to plant biodiversity researchers. Abundance values, like the plant cover, are traditionally collected manually by estimating them directly in the field on vegetation plots by visual inspection (see Fig. 1). However, collecting data this way is laborious, prone to human error, and subjective. Therefore, automated systems performing such estimations offer a significant advantage to these traditional methods, as they can analyze a large number of images of such vegetation plots in a short amount of time and deliver valuable research data at a high temporal resolution. The collected plant abundance data can then be used to determine the influence of environmental changes on the plant communities. The high temporal resolution of the automatically extracted data offers the potential for very fine-grained analyses, such that a shift in the community distribution can be investigated in intervals of days or even hours instead of only weeks [24], months [1] or years [9].

To establish an automated system to perform such an analysis of images, convolutional neural networks (CNNs) are a good choice, as they are powerful image processing models. However, they usually require large amounts of labeled training data to perform well. Körschens et al. [13] demonstrated a way to determine the plant cover by training on the so-called InsectArmageddon dataset [13,24], which we will also investigate in this work and which contains merely 682 labeled images, collected and annotated with plant cover estimates in weekly intervals. As this number of training images is relatively low, especially in conjunction with such a complex task, the quality of the results is very likely limited by the amount of available training data.

To solve the issue of little labeled data, we investigate using unlabeled intermediate images to increase the size of the training set. Plant cover estimates for vegetation plots are very laborious to create. However, additional unlabeled images are not. If an automated camera system exists to gather images for training or automatic analysis of plant cover, it can usually also collect a large number of additional unlabeled images at almost no cost. In the InsectArmageddon dataset, images are collected at a daily basis but only annotated at the weekly one. We leverage this experimental setup to automatically generate weak labels for the intermediate days between two days for which human annotations are given. The key idea is to handle uncertainty in the weak labels by weighting them according to their temporal distance to the next reference estimate. We will refer to this approach as label interpolation.

In addition to this, to enable the network to train on images at their full resolution, we propose a Monte-Carlo sampling approach for training the network, which we will refer to as Monte-Carlo Cropping (MCC). The original image is sampled in equally-sized patches, for each of which the target output is estimated individually. Afterwards, the network output for all patches sampled from a single image is averaged. This kind of sampling empirically seems to have a regularizing effect on the network training, leading to better results on high-resolution images and drastically reducing the training time of such images.

In the following, we will elaborate on related work to our approaches, followed by a detailed explanation of our methods, experimental results, and finally, a conclusion.

2   Related Work

Label Interpolation. In this work, we investigate the problem of utilizing unlabeled images for training in addition to a small number of images with labels. This problem is usually tackled by semi-supervised learning approaches, especially self-training [11,22]. In self-training methods, a model is trained with few annotated images and then used to label available but unannotated images to increase the size of the training set iteratively. In contrast to these approaches, label interpolation heavily utilizes the strong correlation of plant cover values in the time series to generate labels and does not rely on trained models at all. Similarly, the data augmentation method mixup [27] also interpolates labels to generate novel annotations. However, in contrast to our method, the authors do not apply the new labels to unlabeled images but fuse two existing images and their class labels.

Monte-Carlo Cropping (MCC). Another problem we tackle in this work is the utilization of high-resolution images in CNN training. Cropping the original training images into much smaller images is a simple approach to this problem, and is usually applied in tasks like image segmentation and object detection, that also often deal with high-resolution images [4, 15, 16, 25, 26]. For these tasks, cropping is usually done a single time per epoch per image, and the ground-truth data is also adapted in the same way. For image segmentation, the ground-truth data are usually segmentation maps, which have the same dimensions as the original image, and can also be cropped in the same way. The ground-truth for object detection are usually bounding box coordinates in the original images, which can also be easily be adapted to the cropped input image by systematically modifying the coordinates. For plant cover estimation, however, the target data are merely numerical vectors representing the plant cover distribution in the image, and can therefore neither be cropped or simply adapted. To solve this problem, our Monte-Carlo Cropping introduces a stochastical component in order to be able to approximate the underlying plant cover distribution, which does not need to be done for image segmentation and object detection.

3   Methods

3.1   Label Interpolation

The first method we introduce is label interpolation. As shown in Fig. 1, from seven existing images in a single week, only a single one is labeled, leaving the other images unused. Moreover, we can see that the differences between the daily pictures are only minor compared to the weekly differences; however not insignificant. Images of this kind have two advantages. Firstly, the network can learn the growth process of plants in much more fine-grained steps, especially since this kind of data contains more and new information compared to simple augmented images. And secondly, since the differences between the pictures are relatively small, we can infer certain properties of the supposed labels for these images from their neighboring annotations. More formally, for our label interpolation method to work, we take advantage of the fact that plant cover estimates are continuous values. Moreover, we assume that the intermediate value theorem [2] holds for these estimates collected in a time series. That is, if a plant's measured cover value in a certain week was $\text{cover}(t_0)$ and $\text{cover}(t_1)$ in the following week,

$$\forall v \text{ with } \min(\text{cover}(t_0), \text{cover}(t_1)) < v < \max(\text{cover}(t_0), \text{cover}(t_1)), \qquad (1)$$
$$\exists t \in (t_0, t_1) : \text{cover}(t) = v. \qquad (2)$$

Under the assumption that plants grow in a continuous fashion without external interference, this theorem holds.

Here, we will utilize linear interpolation, specifically of the data of two subsequent weeks, which implicitly weights the values respective to their temporal distance to the next annotated data point:

$$\text{cover}(t) = \frac{\text{cover}(t_0)(t_1 - t) + \text{cover}(t_1)(t - t0)}{t_1 - t_0}. \qquad (3)$$

A linear interpolation might not precisely represent the growth process of the plants and discontinuities in the images (like occlusion). However, with such small time steps, the growth process of the plants can be assumed to be approximately linear between two weeks. We are aware of violations of our assumptions in practice. However, empirically such issues play only a minor role when it comes to the overall quality of our suggested approach.

3.2   Monte-Carlo Cropping

The second method we introduce here is Monte-Carlo Cropping (MCC). A significant problem in plant cover prediction is that the images provided by the camera systems usually have a relatively high resolution (e.g., 2688×1520 pixels for the InsectArmageddon dataset). However, networks are usually only applied on rather small, often downscaled images (224×224 for typical ImageNet [21] tasks, and 448×448 or similar for fine-grained ones [5]).

Training on large images is computationally expensive, consumes large amounts of memory, and can take a long time. For the original image $I \in \mathbb{R}^{H \times W \times 3}$ we sample patches $P \in \mathbb{R}^{h \times w \times 3}$ with $h \ll H$ and $w \ll W$. For each patch P, we let the network predict the plant cover separately and then average these values over the number of patches sampled from each image.

Since the patches are sampled from an image with the plant cover values cover_p, the expected value is equal to cover_p for a large number of patches sampled. Therefore, due to the law of large numbers [6], the following holds:

$$\lim_{n \to \infty} \frac{1}{n} \sum_{i=1}^{n} \text{cover}_{i,p} = \text{cover}_p, \qquad (4)$$

with n being the number of patches sampled, i being the index of the randomly sampled patch, and p denoting plant species. I.e., while the plant cover values observed in the smaller patches do not necessarily reflect the values of the total images when selecting a sufficiently large number of patches, they do so on average.

 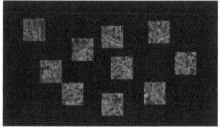

Fig. 2. An example of a random patch selection with Monte-Carlo Cropping.

During training, we sample equally sized square patches from the original image, an example of which can be seen in Fig. 2. It is visible that the number of pixels shown to the network is significantly reduced, depending on the size of the patches and number of patches sampled. Hence, computational complexity can also be reduced with MCC. It should be noted that patches are selected entirely at random, i.e., all pixels can be contained in multiple patches sampled.

4   Experimental Results

4.1   Dataset

In our experiments, we utilize the InsectArmageddon dataset [14,24] from the eponymous iDiv project that took place in 2018 over multiple months. The images were collected in 24 so-called EcoUnits, which are boxes containing small enclosed ecosystems. Each of the EcoUnits was equipped with two cameras that collected daily pictures of these ecosystems. The dataset from the InsectArmageddon experiment comprises estimated plant cover data ("reference estimates") for eight herbaceous plant species in 682 images collected weekly by a single ecologist. The image set with original and interpolated annotations contains about 4900 images, i.e., about seven times the number of images due to one originally labeled image per week, and six with interpolated labels. On this dataset, we perform 12-fold cross-validation by selecting the images of two EcoUnits for testing, and the ones of the remaining 22 EcoUnits for training. For more details on the InsectArmageddon image dataset, we would like to refer to [24] and [14].

4.2   Setup

We use the approach introduced in [13]. i.e., we utilize a ResNet50 [8], architecture with Feature Pyramid Network [17], the 3-phase pre-training pipeline based on freely available images from GBIF[1] to train a classification network (phase 1), which generates simple segmentations with class activation mapping (CAM)

---

[1] http://gbif.org.

[28], on which we then pre-train a segmentation network (phase 2). The weights of this network are then used as initialization for our plant cover prediction network, which we train on the plant cover annotations (phase 3).

During the first phase, we utilize global log-sum-exp-pooling [12,13] with a learning rate of 10^{-4} and a weight decay of 10^{-4}. We use this pooling method, as in [12] it generated better segmentations when used in conjunction with CAM. Moreover, we use a categorical cross-entropy loss during optimization and train with early stopping and dynamic learning rate reduction. The learning rate is reduced by a factor of 10 when there is no improvement in the validation accuracy over four epochs, and the training is stopped, if there is no improvement over six epochs. In the second phase, we use a learning rate of 10^{-5}, a weight decay of 10^{-4}, and a combination of binary-cross-entropy and dice loss, which are summed up and weighted equally as loss. During this training, we also used a dynamic learning rate adaptation and early stopping; however, we monitored the mean Intersection over Union (mIoU) instead of the accuracy. In the third phase, we train with a batch size of 1 and a learning rate of 10^{-5}, which is reduced by a factor of 10 after 50% and 75% of the total epochs, respectively. We are using the mean scaled absolute error (MSAE$_\sigma$) as loss. This error is defined as

$$MSAE_\sigma(t, p) = \frac{1}{n} \sum_{i=1}^{n} \left| \frac{t_i}{\sigma_i} - \frac{p_i}{\sigma_i} \right|, \tag{5}$$

where σ, in our case, is the standard deviation of the species-wise plant cover values calculated over the training dataset. This loss aims to reweight the species to account for the substantial imbalance in the dataset.

In our experiments, we compare the image resolution used in previous works [13] (1536×768 pixels) and the full image resolution (2688×1536 pixels). We investigate several training durations and their effect on the training with weekly and interpolated daily images. For the daily labels we investigate fewer epochs, since the iteration count per epoch is much higher in comparison to the weekly label dataset.

For our experiments on MCC, we investigate different patch sizes as well as several patch counts. We chose the patch sizes of 128^2, 256^2, 512^2, and 1024^2 pixels, and for each patch size, a respective sample count so that the number of pixels sampled is around 50% of the pixel count of the original image. For each sample count selected, we also investigate a pixel count of half or double the number of pixels sampled. For a patch of 512^2 pixels, we investigate sample counts of 8, 4, and 16; for a patch of 256^2 pixels, sample counts of 32, 16, and 64, etc. It should be noted that the cropped image patches are input into the network as-is without any additional resizing.

4.3   Metrics

We investigate three different metrics to analyze our results. The first metric is the aforementioned mean scaled absolute error MSAE$_\sigma$. The second metric

Table 1. Comparison of training with weekly images with only the original labels and daily images with original and interpolated labels. Abbreviations used: MSAE$_\sigma$ - Mean Scaled Absolute Error, IoU - Intersection over Union, DPC - DCA-Procrustes-Correlation. Top results are marked in **bold font**.

Resolution	Epochs	Weekly Images			Daily Images		
		MSAE$_\sigma$	IoU	DPC	MSAE$_\sigma$	IoU	DPC
1536×768	3	0.527	0.158	0.724	0.499	0.198	0.780
	6	0.505	0.192	0.766	0.502	0.204	0.766
	10	0.501	0.196	**0.770**	0.503	0.199	0.772
	15	0.500	0.201	0.768	0.498	0.194	0.773
	25	0.501	0.203	0.760	-	-	-
	40	0.502	0.187	0.765	-	-	-
2688×1536	3	0.545	0.156	0.656	0.494	0.205	0.780
	6	0.510	0.188	0.757	0.493	**0.223**	0.778
	10	0.502	0.204	0.766	0.491	0.208	0.777
	15	0.497	**0.208**	0.757	**0.489**	0.181	**0.781**
	25	**0.493**	0.205	0.763	-	-	-
	40	0.495	0.192	0.761	-	-	-

is the mean Intersection over Union (IoU) metric calculated over the segmentation image subset introduced in [13] containing 14 pixel-wise annotated images from the InsectArmageddon dataset. The last metric we will refer to as the DCA-Procrustes-Correlation (DPC). It is calculated by performing a Detrended Correspondence Analysis (DCA) [10] on the target and predicted outputs, which are then compared with a Procrustes test. This returns a correlation value, where higher values show a higher similarity of the distributions to each other, which is significant for ecological applications.

With the MSAE$_\sigma$, we can evaluate the performance of our models in absolute terms, i.e., how accurate the species-wise predictions are based on the reference estimates. The IoU determines how well the top layer of plants is predicted, disregarding any occluded plants, and the DPC explains how well the predicted species distribution matches with the one estimated by the expert. All experiments are performed in a 12-fold cross-validation over three repetitions.

4.4   Label Interpolation

The results of our experiments with label interpolation are shown in Table 1. Regarding the weekly annotated images, it is visible that the MSAE$_\sigma$ and IoU are increasing with higher epoch counts, and the higher-resolution images also return slightly better results than the low-resolution images. However, after ten epochs, low-resolution images achieve the best DPC value (0.77). This value is not outperformed when using high-resolution images, leading to the conclusion that the network can learn to reduce the prediction error for some more dominant species from the high-resolution images but cannot accurately learn and reflect the actual distribution due to the neglect of less abundant species.

When looking at the results of the experiments using the interpolated daily images in conjunction with the weekly annotations, we notice improvements for both image resolutions, showing that our interpolation method is effective and leads to better results than just using the annotated images. The low-resolution and high-resolution images with daily images outperform their counterparts in all metrics. It should also be noted that the top performance is achieved after a smaller number of epochs for the daily images, likely because the number of iterations per epoch is about seven times the one with weekly images. This way, the top DPC value is achieved after three epochs, while the top IoU is achieved after six epochs. The $MSAE_\sigma$ appears to be still improving for a larger number of epochs.

4.5 Monte-Carlo Cropping

The results of our experiments with MCC on full-resolution images with weekly labels and interpolated daily labels are shown in Fig. 3. The detailed numerical results can be found in the Supplementary Material. Generally, we can see that larger patch sizes lead to better results in terms of $MSAE_\sigma$ and DPC, with the patch sizes 512 and 1024 yielding the top results for the experiments with daily and weekly labels. The patch size of 512 yields the best results for DPC, while the size of 1024 performs best in terms of $MSAE_\sigma$. For the weekly labels, the top DPC value and $MSAE_\sigma$ value are 0.777 and 0.489, which outperform the top results on the full-resolution weekly images with a DPC of 0.766 and $MSAE_\sigma$ of 0.493, respectively. For achieving this performance, for the patch size 512 the optimal sample size is 8, and for 1024 it is 2, representing about 50% of the number of pixels of the original image. The same configurations generate the best $MSAE_\sigma$ and DPC results for the daily images, with 0.487 and 0.784, respectively. The MC training outperforms the full image training also here in terms of $MSAE_\sigma$ (0.487 vs. 0.489) and DPC (0.784 vs. 0.781).

Interestingly, the best top layer prediction results, i.e., segmentation results, were achieved with a much smaller patch size, of 128^2 pixels. For the weekly images and a sample size of 128, the top IoU was 0.220, again outperforming the naive full-resolution approach with an IoU of 0.208. Similarly, with a patch size of 128 and a sample size of 128, the training on the daily images yields an IoU outperforming the full-resolution training (0.232 vs. 0.223).

The discrepancies between the configurations for optimal IoU and optimal $MSAE_\sigma$ and DPC can be explained by what kind of features the network learns for the different patch sizes. With smaller patches, the network is forced to focus on the single plants shown in the top layer and learns little about the relationships of plants between each other, like occlusion. These relationships, however, play a significant role in the accurate prediction of the species-wise values and the entire composition, which are evaluated by $MSAE_\sigma$ and DPC,

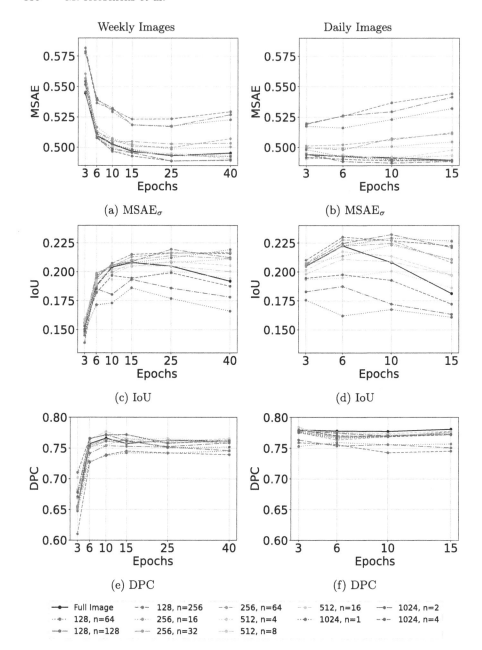

Fig. 3. The development of the different metrics over several training durations for images with weekly labels (left) and images with interpolated (daily) labels (right). Abbreviations used: $MSAE_\sigma$ - Mean Scaled Absolute Error, IoU - Intersection over Union, DPC - DCA-Procrustes-Correlation

Table 2. Comparison of training speed per epoch on the full resolution images using different patches and sample sizes. Times shown are in minutes:seconds.

Patch Size	#Patches	Weekly Images Time per Epoch	Daily Images Time per Epoch
–	–	01:51	16:17
128	64	00:55	09:06
	128	01:34	14:01
	256	03:01	24:25
256	16	00:46	08:22
	32	01:08	10:37
	64	02:10	18:22
512	4	00:46	08:07
	8	01:03	10:16
	16	01:55	16:41
1024	1	00:45	08:15
	2	01:02	10:23
	4	01:52	16:17

respectively. Larger patch sizes capture the relationships and therefore perform better in these aspects.

In summary, our MCC approach can outperform the training with full-resolution images. The results significantly depend on the patch size, with higher patch sizes resulting in better community-based predictions and smaller ones in better individual-based predictions. As training on smaller patches instead of a large image has computational implications, we will compare computation times in the following.

Computation Time Comparison. A comparison of the times per epoch for each setup using the full-resolution images is shown in Table 2. These measurements were taken when training on about 75% of the images of the weekly and daily image sets on an RTX 3090. The training on the original full-resolution images took 1 min and 51 s per epoch for only the weekly images and 16 min and 17 s for daily images. The top results for $MSAE_\sigma$ and DPC were generated by patch size 512 and 8 patches sampled. This setup takes 1 min and 3 s on the weekly images and 10 min and 16 s on daily ones, resulting in a time reduction of about a third. As the setup with patch size 512 and 4 sampled patches performs comparably well, one could even reduce the training time further by about 50%, at little cost in performance. The setup generating the top segmentation results, i.e., patch size 128 and sample sizes 256 and 128, differ in the training durations. Considering the larger numbers of pixels used for sample size 256, the duration is longer for this setup, requiring about 63% more time for an epoch. In contrast, the sample size of 128 reduces the training time again by about 14%. It should be noted that, with MCC, the number of epochs required for the optimal results on the weekly images are similar to the number of epochs for full-resolution training, and on the daily images the training times are usually even shorter for MCC training. For example, with MCC training on daily images the best DPC value is achieved after 3 epochs as opposed to 15 for full-resolution training. Hence, the training times are not only reduced regarding the per-epoch duration, but also the number of epochs in total.

5   Conclusion and Future Work

We introduced two approaches for improving the data efficiency for plant cover estimation training. One method utilizes the unannotated images in the dataset, which can be collected at almost no cost; the other one enables efficient training at high resolution, gathering more information from the high resolution of the images.

Both approaches have proven effective: the label interpolation led to sufficient training data to receive improved results for all investigated metrics when using full-resolution images compared to their lower-resolution counterparts. Therefore, it is advantageous to collect more images than can be labeled, if the images are similar enough to existing images, as we can artificially increase the size of the dataset by interpolating. Furthermore, the Monte-Carlo Cropping improved these results even further, producing better results for different aspects of the plant cover prediction task while decreasing the training time and computation required during training. While, of course, a higher image resolution contains more information, with our MCC approach, especially in combination with label interpolation, such a high resolution can be utilized much more effectively. By increasing the image resolution in future experiments even further than in the InsectArmageddon experiment, with our methods such a high resolution can actually be utilized to improve the cover estimates without additional human effort.

Our approaches will be evaluated further on new plant cover datasets with different image resolutions, more frequent images and more plant species in future work. Moreover, the label interpolation might be improved with a more sophisticated interpolation model instead of linear interpolation, for example, a model that considers the information in the image for interpolation. Similarly, the sample selection of the Monte-Carlo Cropping could be improved by intelligently selecting the patches that contain the most information in the future.

Acknowledgements. Matthias Körschens thanks the Carl Zeiss Foundation for the financial support. We thank Alban Gebler for enabling the image collection process in the iDiv EcoTron and Josephine Ulrich for the data collection. We acknowledge funding from the German Research Foundation (DFG) via the German Centre for Integrative Biodiversity research (iDiv) Halle-Jena-Leipzig (FZT 118) for the support of the FlexPool project PhenEye (09159751).

References

1. Andrzejak, M., Korell, L., Auge, H., Knight, T.M.: Effects of climate change and pollen supplementation on the reproductive success of two grassland plant species. Ecol. Evol. **12**(1), e8501 (2022)
2. Bolzano, B.: Beyträge zu einer begründeteren Darstellung der Mathematik, vol. 1. Im Verlage bey Caspar Widtmann (1810)
3. Bruelheide, H., et al.: Global trait-environment relationships of plant communities. Nat. Ecol. Evol. **2**(12), 1906–1917 (2018)
4. Cheng, B., et al.: Panoptic-deeplab: a simple, strong, and fast baseline for bottom-up panoptic segmentation. In: Proceedings of the IEEE/CVF Conference on Computer Vision and Pattern Recognition, pp. 12475–12485 (2020)
5. Cui, Y., Song, Y., Sun, C., Howard, A., Belongie, S.: Large scale fine-grained categorization and domain-specific transfer learning. In: Proceedings of the IEEE Conference on Computer Vision and Pattern Recognition, pp. 4109–4118 (2018)
6. Evans, M.J., Rosenthal, J.S.: Probability and Statistics: The Science of Uncertainty. Macmillan, New York (2004)
7. Gerstner, K., Dormann, C.F., Stein, A., Manceur, A.M., Seppelt, R.: Editor's choice: review: effects of land use on plant diversity-a global meta-analysis. J. Appl. Ecol. **51**(6), 1690–1700 (2014)
8. He, K., Zhang, X., Ren, S., Sun, J.: Deep residual learning for image recognition. In: Proceedings of the IEEE Conference on Computer Vision and Pattern Recognition (CVPR), pp. 770–778 (2016)
9. Helm, J., Dutoit, T., Saatkamp, A., Bucher, S.F., Leiterer, M., Römermann, C.: Recovery of mediterranean steppe vegetation after cultivation: legacy effects on plant composition, soil properties and functional traits. Appl. Veg. Sci. **22**(1), 71–84 (2019)
10. Hill, M.O., Gauch, H.G.: Detrended correspondence analysis: an improved ordination technique. In: van der Maarel, E. (ed.) Classification and ordination. AIVS, vol. 2, pp. 47–58. Springer, Dordrecht (1980). https://doi.org/10.1007/978-94-009-9197-2_7
11. Kahn, J., Lee, A., Hannun, A.: Self-training for end-to-end speech recognition. In: ICASSP 2020–2020 IEEE International Conference on Acoustics, Speech and Signal Processing (ICASSP), pp. 7084–7088. IEEE (2020)
12. Körschens, M., Bodesheim, P., Denzler, J.: Beyond global average pooling: alternative feature aggregations for weakly supervised localization. In: VISIGRAPP (2022)
13. Körschens, M.: Weakly supervised segmentation pretraining for plant cover prediction. In: Bauckhage, C., Gall, J., Schwing, A. (eds.) DAGM GCPR 2021. LNCS, vol. 13024, pp. 589–603. Springer, Cham (2021). https://doi.org/10.1007/978-3-030-92659-5_38
14. Körschens, M., Bodesheim, P., Römermann, C., Bucher, S.F., Ulrich, J., Denzler, J.: Towards confirmable automated plant cover determination. In: Bartoli, A., Fusiello, A. (eds.) ECCV 2020. LNCS, vol. 12540, pp. 312–329. Springer, Cham (2020). https://doi.org/10.1007/978-3-030-65414-6_22
15. Li, C., et al.: Yolov6 v3. 0: a full-scale reloading. arXiv preprint arXiv:2301.05586 (2023)
16. Li, S., et al.: Efficient multi-order gated aggregation network. arXiv preprint arXiv:2211.03295 (2022)

17. Lin, T.Y., Dollár, P., Girshick, R., He, K., Hariharan, B., Belongie, S.: Feature pyramid networks for object detection. In: Proceedings of the IEEE Conference on Computer Vision and Pattern Recognition (CVPR), pp. 2117–2125 (2017)
18. Liu, H., et al.: Shifting plant species composition in response to climate change stabilizes grassland primary production. Proc. Natl. Acad. Sci. **115**(16), 4051–4056 (2018)
19. Lloret, F., Peñuelas, J., Prieto, P., Llorens, L., Estiarte, M.: Plant community changes induced by experimental climate change: seedling and adult species composition. Perspect. Plant Ecol. Evol. Syst. **11**(1), 53–63 (2009)
20. Rosenzweig, C., Casassa, G., Karoly, D.J., et al.: Assessment of observed changes and responses in natural and managed systems. Climate Change 2007: Impacts, Adaptation and Vulnerability. Contribution of Working Group II to the Fourth Assessment Report of the Intergovernmental Panel on Climate Change, pp. 79–131 (2007)
21. Russakovsky, O., et al.: Imagenet large scale visual recognition challenge. Int. J. Comput. Vision **115**(3), 211–252 (2015)
22. Scudder, H.: Probability of error of some adaptive pattern-recognition machines. IEEE Trans. Inf. Theory **11**(3), 363–371 (1965)
23. Souza, L., Zelikova, T.J., Sanders, N.J.: Bottom-up and top-down effects on plant communities: nutrients limit productivity, but insects determine diversity and composition. Oikos **125**(4), 566–575 (2016)
24. Ulrich, J., et al.: Invertebrate decline leads to shifts in plant species abundance and phenology. Front. Plant Sci. **11**, 1410 (2020)
25. Wang, W., et al.: Internimage: exploring large-scale vision foundation models with deformable convolutions. arXiv preprint arXiv:2211.05778 (2022)
26. Yuan, Y., Chen, X., Chen, X., Wang, J.: Segmentation transformer: object-contextual representations for semantic segmentation. arXiv preprint arXiv:1909.11065 (2019)
27. Zhang, H., Cissé, M., Dauphin, Y., Lopez-Paz, D.: mixup: beyond empirical risk minimization. ArXiv abs/1710.09412 (2017)
28. Zhou, B., Khosla, A., Lapedriza, A., Oliva, A., Torralba, A.: Learning deep features for discriminative localization. In: Proceedings of the IEEE Conference on Computer Vision and Pattern Recognition (CVPR), pp. 2921–2929 (2016)

Learning Channel Importance for High Content Imaging with Interpretable Deep Input Channel Mixing

Daniel Siegismund[(⊠)], Mario Wieser, Stephan Heyse, and Stephan Steigele

Genedata AG, Basel, Switzerland
daniel.siegismund@genedata.com

Abstract. Uncovering novel drug candidates for treating complex diseases remain one of the most challenging tasks in early discovery research. To tackle this challenge, biopharma research established a standardized high content imaging protocol that tags different cellular compartments per image channel. In order to judge the experimental outcome, the scientist requires knowledge about the channel importance with respect to a certain phenotype for decoding the underlying biology. In contrast to traditional image analysis approaches, such experiments are nowadays preferably analyzed by deep learning based approaches which, however, lack crucial information about the channel importance. To overcome this limitation, we present a novel approach which utilizes multi-spectral information of high content images to interpret a certain aspect of cellular biology. To this end, we base our method on image blending concepts with alpha compositing for an arbitrary number of channels. More specifically, we introduce DCMIX, a lightweight, scaleable and end-to-end trainable mixing layer which enables interpretable predictions in high content imaging while retaining the benefits of deep learning based methods. We employ an extensive set of experiments on both MNIST and RXRX1 datasets, demonstrating that DCMIX learns the biologically relevant channel importance without scarifying prediction performance.

Keywords: Biomedical Imaging · Interpretable Machine Learning · Explainable AI · Image Channel Importance

1 Introduction

High-Content Imaging (HCI) has developed to one of the main driving factors in biopharma early discovery research to reveal novel drug candidates for sophisticated treatment strategies such as cancer immunotherapies [21]. HCI is based on a standardized experimental protocol that allow for the systematic acquisition of multi-spectral images, e.g., in form of a cell painting assay protocol that requires a high number of channels with the benefit of a highly generalizable assay [3].

Supplementary Information The online version contains supplementary material available at https://doi.org/10.1007/978-3-031-54605-1_22.

Here, high-content images are recorded by automated instruments on microtiter plates which allow for large-scale drug candidate testing and an automatic analysis procedure to assess the mechanics of a drug candidate for a certain disease. When running such HCI experiments, scientists prepare typically a set of 4 to 15 channels [23,31] with a specific fluorophore that tags a certain cellular protein or compartment. Subsequently, the scientist aims to analyze the experimental outcome with respect to the importance of the fluorescence channels to validate the findings or refine the experiment and, therefore, requires a fast and easy-to-use analysis workflow. This is particularly important as the specific functional or mechanistic knowledge is encoded via the specific staining per image channel [3] and hence required for decoding the underlying biology.

However, to analyze such complex multi-channel cell-painting assays, the scientist requires the ability of sophisticated image analysis to distill the information from the multi-spectral information. In biopharma research, the traditional analysis [5] is gradually replaced by deep learning based approaches [14,39,40,48]. Despite the superior performance of such models in comparison to conventional segmentation based analysis [5], the scientist lacks informative insights in terms of understanding about which fluorescence channel influenced the decision [7].

In the past, various approaches have been proposed to extract the most relevant information from high-dimensional datasets. The most basic approach to determine the most relevant channels is a preprocessing step by applying an unsupervised dimensionality reduction method such as Principal Component Analysis (PCA) [17]. However, employing such a preprocessing step does not guarantee for phenotype-specific channels as the method only optimizes for the directions with the highest variance and not necessarily for the highest phenotypic information. More recently, attention-based approaches have been introduced for image channel selection [4,15,24,32] which suffer from high computational costs and poor scalability. In addition, there are model-agnostic approaches such as Shapely values [19,36] which, however, can suffer from sampling variability [27] and be time consuming in terms of highly complex models [6].

To overcome the aforementioned limitations, we present a simple yet effective method to estimate channel importance for HCI images. More specifically, we introduce a lightweight, easy to use mixing layer that is composed of a generalized image blending mechanism with alpha compositing [1,50] which converts a d-dimensional channel image into a 2D image retaining all phenotype relevant information. This allows not only to incorporate an arbitrary number of channels in a highly scalable fashion but also leads to a reduced network size with faster inference times while being able to facilitate the use of transfer learning of pretrained networks. To summarize, we make the following contributions:

- We extend the imaging blending concepts of [1,50] and apply these to images with an arbitrary number of channels.
- We encapsulate the generalized image blending into a lightweight, scalable and end-to-end trainable mixing layer, called DCMIX, to estimate channel importance for multi-spectral HCI data.

- Experiments on MNIST as well as on the challenging multi-channel real-world imaging data set RXRX1 [42] with 31 different cell phenotype classes demonstrate that the proposed method learns the correct channel importance without sacrificing its model performance.

2 Related Work

In this section, we review related work on interpretable and explainable machine learning [30]. Broadly spoken, we can distinguish between interpretable models that are interpretable by design and explainable models that try to explain existing models post-hoc [30].

Interpretable Machine Learning Methods can be separated into the following model classes: score-based [44], rule-based [9], sparse [43] and neural networks [12], among others [30]. In this review, we focus more closely on sparsity inducing and attention-based interpretable methods. Sparsity-based approaches introduce a sparsity constraint on the model coefficients to determine the feature importance. One of the most basic approaches is the least absolute shrinkage and selection operator (LASSO) introduced by [43] which is employing the L_1-norm to ensure feature sparsity. This approach has subsequently been extended to various lines of research, including dealing with grouped features [33,49], estimating network graphs [13,34] or learning sparse representations in neural networks [26,47]. Most closely related to our work is LassoNet [22] which employs a group lasso constraint based on the feature channels that are obtained from a pretrained feature extraction network. In contrast, our approach is end-to-end trainable and hence does not require a two step approach of feature extraction and importance estimation. More recently, attention-based approaches [45] have emerged in the context of interpretable machine learning. [8] introduced an attention-based model for the analysis of electronic health records and [37] learns important features with an attentive mixture of experts approach. Moreover, attention is used in the context of hyper spherical band/channel selection [4,15,24,32]. In contrast, our approach works on image blending and alpha compositing and hence reducing high computational costs.

Explainable Machine Learning Methods denote approaches that aim to explain decisions of an already trained machine learning model post-hoc by learning a surrogate model [30]. In summary, we distinguish between attribution methods that try to quantify the attribution of a feature to the prediction [41], concept-based explanations trying to explain predictions with high-level concepts [20], symbolic metamodels employing symbolic regression as a surrogate [2] and counterfactual explanations [46]. In the context of our work, we focus on attribution models. [35] learns a surrogate classifier to explain an arbitrary black-box model based on submodular optimization. [38] introduced DeepLIFT to decompose the input contributions on the model prediction. In addition, Shapley values gained a wide adoption in the machine learning domain mainly for feature selection and model explain ability [19,36]. As a result, Lundberg & Lee

[28] introduced Shapely additive explanations (SHAP) to explain model predictions based on Shapely regression values. Finally, Shapley values have been used in the context of HCI channel importance estimation [42]. More specifically, the authors adopt Shapely values to explain the channel importance of HCI images from a pretrained black-box model. Opposed to our approach, this method requires the training of two separate models and hence does not allow for end-to-end training.

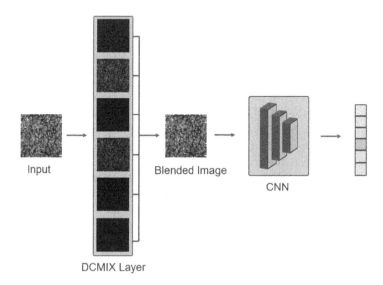

Fig. 1. Blue arrows denote steps and gray boxes actions in our workflow, respectively. In the first step (1.), we take a multi-channel cellular image and split it into single channels. Subsequently, we mix the channel within our DCMIX layer to obtain the most important part of each channel. In the second step (2.), we take the blended image into our classification network. (Color figure online)

3   Model

As illustrated in Fig. 1, we utilize a two step approach for estimating channel importance in multi-spectral bioimage classification settings by introducing a lightweight, easy to use and end-to-end trainable mixing layer. To do so, we propose a blending layer which combines the most important parts of the distinct channels into a new 2D image. After, we perform a classification based on the blended image.

3.1   Conception of the Image Blending Layer

We start with an input image $I \in \mathbb{R}^{h \times w \times c}$ where h denotes the height, w the width and c the number of channels in the multi-spectral image. Subsequently, the image I is split into its distinct channels and processed in the DCMIX layer. The DCMIX layer is inspired by simple image blending and alpha compositing [1,50]. More specifically, the idea behind Alpha blending is to combine two images as follows:

$$C = \alpha_1 \cdot A_1 + (1 - \alpha_1) \cdot A_2, \tag{1}$$

where $A_1 \in \mathbb{R}^{h \times w \times c}$ and $A_2 \in \mathbb{R}^{h \times w \times c}$ are the corresponding image matrices to blend and $C \in \mathbb{R}^{h \times w \times c}$ the blended image matrix. The trainable parameter α_1 determines the transparency of each channel.

In this work, we take advantage of the ideas proposed in [1,50] and generalize the idea by employing the trainable alpha values as weights for each channel that has to be blended with:

$$C = \sum_i^n \alpha_i \cdot A_i \text{ where: } \alpha_i \geq 0, \tag{2}$$

where α_i is multiplied with each channel A_i. The parameter n defines the number of channels and C is the blended image which will be subsequently used for the further analysis.

3.2 Classifying Genetic Perturbations Based on DCMIX-Blended Images

Our goal is to learn a classification model $F_\theta(y \mid C)$ of the blended image C for distinct classes of genetic perturbations y^c where c is the number of genetic perturbations to be predicted. In this work, our model F is a Deep Convolutional Neural Network which extracts a cascade of feature maps M^l where l denotes the current layer. The last feature map is used as an input to the multi-class classification head that predicts the genetic perturbation vector y^c using a softmax output.

3.3 End-to-End Training Algorithm

The model training is described in Algorithm 1. As an input, we use the multi-spectral images X and the genetic perturbation labels y. Subsequently, we draw minibatches from the training data X, y (line 1). For each of the minibatches, we obtain the blended images c_i as well as the corresponding mixing factors α_i. The blended images c_i are fed in the neural network F_θ (line 3) and the corresponding predictions $\hat{y}_i$ are used to calculate the loss in line 5. Finally, we update the parameters θ and α based on the loss by using gradient descent (line 7).

4   Experiments

A description of setups and additional hyperparameters can be found in the supplementary materials.

Algorithm 1. DCMIX training algorithm

INPUT: X images, y labels
OUTPUT: The prediction $\hat{y}$, mixing factors α

1: **for** minibatch x_i, y_i from X, y **do**
2:    $c_i, \alpha_i \leftarrow \text{DCMIX}(x_i)$
3:    $\hat{y}_i \leftarrow F_\theta(c_i)$
4:
5:    loss $\leftarrow$ crossentropy$(\hat{y}_i, y_i)$
6:
7:    update θ, α using gradient descent
8: **end for**

4.1 MNIST

Dataset. To demonstrate the efficacy of DCMIX for estimating channel importance, we generate an artificial dataset based on MNIST [10]. MNIST consists of 70000 samples with images $x \in \mathbb{R}^{28 \times 28 \times 1}$ and labels y that represent numbers from 0 to 9. For our dataset, we randomly select a subset of 10000 samples from MNIST. In order to assess the channel importance, we extend the MNIST images with two additional noise channels. Therefore, we draw two noise matrices with shape 28×28 from a uniform distribution defined on $[0, 255]$. Subsequently, we add the previously generated noise channels to the input image such that we obtain a three channel input image $x \in \mathbb{R}^{28 \times 28 \times 3}$ where the first denotes the most important channel. For training, we split the data into a 70 percent training and a 30 percent hold-out set. The training set is further split into a 80 percent training and 20 percent validation set, respectively.

Models. In order to demonstrate the effectiveness of our approach, we benchmark DCMIX against a plain LCNet050, LassoNet [22] as well as on an attention-based [25,29] LCNet050.

Quantitative Evaluation. Channel Importance. In this experiment, we evaluate the channel importance on the validation set, and the results are reported in Table 1. As we can observe in the channel importance ranking, DCMIX can effectively learn the most important channel one and is in line with the more complex LassoNet and attention-based LCNet050. At the same time, DCMIX requires only a fraction of GFLOPS and model parameters. More specifically, DCMIX requires solely 5.9271 GFLOPS compared to 17.809 GFLOPS for the Attention-LCNet050. In addition, DCMIX need three times less parameters (0.2789 million) in contrast to Attention-LCNet050 (0.9281 million) and requires only the same amount of GFLOPS and parameters as the plain LCNet050.

Quantitative Evaluation. Model Performance. Despite the fact, that the aim of this method is not to improve the model performance but rather learn the

Table 1. Results of the MNIST channel importance and model size. Channel importance ranking denotes the rank of the weights depicted in the second column. The model size is evaluated on GFLOPS and the number of model parameters where lower is better.

Method	Channel importance ranking	Channel weights	GFLOPS	# Parameters (million)
LCNet050	-	-	5.9269	0.2789
LassoNet [22]	1,3,2	120259, 51003, 52318	-	-
Attention [25,29]-LCNet050	1,3,2	1,3.24 × 10^{-11}, 2.33 × 10^{-6}	17.809	0.9281
DCMIX-LCNet050	1,3,2	0.82,0.21,0.22	5.9271	0.2789

most important channel to gain biological insights for a drug discovery experiment, we want to ensure that DCMIX archives competitive performance to state-of-the art approaches. To do so, we compared DCMIX to a plain LCNet050, LassoNet and Attention-LCNet050 in Table 2. Here, we observe that DCMIX obtains competitive results compared to both LCNet050 and Attention-LCNet050 and outperforms LassoNet on accuracy, precision, recall and f1-score measures.

Table 2. Results of model performance for the MNIST dataset on the hold-out dataset. We assess the model performance on four different metrics: accuracy, precision, recall and f1-score where higher is better. Values in brackets denote the standard deviation.

Method	Accuracy	Precision	Recall	F1-Score
LCNet050	0.992 (0.0008)	0.991 (0.002)	0.991 (0.002)	0.991 (0.002)
LassoNet [22]	0.963 (0.012)	0.888 (0.002)	0.888 (0.002)	0.887 (0.002)
Attention [25,29]-LCNet050	0.992 (0.002)	0.991 (0.001)	0.991 (0.001)	0.991 (0.001)
DCMIX-LCNet050	0.991 (0.002)	0.990 (0.002)	0.990 (0.002)	0.990 (0.002)

4.2   RXRX1

Dataset. For our real world experiment, we employ the RXRX1 dataset [42] which consists of 125510 512 × 512 px fluorescence microscopy images (6 channels) of four different human cell lines that are perturbed with 1138 genetic perturbations (including 30 different positive control perturbations). In this study, we used as the training data 30 positive control siRNAs plus the non-active control which lead to 31 classes in total. All images were normalized using the 1 and 99 percent percentile and after, we extract image patches with a size of 192 × 192 px and an offset of 96 px. This step leads to 32776 image patches. For training, we split the data into a 70 percent training and a 30 percent hold-out set. The training set is further split into a 80 percent training and 20 percent validation set, respectively.

Models. For the real-world RXRX1 experiment, we compare DCMIX to LassoNet [22] and the attention-based [25,29] LCNet050.

Table 3. RXRX1 channel importance evaluation for the HepG2 cell line. The importance ranking illustrates the most important channels form left to right based on the weights depicted in the second column. In addition, model statistics are measured in GFLOPS and the number of model parameters (lower is better).

Method	Importance ranking	Channel weights (in Channel order)	GFLOPS	# parameters (millions)
ViT-B16-Imagenet21k [11] + LassoNet [22]	6,4,1,5,2,3	73084, 52526, 31138, 87881, 55612, 107733	-	-
Attention-LCNet050	4,2,5,1,3,6	0.15, 0.17, 0.008, 0.48, 0.16, 0.007	35.61	1.75
DCMIX-LCNet050	4,2,3,5,1,6	0.30, 0.69, 0.38, 1.06, 0.36, 0.21	5.95	0.27

Quantitative Evaluation. Channel Importance. Here, we describe the evaluation results on channel importance for the RXRX1 dataset which is illustrated in Table 3. To do so, we compare the results to the ground truth introduced in [42]. The experiment was manually designed by a scientist in the laboratory such that both channels four and two hold the most important biological information and channel 6 contains no important information for the phenotype. Keeping this information in mind, we assess the channel importance of DCMIX, LassoNet and Attention-LCNet050. Here, we can confirm that DCMIX learns the two most important channels four and two and the least important channel 6. These findings are also supported by Attention-LCNet050 which learned equivalent importance values. In contrast, LassoNet fails to uncover the correct channel importance by selecting the least important channel as the most important one. Despite finding the same important channels, DCMIX possess a 6–8 times higher speed and requires 6 times less parameters compared to the attention based networks and can be used in an end-to-end fashion which is not feasible for LassoNet.

Quantitative Evaluation. Model Performance. In this experiment, we evaluate the model performance of DCMIX to LassoNet and Attention-LCNet050 and illustrate the results in Table 4. Here, we observe that DCMIX outperforms both LassoNet and Attention-LCNet050 in terms of accuracy by five and seven percent, respectively. Furthermore, these finding are confirmed by precision, recall and f1-scores where DCMIX outperforms both competitors by approximately five and seven percent.

Table 4. Results of model performance for the RXRX1 dataset on the hold-out dataset. We asses the model performance on four different metrics: accuracy, precision, recall and f1-score where higher is better. Values in brackets denote the standard deviation.

Method	Accuracy	Precision	Recall	F1-Score
ViT-B16-Imagenet21k [11] + LassoNet [22]	0.695 (0.004)	0.705 (0.005)	0.705 (0.004)	0.704 (0.005)
Attention [25, 29]-LCNet050	0.744 (0.019)	0.753 (0.014)	0.747 (0.014)	0.747 (0.013)
DCMIX-LCNet050	0.765 (0.004)	0.77 (0.037)	0.77 (0.042)	0.764 (0.043)

5   Discussion

DCMIX Demonstrates State-of-the-art Channel Importance Scores in Fluorescence Cellular Imaging. DCMIX employs image blending to estimate the importance of each image channel. In Fig. 2, we provide an overview of the Spearman rank correlation of the channel importance estimates for all tested methods. The results are comparable for all methods (except of LassoNet) with a Spearman ρ always larger than 0.83. Especially the correlations of DCMIX and Attention-LCNet050 to the ground truth shapley values from [42] are evident with a Spearman ρ of 0.89. Both methods estimate the channel 2 and 4 as most important and channel 6 as least important which was the intentionally experimental design and furthermore shown via shapley values [42]. The authors explained their finding with a very large spectral overlap of the fluorescence signal from channel 2 and 4 to any other channel rendering them more important [42].

In contrast, LassoNet does not show any overlap with the rankings selected by all other methods (Fig. 2) with a maximal Spearman ρ value of -0.08.

DCMIX Achieves State-of-the-Art Classification Performance with Lower Model Complexity. Across all classification metrics DCMIX archives competitive results on MNIST and state-of-the-art performances on real-world RXRX1 compared to its competitors. Intuitively, we attribute the competitive results on MINST to the problem simplicity which is further supported by the high classification scores of 99% (Table 2). Concurrently, DCMIX requires merely a fraction of model parameters in all experiments (Tables 1,3) compared to the baselines.

Practical Runtimes for DCMIX Are 6-8 Times Faster Than Attention-Based Approaches. While DCMIX requires only 5.9271 GFLOPS and 5.95 GFLOPS on RXRX1, achieving the same computational performance as plain LCNet050, Attention-LCNet050 needs 17.809 GFLOPS on MNIST and 35.614 GFLOPS on RXRX1, respectively (Table 1 and Table 3). Moreover, even post-hoc approaches such Shapely values that are trained on a black-box model require often more significant computation time. For example, the training time

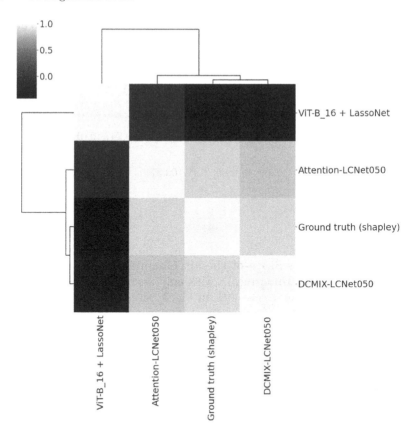

Fig. 2. Visualization of Spearman's rank correlation coefficient of the channel importance estimates for all different methods from Table 3. A value of -1 indicates maximal ranking difference between the channel importance estimates, 1 indicates no difference. Matrix has been sorted using average linkage hierarchical clustering with euclidean distance.

required for the Shapley value explanation are in the range of several minutes for the smaller CIFAR-10 dataset [16]. This demonstrates that the speed of DCMIX outperforms not only interpretable competitors but also explainable post-hoc approaches on a large scale.

DCMIX is Applicable in Real-World Settings Beyond Biomedical Imaging. From an application standpoint we see an advantage of DCMIX over the other tested methods, as the high scalability of DCMIX allows a model training workflow were channel importance is – per default – applied, such that a scientist gets immediate feedback about where the classification relevant information is coming from, and whether it correlates with the known understanding of the underlying biology.

DCMIX scales very well with the number of channels due to the addition of only one additional parameter per additional channel. This is particularly interesting for hyper spectral applications where hundreds of channels exist (e.g. in remote sensing) – a highly interesting application area for subsequent studies.

In addition, DCMIX allows for any arbitrary downstream network which can be fine-tuned/designed for other applications than fluorescence imaging.

DCMIX applies currently a simple addition channel mixing strategy to estimate channel importance without losing any classification performance (see model performance in Table 2 and 4). In principle several other channel blending methods exist, e.g. difference, multiplication or luminosity. Due to the flexibility of DCMIX these other mixing strategies can be easily integrated. Several studies already show the applicability of complex multi-spectral channel blending for visualization and classification in remote sensing [1,18].

6 Conclusion

In this work, we present a novel lightweight framework, DCMIX, which estimates channel importance of fluoresce images based on image blending. This empowers us to estimate phenotype-focused interpretations in a simple yet effective manner. Our experimental results demonstrate that the channel importance scores uncovered by DCMIX are both biologically supported and in line with competitive state-of-the-art approaches on MNIST and RXRX1 datasets. Concurrently, DCMIX is more effective in terms of runtime and scaleable to an arbitrary number of channels without scarifying the model performance.

Limitations. We discuss the limitations of our approach in the following two aspects. (1) The weights of DCMIX which determine the channel importance are solely a proxy and do not explain the absolute importance between channels. (2) DCMIX is based on image blending and hence only supporting image-based datasets. For future work, we plan to investigate how DCMIX can be extended to other data modalities.

References

1. Why Not a Single Image? Combining Visualizations to Facilitate Fieldwork and On-Screen Mapping. Remote Sensing (2019)
2. Alaa, A.M., van der Schaar, M.: Demystifying black-box models with symbolic metamodels. In: Advances in Neural Information Processing Systems (2019)
3. Bray, M.A., et al.: Cell Painting, a high-content image-based assay for morphological profiling using multiplexed fluorescent dyes. Nat. Protoc. **11**(9), 1757–1774 (2016)
4. Cai, Y., Liu, X., Cai, Z.: BS-Nets: an end-to-end framework for band selection of hyperspectral image. IEEE Trans. Geosci. Remote Sens. **58**, 1769–1984 (2020)
5. Carpenter, A.E., et al.: CellProfiler: image analysis software for identifying and quantifying cell phenotypes. Genome Biol. **7**, 1–11 (2006)
6. Carrillo, A., Cantú, L.F., Noriega, A.: Individual explanations in machine learning models: a survey for practitioners. CoRR abs/2104.04144 (2021)
7. Castelvecchi, D.: Can we open the black box of AI? Nat. News **538**, 20 (2016)

8. Choi, E., Bahadori, M.T., Kulas, J.A., Schuetz, A., Stewart, W.F., Sun, J.: Retain: an interpretable predictive model for healthcare using reverse time attention mechanism. In: Advances in Neural Information Processing Systems (2016)

9. Cohen, W.W.: Fast effective rule induction. In: International Conference on Machine Learning (1995)

10. Deng, L.: The MNIST database of handwritten digit images for machine learning research. IEEE Sig. Process. Mag. **29**, 141–142 (2012)

11. Dosovitskiy, A., et al.: an image is worth 16x16 words: transformers for image recognition at scale. In: International Conference on Learning Representations (2020)

12. Feng, J., Simon, N.: Sparse-input neural networks for high-dimensional nonparametric regression and classification (2019)

13. Friedman, J., Hastie, T., Tibshirani, R.: Sparse inverse covariance estimation with the graphical lasso. Biostatistics **9**, 432–441 (2008)

14. Godinez, W.J., Hossain, I., Lazic, S.E., Davies, J.W., Zhang, X.: A multi-scale convolutional neural network for phenotyping high-content cellular images. Bioinformatics **33**, 2010–2019 (2017)

15. He, K., et al.: A dual global-local attention network for hyperspectral band selection. IEEE Trans. Geosci. Remote Sens. **60**, 1–13 (2022)

16. Jethani, N., Sudarshan, M., Covert, I., Lee, S.I., Ranganath, R.: FastSHAP: real-Time Shapley Value Estimation. In: International Conference on Learning Representations (2022)

17. Jolliffe, I.: Principal Component Analysis. Springer, New York (1986). https://doi.org/10.1007/b98835

18. Jordanova, G., Verbovšek, T.: Improved automatic classification of lithogeomorphological units by using raster image blending, Vipava Valley (SW Slovenia). Remote Sens. **15**, 531 (2023)

19. Jullum, M., Redelmeier, A., Aas, K.: groupShapley: efficient prediction explanation with Shapley values for feature groups (2021), arXiv:2106.12228

20. Kim, B., et al.: Interpretability beyond feature attribution: quantitative testing with concept activation vectors (TCAV). In: International Conference on Machine Learning (2018)

21. Kruger, S., et al.: Advances in cancer immunotherapy 2019 - latest trends. J. Exp. Clin. Cancer Res. **38**, 1–11 (2019)

22. Lemhadri, I., Ruan, F., Abraham, L., Tibshirani, R.: Lassonet: a neural network with feature sparsity. J. Mach. Learn. Res. **22**, 5633–5661 (2021)

23. Levenson, R.M., Mansfield, J.R.: Multispectral imaging in biology and medicine: slices of life. Cytometry Part A (2006)

24. Li, W., Chen, H., Liu, Q., Liu, H., Wang, Y., Gui, G.: Attention mechanism and depthwise separable convolution aided 3DCNN for hyperspectral remote sensing image classification. Remote Sens. **14**, 2215 (2022)

25. Lin, Z., et al.: A structured self-attentive sentence embedding. In: International Conference on Learning Representations (2017)

26. Louizos, C., Welling, M., Kingma, D.P.: Learning sparse neural networks through l_0 regularization. In: International Conference on Learning Representations (2018)

27. Lundberg, S.M., et al.: From local explanations to global understanding with explainable AI for trees. Nat. Mach. Intell. **2**, 56–67 (2020)

28. Lundberg, S.M., Lee, S.I.: A unified approach to interpreting model predictions (2017)

29. Luong, T., Pham, H., Manning, C.D.: Effective approaches to attention-based neural machine translation. In: Conference on Empirical Methods in Natural Language Processing (2015)

30. Marcinkevičs, R., Vogt, J.E.: Interpretable and explainable machine learning: a methods-centric overview with concrete examples. WIREs Data Min. Knowl. Discov. (2023)

31. Nalepa, J.: Recent advances in multi- and hyperspectral image analysis. Sensors **21**, 6002 (2021)

32. Nikzad, M., Gao, Y., Zhou, J.: An attention-based lattice network for hyperspectral image classification. IEEE Trans. Geosci. Remote Sens. **60**, 1–15 (2022)

33. Park, T., Casella, G.: The Bayesian lasso. J. Am. Stat. Assoc. **103**, 681–686 (2008)

34. Prabhakaran, S., Metzner, K.J., Böhm, A., Roth, V.: Recovering networks from distance data. In: Asian Conference on Machine Learning (2012)

35. Ribeiro, M.T., Singh, S., Guestrin, C.: "why should i trust you?": explaining the predictions of any classifier. In: ACM SIGKDD International Conference on Knowledge Discovery and Data Mining (2016)

36. Rozemberczki, B., et al.: The shapley value in machine learning. In: International Joint Conference on Artificial Intelligence (2022)

37. Schwab, P., Miladinovic, D., Karlen, W.: Granger-causal attentive mixtures of experts: learning important features with neural networks. In: AAAI Conference on Artificial Intelligence (2019)

38. Shrikumar, A., Greenside, P., Kundaje, A.: Learning important features through propagating activation differences. In: International Conference on Machine Learning (2017)

39. Siegismund, D., Wieser, M., Heyse, S., Steigele, S.: Self-supervised representation learning for high-content screening. In: International Conference on Medical Imaging with Deep Learning (2022)

40. Steigele, S., et al.: Deep learning-based HCS image analysis for the enterprise. Adv. Sci. Drug Discov. SLAS DISCOVERY **25**, 812–821 (2020)

41. Sundararajan, M., Taly, A., Yan, Q.: Axiomatic attribution for deep networks. In: International Conference on Machine Learning (2017)

42. Sypetkowski, M., et al.: RxRx1: A dataset for evaluating experimental batch correction methods. In: IEEE/CVF Conference on Computer Vision and Pattern Recognition Workshops (2023)

43. Tibshirani, R.: Regression shrinkage and selection via the lasso. J. R. Stat. Soc. (Ser. B) **58**, 267–288 (1996)

44. Ustun, B., Rudin, C.: Supersparse linear integer models for optimized medical scoring systems. Mach. Learn. **102**, 349–391 (2015)

45. Vaswani, A., et al.: Attention is all you need. In: Advances in Neural Information Processing Systems (2017)

46. Wachter, S., Mittelstadt, B.D., Russell, C.: Counterfactual explanations without opening the black box: Automated decisions and the gdpr. Cybersecurity (2017)

47. Wieczorek, A., Wieser, M., Murezzan, D., Roth, V.: Learning sparse latent representations with the deep copula information bottleneck. In: International Conference on Learning Representations (2018)

48. Wieser, M., Siegismund, D., Heyse, S., Steigele, S.: Vision transformers show improved robustness in high-content image analysis. In: Swiss Conference on Data Science (2022)

49. Yuan, M., Lin, Y.: Model selection and estimation in regression with grouped variables. J. R. Stat. Soc. Ser. B: Stat. Methodol. **68**, 49–67 (2005)

50. Zhang, L., Wen, T., Shi, J.: Deep image blending. In: IEEE/CVF Winter Conference on Applications of Computer Vision (2020)

Self-supervised Learning in Histopathology: New Perspectives for Prostate Cancer Grading

Markus Bauer[✉] and Christoph Augenstein

Center for Scalable Data Analytics and Artificial Intelligence (ScaDS.AI),
Dresden/Leipzig, Germany
{bauer,augenstein}@wifa.uni-leipzig.de

Abstract. The prostate carcinoma (PCa) is the second most common cause of cancer-deaths among men. To estimate the appropriate therapy pathway after diagnosis, the Gleason score (GS) has been established as an international measure. While the GS has been proven to be a good tool for tumour assessment, it naturally suffers from subjectivity. Especially for cancers of lower to medium severity, this leads to inter- and intra observer variability and a remarkable amount of over- and under therapy. The PCa thus is in the focus of various research works, that aim to improve the grading procedure. With recently emerging AI technologies, solutions have been proposed to automate the GS-based PCa-grading while keeping predictions consistent. Current solutions, however, fail to handle data variability arising from preparation differences among hospitals and typically require a large amount of annotated data, which is often not available. Thus, in this paper, we propose self-supervised learning (SSL) as a new perspective for AI-based PCa grading. Using several thousand PCa cases, we demonstrate that SSL may be a feasible alternative for analysing histopathological samples and pretraining grading models. Our SSL-pretrained models extract features related to the Gleason grades (GGs), and achieve competitive accuracy for PCa downstream classification.

Keywords: Prostate Cancer · Self-Supervised Learning · Artificial Intelligence

1 Introduction

AI technologies are already a widespread choice in various histopathological applications, including those focusing on the PCa. Current research work and emerging commercial solutions use supervised training to create convolutional neural networks (CNNs) that can extract features that match cancer-driven morphological changes and thus can reproduce the GS.

Impressive results for the PCa can be found, even in early works such as the ones of Arvaniti et al. [1] or Nagpal et al. [19], where ∼70% of the expert's GS

© The Author(s), under exclusive license to Springer Nature Switzerland AG 2024
U. Köthe and C. Rother (Eds.): DAGM GCPR 2023, LNCS 14264, pp. 348–360, 2024.
https://doi.org/10.1007/978-3-031-54605-1_23

could be reproduced. Bulten et al. [5] achieve an area under the receiver operating characteristics curve (AUC-ROC) of 0.984 for the tumour vs. non-tumour problem. Tolkach et al. [24] even achieve a binary accuracy of over 95% using a slightly more complex deep learning pipeline. Similar results are achieved by Ström et al. [23] with an AUC-ROC of 0.997. Finally, using CNNs for PCa grading is also part of various international challenges such as the PANDA challenge (c.f. [3] et al.), where a maximum quadratically weighted kappa of 0.86 was achieved by the best team on international validation data. Supervised training methods, however, require huge amounts of labelled data, which is often not available, and suffer from limited annotation quality or missing pathological consensus. Hence, poor generalization is often observed, as results worsen significantly for data which originates from other laboratories (c.f. [22]).

Recent advances in computer vision have shown, that SSL may be of value, to omit these issues, and may even improve performance achieved by supervised models [6,8,13,18,29]. To do so, SSL uses CNNs and visual transformers (ViTs) [16], but generates training signals from the data itself rather than using manual annotations. Early works such as the one of Bulten et al. [4], who applied SSL to PCa data using an autoencoder [26] could show that this method may be feasible for PCa histopathological analysis. Their approach, however, fails to distinguish more groups than benign, stroma and tumour. The problem seems to arise due to the autoencoder's limited capability, to extract robust, discriminative features.

More recent works suggest the definition of pretext tasks, that do not require a generative model, as in the case of an autoencoder. Such tasks may be the prediction of an image's rotation [10], solving of jigsaw puzzles [20], predicting generated pseudo-labels [27], or comparing feature vectors in a contrastive setup using an original and augmented image version [8,13,18,29]. The value of SSL for histopathology is demonstrated by Yan et al. [28], who trained an SSL model on various publicly available histopathology datasets and almost achieved supervised performance on the CAMELYON dataset[1].

Currently, only few works have investigated the value of SSL for PCa histopathological analysis. Thus, we evaluated recent SSL methods using the PANDA dataset. We conclude that SSL may be a good future path and direction to eliminate human bias from cancer grading while keeping a high standard of assessment accuracy and reproducibility. The following sections provide information about our experimental analysis and conclusions.

2   Materials and Methods

To train histopathological PCa models using SSL, we implemented a processing pipeline as depicted in Fig. 1. First, we sample image patches from a few thousand original core needle biopsy (CNB) images and select up to 16 patches per CNB according to the most amount of relevant tissue. Additionally, multiple CNBs are filtered as they are duplicates or contain very noisy labels, as suggested in

---

[1] https://camelyon17.grand-challenge.org.

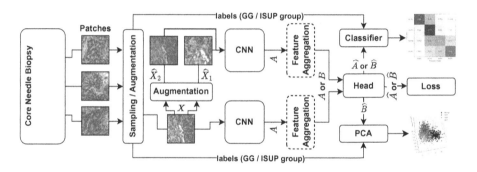

Fig. 1. Overview of the training and validation method.

the winning solution[2] of the PANDA challenge. For each image patch X, we then create multiple augmented versions $\hat{X}$ and process them using a feature encoder. It's noteworthy to say that for one of our approaches (SimCLR) only augmented versions of X will be fed to the CNN. To perform whole-slide-image(WSI)-wide prediction, information from multiple patches needs to be aggregated. Thus, we implement the feature aggregation as suggested by the PANDA baseline[3] as a configurable alternative to processing the individual image patches directly. The key aspect of the feature aggregation is to concatenate multiple CNN-extracted features A of the same WSI in a global feature matrix B, such that

$$B = \text{concat}(A): \ \mathbb{R}^{(BS \cdot N) \times C \times I \times J} \rightarrow \mathbb{R}^{BS \times C \times (N \cdot I) \times J} \qquad (1)$$

whereas BS is the batch size, I and J are the feature shape, C are the kernel map channels and N is a fixed number of patches. The features of the original and augmented patches are then processed by fully connected layers (projection heads) followed by pooling. Afterwards, a contrastive loss is calculated based on these projected feature vectors $\hat{A}$, or $\hat{B}$ respectively, as described in Subsect. 2.1. Finally, we perform multiple downstream tasks for evaluation, as described in Sect. 3.

2.1 Self-supervised Training Methods

The main idea of self-supervised learning (SSL) is to train a neural network in such a way that it learns to capture fundamental morphological properties of images without relying on labelled data. In traditional supervised learning, a neural network is trained on a labelled dataset, where each image is associated with a specific class or label. However, obtaining labelled data can be expensive and time-consuming, especially in domains like medical imaging.

In SSL, instead of using external labels, the network is trained to predict certain image modifications or transformations applied to the original image.

---

[2] kaggle.com/competitions/prostate-cancer-grade-assessment/discussion/169143.
[3] kaggle.com/competitions/prostate-cancer-grade-assessment/discussion/146855.

For example, the network may be trained to predict the rotation angle [10] or to withstand cropping [6–8] applied to the image. Let's denote the unlabelled dataset as $D = x_1, x_2, ..., x_n$, where x_i represents an input image in the dataset and n is the number of images in the dataset. The goal of SSL is to learn a representation function $\phi(x)$ that maps each input image x_i to a feature vector $\phi(x_i)$ in a latent space. The overall SSL objective can be formulated as follows:

$$\theta^* = \arg \min_{\theta} \left(\frac{1}{n} \sum_{i=1}^{n} L\left(\Phi(x_i; \theta), T(x_i)\right) \right) \tag{2}$$

whereas

- θ^* represents the optimal model parameters that minimize the overall loss.
- $\phi(x_i; \theta)$ is the feature vector obtained by applying the representation function ϕ with parameters θ to the input image x_i.
- $T(x_i)$ is the target label or artificial target for the pretext task associated with the input image x_i.
- $L(\phi(x_i; \theta), T(x_i))$ is the loss function that measures the discrepancy between the predicted target $(\phi(x_i; \theta))$ and the actual target $(T(x_i))$ for the pretext task.

The advantage of using SSL in PCa histopathology lies in its potential to extract discriminative features that are not biased by subjective factors, in contrast to directly optimising to the Gleason score. Traditionally, grading PCa involves human pathologists assigning a GS to each tissue sample based on visual appearance. However, this process can be subject to inter-observer variability and lacks objectivity. SSL circumvents the need for GS labels and allows the model to identify intrinsic morphological patterns in the images, which could directly correlate with clinical outcomes like time to biochemical recurrence (BCR) or death of disease (DoD). This opens up new avenues for computer-aided diagnosis and precision medicine in the context of prostate cancer and other medical imaging applications.

SimCLR is one of the earliest, yet still popular, SSL methods. It involves processing images X into augmented versions x_i and x_j that will be fed through a convolutional neural network (CNN) trunk, followed by a fully connected multilayer perceptron (MLP). Augmentations may be colour jitter, cropping and scaling of smaller image parts, or blurring the images, as described in Sect. 3. This process generates feature vectors z_i and z_j of configurable length for all images.

To train the SimCLR model, an important component is the InfoNCE loss [21]. The objective of the InfoNCE loss is to maximize the similarity between feature vectors of the original image's augmented versions (z_i, z_j), while also minimizing the similarity to feature vectors of all other images' augmentations z_k in the batch. This encourages the model to learn representations that effectively capture the essential information present in the original images and their augmented versions. The loss is calculated and used to find optimal parameters ϕ and ω of the trunk and MLP according to (c.f. [8]):

$$\text{InfoNCE}(\phi, \omega) = \arg\min_{\phi,\omega} - \log \frac{e^{sim(z_i, z_j)}}{\sum_{k=1}^{2N} \mathbb{1}_{[k \notin (x_i, x_j)]} e^{sim(z_i, z_k)/\tau}} \tag{3}$$

where

- ϕ and ω are the parameters of the CNN trunk and the MLP, respectively, which need to be learned during training.
- N is the batch size, and $2N$ is the size of the augmented batch.
- z_k represents the feature vectors of the remaining batch images.
- $sim(z_i, z_j)$ is the similarity metric between the feature vectors. It is often computed as the dot product of the feature vectors divided by the product of their norms, which is equivalent to measuring the cosine similarity.
- $\mathbb{1}_{[k \notin (x_i, x_j)]} e^{sim(z_i, z_k)/\tau}$ is an indicator function that equals 1 if k does not belong to the set containing x_i and x_j, and 0 otherwise. This ensures that x_i and x_j are not compared to themselves during the loss calculation.
- τ is a hyperparameter that acts as a temperature parameter, controlling how strongly the feature vectors z_i and z_k are pushed apart in the latent space. It is analogous to the temperature parameter used in a softmax function during training.

By optimizing the SimCLR model with the InfoNCE loss, the CNN trunk and MLP learn to create powerful and transferable image representations, which can be used in downstream tasks like image classification or object detection without the need for labelled data.

DINO is an innovative self-supervised learning method that takes a different approach compared to traditional methods like SimCLR. Instead of using convolutional neural networks (CNNs), DINO employs visual transformers for processing images X and their augmented versions $\hat{X}$. In contrast to SimCLR, which considers multiple images in the batch for comparison, DINO only compares each image with its augmentation within the cost function.

DINO uses two models: a student model $g_{\omega,s}$ and a teacher model $g_{\omega,t}$. These models process the images X and $\hat{X}$ to generate feature representations. Both models are visual transformers, a type of architecture that has shown great success in capturing complex image patterns, and provide good feature capturing capabilities both in spatial and global context.

Before comparing the feature representations, the teacher model $g_{\omega,t}$ processes the original images X to generate the feature vectors $z_t = g_{\omega,t}(X)$). These feature vectors are centred using the batch mean, which helps to remove any biases and normalize the representations. Both the feature vectors of the student model $z_s = g_{\omega,s}(X)$ and the teacher model z_t are sharpened using the Softmax function with an additional temperature parameter τ. The Softmax function amplifies the differences between class probabilities, leading to more discriminative features. The temperature parameter τ controls the concentration of the probability distribution, where higher values result in softer probabilities and vice versa.

The loss is calculated on the probabilities p_t and p_s as in Caron et al. [7]:

$$H = -p_t \cdot \log p_s \tag{4}$$

The objective of the loss function is to iteratively match the probability distributions of the student and teacher models. By minimizing this cross-entropy loss, the student model learns to mimic the teacher model's predictions and aims to achieve similar probabilities for corresponding images and their augmentations.

Another difference between DINO and contrastive SSL like SimCLR is the use of an asymmetric weight update that prevents mode collapse of the extracted features. During training, the student model is updated using standard back-propagation with stochastic gradient descent (SGD) or other optimization algorithms. The goal is to minimize the cross-entropy loss between the teacher's and student's probabilities. The teacher model, on the other hand, is updated differently. Instead of using large batches or memory banks for negative samples as in contrastive methods, DINO employs an elegant solution by updating the teacher model using the exponential moving average (EMA) of the student model's parameters. This technique helps to stabilize and improve the performance of the teacher model over time. By slowly updating the teacher model to follow the student model's latest state, DINO creates a smoother and more reliable teacher model for guiding the student's learning process.

In summary, DINO's setup and cost function leverage visual transformers, distillation, and iterative matching of probability distributions to learn powerful and transferable image representations in a self-supervised manner. This approach presents a promising alternative to CNN-based methods, demonstrating the effectiveness of visual transformers in addressing the challenges of self-supervised learning with impressive performance results.

2.2   Dataset and Training Details

We use data from the PANDA grand challenge, which contains core needle biopsy (CNB) images taken from Radboud (n = 5160), and Karolinska (n = 5456) hospitals. In total, n = 10616 images are available including their annotated primary and secondary GGs and the GS, as well as the ISUP grade groups (IGGs). Furthermore, masks are provided to split the images into tumour, stromal and non-tumour regions, and in the Radboud cases even GG masks. For the Radboud data, the GS distribution is relatively balanced except for GS 10 (2% share), whereas Karolinska data mostly contains cases of low- to medium severity. After cropping and filtering the CNB images, the l_1 (20× magnification at half resolution) region-annotated (:= ROI) training and test set contains 94678 and 31560, and the non-ROI dataset contains 168256 l_2 (20× magnification at quarter resolution) and 157740 l_1 images.

We test two different SSL methods as described above, with residual Networks (ResNet-18 & 50) [14], as suggested in the PANDA challenge, and a

ViT-B-16 for small datasets as suggested by Lee et al. [16]. Additionally, other frameworks that use a joint embedding architecture, namely SwAV [6], BYOL [12], and MOCO [9], have been tested. As their results were inferior to SimCLR and comparable to DINO, we only present the results of those two methodically diverse approaches. For training, we use PyTorch (1.11.0), Python (3.9) and the training frameworks fastAI (2.7.11) [15] and VISSL (0.1.6) [11]. All parameters are tuned using a grid search. Table 1 provides an overview of important augmentation techniques and projection heads, as well as training- and hyperparameters extracted from the grid search. For DINO, using multiple augmentations produced instable training behaviour. Thus, as suggested in [2], we reduced the number of augmentations to reduce the pre-text task complexity. Finally, we only used RandomCrop.

Table 1. Parameter configurations and setup of the SSL algorithms used in this study.

Algorithm	Augmentations	Hyperparameters	Training Parameters	Model
SimCLR	RandomCrop, RandomFlip, ColorDistortion, Gaussian Blur	temperature: 0.7	multi learning rate: • base: 5e−4, • linear: [1e−4, 16e−4], • cosine: [16e−4, 16e−7] SGD/ranger optimizer: • weight decay: 1e−6, • momentum 0.9, • batch size: 32	ResNet-18/50 + MLP: [nc, nc], [nc, 128] nc = 512 / 2048
DINO	RandomCrop	teacher τ: [0.01 - 0.02] student τ: 0.4 ema center: 0.9	multi learning rate: • base: 0.05, • linear: [1e−6, 2e−4], • cosine: [2e−4, 1e−6] AdamW optimizer: • weight decay: 1e−6, • batch size: 32	SmallVit-B16 + MLP: [384, 384], [384, 32]

3 Experiments

To evaluate the potential of the SSL-trained feature encoders, we run multiple downstream tasks. The results are presented in this section. The models are trained using an NVIDIA P100 and V100 card. SSL pretraining takes the most memory and processing time of 28 GB and 96 h, as our setup only allows creating batches up to size 32 for l_1 images, and therefore convergence was only observed after a few hundreds of epochs (c.f. [8]). The supervised models require around quarter the processing time of SSL and converge at around epoch 30. Feature aggregation is used for models in the IGG downstream task and omitted in patch-wise downstream tasks.

Table 2. Overview: Configuration of the self-supervised (SSL) and supervised (SUP) experiments conducted in this study.

No	Training Type	Network Architecture	Concatenated Features	Evaluation Method
1	SSL	SimCLR (ResNet-18)	No	Embedding Visualization
2	SSL	DINO	No	Embedding Visualization
3	SUP	ResNet-18	No	Embedding Visualization
4	SSL	SimCLR (ResNet-18)	No	Patch Downstream Classification
5	SSL	DINO	No	Patch Downstream Classification
6	SUP	ResNet-18	No	Patch Downstream Classification
7	SSL	SimCLR (ResNet-18)	No	Slide Downstream Classification
8	SSL	SimCLR (ResNet-18)	Yes	Slide Downstream Classification
9	SUP	ResNet-18	Yes	Slide Downstream Classification
10	SUP	ResNet-50	Yes	Slide Downstream Classification

We conducted multiple SSL trainings using different algorithms and downstream tasks. In addition, the models were trained in a supervised fashion, to get a fair comparison. Table 2 gives an overview of all conducted experiments. The data for each experiment was structured as in Table 3.

3.1 Qualitative Analysis

To get an initial understanding of SSL's capabilities to extract features that align with the GGs, we first perform qualitative analysis using the principal component analysis (PCA) [17] of the feature vectors. For this first downstream task, we only use the Radboud part of the data, as stain differences among hospitals are known to hinder the model from achieving good results. We thus decided to exclude this influence, as stain normalization is not the focus of this study. If the model extracts features that correlate with known prognostic morphologies, the scatter plot of the features' PCA should show separable clusters for each

Table 3. Data used for the individual experiments, including label amount. For scenarios where patches are processed (1–6) the number of labels equals the input images, and for WSI-processing approaches (7–10) 16 input images equal one label.

No.	Image Size	Quality	No. Training Labels	No. Downstream Labels
1–2	128 × 128	l1	0	-
3	128 × 128	l1	94678	-
4–5	128 × 128	l1	0	5917
6	128 × 128	l1	94678	-
7	128 × 128	l2	0	657
8	128 × 128	l2	0	657
9	128 × 128	l2	10516	-
10	128 × 128	l1	9858	-

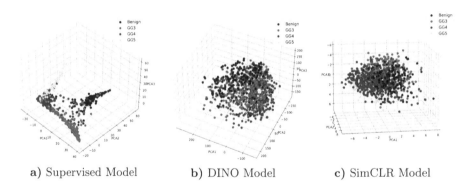

a) Supervised Model   b) DINO Model   c) SimCLR Model

Fig. 2. Scatter plots of the first three PCA main components of patch features generated by the supervised, DINO and SimCLR feature encoders.

of the annotated labels. Figure 2 shows the scatter plot. For the model trained in a supervised fashion, expectations are met. Except for a few cases of low severity which are confused with benign tissue, as well as some confusion between individual GGs, all labels seem to produce separable representations. Yet, the fact that variance among the features seems to be low may be an indicator of missing robustness, as the PCa's heterogenous morphologies should be reflected by the extracted features. The DINO model only produces very rudimentary clusters. In the left part of the plot a cluster of benign tissue can be found which appears to be separable from tumour region patches. Overall, however, a great degree of entangling is observed. This accounts especially for GG5 patches, that can't be distinguished from any of the classes. While the GG5 patches have the lowest class share, this behaviour likely refers to weak features, as at least no overlap should happen with the benign patches (c.f. Fig. 2a). The SimCLR also shows some entangling but generally appears to extract meaningful features, as clusters of the referred GGs can be observed. In contrast to the DINO model, GG5 shows almost no confusion with the benign tissue and also has clearly separable samples. For the remaining tissue samples, we observe a mix between separable samples and entangled ones. From the qualitative analysis, it was already getting obvious that supervised training provides the best feature extractor, while DINO will likely fail to produce features for detection of the highest severity (GG5), and SimCLR probably achieves plausible but mid-tier results.

3.2 Patch-Wise Performance Analysis

To further investigate the effects of SSL training, we analyse the downstream performance using a logistic regression to predict individual patches' GGs. Results are created as the mean of a 3-fold leave-on-out cross validation using the features generated from the ROI test data. Table 4 shows the cross-validation performance results as indicated by mean class balanced accuracy and quadratic

Table 4. Mean patch-wise performance of the different models, in a 3-fold leave-one-out cross validation. The labels refer to benign (B), and Gleason grade 3, 4 and 5 (GG3-5).

Model	resolution	BA	QWK	BBA	BQWK	$f1_B$	$f1_{GG3}$	$f1_{GG4}$	$f1_{GG5}$
Supervised	128^2px@l_1	0.83	0.89	0.94	0.87	0.89	0.89	0.91	0.69
SimCLR	128^2px@l_1	0.63	0.68	0.83	0.65	0.71	0.79	0.78	0.38
DINO	128^2px@l_1	0.52	0.59	0.79	0.59	0.66	0.59	0.73	0.11

weighted kappa (BA; QWK), tumour vs. non-tumour balanced accuracy and quadratic weighted kappa (BBA; BQWK), and $f1$ scores of the individual classes. As expected, the DINO model shows the worst results, with a balanced accuracy (BA) of 0.52 and quadratic weighted kappa (QWK) of 0.59. Especially, the $f1$ score of the GG5 patches was lower than random guessing with 0.11. For the supervised model, BA of 0.83 and QWK of 0.89 was achieved. The GG5 show the lowest $f1$ score here as well. SimCLR performs better than the DINO model, while also struggling to classify GG5 patches correctly. Binary BA (BBA) indicates that most false positives arise from confusing tumour classes with each other. In total, the SimCLR performance slightly improves the results achieved in our earlier works (c.f., [5]) using autoencoders, but still is outperformed by the supervised pendant.

3.3 WSI-Wise Performance Analysis

While the results achieved in patch-wise classification were promising, they are of less practical relevance, as in a real-world setup predictions need to be done for the WSI rather than individual patches. This task is more challenging, as the network also needs to understand the context of a single patch within its WSI. We thus perform a second classification downstream task to predict the WSI's IGG using the non-ROI l_2 dataset and the same preprocessing, validation strategy and split ratio as before. Multiple setups are evaluated, as presented in Table 5. For the SSL models, the encoder part was frozen after training and only the aggregation and projection head are fine-tuned. For fine-tuning and training of the supervised pendants, kappa loss [25] yields the best results. For the SSL part, we focus on the SimCLR model, as DINO didn't appear to deliver useful results.

In general, training by SimCLR without feature aggregation achieves inferior results. For the QWK, the best results at lowest magnification are achieved by the supervised model. The results are in accordance with the PANDA challenge's baseline solution. Table 5 suggests that significant differences between the $f1$ scores of the individual IGG can be found. The worst results are achieved for the IGGs that contain the most heterogenous patterns. This seems plausible, as the training method enforces the network to not only extract meaningful features, but also to decide which features in combination are connected to a certain IGG.

Table 5. Mean WSI-wise performance of the different models, in a 3-fold leave-one-out cross validation. The labels refer to benign (B) and the IGGs 1-5 (I1-I5).

Model	resolution	BA	QWK	BBA	BQWK	$f1_B$	$f1_{I1}$	$f1_{I2}$	$f1_{I3}$	$f1_{I4}$	$f1_{I5}$
SimCLR ResNet-18	128^2px@l_2	0.41	0.57	0.75	0.47	0.63	0.44	0.29	0.24	0.28	0.51
SimCLR ResNet-18 + concat	128^2px@l_2	**0.51**	0.65	**0.85**	0.64	**0.75**	0.54	**0.42**	0.33	**0.46**	0.57
Supervised ResNet-18 + concat	128^2px@l_2	0.50	**0.76**	0.83	0.62	0.74	0.54	0.30	**0.34**	0.25	**0.62**
Supervised ResNet-50 + concat	128^2px@l_2	0.50	0.74	0.83	**0.64**	**0.75**	**0.56**	0.34	0.28	0.40	0.58

Thus, better $f1$ scores are achieved, if less feature variance is present. As the QWK not necessarily captures this behaviour, we also compare for balanced accuracy and individual $f1$ scores. Here, the SimCLR model achieves the best results most of the time, whereas some results are shared with the supervised ResNet-50. The most prominent advantage can be seen for IGGs two and four.

As l_1 images are known to create better accuracies in supervised training (c.f. [3]), we repeat the experiment with non-ROI l_1 images. In this case, similar to the PANDA challenge's results, BA of 0.7+ and QWK of 0.85+ were achieved when using a supervised ResNet-50. For SimCLR, We found that batch size seems to be a critical factor here, but couldn't fully investigate the limits of SSL performance, as the required amount of graphical memory is exceeding our technical capabilities. The results, even though of low BA and QWK, still indicated a balanced behaviour as for the l_2 images.

4   Discussion

In this paper, we showed, that SSL pretraining may be a promising method, to create state-of-the-art PCa grading models, with significantly less effort in annotating cases beforehand. Our models achieve better results in qualitative and quantitative analysis than earlier autoencoder-based works.

Current supervised models are limited by the accuracy of the pathologists themselves (e.g., for PANDA the accuracy of the annotating pathologists against expert consensus, similar to the CNNs, was only at 72%). Our results indicate, that SSL pretraining has the potential to extract prognostic features, which are unaffected by this issue. SSL thus provides a platform to combine morphological information with follow-up-based endpoints as BCR or DoD to directly identify prognostic features after SSL pretraining.

When training the models, we observed, that various hyperparameters such as the batch size and image resolution can have a significant impact on the results. Thus, to fully evaluate the limits of the presented approach, future work should apply a more sophisticated hyperparameter tuning and architecture search. Furthermore, one main issue of the IGG prediction seems to be directly connected to the concatenation-based training. For the SSL approach, this also comes with the downside of high graphical memory consumption. We thus propose, to investigate better strategies for combining various features in future works.

Another important research direction could also lie in using SSL as a data exploration tool. Even though the SSL pretraining reduced the amount of required labels to achieve state-of-the-art classification results to 25% compared to the supervised approach, a total amount of 657 annotated patient cases is still a lot. Our qualitative analyses showed that morphological groups are identified by the algorithm. Hence, SSL may have the capability to reduce the amount of annotated cases even further, by labelling, e.g., the most uncertain cases in an expert-in-the-loop approach.

We conclude that, given the promising results of our work, SSL deserves to get more attention in histopathology. This especially accounts for creating an expert-in-the-loop system, which could also help pathologists to gather new knowledge from the AI, rather than only providing it.

References

1. Arvaniti, E., et al.: Automated Gleason grading of prostate cancer tissue microarrays via deep learning. Sc. Rep. **8**(1), 12054 (2018)
2. Balestriero, R., et al.: A cookbook of self-supervised learning. CoRR abs/2304.12210 (2023)
3. Bulten, W., et al.: Artificial intelligence for diagnosis and Gleason grading of prostate cancer: the PANDA challenge. Nat. Med. **28**(1), 154–163 (2022)
4. Bulten, W., Litjens, G.: Unsupervised prostate cancer detection on h&e using convolutional adversarial autoencoders. CoRR abs/1804.07098 (2018)
5. Bulten, W., et al.: Automated deep-learning system for Gleason grading of prostate cancer using biopsies: a diagnostic study. Lancet Oncol. **21**(2), 233–241 (2020)
6. Caron, M., Misra, I., Mairal, J., Goyal, P., Bojanowski, P., Joulin, A.: Unsupervised learning of visual features by contrasting cluster assignments. In: Proceedings of the 34th International Conference on Neural Information Processing Systems. NIPS'20, Curran Associates Inc., Red Hook, NY, USA (2020)
7. Caron, M., et al.: Emerging properties in self-supervised vision transformers. CoRR abs/2104.14294 (2021)
8. Chen, T., Kornblith, S., Norouzi, M., Hinton, G.: A simple framework for contrastive learning of visual representations. CoRR abs/2002.05709 (2020)
9. Chen, X., Fan, H., Girshick, R., He, K.: Improved baselines with momentum contrastive learning. CoRR abs/2003.04297 (2020)
10. Gidaris, S., Singh, P., Komodakis, N.: Unsupervised representation learning by predicting image rotations. CoRR abs/1803.07728 (2018)
11. Goyal, P., et al.: VISSL (2021). https://github.com/facebookresearch/vissl
12. Grill, J.B., et al.: Bootstrap your own latent a new approach to self-supervised learning. In: Proceedings of the 34th International Conference on Neural Information Processing Systems. NIPS'20, Curran Associates Inc., Red Hook, NY, USA (2020)
13. He, K., Fan, H., Wu, Y., Xie, S., Girshick, R.: Momentum contrast for unsupervised visual representation learning. CoRR abs/1911.05722 (2019)
14. He, K., Zhang, X., Ren, S., Sun, J.: Deep residual learning for image recognition. CoRR abs/1512.03385 (2015)
15. Howard, J., Gugger, S.: Fastai: a layered API for deep learning. CoRR abs/2002.04688 (2020)

16. Lee, S.H., Lee, S., Song, B.C.: Vision transformer for small-size datasets. CoRR abs/2112.13492 (2021)
17. Maćkiewicz, A., Ratajczak, W.: Principal components analysis (PCA). Comput. Geosci. **19**(3), 303–342 (1993). https://doi.org/10.1016/0098-3004(93)90090-r
18. Misra, I., van der Maaten, L.: Self-supervised learning of pretext-invariant representations. CoRR abs/1912.01991 (2019)
19. Nagpal, K., et al.: Development and validation of a deep learning algorithm for Gleason grading of prostate cancer from biopsy specimens. JAMA Oncol. **6**(9), 1372 (2020)
20. Noroozi, M., Favaro, P.: Unsupervised learning of visual representations by solving jigsaw puzzles. CoRR abs/1603.09246 (2016)
21. Oord, A.V.D., Li, Y., Vinyals, O.: Representation learning with contrastive predictive coding. CoRR abs/1807.03748 (2018)
22. Singhal, N., et al.: A deep learning system for prostate cancer diagnosis and grading in whole slide images of core needle biopsies. Sci. Rep. **12**(1), 3383 (2022)
23. Ström, P., et al.: Artificial intelligence for diagnosis and grading of prostate cancer in biopsies: a population-based, diagnostic study. Lancet Oncol. **21**(2), 222–232 (2020)
24. Tolkach, Y., Dohmgörgen, T., Toma, M., Kristiansen, G.: High-accuracy prostate cancer pathology using deep learning. Nat. Mach. Intell. **2**(7), 411–418 (2020)
25. Vaughn, D., Justice, D.: On the direct maximization of quadratic weighted kappa. CoRR abs/1509.07107 (2015)
26. Vincent, P., Larochelle, H., Lajoie, I., Bengio, Y., Manzagol, P.A.: Stacked denoising autoencoders: learning useful representations in a deep network with a local denoising criterion. J. Mach. Learn. Res. **11**, 3371–3408 (2010)
27. Wu, Z., Xiong, Y., Yu, S., Lin, D.: Unsupervised feature learning via nonparametric instance-level discrimination. CoRR abs/1805.01978 (2018)
28. Yan, J., Chen, H., Li, X., Yao, J.: Deep contrastive learning based tissue clustering for annotation-free histopathology image analysis. Comput. Med. Imaging Graph. **97** (2022). N.PAG-N.PAG
29. Zbontar, J., Jing, L., Misra, I., LeCun, Y., Deny, S.: Barlow twins: self-supervised learning via redundancy reduction. CoRR abs/2103.03230 (2021)

Interpretable Machine Learning

DeViL: Decoding Vision features into Language

Meghal Dani[1]([✉]) [iD], Isabel Rio-Torto[3,4] [iD], Stephan Alaniz[1] [iD],
and Zeynep Akata[1,2] [iD]

[1] University of Tübingen, Tübingen, Germany
{meghal.dani,stephan.alaniz,zeynep.akata}@uni-tuebingen.de
[2] MPI for Intelligent Systems, Tübingen, Germany
[3] Faculdade de Ciências da Universidade do Porto, Porto, Portugal
[4] INESC TEC, Porto, Portugal
isabel.riotorto@inesctec.pt

Abstract. Post-hoc explanation methods have often been criticised for abstracting away the decision-making process of deep neural networks. In this work, we would like to provide natural language descriptions for what different layers of a vision backbone have learned. Our *DeViL* method generates textual descriptions of visual features at different layers of the network as well as highlights the attribution locations of learned concepts. We train a transformer network to translate individual image features of any vision layer into a prompt that a separate off-the-shelf language model decodes into natural language. By employing dropout both per-layer and per-spatial-location, our model can generalize training on image-text pairs to generate localized explanations. As it uses a pre-trained language model, our approach is fast to train and can be applied to any vision backbone. Moreover, *DeViL* can create open-vocabulary attribution maps corresponding to words or phrases even outside the training scope of the vision model. We demonstrate that *DeViL* generates textual descriptions relevant to the image content on CC3M, surpassing previous lightweight captioning models and attribution maps, uncovering the learned concepts of the vision backbone. Further, we analyze fine-grained descriptions of layers as well as specific spatial locations and show that *DeViL* outperforms the current state-of-the-art on the neuron-wise descriptions of the MILANNOTATIONS dataset.

Keywords: Explainable AI · Vision-Language Models · Natural Language Explanations · Open-vocabulary Saliency

1 Introduction

Despite the success of deep vision models, the lack of understanding of how they arrive at their predictions inhibits their widespread adoption in safety-critical

---

M. Dani and I. Rio-Torto—Equal contribution.

Supplementary Information The online version contains supplementary material available at https://doi.org/10.1007/978-3-031-54605-1_24.

U. Köthe and C. Rother (Eds.): DAGM GCPR 2023, LNCS 14264, pp. 363–377, 2024.
https://doi.org/10.1007/978-3-031-54605-1_24

fields such as medicine. To better understand arbitrary vision models, post-hoc explanation methods play an important role because they allow inspection a posteriori without any modifications to the architecture or loss function.

One popular strategy to improve the interpretability of vision models are visual attribution maps. Activation-based methods [9,33,35,41,44] take into account the features a vision model produced at a given layer for visualizing the spatial attribution with respect to the network output. However, they are not always reliable [1] and other explanation modalities exist. Natural language explanations (NLEs) have been proposed in the context of vision-language models to extend the language output for a given task with a fitting explanation [32], such as for a VQA task. A less explored direction is directly explaining internal features or neurons of neural networks through natural language [15]. Such explanations would allow a wider reach of application, especially where users are not expected to have expert knowledge and can more easily interpret textual explanations than saliency maps.

In this work, we propose *DeViL* (Decoding Vision features into Language) that can explain features of a vision model through natural language. By employing a general purpose language model, we inherit rich generalization properties, allowing us to additionally perform open-vocabulary saliency analysis. *DeViL* combines providing textual explanations of these visual features with highlighting visual attributions spatially to extract diverse explanations that complement each other. Thus, enabling non-experts to comprehend the network's decision-making process, diagnose potential issues in the model's performance, and enhance user trust and accountability.

With *DeViL*, our key contributions are: i) generating spatial and layerwise natural language explanations for any off-the-shelf vision model, ii) open-vocabulary saliency attributions coherent with textual explanations, and iii) showing how dropout can be used to generalize from image-text pairs on a global level to fine-grained network inspections. To the best of our knowledge, this is the first work to combine these capabilities into a single model while requiring short training times and using abundantly available captioning data instead of explanation specific datasets.

2   Related Work

Inherently Interpretable Models. Apart from post-hoc explanation methods, inherently interpretable models try to modify the network architecture or loss function to make the model more interpretable. For instance, induced alignment pressure on the weights during optimisation, either in a linear [5–7,10] or non-linear manner [22,47], has been shown to produce more interpretable models. While these methods produce more interpretable models, they require adaptation and re-training of existing models and cannot always recover the original task performance. With the increasing size of models, this is not always a scalable solution. Post-hoc methods trade-off the guaranteed faithfulness of the explanation with broader applicability.

Post-hoc Saliency. Saliency attribution is most commonly produced through perturbations [23,28], gradients [37], activations [18,41,44] or their combination [9,33]. Class Activation Mapping (CAM) [44] and its successors, such as Grad-CAM [33] and Grad-CAM++ [9], are one of the most popular attribution methods that make use of network activations, similar to our approach, but additionally use the gradients of the target class. We set ourselves apart from these methods by introducing open-vocabulary saliency maps and also providing directly related natural language explanations.

Natural Language Explanations. Another explanation alternative are NLEs, which provide textual descriptions accompanying the prediction. The approaches are usually divided into predict-explain and explain-predict paradigms: in the first, a language model is finetuned with features and predictions from a pre-trained vision model [17,25], while in the latter a single model is jointly trained to explain and predict [24,29,32]. While these provide a single NLE for the whole image, Bau et al. [4] attempts to label individual highest activated neurons in a network by correlating them with pixel-wise annotations. Building upon that, Hernandez et al. [15] collect the MILANNOTATIONS datasets where humans labeled sets of images that showed high activations for individual neurons of different network architectures. By training a vision-language model on this data, individual neurons of different layers can be described in natural language. In contrast, *DeViL* can generate both types of NLEs (global and local), without requiring a dataset of human annotated descriptions per neuron or layer. Nonetheless, we show that when our model is trained on MILANNOTATIONS, we obtain a higher correspondence with human descriptions.

Captioning Models. Image captioning models [16,26,30,39,46], on the other hand, use large language models (LLMs) to generate free-form captions for the input image. State-of-the-art in captioning is obtained by large-scale pre-training and subsequently finetuning on target datasets [16,46]. On the other hand, lightweight models such as ClipCap [26] perform competitively by relying on pre-trained vision and language models requiring significantly fewer GPU hours to train. *DeViL* is similar to ClipCap in that both models use a translation network between image features and the language model prompt. While ClipCap is capable of generating high-quality captions for images, it cannot be directly used to interpret a model's internal representations. In contrast, by extracting features from multiple layers of the vision model and incorporating dropout, *DeViL* generalizes to more fine-grained descriptions and improves all captioning metrics on CC3M [34].

3   *DeViL* Model

Given a pre-trained vision model g, our goal is to decode the features of several of its L layers into natural language describing what these features encode. These descriptions are specific to the network's activations corresponding to an input image. Let $g_l(x)$ denote the feature map of the lth-layer of g for input image

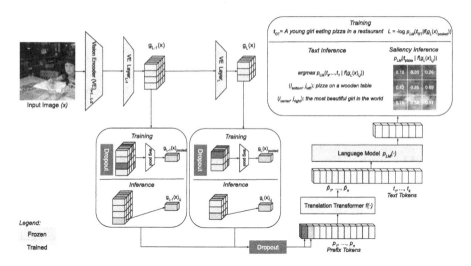

Fig. 1. *DeViL* architecture diagram: Given an input image x and a pre-trained vision encoder with multiple layers (L), we concatenate the average pooling embedding $(g_L(x)_{pooled})$ to learnable prefix tokens (size=10; as in [26]). A translation transformer f then projects prefix tokens $\hat{p}_1, \ldots, \hat{p}_n$ used to condition the language model p_{LM} to get the captions for the entire layer. During inference, we can select individual feature $g_L(x)_{i,j}$ for any arbitrary location i, j of the layer and generate its respective NLE, together with open-vocabulary saliency.

x with spatial size $H_l \times W_l$. We propose *DeViL*, a network that is trained to decode an individual feature vector $g_l(x)_{i,j}$ of an arbitrary spatial location i, j into a natural language description. Since *DeViL* is trained on top of features from a frozen vision model g, we view it as a post-hoc explanation method, that is able to reason about which concepts have been learned by the vision model retrospectively. Figure 1 depicts an overview of the network architecture of *DeViL*, which we describe in more detail in the following sub-sections.

3.1   Translating Vision Features into Language

Our *DeViL* method is designed to be a lightweight model such that it can be trained and applied to existing vision backbones without requiring a long training time. Instead of training a language model, we make use of a pre-trained language model with frozen weights to generate the natural language descriptions for vision features. Specifically, the language model $p_{LM}(t_k|t_1, \ldots, t_{k-1})$ is able to predict the next token t from its tokenizer's vocabulary given a sequence of previous tokens as context. As shown in recent works [26,46], the text generation of language models can be guided by conditioning the model on learned prefix tokens instead of finetuning its weights.

We follow this approach and train only a translation network f that takes image features $g_l(x)_{i,j}$ and produces n prefix tokens $\hat{p} = \{\hat{p}_i\}_{i=1}^{n}$ that are used to condition the language model $p_{\text{LM}}(t_k|\hat{p}_1, \ldots, \hat{p}_n, t_1, \ldots, t_{k-1})$ for generating a description. The translation network uses a standard Transformer architecture. As input, we concatenate the sequence of image features $g_l(x)_{i,j}$ with a set of trained parameters for the initial prefix tokens $\boldsymbol{p}$. From the output, we only keep the transformed prefix tokens $\hat{\boldsymbol{p}}$ to pass on to the language model as prompt in a causal language generation setting.

3.2   Learning to Decode Individual Vision Features

Obtaining fine-grained data on textual descriptions for neurons or activations of the neural networks as done in [15] is costly at scale. Hence, we resort to more commonly available text-image pairs in the form of a captioning dataset to achieve the same goal. Since these image-text pairs relate the global image content to a single sentence, we describe in the following how we can train on these global relations, but evaluate our model on more fine-grained feature locations across the layers of the vision model.

Given a vision model g, we first specify the layers we would like to decode. For every forward pass of g, we extract the features $g_l(x)$ for every layer l in our set of explained layers. At training time, we perform 2D global average pooling over the spatial locations at each feature layer to obtain a single feature vector per layer $g_l(x)_{\text{pooled}}$. After applying a linear projection onto the same dimensionality and adding a positional embedding, the feature vectors are passed to the translation network f as a sequence. Depending on how many layers are being explained, the sequence length for f varies, i.e., it increases by one for each layer that is explained. At inference time, instead of pooling the visual features, we can select a specific location we would like to explain and only pass that particular feature vector $g_l(x)_{i,j}$ to f.

To train our translation network, we optimize the standard causal language modelling task of predicting the next token given previous tokens. In our context, the language model is conditioned on the image features through the translation network. Thus, our loss is $\mathcal{L} = \log p_{\text{LM}}(\boldsymbol{t}|f(g(x))) = \sum_k \log p_{\text{LM}}(t_k|\hat{\boldsymbol{p}}, \{t_i\}_{i=1}^{k-1})$ with trainable parameters only in the translation network f. Once trained, *DeViL* can decode vision features into natural language by conditioning the language model on a vision feature vector and generating a sentence. In practice, we greedily choose the most probable next word with arg max.

3.3   Generalization Through Dropout

The global average pooling at test time is required because we do not have more fine-grained data to train on. However, it creates a discrepancy between training and inference time. To overcome this issue, we introduce two dropout operations. Firstly, we randomly dropout spatial locations i, j of $g_l(x)$ before applying average pooling to obtain $g_l(x)_{\text{pooled}}$. As a result, our translation network observes a larger space of image features that better cover the full distribution of a vision layer's features. Secondly, we randomly subselect the layers from which the translation network f obtains the pooled features. This way, the translation network sometimes receives features only from individual layers during training time. This is crucial because, at inference time, we would like to decode a specific feature of an individual vision layer so this dropout ensures this input configuration is seen during training. Moreover, it allows to train a single network per vision model instead of one per layer.

In contrast to dropout as proposed by [36], we do not remove features element-wise but always remove a full vector to simulate a spatial location or full layer being missing from the input. Hence, we also do not require to perform any rescaling of the features but rather mask the complete vectors from subsequent operations.

3.4   Open-Vocabulary Saliency with *DeViL*

DeViL can be used to obtain the probability of a given word or a phrase conditioned on vision features at layer l and location i, j by evaluating $p_{\mathrm{LM}}(t_{\mathrm{query}}|f(g_l(x)_{i,j}))$. When passing overall features from a layer of interest, we obtain a likelihood of the query for every spatial location that we can visualize as a saliency map. By using a general purpose language model, there are no constraints on the query such that we can obtain saliency maps on concepts that lie outside the original training scope of the vision model. This is useful for seeing whether the vision features encode information about related concepts due to their correlation with training data or obtained as a side-effect.

4   Experiments

We evaluate *DeViL* on both its natural language and saliency generation capabilities. *DeViL* is trained on the CC3M [34] dataset. While our goal is to generalize to more fine-grained descriptions of vision features, *DeViL* can still be used as a captioning model. Thus, we start by evaluating image captioning on CC3M, before discussing explanations of vision features obtained through *DeViL*. For fine-grained analysis, we report both qualitative as well as quantitative results on fine-grained neuron descriptions by training and evaluating on the MILAN-NOTATIONS dataset [15]. Lastly, we evaluate both NLEs and saliency obtained through *DeViL* across different layers to show its generalization capabilities. As we focus on explaining the vision backbone instead of producing captions, all images used for qualitative analysis come from sources outside CC3M, such as ImageNet [11], Places365 [45], and COCO [21]. Details about the *DeViL* architecture and training details can be found in the supplementary.

4.1   Evaluating Feature Descriptions Through Image Captioning

Dataset. We use the official train-validation split of CC3M [34], consisting of 3M image-caption pairs collected from the web. We chose this dataset because it is sufficiently large to cover a large variety in both the vision and language

Table 1. Image captioning results on CC3M [34] with different pre-trained vision backbones and language models, and a comparison with state-of-the-art captioning models, either fully [16,46] or partially-finetuned [26]. We report standard captioning metrics, where higher is better. IN-ResNet50: ImageNet [11] pre-trained ResNet50 [14]. CLIP-ResNet50/ViT: ResNet50/ViT versions of the CLIP [30] vision encoder trained on the CLIP dataset.

Method	Vision Backbone	LM	B4 ↑	M ↑	RL ↑	C ↑	S ↑	#Params (M) ↓
DeViL	IN-ResNet50	OPT	5.851	9.572	23.92	65.73	15.23	88
	CLIP-ResNet50	OPT	6.770	10.68	25.90	78.41	17.38	88
	CLIP-ViT	OPT	**7.506**	**11.22**	**26.82**	**86.29**	**18.37**	88
	CLIP-ViT	GPT2	6.349	10.55	25.70	76.55	17.81	40
ClipCap [26]	CLIP-ViT	GPT2	-	-	25.12	71.82	16.07	43
VLP [46]			-	-	24.35	77.57	16.59	115
LEMON [16]			10.1	12.1	-	104.4	19.0	196.7

modalities. Its successor CC12M [8] is less focused on high conceptual relevance, and more noisy in caption quality, making CC3M more suitable for tasks that require strong semantic alignment between text and image.

Baselines. Although our goal is to translate latent representations of pre-trained vision models into language, *DeViL* can still be used to obtain full image descriptions. Hence, we evaluate *DeViL* generated sentences with standard captioning metrics and compare against captioning methods [16,26,46]. ClipCap [26] is a lightweight model that combines the CLIP vision model with a pre-trained language model. Similar to our approach, ClipCap only trains a translation network to keep the training cost low. Both UnifiedVLP [46] and LEMON [16] are large-scale models pre-trained on several datasets not limited to captioning and subsequently finetuned. Thus, they surpass lightweight models such as ClipCap and *DeViL*, but require a lot of resources to train.

Results. We present our results on common language-based metrics: BLEU@4 [27], METEOR [12], ROUGE-L [20], CIDEr [40], and SPICE [3]. We consider ResNet50 [14] trained on ImageNet and CLIP [30] in both its ResNet50 and ViT variants as our vision backbones.

We report image captioning results in Table 1. Between vision backbones, we observe that CLIP-ViT performs better than its ResNet50 counterpart and ResNet50 trained on ImageNet, which is not surprising given CLIP's contrastive vision-language pre-training. Since the vision encoder of CLIP has in the past depicted strong zero-shot capabilities on a variety of tasks, we would expect it also to have a large coverage of visual concepts when we explain their features.

When using the CLIP-ViT backbone, we further ablate the relevance of the pre-trained language model. We make use of OPT-125M [42] and GPT2 [31] in our pipeline. With CLIP-ViT-B-32 as the vision backbone and OPT as the language model, we obtain our best scores surpassing ClipCap on all by a big margin, e.g. a CIDEr of 86.29 vs. 71.82. Even when using GPT2 and the same

Table 2. Ablating our dropout when evaluated using vision features from all layers or only the very last layer (single) of CLIP-ViT.

Layer	Token Dropout	Feature Dropout	B4 ↑	M ↑	RL ↑	C ↑	S ↑
single			0.3038	3.435	11.76	4.729	1.962
	✓		6.442	10.34	25.14	73.73	16.86
	✓	✓	6.623	10.49	25.50	75.88	17.11
all			7.101	11.16	26.62	82.59	**18.54**
	✓		7.211	11.09	26.70	83.32	18.48
	✓	✓	**7.506**	**11.22**	**26.82**	**86.29**	18.37

translation network architecture as ClipCap, we perform better across the board while using fewer parameters (40M vs. 43M). This is due to our model changes in using multiple layers of the vision backbone and the introduction of both feature-level and layer-level dropouts. Compared to large-scale captioning models that require more resources, we still perform better than UnifiedVLP on all metrics despite it requiring 1200 h of training on a V100 GPU. In comparison, ClipCap reports 72h of training on GTX1080, while *DeViL* requires 24h of training on an A100. LEMON [16] still surpasses our lightweight model as the state-of-the-art model on captioning. Required training resources for LEMON are not reported.

Ablations. We ablate the proposed token and feature dropouts in Table 2 in terms of captioning metrics for the CLIP-ViT model. This table shows 3 different models trained with incremental combinations of both dropouts. While each *DeViL* model is trained to explain multiple vision backbone layers, we evaluate them in two scenarios: using vision features from all layers of the vision backbone it was trained with (all) and when using only the last layer (single). This ablation study confirms that dropout is essential for producing image-relevant captions for individual layers at inference time. Since the model without token dropout has never seen a single layer being passed to the translation network, it performs poorly in this out-of-distribution scenario making CIDEr drop from 75.88 to 4.729. Feature dropout is less essential, but further improves captioning scores and improves generalization. When we compare results on using all layers rather than just using one, we see an improvement in all scores, e.g. CIDEr increases from 75.88 to 86.29. This suggests that complementary information is encoded in the different layers, making it reasonable to assume we can obtain layer-specific explanations even when training on caption data.

Overall, these results show that with our dropout methods, we can train on several layers at once and perform an evaluation on individual layers by themselves, while also avoiding the need to train one model for each layer we might want to explain later on.

4.2 MILAN: Explaining Local Visual Features

Since *DeViL* was designed first and foremost for localized feature inspection in natural language, we strive to compare our method more directly on an explain-

ResNet-ImageNet layer4-1335

Human annotation: long, thin objects
MILAN: long, slender objects
DeViL: animals and chains

AlexNet-Places conv3-196

Human annotation: surfaces that show a pattern
composed of lines
MILAN: grates
DeViL: buildings and windows

ResNet-ImageNet layer3-298

Human annotation: areas that look like keys on a
keyboard
MILAN: Number pads
DeViL: the back of a phone, a computer, a phone

Fig. 2. Qualitative results on MILANNOTATIONS [15] and comparison with the MILAN [15] model.

ability task, and especially on one such task at the local feature level. Thus, we also train *DeViL* on MILANNOTATIONS [15], a dataset of over 50k human descriptions of sets of image regions obtained from the top neuron activating images of several known models like ResNet [14] or AlexNet [19]. For each base model, the authors collect descriptions for the top 15 activated images of each neuron in the network. Each image is masked by its corresponding activation mask, highlighting only the regions for which the corresponding neuron fired.

We compare with ClipCap and the MILAN model [15] trained on MILANNO-TATIONS [15]. Although our model was designed to work with layer-wise feature maps for a single image and not at the neuron level, we adapt *DeViL* by pooling over the 15 masked images given for each neuron. We report the NLP metrics including

Table 3. Evaluating MILAN, Clip-Cap and *DeViL* on MILANNOTA-TIONS.

Method	B4 ↑	M ↑	RL ↑	C ↑	S ↑	BS ↑
MILAN [15]	-	-	-	-	-	0.362
ClipCap [26]	3.99	9.62	27.0	25.1	10.8	0.381
DeViL	**6.28**	**11.3**	**30.6**	**33.7**	**13.3**	**0.382**

BERTScore [43] results in Table 3. The results are averaged over several generalization experiments proposed by [15]. We report a complete comparison in terms of BERTScore of all 13 experiments in the supplementary.

The average BERTScore across scenarios is 0.362, 0.381 and 0.382 for MILAN, ClipCap and *DeViL*, respectively. The margins between all models are small as BERTScore is very sensitive to small differences that can still indicate a reliable ranking [41]. Considering all other language metrics, the difference between ClipCap and *DeViL* is more pronounced and *DeViL* outperforms Clip-Cap consistently. A qualitative comparison with MILAN [15] can be seen in Fig. 2. We refer the reader to examples like "animals and chains" and "building and windows". Both quantitative and qualitative results validate *DeViL's* generalization ability and its primary intended goal: to faithfully decode localized vision features into natural language.

4.3   Diverse Layer-Wise Explanations of Vision Features

Deep neural networks learn to extract meaningful patterns from input data by progressively building up a hierarchy of features. The lower layers tend to detect simple patterns like edges and curves, while the higher layers learn to recognize more complex and abstract concepts [2,14,38,41]. We verify a similar trend in the descriptions generated by *DeViL*. We generate descriptions for each spatial location of the feature map at layer l and produce saliency maps to measure the

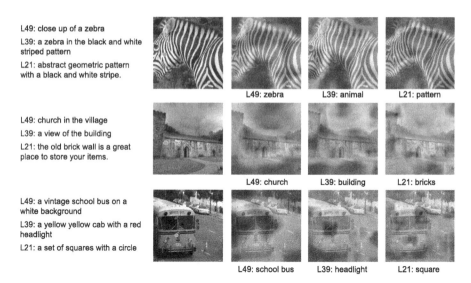

Fig. 3. Generated descriptions at different layers of the CLIP-ResNet50 backbone (L49, L39 & L21) for the location marked with a green dot and corresponding saliency maps for the relevant words in them. (Color figure online)

spatial support of the main subject in the sentence generated at a single location. Our model assigns a probability score to a textual query being generated based on its relevance to the visual features. This score can then be visualized as a heatmap, with higher scores corresponding to areas of the image where the vision model encoded the textual concept.

Qualitative. Figure 3 corresponds to the output generated by the CLIP-ResNet50 model for layers 21, 39, and 49. The green dot in the image shows the location for which the description has been generated. The generated descriptions showcase the aforementioned hierarchy, with lower layers mentioning lower level features like colors (e.g. "red headlight") and shapes (e.g. "squares with a circle") and higher layers mentioning objects (e.g. progression from "building" to "church"). The saliency maps also validate the spatial location of these words, e.g. higher saliency scores for "zebra" at L49, "animal" at L39, and "pattern" at L21.

From Simple to Rich Language Descriptions. To quantify how well *DeViL* captures the differences of what specific vision layers encode, we analyze the generated text descriptions across layers. Specifically, we obtain a single text description per layer by averaging the vision features for each layer and decode them individually with *DeViL*. In Table 4, we take a look at the properties of the language generated by *DeViL* on CC3M. As measured by the CIDEr score, we observe that the text similarity to human captions increases with later layers as more semantically meaningful embeddings are produced by the vision model. We also see that the language shifts from using many adjectives in earlier layers to more verbs and a more comprehensive vocabulary in higher layers. This indicates a shift from describing simple concepts with a limited set of attributes to richer descriptions that also describe relations and actions between objects in the image. In Fig. 4, we show the saliency for the same word across different layers of CLIP-ResNet50. The top layer encodes "Zebra", but not "Pattern", and conversely for a lower layer. These insights can help us better understand intermediate features of a pre-trained model and assist in choosing the right features for a downstream task.

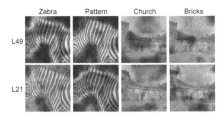

Fig. 4. Semantics are encoded in different layers, CLIP-ResNet50 model.

Table 4. Per-layer statistics of adjectives, verbs, # of unique words.

Model	Layer	Adj (%)	Verbs (%)	#Uniq Words	CIDEr ↑
CLIP-ViT	9	6.37	6.30	4790	61.6
CLIP-ViT	6	7.60	5.78	4115	44.1
CLIP-ViT	3	8.04	5.24	2554	20.2
CLIP-ResNet50	49	6.30	6.66	5228	71.2
CLIP-ResNet50	39	6.69	6.43	4395	54.1
CLIP-ResNet50	21	6.89	5.90	3374	34.6

Quantifying Spatial and Layer Coherence. We want to further analyze how well the spatially localized descriptions generated by *DeViL* capture the content of the underlying image patches. Intuitively, earlier layers encode local information of a smaller underlying patch, while later layers can encode more global information. To test this, we create center crops of sizes 32×32, 64×64, and 128×128 along the full image size of 224×224 and compare their similarity to *DeViL* descriptions of the vision feature closest to the center in each layer's feature map. We use CLIP-ResNet50 to embed the cropped images as well as *DeViL* descriptions and compare their similarities. Figure 6 plots which crop size is most similar with the generated text. We observe that smaller patches have much higher similarity with earlier layer descriptions, and conversely bigger patches with later layers. Descriptions of L21 best match 64×64 patches and this distribution shift progressively to L49 fitting best to the full image content. These results validate that *DeViL* exposes what the vision model encodes both in lower layers describing the content of local patches and global concepts in higher layers.

4.4 Inspecting Different Vision Models Through Saliency

Since *DeViL* incorporates an LLM, it has the ability to produce saliency maps for any word, not being limited by the closed-set of classes of a given dataset. Figure 5 presents a comparison of different vision backbones in terms of saliency maps for different words. The different models can distinguish "cat" and "dog", but also identify both as "animal". Interestingly, since CLIP-based models are

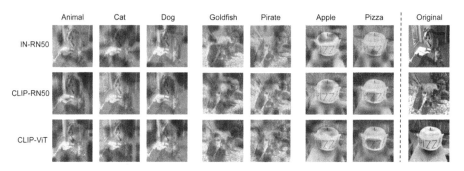

Fig. 5. Open-vocabulary saliency maps for different backbones with the final layer. For CLIP-ViT we use the penultimate layer.

trained with not only images but also text, they can identify the written word "pizza" on the bottom-most image, while an ImageNet trained ResNet50 cannot. Similarly, the word "pirate", written on a stone, is also identified by CLIP-based models for the aquarium image. These failure cases of the CLIP model have been discovered independently (i.e. typography attack [13]) and the explanations of our *DeViL* model expose these as well, highlighting its faithfulness to the vision model. Obtaining saliency maps for open-vocabulary words that did not appear in a model's training data such as the supercategory "animal" or the class "pirate" is a novel contribution of our method. It also allows a more direct comparison with models of different pre-training tasks such as CLIP, which is not possible with methods that rely on the model's output to be the same for direct comparisons. More qualitative results can be found in the supplementary material.

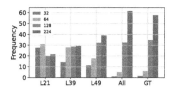

Fig. 6. Frequency of most similar patch size for a given *DeViL* description (L21, L39, L49, All) and human caption (GT) using CLIP-ResNet50.

Table 5. Deletion (↓) and insertion (↑) comparison between Grad-CAM [33] and *DeViL* ResNet50 at different layers (L49, L39, and L21).

Layer	Metric	Grad-CAM [33]	*DeViL* (CC3M)
L49	Del	0.342	0.466
	Ins	0.763	0.697
L39	Del	0.465	0.494
	Ins	0.677	0.661
L21	Del	0.405	0.484
	Ins	0.593	0.635

We also compare our saliency maps quantitatively with Grad-CAM [33], which proposes interpreting a neural network via the gradients for a target class flowing through a given layer. Results are presented in Table 5 for 3 layers of the ResNet50 model (L49, L39, and L11). We report commonly used deletion (Del.)

and insertion (Ins.) metrics [28]. The Del.(Ins.) metric measures the drop(rise) in the probability of a class as relevant pixels given by the saliency map are gradually removed(inserted) from the image. Thus, lower(higher) is better for Del.(Ins.). Although we are unable to outperform Grad-CAM, the latter uses gradients, which provide more information than just activations alone. Furthermore, Grad-CAM is specialized in the network's output classes, while *DeViL* can perform open-vocabulary saliency. An interesting future research direction is to improve and align open-vocabulary saliency with existing approaches.

5   Conclusion

The ability to interpret deep learning models' predictions is crucial for their effective deployment in real-world applications. The visualizations of intermediate feature maps have been shown to be a promising approach for improving model interpretability, but understanding these feature maps often requires further analysis. Our proposed *DeViL* approach for explaining feature maps through natural language is unique as it generates textual descriptions for individual features, and can also produce open-vocabulary saliency attributions. We evaluate the efficacy of our model's language generations on CC3M and MILANNOTATIONS, outperforming competing models, and show extensive qualitative results validating that our open-vocabulary saliency exposes which concepts are understood by each of the model's layers.

Acknowledgments. This work was supported by the ERC (853489-DEXIM), DFG (2064/1 - project number 390727645), BMBF (Tübingen AI Center, FKZ: 01IS18039A), FCT (under PhD grant 2020.07034.BD), Carl Zeiss Stiftung and Else Kröner-Fresenius-Stiftung (EKFS). The authors thank the IMPRS-IS for supporting Meghal Dani.

References

1. Adebayo, J., Gilmer, J., Muelly, M., Goodfellow, I.J., Hardt, M., Kim, B.: Sanity checks for saliency maps. In: NeurIPS (2018)
2. Agrawal, P., Carreira, J., Malik, J.: Learning to see by moving. In: ICCV (2015)
3. Anderson, P., Fernando, B., Johnson, M., Gould, S.: SPICE: semantic propositional image caption evaluation. In: Leibe, B., Matas, J., Sebe, N., Welling, M. (eds.) ECCV 2016. LNCS, vol. 9909, pp. 382–398. Springer, Cham (2016). https://doi.org/10.1007/978-3-319-46454-1_24
4. Bau, D., Zhou, B., Khosla, A., Oliva, A., Torralba, A.: Network dissection: Quantifying interpretability of deep visual representations. In: CVPR (2017)
5. Bohle, M., Fritz, M., Schiele, B.: Convolutional dynamic alignment networks for interpretable classifications. In: CVPR (2021)
6. Böhle, M., Fritz, M., Schiele, B.: B-cos networks: alignment is all we need for interpretability. In: CVPR (2022)
7. Brendel, W., Bethge, M.: Approximating CNNs with bag-of-local-features models works surprisingly well on imageNet. In: ICLR (2019)

8. Changpinyo, S., Sharma, P., Ding, N., Soricut, R.: Conceptual 12m: pushing web-scale image-text pre-training to recognize long-tail visual concepts. In: CVPR (2021)
9. Chattopadhay, A., Sarkar, A., Howlader, P., Balasubramanian, V.N.: Grad-cam++: generalized gradient-based visual explanations for deep convolutional networks. In: WACV (2018)
10. Chen, C., Li, O., Tao, D., Barnett, A., Rudin, C., Su, J.K.: This looks like that: deep learning for interpretable image recognition. In: NeurIPS (2019)
11. Deng, J., Dong, W., Socher, R., Li, L.J., Li, K., Fei-Fei, L.: Imagenet: a large-scale hierarchical image database. In: CVPR (2009)
12. Denkowski, M., Lavie, A.: Meteor universal: Language specific translation evaluation for any target language. In: WMT (2014)
13. Goh, G., et al.: Multimodal neurons in artificial neural networks. Distill **6**, e30 (2021)
14. He, K., Zhang, X., Ren, S., Sun, J.: Deep residual learning for image recognition. In: CVPR (2016)
15. Hernandez, E., Schwettmann, S., Bau, D., Bagashvili, T., Torralba, A., Andreas, J.: Natural language descriptions of deep visual features. In: ICLR (2022)
16. Hu, X., et al.: Scaling up vision-language pre-training for image captioning. In: CVPR (2022)
17. Kayser, M., et al.: e-vil: a dataset and benchmark for natural language explanations in vision-language tasks. In: ICCV (2021)
18. Kim, B., et al.: Interpretability beyond feature attribution: quantitative testing with concept activation vectors (TCAV). In: ICML (2018)
19. Krizhevsky, A., Sutskever, I., Hinton, G.E.: Imagenet classification with deep convolutional neural networks. In: NeurIPS (2012)
20. Lin, C.Y.: Rouge: a package for automatic evaluation of summaries. In: WAS (2004)
21. Lin, T.-Y., et al.: Microsoft COCO: common objects in context. In: Fleet, D., Pajdla, T., Schiele, B., Tuytelaars, T. (eds.) ECCV 2014. LNCS, vol. 8693, pp. 740–755. Springer, Cham (2014). https://doi.org/10.1007/978-3-319-10602-1_48
22. Liu, W., et al.: Decoupled networks. In: CVPR (2018)
23. Lundberg, S.M., Lee, S.: A unified approach to interpreting model predictions. In: Guyon, I., von Luxburg, U., Bengio, S., Wallach, H.M., Fergus, R., Vishwanathan, S.V.N., Garnett, R. (eds.) NeurIPS (2017)
24. Majumder, B.P., Camburu, O., Lukasiewicz, T., Mcauley, J.: Knowledge-grounded self-rationalization via extractive and natural language explanations. In: ICML (2022)
25. Marasović, A., Bhagavatula, C., sung Park, J., Le Bras, R., Smith, N.A., Choi, Y.: Natural language rationales with full-stack visual reasoning: from pixels to semantic frames to commonsense graphs. In: EMNLP (2020)
26. Mokady, R., Hertz, A., Bermano, A.H.: Clipcap: clip prefix for image captioning. arXiv preprint arXiv:2111.09734 (2021)
27. Papineni, K., Roukos, S., Ward, T., Zhu, W.J.: Bleu: a method for automatic evaluation of machine translation. In: ACL (2002)
28. Petsiuk, V., Das, A., Saenko, K.: RISE: randomized input sampling for explanation of black-box models. In: BMVC (2018)
29. Plüster, B., Ambsdorf, J., Braach, L., Lee, J.H., Wermter, S.: Harnessing the power of multi-task pretraining for ground-truth level natural language explanations. arXiv preprint arXiv:2212.04231 (2022)
30. Radford, A., et al.: Learning transferable visual models from natural language supervision. In: ICML (2021)

31. Radford, A., Wu, J., Child, R., Luan, D., Amodei, D., Sutskever, I.: Language models are unsupervised multitask learners (2019)
32. Sammani, F., Mukherjee, T., Deligiannis, N.: NLX-GPT: a model for natural language explanations in vision and vision-language tasks. In: CVPR (2022)
33. Selvaraju, R.R., Cogswell, M., Das, A., Vedantam, R., Parikh, D., Batra, D.: Gradcam: visual explanations from deep networks via gradient-based localization. In: ICCV (2017)
34. Sharma, P., Ding, N., Goodman, S., Soricut, R.: Conceptual captions: a cleaned, hypernymed, image alt-text dataset for automatic image captioning. In: ACL (2018)
35. Smilkov, D., Thorat, N., Kim, B., Viégas, F., Wattenberg, M.: Smoothgrad: removing noise by adding noise (2017)
36. Srivastava, N., Hinton, G.E., Krizhevsky, A., Sutskever, I., Salakhutdinov, R.: Dropout: a simple way to prevent neural networks from overfitting. JMLR **15**, 1929–1958 (2014)
37. Sundararajan, M., Taly, A., Yan, Q.: Axiomatic attribution for deep networks. In: ICML (2017)
38. Szegedy, C., et al.: Going deeper with convolutions. In: CVPR (2015)
39. Tewel, Y., Shalev, Y., Schwartz, I., Wolf, L.: Zerocap: zero-shot image-to-text generation for visual-semantic arithmetic. In: CVPR (2022)
40. Vedantam, R., Lawrence Zitnick, C., Parikh, D.: Cider: consensus-based image description evaluation. In: CVPR (2015)
41. Zeiler, M.D., Fergus, R.: Visualizing and understanding convolutional networks. In: Fleet, D., Pajdla, T., Schiele, B., Tuytelaars, T. (eds.) ECCV 2014. LNCS, vol. 8689, pp. 818–833. Springer, Cham (2014). https://doi.org/10.1007/978-3-319-10590-1_53
42. Zhang, S., et al.: Opt: open pre-trained transformer language models. arXiv preprint arXiv:2205.01068 (2022)
43. Zhang, T., Kishore, V., Wu, F., Weinberger, K.Q., Artzi, Y.: Bertscore: evaluating text generation with Bert. In: ICLR (2020)
44. Zhou, B., Khosla, A., Lapedriza, A., Oliva, A., Torralba, A.: Learning deep features for discriminative localization. In: CVPR (2016)
45. Zhou, B., Lapedriza, A., Khosla, A., Oliva, A., Torralba, A.: Places: a 10 million image database for scene recognition. IEEE T-PAMI (2017)
46. Zhou, L., Palangi, H., Zhang, L., Hu, H., Corso, J., Gao, J.: Unified vision-language pre-training for image captioning and vqa. In: AAAI (2020)
47. Zoumpourlis, G., Doumanoglou, A., Vretos, N., Daras, P.: Non-linear convolution filters for CNN-based learning. In: ICCV (2017)

Zero-Shot Translation of Attention Patterns in VQA Models to Natural Language

Leonard Salewski[1]([⊠])[iD], A. Sophia Koepke[1][iD], Hendrik P. A. Lensch[1][iD], and Zeynep Akata[1,2][iD]

[1] University of Tübingen, Tübingen, Germany
{leonard.salewski,a-sophia.koepke,hendrik.lensch,
zeynep.akata}@uni-tuebingen.de
[2] MPI for Intelligent Systems, Tübingen, Germany

Abstract. Converting a model's internals to text can yield human-understandable insights about the model. Inspired by the recent success of training-free approaches for image captioning, we propose ZS-A2T, a zero-shot framework that translates the transformer attention of a given model into natural language without requiring any training. We consider this in the context of Visual Question Answering (VQA). ZS-A2T builds on a pre-trained large language model (LLM), which receives a task prompt, question, and predicted answer, as inputs. The LLM is guided to select tokens which describe the regions in the input image that the VQA model attended to. Crucially, we determine this similarity by exploiting the text-image matching capabilities of the underlying VQA model. Our framework does not require any training and allows the drop-in replacement of different guiding sources (e.g. attribution instead of attention maps), or language models. We evaluate this novel task on textual explanation datasets for VQA, giving state-of-the-art performances for the zero-shot setting on GQA-REX and VQA-X. Our code is available here.

Keywords: Zero-Shot Translation of Attention Patterns · VQA

1 Introduction

Deep learning systems have become an integral part of our society, both in non-obvious applications, e.g. customer credit scoring, as well as in prominent applications, e.g. ChatGPT [25]. Their impact on the lives of millions of people establishes the need to make these algorithms more transparent and accessible. In the context of Visual Question Answering (VQA) [2, 13], methods for attribution [33] or attention visualization [1] aim to highlight the input image regions that are most relevant for the final decision. However, the actual visual concepts that the model "saw" in the salient regions can remain obscure to the user. In contrast, a natural language description of those visual concepts can be a more intuitive format for a human user.

There is a wide variety of approaches to determine image regions that were relevant for a model's output. Many of those methods do not require training and can be directly

Supplementary Information The online version contains supplementary material available at
https://doi.org/10.1007/978-3-031-54605-1_25.

applied to a given model to generate attribution or attention visualizations. As it is infeasible to train a dedicated model for translating method-specific visual explanations to natural language, we try to address the question: Can we convert the output of any attention or attribution method to natural language without any supervisory data?

Inspired by the impressive capabilities of pre-trained LLMs, we propose a *zero-shot attention-to-text* (ZS-A2T) framework which translates the internal attention of a transformer-based VQA model into natural language without requiring training (see Fig. 1). In particular, ZS-A2T uses a LLM that is steered by visual inputs corresponding to model attribution or attention visualizations. We judge the visual relevance of the LLM's proposals with an image-text matching framework. In contrast to related zero-shot image captioning methods like [37,40,41], ZS-A2T does not

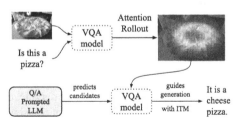

Fig. 1. Our ZS-A2T framework performs training-free translation of attention patterns from VQA models into natural language by combining a pre-trained large language model with language guiding with the VQA model's attention.

exploit CLIP [29], whose image-text understanding would be different from the original task model. Instead, we re-use the encoders of the underlying VQA model for quantifying the agreement between the visual evidence and the candidate word. This guides the text generation without introducing external input into the translation process.

We hypothesize that the content of the verbalizations of the attention patterns for VQA should capture the visual evidence that was used for VQA. This visual evidence should also be described in the corresponding textual explanations. Therefore, we evaluate the quality of our generated attention pattern translations on the VQA-X and GQA-REX datasets. Whilst naturally giving weaker results than methods that were trained to generate explanations in a fully supervised manner along with solving the VQA task, our proposed ZS-A2T outperforms all related methods in this novel zero-shot attention pattern translation setting. Additionally, the training-free setup of our method allows our approach to use different language models without any adaption or training. Similarly, our framework works for any attention aggregation or visual attribution method that can be applied to the underlying VQA model.

To summarize, our contributions are: 1) We introduce the task of converting the internal structures of VQA models to natural language. 2) Our proposed zero-shot ZS-A2T framework is a simple, yet effective method for generating textual outputs with the guidance of the aggregated internal attention and text-image matching capabilities of the VQA model. 3) ZS-A2T can be utilized in conjunction with any pre-trained language model or visual attribution technique, and achieves state-of-the-art results on the GQA-REX and VQA-X textual explanation benchmarks in the zero-shot setting.

2   Related Work

Attention Visualizations and Visual Attribution. Visual attribution methods commonly use backpropagation to trace a model's output to its input, e.g. by visualizing the (slightly modified) gradients on the corresponding input image [4,34–36,46,48]. In addition to that, CAM [50], Grad-CAM [32,33], and variants thereof [9,12,24,28] use model activations in the attribution visualizations. Different to visual attribution methods, perturbation-based methods slightly alter the input and record the resulting changes in the output [10,11]. Unfortunately, it is hard to quantify the quality of attribution visualizations [18]. For modern transformer-based models, a number of studies [1,7,16,45] have investigated the extraction and visualization of attention scores. In particular, attention rollout [1] determines the relevance of input tokens by following the flow of information that is captured in the attention scores and residual connections of the transformer network. However, it is not clear if the resulting visualizations are an intuitive way of explaining deep learning models to human users. Our proposed ZS-A2T framework offers a way of translating such outputs into natural language.

Visual Conditioning for Text Generation with LLMs. Several works have used LLMs for zero-shot image captioning [37,40,41,44,47]. ZeroCap [41] uses CLIP [29] for updating the language model's hidden activations to match the image input. Similarly, MAGIC [37] combines the prediction of the language model, CLIPs rating and a degeneration penalty [38]. EPT [40] only optimizes the hidden activations of a few selected pseudo-tokens for zero-shot video captioning. In contrast to these approaches, Socratic Models [47] generates captions by conditioning the language model on CLIP-detected class names. Another creative approach [44] finetunes a language model to process CLIP text embeddings which at test time can be replaced by CLIP image embeddings. Similarly, [22] finetunes with caption data and addresses the modality gap in a training-free manner. Different to the two aforementioned methods [22,44], ZS-A2T does not require any training (beyond the pre-trained models used) or external models for guiding the language generation, such as CLIP. In particular, the text generation in ZS-A2T is controlled using the VQA model's internal attention along with exploiting the image-text matching capabilities of the same model.

Textual Explanations for VQA. Several VQA datasets with textual explanations have driven research on explaining outputs of models trained for VQA. In particular, the VQA-X [15] dataset extends a subset of VQA v2 [13] with textual explanations from obtained from humans. In contrast, the VQA-E dataset [21] automatically sources explanations from image captions. Recently, the CLEVR-X [30] and GQA-REX [8] extended the CLEVR [17] and GQA [14] datasets with textual explanations by exploiting the corresponding scene graphs. In this work, we evaluate the verbalization of a model's internal attention on textual explanation datasets in the context of VQA, since textual explanations and visual attribution visualizations should both indicate the key features that influenced a VQA model's output.

3 The ZS-A2T Framework

In this section, we explain our proposed framework which is visualized in Fig. 2. We propose the ZS-A2T (**Z**ero-**S**hot **A**ttention **to T**ranslation) framework which converts the internal attention in a VQA model into natural language by translating the visualization of the aggregated attention in the transformer model into natural language

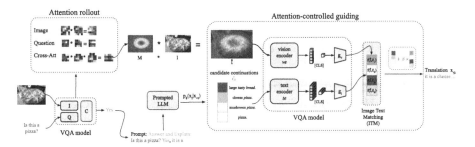

Fig. 2. Our ZS-A2T framework translates the attention rollout [1] of a VQA model into natural language. A pre-trained large language model is prompted with the task description, the question Q, and the predicted answer a. The candidates for the next token x_t along with their continuations (*italic*) are then re-ranked by re-using the image-text matching capabilities of the VQA model. We match the full sentences consisting of already generated tokens, the candidates and their respective continuations with the attention-masked image $\hat{I}$. This information is used to steer the output of a pre-trained language model without requiring any training.

without any supervision. In particular, we prompt a pre-trained large language model for the translation task, and additionally provide the input question and the answer prediction from the VQA model. The text generation is guided by the attention rollout result through the help of the VQA model itself. Token by token, this approach converts visual explanations, i.e. visual attention patterns, into natural language.

Pre-trained Language Model. Our ZS-A2T framework exploits a pre-trained large language model as its text generator. We condition the language model on two different inputs: (i) a task description, (ii) sample specific inputs (i.e. the question Q, and the predicted answer a), and the already generated tokens. We then generate the translation in an autoregressive setup by feeding each predicted token back to the language model. It models the probability

$$p_\theta\big(x_t \mid \underbrace{x_0, \ldots, x_{l-1}}_{\text{task}}, \underbrace{x_l, \ldots, x_{l+s-1}}_{\text{sample }(Q,a)}, \underbrace{x_{l+s}, \ldots, x_{t-1}}_{\text{autoregressive}}\big) \qquad (1)$$

for a token x_t at step t, where l is the number of task tokens and s is the number of sample tokens. θ are the parameters of the pre-trained language model.

The probability of the next token x_t defined in Eq. (1) is independent of the input image. As the pre-trained language model is conditioned on the question and answer, we expect it to predict tokens that fit the question and answer. However, candidate tokens that are likely from a grammatical or statistical point of view, e.g. those that occur frequently in the training text corpus, will be ranked highly. Thus, we argue that the language model predicts the correct tokens for the given question, image, and answer triplet, but not necessarily ranked correctly. To accurately describe the visual concepts, we rely on attention-controlled guiding of the VQA model.

Attention-Controlled Guiding. To generate natural language that actually corresponds to the prediction of the VQA model, we condition the text generation on a masked version of the input image. We obtain an attention-masked image by removing the image information that was not relevant for generating the VQA model's answer prediction a. The removal of information from the image is determined by the internal attention of the VQA model. For this, we use attention rollout which will be described in the following.

Attention Rollout. The attention of the given VQA model is aggregated based on attention rollout [1]. Here, we describe the rollout process for an encoder-decoder VQA model which interlinks the modalities with cross-attention. However, different techniques for obtaining an attention-masked image could be used.

To determine the answer relevant image parts, we record the self-attention scores A_l^{qq} (for the question tokens) and A_l^{ii} (for the image tokens). We also trace the cross-attention scores A_l^{qi}, which model the attention to the image tokens by the question tokens in layer l. The attention scores are saved for each layer l in the VQA model during inference. As attention heads differ in importance [43] we only use the maximum activation $\bar{A}_l = \max(A_l)$ across all heads. Following [1,7], we model how the attention flows throughout the network. We successively multiply the attention scores of a layer with the rolled out values R_l of the previous layer to obtain a final attention rollout map. Additionally, we add the map of the previous layer $\tilde{R}_{l-i}$ to model the residual connection. For self-attention, R_0 is initialized as a diagonal matrix since each token only contains its own information. For cross-attention, R_0^{qi} is initialized to zero, as the tokens have not been contextualized yet.

To roll out the self-attention for the question and visual tokens, we compute the following values for all layers which leverage self-attention before applying normalization,

$$R_l^{qq} = R_{l-i}^{qq} + \bar{A}_l^{qq} \cdot R_{l-i}^{qq}, \qquad R_l^{ii} = R_{l-i}^{ii} + \bar{A}_l^{ii} \cdot R_{l-i}^{ii}. \tag{2}$$

Additionally, we unroll the cross-attention to capture how the VQA model incorporates the visual information into the question representation:

$$R_l^{qi} = R_{l-i}^{qi} + {R_{l-i}^{ii}}^{\mathsf{T}} \cdot \hat{A}_l \cdot R_{l-i}^{qq}. \tag{3}$$

After modelling the residual connection, this captures how the attention rollout of both the question and image tokens is incorporated into the cross-attention. For layers that mix self- and cross-attention we also account for the cross-modal information mixed in at the previous layer:

$$R_l^{qi} = R_{l-i}^{qi} + \hat{A}_l^{qq} \cdot R_{l-i}^{qi}. \tag{4}$$

In the final layer, R_L^{qi} models the importance of each input question token and each visual token for the VQA model's prediction. We average R_L^{qi} over all question tokens to obtain the final aggregated attention map $\bar{R}_L^{qi}$. The threshold τ is applied to get a binary mask which is rescaled to the input image size to obtain M,

$$M = \begin{cases} 1, & \text{if } \tau < \bar{R}_L^{qi}, \\ 0, & \text{otherwise.} \end{cases} \tag{5}$$

The attention-masked image $\hat{I}$ is computed by eliminating irrelevant image parts $\hat{I} = M * I$, where $*$ is the element-wise multiplication.

Visually Guided Text Generation. In the following, we describe the attention-controlled visual guiding of the language decoding process in detail. The language generation at step t starts with the pre-trained language model predicting the probability distribution over all tokens in the vocabulary. We only consider the top-k predictions $c_1, \cdots, c_k$ for the token x_t and refer to those as *candidates*. This subset can be selected for two reasons: a) as argued above it is plausible that a sufficiently large language model conditioned on the question and answer ranks plausible words highly, and b) the weighted sum described in Eq. (7) does not change for sufficiently large k as p_θ is a result of a softmax operation, yielding small values for non-top activations.

In contrast to previous works [37,40,41] which score incomplete sentences with an external image-text matching model (e.g. CLIP), we score a completed sentence with the same task model whose attention patterns we aim to convert to text. Our approach relies on the fact that image-text matching losses used by VQA models are commonly supervised with complete sentences instead of sentence fractions.

We let the language model complete the sentence for each candidate c_i separately based only on the predictions of the language model conditioned on the already generated tokens $x_{\leq t}$ and the candidate c_i. Each continuation is terminated at the first ".", such that the previously generated tokens, the candidate, and the continuation form a complete sentence $\hat{c}_i$. We do not include the question or answer as parts of the candidates. We use top-p sampling to filter the predictions of the language model to get a plausible continuation. Next, the completed sentences $\hat{c}_i$ are ranked by performing image-text matching.

The attention controlled guiding is executed by feeding the text input $\hat{c}_i$ and the masked image $\hat{I}$ as inputs to the VQA model's uni-modal encoders. In particular, we proceed with the contextualized embedding of the [CLS] token $ve(\hat{I})$ of the vision encoder and the corresponding [CLS] token $te(\hat{c}_i)$ of the text encoder. Both tokens are projected into a joint space using the linear maps g_v and g_t provided by the VQA model. This allows to measure the quality of the matching of the image-text pairs.

The matching quality $f(\hat{I}, \hat{c}_i)$ of a candidate sentence $\hat{c}_i$ with respect to the attention rollout-masked image $\hat{I}$ is determined by first computing the cosine similarity $\text{CosSim}(\cdot, \cdot)$ of all possible image-sentence matches,

$$f(\hat{I}, \hat{c}_i) = \frac{e^{\kappa \cdot \text{CosSim}\left(g_v(ve(\hat{I})), g_t(te(\hat{c}_i))\right)}}{\sum_{j \in 1, \ldots, k} e^{\kappa \cdot \text{CosSim}\left(g_v(ve(\hat{I})), g_t(te(\hat{c}_j))\right)}}. \tag{6}$$

Then, we apply a temperature κ in the softmax operation which affects the sharpness of the distribution. Very small values of κ would approximate a uniform distribution, largely disabling the influence of the visual guiding component. On the other hand, too large values may overemphasize highly salient visual concepts, at the cost of grammatical issues (due to overruling the language model). Thus, κ is manually chosen, such that the distribution of the predictions f roughly matches the language model p_θ.

To determine the next token, we compute a weighted sum of the prediction of the language model p_θ and the matching quality f obtained with the VQA model. Thus, at time step t, the next token x_t is computed according to:

$$x_t = \operatorname*{arg\,max}_{i \in 1, \ldots, k} \left\{ p_\theta\left(c_i \mid x_0, \ldots, x_{<t}\right) + \beta \cdot f\left(\hat{I}, \hat{c}_i\right) \right\}, \tag{7}$$

Table 1. Zero-shot model attention to natural language translation results in the context of VQA evaluated on GQA-REX and VQA-X. We report Bleu-4 (B4), Meteor (M), Rouge-L (RL), Cider (C), and Spice (S). Higher is better for all reported metrics. State-of-the-art performances with textual explanation generation methods in the context of VQA are included for reference (supervised). *We adapted the related frameworks to the attention to natural language translation task, and also provided those methods with privileged access to the VQA ground-truth answers.

Setting	Framework↓	GQA-REX [8,14]					VQA-X [15]				
		B4	M	RL	C	S	B4	M	RL	C	S
Zero-shot	ZeroCap $_{GPT\text{-}2}$ [41]*	1.4	4.6	12.3	16.9	5.3	0.7	4.7	14.0	5.8	2.0
	EPT $_{GPT\text{-}2}$ [40]*	0.0	3.3	3.2	2.6	2.8	0.9	6.5	14.9	6.7	2.9
	MAGIC $_{GPT\text{-}2}$ [37]*	2.3	10.8	18.8	41.1	18.8	1.0	8.8	19.3	10.6	7.1
	MAGIC $_{OPT6.7B}$ [37]*	3.3	11.6	22.2	48.8	21.4	1.9	9.5	20.5	14.7	8.9
	Socratic Models $_{OPT6.7B}$ [47]*	3.3	14.1	22.8	40.5	19.3	3.6	12.8	25.7	19.9	10.1
	ZS-A2T $_{OPT6.7B}$ (ours)	**10.2**	**18.2**	**35.0**	**113.5**	**31.4**	**8.5**	**13.8**	**34.2**	**38.1**	**10.5**
Supervised	NLX-GPT [31] $_{GPT\text{-}2}$	-	-	-	-	-	23.8	20.3	47.2	89.2	18.3
	VisualBert-REX [8] $_{LSTM}$	54.6	39.2	78.6	464.2	46.8	-	-	-	-	-

where β is a scalar weighting factor. After selecting the next token x_t, we append it to the original language model prompt and repeat the above process for generating tokens at step $t + 1$ until reaching a stopping criterion (either an [EOS] token, or a period).

4   Experiments

In this section, we describe our experimental setup, including the pre-trained models used in ZS-A2T, the datasets used, and the evaluation metrics. Experimental results generated by ZS-A2T for the zero-shot textual explanation task in the context of VQA are compared to four related training-free methods on the VQA-X and GQA-REX datasets. Although we do not claim that our generated texts are explanations, we do believe that these datasets are well suited for evaluation. Finally, we investigate individual components in our framework in detail, such as the attention-controlled guiding, and the language model prompting before providing qualitative results for ZS-A2T.

Experimental Setup. We used the OPT [49] pre-trained language models for language generation. The transformer-based ALBEF [20] finetuned for VQA, served as our underlying VQA model. The weights for the projection layers are loaded from the non-finetuned, pre-trained ALBEF model, which was trained on an image-text matching objective. Both ALBEF variants were *not* trained to generate texts from the datasets that we test on (VQA-X and GQA-REX). The threshold for the attention rollout scores was set to $\tau = {}^{200}/_{256}$. For guiding, we determine the matching quality for the top-k candidate tokens as $k = 45$ and our continuations are sampled with $p = 0.15$. The guiding temperature is set to $\kappa = 100$. We set the scalar weighting factor between the language model and the attention-controlled guiding to $\beta = 0.7$. To maintain a clean zero-shot protocol, we selected the hyperparameters on the validation split of VQA-X, which is disjoint from the subsets used for the final evaluation. We applied the same settings for GQA-REX without any further tuning.

Datasets. To evaluate all methods, we used the VQA-X [15] and GQA-REX [8,14] datasets for textual explanations in the context of VQA. VQA-X[1] extends a subset of non-trivial VQAv2 [13] questions with human-generated natural language explanations for the ground-truth answer. GQA-REX[2] contains explanations for a subset of the real-world visual reasoning question answering task posed in the GQA dataset. GQA-REX contains one explanation per question-image pair. As two of the related approaches have slow inference speeds (≈ 25 s and ≈ 70 s per sample [40,41] on an NVIDIA v100 GPU), we evaluate all methods on a subset of the test set containing 2000 samples. This is comparable in size to VQA-X's test set. Our approach only needs 7.2 s per sample, and we compare inference speeds of all methods in Section C of the supplementary material.

Evaluation Metrics. Unless stated otherwise, all models are evaluated in the zero-shot setting, i.e. without any training, on the test sets of the respective datasets using commonly reported natural language generation metrics similar to [15]. In particular, we report Bleu-4 (B4) [26], Meteor (M) [5], Rouge-L (RL) [23], Cider (C) [42], and Spice (S) [3] scores. These metrics aim to capture the semantic overlap between sentences by measuring (modified) precision [26] and recall [5,23,26] of n-grams. Additionally, generalizations of n-grams like stemming [5,42], measures of sentence fragmentation [5] or tf-idf weighting [42] are applied to better match human judgement of sentence similarity.

4.1 Comparing to Related Frameworks

To evaluate the quality of the generated translations, we show experimental results on VQA-X and GQA-REX. As there are, to the best of our knowledge, no related works that translate VQA attention patterns into natural language, we adapted a number of zero-shot image captioning methods. For fair comparison, we modified all related works by prompting them with the question and ground-truth answer, as they do not have a dedicated VQA module. This favors the related works, as our framework may base its translation on a wrongly predicted answer. Additionally, we show other common evaluation schemes in Section B of the supplementary material.

First, we compare to the zero-shot image captioning works [37,40,41,47]. For a fair comparison, we adapted the two stronger models (MAGIC and Socratic Models) to operate with the same language model as the one used in our framework (OPT 6.7B). ZS-A2T outperforms all four related approaches for zero-shot translation of attention patterns into natural language by wide margins (see Table 1). Interestingly, the optimization-based approaches ZeroCap and EPT show relatively weak performances (on VQA-X more so than on GQA-REX). This suggests that longer, more complicated prompts (in contrast to the ones used for image captioning) make it hard to optimize helpful starting parameters for the next token prediction (ZeroCap) or next sentence prediction (EPT).

MAGIC gives stronger results, but it is still largely outperformed by our ZS-A2T framework. Similarly, Socratic Models (SMs), the strongest of the adapted related

---

[1] Licensed under the BSD-2 license.

[2] Licensed under the MIT license.

works, is outperformed in all metrics. The generated sentences by ZS-A2T exhibit greater word-by-word overlap with the ground-truth references than those of the related approaches. In particular, this is indicated by the n-gram-based metric Bleu-4 for which ZS-A2T obtains a score of 8.5 compared to 3.6 for SMs on VQA-X. Similarly, ZS-A2T is stronger than SMs in terms of Meteor with 18.2 compared to 14.1 on GQA-REX and 13.8 compared to 12.8 on VQA-X. The same pattern holds true for all other metrics.

For context, we also list results with the recently published supervised models NLX-GPT [31] for VQA-X and VisualBert-REX [8] for GQA-REX. They both employ joint multi-modal transformer models to predict the sentences of the respective datasets. Whilst not strictly comparable, since we translate only the question relevant image regions, it is still interesting to note that our 5-shot variant (c.f. Table 5) significantly shrinks the gap to the supervised models which used 31k VQA-X and 128k GQA-REX training samples respectively, whereas our model does not require any training or just a few in-context examples.

4.2 Ablation Studies on Guiding Inputs

In this section, we study the impact of using different input images in our attention-controlled guiding (see Sect. 3) as well as the effect of guiding with completed sentences (in contrast to incomplete sentences). In addition to this, we provide results for using different visual explanation methods in ZS-A2T, i.e. for visual attribution and perturbation methods. We show additional ablations for the attention thresholding parameter θ and the guiding temperature κ in Section D of the supplementary material.

Influence of Attention Masking. Table 2 shows the effect of using an attention-masked image in the visual guiding. Restricting the guiding of the language generation to the attention-masked image improves the language generation in terms of the Bleu-4, Meteor, Rouge-L, and Cider metrics. Interestingly, the Spice metric is slightly higher (10.8 vs. 10.5) when using the full image for guiding.

Table 2. Ablating the guiding input and text continuation on VQA-X [15]. Our ZS-A2T model uses an attention-masked image, obtained from attention rollout [1], and text continuation.

Guiding Input	B4	M	RL	C	S
Full Image	8.1	13.7	34.1	37.6	**10.8**
No Continuation	6.2	12.5	31.1	28.2	9.4
ZS-A2T (Rel. Masking + Cont.)	**8.5**	**13.8**	**34.2**	**38.1**	10.5

Influence of Using Text Continuations. In Table 2, we also investigate the effect of using the language model to generate text continuations, so that the guiding component can judge completed sentences. Using the continuations increases all metrics, e.g. Cider from 28.2 to 38.1. We hypothesize that this happens for two reasons. First, it reduces the distribution shift between the contrastive image-text matching training of the VQA model. Second, it allows the guiding to judge whether a greedy selection of the visually grounded token at step t may lead to a completed sentence that is not visually supported.

Different Visual Explanation Methods. In addition to using attention rollout to determine relevant image parts (described in Sect. 3), we use five other attribution methods and the perturbation-based visual explanation method RISE [27]. Table 3 (left) showcases that our approach can handle conceptually different visual explanation methods.

Table 3. Ablating different attribution and perturbation methods (left) and type and size of the pre-trained language models (right) in our ZS-A2T framework on VQA-X [15].

Attribution Method	B4	M	RL	C	S
Att. GradCAM [20,33]	7.5	13.3	32.8	33.0	9.2
EigenGradCAM [24]	7.5	13.1	32.8	32.3	9.2
XGradCAM [12]	6.7	12.4	32.1	30.1	9.1
GradCAMElementwise [28]	7.2	12.8	32.5	30.7	9.0
HiResCAM [9]	7.0	12.7	32.5	31.0	9.0
RISE [27]	7.5	13.3	33.1	33.5	9.9
ZS-A2T (attention rollout [1])	**8.5**	**13.8**	**34.2**	**38.1**	**10.5**

LM (#Params)	B4	M	RL	C	S
GPT-2 (125M)	3.6	11.0	26.6	19.8	7.7
OPT (125M)	3.4	10.7	26.5	18.5	7.1
OPT (350M)	3.9	11.6	27.9	20.2	7.9
OPT (1.3B)	7.1	13.0	32.8	28.9	9.2
OPT (2.7B)	7.1	13.3	32.5	31.0	10.1
OPT (6.7B)	**8.5**	**13.8**	**34.2**	**38.1**	**10.5**

The backpropagation-based techniques from the GradCAM family build on the attention probabilities and their respective gradients [20,33] from the same layer of the VQA model ($L = 11$). Thus, the generated sentences using the different methods EigenGradCAM [24], XGradCAM [12], GradCAMElementwise [28] and HiResCAM [9] are of very similar quality in terms of the NLG metrics. Overall, their scores are lower than the scores we obtain when using attention rollout [1].

We additionally show results with the input perturbation-based method RISE [27]. It filters the images applied to the given VQA model and evaluates the VQA model multiple times whilst randomly masking parts of the image. The final importance map is obtained by summing the random masks weighted by the predicted class probability. This indicates the parts in the input that are salient for the VQA models' prediction. We find that the texts generated for RISE are slightly worse than those obtained with attention rollout based attribution method (e.g. Bleu-4 7.5 vs. 8.5 (ours)).

Overall, the visual explanation methods' different abilities to identify the correct relevant image regions is reflected in the quality of the translations to natural language. Attention rollout [7] generally outperforms GradCAM [32] in identifying relevant image regions and the same pattern is found in the quality of the translations. Thus, we conclude that our framework is not tied to a specific visual explanation method, and allows the drop-in replacement of different visual explanation methods for guiding the language generation.

4.3 Language Models

Our framework can be used with different language models without any changes in the setup (c.f. Table 3 (right)). Here, we analyze the performance of ZS-A2T for different language models. We demonstrate that our framework even outperforms other related approaches when using a pre-trained GPT-2 language model. For example, it achieves a Rouge-L value of 26.6 on VQA-X, whereas the previous best model with a GPT-2 backbone (MAGIC) only achieves 19.3 with the same language model. Furthermore, we clearly outperform MAGIC on the n-gram metric Bleu-4 (3.6 vs. 1.0), as well as on Meteor, Rouge-L, Cider, and SPICE (see Table 1). This can be attributed to our temperature κ, which allows for better balancing of the two terms in Eq. (7).

Next, we analyze the impact of the size of the pre-trained language models. Our ZS-A2T framework does benefit from larger, more powerful language models. The performance increase with larger size is consistent across all metrics, e.g. Spice goes from 7.1 to 9.2 when using the OPT model with 125M vs. 1.3B parameters. Using the 6.7B model boosts the Spice performance to 10.5. This suggests that high-quality candidate proposals are beneficial for the generated sentences. Additionally, it also showcases a benefit of our training-free approach: Large or newer language models can be swapped in without additional cost.

4.4 Prompt Ablations

Here, we analyze the effect of different input prompts for the pre-trained language model on the generated text outputs (c.f. Table 4).

Unsurprisingly, providing no task description (row 1) in the input prompt gives the worst outputs. Removing the task description ("Answer and explain:") yields significantly worse results with Bleu-4 decreasing from 8.5 to 3.7, suggesting that the task description is crucial for performance.

Inputting the task in a more structured way ("Question: $\langle q \rangle$? Answer: $\langle a \rangle$. Explanation:") increases the language quality only slightly compared to using no task description. However, the same structured prompt extended

Table 4. Ablating different input prompts on VQA-X [15]. $\langle q \rangle$ and $\langle a \rangle$ are placeholders for the question and answer. Q denotes "Question", A "Answer", and E "Explanation". \n denotes a new line. We show the full prompt templates in Section A of the supplementary material.

Prompt	B4	M	RL	C	S
$\langle q \rangle$? the answer is $\langle a \rangle$ because	3.7	10.3	25.7	21.6	8.4
Q: $\langle q \rangle$? A: $\langle a \rangle$. E:	3.5	11.0	23.2	22.6	9.6
Q: $\langle q \rangle$\n? A: $\langle x \rangle$\n. E:	4.2	11.2	23.7	23.0	9.6
Explain the A: $\langle q \rangle$? The A is $\langle a \rangle$ because	6.9	13.0	32.3	31.7	9.9
A and Explain: $\langle q \rangle$?\n The A is $\langle a \rangle$ because	7.6	13.5	32.9	35.8	**10.6**
A and Explain: $\langle q \rangle$? The A is $\langle a \rangle$ because	**8.5**	**13.8**	**34.2**	**38.1**	10.5

by newline characters \n shows increased or similar metric values for all metrics. A further improvement is achieved by using a meaningful task description ("Explain the answer:") in the input prompt. We used the best prompt ("Answer and explain:") in ZS-A2T.

Impact of In-Context Generation (n-shot prompting). We analyze the effect of prefixing the context with complete examples of questions, answers, and their respective explanations. This enables the language model to better understand the task, as it can see some examples before generating text [6].

We experiment with up to $n = 1$ and $n = 5$ randomly sampled examples from the training set of the respective dataset which are prepended to the context (see Table 5). The full prompts for this setup are included in Section E of the supplementary material.

Using a single example improves the language quality already. For $n = 1$, the natural language generation scores are on average 7.2% higher than for $n = 0$. By just prefixing five in-context learning examples, the generation quality increases on

Table 5. In-context learning with n examples on the VQA-X dataset.

Model	n	B4	M	RL	C	S
ZS-A2T	0	8.5	13.8	34.2	38.1	10.5
ZS-A2T	1	9.8	14.5	34.8	42.7	11.7
ZS-A2T	5	11.9	15.3	37.5	49.6	12.4

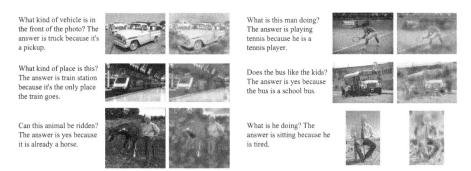

Fig. 3. Qualitative results for ZS-A2T on VQA-X, showing the input image, question, attention rollout [1] output, and generated text. Red indicates higher relevance. The generated text indeed mentions the visual concepts detected by the VQA model. The face regions have been deliberately occluded in this figure.

average by 19.3% over providing no examples. Qualitatively, we find that the language model does not merely copy or modify the texts of the examples when the question and/or answer match, but instead allows to adjust the candidate predictions for the generated sentences accordingly. Additionally, the generated texts better match the language biases in the datasets (e.g. on VQA-X many samples start with "the" or "there").

4.5   Qualitative Results

We provide qualitative examples for natural language translations generated with ZS-A2T for VQA-X in Fig. 3. The attention rollout map is superimposed onto the original image. For each of the examples we show the question, predicted answer and generated sentence that translates the attention patters into natural language. We can observe that attention rollout, used for the attention-controlled guiding, selects relevant image regions that plausibly correspond to the input question. In the bottom left example the main attention is directed towards the *horse*. The generated sentences are fluent (due to the pre-trained language model) and they refer to visual elements (due to the image-text matching). Moreover, the framework can argue with common sense, i.e. it states that *a train station is the only place the train goes*. It combines this prior knowledge from the pre-trained language model with visual concepts detected by the VQA model, such as identifying that the masked image shows *a school bus*. The capability to mention visual elements stems from the attention controlled guiding of the language generation. Additionally, the translations accurately describe the part of the image that the VQA model used to answer the question (e.g. the pickup truck in the top left example).

An observed failure pattern can be seen in the bottom-right example in Fig. 3. It seems very plausible that the person would be *tired*. However, this sentence does not refer to any visual information but instead uses common sense to explain the answer to the input question. In conclusion, the qualitative results in Fig. 3 show that ZS-A2T indeed generates text which mentions visual information contained in the attention patterns that are extracted from the VQA model. Additionally, the generated sentences are overall grammatically correct and fluent.

5   Limitations

Our proposed framework translates the internal attention of a VQA model into natural language. As no datasets exist specifically for this task, we chose to automatically evaluate our text translations of attention maps on textual explanation datasets. Due to the inherent task differences, we do not expect our attention translations to perfectly match the ground-truth explanations (e.g. in terms of writing style), explaining part of the performance gap compared to supervised upper bounds in Table 1. Further research into zero-shot translation methods and the creation of attention translation datasets will be important to better understand attention-based models using natural language.

Our *translation* approach relies on (pre-)trained language models. As a result, the faithfulness of the generated text with respect to the task model is hard to quantify. To address this, we use an attention-controlled visual guiding component for aligning the text generation with the VQA model.

Furthermore, we have only considered the ALBEF VQA model. However, our approach could easily be extended to other models such as LXMERT [39] or ViLT [19].

Our attention-controlled guiding outperforms guiding with the full image by only a slight margin (c.f. Table 2). This could be due to wrong internal reasoning of the task model and attention rollout not identifying the areas causing this. This should be addressed in future work, e.g. by using attention-perturbation to understand the importance of image patches.

Lastly, we hypothesize that the relatively small changes in the ablation studies might be due to the LLM already predicting a common sense translation for the question and answer.

6   Conclusion

In this work, we introduce ZS-A2T, a zero-shot framework for translating the aggregated attention in a VQA model to natural language. In particular, the language generation is guided using the VQA model itself, by means of its internal attention combined with its image-text matching capabilities for selecting word candidates in the language generation. Our proposed method does not require any training and can be flexibly used together with any language model to translate the visual attribution output for an attribution method of choice. Our framework outperforms zero-shot image captioning baselines on textual explanation datasets in the context of VQA.

Acknowledgements. The authors thank IMPRS-IS for supporting Leonard Salewski. This work was partially funded by the Max Planck Society, the BMBF Tübingen AI Center (FKZ: 01IS18039A), DFG (EXC number 2064/1 - Project number 390727645), ERC (853489-DEXIM), and DFG-CRC 1233 (Project number 276693517).

References

1. Abnar, S., Zuidema, W.: Quantifying attention flow in transformers. In: ACL (2020)
2. Agrawal, A., et al.: Vqa: visual question answering. Int. J. Comput. Vis. (2015)
3. Anderson, P., Fernando, B., Johnson, M., Gould, S.: SPICE: semantic propositional image caption evaluation. In: Leibe, B., Matas, J., Sebe, N., Welling, M. (eds.) ECCV 2016. LNCS, vol. 9909, pp. 382–398. Springer, Cham (2016). https://doi.org/10.1007/978-3-319-46454-1_24
4. Bach, S., Binder, A., Montavon, G., Klauschen, F., Müller, K.R., Samek, W.: On pixel-wise explanations for non-linear classifier decisions by layer-wise relevance propagation. PloS one **10**, e0130140 (2015)
5. Banerjee, S., Lavie, A.: Meteor: An automatic metric for MT evaluation with improved correlation with human judgments. In: IEEvaluation@ACL (2005)
6. Brown, T., et al.: Language models are few-shot learners. Adv. Neural. Inf. Process. Syst. **33**, 1877–1901 (2020)
7. Chefer, H., Gur, S., Wolf, L.: Generic attention-model explainability for interpreting bimodal and encoder-decoder transformers. In: ICCV (2021)
8. Chen, S., Zhao, Q.: Rex: Reasoning-aware and grounded explanation. In: CVPR (2022)
9. Draelos, R.L., Carin, L.: Use HiReSCAM instead of grad-cam for faithful explanations of convolutional neural networks (2020)
10. Fong, R., Patrick, M., Vedaldi, A.: Understanding deep networks via extremal perturbations and smooth masks. In: ICCV (2019)
11. Fong, R.C., Vedaldi, A.: Interpretable explanations of black boxes by meaningful perturbation. In: ICCV (2017)
12. Fu, R., Hu, Q., Dong, X., Guo, Y., Gao, Y., Li, B.: Axiom-based grad-cam: towards accurate visualization and explanation of CNNs. In: BMVC (2020)
13. Goyal, Y., Khot, T., Summers-Stay, D., Batra, D., Parikh, D.: Making the V in VQA matter: elevating the role of image understanding in visual question answering. In: CVPR (2017)
14. Hudson, D.A., Manning, C.D.: GQA: a new dataset for real-world visual reasoning and compositional question answering. In: CVPR (2019)
15. Huk Park, D., et al.: Multimodal explanations: justifying decisions and pointing to the evidence. In: CVPR (2018)
16. Jain, S., Wallace, B.C.: Attention is not explanation. In: North American Chapter of the Association for Computational Linguistics (2019)
17. Johnson, J., Hariharan, B., van der Maaten, L., Fei-Fei, L., Zitnick, C.L., Girshick, R.B.: Clevr: a diagnostic dataset for compositional language and elementary visual reasoning. In: CVPR (2017)
18. Kim, S.S., Meister, N., Ramaswamy, V.V., Fong, R., Russakovsky, O.: Hive: evaluating the human interpretability of visual explanations. In: Avidan, S., Brostow, G., Cissé, M., Farinella, G.M., Hassner, T. (eds.) ECCV 2022. LNCS, vol. 13672, pp. 280–298. Springer, Cham (2022). https://doi.org/10.1007/978-3-031-19775-8_17
19. Kim, W., Son, B., Kim, I.: Vilt: vision-and-language transformer without convolution or region supervision. In: International Conference on Machine Learning (2021)
20. Li, J., Selvaraju, R.R., Gotmare, A.D., Joty, S.R., Xiong, C., Hoi, S.C.H.: Align before fuse: vision and language representation learning with momentum distillation. In: NeurIPS (2021)
21. Li, Q., Tao, Q., Joty, S., Cai, J., Luo, J.: VQA-E: explaining, elaborating, and enhancing your answers for visual questions. In: ECCV (2018)
22. Li, W., Zhu, L., Wen, L., Yang, Y.: DeCap: decoding CLIP latents for zero-shot captioning via text-only training. In: The Eleventh International Conference on Learning Representations (2023)

23. Lin, C.Y.: Rouge: a package for automatic evaluation of summaries. In: ACL (2004)
24. Muhammad, M.B., Yeasin, M.: Eigen-cam: class activation map using principal components. In: IJCNN (2020)
25. Ouyang, L., et al.: Training language models to follow instructions with human feedback. NeurIPS **35**, 27730–27744 (2022)
26. Papineni, K., Roukos, S., Ward, T., Zhu, W.J.: Bleu: a method and for automatic and evaluation of machine and translation. In: ACL (2002)
27. Petsiuk, V., Das, A., Saenko, K.: Rise: randomized input sampling for explanation of blackbox models. In: BMVC (2018)
28. Pillai, V., Pirsiavash, H.: Explainable models with consistent interpretations. In: AAAI (2021)
29. Radford, A., et al.: Learning transferable visual models from natural language supervision. In: ICML (2021)
30. Salewski, L., Koepke, A.S., Lensch, H., Akata, Z.: Clevr-x: a visual reasoning dataset for natural language explanations. In: Holzinger, A., Goebel, R., Fong, R., Moon, T., Müller, KR., Samek, W. (eds.) xxAI 2020. LNCS, vol. 13200, pp. 69–88. Springer, Cham (2022). https://doi.org/10.1007/978-3-031-04083-2_5
31. Sammani, F., Mukherjee, T., Deligiannis, N.: Nlx-gpt: a model for natural language explanations in vision and vision-language tasks. In: CVPR (2022)
32. Selvaraju, R.R., Das, A., Vedantam, R., Cogswell, M., Parikh, D., Batra, D.: Grad-CAM: visual explanations from deep networks via gradient-based localization. Int. J. Comput. Vis. (2019)
33. Selvaraju, R.R., Cogswell, M., Das, A., Vedantam, R., Parikh, D., Batra, D.: Grad-cam: visual explanations from deep networks via gradient-based localization. In: ICCV (2017)
34. Simonyan, K., Vedaldi, A., Zisserman, A.: Deep inside convolutional networks: visualising image classification models and saliency maps. In: ICLR workshop (2013)
35. Smilkov, D., Thorat, N., Kim, B., Viégas, F., Wattenberg, M.: Smoothgrad: removing noise by adding noise. arXiv:1706.03825 (2017)
36. Springenberg, J.T., Dosovitskiy, A., Brox, T., Riedmiller, M.: Striving for simplicity: the all convolutional net. In: ICLR (Workshop Track) (2015)
37. Su, Y., et al.: Language models can see: plugging visual controls in text generation. arXiv:2205.02655 (2022)
38. Su, Y., Lan, T., Wang, Y., Yogatama, D., Kong, L., Collier, N.: A contrastive framework for neural text generation. In: Oh, A.H., Agarwal, A., Belgrave, D., Cho, K. (eds.) Advances in Neural Information Processing Systems (2022)
39. Tan, H., Bansal, M.: Lxmert: learning cross-modality encoder representations from transformers. arXiv:1908.07490 (2019)
40. Tewel, Y., Shalev, Y., Nadler, R., Schwartz, I., Wolf, L.: Zero-shot video captioning with evolving pseudo-tokens. arXiv:2207.11100 (2022)
41. Tewel, Y., Shalev, Y., Schwartz, I., Wolf, L.: Zerocap: zero-shot image-to-text generation for visual-semantic arithmetic. In: CVPR (2022)
42. Vedantam, R., Zitnick, C.L., Parikh, D.: Cider: consensus-based image description evaluation. In: CVPR (2015)
43. Voita, E., Talbot, D., Moiseev, F., Sennrich, R., Titov, I.: Analyzing multi-head self-attention: specialized heads do the heavy lifting, the rest can be pruned. In: ACL (2019)
44. Wang, J., Zhang, Y., Yan, M., Zhang, J.C., Sang, J.: Zero-shot image captioning by anchor-augmented vision-language space alignment. arXiv:2211.07275 (2022)
45. Wiegreffe, S., Pinter, Y.: Attention is not not explanation. In: Conference on Empirical Methods in Natural Language Processing (2019)

46. Zeiler, M.D., Fergus, R.: Visualizing and understanding convolutional networks. In: Fleet, D., Pajdla, T., Schiele, B., Tuytelaars, T. (eds.) ECCV 2014. LNCS, vol. 8689, pp. 818–833. Springer, Cham (2014). https://doi.org/10.1007/978-3-319-10590-1_53

47. Zeng, A., et al.: Socratic models: composing zero-shot multimodal reasoning with language. In: ICLR (2023)

48. Zhang, J., Bargal, S.A., Lin, Z., Brandt, J., Shen, X., Sclaroff, S.: Top-down neural attention by excitation backprop. Int. J. Comput. Vis. **126**, 1084–1102 (2018)

49. Zhang, S., et al.: Opt: open pre-trained transformer language models. arXiv:2205.01068 (2022)

50. Zhou, B., Khosla, A., Lapedriza, A., Oliva, A., Torralba, A.: Learning deep features for discriminative localization. In: CVPR (2016)

Beyond Debiasing: Actively Steering Feature Selection via Loss Regularization

Jan Blunk$^{(\boxtimes)}$ iD, Niklas Penzel iD, Paul Bodesheim iD, and Joachim Denzler iD

Computer Vision Group, Friedrich Schiller University Jena, 07743 Jena, Germany
{jan.blunk,niklas.penzel,paul.bodesheim,joachim.denzler}@uni-jena.de
https://inf-cv.uni-jena.de

Abstract. It is common for domain experts like physicians in medical studies to examine features for their reliability with respect to a specific domain task. When introducing machine learning, a common expectation is that machine learning models use the same features as these human experts to solve a task, but that is not always the case. Moreover, datasets often contain features that are known from domain knowledge to generalize badly to the real world, referred to as biases. Current debiasing methods only remove such influences. To additionally integrate the domain knowledge about well-established features into the training of a model, their relevance should be increased. We present a method that allows the manipulation of the relevance of features by actively steering the model's feature selection during the training process. That is, it allows both the discouragement of biases and encouragement of well-established features to incorporate domain knowledge about the feature reliability. We model our objectives for actively steering the feature selection process as a constrained optimization problem, which we implement via a loss regularization that is based on batch-wise feature attributions. We evaluate our approach on a novel synthetic regression dataset and a dataset from the computer vision domain. We observe that it successfully steers the features a model selects during the training process. This is a strong indicator that our method can be used to integrate domain knowledge about well-established features into a model.

Keywords: Feature Steering · Domain Knowledge Integration · Feature Relevance · Trustworthy AI

1 Introduction

Being able to explicitly manipulate how models utilize features to derive their predictions enables diverse opportunities. In particular, it can be used to improve generalization and interpretability [21] of model predictions.

One motivation for the active interference in a model's feature selection process is a training distribution that contains biases. Biases are a common problem

Supplementary Information The online version contains supplementary material available at https://doi.org/10.1007/978-3-031-54605-1_26.

U. Köthe and C. Rother (Eds.): DAGM GCPR 2023, LNCS 14264, pp. 394–408, 2024.
https://doi.org/10.1007/978-3-031-54605-1_26

in computer vision [46]. The term describes features that are only spuriously correlated with the label in the training distribution. If a model bases its predictions on such a bias, it fails to generalize to the real world. If it is known from domain knowledge which features constitute a bias, it is desirable to reduce their influence on the model's prediction process.

In addition to discouraging biases, it can also be desirable to encourage the influence of features on the model's prediction process if they are known from domain knowledge to be particularly well-established. This is not only expected to improve generalization but, similarly to debiasing, it could also increase trust in the model's decisions. An example of such domain knowledge are results from medical studies like the ABCD rule introduced by Nachbar and Stolz [31] for the identification of malignant melanoma. Because State-of-the-art models only base their predictions on some but not all of the features proposed by this rule [39], it provides a suitable illustration of the need for active steering of feature selection.

We show that it is not only possible to discourage but also to encourage the influence of features on a model's prediction process. We present a method that actively steers the influence of features via loss regularization during the training process. Our feature steering approach models the desire for correct predictions and intervention in the model's feature selection process as a multi-objective optimization problem and solves it via the weighted sum method [24]. We evaluate our method on a small regression problem to which we add redundancy and the more complex Colored MNIST dataset [2].

2   Related Work

Most prior work that relates to feature steering has been designed for debiasing [22,38,41,42]. Debiasing describes a special case of feature steering that is limited to discouraging a model from basing its predictions on features that are known to generalize badly to the real world. This situation occurs if a feature is spuriously correlated to the label in the training distribution indicating a causal link between the feature and label, even though this causal link does not exist in the test distribution [18]. We refer to these features as biases. Debiasing covers a diverse set of methods [26,33]. Not all approaches to debiasing are related to our feature steering since their design can be very problem-specific.

Both debiasing and our feature steering method belong to explanation-guided learning (EGL). Gao et al. [13] presented an extensive survey including a theoretical definition for this concept. While explainable AI (XAI) [1,4,17] attempts to generate explanations for model predictions, it does not examine how to improve a model's behavior based on these explanations. EGL attempts to integrate the acquired knowledge by simultaneously optimizing for both generalization and the desired properties of the explanations. In our case, the explanations are batchwise feature attributions, which we attempt to align with the feature steering objectives.

Conceptually, our method shares similarities with an approach proposed by Erion et al. [11]. The authors also proposed a general framework to align feature attributions with domain knowledge. Contrary to our method, they considered the relative importance between features. Moreover, the authors focussed on the integration of domain knowledge about the higher-level properties of the relationships between features to increase performance. We, however, are interested in priors on the selection of features motivated by interpretability and the improvement of generalization.

Implementation-wise, we perform loss regularization to align the feature attributions with domain knowledge. Ross et al. [42] introduced a loss-based regularization approach to EGL. They added a penalty term to the original loss function that integrates domain knowledge via feature attributions generated with input gradients [3]. Rieger et al. proposed contextual decomposition explanation penalization (CDEP) [41], which similarly utilizes penalty terms to perform debiasing. The authors generated their feature attributions with contextual decomposition [30,44], which enabled them to integrate priors about the interaction of features. Reimers et al. also performed debiasing via loss-based regularization [38]. Contrary to the other two approaches, their model-agnostic feature attribution method allowed them to apply their method to features that cannot explicitly be modeled as part of the model inputs. Debiasing via loss-based regularization is also applicable to natural language processing as has been shown by Liu and Avci [22]. We differ from the aforementioned methods with respect to the regularization objective: We are not only interested in decreasing the influence of biases but also in increasing the influence of well-established features.

3   Method

Goal. Our goal is to perform feature steering, that is, to manipulate the influence of specific features on the prediction process of a model during the training process. We want to (1) discourage the usage of undesired features like biases and (2) encourage the usage of desired features identified from domain knowledge. Toward these goals, we implement this via a penalty term that is added to the original loss function.

3.1   Feature Steering

We implement feature steering building upon existing regularization concepts [15, p. 117]. Out of the many different regularization techniques [29], we focus on the modification of the loss function. Specifically, we use penalty terms to incorporate constrained optimization, which allows us to explicitly alter the targeted optimum.

Feature steering can be defined as a constrained optimization problem: On the one hand, we want the model to generate correct predictions via a maximum-likelihood estimation of its parameters and on the other hand we are interested in decreasing or increasing the relevance of certain features. Related debiasing works applied Lagrange multipliers [7] to combine the two objectives of this constraint optimization problem into a single loss function [22,38,41,42]. We generalize this from debiasing to the discouragement and encouragement of arbitrary features, where D refers to the set of features that should be discouraged and E to the set of features that should be encouraged. To model the resulting multi-objective optimization problem, we apply the method of weighted sums [24]. With c_i being a measure of the influence of feature i on the model's prediction process, $\lambda \in \mathbb{R}_{\geq 0}$ as a weight factor and $\mathcal{L}$ as the standard maximum-likelihood loss for network parameters θ, the loss function for general feature steering is defined as:

$$\mathcal{L}'(\theta) = \mathcal{L}(\theta) + \lambda \left(\sum_{i \in D} ||c_i|| - \sum_{i \in E} ||c_i|| \right). \tag{1}$$

For $|| \cdot ||$, we consider the L1 and L2 norms.

3.2   Feature Attribution

To calculate our loss function in practice, the influence c_i of the features whose influence should be steered needs to be determined in every step of the training. The process of determining the influence of specific features is referred to as feature attribution [22].

Contextual decomposition (CD) [30,44] determines the influence of a specific feature by decomposing the output of the model into a linear combination of the influence of the feature and the influence of all other features. This decomposition is iteratively computed from a decomposition of the input within a single forward pass. Therefore, contextual decomposition is designed to determine the influence of features that can be represented as a subset of the inputs of the model.

Reimers et al. [38] model the process of supervised learning via a structural causal model (SCM) [34]. Using this SCM and Reichenbach's Common Cause Principle [37], they derive that the binary question of whether or not a feature influences the prediction of a model boils down to a simple conditional independence test [40]. A feature X_i influences the prediction of a model if it is statistically dependent on the corresponding prediction $\hat{Y}_i$ of the model given the ground truth Y_i:

$$X_i \not\perp\!\!\!\perp \hat{Y}_i \mid Y_i. \tag{2}$$

The authors extend this to a quantitative measure of feature attribution by considering the test statistic of independence tests. We follow their approach and use the conditional mutual information (CMI) [25] and an extended version of the Hilbert Schmidt independence criterion (conditional HSIC) [16,38] to determine the influence of features.

Implementation Details for Reimers et al. The feature attribution obtained with CMI as $I(X_i; \hat{Y}_i | Y_i)$ can take infinite values, which would lead to infinitely large weight changes. This problem occurs if the model's prediction can be fully described by X_i and Y_i since the CMI describes how much additional knowledge of $x \in X_i$ reduces the uncertainty about $\hat{Y}_i$ when $y \in Y_i$ is already known [25, Section 8.1]. Therefore, we transform the CMI into a finite interval with a transformation t that is based on a similar transformation proposed by Linfoot [20] for mutual information. For the CMI $I_i = I(X_i; \hat{Y}_i | Y)$ with respect to feature i we define t as:

$$t(I_i) = \sqrt{1 - e^{-2 \cdot I_i}}. \tag{3}$$

We estimate the CMI with an estimator proposed by Zan et al. [48]. Even though the CMI can generally be considered strictly positive, these estimates may be negative [36]. Due to the definition of the square root, t cannot be applied to these negative estimates. To avoid saturation, we do not set t to a fixed value for negative estimates but instead proceed similarly to straight-through estimators [47] and apply an identity transformation:

$$c_i = \begin{cases} t(I_i) & \text{for } I_i > 0 \\ I_i & \text{for } I_i \leq 0. \end{cases} \tag{4}$$

Consequently, we also apply the identity transformation instead of the L1 or L2 norm to the resulting negative feature attributions. Otherwise, a negative feature attribution would result in a larger loss than positive feature attributions with a smaller magnitude, even though features with negative feature attributions have less influence on the model's prediction process than features with positive feature attributions.

3.3 Theoretical Considerations

Our loss function consists of two components modeling the two separate objectives of feature steering: The maximum-likelihood loss seeks correct predictions for the original distribution while the feature steering part implements the manipulation of the feature influence.

For both very small and very large values of the weight factor λ, one of the two components dominates the loss. In the case of very small values of λ the maximum-likelihood loss dominates and we expect no feature steering to be performed. For very large values of λ, the feature steering component dominates and we expect the model to disregard the desire for correct predictions potentially leading to pathological solutions. Since we are interested in both objectives, we have to select λ as a tradeoff between these two extremes.

4 Datasets

We test our feature steering approach on two datasets of different complexity. Our evaluation starts with a small regression-based example and is then extended to feature steering in an image classification setting.

4.1 Redundant Regression Dataset

We first examine the fundamental behavior of our method on a small regression dataset, to which we add redundant information. That is, we create a low-dimensional linear regression problem and perform a dimensionality expansion of the input variables to add redundant information.

Low-Dimensional Regression Dataset. Our regression-based dataset is generated from a linear regression problem with standard-normal distributed random variables $X_0, ..., X_5$ and standard-uniformly distributed regression coefficients $\beta_0, ..., \beta_5$. That is, the target variable Y is calculated as:

$$Y = \sum_{i=0,...,5} \beta_i X_i. \tag{5}$$

Redundancy. We want to evaluate our method on a dataset that has redundant features because we motivate feature steering as encouraging a model to select particularly favorable features out of multiple alternatives for prediction. To generate redundancy between features in our regression problem, we borrow from latent factor analysis (FA) [5,6]. Concretely, we consider the input variables of our regression problem as unobserved "latent variables" from which the observed redundant "manifest variables" are generated [5, Chapter 1]. Generating the manifest variables is the inverse problem to the common procedure in FA of identifying the latent variables from the manifest variables.

We select the principal component analysis (PCA) [19,35] as our method for FA because contrary to general FA [8, p. 585] it has an explicit inverse. PCA models a special case of FA analysis that assumes that the observations are generated as linear combinations without an additive noise term [5, p. 52].

Because it can be regarded as a method for dimensionality reduction, our approach of performing an inverse PCA can be seen as a dimensionality expansion of a small number of random variables, which introduces redundancy. Afterward, we verify that each considered subset of the created high-dimensional manifest variables still contains all information of the low-dimensional latent variables.

PCA performs a transformation that maximizes the variance of the projected data [8]. For this, the data is made zero-mean and then transformed with the real orthogonal matrix $\mathbf{U}^T$ where the columns of $\mathbf{U} = (u_1, ..., u_n)$ are the eigenvectors corresponding to the sorted eigenvalues of the empirical covariance matrix. When performing a dimensionality reduction from n manifest variables to m latent variables with $n > m$, the data is transformed with $\mathbf{U}'^T$, where $\mathbf{U}' = (u_1, ..., u_m)$ consists of the first m columns of $\mathbf{U}$.

Since we are interested in an inverse PCA with dimensionality expansion, we generate our observations x_n of the manifest variables from the generated instances x_m of the latent variables as:

$$x_n = \mathbf{U}' x_m. \tag{6}$$

That is, to generate the observed manifest variables, we uniformly sample $\mathbb{U} \in \mathbb{R}^{9 \times 9}$ as a random orthogonal matrix with standard-normal distributed coefficients based on the Haar measure [10, 28]. We obtain $\mathbf{U}' \in \mathbb{R}^{9 \times 6}$ by selecting six columns from U to add redundancy of three features.

To guarantee the desired redundancy, we can ensure that no information from the latent variables is lost when only considering 6 out of the 9 manifest variables by proving that the latent variables can be reconstructed from the subset of manifest variables. We achieve this by checking the matrix constructed from the rows of $\mathbf{U}'$ generating the considered manifest variables for left invertibility [45].

4.2   Colored MNIST

Colored MNIST [2] was created by Arjovsky et al. as an adapted version of the MNIST dataset [9] for hand-written digit recognition that is designed for the evaluation of debiasing methods.

The authors introduce colored digits and use the additional color information to propose the following binary task: First, they split the images of MNIST into digits < 5 and ≥ 5. Each group represents one of the binary classification labels. However, the authors flip this label with a probability of 0.25. Then, they color the digits based on the label. Similarly to the label, the color is flipped with a certain probability as well. Following Arjovsky et al. we assign the colors so that red digits are generally associated with label 1 and a digit < 5 and green digits are generally associated with label 0 and a digit ≥ 5.

Arjovsky et al. set the color flip probabilities such that in the training dataset the label is more closely associated with the color than with the digit, but not in the test dataset. That is, a model is driven towards learning the color information as a bias, which hurts generalization to the test distribution. This allows the authors to evaluate their debiasing methods. We follow Arjovsky et al. and create our training environment with a color flip probability of 0.2. To be able to perform hyperparameter tuning, the validation environment is created equally. Then, the test environment is created with a color flip probability of 0.5 so that there is no spurious association between color and label in this environment.

Dataset Statistics. We show that for the training distribution, the maximum performance of a model cannot be improved with additional knowledge of the digits compared to only knowing their color. To demonstrate this, we show the optimal decision strategy does not change with additional knowledge of the digits. As a consequence, the minimal error under the optimal decision strategy is the same under both circumstances. This indicates that only with successful debiasing a model is incentivized to learn digit recognition when trained on the training distribution.

The optimal decision strategy when only knowing a digit's color is predicting the label that has the higher probability given the color. The probabilities can directly be inferred from the color flip probabilities. For red digits label 1 and for green digits label 0 is predicted:

$$\mathbb{P}(\text{Label} = 1|\text{Color} = \text{red}) = 0.8, \tag{7}$$
$$\mathbb{P}(\text{Label} = 0|\text{Color} = \text{green}) = 0.8. \tag{8}$$

With additional knowledge of the digit, the optimal decision strategy consists of predicting the label that has the highest probability given the color and digit. The required conditional probabilities can be calculated via joint probabilities following the definition of the conditional probability of random variables [27, p. 151] (for more details see Appendix A.1):

$$\mathbb{P}(\text{Label} = 1|\text{Color} = \text{red}, \text{Digit} < 5) > 0.5, \tag{9}$$
$$\mathbb{P}(\text{Label} = 1|\text{Color} = \text{red}, \text{Digit} \geq 5) > 0.5, \tag{10}$$
$$\mathbb{P}(\text{Label} = 0|\text{Color} = \text{green}, \text{Digit} \geq 5) > 0.5, \tag{11}$$
$$\mathbb{P}(\text{Label} = 0|\text{Color} = \text{green}, \text{Digit} < 5) > 0.5. \tag{12}$$

The optimal decision strategy still consists of predicting 1 for red digits and 0 for green digits.

Since the optimal decision strategy has not changed, the minimum error E achievable under the optimal decision strategy when only knowing the color and also with additional knowledge of the digit is the same under both circumstances and can be calculated as:

$$E = \sum_{c \in \{\text{red,green}\}} \mathbb{P}(\text{False Prediction}|\text{Color} = c) \cdot \mathbb{P}(\text{Color} = c) \tag{13}$$
$$= 0.2 \cdot 0.5 + 0.2 \cdot 0.5 = 0.2.$$

This shows that a model following the optimal decision strategy can achieve an accuracy of 0.8. In other words, a model reaching a higher accuracy on the training dataset of Colored MNIST must have memorized training samples.

5   Experiments

We test our feature steering method on the two datasets presented in the previous section and demonstrate that it makes both discouragement and encouragement of features possible. Additionally, we examine the model behavior depending on the choice of the weight factor λ.

5.1   Evaluation Metrics

First, we describe how the success of our feature steering method is evaluated. Designing an evaluation metric for feature steering is non-trivial because it has to encompass both objectives of feature steering: Correct predictions and manipulation of the influence of individual features.

Debiasing. In debiasing, it is common to have a training and a test dataset that only differ with respect to the spurious association between bias and label, which is only present in the training distribution. Under the assumption that the model is incentivized to learn the bias when trained on the biased training distribution, debiasing can be evaluated via the performance on the unbiased test dataset. As long as we are only interested in the absolute discouragement of features, we can follow this evaluation approach for feature steering.

General Feature Steering. The evaluation approach for debiasing cannot be applied to general feature steering because it implicitly fixes the desired strength of the feature steering to a total discouragement. Since feature steering also includes partial discouragement or encouragement of features, we choose to evaluate both feature steering objectives separately.

To ensure correct predictions on the original distribution, we consider the generalization error on the test dataset. To evaluate the manipulation of the influence of the specific features on the model's prediction process, similarly to debiasing, we evaluate the performance of the models on a dataset with a distribution shift where there is no spurious association between the feature of interest and the label. For our regression dataset, this can easily be created by replacing the input that corresponds to the feature of interest with random normal-distributed noise with the same mean and variance as the original feature.

To measure the influence of a feature i we consider the difference in performance on the original dataset and the dataset with a distribution shift for i. As both datasets have the same labels, a difference in the maximum-likelihood loss on the datasets can only be attributed to the feature i or its interactions. We additionally normalize this difference to compare the feature steering effect on different datasets.

For a model trained with weight factor λ that achieves a maximum-likelihood loss of $\mathcal{E}(\lambda)$ on the original dataset and $\mathcal{E}_i(\lambda)$ on the version manipulated for feature i, the influence $influence(\lambda, i)$ of this feature on the model's prediction process is calculated as:

$$influence(\lambda, i) = \left| \frac{\mathcal{E}_i(\lambda) - \mathcal{E}(\lambda)}{\mathcal{E}_i(0) - \mathcal{E}(0)} \right|. \tag{14}$$

5.2   Results on Redundant Regression Dataset

We generate 9 instances of the redundant regression dataset presented in Sect. 4.1 with different regression coefficients $\beta_0, ..., \beta_5$ and transformation matrices U'. For each dataset, we generate 1400 training samples and 300 datasets for evaluation. Since we introduce a redundancy of three variables we perform discouragement and encouragement with respect to the first three observed manifest variables.

Our evaluations are conducted with a network that consists of an initial linear layer with rectified linear units (ReLUs) [12,32,43] as activation functions and

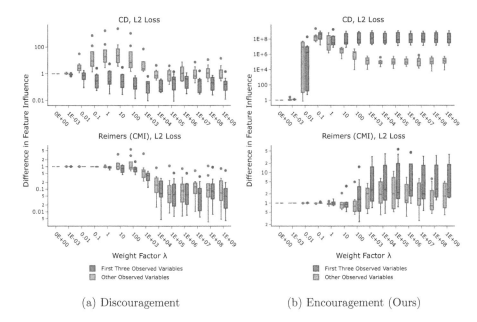

(a) Discouragement   (b) Encouragement (Ours)

Fig. 1. Evaluation of the feature selection. We perform encouragement and discouragement of the first three observed variables for each of the 9 instances of the redundant regression dataset with our feature steering method using L2 loss. The feature steering objective is evaluated based on the feature influences (as described in Sect. 5.1).

the same size as the network input followed by a linear output layer (for more details on the training process see Appendix A.2). The weights are initialized with Xavier initialization [14] and biases to zero. Optimization is performed with PyTorch's default AdamW implementation [23] and learning rate $\delta = 0.01$ for 90 epochs. We follow standard practice for a linear regression problem and train with the mean-squared error as our loss function.

Ablation Study. We examine the model behavior when discouraging and encouraging the first three observed manifest variables with our feature steering method depending on the weight factor. In our experiments, we perform discouragement and encouragement separately. That is, we limit Eq. 1 to either D or E being the empty set. For this, we consider weight factors $\lambda = 10^{-3}, 10^{-2}, ..., 10^9$. The feature attributions for our feature steering method are obtained with contextual decomposition (CD) [30,44] and following Reimers et al. [38] with CMI.

The evolution of the feature influence determined as described in the previous section is shown in Fig. 1. The prediction performance is measured via the mean-squared error on the validation dataset, which can be found in Table 1. In the following, we only consider the observations for the L2 loss but the results for the L1 loss are very similar (see Appendix A.2).

Table 1. Evaluation of the prediction correctness. We consider the maximum-likelihood loss on the test distribution averaged over the instances of the dataset to evaluate the correctness of the predictions generated for encouragement and discouragement of the first three observed variables with L2 loss. In conjunction with Fig. 1, λ can be selected as a tradeoff between feature steering and correct predictions.

λ	Discouragement		Encouragement (Ours)	
	CD	Reimers (CMI)	CD	Reimers (CMI)
$\lambda = 0$	$0.000_{\pm 0.000}$	$0.000_{\pm 0.000}$	$0.000_{\pm 0.000}$	$0.000_{\pm 0.000}$
$\lambda = 0.01$	$0.000_{\pm 0.000}$	$0.000_{\pm 0.000}$	$45.500_{\pm 61.339}$	$0.000_{\pm 0.000}$
$\lambda = 1$	$0.002_{\pm 0.002}$	$0.000_{\pm 0.000}$	$9.373 \cdot 10^6{}_{\pm 6.873 \cdot 10^6}$	$0.005_{\pm 0.001}$
$\lambda = 100$	$0.029_{\pm 0.031}$	$0.032_{\pm 0.009}$	$5.218 \cdot 10^7{}_{\pm 5.903 \cdot 10^6}$	$0.413_{\pm 0.034}$
$\lambda = 10^4$	$0.657_{\pm 0.107}$	$0.911_{\pm 0.117}$	$5.461 \cdot 10^7{}_{\pm 7.410 \cdot 10^6}$	$1.753_{\pm 0.301}$
$\lambda = 10^6$	$0.980_{\pm 0.232}$	$0.957_{\pm 0.102}$	$5.764 \cdot 10^7{}_{\pm 1.087 \cdot 10^7}$	$1.873_{\pm 0.345}$

We find that feature steering generally appears to be successful. However, recall from Sect. 3.3 that extreme values of the weight factor λ are expected to lead to suppression of one of the feature steering objectives. We can particularly observe this pathological behavior for encouragement with CD (see Appendix A.2). Additionally, we observe that the feature steering is very sensitive to λ.

5.3   Results on Colored MNIST

For Colored MNIST, we discourage the color as a spurious bias feature. The experiments are performed with the baseline architecture presented by Arjovsky et al. in their introduction of Colored MNIST [2].

We perform feature attribution for our feature steering method with the conditional-independence-based feature attribution method by Reimers et al. [38]. Because this method expects batched learning, we adapt the training process for batched learning with a batch size of 100, similar to the experiments on the redundant regression dataset. We train the network for 50 epochs (see Appendix A.3).

Ablation Study. We perform discouragement of the color for weight factors $\lambda = 10^{-3}, 10^{-2}, ..., 10^9$ with feature attributions generated with the conditional-independence-based method proposed by Reimers et al. [38]. The feature steering results evaluated as binary accuracies for L2 loss can be found in Fig. 2 (for L1 loss, see Appendix A.3).

Due to the construction of Colored MNIST, a successful feature steering should be indicated by an increase in test accuracy. When applying our method with feature attributions generated with the conditional-independence-based method by Reimers et al. and conditional HSIC, we can observe an increase

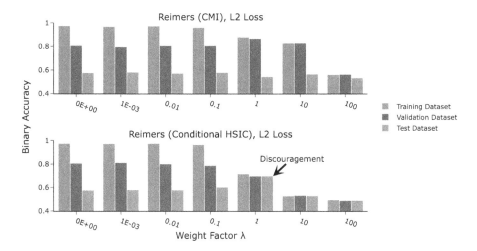

Fig. 2. Evaluation of discouragement on Colored MNIST. For Colored MNIST, we attempt to discourage the model from using the digits' color for prediction. For this, we follow Reimers et al. [38] to generate feature attributions with CMI and conditional HSIC. Because the bias is only present in the training and validation dataset, the success of discouragement can be observed as an increase in test accuracy. An accuracy above 0.8 on the training dataset indicates memorization.

in accuracy from 0.58 to 0.70. With feature attributions based on CMI, we do observe such a clear increase.

Since we have shown in Sect. 4.2 that the maximum accuracy on the training distribution achievable under the optimal decision strategy without memorization is 0.8, we can conclude from the observations that the model overfits to the training data. However, this does not seem to impact the generalization to the validation dataset. Our feature steering method appears to stop this memorization even when performed with CMI without impacting the performance on the validation dataset.

6   Conclusions

In this work, we address the alignment of the feature selection process with domain knowledge. In contrast to prior works from the area of debiasing, we present a method that allows for both the discouragement and encouragement of arbitrary features. Our evaluation indicates that it can be used to integrate domain knowledge about well-established features during the model training, aiming at the improvement of the generalization capabilities of and trust in machine learning models.

We observe that our method is very sensitive to the weight factor λ. Additionally, pathological solutions like extreme model outputs for extreme discouragement or encouragement have to be avoided.

We only consider loss-based feature steering. In the future, we plan to investigate other how feature steering can be achieved by other regularization methods like a manipulation of the sampling process. It would also be beneficial to further investigate the evaluation of feature steering. This includes the development of an evaluation metric that can fairly incorporate both the correctness of predictions and the success of feature steering.

References

1. Adadi, A., Berrada, M.: Peeking inside the black-box: a survey on explainable artificial intelligence (XAI). IEEE Access **6**, 52138–52160 (2018)
2. Arjovsky, M., Bottou, L., Gulrajani, I., Lopez-Paz, D.: Invariant risk minimization (2019)
3. Baehrens, D., Schroeter, T., Harmeling, S., Kawanabe, M., Hansen, K., Müller, K.R.: How to explain individual classification decisions. J. Mach. Learn. Res. **11**, 1803–1831 (2010)
4. Barredo Arrieta, A., et al.: Explainable artificial intelligence (XAI): concepts, taxonomies, opportunities and challenges toward responsible AI. Inf. Fusion **58**, 82–115 (2020)
5. Bartholomew, D.J.: Latent variable models and factor analysis, Griffin's statistical monographs and courses, vol. 40. Oxford Univ. Press and Griffin, New York and London (1987)
6. Basilevsky, A.: Statistical Factor Analysis and Related Methods: Theory and Applications. Wiley series in probability and mathematical statistics. Probability and mathematical statistics, Wiley InterScience, New York, NY, USA and Chichester and Brisbane and Toronto and Singapore (1994)
7. Bertsekas, D.P.: Constrained Optimization and Lagrange Multiplier Methods, Optimization and Neural Computation Series, vol. 4. Athena Scientific, Belmont (1996)
8. Bishop, C.M.: Pattern Recognition and Machine Learning. Springer, Heidelberg (2006)
9. Bottou, L., et al.: Comparison of classifier methods: a case study in handwritten digit recognition. In: Proceedings of the 12th IAPR International Conference on Pattern Recognition (Cat. No.94CH3440-5), pp. 77–82. IEEE Computer Society Press (1994)
10. Diestel, J., Spalsbury, A.: Joys of Haar Measure, Graduate Studies in Mathematics, vol. 150. American Mathematical Society, Providence (2014)
11. Erion, G., Janizek, J.D., Sturmfels, P., Lundberg, S.M., Lee, S.I.: Improving performance of deep learning models with axiomatic attribution priors and expected gradients. Nature Mach. Intell. **3**(7), 620–631 (2021)
12. Fukushima, K.: Cognitron: a self-organizing multilayered neural network. Biol. Cybern. **20**(3–4), 121–136 (1975)
13. Gao, Y., Gu, S., Jiang, J., Hong, S.R., Yu, D., Zhao, L.: Going beyond XAI: a systematic survey for explanation-guided learning (2022)
14. Glorot, X., Bengio, Y.: Understanding the difficulty of training deep feedforward neural networks. In: Teh, Y.W., Titterington, M. (eds.) Proceedings of the Thirteenth International Conference on Artificial Intelligence and Statistics. Proceedings of Machine Learning Research, vol. 9, pp. 249–256. PMLR, Chia Laguna Resort (2010)

15. Goodfellow, I., Bengio, Y., Courville, A.: Deep Learning. MIT Press, Cambridge (2016)
16. Gretton, A., Fukumizu, K., Teo, C.H., Song, L., Schölkopf, B., Smola, A.J.: A Kernel Statistical Test of Independence. In: Proceedings of the 20th International Conference on Neural Information Processing Systems, NIPS 2007, pp. 585–592. Curran Associates Inc, Red Hook (2007)
17. Guidotti, R., Monreale, A., Ruggieri, S., Turini, F., Giannotti, F., Pedreschi, D.: A survey of methods for explaining black box models. ACM Comput. Surv. **51**(5), 1–42 (2019)
18. Hinnefeld, J.H., Cooman, P., Mammo, N., Deese, R.: Evaluating fairness metrics in the presence of dataset bias (2018)
19. Hotelling, H.: Analysis of a complex of statistical variables into principal components. J. Educ. Psychol. **24**(6), 417–441 (1933)
20. Linfoot, E.H.: An informational measure of correlation. Inf. Control **1**(1), 85–89 (1957)
21. Lipton, Z.C.: The mythos of model interpretability. Queue **16**(3), 31–57 (2018)
22. Liu, F., Avci, B.: Incorporating priors with feature attribution on text classification. In: Korhonen, A., Traum, D., Màrquez, L. (eds.) Proceedings of the 57th Annual Meeting of the Association for Computational Linguistics, pp. 6274–6283. Association for Computational Linguistics, Stroudsburg (2019)
23. Loshchilov, I., Hutter, F.: Decoupled weight decay regularization. In: 7th International Conference on Learning Representations, ICLR 2019, New Orleans, LA, USA, 6–9 May 2019 (2019)
24. Marler, R.T., Arora, J.S.: Survey of multi-objective optimization methods for engineering. Struct. Multidiscip. Optim. **26**(6), 369–395 (2004)
25. McKay, D.J.C.: Information Theory, Inference, and Learning Algorithms, 4th edn. Cambridge University Press, Cambridge (2005)
26. Mehrabi, N., Morstatter, F., Saxena, N., Lerman, K., Galstyan, A.: A survey on bias and fairness in machine learning. ACM Comput. Surv. **54**(6), 1–35 (2022)
27. Mendenhall, W., Beaver, R.J., Beaver, B.M.: Introduction to Probability and Statistics. Brooks/Cole, Belmont (2009)
28. Mezzadri, F.: How to generate random matrices from the classical compact groups. Not. AMS **54**(5) (2007)
29. Moradi, R., Berangi, R., Minaei, B.: A survey of regularization strategies for deep models. Artif. Intell. Rev. **53**(6), 3947–3986 (2020)
30. Murdoch, W.J., Liu, P.J., Yu, B.: Beyond word importance: contextual decomposition to extract interactions from LSTMs. In: International Conference on Learning Representations (2018)
31. Nachbar, F., et al.: The ABCD rule of dermatoscopy: high prospective value in the diagnosis of doubtful melanocytic skin lesions. J. Am. Acad. Dermatol. **30**(4), 551–559 (1994)
32. Nair, V., Hinton, G.E.: Rectified Linear Units Improve Restricted Boltzmann Machines. In: Proceedings of the 27th International Conference on International Conference on Machine Learning, ICML 2010, pp. 807–814. Omnipress, Madison (2010)
33. Parraga, O., et al.: Debiasing methods for fairer neural models in vision and language research: a survey (2022)
34. Pearl, J.: Causality: Models, Reasoning, and Inference, 1st edn. Cambridge University Press, Cambridge (2000)
35. Pearson, K.: LIII. On lines and planes of closest fit to systems of points in space. Lond. Edinburgh Dublin Phil. Maga. J. Sci. **2**(11), 559–572 (1901)

36. Polyanskiy, Y., Wu, Y.: Information Theory: From Coding to Learning. Cambridge, MA (2022+)
37. Reichenbach, H.: The Direction of Time. University of California Press, Berkeley (1956)
38. Reimers, C., Bodesheim, P., Runge, J., Denzler, J.: Conditional adversarial debiasing: towards learning unbiased classifiers from biased data. In: Bauckhage, C., Gall, J., Schwing, A. (eds.) DAGM GCPR 2021. LNCS, vol. 13024, pp. 48–62. Springer, Cham (2021). https://doi.org/10.1007/978-3-030-92659-5_4
39. Reimers, C., Penzel, N., Bodesheim, P., Runge, J., Denzler, J.: Conditional dependence tests reveal the usage of ABCD rule features and bias variables in automatic skin lesion classification. In: CVPR ISIC Skin Image Analysis Workshop (CVPR-WS), pp. 1810–1819 (2021)
40. Reimers, C., Runge, J., Denzler, J.: Determining the relevance of features for deep neural networks. In: Vedaldi, A., Bischof, H., Brox, T., Frahm, J.-M. (eds.) ECCV 2020. LNCS, vol. 12371, pp. 330–346. Springer, Cham (2020). https://doi.org/10.1007/978-3-030-58574-7_20
41. Rieger, L., Singh, C., Murdoch, W.J., Yu, B.: Interpretations are useful: penalizing explanations to align neural networks with prior knowledge. In: Proceedings of the 37th International Conference on Machine Learning, ICML 2020 (2020)
42. Ross, A.S., Hughes, M.C., Doshi-Velez, F.: Right for the right reasons: training differentiable models by constraining their explanations. In: Bacchus, F., Sierra, C. (eds.) Proceedings of the Twenty-Sixth International Joint Conference on Artificial Intelligence, pp. 2662–2670. International Joint Conferences on Artificial Intelligence Organization, California (2017)
43. Rumelhart, D.E., McClelland, J.L.: A general framework for parallel distributed processing. In: Parallel Distributed Processing: Explorations in the Microstructure of Cognition: Foundations, pp. 45–76 (1987)
44. Singh, C., Murdoch, W.J., Yu, B.: Hierarchical interpretations for neural network predictions. In: International Conference on Learning Representations (2019)
45. Tan, L.: Generalized inverse of matrix and solution of linear system equation. In: Tan, L. (ed.) A Generalized Framework of Linear Multivariable Control, pp. 38–50. Elsevier Science, Oxford (2017)
46. Wang, A., et al.: REVISE: a tool for measuring and mitigating bias in visual datasets. Int. J. Comput. Vision **130**(7), 1790–1810 (2022)
47. Yin, P., Lyu, J., Zhang, S., Osher, S.J., Qi, Y., Xin, J.: Understanding straight-through estimator in training activation quantized neural nets. In: International Conference on Learning Representations (2019)
48. Zan, L., Meynaoui, A., Assaad, C.K., Devijver, E., Gaussier, E.: A conditional mutual information estimator for mixed data and an associated conditional independence test. Entropy (Basel, Switzerland) **24**(9), 1234 (2022)

Simplified Concrete Dropout - Improving the Generation of Attribution Masks for Fine-Grained Classification

Dimitri Korsch$^{(\boxtimes)}$![ORCID], Maha Shadaydeh ![ORCID], and Joachim Denzler ![ORCID]

Computer Vision Group, Friedrich Schiller University Jena, Jena, Germany
{dimitri.korsch,maha.shadaydeh,joachim.denzler}@uni-jena.de
https://inf-cv.uni-jena.de

Abstract. Fine-grained classification is a particular case of a classification problem, aiming to classify objects that share the visual appearance and can only be distinguished by subtle differences. Fine-grained classification models are often deployed to determine animal species or individuals in automated animal monitoring systems. Precise visual explanations of the model's decision are crucial to analyze systematic errors. Attention- or gradient-based methods are commonly used to identify regions in the image that contribute the most to the classification decision. These methods deliver either too coarse or too noisy explanations, unsuitable for identifying subtle visual differences reliably. However, perturbation-based methods can precisely identify pixels causally responsible for the classification result. *Fill-in of the dropout* (FIDO) algorithm is one of those methods. It utilizes the *concrete dropout* (CD) to sample a set of attribution masks and updates the sampling parameters based on the output of the classification model. A known problem of the algorithm is a high variance in the gradient estimates, which the authors have mitigated until now by mini-batch updates of the sampling parameters. This paper presents a solution to circumvent these computational instabilities by simplifying the CD sampling and reducing reliance on large mini-batch sizes. First, it allows estimating the parameters with smaller mini-batch sizes without losing the quality of the estimates but with a reduced computational effort. Furthermore, our solution produces finer and more coherent attribution masks. Finally, we use the resulting attribution masks to improve the classification performance of a trained model without additional fine-tuning of the model.

Keywords: Perturbation-based counterfactuals · fine-grained classification · attribution masks · concrete dropout · gradient stability

1 Introduction

Fine-grained classification tackles the hard task of classifying objects that share the visual appearance and can only be distinguished by subtle differences, e.g.,

---

Supplementary Information The online version contains supplementary material available at https://doi.org/10.1007/978-3-031-54605-1_27.

U. Köthe and C. Rother (Eds.): DAGM GCPR 2023, LNCS 14264, pp. 409–424, 2024.
https://doi.org/10.1007/978-3-031-54605-1_27

animal species or car makes. Most commonly, fine-grained classification models are employed in the field of animal species recognition or animal individual identification: classification of insects [3,19] and birds [14,21,37], or identification of elephants [24], great apes [4,17,35,45], and sharks [15]. Even though these automated recognition systems surpass humans in terms of recognition performance, in some cases, an explanation of the system's decision might be beneficial even for experts. On the one hand, explanations might help in cases of uncertainty in human decisions. On the other hand, it can help to feedback information to the developer of the system if systematic errors in the decision are observable. Those systematic errors might be spurious biases in the learned models [32] and could be revealed by inspection of a highlighted region that should not be considered by a classification model.

Even though various methods [14,21,24,37] were presented in the context of fine-grained recognition to reliably distinguish classes with subtle visual differences, these methods offer either a too coarse-grained visual explanation or an explanation with many false positives.

Attention-based methods [13,14,47], for example, introduce attention mechanisms to enhance or diminish the values of intermediate features. They operate on intermediate feature representations, which always have a much lower resolution than the input image. Hence, upscaling the low-resolution attention to the higher-resolution image cannot highlight the fine-grained areas, which are often important for a reliable explanation of the decision.

Gradient-based methods [38–40] identify pixel-wise importance by computing the gradients of the classifier's decision w.r.t. the input image. These methods identify much finer areas in the image and enable decision visualization on the fine-grained level. However, these methods may also falsely highlight background pixels as has been shown in the work of Shrikumar et al. [36] and Adebayo et al. [1].

In this paper, we build upon a perturbation-based method, the fill-in of the dropout (FIDO) approach, proposed by Chang et al. [5]. The idea behind FIDO is to perturb the pixel values of the input image and observe the change in the classification decision. The authors realize the perturbation with a binary mask, whose entries model a binary decision whether to perturb a pixel or not. The mask is sampled using a set of trainable parameters and a sampling method introduced as concrete dropout (CD) by Gal et al. [9]. After optimizing the trainable parameters w.r.t. the classification decision, the parameters represent the importance of each pixel for the classification. One drawback of the approach is the high variance in estimating the gradients while optimizing the sampling parameters. Chang et al. mention this drawback in their work, and suggest reducing the variance by averaged gradients over a mini-batch of sampled masks.

We propose a mathematically equivalent but simplified version of CD. As a consequence, we reduce the amount of exponential and logarithm operations during the sampling procedure resulting in more stable gradient computations. We will show that the FIDO algorithm becomes less reliant on the size of the mini-batches, which allows the estimation of the attribution masks with smaller

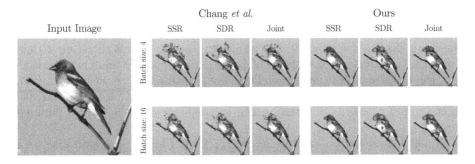

Fig. 1. Visual comparison of the original FIDO method and our proposed improvement. We estimated the masks using 30 optimization steps and two different batch sizes: 4 and 16. Our method produces masks that do not differ much for the visualized batch sizes. In contrast, the method of Chang *et al.* [5] strongly depends on higher batch sizes and produces more wrongly attributed pixels (e.g., the background or the tree branch) if the mini-batch size of 4 or less is used. Similarly to Chang *et al.*, we visualized only the mask values above the threshold of 0.5. *(best viewed in color)*

mini-batch sizes. To summarize our contribution: (1) the estimation of the attribution masks is possible with a smaller mini-batch size without losing quality but with a reduced computational effort; (2) our proposed solution results in more precise and coherent attribution masks, as Fig. 1 shows; (3) most importantly, we demonstrate that the estimated attribution mask can be leveraged for improving the classification performance of a fine-grained classification model. We outperform other baseline methods and achieve classification results comparable to a setup if ground truth bounding boxes are used.

2   Related Work

Attribution methods aim at estimating a saliency (or attribution) map for an input image that defines the importance of each area in the image for the desired task, e.g., for classification. We give a brief overview of three possible attribution methods that are often used in literature.

End-to-end trainable *attention methods* [13,14,47] present different approaches that modify the architecture of a CNN model. In general, these modifications estimate saliency maps, or attentions, for intermediate feature representations. The estimated saliencies are then used to enhance or diminish the feature values. Even though the estimated attention maps improve the classification significantly, they are coarse since they typically operate on intermediate representations right before the final classification layer. Consequently, up-scaling these attentions to the dimension of the original image cannot capture precisely the fine-grained details.

In contrast, *gradient-based methods* [20,38–40] estimate pixel-wise importance by computing gradients of the outputs (logit of the target class) w.r.t. the input pixels. Even though the resulting saliency map is much finer than attention-based saliencies, it often highlights lots of irrelevant areas in the image, e.g., the background of the image. This may be caused by gradient saturation, discontinuity in the activations of the network [36], or an inductive bias due to the convolutional architecture, which is independent of the learned parameters [1].

Finally, *perturbation-based methods* [5,7,8] attribute the importance to a pixel by modifying the pixel's value and observing the change in the network's output. These methods identify image regions that are significantly relevant for a given classification target. Hereby, two different objectives can be used to estimate these regions: (1) the estimation of the smallest region that retains a certain classification score, and (2) the estimation of the smallest region that minimizes the target classification score when this region is changed. Dabkowski and Gal [7] presented a method that follows the mentioned objectives and Chang *et al.* [5] reformulated these objectives in their fill-in of the dropout (FIDO) algorithm. They further presented different infill methods and their effects on the estimated saliency maps.

In this work, we utilize the FIDO algorithm and present a way to enhance the computation stability of the gradients. Furthermore, we propose a way to combine the resulting attribution masks into a joint attribution mask, which we finally use to improve the results of a fine-tuned classification model. As with all perturbation-based methods, we keep the advantage that neither a change of the architecture nor a fine-tuning of the parameters is required.

Fine-grained categorization is a special classification discipline that aims at distinguishing visually very similar objects, e.g., bird species [44], car models [23], moth species [33], or elephant individuals [24]. These objects often differ only in subtle visual features and the major challenge is to build a classification model that identifies these features reliably. On the one hand, it is common to utilize the input image as it is and either perform a smart *pre-training strategy* [6,22] or *aggregate feature* using different techniques [26,37]. On the other hand, there are the *part- or attention-based approaches* [13,14,20,47] that either extract relevant regions, so-called parts, in the input image or enhance and diminish intermediate feature values with attention mechanisms. Finally, *transformer-based approaches* [11,46] are currently at the top in different fine-grained classification benchmarks. However, these methods rely on the parameter-rich transformer architecture and big datasets for fine-tuning. Typically, in the context of automated animal monitoring these resources are not available making such models difficult to deploy in the field.

In this work, we use two widely used CNN architectures [12,41] fine-tuned on the CUB-200-2011 [44] dataset. Without any further modification or fine-tuning, we use the estimated attribution masks to extract an auxiliary crop of the original input image. Finally, we use the extracted crop to enhance the classification decision.

3   Simplified Concrete Dropout - Improved Stability

Our final goal is a pixel-wise attribution of importance for a certain classification output. Perturbation-based methods offer a way to estimate this importance by observing the causal relation between a perturbation of the input and the caused change in the decision of a classification model. One example is the *fill-in of the dropout* (FIDO) algorithm [5] which computes these attribution masks by identifying pixel regions defined as following:

1. Smallest destroying region (SDR) represents an image region that *minimizes* the classification score if this region is changed.
2. Smallest sufficient region (SSR) represents an image region that *maximizes* the classification score if only this region is retained from the original content.

Based on these definitions, the FIDO algorithm optimizes the parameters of a binary dropout mask. The mask identifies whether a pixel value should be perturbed with an alternative representation (*infill*) or not, and can be interpreted as a saliency map. In the following, we formalize the objective functions, illustrate the limitation of the FIDO algorithm, and explain our suggested improvements.

3.1   The FIDO Algorithm and Its Limitations

Given an image $\mathbf{x}$ with N pixels, a class c, a differential classification model $\mathcal{M}$ producing an output distribution $p_{\mathcal{M}}(c|\mathbf{x})$, we are interested in a subset of pixels r that divides the image into two parts $\mathbf{x} = \mathbf{x}_r \cup \mathbf{x}_{\backslash r}$. Observing the classifier's output when $\mathbf{x}_r$ is not visible gives insights into the importance of the region r for the classification decision. Because of the binary division of the image into two parts, the region r can be modeled by a binary dropout mask $\mathbf{z} \in \{0,1\}^N$ with the same size[1] as $\mathbf{x}$ and an infill function ϕ that linearly combines the original image $\mathbf{x}$ and an infill $\hat{\mathbf{x}}$ with an element-wise multiplication $\odot$:

$$\phi(\mathbf{x}, \mathbf{z}) = (1 - \mathbf{z}) \odot \mathbf{x} + \mathbf{z} \odot \hat{\mathbf{x}} \quad . \tag{1}$$

There are different ways to generate an infill image $\hat{\mathbf{x}}$. First, content-independent approaches, like random (uniformly or normally distributed), or fixed (e.g., zeros) pixel values, generate the infill image independently of the input's content. Because these methods are independent of the content of the image, they cause a hard domain shift for the underlying classification model. Chang *et al.* [5] showed that these infill approaches perform worse compared to content-aware methods like GANs [10] or Gaussian blur. Popescu *et al.* [30] used knockoffs [2] to generate infill values and reported in their work superiority of knockoff infills on the MNIST dataset [25]. All of these content-aware methods generate the infill image depending on the pixels of the original image and

---

[1] For sake of simplicity, we consider $\mathbf{x}$ and $\mathbf{z}$ as 1D vectors, instead of 2D matrices with dimensions H and W, and $N = H \cdot W$.

retain the structure and composition of the original image to some degree. In our experiments, we use the Gaussian blur approach to create the infill image $\hat{\mathbf{x}}$. First, it removes the fine-grained details we aim to identify but retains the contents of the image so that the infill is not an out-of-domain input for the classification model. Second, the knockoff generation, proposed by Popescu *et al.*, is suitable for MNIST images because of the low dimensionality of the images (28×28 px) and the binary pixel values. Unfortunately, to this point, there is no way to apply this generation process to real-world RGB images. Finally, the GAN-based infills are computationally intensive and require an additional model that has to be trained on data related to the images we want to analyze.

The search space of all possible binary masks $\mathbf{z}$ grows exponentially with the number of pixels, hence we need an efficient way to estimate the values $z_n \in \mathbf{z}$. Assuming a Bernoulli distribution for the binary mask values allows us to sample the masks from a parametrized distribution $q_\theta(\mathbf{z})$ and optimize the parameters $\theta_n \in \theta$ using the SSR and SDR objectives:

$$L_{SSR}(\theta) = \mathbb{E}_{q_\theta(\mathbf{z})} \left[-s_\mathcal{M}(c|\phi(\mathbf{x}, \mathbf{z})) + \lambda ||\mathbf{1} - \mathbf{z}||_1 \right] \quad \text{and} \tag{2}$$

$$L_{SDR}(\theta) = \mathbb{E}_{q_\theta(\mathbf{z})} \left[\quad s_\mathcal{M}(c|\phi(\mathbf{x}, \mathbf{z})) + \lambda ||\mathbf{z}||_1 \right] \tag{3}$$

with the L_1 regularization factor λ. Following the original work, we set $\lambda = 0.001$. The score $s_\mathcal{M}$ is defined as log-odds of classification probabilities:

$$s_\mathcal{M}(c|\mathbf{x}) = \log \frac{p_\mathcal{M}(c|\mathbf{x})}{1 - p_\mathcal{M}(c|\mathbf{x})} \quad . \tag{4}$$

To be able to optimize θ through a discrete random mask $\mathbf{z}$, the authors relax the discrete Bernoulli distribution and replace it with a continuous approximation: the concrete distribution [16,28]. The resulting sampling, called *concrete dropout* (CD), was proposed by Gal *et al.* [9] and is defined as

$$z_n = \sigma \left(\frac{1}{t} \left(\log \frac{\theta_n}{1 - \theta_n} + \log \frac{\eta}{1 - \eta} \right) \right) \quad \eta \sim \mathcal{U}(0, 1) \tag{5}$$

with the temperature parameter t (we follow the original work and set this parameter to 0.1), σ being the sigmoid function, and η sampled from a uniform distribution.

In the original work, Chang *et al.* [5] proposed two methods to speed up convergence and avoid unnatural artifacts during the optimization process. First, they computed the gradients w.r.t. θ from a mini-batch of dropout masks. They mentioned in Appendix (A.6) that they observed unsatisfactory results with mini-batch sizes less than 4, which they attributed to the *high variance* in the gradient estimates. Second, they sampled a coarser dropout mask (e.g. 56×56) and upsampled the mask using bi-linear interpolation to the dimensions of the input (e.g. 224×224).

In the following, we reflect upon the cause of the high variance in the gradient estimates and propose a way to increase the computational stability. Consequently, our solution reduces the dependency of the FIDO method on the mini-batch size, allowing the estimation of the attribution masks with lower mini-batch sizes which ultimately reduces the computation time. Finally, since we are interested in fine-grained details in the image, the estimation of a coarser attribution mask followed by an upsampling operation would not lead to the desired level of detail. With our solution and the resulting improvement in the gradient computation, we can directly estimate a full-sized attribution mask θ without any unnatural artifacts, as shown in Fig. 1.

3.2   Improving Computational Stability

The sampling of $\mathbf{z}$ using CD requires that all dropout parameters $\theta_n \in \theta$ are in the range $[0, 1]$. One way to achieve this is to initialize the attribution mask with real-valued parameters $\vartheta_n \in \mathbb{R}$ and apply the sigmoid function to those: $\theta_n = \sigma(\vartheta_n)$. As a consequence, the CD sampling procedure for $\mathbf{z}$, as described in Eq. 5, is a chaining of multiple exponential and logarithmic operations. This can be easily implemented in the current deep learning frameworks and is a common practice, e.g., in the reference implementation of Gal *et al.*[2]. However, we hypothesize that exactly this chaining of operations causes a high variance in the gradient estimates, and we validate this assumption in our experiments.

Under the assumption that θ is the output of the sigmoid function, we can simplify the sampling procedure of the attribution mask $\mathbf{z}$ and mitigate the before-mentioned problem. First, for readability reasons, we substitute the uniform noise part with a single variable $\hat{\eta} = \log \frac{\eta}{1-\eta}$ in Eq. 5. Then after using the transformation $\theta_n = \sigma(\vartheta_n)$ from above, expanding the argument of the sigmoid function, and simplifying the terms, the sampling of the binary mask $\mathbf{z}$ using CD transforms to a simple sigmoid function:

$$z_n = \sigma\left(\frac{1}{t}\left(\log\frac{\sigma(\vartheta_n)}{1 - \sigma(\vartheta_n)} + \hat{\eta}\right)\right) \tag{6}$$

$$= \sigma\left(\frac{1}{t}\left(\log\frac{(1 + \exp(-\vartheta_n))^{-1}}{1 - (1 + \exp(-\vartheta_n))^{-1}} + \hat{\eta}\right)\right) \tag{7}$$

$$= \sigma\left(\frac{1}{t}\left(\log\frac{1}{\exp(-\vartheta_n)} + \hat{\eta}\right)\right) = \sigma\left(\frac{\vartheta_n + \hat{\eta}}{t}\right) \quad . \tag{8}$$

The resulting formula is equivalent to the original formulation of CD. However, the reduction of exponential and logarithmic operations, and hence the reduction of the number of operations in the gradient computation, are the major benefits of the simplified version in Eq. 8. As a result, it reduces computational inaccuracies and enhances the propagation of the gradients. Consequently, the

---

[2] https://github.com/yaringal/ConcreteDropout.

optimization of the parameters ϑ, and of the attribution map defined by θ, converges to more precise and better results as we show in Sect. 4.

In Sect. S2 of our supplementary material, we performed an empirical evaluation of this statement and showed that our proposed simplifications result in a lower variance of the gradient estimates. Additionally, you can find in Sect. S1 a Python implementation of the improved Concrete Dropout layer using the PyTorch [29] framework.

3.3   Combined Attribution Mask for Fine-Grained Classification

So far, we only applied operations on the original formulation to simplify Eq. 5 from the original work of Chang *et al.* [5]. However, we can also show that the estimated attribution masks improve the performance of a classification model. First, we follow Chang *et al.* and only consider mask entries with an importance rate above 0.5. Then, we estimate a bounding box around the selected values of the attribution mask. In the end, we use this bounding box to crop a patch from the input image and use it as an additional input to the classification model (see Sect. 4.3). Instead of using the attribution masks separately, we are interested in regions that are important to sustain and should not be deleted. Hence, we propose to combine the attribution masks θ_{SSR} and θ_{SDR} using element-wise multiplication of mask values followed by a square root as a normalization function:

$$\theta_{joint} = \sqrt{\theta_{SSR} \odot (1 - \theta_{SDR})} \quad . \tag{9}$$

With element-wise multiplication, we ensure that if either of the attribution values is low, then the joint attribution is also low. The square root normalizes the joint values to the range where we can apply the same threshold (0.5): for example, if both attribution values are around 0.5, then also the joint attribution will be around 0.5 and not around 0.25.

4   Experiments

We performed all experiments on the CUB-200-2011 [44] dataset. It consists of 5994 training and 5794 test images for 200 different species of birds. It is the most used fine-grained dataset for benchmarking because of its balanced sample distribution. We selected this dataset mainly because it also contains ground truth bounding box annotations, which we used as one of our baselines in Sect. 4.3

Figure 1 shows a qualitative comparison of the estimated masks on one example image of the CUB-200-2011 dataset. Notably, our solution is more stable when we use smaller mini-batch sizes and produces fewer false positive attributions, e.g., in the background or highlighting of the tree branch.

We evaluated two widely used CNN architectures pre-trained on the ImageNet [34] dataset: ResNet50 [12] and InceptionV3 [41]. Additionally, we used

Fig. 2. Examples of the estimated masks for the *Red-winged Blackbird* and the *Yellow-headed Blackbird* using the original FIDO approach and our proposed improved method. Besides the ground-truth segmentation masks, we also reported the intersection over union (IoU) of the estimated mask with the ground-truth. (Color figure online)

an alternative pre-training on the iNaturalist2017 dataset [43] for the InceptionV3 architecture proposed by Cui *et al.* [6] (denoted with INCV3* and INCEPTIONV3* in Tables 1 and 2, respectively). All architectures are fine-tuned for 60 epochs on the CUB-200-2011 dataset using the AdamW [27] optimizer with the learning rate of 1×10^{-3} (and ϵ set to 0.1)[3].

4.1   Evaluating Mask Precision

To quantify the visual observations in Fig. 1, we selected two visually similar classes of Blackbirds from the CUB-200-2011 dataset: the Red-winged Blackbird and the Yellow-headed Blackbird. Both belong to the family of Icterids (New World blackbirds) and have black as a dominant plumage color. However, as the name of the species indicates, the main visual feature distinguishing these birds from other black-feathered birds is the **red wing** or the **yellow head**. Using this information, we created segmentation masks with the *Segment Anything* model [18] for the mentioned regions and used these as ground truth.

We fine-tuned a classification model (ResNet50 [12]) on the entire dataset and estimated the attribution masks using both methods: the original FIDO approach by Chang *et al.* [5] and our improved method. We evaluated different mini-batch sizes and a different number of optimization steps. Both of these parameters strongly affect the runtime of the algorithm. After an attribution mask was estimated, we selected only the values above the threshold of 0.5 and computed the IoU with the ground truth mask. We performed this evaluation for the masks estimated by the SSR and SDR objectives separately as well as using the joint mask as defined in Eq. 9.

In Fig. 3, we report the IoU results of the mentioned setups. First, the plot shows that our solution (solid lines) outperforms the original approach (dashed lines) in every constellation of the hyperparameters. Next, the optimization process becomes less sensitive to the size of the mini-batches. This can be seen either

---

[3] Changing the default parameter smooths the training, as suggested in
   https://www.tensorflow.org/api_docs/python/tf/keras/optimizers/Adam#notes_2.

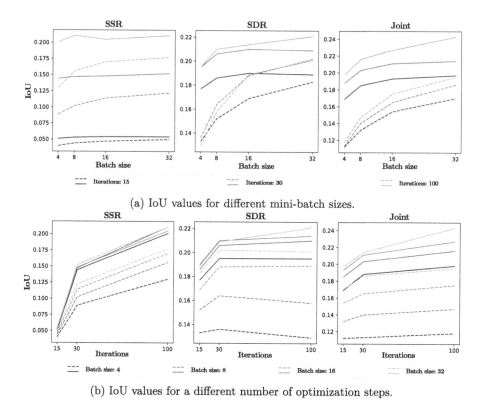

(a) IoU values for different mini-batch sizes.

(b) IoU values for a different number of optimization steps.

Fig. 3. Intersection over union (IoU) of the estimated masks with the ground-truth annotations of a discriminative region. We tested different values for the hyperparameters mini-batch size (a) and the number of optimization steps (b). Our proposed method (solid lines) outperforms the original work (dashed lines) and shows less sensitivity against the mini-batch size. *(best viewed in color)*

by the slope (Fig. 3a) or the variance (Fig. 3b) of the IoU curves. Our method achieved the same quality of the attribution masks with smaller mini-batch sizes. Consequently, by reducing the mini-batch size, the number of sampled dropout masks at every optimization step is also reduced. Hence, by using a mini-batch size of 8 instead of 32, which Chang *et al.* use in their work, we could reduce the computation time per image from 40 to 11 seconds[4] for 100 optimization steps.

In Fig. 2, we visualized four examples of the mentioned classes, our annotated segmentation masks, and the results of both approaches after 100 optimization steps and using a mini-batch size of 8.

---

[4] We processed the images using an Intel i9-10940X CPU, 128GB RAM, and a GeForce RTX 3090 GPU.

Table 1. Comparison of the original solution proposed by Chang *et al.* and our improved implementation in terms of mask coherency. For different model architectures and different mask estimation objectives, we report the total variation as defined in Eq. 10 (*lower is better*).

	SSR			SDR			JOINT		
	RN50	INCV3	INCV3*	RN50	INCV3	INCV3*	RN50	INCV3	INCV3*
CHANG *et al.* [5]	39.74	32.44	27.79	44.21	45.53	37.81	37.61	33.92	28.66
OURS	17.54	18.18	17.37	22.72	21.87	20.20	16.95	15.21	14.06

4.2 Mask Coherency

Following Dabkowski *et al.* [7], Chang *et al.* propose to use total variation regularization with a weighting factor of 0.01, which is defined as

$$\text{TV}(\mathbf{z}) = \sum_{i,j} (z_{i,j} - z_{i,j+1})^2 + \sum_{i,j} (z_{i,j} - z_{i+1,j})^2 \quad . \tag{10}$$

We observed that the high variance in the gradients affects the coherency of the masks (see Fig. 1). Hence, we computed the total variance of the estimated masks and reported the results in Table 1. The total variation is computed for the attribution masks estimated for the entire CUB-200-2011 dataset with the original approach and our proposed solution. The results show that our solution produces more coherent masks, meaning the identified regions are more connected.

4.3 Test-Time Augmentation of a Fine-Grained Classifier

Given a model fine-tuned on the CUB-200-2011 dataset, we evaluated in this experiment how we can use the estimated attribution masks to improve the classification performance of the model. In addition to the prediction of the baseline models, we used different methods to extract one auxiliary crop from the original image and compute the prediction using this crop. Then, we averaged the predictions and report the resulting accuracies in Table 2. This way of classification improvement is widely used to different extent. He *et al.* [12] or Szegedy *et al.* [41], for example, use ten or 144 crops in their work, respectively. Hu *et al.* [14], as another example, perform attention cropping to enhance the prediction of the classifier. In our setup, we extracted a single crop using different methods, which we explain in the following.

Ground-Truth Bounding Boxes: We utilized the bounding box annotations of the CUB-200-2011 dataset. First, we only used the crops identified by the bounding boxes. Second, we combined the predictions from the cropped image and the original image, by averaging the predictions.

Table 2. Comparison of the classification performance using different test-time augmentation (TTA) methods on the CUB-200-2011 dataset. Besides the baselines (no TTA or ground truth bounding boxes), we also evaluated heuristic methods (random or center crop), content-aware methods (GradCam or a bird detector), and two different FIDO implementations (the original work of Chang *et al.* and our proposed improvement). We report the accuracy (in %).

	RESNET50	INCEPTIONV3	INCEPTIONV3*
BASELINE (BL)	82.78	79.86	90.32
GT BOUNDING BOXES ONLY	84.38	81.31	90.18
BL + GT BOUNDING BOXES	84.55	81.65	90.70
BL + RANDOM CROP	83.41	80.45	89.99
BL + CENTER CROP	83.83	81.07	90.16
BL + GRADIENT [20]	83.74	80.76	90.02
BL + BIRDYOLO [42]	83.81	81.12	90.39
BL + FIDO [5]	84.17	81.67	90.47
BL + FIDO (OURS)	**84.67**	**81.77**	**90.51**

Center and Random Crop: Following the motivation behind the crops used by He *et al.* [12] and Szegedy *et al.* [41] that the object of interest is likely to be in the center, we cropped the center of the image. Furthermore, we also extracted a random crop. For both methods, we set the size of the crop to be 75 % of the width and height of the original image. These methods are content-agnostic and use only heuristics to estimate the region to crop.

Gradient Crop: As a first content-aware method, we computed the gradients w.r.t. the input image [38]. We utilized the pre-processing and thresholding of the gradient as presented by Korsch *et al.* [20], estimated a bounding box around the resulting saliency map, and cropped the original image based on the estimated bounding box.

BirdYOLO is a YOLOv3 [31] detection model pre-trained on a bird detection dataset [42]. For each image, we used the bounding box with the highest confidence score, extended it to a square, and cropped the original image accordingly.

FIDO: Finally, we utilized the joint mask computed from the SSR and SDR masks of the FIDO algorithm as defined in Eq. 9. On the one hand, we used the masks estimated by the original work of Chang *et al.* [5], and on the other hand, the masks estimated with our proposed improvements.

The results in Table 2 show that compared to the baseline model the ground truth bounding boxes yield a higher classification accuracy, even if solely using the bounding box crops for classification. Next, we can see that even such content-agnostic methods like center or random cropping can boost classification performance. Similar improvements can be achieved by content-aware methods like gradients or a detection model. We observed the most improvement with the FIDO algorithm, and finally with our proposed solution we achieved the best results that are comparable to using ground-truth bounding boxes.

5   Conclusions

In this paper, we proposed a simplified version of the concrete dropout (CD). The CD is used in the fill-in of the dropout (FIDO) algorithm to sample a set of attribution masks based on an underlying parametrized distribution. Using these masks, one can estimate how relevant a specific image pixel was for the classification decision. The parameters of the distribution are optimized based on the classification score but the optimization process suffers from a high variance in the gradient computation if the original formulation of CD is used. Our solution simplifies the sampling computations and results in more stable gradient estimations. Our approach maintains the quality of the estimated masks while reducing computational effort due to smaller mini-batch sizes during the optimization process. Furthermore, the resulting attribution masks contain fewer falsely attributed regions. We also presented a way of using the estimated fine-grained attribution masks to enhance the classification decision. Compared with other classification baselines, our solution produces the best result and even performs comparably to a setup where ground truth bounding boxes are used.

As an extension, our proposed single-crop TTA can be extended with a part-based approach to further boost the classification performance. Alternatively, a repeated iterative estimation of the masks may be worth an investigation.

References

1. Adebayo, J., Gilmer, J., Muelly, M., Goodfellow, I., Hardt, M., Kim, B.: Sanity checks for saliency maps. Adv. Neural Inf. Process. Syst. **31**, 1–11 (2018)
2. Barber, R.F., Candès, E.J.: Controlling the false discovery rate via knockoffs (2015)
3. Bjerge, K., Nielsen, J.B., Sepstrup, M.V., Helsing-Nielsen, F., Høye, T.T.: An automated light trap to monitor moths (lepidoptera) using computer vision-based tracking and deep learning. Sensors **21**(2), 343 (2021)
4. Brust, C.A., et al.: Towards automated visual monitoring of individual gorillas in the wild. In: ICCV Workshop on Visual Wildlife Monitoring (ICCV-WS), pp. 2820–2830 (2017). https://doi.org/10.1109/ICCVW.2017.333
5. Chang, C.H., Creager, E., Goldenberg, A., Duvenaud, D.: Explaining image classifiers by counterfactual generation. In: International Conference on Learning Representations (2018)
6. Cui, Y., Song, Y., Sun, C., Howard, A., Belongie, S.: Large scale fine-grained categorization and domain-specific transfer learning. In: Proceedings of CVPR (2018). https://doi.org/10.1109/cvpr.2018.00432
7. Dabkowski, P., Gal, Y.: Real time image saliency for black box classifiers. Adv. Neural Inf. Process. Syst. **30**, 1–10 (2017)
8. Fong, R.C., Vedaldi, A.: Interpretable explanations of black boxes by meaningful perturbation. In: Proceedings of the IEEE International Conference on Computer Vision, pp. 3429–3437 (2017)

9. Gal, Y., Hron, J., Kendall, A.: Concrete dropout. Adv. Neural Inf. Process. Syst. **30** (2017)

10. Goodfellow, I., et al.: Generative adversarial networks. Commun. ACM **63**(11), 139–144 (2020)

11. He, J., et al.: Transfg: a transformer architecture for fine-grained recognition. In: Proceedings of the AAAI Conference on Artificial Intelligence, vol. 36, pp. 852–860 (2022)

12. He, K., Zhang, X., Ren, S., Sun, J.: Deep residual learning for image recognition. In: Proceedings of the IEEE Conference on Computer Vision and Pattern Recognition, pp. 770–778 (2016)

13. He, X., Peng, Y., Zhao, J.: Which and how many regions to gaze: focus discriminative regions for fine-grained visual categorization. In: IJCV, pp. 1–21 (2019)

14. Hu, T., Qi, H., Huang, Q., Lu, Y.: See better before looking closer: weakly supervised data augmentation network for fine-grained visual classification. arXiv preprint arXiv:1901.09891 (2019)

15. Hughes, B., Burghardt, T.: Automated visual fin identification of individual great white sharks. Int. J. Comput. Vision **122**(3), 542–557 (2017)

16. Jang, E., Gu, S., Poole, B.: Categorical reparameterization with gumbel-softmax. In: 5th International Conference on Learning Representations, ICLR 2017, Toulon, France, 24–26 April 2017, Conference Track Proceedings. OpenReview.net (2017). https://openreview.net/forum?id=rkE3y85ee

17. Käding, C., Rodner, E., Freytag, A., Mothes, O., Barz, B., Denzler, J.: Active learning for regression tasks with expected model output changes. In: British Machine Vision Conference (BMVC) (2018)

18. Kirillov, A., et al.: Segment anything. arXiv:2304.02643 (2023)

19. Korsch, D., Bodesheim, P., Brehm, G., Denzler, J.: Automated visual monitoring of nocturnal insects with light-based camera traps. In: CVPR Workshop on Fine-grained Visual Classification (CVPR-WS) (2022)

20. Korsch, D., Bodesheim, P., Denzler, J.: Classification-specific parts for improving fine-grained visual categorization. In: Proceedings of the German Conference on Pattern Recognition, pp. 62–75 (2019)

21. Korsch, D., Bodesheim, P., Denzler, J.: End-to-end learning of fisher vector encodings for part features in fine-grained recognition. In: German Conference on Pattern Recognition (DAGM-GCPR), pp. 142–158 (2021). https://doi.org/10.1007/978-3-030-92659-5_9

22. Krause, J., et al.: The unreasonable effectiveness of noisy data for fine-grained recognition. In: Leibe, B., Matas, J., Sebe, N., Welling, M. (eds.) ECCV 2016. LNCS, vol. 9907, pp. 301–320. Springer, Cham (2016). https://doi.org/10.1007/978-3-319-46487-9_19

23. Krause, J., Stark, M., Deng, J., Fei-Fei, L.: 3d object representations for fine-grained categorization. In: 4th International IEEE Workshop on 3D Representation and Recognition (3dRR-13) (2013). https://doi.org/10.1109/iccvw.2013.77

24. Körschens, M., Denzler, J.: Elpephants: a fine-grained dataset for elephant re-identification. In: ICCV Workshop on Computer Vision for Wildlife Conservation (ICCV-WS) (2019)

25. LeCun, Y., Cortes, C., Burges, C., et al.: Mnist handwritten digit database (2010)

26. Lin, T.Y., RoyChowdhury, A., Maji, S.: Bilinear cnn models for fine-grained visual recognition. In: Proceedings of ICCV, pp. 1449–1457 (2015). https://doi.org/10.1109/iccv.2015.170

27. Loshchilov, I., Hutter, F.: Decoupled weight decay regularization. In: International Conference on Learning Representations (2018)

28. Maddison, C., Mnih, A., Teh, Y.: The concrete distribution: a continuous relaxation of discrete random variables. In: Proceedings of the International Conference on Learning Representations. International Conference on Learning Representations (2017)

29. Paszke, A., et al.: Automatic differentiation in pytorch (2017)

30. Popescu, O.I., Shadaydeh, M., Denzler, J.: Counterfactual generation with knock-offs. arXiv preprint arXiv:2102.00951 (2021)

31. Redmon, J., Farhadi, A.: Yolov3: an incremental improvement. arXiv preprint arXiv:1804.02767 (2018)

32. Reimers, C., Penzel, N., Bodesheim, P., Runge, J., Denzler, J.: Conditional dependence tests reveal the usage of abcd rule features and bias variables in automatic skin lesion classification. In: CVPR ISIC Skin Image Analysis Workshop (CVPR-WS), pp. 1810–1819 (2021)

33. Rodner, E., Simon, M., Brehm, G., Pietsch, S., Wägele, J.W., Denzler, J.: Fine-grained recognition datasets for biodiversity analysis. In: CVPR Workshop on Fine-grained Visual Classification (CVPR-WS) (2015)

34. Russakovsky, O., et al.: Imagenet large scale visual recognition challenge. Int. J. Comput. Vision **115**(3), 211–252 (2015)

35. Sakib, F., Burghardt, T.: Visual recognition of great ape behaviours in the wild. In: International Conference on Pattern Recognition (ICPR) Workshop on Visual Observation and Analysis of Vertebrate And Insect Behavior (2021)

36. Shrikumar, A., Greenside, P., Kundaje, A.: Learning important features through propagating activation differences. In: International Conference on Machine Learning, pp. 3145–3153. PMLR (2017)

37. Simon, M., Rodner, E., Darell, T., Denzler, J.: The whole is more than its parts? from explicit to implicit pose normalization. IEEE Trans. Pattern Anal. Mach. Intell. **42**, 749–763 (2018). https://doi.org/10.1109/TPAMI.2018.2885764

38. Simonyan, K., Vedaldi, A., Zisserman, A.: Deep inside convolutional networks: visualising image classification models and saliency maps. In: Proceedings of the International Conference on Learning Representations (ICLR). ICLR (2014)

39. Springenberg, J.T., Dosovitskiy, A., Brox, T., Riedmiller, M.: Striving for simplicity: the all convolutional net. In: ICLR (Workshop Track) (2015)

40. Sundararajan, M., Taly, A., Yan, Q.: Axiomatic attribution for deep networks. In: International Conference on Machine Learning, pp. 3319–3328. PMLR (2017)

41. Szegedy, C., Vanhoucke, V., Ioffe, S., Shlens, J., Wojna, Z.: Rethinking the inception architecture for computer vision. In: Proceedings of the IEEE Conference on Computer Vision and Pattern Recognition (2016)

42. Tran, B.: Bird detection by yolo-v3. https://github.com/xmba15/yolov3_pytorch (2023). Accessed 30 May 2023

43. Van Horn, G., et al.: The inaturalist species classification and detection dataset. In: Proceedings of the IEEE Conference on Computer Vision and Pattern Recognition, pp. 8769–8778 (2018)

44. Wah, C., Branson, S., Welinder, P., Perona, P., Belongie, S.: The caltech-ucsd birds-200-2011 dataset. Technical Report. CNS-TR-2011-001, California Institute of Technology (2011)

45. Yang, X., Mirmehdi, M., Burghardt, T.: Great ape detection in challenging jungle camera trap footage via attention-based spatial and temporal feature blending. In: Proceedings of the IEEE/CVF International Conference on Computer Vision Workshops (2019)

46. Yu, W., et al.: Metaformer is actually what you need for vision. In: Proceedings of the IEEE/CVF Conference on Computer Vision and Pattern Recognition, pp. 10819–10829 (2022)
47. Zhang, L., Huang, S., Liu, W., Tao, D.: Learning a mixture of granularity-specific experts for fine-grained categorization. In: Proceedings of ICCV, pp. 8331–8340 (2019)

Weak Supervision and Online Learning

Best Practices in Active Learning for Semantic Segmentation

Sudhanshu Mittal[1]([⊠]), Joshua Niemeijer[2], Jörg P. Schäfer[2], and Thomas Brox[1]

[1] University of Freiburg, Freiburg im Breisgau, Germany
{mittal,brox}@cs.uni-freiburg.de
[2] German Aerospace Center (DLR), Braunschweig, Germany
{Joshua.Niemeijer,Joerg.Schaefer}@dlr.de

Abstract. Active learning is particularly of interest for semantic segmentation, where annotations are costly. Previous academic studies focused on datasets that are already very diverse and where the model is trained in a supervised manner with a large annotation budget. In contrast, data collected in many driving scenarios is highly redundant, and most medical applications are subject to very constrained annotation budgets. This work investigates the various types of existing active learning methods for semantic segmentation under diverse conditions across three dimensions - data distribution w.r.t. different redundancy levels, integration of semi-supervised learning, and different labeling budgets. We find that these three underlying factors are decisive for the selection of the best active learning approach. As an outcome of our study, we provide a comprehensive usage guide to obtain the best performance for each case. It is the first systematic study that investigates these dimensions covering a wide range of settings including more than 3K model training runs. In this work, we also propose an exemplary evaluation task for driving scenarios, where data has high redundancy, to showcase the practical implications of our research findings.

Keywords: Active Learning · Semantic Segmentation

1 Introduction

The objective of active learning is the reduction of annotation cost by selecting those samples for annotation, which are expected to yield the largest increase in the model's performance. It assumes that raw data can be collected in abundance for most large-scale data applications, such as autonomous driving, but annotation limits the use of this data. Semantic segmentation is particularly costly, as it requires pixel-level annotations. Active learning is, besides weakly supervised and semi-supervised learning, among the best-known ways to deal with this situation.

S. Mittal and J. Niemeijer—These authors contributed equally to this work.

Supplementary Information The online version contains supplementary material available at https://doi.org/10.1007/978-3-031-54605-1_28.

© The Author(s), under exclusive license to Springer Nature Switzerland AG 2024
U. Köthe and C. Rother (Eds.): DAGM GCPR 2023, LNCS 14264, pp. 427–442, 2024.
https://doi.org/10.1007/978-3-031-54605-1_28

Table 1. We study active learning (AL) methods for semantic segmentation over 3 dimensions - dataset distribution, annotation budget, and integration of semi-supervised learning (SSL-AL). Green cells denote newly studied settings in this work. Previous AL works correspond to the grey cells. This work provides a guide to use AL under all shown conditions.

Dataset↓	Annotation Budget			
	Low		High	
Supervision →	AL	SSL-AL	AL	SSL-AL
Diverse	✓	✓	✓	✓
Redundant	✓	✓	✓	✓

In a typical deep active learning process, a batch of samples is acquired from a large unlabeled pool for annotation using an acquisition function and is added to the training scheme. This sampling is done over multiple cycles until an acceptable performance is reached or the annotation budget is exhausted. The acquisition function can be either a single-sample-based acquisition function, where a score is given to each sample individually or a batch-based acquisition function, where a cumulative score is given to the whole selected batch. Existing active learning methods for semantic segmentation assign the score to the sample either based on uncertainty [15,25,35] or representational value [34,35,37]. Most AL methods in the literature are evaluated on datasets like PASCAL-VOC [10], Cityscapes [6], and CamVid [1]. The shared attribute between these AL benchmark datasets is that they are highly diverse, as they were initially curated to provide comprehensive coverage of their corresponding domains. This curation process, however, is a sort of annotation because it is typically not feasible in an entirely automated way.

State-of-the-art active learning methods for segmentation have been evaluated only in a particular experimental setup - highly diverse benchmark datasets with a comparatively large annotation budget; see Table 1. We seek answers to specific missing questions not captured by previous works.

1. How do different active learning methods perform when the dataset has many redundant samples? Samples with highly overlapping information are referred to as redundant samples, for example, the consecutive frames of a video. Many commonly used segmentation datasets were originally collected as videos for practical reasons, e.g., Cityscapes, CamVid, BDD100k [40]. Since active learning methods were only tested on filtered versions of these datasets, their applicability on redundant datasets is open and highly relevant.

2. What happens when the initial unlabeled pool is also used for training along with annotated samples using semi-supervised learning (SSL)? For image classification, many works [13,18,26,28] have shown that integration of SSL into AL is advantageous. For semantic segmentation, this combination is not well studied.

3. What happens when the annotation budget is low? Which methods

scale best in such low-budget settings? Semantic segmentation annotations can be expensive for specific applications, especially in the medical domain. Therefore, it is critical to understand the behavior of the various active learning methods in low-budget settings.

In this work, we report the results of an empirical study designed to find answers to the above-raised questions. We study 5 existing active learning methods across the three dimensions as mentioned above - subject to different data distributions w.r.t. redundancy in the dataset, including the integration of semi-supervised learning, and under low as well as large annotation budget settings, as shown in Table 1. The outcome of this study yields new insights and provides, as the major contribution of this work, a guideline for the best selection of available techniques under the various tested conditions. Additionally, we show that active learning in a low annotation budget setting can be particularly volatile, even nullifying the complete need for it in some cases. This further emphasizes the importance of knowing the underlying data distribution.

We also suggest a new evaluation task (A2D2-3K) for driving scenarios based on the highly redundant A2D2 dataset, which is closer to the raw data collection scheme. The experiment outcome on this task aligns with the findings of our study for redundant dataset type with a high annotation budget setting and shows that there is a strong case for using active learning in this context.

2   Deep Active Learning

We briefly review the state of the art in deep active learning as relevant for our study. In particular, we review the available acquisition methods, the special considerations for segmentation, and the integration of semi-supervised learning.

The acquisition methods can be categorized into single-sample-based and batch-based approaches. They assess the value of new samples for selecting individually and collectively as a batch, respectively.

Single sample acquisition takes the top b samples according to the score of the acquisition function to select a batch of size b. Several methods follow this selection scheme based on either epistemic uncertainty or representation score. For example, uncertainty-based methods try to select the most uncertain samples to acquire a batch. Many methods, such as EquAL [15], Ensemble+AT [24], and CEAL [36], estimate uncertainty based on the output probabilities. Epistemic uncertainty, estimated using Entropy [32], is often used a as strong baseline in several active learning works [15,29,33]. Some methods, namely BALD [17] and DBAL [12] employed a Bayesian approach using Monte Carlo Dropout [11] to measure the epistemic uncertainty. Representation-based methods aim to select the most representative samples of the dataset that are not yet covered by the labeled samples. Numerous adversarial learning-based methods utilize an auxiliary network to score samples based on this measure, including DAAL [37], VAAL [35], and WAAL [34]. For our study, we employ Entropy, EquAL, and BALD to represent single-sample acquisition methods due to their direct applicability to segmentation tasks.

Batch-based acquisition methods acquire the whole batch of size b to maximize cumulative information gain. Sener *et al.* [31] formulated the acquisition function as a core-set selection approach based on the feature representations. It is a representation-based approach that selects the batch of samples jointly to represent the whole data distribution. BatchBALD [23] is a greedy algorithm that selects a batch of points by estimating the joint mutual information between the whole batch and the model parameters. This method was also proposed to remedy the mode collapse issue, where the acquisition function collapses into selecting only similar samples (see Sect. 4.1 for details). However, it is limited to simple image classification datasets like MNIST [8] since its computation complexity grows exponentially with the batch size. Some more recent batch-based methods include k-MEANS++ [41], GLISTER [21], ADS [19], but these methods only evaluate on image classification tasks. For the study, we selected the Coreset method [31] to represent batch-based methods due to its effectiveness, simplicity, and easy scalability to the segmentation task.

2.1 Active Learning for Semantic Segmentation

When applied to semantic segmentation, active learning methods must choose which area of the image is to be considered for the acquisition: the full image [35], superpixels [2], polygons [15,27], or each pixel [33]. Our study uses the straightforward image-wise selection and annotation procedure.

Most existing methods for segmentation are based on the model's uncertainty for the input image, where the average score over all pixels in the image is used to select top-k images. **Entropy** [32] (estimated uncertainty) is a widely used active learning baseline for selection. This function computes per-pixel entropy for the predicted output and uses the averaged entropy as the final score. **EquAL** [15] determines the uncertainty based on the consistency of the prediction on the original image and its horizontally flipped version. The average value over all the pixels is used as the final score. **BALD** [17] is often used as baseline in existing works. It is employed for segmentation by adding dropout layers in the decoder module of the segmentation model and then computing the pixel-wise mutual information using multiple forward passes. **Coreset** [31] is a batch-based approach that was initially proposed for image classification, but it can be easily modified for segmentation. For e.g., the pooled output of the ASPP [4] module in the DeepLabv3+ [5] model can be used as the feature representation for computing distance between the samples. Some other methods [22,34,35] use a GAN model to learn a combined feature space for labeled and unlabeled images and utilize the discriminator output to select the least represented images. Our study includes Entropy, EquAL, BALD, and Coreset approaches for the analysis, along with the random sampling baseline. In this work, these methods are also studied with the integration of semi-supervised learning.

2.2 Semi-supervised Active Learning

Active learning uses a pool of unlabeled samples only for selecting new samples for annotation. However, this pool can also be used for semi-supervised learning (SSL), where the objective is to learn jointly from labeled and unlabeled samples. The combination of SSL and AL has been used successfully in many contexts, such as speech understanding [9,20], image classification [13,27,28,31], and pedestrian detection [30]. Some recent works have also studied active learning methods with the integration of SSL for segmentation, but their scope is limited only to special cases like subsampled driving datasets [29] or low labeling budget [27], both cases with only single-sample acquisition methods. Our work provides a broader overview of the integration of SSL and active learning for the segmentation task. We study this integration over datasets with different redundancy levels, under different labeling budgets, and with single-sample and batch-based methods.

Integration of SSL and AL. A successful integration can also be conceptually explained based on the underlying assumption of semi-supervised learning and the selection principle of the active learning approach. According to the *clustering assumption* of SSL, if two points belong to the same cluster, then their outputs are likely to be close and can be connected by a short curve [3]. In this regard, when labeled samples align with the clusters of unlabeled samples, the cluster assumption of SSL is satisfied, resulting in a good performance. Consequently, to maximize semi-supervised learning performance, newly selected samples must cover the unlabeled clusters that are not already covered by labeled samples. Only acquisition functions that foster this coverage requirement have the potential to leverage the additional benefits that arise from the integration of semi-supervised learning. A batch-based method, e.g., Coreset, selects samples for annotations to minimize the distance to the farthest neighbor. By transitivity, such labeled samples would have a higher tendency to propagate the knowledge to neighboring unlabeled samples in the cluster and utilize the knowledge of unlabeled samples using a semi-supervised learning objective and help boost the model performance. Similar behavior can also be attained using other clustering approaches that optimize for coverage.

3 Experimental Setup

3.1 Tested Approaches

In our study, we test five active learning acquisition functions as discussed in Sect. 2, including Random, Entropy, EquAL, BALD, and Coreset. Here Entropy, EquAL, and BALD approach represent single-sample, and Coreset represents the batch-based approach. All methods select the whole image for annotation. To leverage the unlabeled samples, we use the semi-supervised learning s4GAN method [26]. We consider s4GAN method because it is a simple method that performs close to state-of-the-art methods and works out of the box. We also test another SSL approach, U2PL [38], and find that conclusions do not vary based on the SSL method selection. We pair all the used active learning approaches with SSL using this approach. This is marked by the suffix '-SSL' in the experiments. In particular, we train the model using an SSL objective, which impacts the resulting model and hence the acquisition function.

3.2   Datasets

Active learning methods are often evaluated on PASCAL-VOC and Cityscapes datasets. In this work, we also test on an additional driving dataset, A2D2 and further curate relevant dataset pools from it for extensive experimentation.

Cityscapes [6] is a driving dataset used to benchmark semantic segmentation tasks. The dataset was originally collected as videos from 27 cities, where a diverse set of images were selected for annotation. Due to this selection, Cityscapes is considered a diverse although it was derived from videos. As we will see in the results, the nature of the active learning method changes due to preselection. We find pre-filtering, as done in Cityscapes, is sub-optimal compared to directly applying active learning on the raw data (see Sect. 4.4).

PASCAL-VOC [10] is another widely used segmentation dataset. We use the extended dataset [16], which consists of 10582 training and 1449 validation images. It contains a wide spectrum of natural images with mixed categories like vehicles, animals, furniture, etc. It is the most diverse dataset in this study.

A2D2 [14] is a large-scale driving dataset with 41277 annotated images from 23 sequences. It covers an urban setting from highways, country roads, and three cities. We map the 38 A2D2 categories to the 19 classes of Cityscapes for our experiments. A2D2 provides annotations for every $\sim 10^{th}$ frame in the sequence and contains a lot of overlapping information between frames. It is highly redundant. We utilize 40135 frames from 22 sequences for creating our training sets and one sequence with 1142 images for validation. The validation sequence '20180925_112730' is selected based on the maximum class balance.

A2D2 Pools. To obtain a more continuous spectrum between diverse and redundant datasets, we created five smaller dataset pools by subsampling the A2D2 dataset. Each pool comprises 2640 images, which is comparable in size to the Cityscapes training set. Four pools are curated by subsampling the original dataset, while the fifth pool is created by augmentation. The first four pools, denoted by Pool-Xf (where X is 0, 5, 11, and 21), were created by randomly selecting samples and X consecutive frames for each randomly selected sample from the original A2D2 dataset. Pool-0f contains only randomly selected images. We assume that the consecutive frames contain highly redundant information. Therefore, the pool with more consecutive frames has higher redundancy and lower diversity. The fifth pool, Pool-Aug, contains augmented duplicates in place of the consecutive frames. We create five duplicates of each randomly selected frame by randomly cropping 85% of the image and adding color augmentation.

Diverse vs. Redundant datasets. PASCAL-VOC can be easily tagged as diverse, and A2D2 original and A2D2-Pool-5f/11f/21f can be tagged as redundant. However, it is hard to put a redundant/diverse tag for many datasets in the middle of the spectrum. Cityscapes and A2D2-Pool-0f fall in this spectrum since they are curated by sparsely selecting from large video data. We consider them as diverse for our study since they behave like diverse datasets. Quantifying dataset redundancy is a novel research question that emerged with this work and remains part of future work.

3.3   Experiment Details

Implementation Details. We used the DeepLabv3+ [5] architecture with the Wide-ResNet38 (WRN-38) [39] backbone for all experiments. The backbone WRN-38 is pre-trained using ImageNet [7]. WideResNet is a more efficient and better backbone as compared to ResNet-101. Therefore, we use it for all our experiments. We run all methods on 3 random seeds and report the mean performance. All other training details and hyperparameter information is included in the Supplementary. Since the BALD method requires the introduction of Dropout layers into the architecture, we segregate the methods into two categories: with Monte Carlo Dropout (MCD) and without Monte Carlo Dropout layers. Random, Entropy, EquAL, and Coreset are without MCD. BALD is based on a MCD network. Since the models used in the two categories are not exactly comparable due to different architectures, we also show the fully-supervised performance for both with MCD (100% MCD) and without MCD (100%) architectures.

Evaluation Scheme. We evaluate the methods across different data budget settings, denoted by $\mathcal{I} - \mathcal{S}$, where $\mathcal{I}$ is the initial label budget, $\mathcal{S}$ is the sampling-label budget, and $\mathcal{I}$, $\mathcal{S}$ indicates the percentage of the dataset size. Images are sampled randomly to fulfill the initial label budget. For the subsequent steps, images are sampled using the AL acquisition function up to the allowed sampling-label budget. We test datasets with 10-10, 5-5, and 2-2 budget settings.

Evaluation Metrics. We use mean Intersection over Union (mIoU) to evaluate the performance of the model at each AL cycle step. For the evaluation of the active learning method, we use two metrics: Area Under the Budget Curve (AUC@B) and mean Intersection over Union at a budget B (mIoU@B). **AUC@B** is the area under the performance curves. It captures a cumulative score of the AL performance curve up to a budget B, where B is the percentage of the labeled dataset size. For the experiments on A2D2 pools, we use B = 50 in the 10-10 setting. For PASCAL-VOC, we run three experiments with B = 10, 25, and 50 in 2-2, 5-5, and 10-10 settings, respectively. For Cityscapes, we experiment with B = 50 in the 10-10 setting. **mIoU@B** reports the performance of the model after using a certain labeling budget B. We report performance at an intermediate labeling budget to see the ranking of the AL methods. Dataset-pools / code for all experiments are available here - https://github.com/sud0301/best_practices_ALSS.

4   Results

Here, we answer the three questions raised in Sect. 1 concerning the behavior of active learning methods w.r.t data distribution in terms of redundancy, integration of semi-supervised learning, and different labeling budgets. For each experiment, we compare random, single-sample, or batch-based acquisition.

4.1   Impact of Dataset Redundancy

Table 2. Active Learning results on Cityscapes, A2D2 Pool-0f, PASCAL-VOC. AUC@50 and mIoU@30 metrics are reported. A denotes Acquisition method type. S and B denotes the single-sample and batch-based acquisition.

A	AL Method	SSL	Cityscapes		A2D2 Pool-0f		VOC 5-5		VOC 10-10	
	Metric →		mIoU	AUC	mIoU	AUC	mIoU	AUC	mIoU	AUC
S	Random	✗	58.90	23.29	48.48	19.20	70.70	13.92	72.13	28.85
S	Entropy	✗	61.83	24.25	52.40	**20.37**	70.38	13.94	73.72	29.1
S	EquAL	✗	62.41	24.32	**52.50**	20.35	69.14	13.82	73.40	29.03
B	Coreset	✗	60.89	23.89	51.14	19.88	70.85	13.96	73.63	29.06
S	Random-SSL	✓	60.72	23.85	49.69	19.60	72.57	14.36	75.33	29.87
S	Entropy-SSL	✓	60.61	23.93	50.80	19.90	73.36	14.51	**76.08**	30.01
S	EquAL-SSL	✓	60.26	23.96	51.08	20.02	**73.39**	**14.55**	75.89	**30.06**
B	Coreset-SSL	✓	**63.14**	**24.47**	51.49	20.02	72.88	14.46	75.91	30.03
–	100%	✗	68.42	27.37	56.87	22.75	77.00	15.40	77.00	30.80

Table 3. Active Learning results on A2D2-Pool5f, A2D2-Pool11f, A2D2-Pool-21f, and A2D2-PoolAug. AUC@50 and mIoU@30 metrics are reported. S and B denotes the single-sample and batch-based acquisition, respectively.

A	AL Method	SSL	Pool-5f		Pool-11f		Pool-21f		Pool-Aug	
	Metric →		mIoU	AUC	mIoU	AUC	mIoU	AUC	mIoU	AUC
S	Random	✗	47.58	18.69	44.61	17.76	44.52	17.67	43.80	17.15
S	Entropy	✗	49.96	19.48	47.43	18.52	46.08	18.21	44.51	17.33
S	EquAL	✗	49.50	19.29	47.14	18.44	46.32	18.18	44.24	17.29
B	Coreset	✗	50.08	19.44	47.72	18.69	46.68	18.38	44.70	17.54
S	Random-SSL	✓	47.92	19.03	45.25	18.02	46.27	18.19	44.17	17.29
S	Entropy-SSL	✓	48.78	19.31	47.53	18.56	46.93	18.43	44.50	17.47
S	EquAL-SSL	✓	48.80	19.28	46.50	18.39	47.11	18.54	44.81	17.56
B	Coreset-SSL	✓	**50.44**	**19.69**	**48.99**	**19.01**	**47.62**	**18.69**	**45.81**	**17.74**
–	100%	✗	53.25	21.30	48.85	19.54	49.23	19.69	46.03	18.41
With MC-Dropout decoder										
S	BALD	✗	50.40	19.29	47.85	18.74	46.78	18.57	45.53	17.80
S	BALD-SSL	✓	50.33	19.62	47.34	18.61	47.06	18.57	45.16	17.72
–	100%-MCD	✗	53.82	21.53	50.86	20.34	50.43	20.17	46.62	18.65

Figure 1 and Table 2 shows the results on Cityscapes and A2D2 Pool-0f. For both datasets, the single-sample (S) method, EquAL, performs the best in the supervised-only setting. Table 2 also shows the results obtained on the PASCAL-VOC dataset in 5-5 and 10-10 settings. Single-sample-based methods perform the best in the 10-10 setting, whereas Coreset performs the best in the 5-5 AL setting by a marginal gap w.r.t. random baseline. Figure 1 and Table 3 shows the results for the redundant datasets. The batch-based Coreset method consistently performs the best in all four datasets in the supervised-only setting.

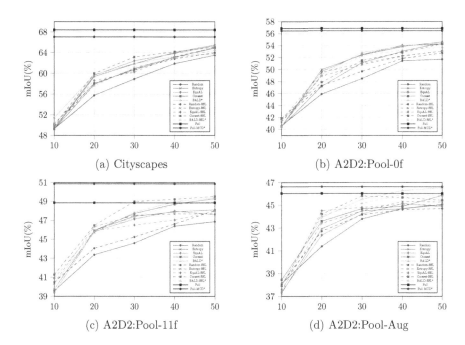

Fig. 1. Results on diverse and redundant datasets. Active Learning performance curves on diverse datasets - Cityscapes and A2D2 Pool-0f, and redundant datasets - A2D2 Pool-11f and Pool-Aug. The X-axis shows the percentage of labeled datasets. The methods which utilize MC-Dropout in their network architecture are marked with ∗.

Diverse Datasets Need a Single-Sample Method and Redundant Datasets Need a Batch-Based Method. We observe that the order of best-performing models changes based on the level of redundancy in the dataset. Single-sample-based acquisition functions perform best on diverse datasets, whereas batch-based acquisition functions perform best on redundant datasets. We attribute this reversed effect to the mode collapse problem, where, for redundant datasets, single-sample acquisition methods select local clusters of similar samples. Diverse datasets are devoid of this issue as they do not possess local clusters due to high diversity across samples. Therefore, the diversity-driven acquisition is not critical for diverse datasets. This observation is consistent for PASCAL-VOC, where single-sample-based uncertainty-type methods perform better than batch-based and random methods in the high-budget setting. The difference between the methods is only marginal here since most acquired samples add ample new information due to the highly diverse nature of the dataset. This difference further diminishes w.r.t. random baseline with a lower labeling budget (*e.g.* 5-5) since any learned useful bias also becomes weaker. The observations for the 5-5 setting tend towards a very low-budget setting which is further analysed in Sect. 4.3.

Mode Collapse Analysis. Here, we analyse and visualize the above mentioned model collapse issue. Mode collapse in active learning refers to the circumstance

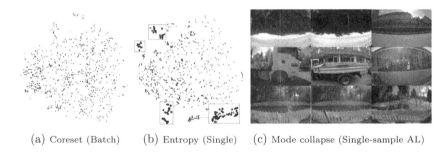

(a) Coreset (Batch)   (b) Entropy (Single)   (c) Mode collapse (Single-sample AL)

Fig. 2. TSNE plots of (a) Coreset and (b) Entropy functions for A2D2 Pool-21f. The yellow points are feature representation from the unlabeled set, the violet point are the acquired points. The batch-based approach has good selection coverage, whereas the single-sample approach selects similar samples from clusters. Figure (c) shows acquired redundant samples from the violet clusters in (b). (Color figure online)

Table 4. Results on A2D2-Pool-0f (diverse) and A2D2-Pool-11f (redundant) in 10-10 budget setting using another SSL [38] method.

A	AL Method	SSL	A2D2 Pool-0f		A2D2 Pool-11f	
			mIoU@30	AUC@50	mIoU@30	AUC@50
S	U2PL-Random	✓	48.32	18.86	44.64	17.60
S	U2PL-Entropy	✓	**50.43**	**19.65**	45.86	18.11
B	U2PL-Coreset	✓	49.51	19.06	**46.28**	**18.23**

that acquisition functions tend to select a set of similar (redundant) samples when acquiring batches of data [23]. This can occur when a single-sample acquisition function gives a high score to at least one of the similar samples in the set. Since similar samples have highly overlapping information, all samples in the set receive a high score. Thus, all similar samples tend to be selected, causing this collapse. Since the selected samples are all very similar, their annotation does not add much more value to the model than if a single sample was added.

We provide a qualitative analysis of the mode collapse issue on the redundant A2D2 Pool-21f. We plot the feature representations using t-SNE to show the selection process for a single-sample-based Entropy function and batch-based Coreset function, shown in Fig. 2. It shows that Entropy acquisition selects many samples within local clusters, which are similar samples with overlapping information. This yields a suboptimal use of the annotation budget. In contrast, Coreset acquisition has a good selection coverage and avoids this mode collapse.

In this work, we argue that mode collapse is a common issue in many real-world datasets, containing similar samples. A good acquisition function for such datasets must be aware of the batch's diversity to address the mode collapse issue. It is largely ignored due to the narrow scope of existing AL benchmarks like PASCAL-VOC and Cityscapes, which only cover diverse datasets.

Table 5. Active Learning results on PASCAL-VOC and A2D2 Pool-0f in 2-2 setting. AUC@10 and mIoU@6 metrics are reported. A denotes Acquisition method type. S and B denotes the single-sample and batch-based acquisition.

A	AL Method	SSL	PASCAL-VOC 2-2		A2D2 Pool-11f 2-2	
	Metric →		mIoU@6	AUC@10	mIoU@6	AUC@10
S	Random	✗	66.41	5.22	37.74	2.93
S	Entropy	✗	66.33	5.11	36.37	2.92
S	EquAL	✗	65.04	5.13	37.28	2.97
B	Coreset	✗	66.24	5.19	**39.63**	**3.10**
S	Random-SSL	✓	**68.60**	**5.37**	36.46	2.90
S	Entropy-SSL	✓	67.26	5.31	36.70	2.93
S	EquAL-SSL	✓	67.44	5.31	36.31	3.06
B	Coreset-SSL	✓	68.03	5.35	39.20	3.06
–	100%	✗	77.00	6.16	48.85	3.91

4.2 Systematic Integration of SSL

For all redundant datasets, the Coreset-SSL approach consistently performs the best; see results in Table 3. For diverse datasets, SSL integration is also helpful, but there is no consistent best approach. For the PASCAL-VOC dataset, single-sample based methods with SSL show the best performance, shown in Table 2. For Cityscapes, Coreset-SSL outperforms all other approaches; see Table 2. For A2D2-Pool0f, Coreset-SSL improves over Coreset, but the single-sample acquisition method BALD approach shows the best performance.

Redundant Datasets Favour the Integration of Batch-Based Active Learning and Semi-supervised Learning. The batch-based acquisition function Coreset always profits from the integration of SSL. Coreset aligns well with the SSL objective since Coreset selects samples from each local cluster, thus covering the whole data distribution. This assists SSL in obtaining maximum information from the unlabeled samples, as discussed in Sect. 2.2. This effect is especially strong in the redundant A2D2 pools, where Coreset-SSL always improves over Coreset and also shows the best performance. In contrast, SSL integration for single-sample methods is either harmful or ineffective, except for the PASCAL-VOC dataset. Interestingly, in Pool-11f, some Coreset-SSL methods even outperform the 100% baseline with less than 30% labeled data. This indicates that some labeled redundant samples can even harm the model , possibly due to data imbalance. For Cityscapes, SSL with Coreset yields significant improvement, and SSL even changes the ranking of the methods. We see that EquAL performs the best in the supervised-only setting, whereas Coreset-SSL surpasses all methods. This slight anomaly in the case of Cityscapes happens because the advantage due to the combination of SSL and batch-based method is greater than the advantage of using single-sample methods in non-redundant datasets. For diverse PASCAL-VOC, all methods align well with SSL. All methods perform well with no clear winner method since all selection criteria select samples providing good coverage of the data distribution.

We tested another latest SSL method called U2PL [38] to show that our observations are not specific to one SSL method. Table 4 shows results on A2D2-pool-0f (diverse) and A2D2-Pool-11f (redundant) datasets. The behavior of the new U2PL methods is similar to the results seen for previous SSL method.

4.3 Low Annotation Budget

Active Learning is Volatile with a Low Budget. Experimenting with PASCAL-VOC in the 2-2 budget setting (see Table 5), Random-SSL performs the best, i.e., semi-supervised learning without active learning component. We believe that active learning fails in this setting because it fails to capture any helpful bias for selection in such a low-data regime with diverse samples. Our observations in this low-budget setting confirm and provide a stronger empirical support for similar behavior observed in [27]. For A2D2 Pool-0f (see Table 5) and Cityscapes in the 2-2 setting, the single-sample acquisition performs the best, while its SSL integration is detrimental. These methods possibly learn some useful bias due to the specialized driving domain. For redundant datasets in low budget settings, batch-based acquisition is still the most effective way. However, SSL does not contribute any additional improvements due to insufficient labeled samples to support learning from unlabeled samples. Overall, we observe a highly volatile nature of active learning in conjunction with a low budget. The ideal policy transitions from random selection towards the batch-based acquisition, as the dataset redundancy goes from low to high. Other result tables are included in the supplementary.

4.4 An Exemplar Case Study: A2D2-3K Task

Previous active learning works on semantic segmentation cover only the combination of a diverse dataset and a high annotation budget. In contrast, the collected raw data can be quite redundant, like in video datasets. To study this missing redundant setting, we propose a new active learning task A2D2-3K for segmentation based on the A2D2 dataset. The new task is to select 3K images (similar size to Cityscapes) from the original A2D2 dataset ($\sim$40K images) to achieve the best performance. We select 3K images using active learning in 3 cycles with 1K images each. We compare 5 acquisition functions, including Random, Entropy, and Coreset, along with SSL integration. Such video datasets are often manually subsampled based on some prior information like time or location, and then used for active learning. Therefore, we also include two such baselines - (a) where 3K samples are uniformly selected based on time information, denoted as Uniform, and (b) where every fifth sample is first selected uniformly to select $\sim 8K$ samples and then applied with Entropy acquisition function, denoted as Uniform(@5)+Entropy. The second approach is closer to previously used active learning benchmarks in the driving context. Results are shown in Table 6. We

Table 6. AL results on the proposed A2D2-3K task. S and B denotes the single-sample and batch-based acquisition. Uniform refers to temporal subsampling selection process and (@5) means every 5th frame.

A	AL Method	without SSL		with SSL	
		mIoU	AUC	mIoU	AUC
B	Uniform	57.75	—	58.93	—
S	Random	56.14	5.35	57.57	5.53
S	Entropy	60.16	5.53	59.91	5.61
B	Coreset	60.30	5.55	**61.13**	**5.72**
S	Uniform (@5) + Entropy	60.40	5.66	59.63	5.59
–	100%	66.65	6.64	—	—

Table 7. Overview showing the best performing AL method for each scenario. Single and Batch refer to single-sample and batch-based method, and Random refers to random selection. Suffix -SSL refers to semi-supervised learning.

Dataset ↓	Annotation Budget			
	Low		High	
Sup. →	AL	SSL-AL	AL	SSL-AL
Diverse	Random	Random-SSL	Single	Single-SSL
Redundant	Batch	Batch	Batch	Batch-SSL

find that the batch-based Coreset-SSL method performs the best, discussed in Sect. 4.2, while the subsampling-based approaches are sub-optimal. This makes an excellent case for active learning in datasets with high redundancy, as active learning filters the data better than time-based subsampling methods.

5   Conclusion

This work shows that active learning is indeed a useful tool for semantic segmentation. However, it is vital to understand the behavior of different active learning methods in various application scenarios. Table 7 provides an overview of the best performing methods for each scenario. Our findings indicate that single-sample-based uncertainty is a suitable measure for sample selection in diverse datasets. In contrast, batch-based diversity-driven measures are better suited for datasets with high levels of redundancy. SSL is successfully integrated with batch-based diversity-driven methods. However, it can have a detrimental impact when combined with single-sample-based uncertainty acquisition functions. Active learning with low annotation budgets is highly sensitive to the level of redundancy in the dataset. These findings have been missing in method development, which are optimized only for a few scenarios. The results of this study facilitate a broader view on the task with positive effects in many applications.

Acknowledgements. The authors would like to thank Philipp Schröppel, Jan Bechtold, and María A. Bravo for their constructive criticism on the manuscript. The research leading to these results is funded by the German Federal Ministry for Economic Affairs and Climate Action within the project "KI Delta Learning" (Forderkennzeichen 19A19013N) and "KI Wissen - Entwicklung von Methoden für die Einbindung von Wissen in maschinelles Lernen". The authors would like to thank the consortium for the successful cooperation. Funded by the Deutsche Forschungsgemeinschaft (DFG) - 401269959, 417962828.

References

1. Brostow, G.J., Fauqueur, J., Cipolla, R.: Semantic object classes in video: a high-definition ground truth database. Pattern Recogn. Lett. **30**, 88–97 (2008)
2. Cai, L., Xu, X., Liew, J.H., Foo, C.S.: Revisiting superpixels for active learning in semantic segmentation with realistic annotation costs. In: Proceedings of the IEEE/CVF Conference on Computer Vision and Pattern Recognition (CVPR) (2021)
3. Chapelle, O., Schölkopf, B., Zien, A. (eds.): Semi-Supervised Learning. The MIT Press, Cambridge (2006)
4. Chen, L., Papandreou, G., Kokkinos, I., Murphy, K., Yuille, A.L.: Deeplab: semantic image segmentation with deep convolutional nets, atrous convolution, and fully connected crfs. TPAMI **40**(4), 834–848 (2018)
5. Chen, L., Zhu, Y., Papandreou, G., Schroff, F., Adam, H.: Encoder-decoder with atrous separable convolution for semantic image segmentation. CoRR arxiv:1802.02611 (2018)
6. Cordts, M., et al.: The cityscapes dataset for semantic urban scene understanding. In: Proceedings of the IEEE Conference on Computer Vision and Pattern Recognition (CVPR) (2016)
7. Deng, J., Dong, W., Socher, R., Li, L.J., Li, K., Fei-Fei, L.: Imagenet: a large-scale hierarchical image database. In: IEEE Conference on Computer Vision and Pattern Recognition (2009)
8. Deng, L.: The mnist database of handwritten digit images for machine learning research. IEEE Signal Process. Maga. **29**, 141–142 (2012)
9. Drugman, T., Pylkkonen, J., Kneser, R.: Active and semi-supervised learning in asr: benefits on the acoustic and language models. In: Interspeech (2016)
10. Everingham, M., van Gool, L., Williams, C.K.I., Winn, J., Zisserman, A.: The pascal visual object classes (voc) challenge. Int. J. Comput. Vision **88**, 303–338 (2010)
11. Gal, Y., Ghahramani, Z.: Dropout as a bayesian approximation: representing model uncertainty in deep learning. In: Proceedings of The 33rd International Conference on Machine Learning (2016)
12. Gal, Y., Islam, R., Ghahramani, Z.: Deep bayesian active learning with image data. In: ICML (2017)
13. Gao, M., Zhang, Z., Yu, G., Arık, S.Ö., Davis, L.S., Pfister, T.: Consistency-based semi-supervised active learning: towards minimizing labeling cost. In: Vedaldi, A., Bischof, H., Brox, T., Frahm, J.-M. (eds.) ECCV 2020. LNCS, vol. 12355, pp. 510–526. Springer, Cham (2020). https://doi.org/10.1007/978-3-030-58607-2_30
14. Geyer, J., et al.: A2D2: audi autonomous driving dataset (2020). https://www.a2d2.audi

15. Golestaneh, S. Alireza, K.K.: Importance of self-consistency in active learning for semantic segmentation. In: BMVC (2020)
16. Hariharan, B., Arbeláez, P., Bourdev, L., Maji, S., Malik, J.: Semantic contours from inverse detectors. In: 2011 International Conference on Computer Vision, pp. 991–998 (2011). https://doi.org/10.1109/ICCV.2011.6126343
17. Houlsby, N., Huszár, F., Ghahramani, Z., Lengyel, M.: Bayesian active learning for classification and preference learning. ArXiv arxiv:1112.5745 (2011)
18. Huang, S., Wang, T., Xiong, H., Huan, J., Dou, D.: Semi-supervised active learning with temporal output discrepancy. In: Proceedings of the IEEE/CVF International Conference on Computer Vision (ICCV) (2021)
19. Jia, R., et al.: Towards efficient data valuation based on the shapley value. In: Proceedings of the Twenty-Second International Conference on Artificial Intelligence and Statistics (2019)
20. Karlos, S., Aridas, C., Kanas, V.G., Kotsiantis, S.: Classification of acoustical signals by combining active learning strategies with semi-supervised learning schemes. In: Neural Computing and Applications, pp. 1–18 (2021)
21. Killamsetty, K., Sivasubramanian, D., Ramakrishnan, G., Iyer, R.: Glister: generalization based data subset selection for efficient and robust learning. In: Proceedings of the AAAI Conference on Artificial Intelligence (2021)
22. Kim, K., Park, D., Kim, K.I., Chun, S.Y.: Task-aware variational adversarial active learning. In: Proceedings of the IEEE/CVF Conference on Computer Vision and Pattern Recognition (CVPR) (2021)
23. Kirsch, A., van Amersfoort, J., Gal, Y.: Batchbald: efficient and diverse batch acquisition for deep bayesian active learning. In: Wallach, H., Larochelle, H., Beygelzimer, A., d' Alché-Buc, F., Fox, E., Garnett, R. (eds.) Advances in Neural Information Processing Systems (2019)
24. Lakshminarayanan, B., Pritzel, A., Blundell, C.: Simple and scalable predictive uncertainty estimation using deep ensembles. In: NeurIPS (2017)
25. Mackowiak, R., Lenz, P., Ghori, O., Diego, F., Lange, O., Rother, C.: Cereals-cost-effective region-based active learning for semantic segmentation. arXiv preprint arXiv:1810.09726 (2018)
26. Mittal, S., Tatarchenko, M., Brox, T.: Semi-supervised semantic segmentation with high-and low-level consistency. IEEE Trans. Pattern Anal. Mach. Intell. **43**(4), 1369–1379 (2019)
27. Mittal, S., Tatarchenko, M., Çiçek, Ö., Brox, T.: Parting with illusions about deep active learning. CoRR abs/1912.05361 (2019). http://arxiv.org/abs/1912.05361
28. Munjal, P., Hayat, N., Hayat, M., Sourati, J., Khan, S.: Towards robust and reproducible active learning using neural networks. In: Proceedings of the IEEE/CVF Conference on Computer Vision and Pattern Recognition (CVPR) (2022)
29. Rangnekar, A., Kanan, C., Hoffman, M.: Semantic segmentation with active semi-supervised learning. In: Proceedings of the IEEE/CVF Winter Conference on Applications of Computer Vision (WACV), pp. 5966–5977 (2023)
30. Rhee, P.K., Erdenee, E., Kyun, S.D., Ahmed, M.U., Jin, S.: Active and semi-supervised learning for object detection with imperfect data. Cogn. Syst. Res. **45**, 109–123 (2017). https://doi.org/10.1016/j.cogsys.2017.05.006
31. Sener, O., Savarese, S.: Active learning for convolutional neural networks: a core-set approach. arXiv preprint arXiv:1708.00489 (2017)
32. Shannon, C.E.: A mathematical theory of communication. ACM SIGMOBILE Mobile Comput. Commun. Rev. **5**(1), 3–55 (2001)

33. Shin, G., Xie, W., Albanie, S.: All you need are a few pixels: semantic segmentation with pixelpick. In: Proceedings of the IEEE/CVF International Conference on Computer Vision (ICCV) Workshops (2021)
34. Shui, C., Zhou, F., Gagné, C., Wang, B.: Deep active learning: unified and principled method for query and training. In: Proceedings of the Twenty Third International Conference on Artificial Intelligence and Statistics (2020)
35. Sinha, S., Ebrahimi, S., Darrell, T.: Variational adversarial active learning. In: Proceedings of the IEEE/CVF International Conference on Computer Vision (ICCV) (2019)
36. Wang, K., Zhang, D., Li, Y., Zhang, R., Lin, L.: Cost-effective active learning for deep image classification. IEEE Trans. Circ. Syst. Video Technol. **27**, 2591–2600 (2017)
37. Wang, S., Li, Y., Ma, K., Ma, R., Guan, H., Zheng, Y.: Dual adversarial network for deep active learning. In: Vedaldi, A., Bischof, H., Brox, T., Frahm, J.-M. (eds.) ECCV 2020. LNCS, vol. 12369, pp. 680–696. Springer, Cham (2020). https://doi.org/10.1007/978-3-030-58586-0_40
38. Wang, Y., et al.: Semi-supervised semantic segmentation using unreliable pseudo-labels. In: CVPR (2022)
39. Wu, Z., Shen, C., van den Hengel, A.: Wider or deeper: revisiting the resnet model for visual recognition. Pattern Recogn. **90**, 119–133 (2019)
40. Yu, F., et al.: BDD100K: a diverse driving video database with scalable annotation tooling. CoRR abs/1805.04687 (2018). http://arxiv.org/abs/1805.04687
41. Zhdanov, F.: Diverse mini-batch active learning. CoRR abs/1901.05954 (2019). http://arxiv.org/abs/1901.05954

COOLer: Class-Incremental Learning for Appearance-Based Multiple Object Tracking

Zhizheng Liu[ID], Mattia Segu[ID], and Fisher Yu[(✉)][ID]

ETH Zürich, 8092 Zürich, Switzerland
{liuzhi,segum}@ethz.ch, i@yf.io

Abstract. Continual learning allows a model to learn multiple tasks sequentially while retaining the old knowledge without the training data of the preceding tasks. This paper extends the scope of continual learning research to class-incremental learning for multiple object tracking (MOT), which is desirable to accommodate the continuously evolving needs of autonomous systems. Previous solutions for continual learning of object detectors do not address the data association stage of appearance-based trackers, leading to catastrophic forgetting of previous classes' re-identification features. We introduce COOLer, a COntrastive- and cOntinual-Learning-based tracker, which incrementally learns to track new categories while preserving past knowledge by training on a combination of currently available ground truth labels and pseudo-labels generated by the past tracker. To further exacerbate the disentanglement of instance representations, we introduce a novel contrastive class-incremental instance representation learning technique. Finally, we propose a practical evaluation protocol for continual learning for MOT and conduct experiments on the BDD100K and SHIFT datasets. Experimental results demonstrate that COOLer continually learns while effectively addressing catastrophic forgetting of both tracking and detection. The project page is available at https://www.vis.xyz/pub/cooler.

Keywords: Continual learning · Multiple object tracking · Re-Identification

1 Introduction

Continual learning aims at training a model to gradually extend its knowledge and learn multiple tasks sequentially without accessing the previous training data [5]. Since merely finetuning a pre-trained model on the new task would result in forgetting the knowledge learned from previous tasks - a problem known in literature as catastrophic forgetting [20]- ad-hoc continual learning solutions are required. As data distributions and practitioners' needs change over time, the practicality of continual learning has made it popular in recent years.

Z. Liu and M. Segu—Equal contribution.

Supplementary Information The online version contains supplementary material available at https://doi.org/10.1007/978-3-031-54605-1_29.

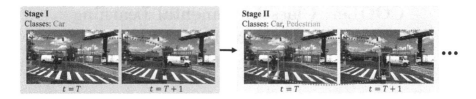

Fig. 1. Illustration of the class-incremental learning problem for multiple object tracking. In a first stage, an MOT model can only track cars (red). When given annotations only for the novel class 'pedestrian' (green), the objective is learning to track the new class without forgetting the previous one. (Color figure online)

This paper addresses class-incremental learning for multiple object tracking (MOT), an important yet novel research problem that, to the best of our knowledge, has not been studied in previous literature. MOT tracks multiple objects simultaneously from a video sequence and outputs their location and category [2]. While prior work [27] explored domain adaptation of MOT to diverse conditions, continual learning for MOT would provide a flexible and inexpensive solution to incrementally expand the MOT model to new classes according to the changing necessities. For example, as illustrated in Fig. 1, one can train an MOT model to track cars and then expand its functionality to track pedestrians with new training data only annotated for pedestrians.

Following the tracking-by-detection paradigm [23], most MOT systems first detect object locations and classes via an object detector, and then associate the detected instances across frames via a data association module. State-the-art trackers often use a combination of motion and appearance cues in their association module [1,30,35]. While motion cues are straight-forward to use with simple heuristics, appearance cues are used for object re-identification (Re-ID) and are more robust to complex object motion and large object displacement across adjacent frames. Appearance-based association typically requires a Re-ID module [8,21,31] for learning Re-ID features. However, it is crucial to make such learned appearance representations flexible to incrementally added categories. Training the appearance extractors only on the new classes would indeed results in catastrophic forgetting of Re-ID features for older classes, and degrade the association performance (Table 2, Fine-tuning). Although previous work [22,28, 37] explores class-incremental learning of object detectors, these approaches are sub-optimal for MOT by not addressing the data association stage.

To address this problem, we introduce COOLer, a COntrastive- and cOntinual-Learning-based multiple object tracker. Building on the state-of-the-art appearance-based tracker QDTrack [21], COOLer represents the first comprehensive approach for continual learning for appearance-based trackers by addressing class-incremental learning of both the building blocks of an MOT system, *i.e.* object detection and data association. To continually learn to track new categories while preventing catastrophic forgetting, we propose to combine the available ground truth labels from the newly added categories with the association pseudo-labels and the temporally-refined detection pseudo-labels generated by the previous-stage tracker on the new training data. Furthermore, adding classes incrementally without imposing any constraint may cause overlapping instance representations from different classes, blurring the decision boundaries and leading to misclassifications. While traditional contrastive learning can disentangle the representations of different classes, they undermine the intra-class discrimination properties of the instance embeddings for data association. To this end, we propose a novel contrastive class-incremental instance representation learning formulation that pushes the embedding distributions of different classes away from each other while keeping the embedding distributions of the same class close to a Gaussian prior. To assess the effectiveness of continual learning strategies for MOT, we propose a practical and comprehensive evaluation protocol and conduct extensive experiments on the BDD100K [34] and SHIFT [29] datasets.

We demonstrate that COOLer can alleviate forgetting of both tracking and detection, while effectively acquiring incremental knowledge. Our key contributions are: (i) we introduce COOLer, the first comprehensive method for class-incremental learning for multiple object tracking; (ii) we propose to use the previous-stage tracker to generate data association pseudo-labels to address catastrophic forgetting of association of previous classes and leverage the temporal information to refine detection pseudo-labels; (iii) we introduce class-incremental instance representation learning to disentangle class representations and further improve both detection and association performance.

2   Related Work

Continual learning aims at learning new knowledge continually while alleviating forgetting. Various continual learning strategies have been proposed, including model growing [26], regularization [14,16], parameter isolation [19], and replay [24]. We here discuss related literature in continual learning for object detection, unsupervised Re-ID learning, and contrastive representation learning.

Continual Learning for Object Detection. Shmelkov et al. [28] propose the first method for continual learning for object detection. It uses the old model as the teacher model which generates pseudo labels for the classification and bounding box regression outputs to prevent forgetting. Later works [17,22] follow this diagram by incorporating the state-of-the-art detectors such as Faster R-CNN [25] and Deformable DETR [38]. While our work also uses detection pseudo-labels, we refine them temporally by leveraging a multiple-object tracker.

Unsupervised Re-ID Learning. As annotating instance IDs is laborious and time-consuming, unsupervised Re-ID learning proposes to learn data association from video sequences without annotations given only a pre-trained detector [13]. Most unsupervised Re-ID learning approaches generate pseudo-identities to train the association module from a simple motion-based tracker [13], image clustering [9,15,32] or contrastive learning of instance representation under data augmentation [27]. In contrast, our class-incremental instance representation learning

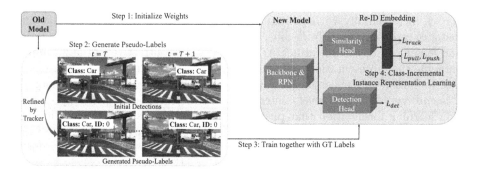

Fig. 2. Pipeline of COOLer for class-incremental learning. 1). Initialize the new model with weights from the old model. 2). Use the previous tracker to refine the initial detections and generate detection and association pseudo-labels. 3). Append them to the ground truth labels to train the new model jointly. 4). During training, apply class-incremental instance representation learning.

approach handles a combination of labeled and unlabeled Re-ID data to continually learn Re-ID of new categories' instances without forgetting the old ones.

Contrastive Representation Learning. Contrastive learning [4,10] aims to attract representations of similar samples and push away representations of dissimilar ones. Previous continual learning methods leverage contrastive learning at a category level. Mai et al. [18] propose supervised contrastive replay and use a nearest-class-mean classifier instead of the softmax classifier. Co2L [3] shows that contrastively-learned representations are more robust to catastrophic forgetting than ones trained with cross-entropy. OWOD [12] introduces a memory queue for updating the class mean prototype vector during training to help contrastive learning. However, such class-contrastive formulations often collapse intra-class representations, hindering Re-ID-based data association in MOT. Our class-incremental instance representation learning approach maintains intra-class variability with a contrastive loss that estimates standard deviation prototype vectors for each class and keeps the class distribution close to a prior.

3   Method

We define the continual learning problem for MOT (Sect. 3.2). We then provide an overview of COOLer (Sect. 3.2) and introduce its two key components, namely continual pseudo-label generation for detection and data association (Sect. 3.3), and class-incremental instance representation learning (Sect. 3.4).

3.1   Problem Definition

We define continual learning for MOT as a class-incremental learning (CIL) problem over a sequence of B training stages $\{\mathcal{S}^0, \mathcal{S}^1, ..., \mathcal{S}^{B-1}\}$, where at each stage b a set of categories Y_b is introduced. $S^b = \{\mathcal{X}^b, \mathcal{D}^b, \mathcal{T}^b\}$ is the set of training videos $\mathcal{X}^b$, detection labels $\mathcal{D}^b$, and tracking labels $\mathcal{T}^b$ for a set of categories Y_b at stage b. Although typical CIL assumes no overlapping classes in different tasks b and b', it is common in real-world applications to observe old classes in new stages [33]. Thus, we assume that categories from another stage b' may occur again at b despite not being in the annotation set, i.e. $Y_b \cap Y_{b'} = \emptyset$. The goal is continually learning an MOT model that can track Y_b without forgetting to track $\bar{Y}_{b-1} = Y_0 \cup ... \cup Y_{b-1}$. During each stage b, only data S^b can be accessed. After each training stage b, the model is evaluated over all seen classes $\mathcal{Y}_b = Y_0 \cup ... \cup Y_b$.

3.2 COOLer

Architecture. COOLer's architecture is based on the representative appearance-based tracker QDTrack [21], which consists of a Faster R-CNN [25] object detector and a similarity head to learn Re-ID embeddings for data association.

Base Training. Given the data $S^0 = \{\mathcal{X}^0, \mathcal{D}^0, \mathcal{T}^0\}$ from the first stage $b = 0$, we train the base model ϕ^0 following QDTrack. Let $\hat{\mathcal{D}}^0$ be the detector predictions and $\hat{\mathcal{V}}^0$ their corresponding Re-ID embeddings. QDTrack is optimized end-to-end with a detection loss $\mathcal{L}_{det}$ to train the object detector, and a tracking loss $\mathcal{L}_{track}$ to learn the Re-ID embeddings for data association. $\mathcal{L}_{det}$ is computed from $\mathcal{D}^0$ and $\hat{\mathcal{D}}^0$ as in Faster R-CNN [25]. As for the tracking loss $\mathcal{L}_{track}$, QDTrack first samples positive and negative pairs of object proposals in adjacent frames using $\mathcal{D}^0$, $\mathcal{T}^0$, and $\hat{\mathcal{D}}^0$. Then, $\mathcal{L}_{track}$ is computed from a contrastive loss using the Re-ID embeddings $\hat{\mathcal{V}}^0$ of the sampled proposals to cluster object embeddings of the same IDs and separate embeddings of different instances. Refer to the original QDTrack paper [21] for more details. The final loss is:

$$\mathcal{L}^0 = \mathcal{L}_{det}(\hat{\mathcal{D}}^0, \mathcal{D}^0) + \mathcal{L}_{track}(\hat{\mathcal{D}}^0, \hat{\mathcal{V}}^0, \mathcal{D}^0, \mathcal{T}^0). \tag{1}$$

Continual Training. Given the old model ϕ^{b-1} trained up to the stage $b - 1$, and the new data S^b for the stage b, COOLer is the first tracker to incrementally learn to track the new classes Y_b without forgetting the old ones $\bar{Y}_{b-1}$. We propose a continual pseudo-label generation strategy for MOT (Sect. 3.3) that uses the previous tracker ϕ^{b-1} to generate pseudo-labels $\{\bar{\mathcal{D}}^b_{old}, \bar{\mathcal{T}}^b_{old}\}$ for the old classes $\bar{Y}_{b-1}$, and combine them with the ground-truth labels $\{\mathcal{D}^b_{new}, \mathcal{T}^b_{new}\}$ for the new ones Y_b to train the new model ϕ^b. To further disentangle the Re-ID embedding space for different classes and instances, we propose a novel class-incremental instance representation learning approach (Sect. 3.4). See Fig. 2 for an overview.

3.3 Continual Pseudo-label Generation for Tracking

While training with detection pseudo-labels generated by the previous object detector has proven effective against catastrophic forgetting in CIL of object

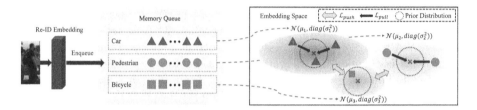

Fig. 3. Illustration of our class-incremental instance representation learning. We keep a memory queue to update the class embedding distributions. The contrastive loss includes an inter-class pushing loss and an intra-class pulling loss.

detection [22,36], detection pseudo-labels lack the instance association information, which is crucial to learn the Re-ID module in appearance-based MOT. We instead propose to use the MOT model ϕ^{b-1} from the previous stage $b-1$ to simultaneously generate temporally-refined detection pseudo-labels $\bar{\mathcal{D}}_{\text{old}}^b$ and instance association pseudo-labels $\bar{\mathcal{T}}_{\text{old}}^b$ for the old classes $\bar{Y}_{b-1}$ in the new stage b. We then train the new tracker ϕ^b on the union of the pseudo-labels $\{\bar{\mathcal{D}}_{\text{old}}^b, \bar{\mathcal{T}}_{\text{old}}^b\}$ for old classes $\bar{Y}_{b-1}$ and ground-truth labels $\{\mathcal{D}_{\text{new}}^b, \mathcal{T}_{\text{new}}^b\}$ for new classes Y_b:

$$\mathcal{L}_{\text{pseudo}}^b = \mathcal{L}_{\text{det}}(\hat{\mathcal{D}}^b, \bar{\mathcal{D}}_{\text{old}}^b \cup \mathcal{D}_{\text{new}}^b) + \mathcal{L}_{\text{track}}(\hat{\mathcal{D}}^b, \hat{\mathcal{V}}^b, \bar{\mathcal{D}}_{\text{old}}^b \cup \mathcal{D}_{\text{new}}^b, \bar{\mathcal{T}}_{\text{old}}^b \cup \mathcal{T}_{\text{new}}^b). \quad (2)$$

It is worth noticing that, unlike detection pseudo-labels in [22,36], our detection pseudo-labels are temporally refined by the tracking algorithm, resulting in a reduced number of false positives and in recovery of initially missed detections. Moreover, the pseudo-identities $\bar{\mathcal{T}}_{\text{old}}^b$ alleviate catastrophic forgetting in data association by training the similarity head on old classes $\bar{Y}_{b-1}$.

3.4   Class-Incremental Instance Representation Learning

Our class-incremental learning strategy based on tracking pseudo-labels (Sect. 3.3) enforces that each instance must be well-separated from others in the embeddings space, but does not constrain where Re-ID features for each class are projected, potentially leading to entangled class distributions that hurt both detection and tracking performance. Previous CIL approaches [3,12,18] ensure separation of class distributions by applying class-contrastive losses during incremental learning. However, naively applying contrastive learning on the instance embedding space would cause the distribution of a class' embeddings to collapse to a single point, undermining the intra-class discrimination properties of the learned Re-ID embeddings necessary for effective data association.

To this end, we introduce a novel contrastive loss for class-incremental instance representation learning that disentangles embeddings of different classes while maintaining the intra-class variability of the embeddings (Fig. 3).

Class Prototype Vectors. First, we model variability of instance embeddings within each class c by approximating each class' embedding distribution as a Gaussian $\mathcal{N}(\boldsymbol{\mu}_c, \text{diag}(\boldsymbol{\sigma}_c^2))$, whose class mean prototype vector $\boldsymbol{\mu}_c$ and class standard deviation prototype vector $\boldsymbol{\sigma}_c$ are approximated online as the exponential moving average of a memory queue with limited size N_{queue} that stores exemplary class embeddings. See Supplement Sec. A for details on the memory queue.

Contrastive Loss. Our contrastive loss consists of a pushing term $\mathcal{L}_{\text{push}}$ that pushes distributions of different classes away from each other, and a pulling term $\mathcal{L}_{\text{pull}}$ that keeps the class distribution close to a prior, ensuring intra-class variability. We derive such losses from the Bhattacharyya distance D_B, which measures the similarity between distributions $\mathcal{N}(\boldsymbol{\mu}_{c_1}, \text{diag}(\boldsymbol{\sigma}_{c_1}^2))$ and $\mathcal{N}(\boldsymbol{\mu}_{c_2}, \text{diag}(\boldsymbol{\sigma}_{c_2}^2))$ of two classes c_1 and c_2. Their Bhattacharyya distance is:

$$D_B(c_1, c_2) = \frac{1}{8}(\boldsymbol{\mu}_{c_1} - \boldsymbol{\mu}_{c_2})^T \boldsymbol{\Sigma}_{c_1,c_2}^{-1}(\boldsymbol{\mu}_{c_1} - \boldsymbol{\mu}_{c_2}) + \frac{1}{2}\ln\frac{\det\boldsymbol{\Sigma}_{c_1,c_2}}{\sqrt{\det\boldsymbol{\Sigma}_{c_1}\det\boldsymbol{\Sigma}_{c_2}}}, \tag{3}$$

where $\boldsymbol{\Sigma}_{c_1,c_2} = \frac{\boldsymbol{\Sigma}_{c_1}+\boldsymbol{\Sigma}_{c_2}}{2}$. As it is hard to back-propagate gradients for the prototype mean and standard deviation $\boldsymbol{\mu}_c, \boldsymbol{\Sigma}_c$, we additionally introduce the per-batch embedding mean $\bar{\boldsymbol{\mu}}_c$ and standard deviation $\bar{\boldsymbol{\sigma}}_c$ for class c:

$$\bar{\boldsymbol{\mu}}_c = \frac{1}{N_c}\sum_{i=1}^{N_c}\boldsymbol{v}_{c,i}, \bar{\boldsymbol{\sigma}}_c = \sqrt{\frac{1}{N_c}\sum_{i=1}^{N_c}(\boldsymbol{v}_{c,i} - \boldsymbol{\mu}_c)^2}, \tag{4}$$

where N_c denotes the number of embedding vectors for class c in the current batch and $\boldsymbol{v}_{c,i}$ is the i_{th} embedding vector for class c.

Pushing Loss. For the pushing loss, the distance between the two class distributions is derived from the first term of Eq. 3 as:

$$D_{\text{push}}(c_1, c_2) = \sqrt{(\bar{\boldsymbol{\mu}}_{c_1} - \bar{\boldsymbol{\mu}}_{c_2})^T \boldsymbol{\Sigma}_{c_1,c_2}^{-1}(\bar{\boldsymbol{\mu}}_{c_1} - \bar{\boldsymbol{\mu}}_{c_2})}. \tag{5}$$

We use the following hinge-based pushing loss to separate the two distributions:

$$\mathcal{L}_{\text{push}} = \frac{1}{C(C-1)}\sum_{c_1=1}^{C}\sum_{\substack{c_2=1 \\ c_2 \neq c_1}}^{C}[\Delta_{\text{push}} - D_{\text{push}}(c_1, c_2)]_+^2, \tag{6}$$

where C is the number of classes, Δ_{push} is the hinge factor, and $[x]_+ = \max(0, x)$.

Pulling Loss. For the pulling loss, we introduce a prior Gaussian distribution $\mathcal{N}(\boldsymbol{\mu}_c, \text{diag}(\boldsymbol{\sigma}_p^2))$ for each class, which has the same class mean prototype vector $\boldsymbol{\mu}_c$ while the standard deviation $\boldsymbol{\sigma}_p$ is fixed. We derive the distance between the class distribution and the prior distribution from the second term of Eq. 3 as:

$$D_{\text{pull}}(c, p) = \frac{1}{2}(\sum_{j=1}^{N_d}\ln(\frac{\bar{\sigma}_{c,j}^2 + \sigma_{p,j}^2}{2}) - \sum_{j=1}^{N_d}\ln(\bar{\sigma}_{c,j}\sigma_{p,j})), \tag{7}$$

where N_d is the dimension of the embedding. We find that directly applying Eq. 7 as the pulling loss will lead to numerical instability during optimization, as the logarithm operator is non-convex. We propose the following surrogate based on the $\mathcal{L}_2$ distance for a smoother optimization landscape as follows:

$$\mathcal{L}_{\text{pull}} = \frac{1}{C} \sum_{c=1}^{C} \sum_{j=1}^{N_d} (\bar{\sigma}_{c,j} - \sigma_{p,j})^2. \tag{8}$$

Total Loss. Finally, we extend Eq. 2 with our pulling and pushing contrastive losses to learn the tracking model ϕ^b at stage b:

$$\mathcal{L}^b = \mathcal{L}_{\text{det}} + \mathcal{L}_{\text{track}} + \beta_1 \mathcal{L}_{\text{pull}} + \beta_2 \mathcal{L}_{\text{push}}, \tag{9}$$

where β_1 and β_2 are weights for the pushing and the pulling loss respectively.

4 Evaluation Protocol

We introduce a protocol for evaluating algorithms for class-incremental MOT.

Datasets. We use the BDD100K [34] and SHIFT [29] tracking datasets for evaluation. BDD100K is a large-scale real-world driving dataset for MOT with 8 classes. SHIFT is a large-scale synthetic driving dataset for MOT with 6 classes. Because of the size of the SHIFT dataset, training multiple stages on it is not feasible with modest computational resources. To ensure practicality for all researchers', we propose to only use its clear-daytime subset. The detailed class statistics for each dataset are reported in Table 1. Note that other popular MOT datasets are unsuitable for our setting. The MOT20 dataset [7] has very few categories. While TAO [6] has hundreds of classes, due to the scarcity of annotations it is intended as an evaluation benchmark and is not suitable for CIL.

Table 1. Class frequencies for the training splits of BDD100K [34] and SHIFT's [29] clear-daytime subset.

Dataset	Car	Ped	Truck	Bus	Bike	Rider	Motor	Train
BDD100K [34]	2098517	369798	149411	57860	25565	20107	12176	1620
SHIFT [29]	677580	749640	145940	65367	52267	–	74469	–

Protocol. The choice of the class ordering during incremental stages may largely impact results and observations. Object detection benchmarks typically add classes by their alphabetical order. However, in real-world MOT applications the annotation order often depends by (i) class frequency or (ii) semantic grouping. We hence propose the practical class splits to mirror the practitioners' needs. First, we propose two *frequency-based splits*. The Most→Least (**M→L**) split incrementally adds classes one-by-one from the most to the least frequent class according to Table 1. General→Specific (**G→S**) only evaluates one incremental step by dividing the classes into two groups: the first half of the most populated classes (General) and the remainder (Specific). Then, we propose a *semantic split*. We group classes into three super-categories according to their semantic similarity: vehicles, bikes, and humans. Therefore, we experiment on the Vehicle→Bike→Human (**V→B→H**) setting with two incremental steps.

Taking BDD100K as example, in the **M→L** setting the classes are added as follows: car→pedestrian→truck→bus→bike→rider→motor→train. In the **G→S** setting, the model is first trained on {car, pedestrian, truck, bus}, and then {bike, rider, motor, train} are added at once. In the **V→B→H** setting, the classes are added as follows: {car, truck, bus, train}→{bike, motor}→{pedestrian, rider}.

5   Experiments

5.1   Baselines

Since no prior work studied class-incremental learning for multiple objcet tracking, we compare COOLer with the following baseline methods:

Fine-tuning. In each incremental step, the model is trained only on the training data of the new classes, without addressing catastrophic forgetting.

Table 2. Class-incremental Learning on BDD100K. We conduct experiments on M→L, G→S and V→B→H settings.We compare COOLer with the Fine-tuning, Distillation, Det PL baselines and the oracle tracker.

Setting		All Classes						
Stage (+New Classes)	Method	mMOTA	mHOTA	mIDF1	MOTA	HOTA	IDF1	mAP
M→L Stage 0 (Car)		67.6	62.1	73.3	67.6	62.1	73.3	58.7
M→L Stage 1 (+Pedestrian)	Fine-tuning	15.6	21.8	27.7	4.5	19.1	14.1	19.9
	Distillation	46.4	51.7	63.0	61.8	59.0	70.1	47.1
	Det PL	46.7	49.5	59.2	56.3	53.9	61.8	46.8
	COOLer	**54.2**	**52.6**	**64.3**	**62.7**	**59.5**	**70.5**	**47.4**
	Oracle	57.4	53.6	65.9	65.1	59.9	71.5	48.3
M→L Stage 2 (+Truck)	Fine-tuning	−11.5	12.8	14.0	−2.2	13.3	6.2	11.7
	Distillation	27.3	47.8	57.3	56.9	56.6	67.4	**42.8**
	Det PL	34.9	47.1	55.6	57.3	55.5	65.1	42.5
	COOLer	**42.8**	**49.2**	**59.6**	**58.6**	**57.9**	**68.7**	42.6
	Oracle	49.8	50.8	62.1	63.2	58.9	70.4	45.0
M→L Stage 3 (+Bus)	Fine-tuning	−24.0	9.2	9.3	−2.0	8.6	2.5	9.9
	Distillation	−11.2	43.4	50.8	54.0	55.1	65.6	40.8
	Det PL	14.1	43.1	49.1	53.6	53.4	61.5	40.9
	COOLer	**34.0**	**47.9**	**57.3**	**55.8**	**56.8**	**67.4**	**41.9**
	Oracle	45.4	50.1	60.9	62.5	58.7	70.2	44.5
M→L Stage 4 (+Bicycle)	Fine-tuning	−16.0	5.6	6.5	−0.8	4.2	0.8	4.6
	Distillation	−19.4	40.1	47.1	51.9	53.2	63.6	35.1
	Det PL	3.6	37.6	42.4	41.2	43.0	46.2	34.3
	COOLer	**28.6**	**44.4**	**53.9**	**53.2**	**55.7**	**66.1**	**36.5**
	Oracle	41.3	47.1	58.0	62.2	58.5	69.9	39.9
G→S Stage 0 (General)		45.6	50.3	61.1	62.4	59.0	70.2	44.6
G→S Stage 1 (+Specific)	Fine-tuning	−24.7	11.7	14.1	−0.5	5.7	1.5	8.4
	Distillation	−32.9	35.4	42.4	59.6	57.3	68.3	29.5
	Det PL	6.0	34.9	41.5	54.1	52.0	59.6	27.9
	COOLer	**28.6**	**38.5**	**48.2**	**60.5**	**58.2**	**69.3**	**29.9**
	Oracle	30.4	38.9	49.0	61.8	58.7	70.0	30.9
V→B→H Stage 0 (Vehicle)		33.1	39.2	46.8	65.1	61.0	72.3	35.0
V→B→H Stage 1 (+Bike)	Fine-tuning	−27.5	9.7	11.2	−0.6	4.9	1.2	7.3
	Distillation	−30.5	34.1	39.6	62.9	59.7	70.6	**29.1**
	Det PL	−3.3	31.3	37.0	53.7	51.4	57.9	26.7
	COOLer	**24.4**	**36.8**	**44.8**	**63.1**	**60.2**	**70.9**	29.1
	Oracle	27.6	38.5	47.8	64.3	60.4	71.6	30.8
V→B→H Stage 2 (+Human)	Fine-tuning	7.4	10.0	13.1	4.4	18.2	13.4	8.2
	Distillation	14.8	35.8	43.9	55.9	55.9	66.4	27.9
	Det PL	15.5	34.6	41.5	52.1	51.4	58.7	27.4
	COOLer	**27.1**	**37.5**	**46.8**	**59.2**	**57.8**	**68.8**	**28.8**
	Oracle	30.4	38.9	49.0	61.8	58.7	70.0	30.9

Distillation. We design a distillation baseline based on Faster-ILOD [22], a state-of-the-art class-incremental object detection method that uses distillation losses from a teacher model of the previous stage to alleviate forgetting. To further address forgetting in data association, we add the following distillation loss on the similarity head of QDTrack to enforce the cosine similarity between teacher and student embeddings for the old classes:

$$\mathcal{L}_{\text{track}}^{\text{dist}} = \left(\frac{\mathbf{v}_{\text{teacher}} \cdot \mathbf{v}_{\text{student}}}{\|\mathbf{v}_{\text{teacher}}\|_2 \cdot \|\mathbf{v}_{\text{student}}\|_2} - 1 \right)^2, \tag{10}$$

where $\mathbf{v}_{\text{teacher}}$ and $\mathbf{v}_{\text{student}}$ are the Re-ID embeddings of the teacher and the student model, computed from the same proposals sampled for Faster-ILOD's ROI head distillation. The final loss is then $\mathcal{L} = \mathcal{L}_{\text{det}} + \mathcal{L}_{\text{track}} + \mu_1 \mathcal{L}_{\text{det}}^{\text{dist}} + \mu_2 \mathcal{L}_{\text{track}}^{\text{dist}}$, where $\mathcal{L}_{\text{det}}^{\text{dist}}$ is the detection distillation loss in [22], and μ_1, μ_2 are set to 1.

Detection Pseudo-Labels (Det PL) . We compare against a baseline that only trains on the joint set of ground-truth labels for the new classes and high-confident (> 0.7) detection pseudo-labels from the old detector for the old classes. Unlike our method, this baseline does not temporally refine the detection pseudo-labels with the tracker, and does not provide association pseudo-labels.

Oracle . We compare the result with an oracle tracker trained in a single stage on the ground truth annotations of all classes.

Table 3. Class-incremental Learning on SHIFT. We conduct experiments on M→L, G→S and V→B→H settings.We compare COOLer with the Fine-tuning and Det PL baselines and the oracle tracker.

Setting		All Classes						
Stage (+New Classes)	Method	mMOTA	mHOTA	mIDF1	MOTA	HOTA	IDF1	mAP
M→L Stage 0 (Pedestrian)		53.7	46.1	54.4	53.7	46.1	54.4	43.0
M→L Stage 1 (+Car)	Fine-tuning	25.8	28.5	30.9	24.2	40.5	37.7	25.3
	Det PL	44.6	46.8	49.7	44.2	47.2	49.1	45.6
	COOLer	**50.9**	**50.9**	**57.0**	**50.9**	**51.0**	**56.8**	**45.7**
	Oracle	53.7	51.8	58.7	53.7	51.4	58.4	46.2
M→L Stage 2 (+Truck)	Fine-tuning	11.7	18.0	19.6	2.7	16.9	8.1	15.5
	Det PL	34.6	44.7	45.9	33.5	43.0	40.4	**44.8**
	COOLer	**45.2**	**51.5**	**57.3**	**48.2**	**50.6**	**56.3**	**44.8**
	Oracle	52.6	53.5	60.7	53.5	51.8	58.9	46.0
G→S Stage 0 (General)		50.8	53.1	60.0	52.4	51.9	58.2	46.0
G→S Stage 1 (+Specific)	Fine-tuning	19.4	24.1	26.9	4.8	18.1	10.1	20.0
	Det PL	45.8	49.8	55.4	48.7	48.9	52.7	**43.2**
	COOLer	**46.0**	**50.8**	**57.0**	**50.8**	**51.4**	**57.5**	42.7
	Oracle	48.8	51.1	57.5	52.5	51.9	58.5	43.8
V→B→H Stage 0 (Vehicle)		47.2	52.1	57.4	51.9	56.4	61.4	45.2
V→B→H Stage 1 (+Bike)	Fine-tuning	16.1	20.4	22.4	5.9	20.5	12.2	16.6
	Det PL	39.4	47.1	51.0	41.4	47.4	48.6	42.0
	COOLer	**44.5**	**51.3**	**57.5**	**49.5**	**55.5**	**60.9**	**42.3**
	Oracle	47.8	52.1	58.0	51.5	55.5	60.8	44.2
V→B→H Stage 2 (+Human)	Fine-tuning	8.9	7.7	9.1	23.0	31.2	30.9	7.1
	Det PL	37.3	41.4	43.7	39.8	40.9	42.6	41.7
	COOLer	**47.0**	**50.6**	**57.5**	**50.7**	**51.3**	**57.7**	**42.2**
	Oracle	48.8	51.1	57.5	52.5	51.9	58.5	43.8

5.2   Implementation Details

COOLer's architecture is based on QDTrack with a ResNet-50 [11] backbone. The model is optimized with SGD with momentum of 0.9 and weight decay of 1e-4. We train the network with 8 NVIDIA 2080Ti GPUs with a total batch size of 16. For all experiments, we train for 6 epochs in each incremental stage. The initial learning rate is 0.02 and decayed to 0.002 after 4 epochs, and to 0.0002 after 5. For BDD100K experiments, the weight for the contrastive losses β_1, β_2 are 0.01; for SHIFT experiments, β_1, β_2 are 0.001. The hinge factor for the pushing loss Δ_{push} is set to 15.0. For the prior distribution $\mathcal{N}(\boldsymbol{\mu}_c, \text{diag}(\boldsymbol{\sigma}_p^2))$ of the pulling loss, we use $\boldsymbol{\sigma}_p = 0.05 \cdot \vec{\mathbf{1}}$, where $\vec{\mathbf{1}}$ is the unit vector. We select hyperparameters from a grid search, and report sensitivity analysis in the supplement.

Table 4. Ablation Study on Method Components. We ablate on the choice of pseudo-labels (PL) and contrastive (CT) loss for COOLer on **M→L** setting on BDD100K. We compare training with our pseudo-labels generated by the tracker (Track) and the pseudo-labels generated by the detector (Det). We also compare our contrastive loss (Ours) with the contrastive loss proposed in OWOD [12].

Setting	Components		All Classes						
Stage (+New Classes)	PL	CT Loss	mMOTA	mHOTA	mIDF1	MOTA	HOTA	IDF1	mAP
M→L Stage 1 (+Pedestrian)	Det	✗	46.7	49.5	59.2	56.3	53.9	61.8	46.8
	Track	✗	54.1	**52.6**	**64.5**	62.5	59.3	70.3	47.2
	Track	OWOD [12]	53.7	52.2	63.9	62.1	58.9	69.8	47.2
	Track	Ours	**54.2**	**52.6**	64.3	**62.7**	**59.5**	**70.5**	**47.4**
M→L Stage 2 (+Truck)	Det	✗	34.9	47.1	55.6	57.3	55.5	65.1	42.5
	Track	✗	**43.4**	49.1	59.5	58.2	57.5	68.3	**42.8**
	Track	OWOD [12]	41.9	48.7	58.9	57.6	57.3	68.0	**42.8**
	Track	Ours	42.8	**49.2**	**59.6**	**58.6**	**57.9**	**68.7**	42.6
M→L Stage 3 (+Bus)	Det	✗	14.1	43.1	49.1	53.6	53.4	61.5	40.9
	Track	✗	32.8	47.6	56.9	54.5	56.3	66.8	**41.9**
	Track	OWOD [12]	33.1	47.5	56.9	53.9	56.1	66.6	**41.9**
	Track	Ours	**34.0**	**47.9**	**57.3**	**55.8**	**56.8**	**67.4**	**41.9**
M→L Stage 4 (+Bicycle)	Det	✗	3.6	37.6	42.4	41.2	43.0	46.2	34.3
	Track	✗	25.7	43.9	52.9	50.8	55.1	65.4	36.1
	Track	OWOD [12]	24.7	43.7	52.7	49.8	54.8	65.0	36.1
	Track	Ours	**28.6**	**44.4**	**53.9**	**53.2**	**55.7**	**66.1**	**36.5**

5.3   Experimental Results

We compare our method to the above-mentioned baselines on the BDD100K and SHIFT datasets. We evaluate the mAP for object detection, and representative tracking metrics for MOT. mMOTA, mHOTA, mIDF1 are averaged across category-specific metrics, while MOTA, HOTA, IDF1 are the overall metrics.

Fig. 4. Qualitative Results of the Det PL baseline and COOLer on a validation video sequence of BDD100K in the fourth step of the **M→L** setting (+Bicycle). Different bounding box colors represent different classes, and the number above the bound box denotes the instance ID. Best viewed in color with zoom.

BDD100K. Table 2 shows the results on the BDD100K dataset. In the **M→L** setting, we show results up to stage 4 (+Bicycle) due to space constraints, and report full results in the supplement. COOLer achieves the best tracking performance among all methods and in all settings. In (**M→L**, Stage 4) COOLer has a noteworthy 48.0%, and 25.0% mMOTA improvement compared to the Distillation and Det PL baselines, showing its effectiveness in class-incremental tracking. Besides boosting the tracking performance, COOLer also improves continual object detection. Compared to the Distillation baseline based on the class-incremental object detector Faster-ILOD [22], COOLer achieves higher mAP thanks to our temporally-refined detection pseudo-labels. COOLer obtains +1.4% and +2.2% mAP wrt. Distillation and Det PL in (**M→L**, Stage 4), and +0.9% and +1.4% mAP wrt. Distillation and Det PL in (**V→B→H**, Stage 2).

SHIFT. We conduct experiments on the SHIFT dataset, and report the results in Table 3. The results confirm the findings and trends observed ob BDD100K. COOLer consistently outperforms all other baselines across all tracking metrics on all classes, further showing the superiority and generality of our approach.

5.4 Ablation Study

We here ablate on method components and analyze qualitative results. In the supplement, we provide an additional analysis of the performance on old classes (model's rigidity) and new classes (model's plasticity) under incremental stages.

Ablation on Method Components. We show the effectiveness of each proposed component of COOLer in Table 4. We compare our detection pseudo-labels refined by the tracker (Track) vs. unrefined detection pseudo-labels from the object detector only (Det). Moreover, we analyze the effect of additional class-incremental contrastive losses, comparing ours (Ours) vs. OWOD's [12] (OWOD). Our components consistently improve over the baselines, and the improvement is more significant as more incremental stages are performed, suggesting that more stages pose a greater challenge in CIL for MOT. Notably, using the tracking pseudo-labels improves over all metrics, with 22.2% mMOTA,

6.9% mHOTA, 10.5% mIDF1, and 1.8% mAP at stage 4. Enabling the class-incremental contrastive loss further boosts 2.9% mMOTA, 0.5% mHOTA, and 1.0% mIDF1, and 0.4% mAP, highlighting the superiority of our contrastive loss. The results confirm that COOLer can (i) utilize the tracker's temporal refinement to produce higher-quality labels for detection, (ii) better preserve the association performance thanks to the association pseudo-labels, and (iii) that our contrastive loss design outperforms OWOD's.

Qualitative Comparison. Figure 4 shows that the Det PL baseline would suffer from ID switches of the car (red) in the middle, due to the misclassification of it as a bus (purple) in the second frame. It can also not associate the pedestrians beside the pole across two frames (ID 322 switches to ID 325). Nevertheless, COOLer can both correctly classify the car and associate the pedestrians. This demonstrates that COOLer can better retain the knowledge of associating objects of the old classes while reducing misclassifications.

6   Conclusion

Our work is the first to address continual learning for MOT, a practical problem as MOT datasets are expensive to collect. We introduce COOLer, the first comprehensive approach to class-incremental learning for multiple object tracking. COOLer adopts a continual pseudo-label generation strategy for tracking that leverages the previous tracker to generate association pseudo-labels and temporally-refine detection pseudo-labels, while introducing class-incremental instance representation learning to further improve the tracking performance. Experimental results demonstrate that COOLer overcomes the drawbacks of detection-oriented methods, improving both detection and association performance. Although highly effective in the proposed setting, COOLer assumes that instances from the previous classes are present in the new training data. We believe experience replay to be a possible solution to this limitation, and we leave its exploration to future work. We hope our work can stimulate future research in this challenging yet practical direction.

Acknowledgments. This work was funded by the Max Planck ETH Center for Learning Systems.

References

1. Aharon, N., Orfaig, R., Bobrovsky, B.Z.: Bot-sort: robust associations multi-pedestrian tracking. arXiv preprint arXiv:2206.14651 (2022)
2. Bernardin, K., Stiefelhagen, R.: Evaluating multiple object tracking performance: the clear mot metrics. EURASIP J. Image Video Process. **2008**, 1–10 (2008)
3. Cha, H., Lee, J., Shin, J.: Co2l: contrastive continual learning. In: Proceedings of the IEEE/CVF International Conference on Computer Vision, pp. 9516–9525 (2021)

4. Chen, T., Kornblith, S., Norouzi, M., Hinton, G.: A simple framework for contrastive learning of visual representations. In: International Conference on Machine Learning, pp. 1597–1607. PMLR (2020)
5. Chen, Z., Liu, B.: Lifelong machine learning. Synth. Lect. Artif. Intell. Mach. Learn. **12**(3), 1–207 (2018)
6. Dave, A., Khurana, T., Tokmakov, P., Schmid, C., Ramanan, D.: TAO: a large-scale benchmark for tracking any object. In: Vedaldi, A., Bischof, H., Brox, T., Frahm, J.-M. (eds.) ECCV 2020. LNCS, vol. 12350, pp. 436–454. Springer, Cham (2020). https://doi.org/10.1007/978-3-030-58558-7_26
7. Dendorfer, P., et al.: Mot20: a benchmark for multi object tracking in crowded scenes. arXiv preprint arXiv:2003.09003 (2020)
8. Du, Y., et al.: Strongsort: make deepsort great again. IEEE Trans. Multimedia **25**, 8725–8737 (2023)
9. Fan, H., Zheng, L., Yan, C., Yang, Y.: Unsupervised person re-identification: clustering and fine-tuning. ACM Trans. Multimedia Comput. Commun. Appl. (TOMM) **14**(4), 1–18 (2018)
10. He, K., Fan, H., Wu, Y., Xie, S., Girshick, R.: Momentum contrast for unsupervised visual representation learning. In: Proceedings of the IEEE/CVF Conference on Computer Vision and Pattern Recognition, pp. 9729–9738 (2020)
11. He, K., Zhang, X., Ren, S., Sun, J.: Deep residual learning for image recognition. In: Proceedings of the IEEE Conference on Computer Vision and Pattern Recognition, pp. 770–778 (2016)
12. Joseph, K., Khan, S., Khan, F.S., Balasubramanian, V.N.: Towards open world object detection. In: Proceedings of the IEEE/CVF Conference on Computer Vision and Pattern Recognition, pp. 5830–5840 (2021)
13. Karthik, S., Prabhu, A., Gandhi, V.: Simple unsupervised multi-object tracking. arXiv preprint arXiv:2006.02609 (2020)
14. Kirkpatrick, J., et al.: Overcoming catastrophic forgetting in neural networks. Proc. Natl. Acad. Sci. **114**(13), 3521–3526 (2017)
15. Li, M., Zhu, X., Gong, S.: Unsupervised tracklet person re-identification. IEEE Trans. Pattern Anal. Mach. Intell. **42**(7), 1770–1782 (2019)
16. Li, Z., Hoiem, D.: Learning without forgetting. IEEE Trans. Pattern Anal. Mach. Intell. **40**(12), 2935–2947 (2017)
17. Liu, Y., Schiele, B., Vedaldi, A., Rupprecht, C.: Continual detection transformer for incremental object detection. In: Proceedings of the IEEE/CVF Conference on Computer Vision and Pattern Recognition, pp. 23799–23808 (2023)
18. Mai, Z., Li, R., Kim, H., Sanner, S.: Supervised contrastive replay: Revisiting the nearest class mean classifier in online class-incremental continual learning. In: Proceedings of the IEEE/CVF Conference on Computer Vision and Pattern Recognition, pp. 3589–3599 (2021)
19. Mallya, A., Lazebnik, S.: Packnet: adding multiple tasks to a single network by iterative pruning. In: Proceedings of the IEEE conference on Computer Vision and Pattern Recognition, pp. 7765–7773 (2018)
20. McCloskey, M., Cohen, N.J.: Catastrophic interference in connectionist networks: the sequential learning problem. In: Psychology of Learning and Motivation, vol. 24, pp. 109–165. Elsevier (1989)
21. Pang, J., et al.: Quasi-dense similarity learning for multiple object tracking. In: Proceedings of the IEEE/CVF Conference on Computer Vision and Pattern Recognition, pp. 164–173 (2021)
22. Peng, C., Zhao, K., Lovell, B.C.: Faster ilod: incremental learning for object detectors based on faster RCNN. Pattern Recogn. Lett. **140**, 109–115 (2020)

23. Ramanan, D., Forsyth, D.A.: Finding and tracking people from the bottom up. In: 2003 IEEE Computer Society Conference on Computer Vision and Pattern Recognition, Proceedings, vol. 2, p. II. IEEE (2003)

24. Rebuffi, S.A., Kolesnikov, A., Sperl, G., Lampert, C.H.: ICARL: incremental classifier and representation learning. In: Proceedings of the IEEE conference on Computer Vision and Pattern Recognition, pp. 2001–2010 (2017)

25. Ren, S., He, K., Girshick, R., Sun, J.: Faster r-cnn: towards real-time object detection with region proposal networks. Adv. Neural Inf. Process. Syst. **28** (2015)

26. Rusu, A.A., et al.: Progressive neural networks. arXiv preprint arXiv:1606.04671 (2016)

27. Segu, M., Schiele, B., Yu, F.: Darth: holistic test-time adaptation for multiple object tracking. In: Proceedings of the IEEE/CVF International Conference on Computer Vision (2023)

28. Shmelkov, K., Schmid, C., Alahari, K.: Incremental learning of object detectors without catastrophic forgetting. In: Proceedings of the IEEE International Conference on Computer Vision, pp. 3400–3409 (2017)

29. Sun, T., et al.: SHIFT: a synthetic driving dataset for continuous multi-task domain adaptation. In: Proceedings of the IEEE/CVF Conference on Computer Vision and Pattern Recognition (CVPR), pp. 21371–21382 (2022)

30. Wang, Y.H.: Smiletrack: similarity learning for multiple object tracking. arXiv preprint arXiv:2211.08824 (2022)

31. Wojke, N., Bewley, A., Paulus, D.: Simple online and realtime tracking with a deep association metric. In: 2017 IEEE International Conference on Image Processing (ICIP), pp. 3645–3649. IEEE (2017). https://doi.org/10.1109/ICIP.2017.8296962

32. Wu, G., Zhu, X., Gong, S.: Tracklet self-supervised learning for unsupervised person re-identification. In: Proceedings of the AAAI Conference on Artificial Intelligence, vol. 34, pp. 12362–12369 (2020)

33. Xie, J., Yan, S., He, X.: General incremental learning with domain-aware categorical representations. In: Proceedings of the IEEE/CVF Conference on Computer Vision and Pattern Recognition, pp. 14351–14360 (2022)

34. Yu, F., et al.: Bdd100k: a diverse driving dataset for heterogeneous multitask learning. In: Proceedings of the IEEE/CVF Conference on Computer Vision and Pattern Recognition, pp. 2636–2645 (2020)

35. Zhang, Y., et al.: Bytetrack: multi-object tracking by associating every detection box. In: European Conference on Computer Vision, pp. 1–21. Springer, Heidelberg (2022). https://doi.org/10.1007/978-3-031-20047-2_1

36. Zheng, K., Chen, C.: Contrast r-cnn for continual learning in object detection. arXiv preprint arXiv:2108.04224 (2021)

37. Zhou, W., Chang, S., Sosa, N., Hamann, H., Cox, D.: Lifelong object detection. arXiv preprint arXiv:2009.01129 (2020)

38. Zhu, X., Su, W., Lu, L., Li, B., Wang, X., Dai, J.: Deformable DETR: deformable transformers for end-to-end object detection. arXiv preprint arXiv:2010.04159 (2020)

Label Smarter, Not Harder: CleverLabel for Faster Annotation of Ambiguous Image Classification with Higher Quality

Lars Schmarje[✉][iD], Vasco Grossmann[iD], Tim Michels[iD], Jakob Nazarenus[iD], Monty Santarossa[iD], Claudius Zelenka[iD], and Reinhard Koch[iD]

Kiel University, Kiel, Germany
{las,vgr,tmi,jna,msa,cze,rk}@informatik.uni-kiel.de

Abstract. High-quality data is crucial for the success of machine learning, but labeling large datasets is often a time-consuming and costly process. While semi-supervised learning can help mitigate the need for labeled data, label quality remains an open issue due to ambiguity and disagreement among annotators. Thus, we use proposal-guided annotations as one option which leads to more consistency between annotators. However, proposing a label increases the probability of the annotators deciding in favor of this specific label. This introduces a bias which we can simulate and remove. We propose a new method CleverLabel for **C**ost-effective **L**ab**E**ling using **V**alidated proposal-guid**E**d annotations and **R**epaired **LABEL**s. CleverLabel can reduce labeling costs by up to 30.0%, while achieving a relative improvement in Kullback-Leibler divergence of up to 29.8% compared to the previous state-of-the-art on a multi-domain real-world image classification benchmark. CleverLabel offers a novel solution to the challenge of efficiently labeling large datasets while also improving the label quality.

Keywords: Ambiguous · data-centric · data annotation

1 Introduction

Labeled data is the fuel of modern deep learning. However, the time-consuming manual labeling process is one of the main limitations of machine learning [54]. Therefore, current research efforts try to mitigate this issue by using unlabeled data [4,55,56] or forms of self-supervision [18,19,22,33]. Following the data-centric paradigm, another approach focuses on improving data quality rather than quantity [15,34,39]. This line of research concludes that one single annotation is not enough to capture ambiguous samples [3,8,10,47], where different annotators will provide different annotations for the same image. These cases are common in most real-world datasets [6,40,46,57] and would require multiple annotations per image to accurately estimate its label distribution. Yet,

---

Supplementary Information The online version contains supplementary material available at https://doi.org/10.1007/978-3-031-54605-1_30.

U. Köthe and C. Rother (Eds.): DAGM GCPR 2023, LNCS 14264, pp. 459–475, 2024.
https://doi.org/10.1007/978-3-031-54605-1_30

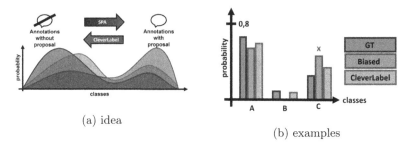

(a) idea

(b) examples

Fig. 1. Illustration of distribution shift – We are interested in the ground-truth label distribution (blue) which is costly to obtain due to multiple required annotations per image. Thus, we propose to use proposals as guidance during the annotation to approximate the distribution more cost efficiently (red). However, this distribution might be shifted toward the proposed class. We provide with CleverLabel (green) a method to improve the biased label distribution (red) to be closer to the original unbiased distribution (blue). Additionally, we provide with SPA an algorithm to simulate and analyze the distribution shift. The concrete effects are shown in the right example for the Mice-Bone dataset on a public benchmark [47] with the proposal marked by x. (Color figure online)

established benchmarks such as ImageNet or CIFAR [23,24] are currently not considering this issue which significantly limits their use in the development of methods that generalize well for ambiguous real-world data.

Acquiring multiple annotations per sample introduces an additional labeling effort, necessitating a trade-off between label quality and quantity. While semi-supervised learning potentially reduces the amount of labeled data, the issue of label quality still arises for the remaining portion of labeled data [28]. One possible solution for handling ambiguous data is using proposal guided annotations [11,41] which have been shown to lead to faster and more consistent annotations [46,50]. However, this approach suffers from two potential issues: (1) Humans tend towards deciding in favor of the provided proposal [20]. This *default effect* introduces a bias, since the proposed class will be annotated more often than it would have been without the proposal. Thus, an average across multiple annotation results in a skewed distribution towards the proposed class as shown in Fig. 1. (2) Real human annotations are required during development which prevents rapid prototyping of proposal systems.

We provide with CleverLabel and SPA two methods to overcome these two issues. Regarding issue (1), we propose Cost-effective LabEling using Validated proposal-guidEd annotations and Repaired LABELs (CleverLabel) which uses a single class per image as proposal to speed-up the annotation process. As noted above, this might skew the label distribution towards the proposed class which can be corrected with CleverLabel. We evaluate the data quality improvement achieved by training a network on labels generated by CleverLabel by comparing the network's predicted label probability distribution to the ground truth label distribution, which is calculated by averaging labels across multiple annotations as in [47]. Improved data quality is indicated by a reduction in the difference between the predicted distribution and the ground truth distribution. In addition, based on a previously published user study [49], we empirically investigate the influence of proposals on the annotator's labeling decisions. Regarding issue (2), we propose Simulated Proposal Acceptance (SPA), a mathematical model that mimics the human behavior during proposal-based labeling. We evaluate CleverLabel and SPA with respect to their technical feasibility and their benefit when applied to simulated and real-world proposal acceptance data. Finally, we evaluate these methods on a real-world benchmark and we provide general guidelines on how to annotate ambiguous data based on the gained insights.

Overall, our contributions commit to three different areas of interest: (1) For improving label quality, we provide the novel method CleverLabel and show across multiple simulated and real world datasets a relative improvement of up to 29.8% with 30.0% reduced costs in comparison to the state of the art. (2) For annotating real-world ambiguous data, we provide annotation guidelines based on our analysis, in which cases to use proposals during the annotation. (3) For researching of countering the effect of proposals on human annotation behavior, we provide our simulation of proposal acceptance (SPA) as an analysis tool. SPA is motivated by theory and shows similar behavior to human annotators on real-world tasks. It is important to note that this research allowed us to achieve the previous contributions.

1.1   Related Work

Data and especially high-quality labeled data is important for modern machine learning [38,63]. Hence, the labeling process is most important in uncertain cases or in ambiguous cases as defined by [47]. However, labeling is also not easy in these cases as demonstrated by the difficulties of melanoma skin cancer classification [36]. The issue of data ambiguity still remains even in large datasets like ImageNet [24] despite heavy cleaning efforts [5,60]. The reasons for this issue can arise for example from image artifacts like low resolution [43], inconsistent definitions [59], uncertainty of the data [1,45] or subjective interpretations [32, 52].

It is important to look at data creation as part of the problem task because it can greatly impact the results. Recent works have shown that differences can depend on the aggregation of labels between annotators [8,62], the selection of image data sources on the web [37], if soft or hard labels are used as label representation [3,8,10,16] or the usage of label-smoothing [30,31,35]. In this work we concentrate on the labeling step issues only. Simply applying SSL only partially solves the problem as it tends to overfit [2]. Hence labeling is necessary and the goal should be to label better and more.

A commonly used idea we want to focus on is proposal-based labeling. It is also known as verification-based labeling [41], label-spreading [11], semi-automatic labeling [29], or suggestion-based annotation [51]. [12] showed that proposal-based data labeling increases both accuracy and speed for their user study (n = 54) which is in agreement with proof-of-concepts by [46,49]. The

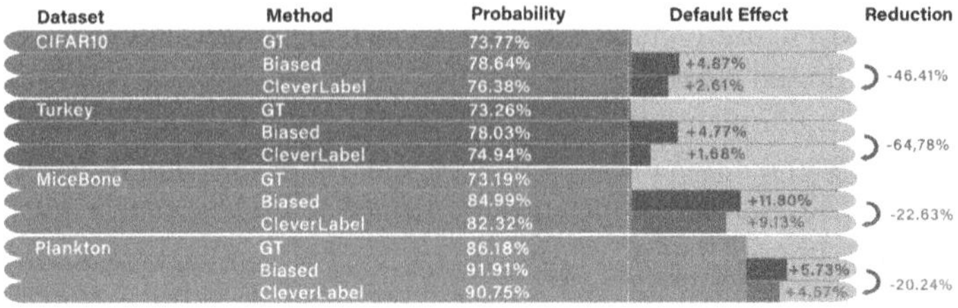

Dataset	Method	Probability	Default Effect	Reduction
CIFAR10	GT	73.77%		
	Biased	78.64%	+4.87%	
	CleverLabel	76.38%	+2.61%	-46.41%
Turkey	GT	73.26%		
	Biased	78.03%	+4.77%	
	CleverLabel	74.94%	+1.68%	-64,78%
MiceBone	GT	73.19%		
	Biased	84.99%	+11.80%	
	CleverLabel	82.32%	+9.13%	-22.63%
Plankton	GT	86.18%		
	Biased	91.91%	+5.73%	
	CleverLabel	90.75%	+4.57%	-20.24%

Fig. 2. Average annotation probability of a proposed class with the proposal unknown (GT, Unbiased) and known (Biased) to the annotators in four evaluated datasets. The proposal increases the probability in all observed cases, revealing a clear default effect in the investigated study. Its value is shown without any further processing (Biased) and with the contributed correction (CleverLabel) which consistently reduces the difference to the unbiased probabilities.

annotation suggestions for the classification in diagnostic reasoning texts had positive effects on label speed and performance without an introduction of a noteworthy bias [51]. We continue this research for the problem of image classification and show that a bias is introduced and how it can be modeled and reversed.

Acceptance or rejection of a proposal was previously modeled e.g. for the review process of scientific publications [9]. They applied a Gaussian process model to simulate the impact of human bias on the acceptance of a paper, but rely on a per annotator knowledge. A simulation framework for instance-dependent noisy labels is presented in [14,17] by using a pseudo-labeling paradigm and [21] uses latent autoregressive time series model for label quality in crowd sourced labeling. Another aspect of labeling are annotation guidelines which can also have an impact on data quality as [53] demonstrate for app reviews. We do not consider guidelines as biases, instead they are a part of data semantics and use only real annotations per image. This has the benefit of avoiding unrealistic synthetic patterns as shown by [61] and simplifies the required knowledge which makes the process more easily applicable.

Note that active learning [44] is a very different approach, in which the model in the loop decides which data-point is annotated next and the model is incrementally retrained. It is outside the scope of this article and it might not be suited for a low number of samples with high ambiguity as indicated by [58]. Consensus processes [1,42] where a joint statement is reached manually or with technical support are also out of scope.

2   Methods

Previous research on proposal-based systems [29,41,51] suggests an influence of the default effect bias on the label distribution. While its impact is assessed as negligible in some cases, it circumvents the analysis of an unbiased annotation distribution [20] which can be desirable, e.g. in medical diagnostics. As we can

---

Algorithm 1. Simulated Proposal Acceptance (SPA)

Require: Proposal ρ_x; $a_i'^x \in \{0\}^K$
  Calculate acceptance probability A
  $r \leftarrow \text{random}(0,1)$
  if $r \leq A$ **then**   ▷ Accept proposal
     $a_{i,\rho_x}'^x \leftarrow 1$
  else   ▷ Sample from remaining classes
     $k \leftarrow$ sampled from $P(L^x = k \mid \rho_x \neq k)$
     $a_{i,k}'^x \leftarrow 1$
  end if

---

identify a significant bias in our own proposal-based annotation pipeline for several datasets (see Fig. 2), two questions arise: how to mitigate the observed default effect and how it was introduced?

In this section, we provide methods to answer both questions. Before we can mitigate the observed default effect, we have to understand how it was introduced. Thus, we introduce simulated proposal acceptance (SPA) with the goal of reproducing the human behavior for annotating images with given proposals. SPA can be used to simulate the labeling process and allow experimental analysis and algorithm development before conducting large scale human annotations with proposals. Building on this understanding, we propose CleverLabel which uses two approaches for improving the biased label distribution to mitigate the default effect: 1. a heuristic approach of class distribution blending (CB) 2. a theoretically motivated bias correction (BC). CleverLabel can be applied to biased distributions generated by humans or to simulated results of SPA.

For a problem with $K \in \mathbb{N}$ classes let L^x and L_b^x be random variables mapping an unbiased or biased annotation of an image x to the selected class k. Their probability distributions $P(L^x = k)$ and $P(L_b^x = k)$ describe the probability that image x is of class k according to a set of unbiased or biased annotations. As discussed in the literature [10,30,31,35], we do not restrict the distribution of L_x further e.g. to only hard labels and instead assume, that we can approximate it via the average of N annotations by $P(L^x = k) \approx \sum_{i=0}^{N-1} \frac{a_{i,k}^x}{N}$ with $a_{i,k}^x \in \{0,1\}$ the i-th annotation for the class k which is one if the class k was selected by the i-th annotator or zero, otherwise. The default effect can cause a bias, $P(L^x = k) \neq P(L_b^x = k)$ for at least one class k. Especially, for the proposed class ρ_x it can be expected that $P(L^x = \rho_x) < P(L_b^x = \rho_x)$.

2.1 Simulated Proposal Acceptance

Given both unbiased as well as biased annotations for the same datasets, we analyze the influence of proposals on an annotator's choice. We notice that a main characteristic is that the acceptance probability increases almost linearly with the ground truth probability of the proposal, $P(L^x = \rho_x)$. If a proposal was rejected, the annotation was mainly influenced by the ground truth probability of the remaining classes. This observation leads to the following model: For a given proposal ρ_x, we calculate the probability A that it gets accepted by an annotator as

$$A = \delta + (\mathbf{1}^* - \delta)P(L^x = \rho_x) \tag{1}$$

with $\delta \in [0,1]$. $\mathbf{1}^*$ is an upper-bound for the linear interpolation which should be close to one. The offset parameter δ can be explained due to the most likely higher probability for the proposed class. We also find that this parameter is dataset dependent because for example with a lower image quality the annotator is inclined to accept a more unlikely proposal. In Subsect. 2.3, we provide more details on how to calculate these values.

With this acceptance probability we can now generate simulated annotations $a'^x_{i,k} \in \{0,1\}$ as in Algorithm 1 and describe the biased distribution similar to the unbiased distribution via $P(L^x_b = k) \approx \sum_{i=0}^{N'-1} \frac{a'^x_{i,k}}{N'}$ with N' describing the number of simulated annotations. The full source-code is in the supplementary and describes all corner cases e.g. $P(L^x \rho_x) = 1$. An experimental validation of this method can be found in the supplementary.

2.2   CleverLabel

Class distribution Blending (CB). A label of an image is in general sample dependent but [7] showed that certain classes are more likely to be confused than others. Thus, we propose to blend the estimated distribution $P(L^x_b = k)$ with a class dependent probability distribution $c(\hat{k}, k)$ to include this information. This class probability distribution describes how likely $\hat{k}$ can be confused with any other given class k. These probabilities can either be given by domain experts or approximated on a small subset of the data as shown in Subsect. 2.3. The blending can be calculated as $\mu P(L^x_b = k) + (1 - \mu)c(\hat{k}, k)$ with the most likely class $\hat{k} = \text{argmax}_{j \in \{1,...,K\}} P(L^x_b = j)$ and blending parameter $\mu \in [0,1]$. This approach can be interpreted as a smoothing of the estimated distribution which is especially useful in cases with a small number of annotations.

Bias Correction (BC). In Subsect. 2.1, we proposed a model to use the knowledge of the unbiased distribution $P(L^x = k)$ to simulate the biased distribution $P(L^x_b = k)$ under the influence of the proposals ρ_x. In this section, we formulate the reverse direction for correcting the bias to a certain degree. According to Eq. 1, for $k = \rho_x$ we can approximate

$$B := P(L^x = \rho_x) = \frac{A - \delta}{\mathbf{1}^* - \delta} \approx \frac{\frac{|M_{\rho_x}|}{N'} - \delta}{\mathbf{1}^* - \delta},$$

with $M_{\rho_x} = \{i \mid i \in \mathbb{N}, i \leq N', a'_{i,\rho_x} = 1\}$ the indices of the annotations with an accepted proposal. Note that we have to clamp the results to the interval $[0,1]$ to receive valid probabilities for numerical reasons.

Table 1. Used offsets (δ) for proposal acceptance

dataset	Benthic	CIFAR10H	MiceBone	Pig	Plankton
User Study	N/A	9.73%	36.36%	N/A	57.84%
Calculated	40.17%	0.00%	41.03%	25.72%	64.81%
dataset	QualityMRI	Synthethic	Treeversity#1	Treeversity#6	Turkey
User Study	N/A	N/A	N/A	N/A	21.64%
Calculated	0.00%	26.08%	26.08%	20.67%	14.17%

For $k \neq \rho_x$ we deduce the probability from the reject case of Algorithm 1

$$P(L^x = k \mid L^x \neq \rho_x) = P(L_b^x = k \mid L^x \neq \rho_x)$$
$$\Leftrightarrow \frac{P(L^x = k, L^x \neq \rho_x)}{P(L^x \neq \rho_x)} = P(L_b^x = k \mid L^x \neq \rho_x)$$
$$\Leftrightarrow P(L^x \neq \rho_x) = (1 - B)P(L_b^x = k \mid L^x \neq \rho_x)$$
$$\approx (1 - B) \cdot \sum_{i \notin M_{\rho_x}} \frac{a'_{i,k}}{N' - |M_{\rho_x}|}.$$

This results in an approximate formula for the original ground truth distribution which relies only on the annotations with proposals. The joint distribution is deducted in the supplementary. It is important to note that the quality of these approximations relies on a large enough number of annotations N'.

2.3   Implementation Details

We use a small user study which was proposed in [49] to develop/verify our proposal acceptance on different subsets. The original data consists of four dataset with multiple annotations per image. We focus on the no proposal and class label proposal annotation approaches but the results for e.g. specific DC3 cluster proposals are similar and can be found in the supplementary.

We calculated the ground-truth dataset dependent offset δ with a light weight approximation described in the supplementary. An overview about the calculated offsets is given in Table 1 in combination with the values of the user study where applicable. Due to the fact, that it can not be expected, that this parameter can approximated in reality with a high precision we use for all experiment except otherwise stated, a balancing threshold $\mu = 0.75$, $\mathbf{1}^* = 0.99$ and $\delta = 0.1$. More details about the selection of these parameters are given in the supplementary.

The class distributions used for blending are approximated on 100 random images with 10 annotations sampled from the ground truth distribution. For a better comparability, we do not investigate different amounts of images and annotations for different datasets but we believe a lower cost solution is possible especially on smaller datasets such as QualityMRI. For this reason, we ignore this static cost in the following evaluations. If not otherwise stated, we use the

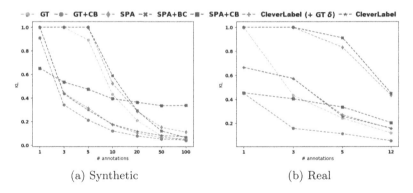

(a) Synthetic   (b) Real

Fig. 3. Label improvement (i.e. smaller Kullback-Leibler divergence (KL) [25]) in regard to the number of annotations per image. Annotations are created synthetically with SPA (a) or with proposals in a real user study (b). Results are clamped for visualization to the range 0 to 1.

method DivideMix [27] and its implementation in [47] to generate the proposals. With other methods the results are very similar and thus are excluded because they do not add further insights. We include the original labels which are used to train the method in the outputted label distribution by blending it with the output in proportion to the used number of annotations. Please see the supplementary for more details about the reproducibility.

3   Evaluation

We show that SPA and our label improvements can be used to create/reverse a biased distribution, respectively. In two subsections, we show that both directions are technically feasible and are beneficial in practical applications. Each section initially gives a short motivation, describes the evaluation metrics and provides the actual results. Additionally, in the supplementary we provide a comparison between our proposed simulation proposal acceptance and other possible simulations. The analysis shows that our chosen simulation is optimal in most cases while remaining easy to reproduce.

3.1   Label Improvement

We show that CB and BC lead to similar improved results on both simulated and real biased distributions. This similarity between CB and BC illustrates the practical benefit of SPA.

Metrics and Comparison. To measure label improvement, we use the Kullback-Leibler divergence (KL) [25] metric between the soft ground truth $P(L^x = k)$ and the estimated distribution. The input for the label improvement methods, i.e. the skewed distributions, are generated either by our method SPA or by use of real proposal acceptance data from [49]. The reported results are the median performance across different annotation offsets or datasets for the synthetic and real data, respectively. For the real data, we used the calculated δ defined in Table 1 for the simulation but as stated above $\delta = 0.1$ for the correction in CleverLabel. The method GT is the baseline and samples annotations directly from $P(L^x = k)$. The full results are in the supplementary.

Results. If we look at the results on the synthetic data created by SPA in Fig. 3a, we see the expected trend that more annotations improve results. While using only CB (SPA+CB) is the best method for one annotation, it is surpassed by all other methods with enough annotations. The baseline (GT), especially in combination with blending (GT+CB), is the best method for higher number of annotations. Our label improvement (CleverLabel) is in most cases the second best method and blending is a major component (SPA+CB). The bias correction (SPA+BC) improves the results further if $\sim$20 or more annotations are available. Using the correct offset (CleverLabel + δ GT) during the correction which was used in the simulation of SPA, is of lower importance. When we look at the full results in the supplementary, wee see benefits of a better δ at an offset larger than 0.4 and more annotations than 5. We conclude that label improvement is possible for synthetic and real data and that the combination of CB and BC with an offset of 0.1 is in most cases the strongest improvement.

Results on real annotations are shown in Fig. 3b. For consistency we keep the previous notation for CleverLabel, even though SPA was not used here to generate biased distributions. The real results show similar trends to the synthetic data. However, the baseline method without blending (GT) performs stronger and some trends are not observable because we only have up to 12 annotations. The correct value for the offsets is even less important for real data, likely because the effect is diminished by the difference of simulation and reality.

Overall, the results on synthetic and real data are similar. Thus, SPA can be used as a valid tool during method development. It is important to point out that the use of proposals will speed up annotations. Hence, different methods should not necessarily be compared for the same number of annotations. E.g. CleverLabel often performs slightly worse than GT in Fig. 3b. Considering a speedup of 2, we would have to compare CleverLabel with 5 annotations to GT with around 3, as explained in the budget calculation in Subsect. 3.2. Due to the similarity of the generated proposals with SPA and the real proposal data from [49], we conclude that experiments can also be verified only on generated proposals with SPA.

3.2   Benchmark Evaluation

Metrics and Comparison. We show the results for CleverLabel on [47]. We compare against the top three benchmarked methods: *Baseline, DivideMix* and *Pseudo v2 soft. Baseline* just samples from the ground-truth but still performed the best with a high number of annotations. *DivideMix* was proposed by [27] and *Pseudo v2 soft (Pseudo soft)* uses Pseudo-Labels [26] of soft labels to improve

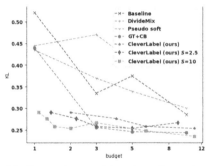
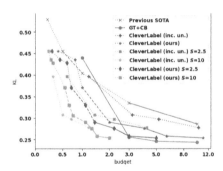

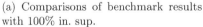

(a) Comparisons of benchmark results with 100% in. sup.

(b) Pareto front visualization of benchmark results with 20,50, 100% in. sup.

Fig. 4. Left: Compares previous state-of-the-art out of 20 evaluated methods reported in [47] (first three), new baseline (GT+CB) and our method (CleverLabel) including different speedups S. Right: The marker and color define the method, while the line style to the next node on the x-axis visualizes the initial supervision, logarithmic scaled budgets, best viewed in color and digitally

the labels. We evaluate the Kullback-Leibler divergence (KL) [25] between the ground truth and the output of the second stage (the evaluation with a fixed model) as well as KL between ground truth and the input of the second stage $(\hat{K}L)$ (for details about the stages please see the original benchmark [47]). We also provide an additional ablation where we replaced the fixed model in the second sage with a visual transformer [13]. The hyperparameters of the transformer were not tuned for each dataset but kept to common recommendations. The speedup S which can be expected due to using proposals depends on the dataset and used approach. For this reason, we include this parameter in our comparison with the values of 1 (no speedup), 2.5 as in [49] or 10 as in [50]. S is used to calculate the *budget* as *initial supervision per image (in. sup.)* $+($ *percentage annotated of $X\cdot$ number of annotations per image* $)/S$). In. sup. describes the percentage of labeled data that is annotated once in phase one of the benchmark. For the skewed distribution generation which is correct by CleverLabel, we used SPA with the calculated δ in Table 1. For CleverLabel a heuristically chosen $\delta = 0.1$ was used if not otherwise stated $(+GT\delta)$. The results are the median scores of all datasets of the averages across three folds. Full results including mean scores are in the supplementary.

Results. We present in Fig. 4a a comparison of our method CleverLabel with previous state-of-the-art methods on the benchmark with an initial supervision of 100%. Even if we assume no speedup, we can achieve lower KL scores than all previous methods, regardless of the used number of annotations. Our proposed label improvement with class blending can also be applied to samples from the ground truth distribution (GT + CB) and achieves the best results in many cases. Due to the fact that it does not leverage proposals it can not benefit from any speedups S. If we take these speedups into consideration, CleverLabel can achieve the best results across all budgets except for outliers.

We investigate lower budgets where the initial supervision could be below 100% in Fig. 4b. The full results can be found in the supplementary. If we compare our method to the combined Pareto front of all previous reported results, we see a clear improvement regardless of the expected speedup. Two additional major interesting findings can be taken from our results. Firstly, the *percentage of labeled data* which is equal to the *initial supervision* for CleverLabel (violet,blue,lightblue) is important as we see improved results from *initial supervision* of 20 to 50 to 100%. This effect is mitigated with higher speedups because then CleverLabel can achieve lower budget results not possible by other initial supervisions. Secondly, we can improve the results further by using proposals also on the unlabeled data (inc. un., red,orange,yellow) after this initialization. This increases the budget because the *percentage of labeled data* is 100% regardless of the *initial supervision* but results in improved scores. With $S = 10$ we can even improve the previous state of the art (Pseudo soft, in. sup 20%, 5 annotations) at the budget of 1.0 from 0.40/0.47 to 0.30/0.33 at a budget of 0.7 which is a relative improvement of 25%/29.8% with median/ mean aggregation.

In Table 2, we conduct several ablations to investigate the impact of individual parts of our method. Comparing KL and $\hat{K}L$ scores, we see similar trends between each other and to Subsect. 3.1. Class blending (CB) is an important part of improved scores but the impact is stronger for $\hat{K}L$. A different blending threshold ($\mu = 0.25$) which prefers the sample independent class distribution leads in most cases to similar or worse results than our selection of 0.75. Bias Correction (BC) and the correct GT offset have a measurable impact on the $\hat{K}L$ while on KL we almost no difference but a saturation at around 0.24 for all approaches most likely due the used network backbone. With a different backbone e.g. a transformer [13] we can verify that BC positively impacts the results. With CleverLabel (the combination of CB and BC) the scores are slightly decreased for example from 0.17 to 0.16.

4 Discussion

In summary, we analyzed the introduced bias during the labeling process when using proposals by developing a simulation of this bias and provided two methods for reducing the proposal-introduced bias. We could show that our methods outperform current state of the art methods on the same or even lower labeling budgets. For low annotation budgets, we have even surpassed our newly proposed baseline of class blending in combination with annotation without proposals. Cost is already a limiting factor when annotating data and thus only results with a better performance for a budget of less than one (which equals the current annotation of every image once) can be expected to be applied in real world applications. We achieved this goal with CleverLabel with speedups larger than 4 which is reasonable based on previously reported values [49].

Table 2. Benchmark results ablation study across different number of annotations per image, the number of annotations is given in the top row, first block of rows KL result on normal benchmark, second block of rows $\hat{K}L$ on benchmark, last block of rows KL results on benchmark but with ViT as backbone, all results are median aggregations across the datasets, the best results per block are marked bold per number of annotations

method	1	3	5	10	20	50	100
CleverLabel (ours)	0.29 ± 0.02	0.28 ± 0.01	0.26 ± 0.02	0.25 ± 0.01	0.27 ± 0.02	0.25 ± 0.02	**0.24 ± 0.01**
CleverLabel (+ GT δ)	0.30 ± 0.02	0.28 ± 0.01	0.27 ± 0.01	0.25 ± 0.02	**0.24 ± 0.01**	**0.24 ± 0.01**	**0.24 ± 0.01**
Only CB	0.34 ± 0.03	**0.28 ± 0.01**	0.27 ± 0.01	0.25 ± 0.02	0.25 ± 0.01	0.25 ± 0.02	0.25 ± 0.02
Only CB ($\mu = 0.25$)	0.33 ± 0.02	**0.28 ± 0.01**	0.33 ± 0.02	0.29 ± 0.01	-	-	-
Only BC	-	0.30 ± 0.02	0.29 ± 0.02	0.26 ± 0.02	-	-	-
CleverLabel (ours)	0.68 ± 0.03	**0.32 ± 0.01**	**0.25 ± 0.01**	**0.16 ± 0.00**	0.11 ± 0.00	0.08 ± 0.00	0.07 ± 0.00
CleverLabel (+ GT δ)	0.68 ± 0.03	0.41 ± 0.01	0.29 ± 0.01	**0.16 ± 0.00**	0.10 ± 0.00	**0.05 ± 0.00**	**0.04 ± 0.00**
Only CB	0.68 ± 0.03	**0.32 ± 0.01**	**0.25 ± 0.01**	0.16 ± 0.01	0.12 ± 0.00	0.09 ± 0.00	0.08 ± 0.00
Only CB ($\mu = 0.25$)	**0.55 ± 0.02**	0.33 ± 0.01	0.29 ± 0.01	0.24 ± 0.01	-	-	-
Only BC	-	1.22 ± 0.04	0.78 ± 0.02	0.36 ± 0.02	-	-	-
CleverLabel (+ GT δ)	-	0.22 ± 0.01	-	0.18 ± 0.01	-	-	0.16 ± 0.01
Only CB	-	0.20 ± 0.01	-	0.18 ± 0.01	-	-	0.17 ± 0.01

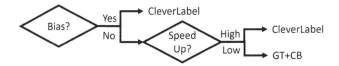

Fig. 5. Flowchart about how to annotate ambiguous data based on the questions if an introduced bias is acceptable and if the expected speedup S is high (> 3)

Based on our research, how should one annotate ambiguous image classification data? While there currently is no strategy for every case, the problem can be broken down into the two major questions as depicted in Fig. 5 and was extended in [48]. Firstly, is a bias in the data acceptable? Be aware that in CleverLabel all labels are human validated and that many consensus processes already use an agreement system [1] with multiple reviewers. If a small bias is acceptable you can directly use proposals and an optional correction like CleverLabel. However, if a bias is not acceptable, the second major question is the expected speedup by using proposals for annotating your specific data. In case of a high expected speedup, the trade-off between the introduced bias and the ability to mitigate it with BC and CB favors CleverLabel. For a low speedup, we recommend avoiding proposals and to rely on class blending which is applicable to any dataset if you can estimate the class transitions as described in Subsect. 2.3. It is difficult to determine the exact trade-off point, because CB improves the results with fewer (10-) annotations, BC improves the results at above (20+) and both each other. Based on this research, we recommend a rough speedup threshold of around three for the trade-off.

The main limitations of this work arise due to the fact that not more than four datasets could be evaluated. We aim at a general approach for different datasets but this results in non-optimal solutions for individual datasets. Multiple extensions for SPA like different kinds of simulated annotators would be possible but would require a larger user study for evaluation. In Subsect. 3.1, we compared our simulation with real data on four datasets, but a larger comparison was not feasible. It is important to note that SPA must not replace human evaluation but should be used for method development and hypothesis testing before an expensive human study which is needed to verify results. We gave a proof of concept about the benefit of bias correction with higher annotation counts with a stronger backbone like transformers. A full reevaluation of the benchmark was not feasible and it is questionable if it would lead to new insights because the scores might be lower but are expected to show similar relations.

5   Conclusion

Data quality is important but comes at a high cost. Proposals can reduce this cost but introduce a bias. We propose to mitigate this issue by simple heuristics and a theoretically motivated bias correction which makes them broader applicable and achieve up to 29.8% relative better scores with reduced cost of 30%. This analysis is only possible due to our new proposed method SPA and results in general guidelines for how to annotate ambiguous data.

Acknowledgments. We acknowledge funding of L. Schmarje by the ARTEMIS project (Grant number 01EC1908E) funded by the Federal Ministry of Education and Research (BMBF, Germany). We further acknowledge the funding of J. Nazarenus by the *OP der Zukunft* project funded by the Business Development and Technlogy Transfer Corporation of Schleswig Holstein (WTSH, Germany) within the REACT-EU program. We also acknowledge the funding of M. Santarossa by the KI-SIGS project (grant number FKZ 01MK20012E) and the funding of V. Grossmann by the Marispace-X project (grant number 68GX21002E), both funded by the Federal Ministry for Economic Affairs and Climate Action (BMWK, Germany).

References

1. Addison, P.F.E.E., et al.: A new wave of marine evidence-based management: emerging challenges and solutions to transform monitoring, evaluating, and reporting. ICES J. Mar. Sci. **75**(3), 941–952 (2018). https://doi.org/10.1093/icesjms/fsx216
2. Arazo, E., Ortego, D., Albert, P., O'Connor, N.E., McGuinness, K.: Pseudo-labeling and confirmation bias in deep semi-supervised learning. In: 2020 International Joint Conference on Neural Networks (IJCNN), pp. 1–8 (2020). https://doi.org/10.1109/IJCNN48605.2020.9207304
3. Basile, V., et al.: We need to consider disagreement in evaluation. In: Proceedings of the 1st Workshop on Benchmarking: Past, Present and Future, pp. 15–21 (2021)
4. Berthelot, D., Carlini, N., Goodfellow, I., Papernot, N., Oliver, A., Raffel, C.A.: Mixmatch: a holistic approach to semi-supervised learning. In: Advances in Neural Information Processing Systems, pp. 5050–5060 (2019)
5. Beyer, L., et al.: Are we done with ImageNet? arXiv preprint arXiv:2006.07159 (2020)

6. Brünger, J., Dippel, S., Koch, R., Veit, C.: 'Tailception': using neural networks for assessing tail lesions on pictures of pig carcasses. Animal **13**(5), 1030–1036 (2019). https://doi.org/10.1017/S1751731118003038

7. Collier, M., Mustafa, B., Kokiopoulou, E., Jenatton, R., Berent, J.: Correlated input-dependent label noise in large-scale image classification. In: Proceedings of the IEEE/CVF Conference on Computer Vision and Pattern Recognition, pp. 1551–1560 (2021)

8. Collins, K.M., Bhatt, U., Weller, A.: Eliciting and learning with soft labels from every annotator. In: Proceedings of the AAAI Conference on Human Computation and Crowdsourcing, vol. 10, no. 1 (2022)

9. Cortes, C., Lawrence, N.D.: Inconsistency in conference peer review: revisiting the 2014 neurips experiment. arXiv preprint arXiv:2109.09774 (2021)

10. Davani, A.M., Díaz, M., Prabhakaran, V.: Dealing with disagreements: looking beyond the majority vote in subjective annotations. Trans. Assoc. Comput. Linguist. **10**, 92–110 (2022). https://doi.org/10.1162/tacl_a_00449

11. Desmond, M., Duesterwald, E., Brimijoin, K., Brachman, M., Pan, Q.: Semi-automated data labeling. In: NeurIPS 2020 Competition and Demonstration Track, pp. 156–169. PMLR (2021)

12. Desmond, M., et al.: Increasing the speed and accuracy of data labeling through an AI assisted interface. In: 26th International Conference on Intelligent User Interfaces, pp. 392–401. Association for Computing Machinery (2021). https://doi.org/10.1145/3397481.3450698

13. Dosovitskiy, A., et al.: An image is worth 16x16 words: transformers for image recognition at scale. In: ICLR (2021)

14. Gao, Z., et al.: Learning from multiple annotator noisy labels via sample-wise label fusion. In: Avidan, S., Brostow, G., Cissé, M., Farinella, G.M., Hassner, T. (eds.) ECCV 2022, Part XXIV. LNCS, vol. 13684, pp. 407–422. Springer, Cham (2022). https://doi.org/10.1007/978-3-031-20053-3_24

15. Gordon, M.L., Zhou, K., Patel, K., Hashimoto, T., Bernstein, M.S.: The disagreement deconvolution: bringing machine learning performance metrics in line with reality. In: Proceedings of the 2021 CHI Conference on Human Factors in Computing Systems, pp. 1–14. ACM (2021). https://doi.org/10.1145/3411764.3445423

16. Grossmann, V., Schmarje, L., Koch, R.: Beyond hard labels: investigating data label distributions. In: ICML 2022 Workshop DataPerf: Benchmarking Data for Data-Centric AI (2022)

17. Gu, K., Masotto, X., Bachani, V., Lakshminarayanan, B., Nikodem, J., Yin, D.: An instance-dependent simulation framework for learning with label noise. Mach. Learn. 1–26 (2022)

18. He, K., Chen, X., Xie, S., Li, Y., Dollár, P., Girshick, R.: Masked autoencoders are scalable vision learners. In: Proceedings of the IEEE/CVF Conference on Computer Vision and Pattern Recognition, pp. 16000–16009 (2022)

19. Hendrycks, D., Mazeika, M., Kadavath, S., Song, D.: Using self-supervised learning can improve model robustness and uncertainty. In: Advances in Neural Information Processing Systems, vol. 32 (2019)

20. Jachimowicz, J.M., Duncan, S., Weber, E.U., Johnson, E.J.: When and why defaults influence decisions: a meta-analysis of default effects. Behavioural Public Policy **3**(2), 159–186 (2019)

21. Jung, H., Park, Y., Lease, M.: Predicting next label quality: a time-series model of crowdwork. In: Proceedings of the AAAI Conference on Human Computation and Crowdsourcing, vol. 2, no. 1, pp. 87–95 (2014). https://doi.org/10.1609/hcomp.v2i1.13165

22. Kolesnikov, A., et al.: Big transfer (BiT): general visual representation learning. In: Vedaldi, A., Bischof, H., Brox, T., Frahm, J.M. (eds.) ECCV 2020. LNCS, vol. 12350, pp. 491–507. Springer, Cham (2020). https://doi.org/10.1007/978-3-030-58558-7_29

23. Krizhevsky, A., Hinton, G.: Learning multiple layers of features from tiny images. Technical report, Citeseer (2009)

24. Krizhevsky, A., Sutskever, I., Hinton, G.E.: Imagenet classification with deep convolutional neural networks. In: Advances in Neural Information Processing Systems, vol. 60, pp. 1097–1105. Association for Computing Machinery (2012). https://doi.org/10.1145/3065386

25. Kullback, S., Leibler, R.A.: On information and sufficiency. Ann. Math. Statist. 22(1), 79–86 (1951). https://doi.org/10.1214/aoms/1177729694

26. Lee, D.H.: Pseudo-label: the simple and efficient semi-supervised learning method for deep neural networks. In: Workshop on Challenges in Representation Learning, ICML, vol. 3, p. 2 (2013)

27. Li, J., Socher, R., Hoi, S.C.H.: DivideMix: learning with noisy labels as semi-supervised learning. In: International Conference on Learning Representations, pp. 1–14 (2020)

28. Li, Y.F., Liang, D.M.: Safe semi-supervised learning: a brief introduction. Front. Comp. Sci. 13(4), 669–676 (2019)

29. Lopresti, D., Nagy, G.: Optimal data partition for semi-automated labeling. In: Proceedings of the 21st International Conference on Pattern Recognition (ICPR 2012), pp. 286–289. IEEE (2012)

30. Lukasik, M., Bhojanapalli, S., Menon, A.K., Kumar, S.: Does label smoothing mitigate label noise? In: International Conference on Machine Learning, pp. 6448–6458. PMLR (2020)

31. Lukov, T., Zhao, N., Lee, G.H., Lim, S.N.: Teaching with soft label smoothing for mitigating noisy labels in facial expressions. In: Avidan, S., Brostow, G., Cissé, M., Farinella, G.M., Hassner, T. (eds.) ECCV 2022, Part XII. LNCS, vol. 13672, pp. 648–665. Springer, Cham (2022). https://doi.org/10.1007/978-3-031-19775-8_38

32. Mazeika, M., et al.: How would the viewer feel? Estimating wellbeing from video scenarios. Adv. Neural. Inf. Process. Syst. 35, 18571–18585 (2022)

33. Misra, I., van der Maaten, L., van der Maaten, L.: Self-supervised learning of pretext-invariant representations. In: Proceedings of the IEEE/CVF Conference on Computer Vision and Pattern Recognition, pp. 6707–6717 (2020)

34. Motamedi, M., Sakharnykh, N., Kaldewey, T.: A data-centric approach for training deep neural networks with less data. In: NeurIPS 2021 Data-Centric AI workshop (2021)

35. Müller, R., Kornblith, S., Hinton, G.: When does label smoothing help? In: Advances in Neural Information Processing Systems, vol. 32 (2019)

36. Naeem, A., Farooq, M.S., Khelifi, A., Abid, A.: Malignant melanoma classification using deep learning: datasets, performance measurements, challenges and opportunities. IEEE Access 8, 110575–110597 (2020)

37. Nguyen, T., Ilharco, G., Wortsman, M., Oh, S., Schmidt, L.: Quality Not Quantity: On the Interaction between Dataset Design and Robustness of CLIP, pp. 1–46 (2022)

38. Northcutt, C.G., Athalye, A., Mueller, J.: Pervasive label errors in test sets destabilize machine learning benchmarks. In: 35th Conference on Neural Information Processing Systems (NeurIPS 2021) Track on Datasets and Benchmarks (2021)

39. Northcutt, C.G., Jiang, L., Chuang, I.L.: Confident learning: estimating uncertainty in dataset labels. J. Artif. Intell. Res. **70**, 1373–1411 (2021). https://doi.org/10.1613/JAIR.1.12125
40. Ooms, E.A., et al.: Mammography: interobserver variability in breast density assessment. Breast **16**(6), 568–576 (2007). https://doi.org/10.1016/j.breast.2007.04.007
41. Papadopoulos, D.P., Weber, E., Torralba, A.: Scaling up instance annotation via label propagation. In: Proceedings of the IEEE/CVF International Conference on Computer Vision, pp. 15364–15373 (2021)
42. Patel, B.N., et al.: Human-machine partnership with artificial intelligence for chest radiograph diagnosis. NPJ Digit. Med. **2**(1), 1–10 (2019). https://doi.org/10.1038/s41746-019-0189-7
43. Peterson, J., Battleday, R., Griffiths, T., Russakovsky, O.: Human uncertainty makes classification more robust. In: Proceedings of the IEEE International Conference on Computer Vision 2019-October, pp. 9616–9625 (2019). https://doi.org/10.1109/ICCV.2019.00971
44. Ren, P., et al.: A survey of deep active learning. ACM Comput. Surv. (CSUR) **54**(9), 1–40 (2021)
45. Saleh, A., Laradji, I.H., Konovalov, D.A., Bradley, M., Vazquez, D., Sheaves, M.: A realistic fish-habitat dataset to evaluate algorithms for underwater visual analysis. Sci. Rep. **10**(1), 1–10 (2020). https://doi.org/10.1038/s41598-020-71639-x
46. Schmarje, L., Brünger, J., Santarossa, M., Schröder, S.M., Kiko, R., Koch, R.: Fuzzy overclustering: semi-supervised classification of fuzzy labels with overclustering and inverse cross-entropy. Sensors **21**(19), 6661 (2021). https://doi.org/10.3390/s21196661
47. Schmarje, L., et al.: Is one annotation enough? A data-centric image classification benchmark for noisy and ambiguous label estimation. Adv. Neural. Inf. Process. Syst. **35**, 33215–33232 (2022)
48. Schmarje, L., Grossmann, V., Zelenka, C., Koch, R.: Annotating Ambiguous Images: General Annotation Strategy for High-Quality Data with Real-World Biomedical Validation. arXiv preprint arXiv:2306.12189 (2023)
49. Schmarje, L., et al.: A data-centric approach for improving ambiguous labels with combined semi-supervised classification and clustering. In: Proceedings of the European Conference on Computer Vision (ECCV) (2022)
50. Schröder, S.M., Kiko, R., Koch, R.: MorphoCluster: efficient annotation of plankton images by clustering. Sensors **20** (2020)
51. Schulz, C., et al.: Analysis of automatic annotation suggestions for hard discourse-level tasks in expert domains. In: Proceedings of the 57th Annual Meeting of the Association for Computational Linguistics, pp. 2761–2772. Association for Computational Linguistics (2019). https://doi.org/10.18653/v1/P19-1265
52. Schustek, P., Moreno-Bote, R.: Instance-based generalization for human judgments about uncertainty. PLoS Comput. Biol. **14**(6), e1006205 (2018). https://doi.org/10.1371/journal.pcbi.1006205
53. Shah, F.A., Sirts, K., Pfahl, D.: The impact of annotation guidelines and annotated data on extracting app features from app reviews. arXiv preprint arXiv:1810.05187 (2018)
54. Sheng, V.S., Provost, F.: Get another label? Improving Data Quality and Data Mining Using Multiple, Noisy Labelers Categories and Subject Descriptors, New York, pp. 614–622 (2008)
55. Singh, A., Nowak, R., Zhu, J.: Unlabeled data: now it helps, now it doesn't. In: Advances in Neural Information Processing Systems, vol. 21 (2008)

56. Sohn, K., et al.: FixMatch: simplifying semi-supervised learning with consistency and confidence. In: Advances in Neural Information Processing Systems 33 pre-proceedings (NeurIPS 2020) (2020)

57. Tarling, P., Cantor, M., Clapés, A., Escalera, S.: Deep learning with self-supervision and uncertainty regularization to count fish in underwater images. PLoS ONE **17**(5), 1–22 (2021)

58. Tifrea, A., Clarysse, J., Yang, F.: Uniform versus uncertainty sampling: when being active is less efficient than staying passive. arXiv preprint arXiv:2212.00772 (2022)

59. Uijlings, J., Mensink, T., Ferrari, V.: The Missing Link: Finding label relations across datasets (2022)

60. Vasudevan, V., Caine, B., Gontijo-Lopes, R., Fridovich-Keil, S., Roelofs, R.: When does dough become a bagel? Analyzing the remaining mistakes on ImageNet. Adv. Neural. Inf. Process. Syst. **35**, 6720–6734 (2022)

61. Wei, J., Zhu, Z., Cheng, H., Liu, T., Niu, G., Liu, Y.: Learning with noisy labels revisited: a study using real-world human annotations. In: ICLR, pp. 1–23 (2021)

62. Wei, X., Cong, H., Zhang, Z., Peng, J., Chen, G., Li, J.: Faint Features Tell: Automatic Vertebrae Fracture Screening Assisted by Contrastive Learning (2022)

63. Yun, S., Oh, S.J., Heo, B., Han, D., Choe, J., Chun, S.: Re-labeling imagenet: from single to multi-labels, from global to localized labels. In: Proceedings of the IEEE/CVF Conference on Computer Vision and Pattern Recognition (CVPR), pp. 2340–2350 (2021)

Speeding Up Online Self-Supervised Learning by Exploiting Its Limitations

Sina Mokhtarzadeh Azar$^{(\boxtimes)}$ and Radu Timofte

Computer Vision Lab, CAIDAS & IFI, University of Würzburg, Würzburg, Germany
{sina.mokhtarzadeh-azar,radu.timofte}@uni-wuerzburg.de

Abstract. Online Self-Supervised Learning tackles the problem of learning Self-Supervised representations from a stream of data in an online fashion. This is the more realistic scenario of Self-Supervised Learning where data becomes available continuously and must be used for training straight away. Contrary to regular Self-Supervised Learning methods where they need to go hundreds of times through a dataset to produce suitable representations, Online Self-Supervised Learning has a limited budget for training iterations for the new data points from the stream. Additionally, the training can potentially continue indefinitely without a specific end. We propose a framework for Online Self-supervised Learning with the goal of learning as much as possible from the newly arrived batch of data in a limited amount of training iterations before the next batch becomes available. To achieve this goal we use a cycle of aggressive learning rate increase for every batch of data which is combined with a memory to reduce overfitting on the current batch and forgetting the knowledge gained from previous batches. Additionally, we propose Reducible Anchor Loss Selection (RALS) to intelligently select the most useful samples from the combination of the new batch and samples from the memory. Considering the limitation of a smaller number of iterations over the data, multiple empirical results on CIFAR-100 and ImageNet-100 datasets show the effectiveness of our approach.

Keywords: Self-Supervised Learning · Continual Learning

1 Introduction

Large amounts of unlabeled visual data are being generated every day from multiple sources like smartphones, surveillance cameras, self-driving cars, etc. Self-supervised Learning (SSL) can make use of this limitless data to learn strong representations that can be used to improve various downstream tasks. However, training on the possibly infinite data is a real challenge. Recent methods like [10, 17] provide models that are able to learn continually from unlabeled data. These methods process large chunks of data in the form of new tasks on which they

---

Supplementary Information The online version contains supplementary material available at https://doi.org/10.1007/978-3-031-54605-1_31.

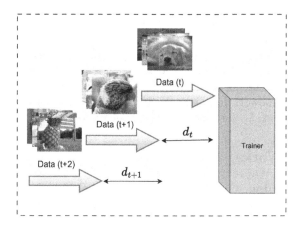

Fig. 1. Illustration of a scenario where a stream is generating batches of data with a time difference between each batch. Trainer has a limited amount of time to learn from the currently available batch of data before the next batch arrives.

usually spend a significant amount of training epochs. In a scenario where new data arrives in an online fashion from a stream, these approaches are not usable due to the long training process. Therefore, Online Self-Supervised Learning (OSSL) methods capable of learning from streaming data must be developed.

Considering a stream of data where there is limited time between the preparation of each data batch from the stream (see Fig. 1), we need to restrict the number of training iterations on the batch in order for the training to continue on the new batch. With a potentially infinite data stream, the end of training is unknown. Therefore, another challenge is that the usual learning rate schedulers requiring the end of training to be specified can not be used out of the box in the online learning setting.

We propose Single Local Cycle Learning Rate Scheduler (SLCLRS) in order to tackle the challenges of infinite data with an unknown ending and the need for faster learning from the currently available batch of data with limited training steps. This is inspired by [28] which uses the One Cycle Learning Rate Scheduler (OCLRS) to increase the learning rate to a large value midway through the training epochs and then gradually decrease it to a very small value towards the ending epoch which in turn speeds up the training process. However, this scheduler works based on the whole training process. In order to tackle the online scenario we use SLCLRS with a limited number of training steps for every new batch that arrives to address the previous challenges.

Additionally, we propose Reducible Anchor Loss Selection (RALS) to select the most suitable samples in the online learning setting considering the change of the loss for the samples based on the current model and the anchor model trained prior to getting the current batch of data. This is based on Reducible Holdout Loss Selection (RHO-LOSS) [19] that follows the direction of choosing the most suitable samples for training based on a loss increase from a pre-trained model on a hold-out set. However, RHO-LOSS works in an offline setting with a static model. RALS on the other hand uses a dynamic anchor model to calculate the selection criteria.

The rest of the paper is organized as follows. First, in Sect. 2, the related works are briefly discussed. A formalized problem definition is provided in Sect. 3. Details of our framework are given in Sect. 4. This is followed by experiments and analysis in Sect. 5. We conclude the paper in Sect. 6.

2   Related Works

Continual Learning. Continual Learning has the goal of learning new tasks continually without forgetting the previously learned tasks. The main techniques used to tackle the Continual Learning problem are Regularization-based, Memory-based, or Parameter Isolation-based.

Regularization-based methods simply add a regularization term to limit the changes happening to the parameters of the model to stop it from forgetting the previous tasks [1,3,6,12,15,16,23,32].

Memory-based methods keep a portion of data in a memory [2,4,5,22,24]. By combining the samples in the memory with the samples in the new task, catastrophic forgetting can be mitigated.

Among memory-based methods, Maximally Interfered Retrieval (MIR) [2] is the most similar to our work. They use a combination of samples from memory and the new task to train a supervised model. An optimization step is performed using only the new samples to find the samples in the memory with the highest increase in loss to be retrieved for training.

Parameter Isolation based methods tackle forgetting by using different parameters for each task [9,18,26,27,30]. This can be achieved by using different parameters inside a fixed model for each task or by adding new parameters for every new task.

Continual Self-Supervised Learning. Continual Self-Supervised Learning is a relatively new topic. Lifelong Unsupervised Mixup (LUMP) [17] shows that features learned using unsupervised continual learning provide better generalization and suffer less from catastrophic forgetting. They also propose to interpolate samples from a memory with the current task samples to reduce forgetting.

CaSSLe [10] proposes a Continual Self-Supervised Learning approach that utilizes a distillation mechanism compatible with various self-supervised Learning algorithms instead of a memory to reduce forgetting and it achieves impressive results. However, the training process takes a lot of epochs which makes it unable to work in an online setting.

Most recently, in the concurrent work of [21] the problem of Continuous Self-Supervised Learning is studied. They mainly address the Non-IID nature of correlated streaming data through the use of a Minimum Redundancy Buffer. Our method is similar to this work with the difference that we focus on speeding up the self-supervised Learning convergence on the provided data stream without explicitly handling Non-IID data. Similar ideas like [21] can be used in

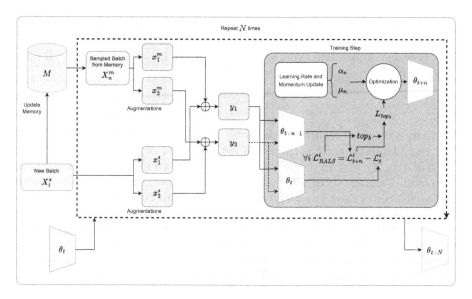

Fig. 2. Overview of our proposed method. Every batch of data X_t^s that arrives at time t from the stream is used in combination with a batch of data X_n^m from a memory M for training a model for a limited number of steps N using the single local cycle learning rate scheduler before the next batch gets ready. Reducible anchor loss selection is also used to find the best possible subset of samples in order to provide even more speed up for training.

combination with our approach to implicitly consider the Non-IID data but it is not the focus of this paper.

3   Problem Definition

Regular Self-Supervised Learning methods have access to all the samples in the dataset D during training. In each training step, a batch of images X is sampled from D and two augmentations x_1 and x_2 are generated from it. These augmentations are fed to a model f to produce representations z_1 and z_2. f is parameterized by $\theta = (\theta_b, \theta_p)$ where θ_b and θ_p are the parameters for backbone and projection layers, respectively. A self-supervised loss function $\mathcal{L}_S(z_1, z_2)$ is used to optimize the parameters θ based on z_1 and z_2:

$$\sum_b^B \mathcal{L}_S(z_1^b, z_2^b). \tag{1}$$

In Continual Self-supervised Learning (CSSL) the model is trained on a sequence of T tasks on different corresponding chunks of the dataset $D = (D_1, D_2, ..., D_T)$. These chunks of data are sequentially provided to the model without access to the other chunks. However, it considers no limits on the time and epochs to train the model on every subset of D. The model must be trained in a way that in addition to learning from new data chunks, it does not forget what was learned from previous chunks. Therefore self-supervised loss on all the subsets of D must be minimized:

$$\sum_{t}^{T}\sum_{b}^{B_t}\mathcal{L}_S(z_1^{b,t}, z_2^{b,t}). \tag{2}$$

We address the more realistic setting where data source D is a stream (with possibly non i.i.d data) and the training must happen in an online approach. Every batch of data X_t^s that arrives at time t from the stream must be used for training for a limited amount of time before the next batch gets ready. The objective for Online Self-Supervised Learning (OSSL) can be considered as an extreme case of CSSL where the chunks of data are small and the number of OSSL tasks T_O is much larger than CSSL ones ($T_O \gg T$). Therefore, the objective will be similar to CSSL:

$$\sum_{t}^{T_O}\sum_{b}^{B_t}\mathcal{L}_S(z_1^{b,t}, z_2^{b,t}). \tag{3}$$

Our goal is to learn representations using X_t^s as fast as possible without having access to future data or the past data except the ones stored in a memory M. Additionally, we avoid using learning rate schedulers that consider an end for the data stream.

4   Proposed Method

The goal of our approach is to improve the speed of convergence for Online Self-Supervised Learning considering the challenges of the unknown end of training and a limited number of training iterations per new batch of data from the stream. In this section, we describe the proposed framework and describe how SLCLRS and RALS are incorporated into it. An overview of our approach is presented in Fig. 2.

4.1   Single Local Cycle Learning Rate Scheduler

In a regular training setting OCLRS is used to achieve comparable performance with fewer training epochs by increasing the learning rate to a high value at the beginning of the training and reducing it to a much smaller value at the end. We suggest that a batch of data is the small version of the dataset and we can use a single cycle of increasing and decreasing the learning rate in the current local iteration corresponding to the new batch of data X_t^s in order to speed up learning this batch. The duration of this cycle is based on the available budget for the training steps in the current local iteration.

Using an aggressive scheduler on just the new batch X_t^s will lead to overfitting on that batch and possibly forgetting the previously learned representations. Therefore, we store a portion of data in the memory M and combine a batch from memory X_n^m with the new batch from stream X_t^s in every training step n (similar to [2]). Given the optimizer o and scheduler s for $n \in 1, ..., N$ where N is the number of training steps for each batch of data, the training process can be written as follows:

$$y_1 = x_1^m \oplus x_1^s,$$
$$y_2 = x_2^m \oplus x_2^s,$$
(4)

$$z_1^{n-1} = f_{\theta_{t+n-1}}(y_1),$$
$$z_2^{n-1} = f_{\theta_{t+n-1}}(y_2),$$
(5)

$$\mathcal{L}_{t+n} = \mathcal{L}_S(z_1^{n-1}, z_2^{n-1}),$$
(6)

$$\alpha_n, \mu_n = s(n),$$
$$\theta_{t+n} = o(\mathcal{L}_{t+n}, \theta_{t+n-1}, \alpha_n, \mu_n).$$
(7)

Here, (x_1^m, x_2^m) and (x_1^s, x_2^s) are the augmentations created from X_n^m and X_t^s, respectively. $\oplus$ shows the concatenation along the batch dimension and (y_1, y_2) are the concatenated augmentations. $f_{\theta_{t+n-1}}$ is the model optimized for $n-1$ steps after receiving the batch of data at step t. This model is used to produce the representations (z_1^{n-1}, z_2^{n-1}) which in turn are used to calculate the loss $\mathcal{L}_{t+n}$ at step n. The scheduler updates the learning rate α_n and momentum μ_n based on step n then the optimizer calculates the new set of parameters θ_{t+n} for step n. The reason we also update the momentum is that the positive effect of reducing it while increasing the learning rate was observed in [28].

The scheduler in [28] uses linear functions for increasing and decreasing the learning rate. However, we utilize the cosine function version provided in PyTorch [20] which is in turn based on Fastai's implementation [13]. An illustration of the learning rate and momentum schedules we use with a different number of training steps per batch is provided in the Appendix.

As previously mentioned, one of the challenges of OSSL is the possibly unknown ending. The benefit of using SLCLRS with every new batch is that we do not need to consider an ending for the training and this procedure can continue indefinitely given a data stream. The training can stop at the end of every iteration knowing sufficient optimization was performed on the latest data from the stream.

It should be noted that we use simple random sampling for both memory update and retrieval. More complex strategies to handle the memory can be used for more efficient memory management but it was not the focus of our work.

4.2   Reducible Anchor Loss Selection

The use of memory in combination with different augmentations (x_1^s, x_2^s) at each training step n can reduce the chances of overfitting on the new batch X_t^s but it can still happen. Additionally, we suggest a scenario exists that the loss for some samples of X_t^s stops decreasing which in turn slows down the convergence on the combined set of samples. Therefore, selecting samples with the highest increase in loss compared to the beginning step of this iteration can help speed up the convergence. The inspiration for this idea comes from the reducible holdout loss selection of Mindermann *et al* [19]. Given a model for training, this method finds the data points with the highest increase in loss compared to the loss of the pre-trained model on a holdout set. These points are then used for training. However, in our use case, we do not necessarily have a holdout set. Instead, we consider the model at the beginning of the iteration f_{θ_t} as an anchor model to also limit the divergence of parameters from the anchor point. Our method with RALS can be described as follows:

$$
\begin{aligned}
z_1^0 &= f_{\theta_t}(y_1), \\
z_2^0 &= f_{\theta_t}(y_2),
\end{aligned}
\tag{8}
$$

$$
\begin{aligned}
\mathcal{L}_t^i &= \mathcal{L}_S^i(z_1^0, z_2^0), \\
\mathcal{L}_{RALS}^i &= \mathcal{L}_{t+n}^i - \mathcal{L}_t^i, \\
\mathcal{L}_{top_k} &= \frac{1}{k} \sum_{j \in top_k(\mathcal{L}_{RALS}^i)} \mathcal{L}_{t+n}^j
\end{aligned}
\tag{9}
$$

Here, $\mathcal{L}_{t+n}^i$ shows the loss at step n for the individual sample i. Reducible anchor loss $\mathcal{L}_{RALS}^i$ is the increase in loss for sample i and it is used as the metric for the selection process. Finally, based on the reducible anchor loss metric, the average loss over top k samples is calculated as $\mathcal{L}_{top_k}$, and the optimization is performed based on this loss. This approach should lead to faster convergence by focusing on the more important points. In practice in order to find the top k samples, initially we run the models in inference mode without calculating gradients. Then only the selected samples are fed again to the model for training.

Multiple scenarios can lead to a data sample having high reducible anchor loss. First, if the model started overfitting on a sample at step n, its loss value for that sample will start to decrease compared to the frozen anchor model. Therefore, due to lower $\mathcal{L}_{RALS}^i$, the probability of being selected among the top RALS samples would decrease leading to less overfitting on that sample. Second, a sample from the memory would probably have a lower loss with f_{θ_t}. If this loss increases at step n, it could mean that the model has started to forget the representations learned from this sample. Therefore, it will be selected based on reducible anchor loss for training which in turn will lead to less forgetting. Finally, similar to [19], less relevant and noisy samples will also not get into selected samples due to already high $\mathcal{L}_t^i$.

4.3   Integration of SSL Methods

We studied two popular Self-Supervised Learning methods of SimCLR [7], and Barlow Twins [31] in our proposed framework. A summary of each method and the approach taken to calculate individual loss values is provided next.

SimCLR [7] is a contrastive Self-Supervised Learning method that uses a contrastive loss to learn representations from two augmentations of a set of images. The contrastive loss for a pair of positive samples i, j is written as follows:

$$l_{i,j} = -log \frac{exp(sim(z_i, z_j)/\tau)}{\sum_{k=1}^{2N} \mathbb{1}_{[k \neq i]} exp(sim(z_i, z_k)/\tau)}. \tag{10}$$

The total loss for SimCLR is calculated by summing all the positive pairs in the batch [7]. Here, the sum of elements $l_{i,j}$, and $l_{j,i}$ corresponding to the augmentations of the same image is used as the loss term for the reducible anchor loss calculation.

Barlow Twins [31] uses a different loss function based on a cross-correlation matrix which computes a single combined output for all the samples in the batch without providing individual loss values. Given the mean-centered representations Z^A and Z^B from two augmented views of a batch of images, the cross-correlation matrix C_{ij} is calculated as follows:

$$C_{ij} = \frac{\sum_b z_{b,i}^A z_{b,j}^B}{\sqrt{\sum_b \left(z_{b,i}^A\right)^2} \sqrt{\sum_b \left(z_{b,j}^B\right)^2}}, \tag{11}$$

Then the loss function for Barlow Twins $\mathcal{L}_{BT}$ is calculated as:

$$\mathcal{L}_{BT} = \sum_i (1 - C_{ij})^2 + \lambda \sum_i \sum_{j \neq i} C_{ij}^2 \tag{12}$$

It is not straightforward to extract individual loss terms from this loss function. In order to calculate reducible anchor loss, we divide the available batch of data into multiple smaller parts with N_p images in each part p. Then we can calculate $\mathcal{L}_{BT}$ on these parts which are treated as a group and the selection of the whole group depends on the calculated reducible anchor loss of each part.

5   Experimental Results

In this section, we provide details about datasets, experiment settings, and implementation followed by results and various analyses on the mentioned datasets with our method. Additional details and experiments can be found in the supplementary material.

5.1   Datasets

CIFAR-100. This dataset consist of 60,000 small 32×32 images from 100 classes [14]. 50,000 of these images are used for training leaving the rest for testing. Although our method does not need to know the task boundaries, in order to have fair comparisons, we use the same 5-task class incremental setting as [10] for training. Therefore, the dataset is divided into 5 subsets of 20 classes and each chunk is fed in the same sequence to our model.

ImageNet-100. This dataset [29] is a 100 class subset of ImageNet [25] large-scale dataset. Training data consists of approximately 127k images (maximum of 1300 per class). 5000 images are also used for evaluation (50 per class). Similar to CIFAR-100, we feed the data in a 5-class class incremental setting to the models.

5.2   Settings

We follow the same setting as [10] to train and evaluate the models. All the models and baselines are trained with self-supervision on the training parts of the datasets. For the evaluation, the backbones are frozen and a linear model is trained on the outputs of the frozen backbone using the train set. Then the accuracy of the validation set is reported. In addition to our method, we conduct experiments using the CaSSLe [10] and an offline approach. To the best of our knowledge, the CaSSLe is the closest work to our method on CIFAR-100 and ImageNet-100 datasets. Our method has the disadvantage of being limited by the online setting but it also uses a larger batch of data in each step due to the use of memory. Therefore, a completely fair comparison is not possible and we mostly treat CaSSLe as a good base point to compare our approach.

The data of the first task in both datasets are used for offline pretraining in order to make comparisons with [10]. All the methods are initialized with the pre-trained weights of the offline model. In all the settings, training is executed for a varying number of steps to analyze the speed of convergence.

Offline. This setting is the regular training with access to the whole dataset. Since it does not have a method to prevent forgetting, we also include the data from the first task in this setting.

CaSSLe. The method proposed in [10] where the data from each task is processed multiple times separately without having access to the data from other tasks. A distillation mechanism is used to prevent forgetting.

Ours. Our proposed method in which the data is processed in an online approach. We include experiments with and without using RALS to analyze the effects of different parts of our work.

5.3   Implementation Details

We build upon the implementation provided by [10] which is itself based on [8]. The source code will be available at https://github.com/sinaazar/SpeedOSSL We adopt the same data preparation process as [10]. We use a batch size of 128 for streaming data. When training without RALS, the same 128 value is used to get a batch of data from the Memory. This value is increased to 256 when using RALS. While using RALS with Barlow Twins and SimCLR we choose $k = 256$

out of 384 samples in each step. Part size N_p for Barlow Twins is set to 16 in all the experiments. We use ResNet18 [11] as the backbone model.

The maximum learning rate for the scheduler is set to 0.1 in ImageNet-100 experiments for both the Barlow Twins and SimCLR. On CIFAR-100, we use 0.05 and 1.0 for Barlow Twins and SimCLR, respectively. The initial learning rate is set to 0.1 of the maximum learning rate in all the settings. Maximum and minimum amounts for momentum are set to 0.95 and 0.85. All the experiments increase/decrease learning rate/momentum halfway through the training steps on each batch except the 50 steps experiments which the increase lasts for a quarter of the training steps. The default memory size for experiments on CIFAR-100 and ImageNet-100 is 10000 and 20000, respectively.

Table 1. Comparison of results of SimCLR (SCLR) [7] and Barlow Twins (BT) [31] methods with various approaches and training steps on CIFAR-100 and ImageNet-100. The focus of this work is on a smaller number of steps but the longer trained versions of CaSSLe [10] are also reported for more insights.

Steps	Strategy	CIFAR-100 Acc		ImageNet-100 Acc	
		BT [31]	SCLR [7]	BT [31]	SCLR [7]
10	Offline	48.5	50.68	44.74	58.94
	CaSSLe [10]	50.89	49.48	49.70	59.70
	Ours Without RALS	55.39	50.39	66.10	64.64
	Ours	55.75	50.63	66.94	64.86
20	Offline	56.23	51.71	67.94	67.84
	CaSSLe [10]	54.35	50.34	64.48	63.74
	Ours Without RALS	55.95	52.44	67.02	66.26
	Ours	56.64	52.77	68.18	66.78
50	Offline	59.64	54.29	69.24	71.26
	CaSSLe [10]	56.25	51.83	67.56	65.56
	Ours Without RALS	57.15	53.25	66.92	67.48
	Ours	58.48	54.76	68.40	67.98
100	Offline	62.93	56.64	74.66	73.28
	CaSSLe [10]	57.48	53.19	69.74	66.94
Full	CaSSLe [10]	58.26	55.91	69.90	67.96

5.4   CIFAR-100 Results

The results for CIFAR-100 [14] and ImageNet-100 dataset [29] datasets are presented in Table 1. Here, the linear evaluation accuracies for different strategies with a varying number of training steps are provided for SimCLR and Barlow Twins. Starting from SimCLR with 10 steps, our method outperforms CaSSLe trained for 10 and 20 steps with or without using RALS. This holds when the 20 steps version is compared with CaSSLe trained for 20 and 50 steps. Generally, increasing the number of steps shows similar improvements for our approach compared to CaSSLe. This compensates for the fact that an additional batch from memory is added to the streaming batch during the training of our method.

We observe similar results to SimCLR when training the model with the Barlow Twins method. Here, the difference in accuracy with CaSSLe becomes even larger in the 10-step setting. Again in all the step numbers, we see improvements over CaSSLe. It is also interesting to see that our method with RALS slightly outperforms the fully trained CaSSLe. The offline setting starts to dominate the results starting from 50 steps.

In all the experiments, including RALS leads to better performance than not including it albeit marginally in some scenarios. Generally, it can be observed that with more training steps we see higher improvements with RALS compared to only using the SLCLRS.

5.5   ImageNet-100 Results

Similar to CIFAR-100, we can see consistent improvements in all the training step numbers for both SimCLR and Barlow Twins. In all cases, using RALS leads to improvements compared to not using it. The improvements are more noticeable when using Barlow Twins. Based on these results and the reported accuracies from CIFAR-100, we can confidently validate the impact of RALS.

Similar to CIFAR-100 results, we see better performance from our method with RALS compared to CaSSLe in a higher step number setting. SimCLR results show the 50-step training version of our method performing on par with the fully trained version of the CaSSLe.

Overall, it can be seen that with steps as little as 10, noticeable results like 64.86% with SimCLR and 66.94% with Barlow Twins can be achieved in an online training scenario while using the ImageNet-100 dataset.

Table 2. Comparison of results of our approach with different backbone methods and memory sizes on CIFAR-100 while training the full model for 20 steps.

Memory Size	SimCLR [7] Acc	Barlow Twins [31] Acc
2000	50.43	55.68
5000	52.47	55.63
10000	52.77	56.64
20000	53.41	56.29

5.6   Analysis

Memory. The main goal of our method is to learn from a stream of data as fast as possible. Therefore, we are tackling a more challenging setup than offline Continual Self-Supervised Learning. Generally, it is not expected to be able

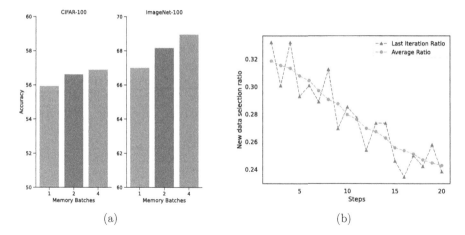

(a)   (b)

Fig. 3. (a) Comparison of the accuracy of our method trained with different numbers of batches sampled from the memory in each iteration. The training was performed for 20 steps in each iteration with the Barlow Twins SSL algorithm on both CIFAR-100 and ImageNet-100 datasets. (b) Progression of selection ratio of the new batch to the combination of the new batch and samples drawn from the memory. The average ratio for the past 100 iterations in addition to the last iteration ratio for a 20-step training is shown here.

to outperform offline CSSL. However, with a big enough memory, we observed improvements when only a small number of training steps are allowed. Table 2 shows the results on CIFAR-100 datasets for our full model trained for 20 steps with varying memory sizes. It can be observed that generally the bigger the memory the better the results.

Considering the advantage of being online trainable, our approach is still interesting even with smaller memory size.

In Fig. 3 (a), we can see the effect of increasing the number of batches sampled from the memory relative to the newly arrived batch of data. Based on the available training time between two iterations, the number of batches sampled from the memory can be increased to improve performance. The intuition behind it is that the RALS will have more samples to select from which in turn will lead to the selection of samples with higher reducible anchor loss.

Selection Behaviour. In order to get a better understanding of the distribution of the samples prioritized by the RALS during the local training steps, we keep track of the number of images selected from the new batch and the samples randomly selected from the memory. More specifically, we calculate the ratio of samples selected from the new batch to the total number of samples used in the current iteration. A visualization is provided in Fig. 3 (b) where it shows the average ratio over a period of 100 iterations during training and the ratio of the last iteration. We can see that on average, during the initial steps of each local training session, the samples from the new batch are randomly selected.

However, when the current model starts to deviate from the anchor model, the RALS starts to select samples more intelligently and it is easy to see that the more the new samples are used for training the less likely they are to be selected. This means the reducible anchor loss is indeed reducing for these samples and the model is learning quickly from them. It is also worth mentioning that the last iteration ratio is not necessarily monotonically decreasing like the average ratio which shows the flexibility of RALS based on the current distribution of samples.

6 Conclusion

In this work, we discussed the challenge of speeding up Online Self-Supervised Learning. We proposed using Single Local Cycle Learning Rate Scheduler to learn from the new samples of a stream of images as fast as possible. Additionally, the idea of Reducible Anchor Loss Selection was proposed to speed up training by selecting more useful samples. The results on both CIFAR-100 and ImageNet-100 with self-supervised learning methods of SimCLR and Barlow Twins showed consistent improvements on the speed of convergence.

Acknowledgements. This work was partly supported by the Alexander von Humboldt Foundation.

References

1. Aljundi, R., Babiloni, F., Elhoseiny, M., Rohrbach, M., Tuytelaars, T.: Memory aware synapses: learning what (not) to forget. In: Proceedings of the European Conference on Computer Vision (ECCV), pp. 139–154 (2018)
2. Aljundi, R., et al.: Online continual learning with maximal interfered retrieval. In: Wallach, H., Larochelle, H., Beygelzimer, A., d'Alché-Buc, F., Fox, E., Garnett, R. (eds.) Advances in Neural Information Processing Systems, vol. 32, pp. 11849–11860. Curran Associates, Inc. (2019). http://papers.nips.cc/paper/9357-online-continual-learning-with-maximal-interfered-retrieval.pdf
3. Aljundi, R., Kelchtermans, K., Tuytelaars, T.: Task-free continual learning. In: Proceedings of the IEEE/CVF Conference on Computer Vision and Pattern Recognition, pp. 11254–11263 (2019)
4. Aljundi, R., Lin, M., Goujaud, B., Bengio, Y.: Gradient based sample selection for online continual learning. In: Advances in Neural Information Processing Systems, vol. 32 (2019)
5. Buzzega, P., Boschini, M., Porrello, A., Abati, D., Calderara, S.: Dark experience for general continual learning: a strong, simple baseline. Adv. Neural. Inf. Process. Syst. **33**, 15920–15930 (2020)
6. Chaudhry, A., Ranzato, M., Rohrbach, M., Elhoseiny, M.: Efficient lifelong learning with a-gem. arXiv preprint arXiv:1812.00420 (2018)
7. Chen, T., Kornblith, S., Norouzi, M., Hinton, G.: A simple framework for contrastive learning of visual representations. In: International Conference on Machine Learning, pp. 1597–1607. PMLR (2020)

8. da Costa, V.G.T., Fini, E., Nabi, M., Sebe, N., Ricci, E.: solo-learn: a library of self-supervised methods for visual representation learning. J. Mach. Learn. Res. **23**, 56:1–56:6 (2022)

9. Fernando, C., et al.: Pathnet: evolution channels gradient descent in super neural networks. arXiv preprint arXiv:1701.08734 (2017)

10. Fini, E., da Costa, V.G.T., Alameda-Pineda, X., Ricci, E., Alahari, K., Mairal, J.: Self-supervised models are continual learners. In: Proceedings of the IEEE/CVF Conference on Computer Vision and Pattern Recognition, pp. 9621–9630 (2022)

11. He, K., Zhang, X., Ren, S., Sun, J.: Deep residual learning for image recognition. In: Proceedings of the IEEE Conference on Computer Vision and Pattern Recognition, pp. 770–778 (2016)

12. He, X., Jaeger, H.: Overcoming catastrophic interference using conceptor-aided backpropagation. In: International Conference on Learning Representations (2018)

13. Howard, J., Gugger, S.: Fastai: a layered API for deep learning. Information **11**(2), 108 (2020)

14. Krizhevsky, A., Hinton, G., et al.: Learning multiple layers of features from tiny images (2009)

15. Lee, S.W., Kim, J.H., Jun, J., Ha, J.W., Zhang, B.T.: Overcoming catastrophic forgetting by incremental moment matching. In: Advances in Neural Information Processing Systems, vol. 30 (2017)

16. Lopez-Paz, D., Ranzato, M.: Gradient episodic memory for continual learning. In: Advances in Neural Information Processing Systems, vol. 30 (2017)

17. Madaan, D., Yoon, J., Li, Y., Liu, Y., Hwang, S.J.: Representational continuity for unsupervised continual learning. In: International Conference on Learning Representations (2021)

18. Mallya, A., Lazebnik, S.: Piggyback: adding multiple tasks to a single, fixed network by learning to mask. arXiv preprint arXiv:1801.06519, vol. 6, no. 8 (2018)

19. Mindermann, S., et al.: Prioritized training on points that are learnable, worth learning, and not yet learnt. In: International Conference on Machine Learning, pp. 15630–15649. PMLR (2022)

20. Paszke, A., et al.: Pytorch: an imperative style, high-performance deep learning library. In: Advances in Neural Information Processing Systems, vol. 32, pp. 8024–8035. Curran Associates, Inc. (2019). http://papers.neurips.cc/paper/9015-pytorch-an-imperative-style-high-performance-deep-learning-library.pdf

21. Purushwalkam, S., Morgado, P., Gupta, A.: The challenges of continuous self-supervised learning. In: Avidan, S., Brostow, G.J., Cissé, M., Farinella, G.M., Hassner, T. (eds.) ECCV 2022, Part XXVI. LNCS, vol. 13686, pp. 702–721. Springer, Cham (2022). https://doi.org/10.1007/978-3-031-19809-0_40

22. Rebuffi, S.A., Kolesnikov, A., Sperl, G., Lampert, C.H.: ICARL: incremental classifier and representation learning. In: Proceedings of the IEEE Conference on Computer Vision and Pattern Recognition, pp. 2001–2010 (2017)

23. Ritter, H., Botev, A., Barber, D.: Online structured laplace approximations for overcoming catastrophic forgetting. In: Advances in Neural Information Processing Systems, vol. 31 (2018)

24. Robins, A.: Catastrophic forgetting, rehearsal and pseudorehearsal. Connect. Sci. **7**(2), 123–146 (1995)

25. Russakovsky, O., et al.: Imagenet large scale visual recognition challenge. Int. J. Comput. Vision **115**(3), 211–252 (2015)

26. Rusu, A.A., et al.: Progressive neural networks. arXiv preprint arXiv:1606.04671 (2016)

27. Serra, J., Suris, D., Miron, M., Karatzoglou, A.: Overcoming catastrophic forgetting with hard attention to the task. In: International Conference on Machine Learning, pp. 4548–4557. PMLR (2018)
28. Smith, L.N., Topin, N.: Super-convergence: Very fast training of neural networks using large learning rates. In: Artificial Intelligence and Machine Learning for Multi-Domain Operations Applications, vol. 11006, pp. 369–386. SPIE (2019)
29. Tian, Y., Krishnan, D., Isola, P.: Contrastive multiview coding. In: Vedaldi, A., Bischof, H., Brox, T., Frahm, J.M. (eds.) ECCV 2020. LNCS, vol. 12356, pp. 776–794. Springer, Cham (2020). https://doi.org/10.1007/978-3-030-58621-8_45
30. Yoon, J., Yang, E., Lee, J., Hwang, S.J.: Lifelong learning with dynamically expandable networks. arXiv preprint arXiv:1708.01547 (2017)
31. Zbontar, J., Jing, L., Misra, I., LeCun, Y., Deny, S.: Barlow twins: self-supervised learning via redundancy reduction. In: International Conference on Machine Learning, pp. 12310–12320. PMLR (2021)
32. Zenke, F., Poole, B., Ganguli, S.: Continual learning through synaptic intelligence. In: International Conference on Machine Learning, pp. 3987–3995. PMLR (2017)

Text-to-Feature Diffusion for Audio-Visual Few-Shot Learning

Otniel-Bogdan Mercea[1]([✉])[ID], Thomas Hummel[1][ID], A. Sophia Koepke[1][ID],
and Zeynep Akata[1,2][ID]

[1] University of Tübingen, Tübingen, Germany
{otniel-bogdan.mercea,thomas.hummel,a-sophia.koepke,
zeynep.akata}@uni-tuebingen.de
[2] MPI for Intelligent Systems, Tübingen, Germany

Abstract. Training deep learning models for video classification from audio-visual data commonly requires vast amounts of labeled training data collected via a costly process. A challenging and underexplored, yet much cheaper, setup is few-shot learning from video data. In particular, the inherently multi-modal nature of video data with sound and visual information has not been leveraged extensively for the few-shot video classification task. Therefore, we introduce a unified audio-visual few-shot video classification benchmark on three datasets, i.e. the VGGSound-FSL, UCF-FSL, ActivityNet-FSL datasets, where we adapt and compare ten methods. In addition, we propose AV-DIFF, a text-to-feature diffusion framework, which first fuses the temporal and audio-visual features via cross-modal attention and then generates multi-modal features for the novel classes. We show that AV-DIFF obtains state-of-the-art performance on our proposed benchmark for audio-visual (generalised) few-shot learning. Our benchmark paves the way for effective audio-visual classification when only limited labeled data is available. Code and data are available at https://github.com/ExplainableML/AVDIFF-GFSL.

Keywords: audio-visual learning · few-shot learning

1 Introduction

The use of audio-visual data can yield impressive results for video classification [55,61,84]. The complementary knowledge contained in the two modalities results in a richer learning signal than using unimodal data. However, video classification frameworks commonly rely on significant amounts of costly training data and computational resources. To mitigate the need for large amounts of labeled data, we consider the few-shot learning (FSL) setting where a model is tasked to recognise new classes with only few labeled examples. Moreover,

Supplementary Information The online version contains supplementary material available at https://doi.org/10.1007/978-3-031-54605-1_32.

the need for vast computational resources can be alleviated by operating on the feature level, using features extracted from pre-trained visual and sound classification networks.

In this work, we tackle the task of few-shot action recognition in videos from audio and visual data which is an understudied problem in computer vision. In the few-shot setting, a model has to learn a transferable audio-visual representation which can be adapted to new classes with few annotated data samples. In particular, we focus on the more practical generalised FSL (GFSL) setting, where the aim is to recognise samples from both the base classes, i.e. classes with many training samples, and from novel classes which contain only few examples. Additional modalities, such as text and audio, are especially useful for learning transferable and robust representations from few samples (Fig. 1).

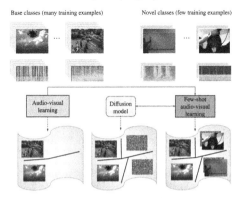

To the best of our knowledge, the FSL setting with audio-visual data has only been considered for speech recognition [87], and for learning an acoustic model of 3D scenes [50]. Moreover, existing video FSL benchmarks are not suitable for the audio-visual setting. In particular, the SomethingV2 and HMDB51 benchmarks proposed in [15] and [86] do not contain audio and about 50% of the classes in the UCF101 benchmark from [82] have no sound either. The Kinetics split in [89] suffers from an overlap with the classes used to pre-train the feature extractors [82], and [55,84] show that the audio modality in Kinetics is less class-relevant than the visual modality. Existing audio-visual zero-shot learning benchmarks [51,52] cannot directly be used for few-shot learning due to their distinct training and testing protocols. Moreover, the baselines in both set-

Fig. 1. AV-DIFF learns to fuse the audio-visual inputs into multi-modal representations in the audio-visual learning stage (left). In the few-shot learning stage (right), the multi-modal representations from the previous stage are used to concurrently train (double arrow line) a text-conditioned diffusion model on all the classes (middle) and a classifier. The classifier is trained on real features from base classes and real and synthetic features from novel classes.

tings differ significantly as state-of-the-art few-shot learning methods usually necessitate knowledge of novel classes through classification objectives and generative models, a condition that is not possible in zero-shot learning. Thus, we introduce a new benchmark for generalised audio-visual FSL for video classification that is comprised of three audio-visual datasets and ten methods carefully adapted to this challenging, yet practical task.

To tackle our new benchmark, we propose AV-DIFF which uses a novel hybrid cross-modal attention for fusing audio-visual information. Different to various attention fusion techniques in the audio-visual domain [51,52,55] which use a single attention type or different transformers for each modality, our model makes use of a novel combination of within-modality and cross-modal attention in a multi-modal transformer. This allows the effective fusion of information from both modalities and across the temporal dimension of the inputs. Furthermore, we introduce a novel text-conditioned diffusion model for generating audio-visual features to augment the few samples in the novel classes. In the image and video domain, generative adversarial networks (GANs) have been used to generate uni-modal features for data augmentation in the FSL setting [32,46,57,82,83]. However, we are not aware of prior works that have used diffusion models for multi-modal (audio-visual) feature generation in FSL. Both, cross-modal fusion and the text-to-feature diffusion contribute to significant boosts in performance on our proposed benchmark.

To summarise, our contributions are: 1) We introduce the audio-visual generalised few-shot learning task for video classification and a benchmark on three audio-visual datasets. We additionally adapt and compare ten methods for this task. 2) We propose a hybrid attention mechanism to fuse multi-modal information, and a diffusion model for multi-modal feature generation to augment the training dataset with additional novel-class samples. 3) We obtain state-of-the-art performance across all three datasets, outperforming the adapted multi-modal zero-shot learning and video FSL models.

2   Related Work

We discuss prior works in learning from audio-visual data, FSL, and feature generation in low-shot learning.

Audio-Visual Learning. Multi-modal inputs, such as audio and visual data, provide significantly more information than unimodal data, resulting in improved overall performance for video classification and acoustic scene classification [7,10,45,59–61]. Approaches, such as [21,25], use class-label supervision between modalities without requiring temporal alignment between the input modalities. Besides audio and video classification, other domains also benefit from multi-modal data, such as lip reading [4,5], audio synthesis based on visual information [27,30,43,44,56,71,88], and localisation and separation of sounds in videos [3,6,8,18,28,58,74]. Recently, transformer models have gained popularity in audio-visual learning, e.g. for classification [14], event localization [48], dense video captioning [36], and text-based video retrieval [26,79]. As shown in these works, transformers can effectively process multi-modal input. Thus, our proposed framework fuses audio-visual information using a transformer-based mechanism.

FSL has been explored in the image domain [20,23,32,47,49,63,64,67,69,72,78, 80,81,85] and in the video domain [11,15,41,82,89]. The popular meta-learning paradigm in FSL [11,15,47,49,64,72,78,80,85,89] has been criticised by recent works [20,39,80,82]. In the video domain, commonly a query and support set is used and each query sample is compared to all the support samples [11,15,62,89]. The number of comparisons grows exponentially with the number of ways and shots. These methods become prohibitively expensive for GFSL, where models are evaluated on both the base and the novel classes. Hence, we focus on the non-meta learning approach in this work. Some non-meta learning approaches have addressed the more challenging and practical GFSL setting for videos [46,82] using unimodal visual data. In contrast, we propose to use multi-modal data in our novel (G)FSL benchmark for audio-visual video classification which provides the possibility to test a model in both scenarios (FSL and GFSL).

Feature Generation. Due to the progress of generative models, such as GANs [2,29,31,37,54] and diffusion models [12,24,66], different works have tried to adapt these systems to generate features as a data augmentation mechanism. GANs have been used in zero-shot learning (ZSL) and FSL [46,57,82,83] to increase the number and diversity of samples especially for unseen or novel classes. Diffusion models have also been applied to image generation in the feature space, such as [66,76], but not in the ZSL or FSL setting. It is known that GANs are hard to optimize [68] while diffusion models appear to be more stable, leading to better results [22]. Therefore, our proposed framework uses a text-conditioned diffusion model to generate features for the novel classes in the FSL setting.

3   Audio-Visual (G)FSL Benchmark

We describe the audio-visual (G)FSL setting, present our proposed benchmark that we construct from audio-visual datasets, and explain the methods that we used to establish baselines for this task.

3.1   Audio-Visual (G)FSL Setting

We address the tasks of (G)FSL using audio-visual inputs. The aim of FSL is to recognise samples from classes that contain very few training samples, so-called *novel classes*. In addition, the goal of GFSL is to recognise both *base classes*, which contain a significant amount of samples, and novel classes.

Given an audio-visual dataset $\mathcal{V}$ with M samples and C classes, containing base and novel classes, we have $\mathcal{V} = \{\mathcal{X}_{a[i]}, \mathcal{X}_{v[i]}, y_{[i]}\}_{i=1}^{M}$, where $\mathcal{X}_{a[i]}$ represents the audio input, $\mathcal{X}_{v[i]}$ the video input and $y_{[i]} \in \mathbb{R}^{C}$ the ground-truth class label. Both the audio and the video inputs contain temporal information. Two frozen, pretrained networks are used to extract features from the inputs, VGGish [34] for the audio features $a_{[i]} = \{a_1, \ldots, a_t, \ldots, a_{F_a}\}_i$ and C3D [75] for video features $v_{[i]} = \{v_1, \ldots, v_t, \ldots, v_{F_v}\}_i$. We use these specific feature extractors to ensure that there is no leakage to the novel classes from classes seen when training the feature extractors (Sports1M [40] for the visual and Youtube-8M [1] for the audio modality), similar to [52]. A potential leakage is harmful as it would artificially increase the performance and will not reflect the true performance.

All models are evaluated in the FSL and GFSL settings for k samples in the novel classes (called shots), with $k \in \{1, 5, 10, 20\}$. During inference, in the FSL setting, the class search space is composed only of the novel class labels and

Table 1. Statistics for our VGGSound-FSL **(1)**, UCF-FSL **(2)**, and ActivityNet-FSL **(3)** benchmark datasets, showing the number of classes and videos in our proposed splits in the 5-shot setting. $\mathcal{V}_{B_1} \cup \mathcal{V}_{N_1}$ are used for training, Val_B and Val_N for validation in the first training stage. $\mathcal{V}_{B_2} \cup \mathcal{V}_{N_2}$ serves as training set in the second stage, and evaluation is done on $Test_B$ and $Test_N$.

| | # classes | | | | # videos *stage 1* | | | | # videos *stage 2* | | | |
	all	$\mathcal{V}_{B_1}$	$\mathcal{V}_{N_1}$	$\mathcal{V}_{N_2}$	$\mathcal{V}_{B_1}$	$\mathcal{V}_{N_1}$	Val_B	Val_N	$\mathcal{V}_{B_2}$	$\mathcal{V}_{N_2}$	$Test_B$	$Test_N$
(1)	271	138	69	64	70351	345	7817	2757	81270	320	9032	2880
(2)	48	30	12	6	3174	60	353	1407	4994	30	555	815
(3)	198	99	51	48	9204	255	1023	4052	14534	240	1615	3812

the samples belonging to these classes. In the GFSL setting, the search space contains both the novel and base class labels and their corresponding samples.

Meta-learning approaches commonly use the notion of episodes, where each episode only uses P novel classes randomly sampled from the total number of novel classes in a dataset, usually $P \in \{1,5\}$ (coined P-way). However, similar to [82], we suggest to use higher values for P (e.g. all the classes in the dataset), so that the evaluation is closer to the real-world setting, as argued in [32,82]. In our proposed FSL setting, P corresponds to the total number of novel classes $P = N$, while for GFSL $P = C$. Our evaluation protocol is in line with [32].

3.2 Dataset Splits and Training Protocol

We provide training and evaluation protocols for audio-visual (G)FSL along with splits for UCF-FSL, ActivityNet-FSL and VGGSound-FSL. These are based on the UCF-101 [70], ActivityNet [33] and VGGSound [19] datasets.

Our proposed training and evaluation protocol is similar to [32,51,52]. The training protocol is composed of two stages, indicated by subscripts $_{1,2}$. In the first stage, a model is trained on the training set $Train_1 = \mathcal{V}_{B_1} \cup \mathcal{V}_{N_1}$ where $\mathcal{V}_{B_1}$ consists of dataset samples from base classes, and $\mathcal{V}_{N_1}$ contains k samples for each of the classes N_1. The trained model is then evaluated on $Val = Val_B \cup Val_N$, where Val is the validation dataset which contains the same classes as $Train_1$. In the first stage, the hyperparameters for the network are determined, such as the number of training epochs and the learning rate scheduler parameters.

In the second stage, the model is retrained on the training set $Train_2$, using the hyperparameters determined in the first stage. Here, $Train_2 = \mathcal{V}_{B_2} \cup \mathcal{V}_{N_2}$ with $\mathcal{V}_{B_2} = Train_1 \cup Val$, and $\mathcal{V}_{N_2}$ contains k samples for the novel classes in the $Test$ set. The final model is evaluated on $Test = Test_B \cup Test_N$ with $Train_2 \cap Test = \emptyset$. With a small number of shots, e.g. $k = 1$, models risk a bias towards the novel samples in $Train_2$. To obtain robust evaluation results, the second stage is repeated three times with k randomly selected, but fixed samples from $\mathcal{V}_{N_2}$. We provide dataset statistics in Table 1.

3.3   Benchmark Comparisons

To establish benchmark performances for audio-visual GFSL task, we adapt ten recent state-of-the-art methods for video FSL from visual information only, from audio-visual representation learning, and from audio-visual ZSL.

We provide results with several few-shot video recognition frameworks adapted to the multimodal audio-visual setting.

ProtoGan [46] uses GANs conditioned on the visual prototypes of classes that are obtained by averaging the features of all videos in that class. We adapt it to audio-visual inputs by concatenating the visual and audio features before passing them into the model.

SLDG [13] is a multi-modal video FSL that uses video frames and optical flow as input. It weighs the frame features according to normal distributions. We replace the optical flow in [13] with audio features.

TSL [82] is the current state-of-the-art video FSL which uses a GAN to generate synthetic samples for novel classes. It does not fully use temporal information, as the final score is the average of scores obtained on multiple short segments. We adapt it to the multi-modal setting by concatenating input features from the audio and visual modalities.

Moreover, we have adapted audio-visual representation learning methods to the few-shot task as can be seen below.

Perceiver [38], **Hierarchical Perceiver (HiP)** [16], and **Attention Fusion** [25] are versatile video classification methods and we provide comparisons with them. We use the implementations of the adapted Perceiver and Attention Fusion frameworks provided by [51] and we implement HiP in a similar way.

MBT [55] learns audio-visual representations for video recognition. It uses a transformer for each modality and these transformers can only exchange information using bottleneck attention.

Zorro [65], in contrast to MBT, uses two transformers that do not have access to the bottleneck attention. We adapt it by using a classifier on top of the averaged bottleneck attention tokens.

Finally, we have adapted the state-of-the-art methods in the audio-visual zero-shot learning domain, as shown below.

AVCA [52] is an audio-visual ZSL method which uses temporally averaged features for the audio and visual modalities. We adapt it by using a classifier on the video output, which is the strongest of the two outputs in [52].

TCaF [51] is the state-of-the-art audio-visual ZSL method. It utilizes a transformer architecture with only cross-modal attention, leveraging temporal information in both modalities. As it does not use a classifier, TCaF outputs embeddings, and we determine the class by computing the distance to the semantic descriptors and selecting the closest one.

4   AV-Diff Framework

In this section, we provide details for our proposed cross-modal AV-Diff framework which employs cross-modal fusion (Sect. 4.1) and a diffusion model to

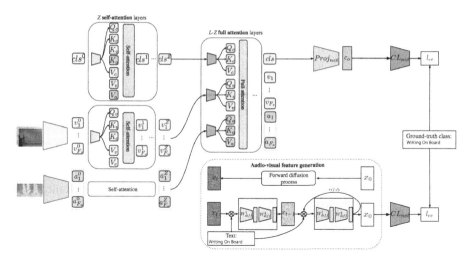

Fig. 2. Our AV-Diff model for audio-visual (G)FSL takes audio and visual features extracted from pre-trained audio and video classification models as inputs. During training, the features from both modalities are fused into a classification token, denoted by cls. At the same time, our diffusion model (bottom) generates additional synthetic features for the novel classes (denoted by x_0). Finally, we train our classifier CL_{net} (right) on fused real features c_o of both novel and base classes and synthetic features of novel classes. $\otimes$ is the concatenation operator.

generate audio-visual features (Sect. 4.2). Then, we describe the training curriculum in Sect. 4.3. Figure 2 illustrates AV-Diff's full architecture.

4.1   Audio-Visual Fusion with Cross-Modal Attention

Audio-Visual Fusion. We project the audio $a_{[i]}$ and visual features $v_{[i]}$ to a shared embedding space. Then we use Fourier features [73] as temporal positional embeddings and modality embeddings respectively and obtain positional aware video v_t^E and audio a_t^E tokens for timestep t. We prepend a classification token $cls^0 \in \mathbb{R}^{d_{dim}}$ to the audio and visual tokens. The output token cls corresponding to cls^0 is the final fused audio-visual representation which is input to $Proj_{net}$. Our audio-visual fusion mechanism contains L layers, which are based on multi-head attention [77] Att^l, followed by a feed forward function $\mathrm{FF}^l : \mathbb{R}^{d_{dim}} \rightarrow \mathbb{R}^{d_{dim}}$. The input to the first layer is $x_{in}^1 = [cls^0, a_1^E, \cdots, a_{T_a}^E, v_1^E, \cdots, v_{T_v}^E]$. The output of a layer is:

$$x_{out}^l = \mathrm{FF}^l(\mathrm{Att}^l(x_{in}^l) + x_{in}^l) + \mathrm{Att}^l(x_{in}^l) + x_{in}^l. \tag{1}$$

In the following, we describe the first layer of the audio-visual fusion. The other layers work similarly. Our input x_{in}^1 is projected to queries, keys and values with linear maps $s : \mathbb{R}^{d_{dim}} \rightarrow \mathbb{R}^{d_{dim}}$ for $s \in \{q, k, v\}$. The outputs of the projection are written as zero-padded query, key and value features. For the keys we get:

$$\mathbf{K}_c = [k(cls^0), 0, \cdots, 0], \tag{2}$$

$$\mathbf{K}_a = [0, \cdots, 0, k(a_1^E), \cdots, k(a_{F_a}^E), 0, \cdots, 0], \tag{3}$$

$$\mathbf{K}_v = [0, \cdots, 0, k(v_1^E), \cdots, k(v_{F_v}^E)]. \tag{4}$$

The final keys are obtained as $\mathbf{K} = \mathbf{K}_c + \mathbf{K}_a + \mathbf{K}_v$. The queries and values are obtained in a similar way. We define full attention as $\mathbf{A} = \mathbf{A}_c + \mathbf{A}_{cross} + \mathbf{A}_{self}$:

$$\mathbf{A}_c = \mathbf{Q}_c\,\mathbf{K}^T + \mathbf{K}\,\mathbf{Q}_c^T, \qquad \mathbf{A}_{cross} = \mathbf{Q}_a\,\mathbf{K}_v^T + \mathbf{Q}_v\,\mathbf{K}_a^T,$$
$$\mathbf{A}_{self} = \mathbf{Q}_a\,\mathbf{K}_a^T + \mathbf{Q}_v\,\mathbf{K}_v^T. \tag{5}$$

The novelty in the attention mechanism in AV-DIFF is that it exploits a hybrid attention mechanism composed of two types of attention: within-modality self-attention and full-attention. The first Z layers use self-attention $\mathbf{A}_{self} + \mathbf{A}_c$, the subsequent $L - Z$ layers leverage full attention $\mathbf{A}$.

Audio-Visual classification. We project cls to $\mathbb{R}^{d_{out}}$ by using a projection network, $c_o = Proj_{net}(cls)$. Then, we apply a classification layer to c_o, $logits = CL_{net}(c_o)$. Given the ground-truth labels gt, we use a cross-entropy loss, $L_{ce} = CE(logits, gt)$ to train the full architecture.

4.2   Text-Conditioned Feature Generation

AV-DIFF uses a diffusion process to generate audio-visual features which is based on the Denoising Diffusion Probabilistic Models (DDPM) [35]. In particular, we condition the generation of features for novel classes on a conditioning signal, such as the word embedding (e.g. word2vec [53]) of a class name. The diffusion framework consists of a forward process and a reverse process.

The forward process adds noise to the data sample x_0 for T timesteps:

$$q(x_{1:T}|x_0) = \prod_{t=1}^{T} q(x_t|x_{t-1}) = \prod_{t=1}^{T} \mathcal{N}\left(x_t; \sqrt{1 - \beta_t}x_{t-1}, \beta_t \mathbf{I}\right), \tag{6}$$

where $\beta_1, \ldots, \beta_T$ is the variance schedule.

As the **reverse process** $q(x_{t-1}|x_t)$ is intractable, we approximate it with a parameterised model p_θ:

$$p_\theta(x_{0:T}) = p_\theta(x_T)\prod_{t=1}^{T} p_\theta(x_{t-1}|x_t) = p_\theta(x_T)\prod_{t=1}^{T} \mathcal{N}(x_{t-1}; \mu_\theta(x_t, t), \Sigma_\theta(x_t, t)). \tag{7}$$

We condition the model on the timestep t and the class label embedding w,

$$L_{\text{diff},w} = E_{x_0, t, w, \epsilon}[||\epsilon - \epsilon_\theta(\sqrt{\bar{a}_t}x_0 + \sqrt{1 - \bar{a}_t}\epsilon, w, t)||^2], \tag{8}$$

where ϵ is the noise added at each timestep and ϵ_θ is a model that predicts this noise. The sample at timestep $t - 1$ is obtained from timestep t as:

$$p_\theta(x_{t-1}|x_t, w) = \mathcal{N}(x_{t-1}; \frac{1}{\sqrt{\alpha_t}}(x_t - \frac{\beta_t}{\sqrt{1 - \bar{\alpha}_t}}\epsilon_\theta(x_t, w, t)), \sigma_t^2 \mathcal{I}). \tag{9}$$

The input to ϵ_θ at timestep t is obtained by concatenating x_t, w, and t. We optimize $L_{\text{diff},w}$ to learn p_θ.

4.3 Training Curriculum and Evaluation

Each training stage (explained in Sect. 3.2) is split into two substages. In the first substage, we train the full architecture (the fusion mechanism, the diffusion model, $Proj_{net}$ and the classifier CL_{net}) on base classes $\mathcal{V}_{B_1}$ (or $\mathcal{V}_{B_2}$ in the second stage) by minimizing $L_{ce} + L_{\text{diff},w}$. The classifier CL_{net} is trained only on real features for the base classes in $\mathcal{V}_{B_1}$ (or $\mathcal{V}_{B_2}$ for the second stage) in the first substage.

During the second substage, we freeze the fusion mechanism and continue to train the diffusion model, $Proj_{net}$ and CL_{net} with the same training objective $L_{ce} + L_{\text{diff},w}$. Here we consider both base and novel classes $\mathcal{V}_{B_1}$ and $\mathcal{V}_{N_1}$ classes (or $\mathcal{V}_{B_2}$ and $\mathcal{V}_{N_2}$ in the second stage), unlike in the first substage where we only used base classes. For each batch composed of real samples from novel classes, we generate a corresponding batch of the same size with synthetic samples using our diffusion model. CL_{net} is then trained on real features from $\mathcal{V}_{B_1}$ (or $\mathcal{V}_{B_2}$ in the second stage) and on real and synthetic features for the classes in $\mathcal{V}_{N_1}$ (or $\mathcal{V}_{N_2}$ in the second stage). Freezing the audio-visual transformer ensures that its fusion mechanism does not overfit to the few samples from the novel classes.

The diffusion model is not used for inference, and the output of the classifier CL_{net} for c_0 provides the predicted score for each class (including the novel classes). The class with the highest score is selected as the predicted class.

5 Experiments

In this section, we first provide the implementation details for obtaining the presented results (Sect. 5.1). We then report results for our proposed AV-DIFF in our benchmark study (Sect. 5.2). Finally, we analyse the impact of different components of AV-DIFF (Sect. 5.3).

5.1 Implementation Details

AV-DIFF uses features extracted from pre-trained audio and visual classification networks as inputs (details provided in the suppl. material). AV-DIFF is trained using $d_{dim} = 300$ and $d_{out} = 64$. Our fusion network has $L = 5, 4, 8$ transformer layers, the layer after which the attention changes is set to $Z = 3, 2, 5$ on ActivityNet-FSL, UCF-FSL and VGGSound-FSL respectively. We train all models on a single NVIDIA RTX 2080-Ti GPU. The first substage uses 30 epochs while the second one uses 20 epochs. We use the Adam optimizer [42], and $\beta_1 = 0.9$, $\beta_2 = 0.999$, and weight decay of $1e^{-5}$. We use a learning rate of $7e^{-5}$ for UCF-FSL and ActivityNet-FSL, and $6e^{-5}$ for VGGSound-FSL. For ActivityNet-FSL and UCF-FSL, we use a scheduler that reduces the learning rate by a factor of 0.1 when the performance has not improved for 3 epochs. We use a batch size of 32 for ActivityNet-FSL, and 64 for UCF-FSL and VGGSound-FSL. Each epoch consists of 300 batches. As ActivityNet-FSL has very long videos, we randomly trim the number of features during training to 60. During evaluation, we also

Table 2. Our benchmark study for audio-visual (G)FSL: 1,5,10-shot performance of our AV-DIFF and compared methods on (G)FSL. The harmonic mean (HM) of the mean class accuracies for base and novel classes are reported for GFSL. For the FSL performance, only the test subset of the novel classes is considered. Base, novel, and 20-shots performances are included in the suppl. material.

Model ↓	VGGSound-FSL						UCF-FSL						ActivityNet-FSL					
	1-shot		5-shot		10-shot		1-shot		5-shot		10-shot		1-shot		5-shot		10-shot	
	HM	FSL	HM	FSL	HM	FSL	HM	FSL	HM	FSL	HM	FSL	HM	FSL	HM	FSL	HM	FSL
Att. Fusion [25]	15.46	16.37	28.22	31.57	30.73	39.02	37.39	36.88	51.68	47.18	57.91	52.19	4.35	5.82	6.17	8.13	10.67	10.78
Perceiver [38]	17.97	18.51	29.92	33.58	33.65	40.73	44.12	33.73	48.60	40.47	55.33	47.86	17.34	12.53	25.75	21.50	29.88	26.46
MBT [55]	14.70	21.96	27.26	34.95	30.12	38.93	39.65	27.99	46.55	34.53	50.04	39.73	14.26	12.63	23.26	22.38	26.86	26.03
TCaF [51]	19.54	20.01	26.09	32.22	28.95	36.43	44.61	35.90	46.29	37.39	54.19	47.61	16.50	13.01	22.79	21.81	24.78	23.33
ProtoGan [46]	10.74	14.08	25.17	28.87	29.85	34.80	37.95	28.08	42.42	33.63	51.01	40.68	2.77	4.40	2.67	7.81	4.05	8.81
SLDG [13]	16.83	17.57	20.79	25.17	24.11	29.48	39.92	28.91	36.47	28.56	34.31	26.96	13.57	10.30	22.29	19.16	27.81	25.35
TSL [82]	18.73	22.44	19.49	29.50	21.93	31.29	44.51	35.17	51.08	42.42	60.93	55.63	9.53	10.77	10.97	12.77	10.39	12.18
HiP [16]	19.27	18.64	26.82	30.67	29.25	35.13	21.79	34.88	36.44	42.23	50.69	43.29	13.80	10.31	18.10	16.25	19.37	17.06
Zorro [65]	18.88	21.79	29.56	35.17	32.06	40.66	44.35	34.52	51.86	42.59	58.89	49.06	14.56	11.94	23.14	21.94	27.35	26.33
AVCA [52]	6.29	10.29	15.98	20.50	18.08	28.27	43.61	31.24	49.19	36.70	50.53	39.17	12.83	12.22	20.09	21.65	26.02	26.76
AV-DIFF	**20.31**	**22.95**	**31.19**	**36.56**	**33.99**	**41.39**	**51.50**	**39.89**	**59.96**	**51.45**	**64.18**	**57.39**	**18.47**	**13.80**	**26.96**	**23.00**	**30.86**	**27.81**

trim the videos to a maximum length of 300 features, and the trimmed features are centered in the middle of the video. To reduce the bias towards base classes, we use calibrated stacking [17] on the search space composed of the interval [0,1] with a step size of 0.1. This value is obtained on the validation dataset.

5.2 Audio-Visual GFSL Performance

For each of the models featuring in our benchmark, we report results for three different numbers of shots, i.e. 1-shot, 5-shot, 10-shot on all three datasets in Table 2. AV-DIFF outperforms all the methods across all shots and datasets for few-shot learning (FSL) and generalised few-shot learning (HM).

For 1-shot, AV-DIFF achieves a HM/FSL of 20.31%/22.95% vs. HM of 19.54% for TCAF and FSL score of 22.44% for TSL on VGGSound-FSL. On 5-shot, our model obtains a HM/FSL of 31.19%/36.56% vs. 29.92% for the Perceiver and FSL of 35.17% for Zorro. Furthermore, AV-DIFF yields slightly better results than the Perceiver in both HM and FSL for 10 shots, with HM/FSL of 33.99%/41.39% vs. 33.65%/40.73% for the Perceiver. Thus, combining our hybrid attention and the diffusion model is superior to systems that rely solely on powerful attention mechanisms without incorporating generative modeling (Perceiver, TCAF) and systems that incorporate generative modelling, but that do not employ powerful attention mechanisms (TSL, ProtoGan).

Similar trends are observed on UCF-FSL, while on ActivityNet-FSL, the ranking of methods changes dramatically. Methods that perform well on UCF-FSL and VGGSound-FSL, but which do not fully use the temporal information (e.g. Attention Fusion, ProtoGan and TSL) perform weakly on ActivityNet-FSL which contains videos with varying length, including some very long videos, making the setting more challenging. Our AV-DIFF can process temporal information effectively, resulting in robust state-of-the-art results on ActivityNet-FSL.

Table 3. Impact of different audio-visual fusion mechanisms in the 5-shot setting.

Model ↓	VGGSound-FSL				UCF-FSL				ActivityNet-FSL			
	B	N	HM	FSL	B	N	HM	FSL	B	N	HM	FSL
A	28.56	31.52	29.98	36.55	78.95	42.07	54.90	43.75	23.10	22.06	22.57	22.53
$\mathbf{A}_{cross} + \mathbf{A}_c$	28.44	32.48	30.33	36.85	82.89	44.33	57.77	47.02	27.02	21.25	23.79	21.98
$\mathbf{A}_{self} + \mathbf{A}_c$	26.68	33.23	29.60	**37.06**	50.10	44.58	47.18	45.03	31.61	21.48	25.58	22.65
Alternate AV-Diff	27.40	32.60	29.78	36.82	80.25	43.01	56.00	45.81	31.15	21.57	25.49	22.59
AV-Diff	30.88	31.50	**31.19**	36.56	74.11	50.35	**59.96**	**51.45**	35.84	21.61	**26.96**	**23.00**

Interestingly, VGGSound-FSL contains the most classes among the datasets considered, resulting in a significantly lower N (suppl. material, Tab. 1) than FSL. This also lowers the HM (computed from B, N). On VGGSound-FSL, methods tend to be biased towards novel classes (N $\geq$ B) due to calibration [17]. In this case, HM $\leq$ N $\leq$ FSL. Moreover, some baselines that were also used in audio-visual zero-shot learning [51,52] (e.g. TCAF) exhibit significant increases in performance even in the 1-shot setting. This is expected as for 1-shot learning, one training example is used from each novel class. This reduces the bias towards base classes, leading to more balanced B and N scores, and thereby better HM and FSL results. Base, novel, and 20-shot performances are included in the suppl. material.

5.3 AV-Diff Model Ablations

Here, we analyse the benefits of the main components of AV-Diff, i.e. our proposed audio-visual fusion mechanism, and the diffusion model for feature generation. Furthermore, we analyse the importance of using multiple modalities, and the effect of different semantic representations.

Audio-Visual Fusion Mechanism. Table 3 ablates our cross-modal fusion mechanism for generating rich audio-visual representations. As shown in Sect. 4.1, AV-Diff uses two types of attention: $\mathbf{A}_{self} + \mathbf{A}_c$ for the first few layers and $\mathbf{A}$ for the later layers. For *Alternate* AV-Diff, we alternate the two types of attention used in AV-Diff in subsequent layers. We also show our model with $\mathbf{A}_{cross} + \mathbf{A}_c$ which is the same attention used by the SOTA audio-visual GZSL framework [51]. On ActivityNet-FSL, AV-Diff obtains a HM/FSL of 26.96%/23.00% vs. 25.58%/22.65% for $\mathbf{A}_{self} + \mathbf{A}_c$. The same trend is seen on UCF-FSL. On VGGSound-FSL we outperform *Alternate* AV-Diff on HM, but are slightly weaker than $\mathbf{A}_{self} + \mathbf{A}_c$ in FSL. Overall, our fusion mechanism is the best across both metrics and datasets.

Feature Generation Model. In Table 4, we investigate the impact of different generative models to produce audio-visual features for the novel classes. We compare the diffusion model in AV-Diff to a GAN similar to the one used by TSL [82], which optimizes a Wasserstein GAN loss [9]. On ActivityNet-FSL, we observe that AV-Diff outperforms the GAN variant, with a HM/FSL of

Table 4. Influence of using different feature generators in the 5-shot setting.

Model ↓	VGGSound-FSL				UCF-FSL				ActivityNet-FSL			
	B	N	HM	FSL	B	N	HM	FSL	B	N	HM	FSL
AV-GAN	27.80	31.75	29.64	36.53	83.79	36.20	50.56	37.33	35.12	19.53	25.10	21.35
AV-Diff	30.88	31.50	**31.19**	**36.56**	74.11	50.35	**59.96**	**51.45**	35.84	21.61	**26.96**	**23.00**

Table 5. Influence of using multi-modal input in the 5-shot setting.

Model ↓	VGGSound-FSL				UCF-FSL				ActivityNet-FSL			
	B	N	HM	FSL	B	N	HM	FSL	B	N	HM	FSL
Audio	28.30	30.56	29.39	**36.64**	55.31	39.18	45.87	44.44	13.74	15.23	14.45	17.58
Visual	7.83	8.92	8.35	9.51	67.13	30.70	42.14	30.98	20.80	17.49	19.01	17.84
AV-Diff	30.88	31.50	**31.19**	36.56	74.11	50.35	**59.96**	**51.45**	35.84	21.61	**26.96**	**23.00**

26.96%/23.00% vs. 25.10%/21.35% for the GAN. The same can be seen on UCF-FSL and VGGSound-FSL. This shows that our generative diffusion model is better suited for audio-visual GFSL than a GAN.

Multi-modal Input. We explore the impact of using multi-modal inputs for AV-Diff in Table 5. For unimodal inputs, we adapt AV-Diff to only employ full attention which is identical to self-attention in this case. On ActivityNet-FSL, using multi-modal inputs provides a significant boost in performance compared to unimodal inputs, with a HM/FSL of 26.96%/23.00% vs. 19.01%/17.84% when using only visual information. The same trend can be observed on UCF-FSL. In contrast, on VGGSound-FSL, using multi-modal inputs gives stronger GFSL but slightly weaker results in FSL than using the audio modality. This might be due to the focus on the audio modality in the data curation process for VGGSound. As a result, significant portions of the visual information can be unrelated to the labelled class. Overall, the use of multi-modal inputs from the audio and visual modalities significantly boosts the (G)FSL performance for AV-Diff.

However, one interesting aspect is that using both modalities leads to better B and N performances across all three datasets. For example, on ActivityNet-FSL, AV-Diff obtains a B score of 35.84% and an N score of 21.61% compared to 20.80% and 17.49% when using only the visual modality. On UCF-FSL, AV-Diff achieves a score of 74.11% for B and 50.35% for N compared to 67.13% and 39.18% for the visual and audio modalities respectively. Finally, on VGGSound-FSL, AV-Diff achieves a B score of 30.88% and an N score of 31.50% compared to 28.30% and 30.56% for unimodal audio inputs. This shows that using multi-modal inputs decreases the bias towards either of the metrics, leading to a more robust and balanced system.

Semantic Class Representations. We consider using different semantic class representations in Table 6. In FSL, the most common semantic descriptor is word2vec [53] which is used to condition the audio-visual feature generation in AV-Diff. However, related works (e.g. ProtoGan [46]), use prototypes which

Table 6. Influence of different semantic class representations in the 5-shot setting.

Model ↓	VGGSound-FSL				UCF-FSL				ActivityNet-FSL			
	B	N	HM	FSL	B	N	HM	FSL	B	N	HM	FSL
AV-DIFF av_{prot}	25.74	33.00	28.92	35.76	83.38	42.46	56.26	44.78	32.22	21.50	25.79	22.73
AV-DIFF	30.88	31.50	**31.19**	**36.56**	74.11	50.35	**59.96**	**51.45**	35.84	21.61	**26.96**	**23.00**

average the visual features of all the training videos in a class to obtain the semantic representation of that class. In the multi-modal setting, we can concatenate the audio and visual prototypes to obtain multi-modal prototypes av_{prot} which is used as a conditioning signal for our diffusion model. On ActivityNet-FSL, using word2vec embeddings leads to better results than using the audio-visual prototypes av_{prot}, with a HM/FSL of 26.96%/23.00% vs. 25.79%/22.73% for av_{prot}. The same can be seen on UCF-FSL and VGGSound-FSL, demonstrating that the word2vec embeddings provide a more effective conditioning signal.

6 Conclusion

In this work, we propose an audio-visual (generalised) few-shot learning benchmark for video classification. Our benchmark includes training and evaluation protocols on three datasets, namely VGGSound-FSL, UCF-FSL and ActivityNet-FSL, and baseline performances for ten state-of-the-art methods adapted from different fields. Moreover, we propose AV-DIFF which fuses multi-modal information with a hybrid attention mechanism and uses a text-conditioned diffusion model to generate features for novel classes. AV-DIFF outperforms all related methods on the new benchmark. Finally, we provided extensive model ablations to show the benefits of our model's components. We hope that our benchmark will enable significant progress for audio-visual generalised few-shot learning.

Acknowledgements. This work was supported by BMBF FKZ: 01IS18039A, DFG: SFB 1233 TP 17 - project number 276693517, by the ERC (853489 - DEXIM), and by EXC number 2064/1 - project number 390727645. The authors thank the International Max Planck Research School for Intelligent Systems (IMPRS-IS) for supporting O.-B. Mercea and T. Hummel.

References

1. Abu-El-Haija, S., et al.: Youtube-8m: a large-scale video classification benchmark. arXiv:1609.08675 (2016)
2. Adler, J., Lunz, S.: Banach Wasserstein GAN. In: NeurIPS (2018)
3. Afouras, T., Asano, Y.M., Fagan, F., Vedaldi, A., Metze, F.: Self-supervised object detection from audio-visual correspondence. In: CVPR (2022)

4. Afouras, T., Chung, J.S., Senior, A., Vinyals, O., Zisserman, A.: Deep audio-visual speech recognition. IEEE TPAMI **44**(12), 8717–8727 (2018)
5. Afouras, T., Chung, J.S., Zisserman, A.: ASR is all you need: cross-modal distillation for lip reading. In: ICASSP (2020)
6. Afouras, T., Owens, A., Chung, J.S., Zisserman, A.: Self-supervised learning of audio-visual objects from video. In: ECCV (2020)
7. Alwassel, H., Mahajan, D., Torresani, L., Ghanem, B., Tran, D.: Self-supervised learning by cross-modal audio-video clustering. In: NeurIPS (2020)
8. Arandjelovic, R., Zisserman, A.: Objects that sound. In: ECCV (2018)
9. Arjovsky, M., Chintala, S., Bottou, L.: Wasserstein generative adversarial networks. In: ICML (2017)
10. Aytar, Y., Vondrick, C., Torralba, A.: Soundnet: learning sound representations from unlabeled video. In: NeurIPS (2016)
11. Bishay, M., Zoumpourlis, G., Patras, I.: Tarn: Temporal attentive relation network for few-shot and zero-shot action recognition. In: BMVC (2019)
12. Blattmann, A., Rombach, R., Oktay, K., Müller, J., Ommer, B.: Semi-parametric neural image synthesis. In: NeurIPS (2022)
13. Bo, Y., Lu, Y., He, W.: Few-shot learning of video action recognition only based on video contents. In: WACV (2020)
14. Boes, W., Van hamme, H.: Audiovisual transformer architectures for large-scale classification and synchronization of weakly labeled audio events. In: ACM MM (2019)
15. Cao, K., Ji, J., Cao, Z., Chang, C.Y., Niebles, J.C.: Few-shot video classification via temporal alignment. In: CVPR (2020)
16. Carreira, J., et al.: Hierarchical perceiver. arXiv preprint arXiv:2202.10890 (2022)
17. Chao, W.L., Changpinyo, S., Gong, B., Sha, F.: An empirical study and analysis of generalized zero-shot learning for object recognition in the wild. In: ECCV (2016)
18. Chen, H., Xie, W., Afouras, T., Nagrani, A., Vedaldi, A., Zisserman, A.: Localizing visual sounds the hard way. In: CVPR (2021)
19. Chen, H., Xie, W., Vedaldi, A., Zisserman, A.: Vggsound: a large-scale audio-visual dataset. In: ICASSP (2020)
20. Chen, W.Y., Liu, Y.C., Kira, Z., Wang, Y.C.F., Huang, J.B.: A closer look at few-shot classification. arXiv:1904.04232 (2019)
21. Chen, Y., Xian, Y., Koepke, A.S., Shan, Y., Akata, Z.: Distilling audio-visual knowledge by compositional contrastive learning. In: CVPR (2021)
22. Dhariwal, P., Nichol, A.: Diffusion models beat GANs on image synthesis. In: NeurIPS (2021)
23. Douze, M., Szlam, A., Hariharan, B., Jégou, H.: Low-shot learning with large-scale diffusion. In: CVPR (2018)
24. Esser, P., Rombach, R., Blattmann, A., Ommer, B.: Imagebart: bidirectional context with multinomial diffusion for autoregressive image synthesis. In: NeurIPS (2021)
25. Fayek, H.M., Kumar, A.: Large scale audiovisual learning of sounds with weakly labeled data. In: IJCAI (2020)
26. Gabeur, V., Sun, C., Alahari, K., Schmid, C.: Multi-modal transformer for video retrieval. In: ECCV (2020)
27. Gan, C., Huang, D., Chen, P., Tenenbaum, J.B., Torralba, A.: Foley music: learning to generate music from videos. In: ECCV (2020)
28. Gao, R., Grauman, K.: Co-separating sounds of visual objects. In: ICCV (2019)
29. Gatys, L.A., Ecker, A.S., Bethge, M.: A neural algorithm of artistic style. arXiv:1508.06576 (2015)

30. Goldstein, S., Moses, Y.: Guitar music transcription from silent video. In: BMVC (2018)
31. Goodfellow, I., et al.: Generative adversarial networks. Commun. ACM **63**(11), 139–144 (2020)
32. Hariharan, B., Girshick, R.: Low-shot visual recognition by shrinking and hallucinating features. In: ICCV (2017)
33. Heilbron, F.C., Escorcia, V., Ghanem, B., Niebles, J.C.: Activitynet: a large-scale video benchmark for human activity understanding. In: CVPR (2015)
34. Hershey, S., et al.: CNN architectures for large-scale audio classification. In: ICASSP (2017)
35. Ho, J., Jain, A., Abbeel, P.: Denoising diffusion probabilistic models. In: NeurIPS (2020)
36. Iashin, V., Rahtu, E.: A better use of audio-visual cues: Dense video captioning with bi-modal transformer. In: BMVC (2020)
37. Isola, P., Zhu, J.Y., Zhou, T., Efros, A.A.: Image-to-image translation with conditional adversarial networks. In: CVPR (2017)
38. Jaegle, A., Gimeno, F., Brock, A., Vinyals, O., Zisserman, A., Carreira, J.: Perceiver: general perception with iterative attention. In: ICML (2021)
39. Kang, B., et al.: Decoupling representation and classifier for long-tailed recognition. In: ICLR (2020)
40. Karpathy, A., Toderici, G., Shetty, S., Leung, T., Sukthankar, R., Fei-Fei, L.: Large-scale video classification with convolutional neural networks. In: CVPR (2014)
41. Kim, S., Choi, D.W.: Better generalized few-shot learning even without base data. arXiv:2211.16095 (2022)
42. Kingma, D.P., Ba, J.: Adam: a method for stochastic optimization. arXiv:1412.6980 (2014)
43. Koepke, A.S., Wiles, O., Moses, Y., Zisserman, A.: Sight to sound: an end-to-end approach for visual piano transcription. In: ICASSP (2020)
44. Koepke, A.S., Wiles, O., Zisserman, A.: Visual pitch estimation. In: SMC (2019)
45. Korbar, B., Tran, D., Torresani, L.: Cooperative learning of audio and video models from self-supervised synchronization. In: NeurIPS (2018)
46. Kumar Dwivedi, S., Gupta, V., Mitra, R., Ahmed, S., Jain, A.: Protogan: towards few shot learning for action recognition. In: ICCVW (2019)
47. Li, X., et al.: Learning to self-train for semi-supervised few-shot classification. In: NeurIPS (2019)
48. Lin, Y.B., Wang, Y.C.F.: Audiovisual transformer with instance attention for audio-visual event localization. In: ACCV (2020)
49. Liu, Y., et al.: Learning to propagate labels: transductive propagation network for few-shot learning. arXiv:1805.10002 (2018)
50. Majumder, S., Chen, C., Al-Halah, Z., Grauman, K.: Few-shot audio-visual learning of environment acoustics. In: NeurIPS (2022)
51. Mercea, O.B., Hummel, T., Koepke, A.S., Akata, Z.: Temporal and cross-modal attention for audio-visual zero-shot learning. In: ECCV (2022)
52. Mercea, O.B., Riesch, L., Koepke, A.S., Akata, Z.: Audio-visual generalised zero-shot learning with cross-modal attention and language. In: CVPR (2022)
53. Mikolov, T., Chen, K., Corrado, G., Dean, J.: Efficient estimation of word representations in vector space. In: ICLR (2013)
54. Mirza, M., Osindero, S.: Conditional generative adversarial nets. arXiv:1411.1784 (2014)
55. Nagrani, A., Yang, S., Arnab, A., Jansen, A., Schmid, C., Sun, C.: Attention bottlenecks for multimodal fusion. In: NeurIPS (2021)

56. Narasimhan, M., Ginosar, S., Owens, A., Efros, A.A., Darrell, T.: Strumming to the beat: audio-conditioned contrastive video textures. arXiv:2104.02687 (2021)
57. Narayan, S., Gupta, A., Khan, F.S., Snoek, C.G., Shao, L.: Latent embedding feedback and discriminative features for zero-shot classification. In: ECCV (2020)
58. Owens, A., Efros, A.A.: Audio-visual scene analysis with self-supervised multisensory features. In: ECCV (2018)
59. Owens, A., Wu, J., McDermott, J.H., Freeman, W.T., Torralba, A.: Ambient sound provides supervision for visual learning. In: ECCV (2016)
60. Owens, A., Wu, J., McDermott, J.H., Freeman, W.T., Torralba, A.: Learning sight from sound: ambient sound provides supervision for visual learning. In: IJCV (2018)
61. Patrick, M., Asano, Y.M., Fong, R., Henriques, J.F., Zweig, G., Vedaldi, A.: Multimodal self-supervision from generalized data transformations. In: NeurIPS (2020)
62. Perrett, T., Masullo, A., Burghardt, T., Mirmehdi, M., Damen, D.: Temporal-relational crosstransformers for few-shot action recognition. In: CVPR (2021)
63. Qi, H., Brown, M., Lowe, D.G.: Low-shot learning with imprinted weights. In: CVPR (2018)
64. Ravi, S., Larochelle, H.: Optimization as a model for few-shot learning. In: ICLR (2017)
65. Recasens, A., et al.: Zorro: the masked multimodal transformer. arXiv preprint arXiv:2301.09595 (2023)
66. Rombach, R., Blattmann, A., Lorenz, D., Esser, P., Ommer, B.: High-resolution image synthesis with latent diffusion models. In: CVPR (2022)
67. Roy, A., Shah, A., Shah, K., Roy, A., Chellappa, R.: Diffalign: few-shot learning using diffusion based synthesis and alignment. arXiv preprint arXiv:2212.05404 (2022)
68. Saxena, D., Cao, J.: Generative adversarial networks (GANs) challenges, solutions, and future directions. ACM Comput. Surv. (CSUR) **54**(3), 1–42 (2021)
69. Snell, J., Swersky, K., Zemel, R.: Prototypical networks for few-shot learning. In: NeurIPS (2017)
70. Soomro, K., Zamir, A.R., Shah, M.: UCF101: a dataset of 101 human actions classes from videos in the wild. arXiv:1212.0402 (2012)
71. Su, K., Liu, X., Shlizerman, E.: Multi-instrumentalist net: unsupervised generation of music from body movements. arXiv:2012.03478 (2020)
72. Sung, F., Yang, Y., Zhang, L., Xiang, T., Torr, P.H., Hospedales, T.M.: Learning to compare: relation network for few-shot learning. In: CVPR (2018)
73. Tancik, M., et al.: Fourier features let networks learn high frequency functions in low dimensional domains. In: NeurIPS (2020)
74. Tian, Y., Shi, J., Li, B., Duan, Z., Xu, C.: Audio-visual event localization in unconstrained videos. In: ECCV (2018)
75. Tran, D., Bourdev, L., Fergus, R., Torresani, L., Paluri, M.: Learning spatiotemporal features with 3D convolutional networks. In: ICCV (2015)
76. Vahdat, A., Kreis, K., Kautz, J.: Score-based generative modeling in latent space. In: NeurIPS (2021)
77. Vaswani, A., et al.: Attention is all you need. In: NeurIPS (2017)
78. Vinyals, O., Blundell, C., Lillicrap, T., Wierstra, D., et al.: Matching networks for one shot learning. In: NeurIPS (2016)
79. Wang, X., Zhu, L., Yang, Y.: T2VLAD: global-local sequence alignment for text-video retrieval. In: CVPR (2021)
80. Wang, Y., Chao, W.L., Weinberger, K.Q., van der Maaten, L.: Simpleshot: revisiting nearest-neighbor classification for few-shot learning. arXiv:1911.04623 (2019)

81. Wang, Y.X., Girshick, R., Hebert, M., Hariharan, B.: Low-shot learning from imaginary data. In: CVPR (2018)
82. Xian, Y., Korbar, B., Douze, M., Torresani, L., Schiele, B., Akata, Z.: Generalized few-shot video classification with video retrieval and feature generation. IEEE TPAMI **44**(12), 8949–8961 (2021)
83. Xian, Y., Sharma, S., Schiele, B., Akata, Z.: F-VAEGAN-D2: a feature generating framework for any-shot learning. In: CVPR (2019)
84. Xiao, F., Lee, Y.J., Grauman, K., Malik, J., Feichtenhofer, C.: Audiovisual slowfast networks for video recognition. arXiv:2001.08740 (2020)
85. Ye, H.J., Hu, H., Zhan, D.C., Sha, F.: Few-shot learning via embedding adaptation with set-to-set functions. In: CVPR (2020)
86. Zhang, H., Zhang, L., Qi, X., Li, H., Torr, P.H., Koniusz, P.: Few-shot action recognition with permutation-invariant attention. In: ECCV (2020)
87. Zhang, Y.K., Zhou, D.W., Ye, H.J., Zhan, D.C.: Audio-visual generalized few-shot learning with prototype-based co-adaptation. In: Proceedings of Interspeech 2022 (2022)
88. Zhou, H., Liu, Z., Xu, X., Luo, P., Wang, X.: Vision-infused deep audio inpainting. In: ICCV (2019)
89. Zhu, L., Yang, Y.: Compound memory networks for few-shot video classification. In: ECCV (2018)

Correlation Clustering of Bird Sounds

David Stein$^{(\boxtimes)}$ and Bjoern Andres

Technische Universität Dresden, Dresden, Germany
{david.stein1,bjoern.andres}@tu-dresden.de

Abstract. Bird sound classification is the task of relating any sound recording to those species of bird that can be heard in the recording. Here, we study bird sound clustering, the task of deciding for any pair of sound recordings whether the same species of bird can be heard in both. We address this problem by first learning, from a training set, probabilities of pairs of recordings being related in this way, and then inferring a maximally probable partition of a test set by correlation clustering. We address the following questions: How accurate is this clustering, compared to a classification of the test set? How do the clusters thus inferred relate to the clusters obtained by classification? How accurate is this clustering when applied to recordings of bird species not heard during training? How effective is this clustering in separating, from bird sounds, environmental noise not heard during training?

Keywords: Correlation clustering · Bird sound classification

1 Introduction

The abundance and variety of bird species are well-established markers of biodiversity and the overall health of ecosystems [10]. Traditional approaches to measuring these quantities rely on human experts counting bird species at select locations by sighting and hearing [34]. This approach is labor-intensive, costly and biased by the experience of individual experts. Recently, progress has been made toward replacing this approach by a combination of passive audio monitoring [8,29,40] and automated bird sound classification [21]. The effectiveness of this automated approach can be seen, for instance, in [22,45]. Bird sound classification is the task of relating any sound recording to those species of bird that can be heard in the recording [12,21]. Models and algorithms for bird sound classification are a topic of the annual BirdCLEF Challenge [11,16,17,19,20]. Any model for bird sound classification is defined and learned for a fixed set of bird species. At the time of writing, the most accurate models developed for this task all have the form of a neural network [11,12,18,20–22,37,39].

Here, we study bird sound clustering, the task of deciding for any pair of bird sound recordings whether the same species of bird can be heard in both.

Supplementary Information The online version contains supplementary material available at https://doi.org/10.1007/978-3-031-54605-1_33.

We address this task in three steps. Firstly, we define a probabilistic model of bird sound clusterings. Secondly, we learn from a training set a probability mass function of the probability of pairs of sound recordings being related. Thirdly, we infer a maximally probable partition of a test set by solving a correlation clustering problem locally. Unlike models for bird sound classification, the model we define for bird sound clustering is agnostic to the notion of bird species.

In this article, we make four contributions: Firstly, we quantify empirically how accurate bird sound correlation clustering is compared to bird sound classification. To this end, we compare in terms of a metric known as the variation of information [3,31] partitions of a test set inferred using our model to partitions of the same test set induced by classifications of this set according to a fixed set of bird species. Secondly, we measure empirically how the clusters of the test set inferred using our model relate to bird species. To this end, we relate each cluster to an optimally matching bird species and count, for each bird species, the numbers of false positives and false negatives. Thirdly, we quantify empirically how accurate correlation clustering is when applied to recordings of bird species not heard during training. Fourthly, we quantify empirically the effectiveness of correlation clustering in separating from bird sounds environmental noise not heard during training.

2 Related Work

Metric-based clustering of bird sounds with prior knowledge of the number of clusters is studied in [7,30,38]: k means clustering in [38], k nearest neighbor clustering in [7], and clustering with respect to the distance to all elements of three given clusters in [30, Section 2.2]. In contrast, we study *correlation clustering* [4] of bird sounds without prior knowledge of the number of clusters.

In [7], the coefficients in the objective function of a clustering problem are defined by the output of a Siamese network. Siamese networks, introduced in [6] and described in the recent survey [27], are applied to the tasks of classifying and embedding bird sounds in [7,36]. We follow [7] in that we also define the coefficients in the objective function of a clustering problem by the output of a Siamese network. However, as we consider a correlation clustering problem, we learn the Siamese network by minimizing a loss function fundamentally different from that in [7]. Beyond bird sounds, correlation clustering with respect to costs defined by the output of a Siamese network is considered in [14,26,41] for the task of clustering images, and in [43] for the task of tracking humans in a video. We are unaware of prior work on correlation clustering of bird sounds.

Probabilistic models of the partitions of a set, and, more generally, the decompositions of graphs, without priors or constraints on the number or size of clusters, are studied for various applications, including image segmentation [1,2,23,25], motion trajectory segmentation [24] and multiple object tracking [42,43]. The Bayesian network we introduce here for bird sound clustering is analogous to the specialization to complete graphs of the model introduced in [2] for image segmentation. Like in [43] and unlike in [2], the probability mass

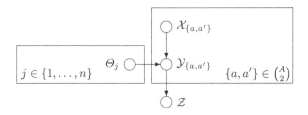

Fig. 1. Depicted above is a Bayesian network defining conditional independence assumptions of a probabilistic model for bird sound clustering we introduce in Sect. 3.2.

function we consider here for the probability of a pair of bird sounds being in the same cluster has the form of a Siamese network. Like in [2] and unlike in [43], we cluster all elements, without the possibility of choosing a subset.

Complementary to prior work and ours on either classification or clustering of bird sounds are models for sound separation [44] that can separate multiple bird species audible in the same sound recoding and have been shown to increase the accuracy of bird sound classification [9].

General theoretical connections between clustering and classification are established in [5, 47].

3   Model

3.1   Representation of Clusterings

We consider a finite, non-empty set A of sound recordings that we seek to cluster. The feasible solutions to this task are the partitions of the set A. Recall that a partition Π of A is a collection $\Pi \subseteq 2^A$ of non-empty and pairwise disjoint subsets of A whose union is A. Here, 2^A denotes the power set of A. We will use the terms *partition* and *clustering* synonymously for the purpose of this article and refer to the elements of a partition as *clusters*.

Below, we represent any partition Π of the set A, by the function $y^\Pi : \binom{A}{2} \rightarrow \{0, 1\}$ that maps any pair $\{a, a'\} \in \binom{A}{2}$ of distinct sound recordings $a, a' \in A$ to the number $y^\Pi_{\{a,a'\}} = 1$ if a and a' are in the same cluster, i.e. if there exists a cluster $U \in \Pi$ such that $a \in U$ and $a' \in U$, and maps the pair to the number $y^\Pi_{\{a,a'\}} = 0$, otherwise.

Importantly, not every function $y : \binom{A}{2} \rightarrow \{0, 1\}$ well-defines a partition of the set A. Instead, there can be three distinct elements a, b, c such that $y_{\{a,b\}} = y_{\{b,c\}} = 1$ and $y_{\{a,c\}} = 0$. However, it is impossible to put a and b in the same cluster, and put b and c in the same cluster, and not put a and c in the same cluster, as this violates transitivity. The functions $y : \binom{A}{2} \rightarrow \{0, 1\}$ that well-define a partition of the set A are precisely those that hold the additional property

$$\forall a \in A \; \forall b \in A \setminus \{a\} \; \forall c \in A \setminus \{a, b\}: \quad y_{\{a,b\}} + y_{\{b,c\}} - 1 \leq y_{\{a,c\}}. \tag{1}$$

We let Z_A denote the set of all such functions. That is:

$$Z_A := \left\{ y^{\Pi} : \tbinom{A}{2} \to \{0,1\} \mid (1) \right\}. \tag{2}$$

3.2 Bayesian Model

With the above representation of clusterings in mind, we define a probabilistic model with four classes of random variables. This model is depicted in Fig. 1.

For every $\{a, a'\} \in \binom{A}{2}$, let $\mathcal{X}_{\{a,a'\}}$ be a random variable whose value is a vector $x_{\{a,a'\}} \in \mathbb{R}^{2m}$, with $m \in \mathbb{N}$. We call the first m coordinates a *feature vector* of the sound recording a, and we call the last m coordinates a feature vector of the sound recording a'. These feature vectors are described in more detail in Sect. 6.

For every $\{a, a'\} \in \binom{A}{2}$, let $\mathcal{Y}_{\{a,a'\}}$ be a random variable whose value is a binary number $y_{\{a,a'\}} \in \{0,1\}$, indicating whether the recordings a and a' are in the same cluster, $y_{\{a,a'\}} = 1$, or distinct clusters, $y_{\{a,a'\}} = 0$.

For a fixed number $n \in \mathbb{N}$ and every $j \in \{1, \ldots, n\}$, let Θ_j be a random variable whose value is a real number $\theta_j \in \mathbb{R}$ that we call a *model parameter*.

Finally, let $\mathcal{Z}$ be a random variable whose value is a set $Z \subseteq \{0,1\}^{\binom{A}{2}}$ of feasible maps from the set $\binom{A}{2}$ of pairs of distinct sound recordings to the binary numbers. We will fix this random variable to the set Z_A defined in (2) of those functions that well-define a partition of the set A.

Among these random variables, we assume conditional independencies according to the Bayesian Net depicted in Fig. 1. This implies the factorization:

$$P(\mathcal{X}, \mathcal{Y}, \mathcal{Z}, \Theta) = P(\mathcal{Z} \mid \mathcal{Y}) \prod_{\{a,a'\} \in \binom{A}{2}} P(\mathcal{Y}_{\{a,a'\}} \mid \mathcal{X}_{\{a,a'\}}, \Theta) \prod_{\{a,a'\} \in \binom{A}{2}} P(\mathcal{X}_{\{a,a\}}) \prod_{j=1}^{2m} P(\Theta_j) \tag{3}$$

For the conditional probabilities on the right-hand side, we define probability measures:

First is a probability mass function that assigns a probability mass of zero to all $y \notin Z$ and assigns equal and positive probability mass to all $y \in Z$. For any $Z \subseteq \{0,1\}^{\binom{A}{2}}$ and any $y \in \{0,1\}^{\binom{A}{2}}$:

$$p_{\mathcal{Z}|\mathcal{Y}}(Z, y) \propto \begin{cases} 1 & \text{if } y \in Z \\ 0 & \text{otherwise} \end{cases}. \tag{4}$$

Recall that we fix $Z = Z_A$, i.e. we assign positive and equal probability mass to those binary labelings of pairs of audio recordings that well-define a clustering of the set A.

Second is a logistic distribution: For any $\{a, a'\} \in \binom{A}{2}$, any $x_{\{a,a'\}} \in \mathbb{R}^{2m}$ and any $\theta \in \mathbb{R}^n$:

$$p_{\mathcal{Y}_{\{a,a'\}}|\mathcal{X}_{\{a,a'\}}, \Theta}(1, x_{\{a,a'\}}, \theta) = \frac{1}{1 + 2^{-f_\theta\left(x_{\{a,a'\}}\right)}}. \tag{5}$$

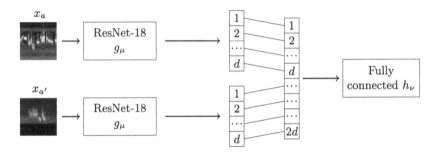

Fig. 2. In order to decide if the same species of bird can be heard in the spectrograms $x_a, x_{a'} \in \mathbb{R}^m$ of two distinct sound recordings $a, a' \in A$, we learn a Siamese neural network. In this network, each spectrogram is mapped to a d-dimensional vector via the same ResNet-18 [13], $g_\mu \colon \mathbb{R}^m \to \mathbb{R}^d$, with output dimension $d = 128$ and parameters $\mu \in \mathbb{R}^{11235905}$. These vectors are then concatenated and put into a fully connected layer $h_\theta \colon \mathbb{R}^d \times \mathbb{R}^d \to \mathbb{R}$ with a single linear output neuron and parameters $\nu \in \mathbb{R}^{33025}$. Overall, this network defines the function $f_\theta \colon \mathbb{R}^{2m} \to \mathbb{R}$ in the logistic distribution (5), with parameters $\theta := (\mu, \nu)$, such that for any input pair $(x_a, x_{a'}) = x_{a,a'}$, we have $f_\theta(x_{\{a,a'\}}) = h_\nu(g_\mu(x_a), g_\mu(x_{a'}))$.

Here, the function $f_\theta \colon \mathbb{R}^{2m} \to \mathbb{R}$ has the form of the Siamese neural network depicted in Fig. 2.

Third is a uniform distribution on a finite interval. For a fixed $\tau \in \mathbb{R}^+$, any $j \in \{1, \ldots, n\}$ and any $\theta_j \in \mathbb{R}$:

$$p_{\Theta_j}(\theta_j) \propto \begin{cases} 1 & \text{if } \theta_j \in [-\tau, \tau] \\ 0 & \text{otherwise} \end{cases}. \tag{6}$$

4   Learning

Training data consists of (i) a set A of sound recordings, (ii) for each sound recording $a \in A$, a feature vector x_a, (iii) for each pair $\{a, a'\} \in \binom{A}{2}$ of distinct sound recordings, a binary number $y_{\{a,a'\}} \in \{0, 1\}$ that is 1 if and only if a human annotator has labeled both a and a' with the same bird species. This training data fixes the values of the random variables X and Y in the probabilistic model. In addition, we fix $Z = Z_A$, as described above.

We learn model parameters by maximizing the conditional probability

$$P(\Theta \mid \mathcal{X}, \mathcal{Y}, \mathcal{Z}) \propto \prod_{\{a,a'\} \in \binom{A}{2}} P(\mathcal{Y}_{\{a,a'\}} \mid \mathcal{X}_{\{a,a'\}}, \Theta) \prod_{j=1}^{n} P(\Theta_j). \tag{7}$$

With the logistic distribution (5) and the prior distribution (6), and after elementary arithmetic transformations, this problem takes the form of the linearly constrained non-linear logistic regression problem

$$\inf_{\theta \in \mathbb{R}^n} \quad \sum_{\{a,a'\} \in \binom{A}{2}} \left(-y_{\{a,a'\}} f_\theta(x_{\{a,a'\}}) + \log_2(1 + 2^{f_\theta(x_{\{a,a'\}})}) \right) \quad (8)$$

$$\text{subject to} \quad \forall j \in \{1, \dots, n\}: \quad -\tau \leq \theta_j \leq \tau. \quad (9)$$

In practice, we choose τ large enough for the constraints (9) to be inactive for the training data we consider, i.e. we consider an uninformative prior over the model parameters. We observe that the unconstrained problem (8) is non-convex, due to the non-convexity of f_θ. In practice, we do not solve this problem, not even locally. Instead, we compute a feasible solution $\hat{\theta} \in \mathbb{R}^n$ heuristically, by means of stochastic gradient descent with an adaptive learning rate. More specifically, we employ the algorithm AdamW [28] with mini-batches $B_A \subseteq \binom{A}{2}$ and the loss

$$\frac{1}{|B_A|} \sum_{\{a,a'\} \in B_A} \left(-y_{\{a,a'\}} f_\theta(x_{\{a,a'\}}) + \log_2(1 + 2^{f_\theta(x_{\{a,a'\}})}) \right). \quad (10)$$

We set the initial learning rate to 10^{-4}, the batch size to 64, and the number of iterations to 380,000. Moreover, we balance the batches in the sense that there are exactly $|B_A|/2$ elements in B_A with $y_{\{a,a'\}} = 1$ and exactly $|B_A|/2$ elements in B_A with $y_{\{a,a'\}} = 0$. All learning is carried out on a single NVIDIA A100 GPU with 16 AMD EPYC 7352 CPU cores, equipped with 32 GB of RAM. Our implementation can be here.

5 Inference

We assume to have learned and now fixed model parameters $\hat{\theta}$. In addition, we are given a feature vector x_a for every sound recording $a \in A$ of a test set A. This fixes the values of the random variables Θ and X in the probabilistic model. In addition, we fix $Z = Z_A$, as described above, so as to concentrate the probability measure on those binary decisions for pairs of recordings that well-define a partition of the set A.

We infer a clustering of the set A by maximizing the conditional probability

$$P(\mathcal{Y} \mid \mathcal{X}, \mathcal{Z}, \Theta) \propto P(\mathcal{Z} \mid \mathcal{Y}) \prod_{\{a,a'\} \in \binom{A}{2}} P(\mathcal{Y}_{\{a,a'\}} \mid \mathcal{X}_{\{a,a'\}}, \Theta) \quad (11)$$

For the uniform distribution (4) on the subset Z_A, and for the logistic distribution (5), the maximizers of this probability mass can be found by solving the correlation clustering problem

$$\max_{y: \binom{A}{2} \to \{0,1\}} \quad f_\theta(x_{\{a,a'\}}) \, y_{\{a,a'\}} \quad (12)$$

$$\text{subject to} \quad \forall a \in A \, \forall b \in A \setminus \{a\} \, \forall c \in A \setminus \{a, b\}: \quad y_{\{a,b\}} + y_{\{b,c\}} - 1 \leq y_{\{a,c\}} \quad (13)$$

In practice, we compute a locally optimal feasible solution $\hat{y}\colon \binom{A}{2} \to \{0,1\}$ to this NP-hard problem by means of the local search algorithm GAEC, until convergence, and then the local search algorithm KLj, both from [25]. The output $\hat{y}$ is guaranteed to well-define a clustering of the set A such that any distinct sound recordings $a, a' \in A$ belong to the same cluster if and only if $\hat{y}_{\{a,a'\}} = 1$.

6 Experiments

6.1 Dataset

We start from those 17,313 audio recordings of a total of 316 bird species from the collection Xeno-Canto [46] of quality A or B that are recorded in Germany, contain bird songs and do not contain background species. The files are re-sampled to 44,100 Hz and split into chunks of 2 s. For each chunk, we compute the mel spectrogram with a frame width of 1024 samples, an overlap of 768 samples and 128 mel bins and re-scale it to 128×384 entries. Finally, to distinguish salient from non-salient chunks, we apply the signal detector proposed in [22]. Bird species with less than 100 salient audio chunks are excluded. This defines a first dataset of 68 bird species with at least 10 min of audio recordings in total. We split this set according to the proportions 8/1/1 into disjoint subsets Train-68, Val-68 and Test-68. In addition, we consider a set Test-0,87 of 87 bird species with less than 10 min but more than one minute of audio data. We call the union of both test sets Test-68,87. In addition, we define a set Test-N containing 39 classes of environmental noise not used for augmentation from the collection ESC-50 [33]. We refer to the union of Test-68 and Test-N as Test-68,N. During learning, we employ augmentation techniques, specifically: horizontal and vertical roll, time shift, SpecAugment [32], as well as the addition of white noise, pink noise and some environmental noise from ESC-50.

6.2 Metrics

In order to measure the distance between a predicted partition $\hat{\Pi}$ of a finite set A, on the one hand, and a true partition Π of the same set A, on the other hand, we evaluate a metric known as the variation of information [3,31]:

$$\mathrm{VI}(\Pi, \hat{\Pi}) = H(\Pi \mid \hat{\Pi}) + H(\hat{\Pi} \mid \Pi) \tag{14}$$

Here, the conditional entropy $H(\Pi \mid \hat{\Pi})$ is indicative of false joins, whereas the conditional entropy $H(\hat{\Pi} \mid \Pi)$ is indicative of false cuts.

In order to measure the accuracy of decisions $\hat{y}\colon \binom{A}{2} \to \{0,1\}$ for all pairs $\{a, a'\} \in \binom{A}{2}$ of sound recordings also for decisions that do not well-define a clustering of A, we calculate the numbers of true joins (TJ), true cuts (TC), false cuts (FC) and false joins (FJ) of these pairs according to Eqs. (15) and (16) below. From these, we calculate in the usual way the precision and recall of cuts, the precision and recall of joins, and Rand's index [35].

$$\text{TJ}(y^{\Pi}, \hat{y}) = \sum_{ij \in \binom{A}{2}} y_{ij}^{\Pi} \hat{y}_{ij}, \quad \text{TC}(y^{\Pi}, \hat{y}) = \sum_{ij \in \binom{A}{2}} (1 - y_{ij}^{\Pi})(1 - \hat{y}_{ij}) \quad (15)$$

$$\text{FC}(y^{\Pi}, \hat{y}) = \sum_{ij \in \binom{A}{2}} (1 - \hat{y}_{ij}) y_{ij}^{\Pi}, \quad \text{FJ}(y^{\Pi}, \hat{y}) = \sum_{ij \in \binom{A}{2}} \hat{y}_{ij}(1 - y_{ij}^{\Pi}). \quad (16)$$

6.3 Clustering vs Classification

Here, we describe the experiments we conduct in order to compare the accuracy of a clustering of bird sounds with the accuracy of a classification of bird sounds. The results are shown in Table 1 and Fig. 3.

Procedure and Results. Toward clustering, we learn the model f_θ defined in Sect. 3.2, as described in Sect. 4, from the data set Train-68, with and without data augmentation, and apply it to the independent data set Test-68 in two different ways: Firstly, we infer an independent decision $y_{\{a,a'\}} \in \{0,1\}$ for every pair of distinct sound recordings a, a', by asking whether $f_\theta(x_{\{a,a'\}}) \geq 0$ ($y_{\{a,a'\}} = 1$) or $f_\theta(x_{\{a,a'\}}) < 0$ ($y_{\{a,a'\}} = 0$). These decisions together do not necessarily well-define a clustering of Test-68. Yet, we compare these decisions independently to the truth, in Rows 1–2 of Table 1. Secondly, we infer a partition of Test-68 by correlation clustering, as described in Sect. 5 (Rows 3–4 of Table 1). Thirdly, we infer a partition of Test-68 and a subsample of Train-68, which contains 128 randomly chosen recordings per species, jointly by locally solving the correlation clustering problem for the union of these data sets, also as described in Sect. 5 (Rows 5–6 of Table 1).

Toward classification, we learn a ResNet-18 on Train-68, with and without data augmentation. Using this model, we infer a classification of Test-68 (Rows

Table 1. Above, we report, for models trained on Train-68 and evaluated on Test-68, whether the inferred solution well-defines a partition of Test-68 (Π) and how this solution compares to the truth in terms of Rand's index (RI), the variation of information (VI), conditional entropies due to false cuts (VI$_{FC}$) and false joins (VI$_{FJ}$), the precision (P) and recall (R) of cuts (C) and joins (J), and the classification accuracy (CA).

	Model	Π	RI	VI	VI$_{FC}$	VI$_{FJ}$	PC	RC	PJ	RJ	CA
1.	f_θ	no	0.89	-	-	-	97.9%	89.9%	42.6%	79.5%	-
2.	f_θ + Aug	no	0.87	-	-	-	**98.7%**	86.9%	38.7%	**87.6%**	-
3.	f_θ + CC	yes	0.93	4.21	1.99	2.22	97.3%	95.0%	57.6%	72.1%	-
4.	f_θ + Aug + CC	yes	0.91	3.28	1.34	1.95	98.1%	92.0%	48.9%	81.3%	-
5.	f_θ + CC + T	yes	0.93	4.21	2.02	2.19	97.3%	95.2%	58.5%	71.7%	-
6.	f_θ + Aug + CC + T	yes	0.91	3.27	1.35	1.91	98.1%	92.2%	49.4%	80.8%	-
7.	ResNet18	yes	0.94	4.67	2.33	2.34	96.7%	96.9%	66.2%	64.8%	59.6%
8.	ResNet18 + Aug	yes	**0.96**	**3.20**	1.68	**1.72**	97.3%	**97.8%**	**75.3%**	71.8%	72.7%
9.	BirdNET Analyzer	yes	0.77	3.50	**1.22**	2.28	94.3%	79.4%	18.3%	48.9%	49.7%
10.	f_θ + T	yes	0.93	4.26	1.97	2.29	97.3%	95.0%	57.8%	72.2%	64.1%
11.	f_θ + Aug + T	yes	0.94	3.31	1.48	1.83	97.8%	95.6%	62.6%	77.3%	**73.1%**

7–8 of Table 1). In addition, we classify Test-68 by means of BirdNET analyzer [22] (Row 9 of Table 1). We remark that BirdNET is defined for 3-second sound recordings while we work with 2-second sound recordings. When applying BirdNET to these 2-second recordings, they are padded with random noise as described in [15]. Finally, we infer a classification of Test-68 by assigning each sound recording to one of the true clusters of Train-68 for which this assignment is maximally probable according to the model f_θ learned on Train-68. We report the accuracy of this classification with respect to f_θ in Rows 10–11 of Table 1. For each classification of Test-68, we report the distance from the truth of the *clustering* of Test-68 induced by the classification. This allows for a direct comparison of classification with clustering.

Discussion. Closest to the truth by a variation of information of 3.20 is the clustering of Test-68 induced by the classification of Test-68 by means of the ResNet-18 learned from Train-68, with data augmentation (Row 8 in Table 1). This result is expected, as classification is clustering with a constrained set of clusters, and this constraint constitutes additional prior knowledge. Dropping this information during learning but not during inference (Row 6 in Table 1) leads to the second best clustering that differs from the true clustering of Test-68 by a variation of information of 3.27. Dropping this knowledge during learning and inference (Row 4 in Table 1) leads to a variation of information 3.28. It can be seen from these results that a clustering of this bird sound data set is less accurate than a classification, but still informative. From a comparison of Rows 2 and 4 of Table 1, it can bee seen that the local solution of the correlation clustering problem not only leads to decisions for pairs of sound recordings that well-define a clustering of Test-68 but also increases the accuracy of these decisions in terms of Rand's index, from 0.87 to 0.91. Looking at these two experiments in more detail, we observe an increase in the recall of cuts and precision of joins due to correlation clustering, while the precision of cuts decreases slightly and the recall of joins decreases strongly. Indeed, we observe more clusters than bird species (see Fig. 3). There are two possible explanations for this effect. Firstly, the local search algorithm we apply starts from the finest possible clustering into singleton sets and is therefore biased toward excessive cuts (more clusters). Secondly, there might be different types of sounds associated with the same bird species. We have not been able to confirm or refute this hypothesis and are encouraged to collaborate with ornithologists to gain additional insight.

6.4   Clustering Unseen Data

Next, we describe the experiments we conduct in order to quantify the accuracy of the learned model for bird sound clustering when applied to sounds of bird species not heard during training. The results are shown in Table 2. Additional results for a combination of bird species heard and not heard during training are shown in Table 3.

Procedure and Results. To begin with, we learn f_θ on Train-68 as described in Sect. 4. Then, analogously to Sect. 6.3, we infer an independent decision

$y_{\{a,a'\}} \in \{0,1\}$ for every pair of distinct sound recordings a, a' from the data set Test-0,87, by asking whether $f_\theta(x_{\{a,a'\}}) \geq 0$. We compare these independent decisions to the truth, in Rows 1–2 of Table 2. Next, we infer a partition of Test-0,87 by correlation clustering, as described in Sect. 5; see Rows 3–4 of Table 2. Analogously to these two experiments, we infer decisions and a partition of the joint test set Test-68,87; see Table 3.

Discussion. It can be seen from Rows 3 and 4 of Table 2 that a clustering inferred using the model f_θ of the bird sounds of the data set Test-0,87 of 87 bird species not contained in the training data Train-68 is informative, i.e. better than random guessing. Furthermore, it can be seen from a comparison of Rows 1 and 3 as well as from a comparison of Rows 2 and 4 of Table 2 that correlation clustering increases the recall of cuts and the precision of joins, but decreases the precision of cuts and the recall of joins. Precision and recall of cuts are consistently higher than precision and recall of joins. This observation is consistent with the excessive cuts we have observed also for bird species seen during training, cf. Sect. 6.3. Possible explanations are, firstly, the bias toward excessive cuts in clusterings output by the local search algorithm we use for the correlation clustering problem and, secondly, the presence of different types of

Table 2. Above, we report the accuracy of the learned model f_θ when applied to the task of clustering the data set Test-0,87 of bird sounds of 87 bird species not heard during training.

	Model	Π	RI	VI	$\mathrm{VI_{FC}}$	$\mathrm{VI_{FJ}}$	PC	RC	PJ	RJ	CA
1.	f_θ	no	0.82	-	-	-	97.5%	83.5%	14.6%	57.1%	-
2.	$f_\theta + \mathrm{Aug}$	no	0.78	-	-	-	**97.8%**	79.2%	13.1%	**64.0%**	-
3.	$f_\theta + \mathrm{CC}$	yes	**0.90**	5.42	2.30	**3.12**	96.9%	**92.4%**	**20.8%**	40.9%	37.7%
4.	$f_\theta + \mathrm{Aug} + \mathrm{CC}$	yes	0.86	**5.06**	**1.83**	3.23	97.2%	88.4%	16.7%	47.5%	39.4%

Table 3. Above, we report the accuracy of the learned model f_θ when applied to the task of clustering the data set Test-68,87 of bird sounds of 68 bird species heard during training and 87 bird species not heard during training. More specifically, we report precision and recall of cuts and joins, separately for pairs of sound recordings both belonging to Test-0,87 (UU), both belonging to Test-68 (BB) or containing one from the set Test-0,87 and one from the set Test-68 (UB).

	Model	Π		J_{UU}	C_{UU}	J_{UB}	C_{UB}	J_{BB}	C_{BB}
1.	f_θ	no	P:	14.6%	97.5%	0%	100%	42.6%	97.9%
			R:	57.1%	83.5%	100%	84.6%	79.5%	89.9%
2.	$f_\theta + \mathrm{Aug}$	no	P:	13.1%	**97.8%**	0%	100%	38.7%	**98.7%**
			R:	**64.0%**	79.2%	100%	81.1%	**87.6%**	86.9%
3.	$f_\theta + \mathrm{CC}$	yes	P:	14.3%	96.1%	0%	100%	**59.7%**	97.1%
			R:	23.2%	**93.2%**	100%	**91.7%**	70.1%	**95.5%**
4.	$f_\theta + \mathrm{CC} + \mathrm{Aug}$	yes	P:	**17.7%**	96.8%	0%	100%	47.7%	98.1%
			R:	39.0%	91.1%	100%	89.0%	81.3%	91.6%

sounds for the same bird species in the data set Test-0,87. From Table 3, it can be seen that the clustering inferred using f_θ separates heard from unheard bird species accurately. From a comparison of Tables 1 to 3, it can be seen for pairs of bird sounds both from species heard during training (BB) or both from species not heard during training (UU), that the accuracy degrades little in a clustering of the joint set Test-68,87, compared to clusterings of the separate sets Test-68 and Test-0,87.

6.5 Clustering Noise

Next, we describe the experiments we conduct in order to quantify the accuracy of clusterings, inferred using the learned model, of bird sounds and environmental noise not heard during training. The results are shown in Table 4.

Procedure and Results. To begin with, we learn f_θ on the data set Train-68 as described in Sect. 4. Then, analogously to Sect. 6.4, we infer an independent decision $y_{\{a,a'\}} \in \{0,1\}$ for every pair of distinct sound recordings a, a' from the data set Test-68,N, by asking whether $f_\theta(x_{\{a,a'\}}) \geq 0$. We compare these independent decisions to the truth, in Rows 1–2 of Table 4. Next, we infer a partition of Test-68,N by correlation clustering, as described in Sect. 5; see Rows 3–4 of Table 4.

Discussion. From Table 4, it can be seen that f_θ separates environmental noise from the set Test-N accurately from bird sounds from the set Test-68, with or without correlation clustering, and despite the fact that the noise has not been heard during training on Train-68. From a comparison of Tables 1 and 4, it can be seen that the clustering of those sound recordings that both belong to Test-68 (BB) degrades only slightly when adding the environmental noise from the set Test-N to the problem. From the column J_{NB} and C_{NB} of Table 4, it can be seen that clustering the 39 types of noise is more challenging. This is expected, as environmental noise is different from bird sounds and has not been heard during training.

Table 4. Above, we report the accuracy of the learned model f_θ on Test-68,N. This includes precision and recall of cuts and joins for pairs of recordings both from Test-N (NN), both from Test-68 (BB) or one from Test-N and one from Test-68 (NB).

Model	Π		J_{NN}	C_{NN}	J_{NB}	C_{NB}	J_{BB}	C_{BB}
f_θ	no	P:	**3.9%**	98.5%	0%	**100%**	42.6%	97.9%
		R:	64.1%	59.2%	100%	78.4%	79.5%	89.9%
f_θ + Aug	no	P:	3.2%	**98.9%**	0%	**100%**	38.7%	**98.7%**
		R:	**84.9%**	34.2%	100%	77.9%	**87.6%**	86.9%
f_θ + CC	yes	P:	3.3%	97.7%	0%	**100%**	**57.5%**	97.3%
		R:	25.0%	**81.4%**	100%	87.0%	72.0%	**95.0%**
f_θ + CC + Aug	yes	P:	3.5%	98.0%	0%	**100%**	47.7%	98.2%
		R:	47.5%	66.8%	100%	**88.2%**	82.3%	91.5%

Bird species (truth)

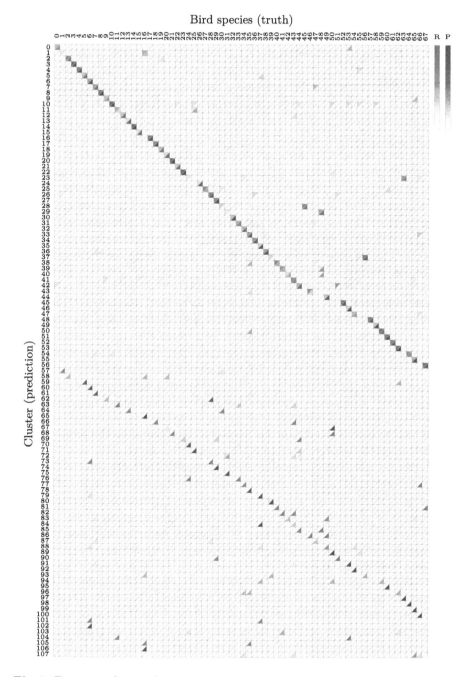

Fig. 3. For a correlation clustering of the set Test-68 with respect to the model f_θ trained on Train-68, the relation between predicted clusters (rows) and true bird species (columns) is shown in terms of precision (blue, ◢) and recall (red, ◤). (Color figure online)

7   Conclusion

We have defined a probabilistic model, along with heuristics for learning and inference, for clustering sound recordings of birds by estimating for pairs of recordings whether the same species of bird can be heard in both. For a public collection of bird sounds, we have shown empirically that partitions inferred by our model are less accurate than classifications with a known and fixed set of bird species, but are still informative. Specifically, we have observed more clusters than bird species. This observation encourages future work toward solving the instances of the inference problem exactly, with the goal of eliminating a bias toward additional clusters introduced by the inexact local search algorithm we employ here. This observation also encourages future collaboration with ornithologists toward an analysis of the additional clusters. Finally, our model has proven informative when applied to sound recordings of 87 bird species not heard during training, and in separating from bird sounds 39 types of environmental noise not used for training. Further work is required to decide if this can be exploited in practice, e.g. for rare species with little training data.

Acknowledgement. The authors acknowledge funding by the Federal Ministry of Education and Research of Germany, from grant 16LW0079K.

References

1. Andres, B., Kappes, J.H., Beier, T., Köthe, U., Hamprecht, F.A.: Probabilistic image segmentation with closedness constraints. In: ICCV (2011). https://doi.org/10.1109/ICCV.2011.6126550
2. Andres, B., et al.: Globally optimal closed-surface segmentation for connectomics. In: ECCV (2012). https://doi.org/10.1007/978-3-642-33712-3_56
3. Arabie, P., Boorman, S.A.: Multidimensional scaling of measures of distance between partitions. J. Math. Psychol. **10**(2), 148–203 (1973). https://doi.org/10.1016/0022-2496(73)90012-6
4. Bansal, N., Blum, A., Chawla, S.: Correlation clustering. Mach. Learn. **56**(1), 89–113 (2004). https://doi.org/10.1023/B:MACH.0000033116.57574.95
5. Bao, H., Shimada, T., Xu, L., Sato, I., Sugiyama, M.: Pairwise supervision can provably elicit a decision boundary. In: AISTATS (2022). https://proceedings.mlr.press/v151/bao22a.html
6. Bromley, J., Guyon, I., LeCun, Y., Säckinger, E., Shah, R.: Signature verification using a "siamese" time delay neural network. In: NIPS (1993). https://proceedings.neurips.cc/paper_files/paper/1993/file/288cc0ff022877bd3df94bc9360b9c5d-Paper.pdf
7. Clementino, T., Colonna, J.: Using triplet loss for bird species recognition on BirdCLEF 2020. In: Conference and Labs of the Evaluation Forum (working notes) (2020)
8. Darras, K., et al.: Comparing the sampling performance of sound recorders versus point counts in bird surveys: a meta-analysis. J. Appl. Ecol. **55**(6), 2575–2586 (2018). https://doi.org/10.1111/1365-2664.13229

9. Denton, T., Wisdom, S., Hershey, J.R.: Improving bird classification with unsupervised sound separation. In: International Conference on Acoustics, Speech and Signal Processing (2022). https://doi.org/10.1109/ICASSP43922.2022.9747202
10. Fitzpatrick, J.W., Lovette, I.J.: Handbook of Bird Biology. Wiley, Hoboken (2016)
11. Goëau, H., Kahl, S., Glotin, H., Planqué, R., Vellinga, W.P., Joly, A.: Overview of BirdCLEF 2018: monospecies vs. soundscape bird identification. In: Conference and Labs of the Evaluation Forum (2018)
12. Gupta, G., Kshirsagar, M., Zhong, M., Gholami, S., Ferres, J.L.: Comparing recurrent convolutional neural networks for large scale bird species classification. Sci. Rep. **11**(1), 17085 (2021). https://doi.org/10.1038/s41598-021-96446-w
13. He, K., Zhang, X., Ren, S., Sun, J.: Deep residual learning for image recognition. In: CVPR (2016). https://doi.org/10.1109/CVPR.2016.90
14. Ho, K., Keuper, J., Pfreundt, F.J., Keuper, M.: Learning embeddings for image clustering: an empirical study of triplet loss approaches. In: International Conference on Pattern Recognition (2021). https://doi.org/10.1109/ICPR48806.2021.9412602
15. Kahl, S.: BirdNET Analyzer. https://github.com/kahst/BirdNET-Analyzer
16. Kahl, S., et al.: Overview of BirdCLEF 2020: bird sound recognition in complex acoustic environments. In: Conference and Labs of the Evaluation Forum (2020)
17. Kahl, S., et al.: Overview of BirdCLEF 2021: bird call identification in soundscape recordings. In: Conference and Labs of the Evaluation Forum (working notes) (2021)
18. Kahl, S., et al.: Acoustic event classification using convolutional neural networks. In: Informatik 2017. Gesellschaft für Informatik, Bonn (2017). https://doi.org/10.18420/in2017_217
19. Kahl, S., et al.: Overview of BirdCLEF 2022: endangered bird species recognition in soundscape recordings. In: Conference and Labs of the Evaluation Forum (working notes) (2022)
20. Kahl, S., et al.: Overview of BirdCLEF 2019: large-scale bird recognition in soundscapes. In: Conference and Labs of the Evaluation Forum (2019)
21. Kahl, S., et al.: Large-scale bird sound classification using convolutional neural networks. In: Conference and Labs of the Evaluation Forum (working notes) (2017)
22. Kahl, S., Wood, C.M., Eibl, M., Klinck, H.: BirdNET: a deep learning solution for avian diversity monitoring. Eco. Inform. **61**, 101236 (2021). https://doi.org/10.1016/j.ecoinf.2021.101236
23. Kappes, J.H., Swoboda, P., Savchynskyy, B., Hazan, T., Schnörr, C.: Multicuts and perturb & MAP for probabilistic graph clustering. J. Math. Imaging Vis. **56**(2), 221–237 (2016). https://doi.org/10.1007/s10851-016-0659-3
24. Keuper, M., Andres, B., Brox, T.: Motion trajectory segmentation via minimum cost multicuts. In: ICCV (2015). https://doi.org/10.1109/ICCV.2015.374
25. Keuper, M., Levinkov, E., Bonneel, N., Lavoué, G., Brox, T., Andres, B.: Efficient decomposition of image and mesh graphs by lifted multicuts. In: ICCV (2015). https://doi.org/10.1109/ICCV.2015.204
26. Levinkov, E., Kirillov, A., Andres, B.: A comparative study of local search algorithms for correlation clustering. In: GCPR (2017). https://doi.org/10.1007/978-3-319-66709-6_9
27. Li, Y., Chen, C.L.P., Zhang, T.: A survey on siamese network: methodologies, applications, and opportunities. Trans. Artif. Intell. **3**(6), 994–1014 (2022). https://doi.org/10.1109/TAI.2022.3207112

28. Loshchilov, I., Hutter, F.: Decoupled weight decay regularization. In: ICLR (2019). https://openreview.net/forum?id=Bkg6RiCqY7
29. Markova-Nenova, N., Engler, J.O., Cord, A.F., Wätzold, F.: A cost comparison analysis of bird-monitoring techniques for result-based payments in agriculture. Technical report, University Library of Munich, Germany (2023). https://EconPapers.repec.org/RePEc:pra:mprapa:116311
30. McGinn, K., Kahl, S., Peery, M.Z., Klinck, H., Wood, C.M.: Feature embeddings from the BirdNET algorithm provide insights into avian ecology. Eco. Inform. **74**, 101995 (2023). https://doi.org/10.1016/j.ecoinf.2023.101995
31. Meilă, M.: Comparing clusterings-an information based distance. J. Multivar. Anal. **98**(5), 873–895 (2007). https://doi.org/10.1016/j.jmva.2006.11.013
32. Park, D.S., et al.: SpecAugment: a simple data augmentation method for automatic speech recognition. In: Interspeech 2019 (2019). https://doi.org/10.21437/Interspeech
33. Piczak, K.J.: ESC: dataset for environmental sound classification. In: ACM Conference on Multimedia (2015). https://doi.org/10.1145/2733373.2806390
34. Ralph, C.J., Sauer, J.R., Droege, S.: Monitoring bird populations by point counts. Pacific Southwest Research Station (1995)
35. Rand, W.M.: Objective criteria for the evaluation of clustering methods. J. Am. Stat. Assoc. **66**(336), 846–850 (1971). https://doi.org/10.1080/01621459.1971.10482356
36. Rentería, S., Vallejo, E.E., Taylor, C.E.: Birdsong phrase verification and classification using siamese neural networks. bioRxiv (2021). https://doi.org/10.1101/2021.03.16.435625, (preprint)
37. Salamon, J., Bello, J.P.: Deep convolutional neural networks and data augmentation for environmental sound classification. Signal Process. Lett. **24**(3), 279–283 (2017). https://doi.org/10.1109/LSP.2017.2657381
38. Seth, H., Bhatia, R., Rajan, P.: Feature learning for bird call clustering. In: International Conference on Industrial and Information Systems (2018). https://doi.org/10.1109/ICIINFS.2018.8721418
39. Sevilla, A., Glotin, H.: Audio bird classification with inception-v4 extended with time and time-frequency attention mechanisms. In: Conference and Labs of the Evaluation Forum (working notes) (2017)
40. Shonfield, J., Bayne, E.M.: Autonomous recording units in avian ecological research: current use and future applications. Avian Conserv. Ecol. **12**(1) (2017). https://doi.org/10.5751/ACE-00974-120114
41. Song, J., Andres, B., Black, M.J., Hilliges, O., Tang, S.: End-to-end learning for graph decomposition. In: ICCV (2019). https://doi.org/10.1109/ICCV.2019.01019
42. Tang, S., Andres, B., Andriluka, M., Schiele, B.: Subgraph decomposition for multi-target tracking. In: CVPR (2015). https://doi.org/10.1109/CVPR.2015.7299138
43. Tang, S., Andriluka, M., Andres, B., Schiele, B.: Multiple people tracking by lifted multicut and person re-identification. In: CVPR (2017). https://doi.org/10.1109/CVPR.2017.394
44. Wisdom, S., Tzinis, E., Erdogan, H., Weiss, R.J., Wilson, K., Hershey, J.R.: Unsupervised sound separation using mixture invariant training. In: NeurIPS (2020). https://proceedings.neurips.cc/paper/2020/file/28538c394c36e4d5ea8ff5ad60562a93-Paper.pdf

45. Wood, C.M., Gutiérrez, R.J., Peery, M.Z.: Acoustic monitoring reveals a diverse forest owl community, illustrating its potential for basic and applied ecology. Ecology **100**(9), 1–3 (2019). https://doi.org/10.1002/ecy.2764
46. Xeno-canto: Sharing wildlife sounds from around the world (2023). https://xeno-canto.org/about/xeno-canto
47. Zhang, J., Yan, R.: On the value of pairwise constraints in classification and consistency. In: ICML (2007). https://doi.org/10.1145/1273496.1273636

MargCTGAN: A "Marginally" Better CTGAN for the Low Sample Regime

Tejumade Afonja$^{(\boxtimes)}$ [ID], Dingfan Chen [ID], and Mario Fritz [ID]

CISPA Helmholtz Center for Information Security, Saarbrücken, Germany
{tejumade.afonja,dingfan.chen,fritz}@cispa.de

Abstract. The potential of realistic and useful synthetic data is significant. However, current evaluation methods for synthetic tabular data generation predominantly focus on downstream task usefulness, often neglecting the importance of statistical properties. This oversight becomes particularly prominent in low sample scenarios, accompanied by a swift deterioration of these statistical measures. In this paper, we address this issue by conducting an evaluation of three popular synthetic tabular data generators based on their marginal distribution, column-pair correlation, joint distribution and downstream task utility performance across high to low sample regimes. The popular `CTGAN` model shows strong utility, but underperforms in low sample settings in terms of utility. To overcome this limitation, we propose `MargCTGAN` that adds feature matching of de-correlated marginals, which results in a consistent improvement in downstream utility as well as statistical properties of the synthetic data.

Keywords: Synthetic Data · GAN · Tabular Data · Evaluation Metrics

1 Introduction

Tabular data, despite being the most widely used data type [12], presents substantial challenges ranging from data heterogeneity and quality measurement to imbalance and privacy concerns. Encouragingly, recent advancements in synthetic tabular data generators have shown considerable promise in tackling these issues. These models have shown effectiveness in handling heterogeneous data attributes [22,25], facilitating the safe sharing of personal records [5,18,19], and mitigating class imbalance [8]. Nonetheless, the evaluation of existing models predominantly focuses on downstream machine learning tasks and large datasets. This evaluation paradigm overlooks their utility in broader practical scenarios, especially the data-limited, low-resource settings, and fails to consider other crucial aspects of synthetic datasets including fidelity, diversity, and authenticity [1].

Supplementary Information The online version contains supplementary material available at https://doi.org/10.1007/978-3-031-54605-1_34.

U. Köthe and C. Rother (Eds.): DAGM GCPR 2023, LNCS 14264, pp. 524–537, 2024.
https://doi.org/10.1007/978-3-031-54605-1_34

In response to these challenges, we introduce a comprehensive evaluation framework, integrating nine distinct metrics across four critical dimensions: downstream task utility, joint fidelity, preservation of attribute correlations, and alignment of marginals (Sect. 5). Our objective is to thoroughly evaluate the representative models using diverse metrics, aiming at a comprehensive understanding of their quality and adaptability, particularly for scenarios that are underexplored in existing literature.

Our evaluation uncovers intriguing insights into the characteristics of three popular synthetic tabular data generators: TableGAN [19], CTGAN [22], TVAE [22]. For instance, CTGAN model typically demonstrates high attribute fidelity but falls short in utility for low-data scenarios. Conversely, TableGAN exhibits better utility but lacks performance in other dimensions. To capitalize on the strengths of both models, we propose MargCTGAN that improves upon CTGAN by introducing feature matching of decorrelated marginals in the principal component space. This approach consistently improves utility without compromising other fidelity measures, especially in the data-limited settings.

In summary, we make the following contributions:

- We conduct an extensive investigation into the performance of representative tabular data generators across various contexts, with a specific focus on the low-sample regime that is underexplored in existing literature. This investigation is carried out using a comprehensive evaluation framework, which assesses the models across four critical dimensions: downstream task utility, joint fidelity, column-pair fidelity, and marginal fidelity.
- Our comprehensive evaluation framework is released[1] as an open-source tool, with the aim of facilitating reproducible research, encouraging fair and extensive comparisons among methods, as well as providing a deeper understanding of the models' performance, quality, and fidelity.
- Prompted by the suboptimal performance of existing tabular generators in low-sample scenarios, we propose MargCTGAN. This model improves upon CTGAN by introducing a moment-matching loss within a decorrelated feature space, which effectively steers the generator towards capturing the statistical characteristics intrinsic to the data distribution.

2   Related Works

2.1   Tabular Data Generators

In recent years, deep generative models have seen significant advancements in their application to diverse forms of tabular data, including discrete attributes [5], continuous values [18], and heterogeneous mixtures [19,22,23,25]. Notably, TableGAN [19], CTGAN [22], and TVAE [22] stand out as the most popular benchmark models and will be the focus of our empirical evaluation. On the other hand, the issue of limited data availability remains underexplored in literature, despite

---

[1] https://github.com/tejuafonja/margctgan/.

several attempts to bypass such challenges by effectively combining multiple data sources [4, 17, 24]. Our work aims to fill this research gap by introducing a systematic evaluation across various scenarios, ranging from full-resource to data-limited cases. Additionally, we propose model improvements that designed to effectively capture the underlying data structure in low-sample settings.

2.2   Evaluation of Tabular Data Generators

The evaluation of generators, particularly for tabular data, is a challenging area due to its requirement for complex metrics, unlike simpler visual inspection for image data [21]. Recent studies have introduced a variety of metrics: prominent among these are downstream machine learning efficacy, unified metrics evaluation [6], and evaluations focusing on distinct aspects [1, 7]. In this work, we consider comprehensive evaluation methods encompassing machine learning efficacy, statistical properties such as divergence on marginals, column correlations, and joint distance.

3   Background

We examine three leading tabular data generators with diverse architectures and preprocessing schemes. Here, we present an overview of each model.

3.1   Tabular GAN (TableGAN)

TableGAN is a GAN-based method for synthesizing tabular data [19]. It converts categorical columns into numerical representations using label encoding and applies min-max normalization to numerical columns. Each record is transformed into a 2D image represented as a square matrix, allowing the use of the DCGAN model [20] for generating synthetic data. The architecture consists of a generator network ($\mathcal{G}$), a discriminator network ($\mathcal{D}$), and a classifier network ($\mathcal{C}$). $\mathcal{G}$ generates synthetic data resembling real data, while $\mathcal{D}$ distinguishes between real and synthetic data. $\mathcal{C}$ helps generate data suitable for downstream tasks by predicting labels. Training follows standard GAN techniques [10], optimizing $\mathcal{G}$ and $\mathcal{D}$ using the GAN loss. Information loss ($\mathcal{L}_{\text{info}}^{\mathcal{G}}$) minimizes statistical differences between real and synthetic data. The final loss objective optimized by $\mathcal{G}$ is $\mathcal{L}^{\mathcal{G}} = \mathcal{L}_{\text{orig}}^{\mathcal{G}} + \mathcal{L}_{\text{info}}^{\mathcal{G}} + \mathcal{L}_{\text{class}}^{\mathcal{G}}$, where $\mathcal{L}_{\text{orig}}^{\mathcal{G}}$ minimizes $\log(1 - \mathcal{D}(\mathcal{G}(z)))$, and $\mathcal{L}_{\text{info}}^{\mathcal{G}}$ minimizes statistical properties with privacy control.

3.2   Conditional Tabular GAN (CTGAN)

CTGAN [22] is a GAN-based model designed to tackle challenges in data synthesis, including generating multi-modal numerical columns and balancing categorical columns. It introduces novel preprocessing schemes: mode-specific normalization and training-by-sampling. Mode-specific normalization uses a variational Gaussian mixture model to estimate the number of modes in numerical columns and samples normalized values accordingly. Training-by-sampling addresses imbalanced categorical columns by conditioning the generator ($\mathcal{G}$) and discriminator ($\mathcal{D}$) on a condition vector, which resamples the categorical column during training iterations. CTGAN is based on the PacGAN [16] framework and uses fully connected neural networks for $\mathcal{G}$ and $\mathcal{D}$. It optimizes the Wasserstein loss with gradient penalty (WGP) [2] . The final loss objective optimized by $\mathcal{G}$ includes the Wasserstein loss and a generator condition loss.

3.3 Tabular VAE Model (TVAE)

TVAE [22] is a variant of the variational autoencoder (VAE), a generative model based on encoder-decoder neural networks. It employs fully connected neural networks for the encoder (enc) and decoder (dec) networks. The encoder maps the input data to a latent code, which serves as a compressed representation. The decoder reconstructs the original data from this latent code. Both networks are trained simultaneously using the evidence lower-bound (ELBO) [13] objective, promoting effective latent space distribution learning and accurate data reconstruction. By training the encoder and decoder together, TVAE learns a compact representation capturing the data structure and generating realistic samples. Numerical columns undergo similar preprocessing as CTGAN, while categorical columns are one-hot encoded.

4   Method: MargCTGAN

MargCTGAN adheres to the standard Generative Adversarial Networks (GANs) paradigm [10], which involves training a generator $\mathcal{G}$ and a discriminator $\mathcal{D}$ in an adversarial manner. The training target is to enhance the discriminator's ability to distinguish between real and fake data, while simultaneously updating the generator to produce samples that are increasingly realistic. We adopt the WGAN-GP objective [11] in which the overall training process can be interpreted as optimizing the generator to minimize the Wasserstein distance between the distributions of the generated and real data:

$$\mathcal{L}_{\text{WGP}} = \underset{z \sim p_z}{\mathbb{E}} \big[\mathcal{D}\big(\mathcal{G}(z)\big) \big] - \underset{x \sim p_{\text{data}}}{\mathbb{E}} \big[\mathcal{D}(x) \big] + \lambda \big(\| \nabla_{\hat{x}} \mathcal{D}(\hat{x}) \|_2 - 1 \big)^2 \qquad (1)$$

where $\hat{x}$ is constructed by interpolating real and generated samples and λ denotes the weight for the gradient penalty. The discriminator is trained to minimize $\mathcal{L}_{\text{WGP}}$, while the generator is trained to maximize it.

Following the CTGAN [22] framework, we adopt several key techniques to adapt GAN models for tabular data. Firstly, one-hot encoding is applied to pre-process categorical attributes, paired with the Gumbel-softmax function serving as the network output activation function, thereby ensuring differentiability. Secondly, for numerical attributes, we apply a technique known as *mode-specific normalization* in the pre-processing phase, enabling an accurate reflection of the multimodality in the values distribution. Lastly, we employ the *training-by-sampling* strategy during the training process, which effectively balances the occurrences of different classes in the categorical columns to match their real distribution. This strategy introduces an additional loss term on the generator, which we denote as $\mathcal{L}_{\text{cond}}$.

While CTGAN generally demonstrates promising utility for training downstream machine learning classifiers, it often falls short in capturing low-level distribution statistics, particularly in low-sample scenarios (See Fig. 2). Drawing inspiration from TableGAN, we propose a moment matching loss that proactively encourages the generator to learn and mirror the first and second-order data statistics. Notably, unlike TableGAN which attempts to match statistics on the features extracted by the discriminator, we compute the first and second moments after conducting the Principal Component Analysis (PCA) on the data. Specifically, the transform is performed while maintaining the original data dimensionality, i.e., we simply decorrelate without down-projection. Intriguingly, this straightforward technique proves effective (Fig. 4), likely because the decorrelated feature representation supports the independent moment matching. Formally,

$$\mathcal{L}_{\text{mean}} = \left\| \underset{x \sim p_{\text{data}}}{\mathbb{E}} \left[f(x) \right] - \underset{z \sim p_z}{\mathbb{E}} \left[f\big(\mathcal{G}(z)\big) \right] \right\|_2$$

$$\mathcal{L}_{\text{std}} = \left\| \underset{x \sim p_{\text{data}}}{\text{SD}} \left[f(x) \right] - \underset{z \sim p_z}{\text{SD}} \left[f\big(\mathcal{G}(z)\big) \right] \right\|_2$$

$$\mathcal{L}_{\text{marg}} = \mathcal{L}_{\text{mean}} + \mathcal{L}_{\text{std}}$$

$$\mathcal{L}^{\mathcal{G}} = -\mathcal{L}_{\text{WGP}} + \mathcal{L}_{\text{cond}} + \mathcal{L}_{\text{marg}} \tag{2}$$

where $f(\cdot)$ denotes the PCA transformation function. $\mathcal{L}_{\text{mean}}$ targets the mean, while $\mathcal{L}_{\text{std}}$ focuses on the standard deviation. The total training losses for the generator and discriminator are $\mathcal{L}^{\mathcal{G}}$ and $\mathcal{L}_{\text{WGP}}$, respectively.

5   Multi-dimensional Evaluation Metrics

We present a comprehensive evaluation that accesses tabular data generators performance across four critical dimensions: downstream task utility, joint fidelity, column-pair fidelity, and marginal fidelity. The implementation details can be found in Sect. 6.

Downstream Task Utility. This dimension focuses on the efficacy of synthetic data as a substitute for real data in specific tasks. This effectiveness is typically quantified by *machine learning efficacy* that evaluates the performance (e.g., F1-score or accuracy) on a distinct real test dataset when training predictive ML models on synthetic data. In situations where knowledge of the target downstream task is unavailable, an alternate methodology known as *dimension-wise prediction* (or *all-models test*) may be employed. This methodology considers each column as a potential target variable for the task and reports the mean performance across all cases.

Joint Fidelity. This category aims to quantify the similarity between the overall *joint* distributions of real and synthetic data. While an exact measurement is always intractable, the most commonly used approximation is the *distance to closest record*. This computes the Euclidean distance between each synthetic data sample and its nearest neighbors in the real test dataset, intending to assess the possibility of each synthetic sample being real. Conversely, the *likelihood approximation* computes the distance between each real test sample and its closest synthetic sample. This mirrors the probability of each real sample being potentially generated by the model, thereby encapsulating a concept of data likelihood.

Column-Pair Fidelity. This dimension investigates the preservation of feature interactions, specifically focusing on the direction and strength of correlations between pairs of columns in the synthetic dataset as compared to the real dataset. A commonly used metric for this purpose is the *association difference*, also referred to as the *pairwise correlation difference*. This measure quantifies the discrepancy between the correlation matrices of the real and synthetic datasets, where the correlation matrix encapsulates the pairwise correlation of columns within the data.

Marginal Fidelity. Accurately replicating the real data distribution requires aligning the marginals, ensuring a match in the distribution of each individual column. Evaluating this criterion involves quantifying the disparity between two one-dimensional variables. Commonly used metrics for this purpose include the *Jensen-Shannon divergence*, *Wasserstein distance*, and *column correlation*. Additionally, we propose *histogram intersection*, widely used in various other fields. The metric calculates the sum of the minimum probabilities between the synthetic and real data distributions, expressed as $HI(p,q) = \sum_i \min(p_i, q_i)$. A perfect match between p and q yields $HI(p,q) = 1$, while $HI(p,q) = 0$ indicates no overlap between the two distributions. For numerical columns, discretization via binning is typically performed prior to calculating divergence measures to ensure tractability.

6   Implementation Details

6.1   Metrics

Downstream Task Utility. For the *machine learning efficacy* and *all models test* metrics, we used the SDMetrics package[2] with logistic regression, decision tree classifier, and multilayer perceptron models for classification tasks, and linear regression, decision tree regressor, and multilayer perceptron models for regression tasks. We standardized numerical columns for classification models and performed one-hot encoding for categorical columns. F1-score was used for classification models, and R^2-score was normalized to $[0, 1]$ for regression models.

Joint Fidelity. Numerical columns were min-max normalized to range between 0 and 1, and categorical columns were one-hot encoded. We used the

---

[2] https://docs.sdv.dev/sdmetrics/metrics/metrics-in-beta/ml-efficacy-single-table/binary-classification.

Table 1. Summary of Datasets. **Col** refers to number of columns. **N/B/M** correspond to the number of numerical, binary, and multi-class categorical columns, respectively.

Dataset	Train/Test Size	Col	N/B/M	Task
Adult	34118/14622	15	7/2/6	classification
Census	199523/99762	41	7/3/31	classification
News	31644/8000	60	45/15/0	classification
Texas	60127/15032	18	7/1/10	classification

scikit-learn nearest-neighbor implementation[3] with Euclidean distance and different numbers of nearest neighbors ($[1, 2, 3, \ldots, 9]$). For the *likelihood approximation*, we calculated the distance between each of 5000 random test samples to its closest synthetic sample and report the average over real test samples. For the *distance to closest record* metric, we compute the distance of each sample in the synthetic set to its nearest neighbor in a set of 5000 random test samples and report the average over the synthetic samples.

Column-Pair Fidelity. The *associations difference* metric was inspired by the "plot correlation difference" function from the tabular-evaluator package[4] and implemented using the dython package[5]. We used Pearson correlation coefficient for numerical columns, Cramer's V for categorical columns, and the Correlation Ratio for numerical-categorical columns. The range of Cramer's V and Correlation Ratio is between 0 and 1, while Pearson correlation coefficient ranges from -1 to 1. We calculated the absolute difference between the association matrices of the synthetic data and the real data, reporting the mean absolute difference.

Marginal Fidelity. Numerical columns were min-max normalized to range between 0 and 1, and categorical columns were one-hot encoded. The marginal metrics were applied to each column in the dataset. Binning followed a uniform grid between 0 and 1, using bin widths sizes of 25, 50, or 100 for the real data. For the *histogram intersection*, *Wasserstein distance*, and *Jenson-Shannon distance* metrics, the same binning strategy was used for numerical columns. The SciPy package[6] was used to calculate *Wasserstein distance* and *Jenson-Shannon distance* with the base=2 setting. The Dython package was used to compute the *column correlation* metric and provided an implementation for the *histogram intersection* metric, which was not available in prior work.

7   Experiments

Setup. We conducted evaluations on four benchmark tabular datasets: Adult [14], Census [15], News [9], and Texas. These datasets exhibit diverse

---

[3] https://scikit-learn.org/stable/modules/generated/sklearn.neighbors.KNeighborsClassifier.html.

[4] https://github.com/Baukebrenninkmeijer/table-evaluator.

[5] http://shakedzy.xyz/dython/modules/nominal/.

[6] https://docs.scipy.org/.

properties in terms of size (spanning 30-199 thousand samples), column heterogeneity, and distinct characteristics (Refer to Table 1 and Appendix B for details). Our investigation spans a geometric progression of sample sizes, extending from 40 to the full dataset size (notated as "all"), to emulate a range from low to high resource settings. In line with existing studies [22], models were trained for 300 epochs. The evaluations were conducted on a separate test set that was never used during the whole training process of the tabular data generators. To account for potential randomness, experiments were conducted over three different random seeds for model training and repeated across five trials for generating synthetic datasets. All the code was implemented in the Python and all experiments are conducted on a single Titan RTX GPU. See details in Appendix A.

7.1 Correlation of Metrics

In order to evaluate the tabular data generators comprehensively across various dimensions, we conducted a thorough correlation analysis of the metrics discussed in Sect. 5, as illustrated in Fig. 1. Our analysis revealed a significant degree of correlation among metrics within each dimension. This was particularly evident for the marginal-based metrics, with Pearson coefficients ranging from 0.74 to 0.98. Consequently, any of these metrics could effectively represent their respective dimension. To ensure clarity and computational efficiency, we specifically selected the **efficacy test (machine learning efficacy)**, **closeness approximation (distance to closest record)**, **associations difference**, and **histogram intersection** as representative metrics for summarizing each crucial dimension discussed in Sect. 5.

7.2 Performance Comparison

Downstream Task Utility. The *efficacy score* measures the utility of synthetic data in downstream tasks, as illustrated in the top-left plot of Fig. 2. In the best-case scenario (marked as "all" in x-axis), the performances of CTGAN, TVAE, and MargCTGAN are comparable. Performance generally degrades in low-sample settings, with the most significant drop around the size of 640. This decline is particularly notable for CTGAN, which exhibits a relative error up to 57%. While TVAE generally outperforms the other models across varying sample sizes, our MargCTGAN performs robustly, demonstrating particular advantages in low-sample settings. Notably, MargCTGAN consistently outperforms its backbone model, CTGAN, across all settings.

Joint Fidelity and Memorization. The *distance to the closest record* metric, depicted in the bottom-left subplot of Fig. 2, measures the alignment between the real and synthetic joint distribution and simultaneously illustrates the memorization effects of the generators. Striking a balance is crucial as over-memorization might compromise privacy. TableGAN consistently maintains the most substantial distance from the real data reference, aligning with its design objective of privacy

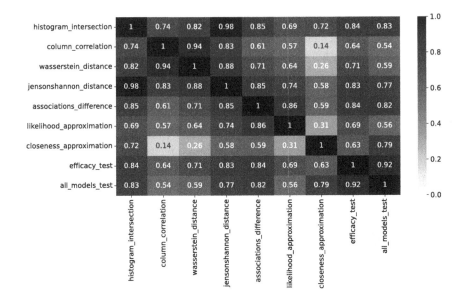

Fig. 1. Pearson correlation coefficients (in absolute value) among different metrics across multiple experimental trials on all datasets.

preservation. Conversely, TVAE displays the closest proximity, even exceeding the real reference, indicating a potential overfitting risk and privacy leakage. This may be attributed to its use of reconstruction loss in its training objective [3]. As the training size reduces, the distance between the synthetic and real data first increases then decreases, potentially signifying the generator's shift from generalization to memorization. While both CTGAN and MargCTGAN maintain a moderate distance from real data, our MargCTGAN generally demonstrates a closer proximity to the reference, presenting an appropriate balance between alignment and privacy protection.

Pairwise Correlation. The *association difference* metric (bottom-right subplot in Fig. 2) quantifies the disparity between the correlation matrices of the real and synthetic data. As expected, this disparity increases as the sample size decreases, a trend also seen in the real data reference. This could be attributed to data diversity, where different smaller subsets might not retain the same statistical characteristics while the sampling randomness is accounted for in our repeated experiments. Among all models, TableGAN exhibits the largest associations difference score, particularly in the low-sample regime, indicating challenges in capturing associations with limited training samples. Both MargCTGAN and TVAE display similar behavior, with our MargCTGAN following the trend of real data reference more precisely, specifically in low-sample settings.

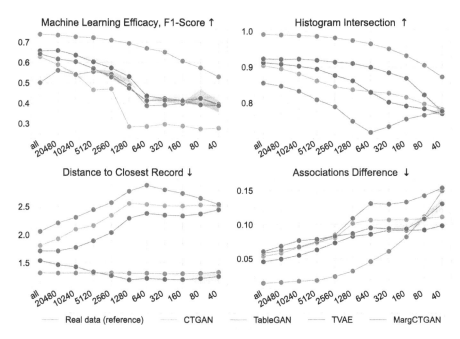

Fig. 2. Averaged score across datasets. The **X-axis** represents the size of the training dataset, with "all" indicating the full dataset size. **Real data (reference)** corresponds to the metrics directly measured on the real (train vs. test) data, serving as the reference (oracle score) for optimal performance.

Marginal Matching. The *histogram intersection* metric, depicted in the top-right subfigure in Fig. 2, assessing the overlap of real and synthetic marginal distributions. Our moment matching objective within MargCTGAN explicitly encourages such coverage of low-level statistics, leading to consistent superior performance of MargCTGAN across various settings. A more detailed analysis, presented in Fig. 3, reveals performance differences across numerical and categorical columns. Here, TVAE demonstrates good performance with numerical attributes but exhibits limitations in handling categorical ones, whereas CTGAN excels in handling categorical columns, possibly due to its training-by-sampling approach, but falls short with the numerical ones. Notably, MargCTGAN balances both aspects, outperforming CTGAN in numerical columns while matching its performance in categorical ones. Moreover, while most models show decreased performance in low-resource settings, TableGAN exhibits improvement, potentially due to its similar moment matching approach to ours, thereby further validating our design choice.

Insights into Performance and Behavior of Histogram Intersection Metric. Figure 3 highlighted that TVAE excels in datasets with numerical columns but struggles with categorical columns, resulting in subpar marginal performance due to its inability to accurately reproduce different categories.

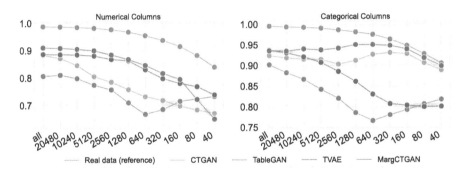

Fig. 3. Histogram intersection score for numerical and categorical columns respectively, which is averaged across datasets. The **X-axis** represents the size of the training dataset, with "all" indicating the full dataset size. **Real data (reference)** corresponds to the metrics directly measured on the real (train vs. test) data, serving as the reference (oracle score) for optimal performance.

Surprisingly, despite this limitation, the synthetic datasets generated by TVAE showed high utility in downstream tasks, suggesting that a good marginal distribution is not always a prerequisite for usefulness. On the other hand, CTGAN demonstrated superior performance in capturing associations within categorical columns, showcasing the effectiveness of its training-by-sampling approach. Notably, MargCTGAN achieved similar performance to CTGAN in categorical columns while outperforming it in numerical columns, aligning more closely with TVAE in this aspect.

It is important to note that all models experienced degraded performance in low-resource settings. However, interestingly, TableGAN exhibited improved performance in such scenarios. This improvement may be attributed to its information loss, which share similar idea of our moment matching objective. Figures 5(a), 5(b), 5(c), 5(d) in Appendix C further shows the breakdown across the different datasets.

Ablation of Moment Matching in Raw Data Space. We conducted an additional ablation study to investigate the effect of the moment matching technique with and without applying PCA in MargCTGAN. As shown in Fig. 4, while both moment matching without PCA (CTGAN+Raw) and with PCA (MargCTGAN) performs generally better than the baseline CTGAN, the PCA adopted in our MargCTGAN does provide additional notable improvement consistently across different metrics considered in our study.

8   Discussion

While our MargCTGAN shows consistent improvements over a broad range of settings, we discuss additional observations and limitations below. The ablation study examined the effect of the moment matching technique with and without

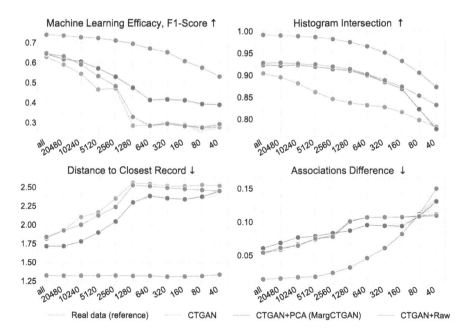

Fig. 4. Comparison between CTGAN trained with PCA loss objective (MargCTGAN) and CTGAN trained with raw moment matching loss objective. The **X-axis** represents the size of the training dataset, with "all" indicating the full dataset size. **Real data (reference)** corresponds to the metrics directly measured on the real (train vs. test) data, serving as the reference (oracle score) for optimal performance.

applying PCA in MargCTGAN. Both approaches outperformed the baseline CTGAN, but the PCA-moment matching in MargCTGAN provided notable improvement across different metrics. However, in extremely low-sample scenarios, MargCTGAN showed a performance drop compared to CTGAN in terms of capturing associations and reproducing marginal distributions. We attribute this to the rank-deficiency issue in the PCA-moment matching approach when the sample size is smaller than the number of features. In such cases, models like CTGAN with the raw feature moment matching (CTGAN+Raw) method may be more suitable. Understanding the strengths and weaknesses of different models under varying resource constraints helps in selecting the appropriate synthetic data generation approach.

9   Conclusion

In conclusion, our comprehensive evaluation of three popular tabular data generators across different dataset sizes underscores the importance of developing models that excel in low-sample regimes. Consequently, we propose MargCTGAN, an adaptation of the popular CTGAN model, which consistently exhibits performance improvements in various dataset sizes and setups. This further emphasizes the significance of incorporating statistical moment matching techniques in the optimization process to enhance the model's learning capabilities. To ensure the impact and reproducibility of our work, we release our code and setup[7]. We hope that the availability of our evaluation framework will contribute to the advancement of the current state of evaluating tabular data generators and facilitate future research in this evolving field.

Acknowledgements. This work was partially funded by ELSA - European Lighthouse on Secure and Safe AI funded by the European Union under grant agreement No. 101070617. Additionally, this work is supported by the Helmholtz Association within the project "Protecting Genetic Data with Synthetic Cohorts from Deep Generative Models (PRO-GENE-GEN)" (ZT-I-PF-5-23) and Bundesministeriums für Bildung und Forschung "PriSyn" (16KISAO29K). Views and opinions expressed are however those of the authors only and do not necessarily reflect those of the European Union or European Commission. Neither the European Union nor the European Commission can be held responsible for them. Moreover, Dingfan Chen was partially supported by Qualcomm Innovation Fellowship Europe. We also thank the team from synthetic data vault project for open-sourcing their code.

References

1. Alaa, A., Van Breugel, B., Saveliev, E.S., van der Schaar, M.: How faithful is your synthetic data? Sample-level metrics for evaluating and auditing generative models. In: International Conference on Machine Learning (ICML). PMLR (2022)
2. Arjovsky, M., Chintala, S., Bottou, L.: Wasserstein GAN (2017)
3. Chen, D., Yu, N., Zhang, Y., Fritz, M.: Gan-leaks: A taxonomy of membership inference attacks against generative models. In: Proceedings of the 2020 ACM SIGSAC Conference on Computer and Communications Security (ACM CCS) (2020)
4. Chen, H., Jajodia, S., Liu, J., Park, N., Sokolov, V., Subrahmanian, V.: FakeTables: using GANs to generate functional dependency preserving tables with bounded real data. In: IJCAI (2019)
5. Choi, E., Biswal, S., Malin, B., Duke, J., Stewart, W.F., Sun, J.: Generating multi-label discrete patient records using generative adversarial networks. In: Machine Learning for Healthcare Conference. PMLR (2017)
6. Chundawat, V.S., Tarun, A.K., Mandal, M., Lahoti, M., Narang, P.: A universal metric for robust evaluation of synthetic tabular data. IEEE Transactions on Artificial Intelligence, 1–11 (2022). https://doi.org/10.1109/TAI.2022.3229289
7. Dankar, F.K., Ibrahim, M.K., Ismail, L.: A multi-dimensional evaluation of synthetic data generators. IEEE Access **10**, 11147–11158 (2022)
8. Engelmann, J., Lessmann, S.: Conditional Wasserstein GAN-based oversampling of tabular data for imbalanced learning. Expert Syst. Appl. **174**, 114582 (2021)
9. Fernandes, K., Vinagre, P., Cortez, P.: A proactive intelligent decision support system for predicting the popularity of online news. In: Pereira, F., Machado, P., Costa, E., Cardoso, A. (eds.) Progress in Artificial Intelligence. EPIA 2015. LNCS, vol. 9273, pp. 535–546. Springer, Cham (2015). https://doi.org/10.1007/978-3-319-23485-4_53

---

[7] https://github.com/tejuafonja/margctgan/.

10. Goodfellow, I., et al.: Generative adversarial nets. In: Ghahramani, Z., Welling, M., Cortes, C., Lawrence, N., Weinberger, K. (eds.) Advances in Neural Information Processing Systems, vol. 27. Curran Associates, Inc. (2014)
11. Gulrajani, I., Ahmed, F., Arjovsky, M., Dumoulin, V., Courville, A.C.: Improved training of Wasserstein GANs. In: Advances in Neural Information Processing Systems (NeurIPS), vol. 30 (2017)
12. Kaggle: 2018 Kaggle machine learning & data science survey
13. Kingma, D.P., Welling, M.: Auto-encoding variational Bayes. arXiv preprint arXiv:1312.6114 (2013)
14. Kohavi, R., Becker, B.: UCI machine learning repository: adult data set. UCI machine learning repository (1996). Accessed 10 May 2022
15. Lane, T., Kohavi, R.: Census-income (KDD) data set. UCI machine learning repository (2010). Accessed 10 May 2022
16. Lin, Z., Khetan, A., Fanti, G., Oh, S.: PacGAN: the power of two samples in generative adversarial networks (2018)
17. Ma, C., Tschiatschek, S., Turner, R., Hernández-Lobato, J.M., Zhang, C.: VAEM: a deep generative model for heterogeneous mixed type data. In: Advances in Neural Information Processing Systems (NeurIPS), vol. 33 (2020)
18. Mottini, A., Lheritier, A., Acuna-Agost, R.: Airline passenger name record generation using generative adversarial networks. arXiv preprint arXiv:1807.06657 (2018)
19. Park, N., Mohammadi, M., Gorde, K., Jajodia, S., Park, H., Kim, Y.: Data synthesis based on generative adversarial networks. Proceedings of the VLDB Endowment (2018). https://doi.org/10.14778/3231751.3231757
20. Radford, A., Metz, L., Chintala, S.: Unsupervised representation learning with deep convolutional generative adversarial networks. In: Bengio, Y., LeCun, Y. (eds.) 4th International Conference on Learning Representations, ICLR 2016, San Juan, Puerto Rico, 2–4 May 2016, Conference Track Proceedings (2016)
21. Theis, L., van den Oord, A., Bethge, M.: A note on the evaluation of generative models. In: International Conference on Learning Representations (ICLR 2016) (2016)
22. Xu, L., Skoularidou, M., Cuesta-Infante, A., Veeramachaneni, K.: Modeling tabular data using conditional GAN. In: Advances in Neural Information Processing Systems (NeurIPS), vol. 32 (2019)
23. Xu, L., Veeramachaneni, K.: Synthesizing tabular data using generative adversarial networks. arXiv preprint arXiv:1811.11264 (2018)
24. Yoon, J., Jordon, J., Schaar, M.: Radialgan: Leveraging multiple datasets to improve target-specific predictive models using generative adversarial networks. In: International Conference on Machine Learning (ICML). PMLR (2018)
25. Zhao, Z., Kunar, A., Birke, R., Chen, L.Y.: CTAB-GAN: effective table data synthesizing. In: Asian Conference on Machine Learning. PMLR (2021)

Robust Models

Detecting Model Misspecification in Amortized Bayesian Inference with Neural Networks

Marvin Schmitt[1]([envelope]) [ID], Paul-Christian Bürkner[1,2] [ID], Ullrich Köthe[3] [ID], and Stefan T. Radev[4] [ID]

[1] Cluster of Excellence SimTech, University of Stuttgart, Stuttgart, Germany
mail.marvinschmitt@gmail.com
[2] Department of Statistics, TU Dortmund University, Dortmund, Germany
[3] Visual Learning Lab, Heidelberg University, Heidelberg, Germany
[4] Cluster of Excellence STRUCTURES, Heidelberg University, Heidelberg, Germany

Abstract. Recent advances in probabilistic deep learning enable efficient amortized Bayesian inference in settings where the likelihood function is only implicitly defined by a simulation program (simulation-based inference; SBI). But how faithful is such inference if the simulation represents reality somewhat inaccurately—that is, if the true system behavior at test time deviates from the one seen during training? We conceptualize the types of model misspecification arising in SBI and systematically investigate how the performance of neural posterior approximators gradually deteriorates under these misspecifications, making inference results less and less trustworthy. To notify users about this problem, we propose a new misspecification measure that can be trained in an unsupervised fashion (i.e., without training data from the true distribution) and reliably detects model misspecification at test time. Our experiments clearly demonstrate the utility of our new measure both on toy examples with an analytical ground-truth and on representative scientific tasks in cell biology, cognitive decision making, and disease outbreak dynamics. We show how the proposed misspecification test warns users about suspicious outputs, raises an alarm when predictions are not trustworthy, and guides model designers in their search for better simulators.

Keywords: Simulation-Based Inference · Model Misspecification · Robustness

1 Introduction

Computer simulations play a fundamental role in many fields of science. However, the associated *inverse* problems of finding simulation parameters that accurately reproduce or predict real-world behavior are generally difficult and analytically

Supplementary Information The online version contains supplementary material available at https://doi.org/10.1007/978-3-031-54605-1_35.

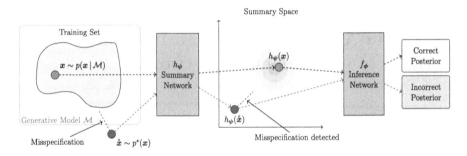

Fig. 1. Conceptual overview of our neural approach. The summary network h_ψ maps observations x to summary statistics $h_\psi(x)$, and the inference network f_ϕ estimates the posterior $p(\theta \mid x, \mathcal{M})$ from the summary statistics. The generative model $\mathcal{M}$ creates training data x in the green region, and the networks learn to map these data to well-defined summary statistics and posteriors (green regions/dot/box). If the generative model $\mathcal{M}$ is misspecificed, real observations $\mathring{x}$ fall outside the training region and are therefore mapped to outlying summary statistics and potentially incorrect posteriors (red dots/box). Since our learning approach enforces a known inlier summary distribution (e.g., Gaussian), misspecification can be detected by a distribution mismatch in summary space, as signaled by a high maximum mean discrepancy [22] score. (Color figure online)

intractable. Here, we consider *simulation-based inference* (SBI) [9] as a general approach to overcome this difficulty within a Bayesian inference framework. That is, given an assumed generative model $\mathcal{M}$ (as represented by the simulation program, see Sect. 3.2 for details) and observations x (real or simulated outcomes), we estimate the posterior distribution $p(\theta \mid x, \mathcal{M})$ of the simulation parameters θ that would reproduce the observed x. The recent introduction of efficient neural network approximators for this task has inspired a rapidly growing literature on SBI solutions for various application domains [4,6,18,20,29,33,48]. These empirical successes call for a systematic investigation of the trustworthiness of SBI, see Fig. 1.

We conduct an extensive analysis of neural posterior estimation (NPE) and sequential neural posterior estimation (SNPE), two deep learning algorithms to approximate the posterior distribution $p(\theta \mid x, \mathcal{M})$. In particular, we study their accuracy under model misspecification, where the generative model $\mathcal{M}^*$ at test time (the "true data generating process") deviates from the one assumed during training (i.e., $\mathcal{M}^* \neq \mathcal{M}$), a situation commonly known as *simulation gap*. As a consequence of a simulation gap, the observed data of interest might lie outside of the simulated data from the training phase of SBI. Paralleling the notion of "out-of-distribution" in anomaly detection and representation learning, simulation gaps may lead to "out-of-simulation" samples, and ultimately to wrong posterior estimates.

In this work, we propose a new misspecification measure that can be trained in an unsupervised fashion (i.e., without knowledge of $\mathcal{M}^*$ or training data from the true data distribution) and reliably quantifies by how much $\mathcal{M}^*$ deviates from $\mathcal{M}$ at test time. Our experiments clearly demonstrate the power of our new measure both on toy examples with an analytical ground-truth, and on representative scientific tasks in cell biology, cognitive decision making, and disease outbreak dynamics. We show how simulation-based posterior inference gradually deteriorates as the simulation gap widens and how the proposed misspecification test warns users about suspicious outputs, raises an alarm when predictions are not trustworthy, and guides model designers in their search for better simulators. Thus, our investigations complement existing work on deep amortized SBI, whose main focus has been on network architectures and training algorithms for high accuracy in the well-specified case $\mathcal{M}^* = \mathcal{M}$ [14,21,35,38,41,45,46]. In particular, our paper makes the following key contributions:

(i) We systematically conceptualize different sources of model misspecification in amortized Bayesian inference with neural networks and propose a new detection criterion that is widely applicable to different model structures, inputs, and outputs.
(ii) We incorporate this criterion into existing neural posterior estimation methods, with hand-crafted and learned summary statistics, with sequential or amortized inference regimes, and we extend the associated learning algorithms in a largely non-intrusive manner.
(iii) We conduct a systematic empirical evaluation of our detection criterion, the influence of the summary space dimension, and the relationship between summary outliers and posterior distortion under various types and strengths of model misspecification.

2   Related Work

Model misspecification has been studied both in the context of standard Bayesian inference and generalizations thereof [28,47]. To alleviate model misspecification in generalized Bayesian inference, researchers have investigated probabilistic classifiers [52], second-order PAC-Bayes bounds [36], scoring rules [19], priors over a class of predictive models [31], or Stein discrepancy as a loss function [37]. Notably, these approaches deviate from the standard Bayesian formulation and investigate alternative schemes for belief updating and learning (e.g., replacing the likelihood function with a generic loss function). In contrast, our method remains grounded in the standard Bayesian framework embodying an implicit likelihood principle [3]. Differently, power scaling methods incorporate a modified likelihood (raised to a power $0 < \alpha < 1$) in order to prevent potentially overconfident Bayesian updating [23,26]. However, the SBI setting assumes that the likelihood function is not available in closed-form, which makes an explicit modification of the implicitly defined likelihood less obvious.

Neural approaches to amortized SBI can be categorized as either targeting the posterior [21,45], the likelihood [24,43], or both [56]. These methods employ simulations for training amortized neural approximators which can either generate samples from the posterior directly [21,45,56] or in tandem with Markov chain Monte Carlo (MCMC) sampling algorithms [24,43]. Since the behavior of these methods depends on the fidelity of the simulations used as training data, we hypothesize that their estimation quality will be, in general, unpredictable, when faced with atypical real-world data. Indeed, the critical impact of model misspecification in neural SBI has been commonly acknowledged in the scientific research community [1,8,15,16,39,58].

Recent approaches to detect model misspecification in simulation-based inference are usually based on the obtained approximate posterior distribution [12,25,30]. However, we show in **Experiment 1** and **Experiment 5** **(Appendix)** that the approximate posteriors in simulation-based inference tend to show pathological behavior under misspecified models. Posteriors from misspecified models may erroneously look legitimate, rendering diagnostic methods on their basis unreliable. Moreover, the same applies for approaches based on the *posterior predictive distribution* [7,17,53] since these also rely on the fidelity of the posterior distribution and can therefore only serve as an indirect measure of misspecification.

A few novel techniques aim to *mitigate* model misspecification in simulation-based inference to achieve robust inference. [11] equip neural ratio estimation [24] with a balancing condition which tends to produce more conservative posterior approximations. [54] explore a way to alleviate model misspecification with two neural approximators and subsequent MCMC. While both approaches are appealing in theory, the computational burden of MCMC sampling contradicts the idea of amortized inference and prohibits their use in complex applications with learned summary statistics and large amounts of data. In fact, [29] used amortized neural SBI on more than a million data sets of multiple observations each and demonstrated that an alternative inference method involving non-amortized MCMC would have taken years of sampling.

For robust non-amortized ABC samplers, the possibility of utilizing hand-crafted summary statistics as an important element of misspecification analysis has already been explored [15,16]. Our work parallels these ideas and extends them to the case of *learnable summary statistics* in amortized SBI on potentially massive data sets, where ABC becomes infeasible. However, we show in **Experiment 2** that our method also works with hand-crafted summary statistics.

Finally, from the perspective of deep anomaly detection, our approach for learning informative summary statistics can be viewed as a special case of *generic normality feature learning* [40]. Standard learned summary statistics are optimized with a generic feature learning objective which is not primarily designed for anomaly detection [45]. However, since learned summary statistics are also optimized to be maximally informative for posterior inference, they will likely capture underlying data regularities [40].

3   Method

For simulation-based Bayesian inference, we define a generative model as a triple $\mathcal{M} = \big(g(\boldsymbol{\theta}, \boldsymbol{\xi}), p(\boldsymbol{\xi} \,|\, \boldsymbol{\theta}), p(\boldsymbol{\theta})\big)$. A generative model $\mathcal{M}$ generates data $\boldsymbol{x} \in \mathcal{X}$ according to the system

$$\boldsymbol{x} = g(\boldsymbol{\theta}, \boldsymbol{\xi}) \quad \text{with} \quad \boldsymbol{\xi} \sim p(\boldsymbol{\xi} \,|\, \boldsymbol{\theta}), \; \boldsymbol{\theta} \sim p(\boldsymbol{\theta}), \tag{1}$$

where g denotes a (randomized) simulator, $\boldsymbol{\xi} \in \Xi$ is a source of randomness (i.e., noise) with density function $p(\boldsymbol{\xi} \mid \boldsymbol{\theta})$, and $p(\boldsymbol{\theta})$ encodes prior knowledge about plausible simulation parameters $\boldsymbol{\theta} \in \Theta$. Throughout the paper, we use the decorated symbol $\overset{*}{x}$ to mark data that was in fact *observed* in the real world and not merely simulated by the assumed model $\mathcal{M}$. The parameters $\boldsymbol{\theta}$ consist of hidden properties whose role in g we explicitly understand and model, and $\boldsymbol{\xi}$ takes care of nuisance effects that we only treat statistically. The abstract spaces $\mathcal{X}, \Xi$, and Θ denote the domain of possible output data (possible worlds), the scope of noise, and the set of admissible model parameters, respectively. The distinction between hidden properties $\boldsymbol{\theta}$ and noise $\boldsymbol{\xi}$ is not entirely clear-cut, but depends on our modeling goals and may vary across applications.

Our generative model formulation is equivalent to the standard factorization of the Bayesian joint distribution into likelihood and prior, $p(\boldsymbol{\theta}, \boldsymbol{x} \mid \mathcal{M}) = p(\boldsymbol{x} \mid \boldsymbol{\theta}, \mathcal{M}) \, p(\boldsymbol{\theta} \mid \mathcal{M})$, where $\mathcal{M}$ expresses the prior knowledge and assumptions embodied in the model. The likelihood is obtained by marginalizing the joint distribution $p(\boldsymbol{\xi}, \boldsymbol{x} \mid \boldsymbol{\theta}, \mathcal{M})$ over all possible values of the nuisance parameters $\boldsymbol{\xi}$, that is, over all possible execution paths of the simulation program, for fixed $\boldsymbol{\theta}$:

$$p(\boldsymbol{x} \mid \boldsymbol{\theta}, \mathcal{M}) = \int_{\Xi} p(\boldsymbol{\xi}, \boldsymbol{x} \mid \boldsymbol{\theta}, \mathcal{M}) \, \mathrm{d}\boldsymbol{\xi}. \tag{2}$$

This integral is typically intractable [9], but we assume that it exists and is non-degenerate, that is, it defines a proper density over the constrained manifold $(g(\boldsymbol{\theta}, \boldsymbol{\xi}), \boldsymbol{\xi})$, and this density can be learned. A major challenge in Bayesian inference is approximating the posterior distribution $p(\boldsymbol{\theta} \mid \boldsymbol{x}, \mathcal{M}) \propto p(\boldsymbol{x} \mid \boldsymbol{\theta}, \mathcal{M}) \, p(\boldsymbol{\theta} \mid \mathcal{M})$. Below, we focus on *amortized* posterior approximation with neural networks, which aims to achieve zero-shot posterior sampling for any input data $\boldsymbol{x}$ compatible with the reference model $\mathcal{M}$.[1]

3.1 Neural Posterior Estimation

Neural Posterior Estimation (NPE) with learned summary statistics $h_\psi(\boldsymbol{x})$ involves a posterior network and a summary network which jointly minimize the expected KL divergence between analytic and approximate posterior

$$\boldsymbol{\psi}^*, \boldsymbol{\phi}^* = \operatorname*{argmin}_{\boldsymbol{\psi}, \boldsymbol{\phi}} \mathbb{E}_{p(\boldsymbol{x} \mid \mathcal{M})} \Big[\mathbb{KL} \big[p(\boldsymbol{\theta} \mid \boldsymbol{x}, \mathcal{M}) \, \| \, q_\phi(\boldsymbol{\theta} \mid h_\psi(\boldsymbol{x}), \mathcal{M}) \big] \Big], \tag{3}$$

where the expectation runs over the prior predictive distribution $p(\boldsymbol{x} \mid \mathcal{M})$. The above criterion simplifies to

$$\boldsymbol{\psi}^*, \boldsymbol{\phi}^* = \operatorname*{argmin}_{\boldsymbol{\psi}, \boldsymbol{\phi}} \mathbb{E}_{p(\boldsymbol{\theta}, \boldsymbol{x} \mid \mathcal{M})} \Big[-\log q_\phi(\boldsymbol{\theta} \mid h_\psi(\boldsymbol{x}), \mathcal{M}) \Big], \tag{4}$$

since the analytic posterior $p(\boldsymbol{\theta} \mid \boldsymbol{x}, \mathcal{M})$ does not depend on the trainable neural network parameters $(\boldsymbol{\psi}, \boldsymbol{\phi})$. This criterion optimizes a summary (aka embedding)

---

[1] We demonstrate in **Experiment 1** that model misspecification also affects the performance of non-amortized sequential neural posterior estimation.

network with parameters ψ and an inference network with parameters ϕ which learn to perform zero-shot posterior estimation over the generative scope of $\mathcal{M}$. The summary network transforms input data $\boldsymbol{x}$ of variable size and structure to a fixed-length representation $\boldsymbol{z} = h_\psi(\boldsymbol{x})$. The inference network f_ϕ generates random draws from an approximate posterior q_ϕ via a normalizing flow, for instance, realized by a conditional invertible neural network [2] or a conditional masked autoregressive flow [42].

We approximate the expectation in Eq. 4 via simulations from the generative model $\mathcal{M}$ and repeat the process until convergence, which enables us to perform fully amortized inference (i.e., the posterior functional can be evaluated for any number of observed data sets $\boldsymbol{x}$). Moreover, this objective is self-consistent and results in correct amortized inference under optimal convergence [21,45].

3.2   Model Misspecification in Simulation-Based Inference

When modeling a complex system or process, we typically assume an unknown (true) generator $\mathcal{M}^*$, which yields an unknown (true) distribution $\mathring{\boldsymbol{x}} \sim p^*(\boldsymbol{x})$ and is available to the data analyst only via a finite realization (i.e., actually observed data $\mathring{\boldsymbol{x}}$). According to a common definition [16,32,36,55], the generative model $\mathcal{M}$ is well-specified if a "true" parameter $\theta^* \in \Theta$ exists, such that the (conditional) likelihood matches the data-generating distribution,

$$p(\boldsymbol{x} \mid \boldsymbol{\theta}^*, \mathcal{M}) = p^*(\boldsymbol{x}), \tag{5}$$

and misspecified otherwise. This likelihood-centered definition is well-established and sensible in many domains of Bayesian inference.

In *simulation-based* inference, however, there is an additional difficulty regarding model specification: Simulation-based training (see Eq. 3) takes the expectation with respect to the model-implied prior predictive distribution $p(\boldsymbol{x} \mid \mathcal{M})$, not necessarily the "true" real-world distribution $p^*(\boldsymbol{x})$. Thus, optimal convergence does not imply correct amortized inference or faithful prediction in the real world when there is a simulation gap, that is, when the assumed training model $\mathcal{M}$ deviates critically from the unknown true generative model $\mathcal{M}^*$.

Crucially, even if the generative model $\mathcal{M}$ is well-specified according to the likelihood-centered definition in Eq. 5, finite training with respect to a "wrong" prior (predictive) distribution will likely result in insufficient learning of relevant parameter (and data) regions. This scenario could also be framed as "out-of-simulation" (OOSim) by analogy with the common out-of-distribution (OOD) problem in machine learning applications [57]. In fact, we observe in **Experiment 1** that a misspecified prior distribution worsens posterior inference just like a misspecified likelihood function does.

Thus, our adjusted definition of model misspecification *in the context of simulation-based inference* considers the entire prior predictive distribution $p(\boldsymbol{x} \mid \mathcal{M})$: A generative model $\mathcal{M}$ is well-specified if the information loss through modeling $p^*(\boldsymbol{x})$ with $p(\boldsymbol{x} \mid \mathcal{M})$ falls below an acceptance threshold ϑ,

$$\mathbb{D}\big[p(\boldsymbol{x} \mid \mathcal{M}) \,\|\, p^*(\boldsymbol{x})\big] < \vartheta, \tag{6}$$

and misspecified otherwise. The symbol $\mathbb{D}$ denotes a divergence metric quantifying the "distance" between the data distributions implied by reality and by the model (i.e., the marginal likelihood). A natural choice for $\mathbb{D}$ would stem from the family of $\mathcal{F}$-divergences, such as the KL divergence. However, we choose the Maximum Mean Discrepancy (MMD) because we can tractably estimate it on finite samples from $p(\boldsymbol{x} \mid \mathcal{M})$ and $p^*(\boldsymbol{x})$ and its analytic value equals zero if and only if the two densities are equal [22].

Our adjusted definition of model misspecification no longer assumes the existence of a *true* parameter vector $\boldsymbol{\theta}^*$ (cf. Eq. 5). Instead, we focus on the *marginal likelihood* $p(\boldsymbol{x} \mid \mathcal{M})$ which represents the entire prior predictive distribution of a model and does not commit to a single most representative parameter vector. In this way, multiple models whose marginal distributions are representative of $p^*(\boldsymbol{x})$ can be considered well-specified without any reference to some hypothetical ground-truth $\boldsymbol{\theta}^*$, which may not even exist for opaque systems with unknown properties.

3.3 Structured Summary Statistics

In simulation-based inference, summary statistics have a dual purpose because (i) they are fixed-length vectors, even if the input data $\boldsymbol{x}$ have variable length; and (ii) they usually contain crucial features of the data, which simplifies neural posterior inference. However, in complex real-world scenarios such as COVID-19 modeling (see **Experiment 3**), it is not feasible to rely on hand-crafted summary statistics. Thus, combining neural posterior estimation with *learned summary statistics* leverages the benefits of summary statistics (i.e., compression to fixed-length vectors) while avoiding the virtually impossible task of designing hand-crafted summary statistics for complex models.

In simulation-based inference, the summary network h_ψ acts as an interface between the data $\boldsymbol{x}$ and the inference network f_ϕ. Its role is to learn maximally informative summary vectors of fixed size S from complex and structured observations (e.g., sets of *i.i.d.* measurements or multivariate time series). Since the learned summary statistics are optimized to be maximally informative for posterior inference, they are forced to capture underlying data regularities (see Sect. 2). Therefore, we deem the summary network's representation $\boldsymbol{z} = h_\psi(\boldsymbol{x})$ as an adequate target to detect simulation gaps.

Specifically, we prescribe an S-dimensional multivariate unit (aka. standard) Gaussian distribution to the summary space, $p(\boldsymbol{z} = h_\psi(\boldsymbol{x}) \mid \mathcal{M}) \approx \mathcal{N}(\boldsymbol{z} \mid \boldsymbol{0}, \mathbb{I})$, by minimizing the MMD between summary network outputs and random draws from a unit Gaussian distribution. To ensure that the summary vectors comply with the support of the Gaussian density, we use a linear (bottleneck) output layer with S units in the summary network. A random vector in summary space takes the form $h_\psi(\boldsymbol{x}) \equiv \boldsymbol{z} \equiv (z_1, \ldots, z_S) \in \mathbb{R}^S$. The extended optimization objective follows as

$$\psi^*, \phi^* = \underset{\psi, \phi}{\operatorname{argmin}} \, \mathbb{E}_{p(\boldsymbol{\theta}, \boldsymbol{x} \,|\, \mathcal{M})} \left[-\log q_\phi\big(\boldsymbol{\theta} \,|\, h_\psi(\boldsymbol{x}), \mathcal{M}\big) \right]$$
$$+ \gamma \operatorname{MMD}^2 \big[p\big(h_\psi(\boldsymbol{x}) \,|\, \mathcal{M}\big) \,||\, \mathcal{N}(\boldsymbol{0}, \mathbb{I}) \big] \tag{7}$$

with a hyperparameter γ to control the relative weight of the MMD term. Intuitively, this objective encourages the approximate posterior $q_\phi\big(\boldsymbol{\theta} \,|\, h_\psi(\boldsymbol{x}), \mathcal{M}\big)$ to match the correct posterior and the summary distribution $p\big(h_\psi(\boldsymbol{x}) \,|\, \mathcal{M}\big)$ to match a unit Gaussian. The extended objective does not constitute a theoretical trade-off between the two terms, since the MMD merely reshapes the summary distribution in an information-preserving manner. In practice, the extended objective may render optimization of the summary network more difficult, but our experiments suggest that it does not restrict the quality of the amortized posteriors.

This method is also directly applicable to hand-crafted summary statistics. Hand-crafted summary statistics already have fixed length and usually contain rich information for posterior inference. Thus, the task of the summary network h_ψ simplifies to transforming the hand-crafted summary statistics to a unit Gaussian (Eq. 7) to enable model misspecification via distribution matching during test time (see below). We apply our method to a problem with hand-crafted summary statistics in **Experiment 2**.

3.4 Detecting Model Misspecification with Finite Data

Once the simulation-based training phase is completed, we can generate M validation samples $\{\boldsymbol{\theta}^{(m)}, \boldsymbol{x}^{(m)}\}$ from our generative model $\mathcal{M}$ and pass them through the summary network to obtain a sample of latent summary vectors $\{\boldsymbol{z}^{(m)}\}$, where $\boldsymbol{z} = h_\psi(\boldsymbol{x})$ denotes the output of the summary network. The properties of this sample contain important convergence information: If $\boldsymbol{z}$ is approximately unit Gaussian, we can assume a structured summary space given the training model $\mathcal{M}$. This enables model misspecification diagnostics via distribution checking during inference on real data (see the Appendix for the detailed algorithm).

Let $\{\overset{\circ}{\boldsymbol{x}}{}^{(n)}\}$ be an *observed* sample, either simulated from a different generative model, or arising from real-world observations with an unknown generator. Before invoking the inference network, we pass this sample through the summary network to obtain the summary statistics for the sample: $\{\overset{\circ}{\boldsymbol{z}}{}^{(n)}\}$. We then compare the validation summary distribution $\{\boldsymbol{z}^{(m)}\}$ with the summary statistics of the observed data $\{\overset{\circ}{\boldsymbol{z}}{}^{(n)}\}$ according to the sample-based MMD estimate $\widehat{\operatorname{MMD}}^2 (p(\boldsymbol{z}) \,||\, p(\overset{\circ}{\boldsymbol{z}}))$ [22]. Importantly, we are not limited to pre-determined sizes of simulated or real-world data sets, as the MMD estimator is defined for arbitrary M and N. To allow MMD estimation for data sets with single instances ($N = 1$ or $M = 1$), we do not use the unbiased MMD version from [22]. Singleton data sets are an important use case for our method in practice, and potential advantages of unbiased estimators do not justify exclusion of such data. To enhance visibility, the figures in the experimental section will depict the square root of the originally squared MMD estimate.

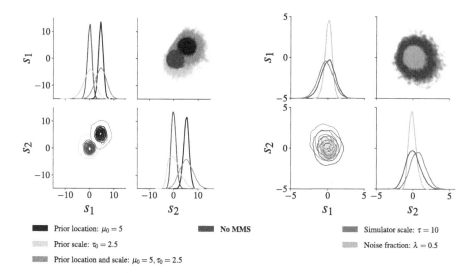

Fig. 2. Experiment 1. Summary space samples for the minimal sufficient summary network ($S = 2$) from a well-specified model $\mathcal{M}$ (blue) and several misspecified configurations. **Left:** Prior misspecification can be detected. **Right:** Noise misspecification can be detected, while simulator scale misspecification is indistinguishable from the validation summary statistics.

Whenever we estimate the MMD from finite data, its estimates vary according to a sampling distribution and we can resort to a frequentist hypothesis test to determine the probability of observed MMD values under well-specified models. Although this sampling distribution under the null hypothesis is unknown, we can estimate it from multiple sets of simulations from the generative model, $\{z^{(m)}\}$ and $\{z^{(n)}\}$, with M large and N equal to the number of real data sets. Based on the estimated sampling distribution, we can obtain a critical MMD value for a fixed Type I error probability (α) and compare it to the one estimated with the observed data. In general, a larger α level corresponds to a more conservative modeling approach: A larger type I error implies that more tests reject the null hypothesis, which corresponds to more frequent model misspecification alarms and a higher chance that incorrect models will be recognised. The Type II error probability (β) of this test will generally be high (i.e., the *power* of the test will be low) whenever the number of real data sets N is very small. However, we show in **Experiment 3** that even as few as 5 real data sets suffice to achieve $\beta \approx 0$ for a complex model on COVID-19 time series.

4   Experiments

4.1   Experiment 1: 2D Gaussian Means

We set the stage by estimating the means of a 2-dimensional conjugate Gaussian model with $K = 100$ observations per data set and a known analytic posterior in

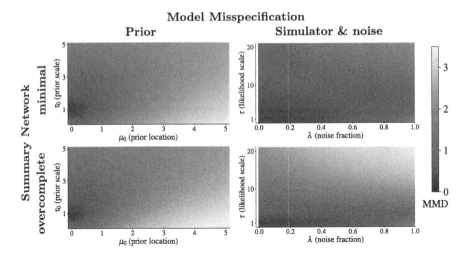

Fig. 3. Experiment 1. Summary space MMD as a function of misspecification severity. White stars indicate the well-specified model configuration (i.e., equal to the training model $\mathcal{M}$).

order to illustrate our method. This experiment contains the Gaussian examples from [16] and [54], and extends them by (i) studying misspecifications beyond the likelihood variance (see below); and (ii) implementing continuously widening simulation gaps, as opposed to a single discrete misspecification. The data generating process is defined as

$$x_k \sim \mathcal{N}(x \,|\, \mu, \Sigma) \quad \text{for } k = 1, ..., K \qquad \text{with} \quad \mu \sim \mathcal{N}(\mu \,|\, \mu_0, \Sigma_0). \qquad (8)$$

As a summary network, we use a permutation invariant network [5] with $S = 2$ output dimensions, which equal the number of minimal sufficient statistics implied by the analytic posterior. The terms "minimal", "sufficient", and "overcomplete" refer to the inference task and *not* to the data. Thus, $S = 2$ summary statistics are *sufficient* to solve the inference task, namely recover two means. For training the posterior approximator, we set the prior of the generative model $\mathcal{M}$ to a unit Gaussian and the likelihood covariance Σ to an identity matrix.

We induce prior misspecification by altering the prior location μ_0 and covariance $\Sigma_0 = \tau_0 \mathbb{I}$ (only diagonal covariance, controlled through the factor τ_0). Further, we achieve misspecified likelihoods by manipulating the likelihood covariance $\Sigma = \tau \mathbb{I}$ (only diagonal covariance, controlled through τ). We induce noise misspecification by replacing a fraction $\lambda \in [0, 1]$ of the data x with samples from a scaled Beta$(2, 5)$ distribution.

Results. The neural posterior estimator trained to minimize the augmented objective (Eq. 7) exhibits excellent recovery and calibration [49,50] in the well-specified case, as shown in the Appendix. All prior misspecifications manifest themselves in anomalies in the summary space which are directly detectable

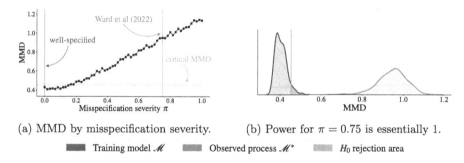

(a) MMD by misspecification severity.   (b) Power for $\pi = 0.75$ is essentially 1.

▬ Training model $\mathcal{M}$ ▬ Observed process $\mathcal{M}^*$ ▬ H_0 rejection area

Fig. 4. Experiment 2. MMD increases with misspecification severity (a; mean, SD of 20 repetitions). Our test easily detects the setting from [54] (b).

through visual inspection of the 2-dimensional summary space in Fig. 2 (left). Note that the combined prior misspecification (location and scale) exhibits a summary space pattern that combines the location and scale of the respective location and scale misspecifications. However, based on the 2-dimensional summary space, misspecifications in the fixed parameters of the likelihood (τ) and mixture noise are not detectable via an increased MMD (see Fig. 3, top right).

We further investigate the effect of an *overcomplete* summary space with respect to the inference task, namely $S = 4$ learned summary statistics with an otherwise equal architecture. In addition to prior misspecifications, the overcomplete summary network also captures misspecifications in the noise and simulator via the MMD criterion (see Fig. 3, bottom row). Furthermore, the induced misspecifications in the noise and simulator are visually detectable in the summary space samples (see Appendix). Recall that the 2-dimensional summary space fails to capture these misspecifications (see Fig. 3, top right). The effect of model misspecificaiton on the posterior recovery error is described in the Appendix.

SNPE-C. Our method successfully detects model misspecification using SNPE-C [21] with a structured summary space (see Appendix). The results are largely equivalent to those obtained with NPE, as implemented in the BayesFlow framework [45].

4.2 Experiment 2: Cancer and Stromal Cell Model

This experiment illustrates model misspecification detection in a marked point process model of cancer and stromal cells [27]. We use the original implementation of [54] with hand-crafted summary statistics and showcase the applicability of our method in scenarios where good summary statistics are known. The inference parameters are three Poisson rates $\lambda_c, \lambda_p, \lambda_d$, and the setup in [54] extracts four hand-crafted summary statistics from the 2D plane data: (1–2) number of cancer and stromal cells; (3–4) mean and maximum distance from stromal cells to the nearest cancer cell. All implementation details are described in the Appendix.

We achieve misspecification during inference by mimicking necrosis, which often occurs in core regions of tumors. A Bernoulli distribution with parameter π controls whether a cell is affected by necrosis or not. Consequently, $\pi = 0$ implies no necrosis (and thus no simulation gap), and $\pi = 1$ entails that all cells are affected. The experiments by [54] study a single misspecification, namely the case $\pi = 0.75$ in our implementation. In order to employ our proposed method for model misspecification detection, we add a small summary network $h_\psi : \mathbb{R}^4 \to \mathbb{R}^4$ consisting of three hidden fully connected layers with 64 units each. This network h_ψ merely transforms the hand-crafted summary statistics into a 4-D unit Gaussian, followed by NPE for posterior inference.

Results. Our MMD misspecification score increases with increasingly severe model misspecification (i.e., increasing necrosis rate π), see Fig. 4a. What is more, for the single misspecification $\pi = 0.75$ studied by [54], we illustrate (i) the power of our proposed hypothesis test; and (ii) the summary space distribution for misspecified data. The power $(1 - \beta)$ essentially equals 1, as shown in Fig. 4b: The MMD sampling distributions under the training model (H_0) and under the observed data generating process $(\mathcal{M}^*)$ are completely separated.

4.3   Experiment 3: Epidemiological Model for COVID-19

As a final real-world example, we treat a high-dimensional compartmental model representing the early months of the COVID-19 pandemic in Germany [44]. We investigate the utility of our method to detect simulation gaps in a much more realistic and non-trivial extension of the SIR settings in [34] and

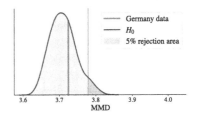

[54] with substantially increased complexity. Moreover, we perform inference on real COVID-19 data from Germany

Fig. 5. Representation of Germany's COVID-19 time series w.r.t. the MMD distribution under $H_0 : p^*(\boldsymbol{x}) = p(\boldsymbol{x} \mid \mathcal{M})$.

and use our new method to test whether the model used in [44] is misspecified, possibly undermining the trustworthiness of political conclusions that are based on the inferred posteriors. To achieve this, we train an NPE setup with the BayesFlow framework [45] identical to [44] but using our new optimization objective (Eq. 7) to encourage a structured summary space. We then simulate 1000 time series from the training model $\mathcal{M}$ and 1000 time series from three misspecified models: (i) a model $\mathcal{M}_1$ without an intervention sub-model; (ii) a model $\mathcal{M}_2$ without an observation sub-model; (iii) a model $\mathcal{M}_3$ without a "carrier" compartment [10].

Results. Table 1 shows the MMD between the summary representation of $N = 1, 2, 5$ bootstrapped time series from each model and the summary representation of the 1000 time series from model $\mathcal{M}$ (see the Appendix for bootstrapping details). We also calculate the power $(1 - \beta)$ of our hypothesis test for each misspecified model under the sampling distribution estimated from 1000 samples of the 1000 time series from $\mathcal{M}$ at a type I error probability of $\alpha = .05$. We

Table 1. Experiment 3. Results for different variations of the COVID-19 compartmental model. We report the median and 95% CI of 100 bootstrap samples.

Model	Bootstrap MMD			Power $(1 - \beta)$		
	$N = 1$	$N = 2$	$N = 5$	$N = 1$	$N = 2$	$N = 5$
$\mathcal{M}$	$3.70\,[3.65, 3.79]$	$2.61\,[2.54, 2.91]$	$1.66\,[1.59, 1.84]$	—	—	—
$\mathcal{M}_1$	$3.76\,[3.72, 3.80]$	$2.86\,[2.62, 3.16]$	$2.11\,[1.82, 2.50]$	.998	.958	≈ 1.0
$\mathcal{M}_2$	$3.80\,[3.73, 3.83]$	$2.81\,[2.65, 3.00]$	$2.01\,[1.82, 2.19]$	.789	.804	≈ 1.0
$\mathcal{M}_3$	$3.78\,[3.74, 3.83]$	$2.81\,[2.68, 3.11]$	$2.07\,[1.92, 2.41]$	.631	.690	≈ 1.0

observe that the power of the test rapidly increases with more data sets and the Type II error probability (β) is essentially zero for as few as $N = 5$ time series.

As a next step, we pass the reported COVID-19 data between 1 March and 21 April 2020 [13] through the summary network and compute the critical MMD value for a sampling-based hypothesis test with an α level of .05 (see Fig. 5). The MMD of the Germany data is well below the critical MMD value (it essentially lies in the bulk of the distribution), leading to the conclusion that the assumed training model $\mathcal{M}$ is well-specified for this time period.

5 Conclusions

This paper approached a fundamental problem in amortized simulation-based Bayesian inference, namely, flagging potential posterior errors due to model misspecification. We argued that misspecified models might cause so-called *simulation gaps*, resulting in deviations between simulations during training time and actual observed data at test time. We further showed that simulation gaps can be detrimental for the performance and faithfulness of simulation-based inference relying on neural networks. We proposed to increase the networks' awareness of posterior errors by compressing simulations into a structured latent summary space induced by a modified optimization objective in an unsupervised fashion. We then applied the maximum mean discrepancy (MMD) estimator, equipped with a sampling-based hypothesis test, as a criterion to spotlight discrepancies between model-implied and actually observed distributions in summary space. While we focused on the application to NPE (BayesFlow implementation [45]) and SNPE (sbi implementation [51]), the proposed method can be easily integrated into other inference algorithms and frameworks as well. Our software implementations are available in the BayesFlow library (http://www.bayesflow.org) and can be seamlessly integrated into an end-to-end workflow for amortized simulation-based inference.

Acknowledgments. MS and PCB were supported by the Cyber Valley Research Fund (grant number: CyVy-RF-2021-16) and the Deutsche Forschungsgemeinschaft (DFG, German Research Foundation) under Germany's Excellence Strategy EXC-2075

- 390740016 (the Stuttgart Cluster of Excellence SimTech). UK was supported by the Informatics for Life initiative funded by the Klaus Tschira Foundation. STR was funded by the Deutsche Forschungsgemeinschaft (DFG, German Research Foundation) under Germany's Excellence Strategy - EXC-2181 - 390900948 (the Heidelberg Cluster of Excellence STRUCTURES).

References

1. Alquier, P., Ridgway, J.: Concentration of tempered posteriors and of their variational approximations. arXiv:1706.09293 [cs, math, stat] (2019). arXiv: 1706.09293
2. Ardizzone, L., Lüth, C., Kruse, J., Rother, C., Köthe, U.: Guided image generation with conditional invertible neural networks (2019)
3. Berger, J.O., Wolpert, R.L.: The Likelihood Principle. No. v. 6 in Lecture Notes-Monograph Series. 2nd edn. Institute of Mathematical Statistics, Hayward (1988)
4. Bieringer, S., et al.: Measuring QCD splittings with invertible networks. SciPost Phys. Proc. **10**(6), 126 (2021)
5. Bloem-Reddy, B., Teh, Y.W.: Probabilistic symmetries and invariant neural networks. J. Mach. Learn. Res. **21**, 90–1 (2020)
6. Butter, A., et al.: Machine learning and LHC event generation. arXiv preprint arXiv:2203.07460 (2022)
7. Bürkner, P.C., Gabry, J., Vehtari, A.: Approximate leave-future-out cross-validation for Bayesian time series models. J. Stat. Comput. Simul. **90**(14), 2499–2523 (2020). https://doi.org/10.1080/00949655.2020.1783262. arXiv:1902.06281 [stat]
8. Cannon, P., Ward, D., Schmon, S.M.: Investigating the impact of model misspecification in neural simulation-based inference (2022). arXiv:2209.01845 [cs, stat]
9. Cranmer, K., Brehmer, J., Louppe, G.: The frontier of simulation-based inference. Proc. Natl. Acad. Sci. **117**(48), 30055–30062 (2020)
10. Dehning, J., et al.: Inferring change points in the spread of COVID-19 reveals the effectiveness of interventions. Science **369**(6500) (2020)
11. Delaunoy, A., Hermans, J., Rozet, F., Wehenkel, A., Louppe, G.: Towards reliable simulation-based inference with balanced neural ratio estimation (2022). arXiv:2208.13624 [cs, stat]
12. Dellaporta, C., Knoblauch, J., Damoulas, T., Briol, F.X.: Robust Bayesian inference for simulator-based models via the MMD Posterior Bootstrap (2022). https://doi.org/10.48550/ARXIV.2202.04744
13. Dong, E., Du, H., Gardner, L.: An interactive web-based dashboard to track COVID-19 in real time. Lancet. Infect. Dis **20**(5), 533–534 (2020). https://doi.org/10.1016/S1473-3099(20)30120-1
14. Durkan, C., Murray, I., Papamakarios, G.: On contrastive learning for likelihood-free inference. In: International Conference on Machine Learning, pp. 2771–2781. PMLR (2020)
15. Frazier, D.T., Drovandi, C.: Robust approximate Bayesian inference with synthetic likelihood. J. Comput. Graph. Stat. **30**(4), 958–976 (2021). https://doi.org/10.1080/10618600.2021.1875839
16. Frazier, D.T., Robert, C.P., Rousseau, J.: Model misspecification in approximate Bayesian computation: consequences and diagnostics. J. Royal Stat. Soc. Ser. B (Stat. Method.) **82**(2), 421–444 (2020). https://doi.org/10.1111/rssb.12356

17. Gabry, J., Simpson, D., Vehtari, A., Betancourt, M., Gelman, A.: Visualization in Bayesian workflow. J. Royal Stat. Soc. Ser. A (Stat. Soc.) **182**(2), 389–402 (2019)
18. Ghaderi-Kangavari, A., Rad, J.A., Nunez, M.D.: A general integrative neurocognitive modeling framework to jointly describe EEG and decision-making on single trials. Comput. Brain Behav. (2023). https://doi.org/10.1007/s42113-023-00167-4
19. Giummolè, F., Mameli, V., Ruli, E., Ventura, L.: Objective Bayesian inference with proper scoring rules. TEST **28**(3), 728–755 (2019)
20. Gonçalves, P.J., et al.: Training deep neural density estimators to identify mechanistic models of neural dynamics. Elife **9**, e56261 (2020)
21. Greenberg, D., Nonnenmacher, M., Macke, J.: Automatic posterior transformation for likelihood-free inference. In: International Conference on Machine Learning, pp. 2404–2414. PMLR (2019)
22. Gretton, A., Borgwardt, K., Rasch, M., Schölkopf, B., Smola, A.: A Kernel two-sample test. J. Mach. Learn. Res. **13**, 723–773 (2012)
23. Grünwald, P., Van Ommen, T., et al.: Inconsistency of Bayesian inference for misspecified linear models, and a proposal for repairing it. Bayesian Anal. **12**(4), 1069–1103 (2017)
24. Hermans, J., Begy, V., Louppe, G.: Likelihood-free MCMC with amortized approximate ratio estimators. In: International Conference on Machine Learning, pp. 4239–4248. PMLR (2020)
25. Hermans, J., Delaunoy, A., Rozet, F., Wehenkel, A., Louppe, G.: Averting a crisis in simulation-based inference. arXiv preprint arXiv:2110.06581 (2021)
26. Holmes, C.C., Walker, S.G.: Assigning a value to a power likelihood in a general Bayesian model. Biometrika **104**(2), 497–503 (2017)
27. Jones-Todd, C.M., et al.: Identifying prognostic structural features in tissue sections of colon cancer patients using point pattern analysis: Point pattern analysis of colon cancer tissue sections. Stat. Med. **38**(8), 1421–1441 (2019). https://doi.org/10.1002/sim.8046
28. Knoblauch, J., Jewson, J., Damoulas, T.: Generalized variational inference: three arguments for deriving new posteriors. arXiv preprint arXiv:1904.02063 (2019)
29. von Krause, M., Radev, S.T., Voss, A.: Mental speed is high until age 60 as revealed by analysis of over a million participants. Nat. Hum. Behav. **6**(5), 700–708 (2022). https://doi.org/10.1038/s41562-021-01282-7
30. Leclercq, F.: Simulation-based inference of Bayesian hierarchical models while checking for model misspecification (2022). arXiv:2209.11057 [astro-ph, q-bio, stat]
31. Loaiza-Maya, R., Martin, G.M., Frazier, D.T.: Focused Bayesian prediction. J. Appl. Economet. **36**(5), 517–543 (2021)
32. Lotfi, S., Izmailov, P., Benton, G., Goldblum, M., Wilson, A.G.: Bayesian model selection, the marginal likelihood, and generalization. arXiv preprint arXiv:2202.11678 (2022)
33. Lueckmann, J.M., Boelts, J., Greenberg, D., Goncalves, P., Macke, J.: Benchmarking simulation-based inference. In: International Conference on Artificial Intelligence and Statistics, pp. 343–351. PMLR (2021)
34. Lueckmann, J.M., Boelts, J., Greenberg, D., Goncalves, P., Macke, J.: Benchmarking simulation-based inference. In: Banerjee, A., Fukumizu, K. (eds.) Proceedings of The 24th International Conference on Artificial Intelligence and Statistics. Proceedings of Machine Learning Research, vol. 130, pp. 343–351. PMLR (2021)
35. Lueckmann, J.M., Goncalves, P.J., Bassetto, G., Öcal, K., Nonnenmacher, M., Macke, J.H.: Flexible statistical inference for mechanistic models of neural dynamics. In: Advances in Neural Information Processing Systems, vol. 30 (2017)

36. Masegosa, A.: Learning under model misspecification: applications to variational and ensemble methods. In: Advances in Neural Information Processing Systems, vol. 33, pp. 5479–5491 (2020)
37. Matsubara, T., Knoblauch, J., Briol, F.X., Oates, C.J.: Robust generalised bayesian inference for intractable likelihoods (2022). arXiv:2104.07359 [math, stat]
38. Pacchiardi, L., Dutta, R.: Likelihood-free inference with generative neural networks via scoring rule minimization. arXiv preprint arXiv:2205.15784 (2022)
39. Pacchiardi, L., Dutta, R.: Score matched neural exponential families for likelihood-free inference (2022). arXiv:2012.10903 [stat]
40. Pang, G., Shen, C., Cao, L., Hengel, A.V.D.: Deep learning for anomaly detection: a review. ACM Comput. Surv. **54**(2), 1–38 (2022). https://doi.org/10.1145/3439950. arXiv:2007.02500 [cs, stat]
41. Papamakarios, G., Murray, I.: Fast ε-free inference of simulation models with Bayesian conditional density estimation. In: Advances in Neural Information Processing Systems, vol. 29 (2016)
42. Papamakarios, G., Pavlakou, T., Murray, I.: Masked autoregressive flow for density estimation. In: Advances in Neural Information Processing Systems, vol. 30 (2017)
43. Papamakarios, G., Sterratt, D., Murray, I.: Sequential neural likelihood: fast likelihood-free inference with autoregressive flows. In: The 22nd International Conference on Artificial Intelligence and Statistics, pp. 837–848. PMLR (2019)
44. Radev, S.T., et al.: OutbreakFlow: model-based Bayesian inference of disease outbreak dynamics with invertible neural networks and its application to the COVID-19 pandemics in Germany. PLoS Comput. Biol. **17**(10), e1009472 (2021)
45. Radev, S.T., Mertens, U.K., Voss, A., Ardizzone, L., Köthe, U.: BayesFlow: learning complex stochastic models with invertible neural networks. IEEE Trans. Neural Netw. Learn. Syst. **33**, 1452–1466 (2020)
46. Ramesh, P., et al.: GATSBI: generative adversarial training for simulation-based inference. arXiv preprint arXiv:2203.06481 (2022)
47. Schmon, S.M., Cannon, P.W., Knoblauch, J.: Generalized posteriors in approximate Bayesian computation (2021). arXiv:2011.08644 [stat]
48. Shiono, T.: Estimation of agent-based models using Bayesian deep learning approach of BayesFlow. J. Econ. Dyn. Control **125**, 104082 (2021)
49. Säilynoja, T., Bürkner, P.C., Vehtari, A.: Graphical test for discrete uniformity and its applications in goodness of fit evaluation and multiple sample comparison (2021). arXiv:2103.10522 [stat]
50. Talts, S., Betancourt, M., Simpson, D., Vehtari, A., Gelman, A.: Validating Bayesian inference algorithms with simulation-based calibration (2020). arXiv:1804.06788 [stat]
51. Tejero-Cantero, A., et al.: SBI-a toolkit for simulation-based inference. arXiv preprint arXiv:2007.09114 (2020)
52. Thomas, O., Corander, J.: Diagnosing model misspecification and performing generalized Bayes' updates via probabilistic classifiers. arXiv preprint arXiv:1912.05810 (2019)
53. Vehtari, A., Ojanen, J.: A survey of Bayesian predictive methods for model assessment, selection and comparison. Stat. Surv. **6** (2012). https://doi.org/10.1214/12-SS102
54. Ward, D., Cannon, P., Beaumont, M., Fasiolo, M., Schmon, S.M.: Robust neural posterior estimation and statistical model criticism (2022). arXiv:2210.06564 [cs, stat]
55. White, H.: Maximum likelihood estimation of misspecified models. Econometrica **50**(1), 1–25 (1982)

56. Wiqvist, S., Frellsen, J., Picchini, U.: Sequential neural posterior and likelihood approximation. arXiv preprint arXiv:2102.06522 (2021)
57. Yang, J., Zhou, K., Li, Y., Liu, Z.: Generalized out-of-distribution detection: a survey. arXiv:2110.11334 (2021)
58. Zhang, F., Gao, C.: Convergence rates of variational posterior distributions. Ann. Stat. **48**(4), 2180–2207 (2020). https://doi.org/10.1214/19-AOS1883

Adversarial Perturbations Straight on JPEG Coefficients

Kolja Sielmann(ID) and Peer Stelldinger(✉)(ID)

Hamburg University of Applied Sciences, 20099 Hamburg, Germany
{kolja.sielmann,peer.stelldinger}@haw-hamburg.de

Abstract. Adversarial examples are samples that are close to benign samples with respect to a distance metric, but misclassified by a neural network. While adversarial perturbations of images are usually computed for RGB images, we propose perturbing straight on JPEG coefficients with the ability to individually control the perturbation applied on each color channel and frequency. We find that perturbation as a function of perceptual distance is most efficient for medium frequencies, especially when JPEG compression is used in defense. Overall, we show that attacks on JPEG coefficients are more efficient than state-of-the-art methods that (mainly) apply their perturbation in RGB pixel space. This is partly due to the use of the YC_bC_r color space, which allows to perturb luma information exclusively, but also due to perturbing the cosine transform coefficients instead of pixels. Moreover, adversarial training using such JPEG attacks with various frequency weighting vectors results in generally strong robustness against RGB and YC_bC_r attacks as well.

Keywords: Adversarial Attacks · JPEG · Perceptual Distance

1 Introduction

There has been a large amount of research in recent years on image adversarial attacks and how to defend neural networks against them [3,8,18,29]. Generally, images are represented using RGB pixels and while there has been some research on attacks that try to bypass JPEG compression in defense or when saving the adversarial images [32,33], the main perturbation is mostly still applied in RGB representations. Perturbing straight on JPEG coefficients has only been used as an example of an unforeseen threat model [15,19], but never been analyzed in detail, although there are several advantages. Adversarial examples exist because neural network classifiers are relying on properties of the data different from those used by humans. In contrast, lossy image compression algorithms like JPEG aim to remove properties of the data which are imperceptible for humans. Thus, a representation of images which separates perceivable from imperceptible parts of the data and enables to control the applied perturbations across frequencies could be a better basis for generating adversarial examples as well as for an adversarial defense.

U. Köthe and C. Rother (Eds.): DAGM GCPR 2023, LNCS 14264, pp. 558–573, 2024.
https://doi.org/10.1007/978-3-031-54605-1_36

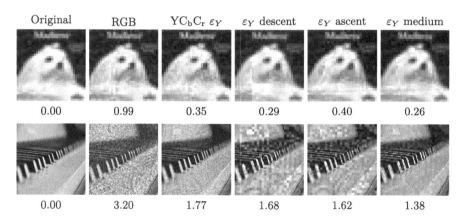

Original	RGB	YC_bC_r ε_Y	ε_Y descent	ε_Y ascent	ε_Y medium
0.00	0.99	0.35	0.29	0.40	0.26
0.00	3.20	1.77	1.68	1.62	1.38

Fig. 1. Adversarial examples with minimum perturbation to force a misclassification on a Densenet^{jq50} for CIFAR10 (top) and IMAGENET (bottom) for attacks on RGB, YC_bC_r pixels and JPEG coefficients (jq 100) using different frequency weighting vectors. The LPIPS distance is given below each image.

JPEG compression is known to be a weak defence strategy against adversarial attacks [5,6,10,28]. Attacking straight on JPEG coefficients could increase the success on nets that use JPEG compression in defense, as it could prevent that perturbations are removed during JPEG compression. Moreover, using a YC_bC_r representation of the image pixels, which is also part of the JPEG compression pipeline, is beneficial for both adversarial attacks and adversarial defense [25]. This leads us to the following questions: Can perturbing straight on JPEG coefficients result in adversarial attacks that are more efficient, i.e. show the same or higher success while being perceptually closer to the original? Can such JPEG attacks indeed bypass JPEG compression with more efficiency than state-of-the-art attacks? Is there a difference between the impact of low-, medium- and high-frequency perturbations on JPEG adversarial attacks? And can these differences be used to achieve more generalising robustness with adversarial training?

Our work is structured as follows: All necessary background on adversarial attacks and defenses, JPEG compression and perceptual metrics is given in Sect. 2. In Sect. 3, we explain our attack method in detail. Section 4 includes the analysis of the efficiency of our approach in comparison with state-of-the-art attacks, followed by a conclusion in Sect. 5. Our implementation is available at https://github.com/KoljaSmn/jpeg-adversarial-attacks.

2   Related Work

2.1   Adversarial Attacks

Following Szegedy et al. [34], given an original input image x with the corresponding ground-truth label y, an image $x' = x + \delta$ is called an adversarial example, if and only if $D(x, x') \leq \varepsilon \wedge f(x') \neq y$, where ε is a hyperparameter limiting the perturbation δ on the original image, D is a distance metric and f

is the neural net's output class for a given input. Usually, L_p norms are used as distance metric. We focus on untargeted attacks that are limited by the L_∞ norm, i.e. attacks that search for an adversarial example x' with a maximum pixel-wise perturbation of ε: $L_\infty(x' - x) = \max_i |x'_i - x_i| \leq \varepsilon$. For generating adversarial examples, we use the BASIC ITERATIVE METHOD (BIM) [18] which iteratively updates the image in the direction of the loss gradient by step size α,

$$x'_t = \text{Clip}_{x,\varepsilon}(x'_{t-1} + \alpha \cdot \text{sign}(\nabla_{x'_{t-1}} \text{J}(x'_{t-1}, y))), \tag{1}$$

where J is the categorical crossentropy loss for some source model.

2.2 Perceptual Metrics

Usually, L_p norms measured in the images' RGB representations are used to evaluate the success of adversarial attacks. These are not really suitable for measuring perceptual differences in real-world scenarios though: First, the RGB color model is based more on physiological properties [26], than on perceptual ones, and it is not perceptually uniform [21]. Second, L_p norms only compute pixel-wise differences and cannot measure structural differences.

Recently, there has been a development towards using perceptually more meaningful distances for measuring and minimizing the distortions created by adversarial attacks: Zhao et al. [39] minimize the CIEDE2000 distance which has been designed to measure perceived color distances [20]. Others have used the Learned Perceptual Image Patch Similarity (LPIPS) to either measure or minimize the perceptual distortion [13,19]. LPIPS is a perceptual loss function that was proposed by Zhang et al. [38] and uses the differences between activations of some convolutional layers in a pretrained network. By relying on differences in feature spaces, LPIPS can also measure structural differences and it has shown to be closer to human perception than pixel-wise distance metrics [38].

The superiority of LPIPS as a perceptual metric can also be illustrated using a simple example, shown in Fig. 2, where every pixel in the background was disturbed by adding/subtracting 3 from every RGB channel in two different patterns. On the left, the direction was arranged as a chessboard and on the right it was chosen randomly. The randomly arranged perturbation is not visible without zooming in, while the left image is clearly distinguishable. As the background contains the same pixels on both perturbed images, but the arrangement varies, pixel-wise distances like CIEDE2000 L_2 do not vary, while LPIPS does, corresponding to human perception. In our experiments, we use a VGG-16 net and train the LPIPS model in the same way as in the original paper [38].

2.3 JPEG Compression and JPEG-Resistant Attacks

JPEG compression builds on the idea that high frequency image content can be altered more before becoming noticeable. In addition to that it takes advantage of human color perception being of lower resolution than human brightness perception. JPEG compression consists of the following steps: First, the pixels are

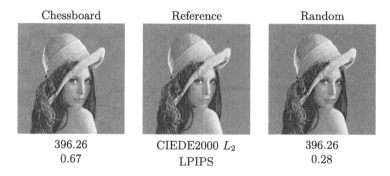

Chessboard   Reference   Random

396.26   CIEDE2000 L_2 396.26
0.67   LPIPS   0.28

Fig. 2. The reference image's unicoloured background was perturbed with some noise, by adding or subtracting 3 from each RGB channel value. The arrangement of subtracting/adding varies between both patches.

transformed from RGB to YC_bC_r color space. Second, usually the color channels are subsampled. Third, the three channels are each divided into blocks of size 8×8 pixels which are then replaced by their 64 discrete cosine transform (DCT) [1] coefficients. The main part of the lossy data reduction follows in step four, where the coefficients are divided by some quantization thresholds, which depend on the JPEG quality, and then quantized.

There has been little research on attacks that perturb JPEG coefficients or try to bypass JPEG compression. Kang et al. used JPEG attacks as an example of an unforeseen threat model, but do not give much detail on their attack and do not analyze the attack's success for different parameters [15].

Shin & Song [33] proposed an attack that perturbs the images' RGB pixel representation, but includes an approximation of JPEG compression in the source model. The perturbation of their BIM variant is then given by

$$x'_t = x'_{t-1} + \alpha \cdot \text{sign}(\nabla_{x'_{t-1}} J(JPEG^{jq}_{\text{approx}}(x'_{t-1}), y)), \qquad (2)$$

where $JPEG^{jq}_{\text{approx}}(x)$ is an approximation of JPEG compression, where the rounding during the quantization step is replaced by a differentiable approximation. They also propose an ensemble attack that combines gradients using different JPEG qualities.

Shi et al. [32] proposed an attack that first applies an RGB attack (e.g. BIM) and then compresses the image using a fast adversarial rounding scheme[1] that performs JPEG compression but does not round every coefficient to the nearest integer, but the most important ones in the gradient's direction.

While both approaches can make the perturbation more robust towards JPEG compression, the perturbation is still applied in the RGB pixel representation though. As our attack perturbs straight on JPEG coefficients, it does not have to include an approximation of JPEG compression in the target model or

---

[1] For targeted attacks, they also propose an iterative rounding scheme. As we only consider untargeted attacks, we will only use the fast adversarial rounding.

make the perturbation robust against JPEG compression using a sophisticated rounding scheme. Thus, our approach is technically straightforward.

2.4   Adversarial Defenses

Goodfellow et al. introduced the concept of defending a neural network against adversarial attacks by adversarial training [8]. The simple idea is to use adversarial examples constructed on the network itself in addition to benign samples for training. In this work, we will use the adversarial training approach by Madry et al., that uses BIM images during training [22].

Since adversarial attacks rely on adding small perturbations to images, other defense methods try to alter or remove such perturbations. I.e. it has been shown, that JPEG compression can reverse the drop in classification accuracy for FGSM [8] attacks as long as the maximal perturbation ε is small enough [6]. It is also known, that training on images of different JPEG compression rates can be used as defense strategy [5,10], although these defenses are only regarded as weak defense strategies [28].

2.5   Adversarial Attacks and Defenses from a Frequency Perspective

By selectively adding noise to different frequencies, Tsuzuku and Sato showed that neural networks are sensitive to the directions of fourier basis functions [36]. Guo et al. and Sharma et al. both masked gradients for high DCT frequencies during RGB pixel perturbation [9,31] and argue that low-frequency perturbations can circumvent certain defenses. Both do not use perceptual distances to evaluate the attacks though, but RGB L_2 distances, or respectively, the input parameter ε, which does not reflect the structural difference of low- and high-frequency perturbations though. Yin et al. argue that adversarial training does increase the robustness on high DFT frequencies, but leads to vulnerability on low frequencies. They also find that neural networks can be successfully trained using high-frequency information that is barely visible to human [37].

Bernhard et al. [2] showed that networks that rely on low frequency information tend to achieve higher adversarial robustness. The intuition behind this is that humans mainly rely on low-frequency information as well. A classifier that uses low-frequency information instead of high frequency components that are barely visible for humans, should thus be more aligned to the human perception; a network relying on exactly the same information as humans, would contradict the existence of adversarial examples. Additionally, Bernhard et al. found that adversarial perturbations are inefficient when limited to high frequencies. Similarly, Maiya et al. [23] state that adversarial perturbations are not necessarily a high-frequency phenomenon, but their distribution across frequencies is dataset-dependent. For CIFAR10 [17], the undefended models are most sensitive on high frequencies, while for IMAGENET [30] they are more sensitive for lower frequencies. For the adversarially trained models the robustness across the whole spectrum increases and in case of CIFAR10 the sensitivity even reverses towards low frequencies.

However, none of these works [2,9,23,31,36,37] are JPEG-related, as they still perturb RGB pixels and perform the DCT/DFT on the whole image and not on 8×8 blocks. Another difference is that they mask some frequencies, while we just weight the perturbations differently.

3   Proposed Method

Let $x^{jq} = (Y, C_b, C_r)$ be a quantized JPEG image of quality jq. For an image of shape $h \times w$, the luma channel Y has shape $(h/8, w/8, 64)$, and the chroma channels also have shape $(h/8, w/8, 64)$, as we do not use chroma subsampling in our attacks in order to focus on the distortion created by the adversarial perturbation. To enable individual control over the perturbation made on each channel, we define three L_∞-balls that limit the relative perturbation made on each channel. For that, we define nine variables, three relative perturbation budgets $\varepsilon_Y^{\mathrm{rel}}, \varepsilon_{C_b}^{\mathrm{rel}}, \varepsilon_{C_r}^{\mathrm{rel}} \in \mathcal{R}_{\geq 0}$, relative step sizes $\alpha_Y^{\mathrm{rel}}, \alpha_{C_b}^{\mathrm{rel}}, \alpha_{C_r}^{\mathrm{rel}} \in \mathcal{R}_{\geq 0}$ and three weighting vectors $\lambda_Y, \lambda_{C_b}, \lambda_{C_r} \in [0,1]^{64}$, where the ε values control the amount of perturbation made on each channel and the λ values determine how much perturbation is permitted for every DCT frequency component. From these relative budgets and the masking vectors, we then compute absolute limits $\varepsilon_Y^{\mathrm{abs}}, \varepsilon_{C_b}^{\mathrm{abs}}, \varepsilon_{C_r}^{\mathrm{abs}} \in \mathcal{R}_{\geq 0}^{(h/8) \times (w/8) \times 64}$ by

$$\varepsilon_Y^{\mathrm{abs}} = \varepsilon_Y^{\mathrm{rel}} \cdot \lambda_Y \cdot |Y|, \quad \varepsilon_{C_b}^{\mathrm{abs}} = \varepsilon_{C_b}^{\mathrm{rel}} \cdot \lambda_{C_b} \cdot |C_b|, \quad \varepsilon_{C_r}^{\mathrm{abs}} = \varepsilon_{C_r}^{\mathrm{rel}} \cdot \lambda_{C_r} \cdot |C_r|. \tag{3}$$

The absolute step sizes $\alpha_Y^{\mathrm{abs}}, \alpha_{C_b}^{\mathrm{abs}}, \alpha_{C_r}^{\mathrm{abs}} \in \mathcal{R}_{\geq 0}^{(h/8) \times (w/8) \times 64}$ are computed correspondingly. For BIM, a single perturbation step is defined by

$$Y_t' = Y_{t-1}' + \mathrm{sign}(\nabla_{Y_{t-1}'}(J(\mathrm{rgb}(x_t'), y))) \cdot \alpha_Y^{\mathrm{abs}}$$
$$C_{bt}' = C_{bt-1}' + \mathrm{sign}(\nabla_{C_{bt-1}'}(J(\mathrm{rgb}(x_t'), y))) \cdot \alpha_{C_b}^{\mathrm{abs}}$$
$$C_{rt}' = C_{rt-1}' + \mathrm{sign}(\nabla_{C_{rt-1}'}(J(\mathrm{rgb}(x_t'), y))) \cdot \alpha_{C_r}^{\mathrm{abs}}, \tag{4}$$

where $\mathrm{rgb}(x)$ denotes the transformation from JPEG to unquantized RGB data for JPEG image x. The JPEG to RGB conversion is implemented in a differentiable way using standard convolutional layers with fixed weights. After each update step, the coefficients are clipped to be within each L_∞-ball. After T iterations, the coefficients are rounded to the nearest integer.

4   Experiments and Results

We assume a black-box setting in which a ResNet [11] is used as a source model, and several, partially defended, DenseNets [12] are used as transfer models. Densenet^{jqQ} denotes a normally trained DenseNet, where the input is JPEG compressed with quality Q at inference time. Densenet$_M^{RGB}$ denotes a net that is adversarially trained with Madry et al.'s method [22] that uses RGB BIM to create adversarial images during training. In our experiments, we use all 10000 test images for CIFAR10 and a 10000 image subset of the validation dataset for IMAGENET. We incrementally increase the perturbation bound ε or, respectively, $\varepsilon_Y^{rel}, \varepsilon_{C_b}^{rel}, \varepsilon_{C_r}^{rel},$ [2] measure the success rates and perceptual distances for each attack and then, plot the success rate in dependence of the perceptual distance, which we call the efficiency of an attack.[3]

4.1 Varying Luma and Chroma Perturbations

In our first experiment, we compare the success of our JPEG attacks across color channels. Figure 3 illustrates the attack efficiency on each channel. ε_{all} implies that the same $\varepsilon_Y^{rel} = \varepsilon_{C_b}^{rel} = \varepsilon_{C_r}^{rel}$ is used for all three channels. The other attacks are performed on just one channel each, while the other ε's are set to 0.

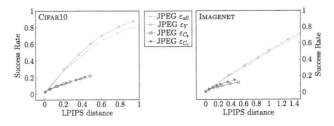

Fig. 3. LPIPS efficiency for unmasked ($\lambda_{all} = 1$) BIM on a Densenet^{jq50}.

The results confirm Pestana et al. [25], in that adversarial perturbations are much more efficient in the luma than in the chroma channels for both datasets. This is in accordance to neural networks being known to primarily classify based on the image's shapes and textures [7,25]. As luma attacks perform best, our JPEG attacks will only perturb the luma channel in the following.

4.2 Varying Perturbations Across Frequencies

Up to now, we applied the same relative perturbation bounds to all JPEG coefficients of one channel although their impact may be very different. One could assume that high frequency perturbations are perceived as noise and are thus less visible than low frequency perturbations. This is in accordance to the behaviour of JPEG compression, which preferably removes high frequency components. On the other hand, low frequency components are perceived as less prominent when high frequency components are visible at the same time, which is the basis of e.g. hybrid image optical illusions [24]. We test this in a second experiment by applying different weighting vectors λ_Y that are illustrated in Fig. 4. The

---

[2] The step sizes are chosen as $\alpha = \frac{\varepsilon}{T}$ for RGB and correspondingly for JPEG attacks. We always use $T = 10$ iterations in our experiments.

[3] For comparison, attacking images with RGB FGSM/BIM and $\varepsilon = 8$ results in an average CIEDE2000 L_2 distance of 203.61/107.17 and a LPIPS distance of 0.85/0.37.

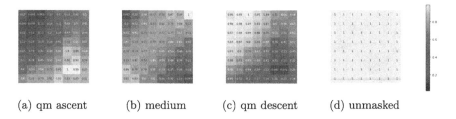

(a) qm ascent   (b) medium   (c) qm descent   (d) unmasked

Fig. 4. DCT weighting vectors (λ). Frequencies increase from top-left to bottom-right.eps

qm descent/ascent weighting vectors are based on the luma quantization matrix for JPEG quality 50, the medium vector was determined by applying absolute perturbations using the qm descent vector and then extracting the resulting relative perturbations. Figure 5 summarizes the results of the experiment for both datasets. For CIFAR10, we observe that the ascent weighting vector that concentrates perturbations on high frequencies is the most efficient on the undefended DenseNet, closely followed by the medium masking vector. When Densenet^{jq50} is considered, the ascent vector becomes least successful because the perturbation made on high frequencies is removed during JPEG compression. The JPEG quality used for computing the qm descent/ascent weighting vectors does only slightly influence the resulting weighting vectors and thus, the attack's efficiency. I.e., weighting vectors that use JPEG qualities that are different from the one used in defense (50 in this case) do not yield a significant reduction in efficiency. On the adversarially trained net, the order is reversed compared to the undefended net. As already stated by Yin et al. [37], adversarial training does lead to more robustness on high frequencies but vulnerability on low ones, at least for CIFAR10.

For IMAGENET, the difference between the efficiency of low-frequency and high-frequency perturbations is smaller which indicates that the undefended net is indeed more sensitive towards low-frequency perturbations than nets trained on CIFAR10 as already found by Maiya et al. [23], but the medium vector shows even more success. Again, we observe that using JPEG compression in defense decreases the success of high-frequency perturbations as the ascent vector's efficiency is decreased, while the efficiency of medium and low frequency perturbation is less affected by JPEG compression. While a lower JPEG quality could reduce their efficiency too, the relative results should remain the same. Here, we can not observe any outstanding vulnerabilities resulting from the adversarial training as all vectors are similarly successful.

Contrary to the general assumption that adversarial perturbations are mainly a high-frequency phenomenon, the experiments show that medium frequency perturbations are the most efficient (IMAGENET), or at least approximately on par with the best other perturbations (CIFAR10). Note that these observation should apply for perturbations in the medium frequencies in general and we do not state that our selection of the medium vector is optimal. The results also

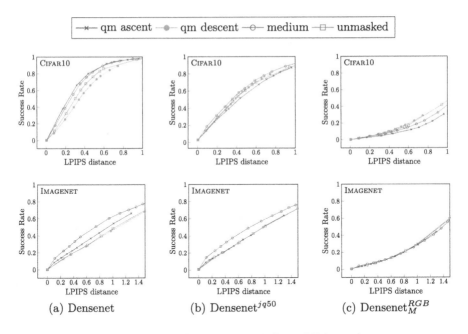

Fig. 5. LPIPS efficiency of JPEG luma BIM attacks.

correspond to findings in steganography and watermarking [4,14,16,27], where information is preferably added in medium frequency components since these have less contribution towards energy and perceived image details. Following these results, we will use the medium weighting vector in the following experiments for comparison with state-of-the-art attacks.

4.3 Comparison of Adversarial Attacks on JPEG Coefficients to YC_bC_r and RGB Pixel Representations

In this section, we will analyze whether our attacks straight on JPEG coefficients are advantageous over attacks on pixel representations, such as the usual RGB attacks. However, to determine whether the advantages of JPEG attacks are due to using the YC_bC_r color model or using DCT coefficients, our experiments also include pure YC_bC_r pixel attacks, where we only perturb the luma channel but perform absolute perturbations on pixel values similar to standard RGB attacks.

The results (Fig. 6) show, that our JPEG attack is more successful than the YC_bC_r and RGB attack on both CIFAR10 and IMAGENET, especially on the net defended with JPEG compression. There are two main reasons for the superiority of the JPEG approach: First, as shown in Sect. 4.1 and already stated by Pestana et al. [25], adversarial attacks are much more effective when only luma information is perturbed, as the shape and textures that neural networks rely on for classification are mainly located here. Attacking RGB pixels always implies that color information is also changed, resulting in more perceptual difference than needed and thus, less efficiency. Second, perturbing JPEG coefficients allows to control how perturbations are distributed across frequencies and fixing 0-coefficients (as being done implicitly by our approach) avoids perturbing high-frequency information that would be removed during the JPEG compression in defense anyway. This proofs that the advantage of attacking on JPEG coefficients is not exclusively reasoned by the use of the YC_bC_r color model, but also because of the DCT representation.

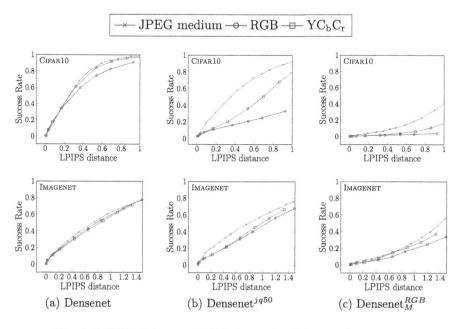

Fig. 6. LPIPS efficiency of JPEG (jq 100), RGB and YC_bC_r BIM.

The $Densenet_M^{RGB}$s are basically robust against the RGB attack, while they still are vulnerable towards our JPEG attack. This alone is not surprising as this RGB attack is what is used during the adversarial training and adversarially trained nets are known to be vulnerable towards unseen threat models [15,19], but the difference between the JPEG and the YC_bC_r attack is worth mentioning as both are attacking on luma exclusively. For CIFAR10, we also adversarially trained a net with JPEG ε_{all} and ε_Y attacks using our four frequency vectors with probability ratios medium:ascent:descent:unmasked 8:5:4:1. The ε_{all}-attacks are weighted twice as much as the ε_Y-attacks. The JPEG adversarial training leads to high overall robustness regarding not only JPEG but also YC_bC_r and RGB attacks: the success rates for $\sim$ 0.9 LPIPS distance are 8.60% (JPEG medium), 2.14% (YC_bC_r) and 6.01% (RGB), compared to 32.53%, 10.72% and 3.97% for an RGB defense. However, the clean accuracy drops from 82.09% ($Densenet_M^{RGB}$) to 74.74%, as expected, since "robustness may be at odds with accuracy" [35]. The adversarial training using JPEG attacks leads to the net

Airplane Automobile   Cat   Deer   Dog   Horse   Ship

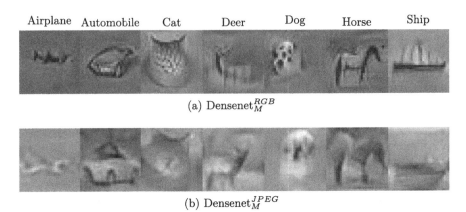

(a) Densenet$_M^{RGB}$

(b) Densenet$_M^{JPEG}$

Fig. 7. Starting from unicolored images (R=G=B=128), each model's loss was minimized in 100 steps of gradient descent for some of CIFAR10's classes.

relying on low-frequency information even more than the Densenet$_M^{RGB}$, as Fig. 7 illustrates. The reliance on the general composition of images and abstract, coarse structures rather than superficial high-frequency information results in better robustness against small perturbations and better generalization.

As the examples in Fig. 1 show, RGB and YC$_b$C$_r$ pixel attacks often result in clearly visible colour or high-frequency noise, while the perturbations from the JPEG medium attack are generally less visible. One problem of our JPEG attacks is that some 8 × 8 JPEG blocks are clearly visible when there are too strong perturbations on low frequencies.

4.4   Comparison with JPEG-Resistant Attacks

One of our main motivations for proposing attacks straight on JPEG coefficients was bypassing JPEG compression in defense, or when saving the adversarial images. Thus, we compare our approach to Shin & Song's [33] and Shi et al.'s [32] attacks, for three JPEG qualities used in attack. The experiment is conducted for both CIFAR10 and IMAGENET (Fig. 8). As Shin & Song return uncompressed images, we compress them to the same JPEG qualities for comparison.

On both datasets, we observe that our attack is superior compared to Shi et al.'s approach for all three JPEG qualities. Although the fast adversarial rounding in their attack makes the perturbations more robust towards JPEG compression for a given ε, it also induces a significant perceptual distortion even if $\varepsilon = 0$. Additionally, their attack still perturbs mainly on RGB pixels which results in color perturbations that are partially removed during the chroma subsampling in the JPEG compression in defense anyway.

In comparison with Shin & Song's approach the results are less clear. As it always shows better performance, we only include the ensemble attack from Shin

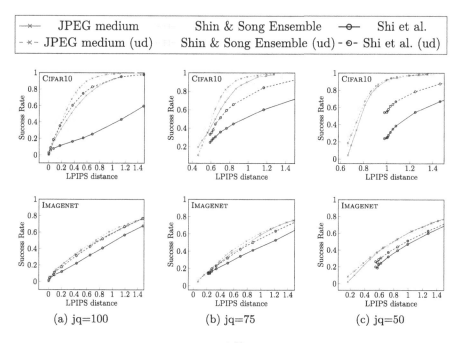

Fig. 8. LPIPS efficiency on the Densenet^{jq50} and the undefended (ud) DenseNet for BIM attacks, for different JPEG qualities used in attack.

& Song [33] in our experiments.[4] For very small perturbations, the attacks from Shin & Song show more efficiency, while for larger perturbations our attack is often more efficient, especially on IMAGENET. Moreover, the ensemble attack's efficiency is significantly worse than ours when the target model is undefended. We explain this by the chroma subsampling that is used in the attack but not in the undefended net. Thus, the attack could induce color perturbations that are ideal to fool nets that use chroma subsampling in defense. In a black-box setting though, it would be unknown whether and how the target model is defended. Therefore, generalizing for a number of target models is an important measure of an attack's success in the black-box setting. In total, our JPEG attack though seems to generalize very well, as it performs well on both undefended and defended nets, and efficiency barely differs between the attack qualities used in attack. Another advantage is our attack's smaller computation time: On a NVIDIA P6000, attacking the whole CIFAR10 test dataset with 10 iterations took only 72*s* compared to 218*s* for Shin & Song's ensemble attack.

As the sample images in Fig. 9 show, both Shin & Song's and Shi et al.'s attacks show significant perturbations (colour noise, high-frequency noise and/or block artifacts), while the medium frequency attack shows less perceptual distortions and a smaller LPIPS distance.

---

[4] For Shin & Song's ensemble attack, jpeg qualities 90, 75 and 50 were used for all three subfigures.

Original	Shi et al.	Shin & Song	ε_Y descent	ε_Y ascent	ε_Y medium

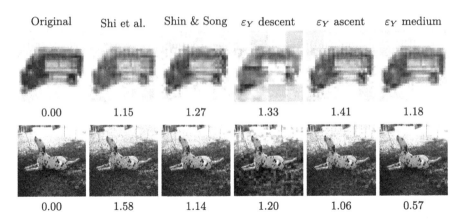

0.00	1.15	1.27	1.33	1.41	1.18
0.00	1.58	1.14	1.20	1.06	0.57

Fig. 9. Adversarial examples with minimum perturbation to force a misclassification on a Densenet^{jq50} for CIFAR10 (top) and IMAGENET. Images are created on a ResNet. The LPIPS distance is given below each image.

5   Conclusion

We introduced a JPEG version of the BASIC ITERATIVE METHOD that allows individual control over the allowed perturbation on each channel and frequency. We found that applying perturbations straight on JPEG coefficients has several advantages that lead to superiority over perturbing straight on RGB or YC_bC_r pixels:

First, JPEG uses the YC_bC_r color model which is well-suited for adversarial attacks as it separates chroma and luma information which is often more important for neural networks and thus more efficient to perturb than color channels.

Second, the ability to control the perturbation applied on each frequency allowed us to find that adversarial perturbations on medium frequencies are often more efficient than when they are concentrated on the highest frequencies, especially when JPEG compression is used in defense.

Third, perturbing straight on JPEG coefficients and fixing 0-coefficients allows to apply only perturbations that are not removed during JPEG compression such that it can often bypass JPEG compression more efficiently than state-of-the-art attacks.

Fourth, our approach is much simpler than other methods which try to bypass JPEG compression [32,33], but still generally outperforms them regarding success rate.

Finally, we observed that RGB adversarial training can indeed lead to vulnerability on low frequencies, while adversarial training using multiple, weighted JPEG attacks results in strong overall robustness – not only against JPEG attacks, but also against RGB and YC_bC_r pixel attacks.

Thus, adversarial perturbations straight on JPEG coefficients leads to more successful attacks and can be used for a generally robust defence strategy.

References

1. Ahmed, N., Natarajan, T., Rao, K.: Discrete cosine transform. IEEE Trans. Comput. C-23(1), 90–93 (1974). https://doi.org/10.1109/T-C.1974.223784
2. Bernhard, R., et al.: Impact of spatial frequency based constraints on adversarial robustness. In: International Joint Conference on Neural Networks, IJCNN (2021). https://doi.org/10.1109/IJCNN52387.2021.9534307
3. Carlini, N., Wagner, D.: Towards evaluating the robustness of neural networks. In: 2017 IEEE Symposium on Security and Privacy (SP). IEEE (2017). https://doi.org/10.1109/SP.2017.49
4. Chang, C.C., Lin, C.C., Tseng, C.S., Tai, W.L.: Reversible hiding in DCT-based compressed images. Inf. Sci. **177**(13), 2768–2786 (2007). https://www.sciencedirect.com/science/article/pii/S0020025507001016
5. Das, N., et al.: Keeping the bad guys out: Protecting and vaccinating deep learning with JPEG compression. CoRR (2017). http://arxiv.org/abs/1705.02900
6. Dziugaite, G.K., Ghahramani, Z., Roy, D.M.: A study of the effect of JPG compression on adversarial images. CoRR (2016). http://arxiv.org/abs/1608.00853
7. Geirhos, R., Rubisch, P., Michaelis, C., Bethge, M., Wichmann, F.A., Brendel, W.: ImageNet-trained CNNs are biased towards texture; increasing shape bias improves accuracy and robustness. In: International Conference on Learning Representations, ICLR (2019). https://openreview.net/forum?id=Bygh9j09KX
8. Goodfellow, I.J., Shlens, J., Szegedy, C.: Explaining and harnessing adversarial examples. In: International Conference on Learning Representations, ICLR (2015)
9. Guo, C., Frank, J.S., Weinberger, K.Q.: Low frequency adversarial perturbation. In: Uncertainty in Artificial Intelligence Conference. PMLR 115 (2020). https://proceedings.mlr.press/v115/guo20a.html
10. Guo, C., Rana, M., Cissé, M., van der Maaten, L.: Countering adversarial images using input transformations. In: International Conference on Learning Representations, ICLR (2018). https://openreview.net/forum?id=SyJ7ClWCb
11. He, K., Zhang, X., Ren, S., Sun, J.: Deep residual learning for image recognition. In: IEEE Conference on Computer Vision and Pattern Recognition, CVPR (2016). https://doi.org/10.1109/CVPR.2016.90
12. Huang, G., Liu, Z., van der Maaten, L., Weinberger, K.Q.: Densely connected convolutional networks. In: IEEE Conference on Computer Vision and Pattern Recognition, CVPR (2017). https://doi.org/10.1109/CVPR.2017.243
13. Jordan, M., Manoj, N., Goel, S., Dimakis, A.G.: Quantifying perceptual distortion of adversarial examples. CoRR (2019). https://arxiv.org/abs/1902.08265
14. Kahlessenane, F., Khaldi, A., Kafi, R., Euschi, S.: A robust blind medical image watermarking approach for telemedicine applications. Clust. Comput. **24**(3), 2069–2082 (2021)
15. Kang, D., Sun, Y., Hendrycks, D., Brown, T., Steinhardt, J.: Testing robustness against unforeseen adversaries. CoRR **abs/1908.08016** (2019). http://arxiv.org/abs/1908.08016
16. Khan, S., et al.: On hiding secret information in medium frequency DCT components using least significant bits steganography. CMES-Comput. Model. Eng. Sci. **118**(3) (2019)
17. Krizhevsky, A.: Learning multiple layers of features from tiny images. University of Toronto (2012). https://www.cs.toronto.edu/~kriz/cifar.html
18. Kurakin, A., Goodfellow, I.J., Bengio, S.: Adversarial examples in the physical world. In: International Conference on Learning Representations, ICLR (2017). https://openreview.net/forum?id=HJGU3Rodl

19. Laidlaw, C., Singla, S., Feizi, S.: Perceptual adversarial robustness: defense against unseen threat models. In: International Conference on Learning Representations, ICLR (2021). https://openreview.net/forum?id=dFwBosAcJkN

20. Luo, M.R., Cui, G., Rigg, B.: The development of the CIE 2000 colour-difference formula: CIEDE2000. Color Res. Appl. **26**(5), 340–350 (2001). https://doi.org/10.1002/col.1049

21. MacDonald, L.: Using color effectively in computer graphics. IEEE Comput. Graph. Appl. **19**(4), 20–35 (1999). https://doi.org/10.1109/38.773961

22. Madry, A., Makelov, A., Schmidt, L., Tsipras, D., Vladu, A.: Towards deep learning models resistant to adversarial attacks. In: International Conference on Learning Representations, ICLR (2018). https://openreview.net/forum?id=rJzIBfZAb

23. Maiya, S.R., Ehrlich, M., Agarwal, V., Lim, S., Goldstein, T., Shrivastava, A.: A frequency perspective of adversarial robustness. CoRR (2021). https://arxiv.org/abs/2111.00861

24. Oliva, A., Torralba, A., Schyns, P.G.: Hybrid images. ACM Trans. Graph. **25**(3), 527–532 (2006). https://doi.org/10.1145/1141911.1141919

25. Pestana, C., Akhtar, N., Liu, W., Glance, D., Mian, A.: Adversarial attacks and defense on deep learning classification models using YCbCr color images. In: International Joint Conference on Neural Networks, IJCNN (2021). https://doi.org/10.1109/IJCNN52387.2021.9533495

26. Plataniotis, K., Venetsanopoulos, A.N.: Color Image Processing and Applications. Springer, Heidelberg (2000). https://doi.org/10.1007/978-3-662-04186-4

27. Pradhan, C., Saxena, V., Bisoi, A.K.: Non blind digital watermarking technique using DCT and cross chaos map. In: International Conference on Communications, Devices and Intelligent Systems, CODIS (2012). https://doi.org/10.1109/CODIS.2012.6422191

28. Raff, E., Sylvester, J., Forsyth, S., McLean, M.: Barrage of random transforms for adversarially robust defense. In: IEEE/CVF Conference on Computer Vision and Pattern Recognition, CVPR (2019)

29. Ren, K., Zheng, T., Qin, Z., Liu, X.: Adversarial attacks and defenses in deep learning. Engineering **6**(3), 346–360 (2020). https://doi.org/10.1016/j.eng.2019.12.012

30. Russakovsky, O., et al.: ImageNet large scale visual recognition challenge. Int. J. Comput. Vis. **115**, 211–252 (2014). https://www.image-net.org/

31. Sharma, Y., Ding, G.W., Brubaker, M.A.: On the effectiveness of low frequency perturbations. In: International Joint Conference on Artificial Intelligence, IJCAI (2019)

32. Shi, M., Li, S., Yin, Z., Zhang, X., Qian, Z.: On generating JPEG adversarial images. In: IEEE International Conference on Multimedia and Expo, ICME (2021). https://doi.org/10.1109/ICME51207.2021.9428243

33. Shin, R., Song, D.: JPEG-resistant adversarial images. In: NIPS 2017 Workshop on Machine Learning and Computer Security, NeuRIPS (2017)

34. Szegedy, C., et al.: Intriguing properties of neural networks. In: International Conference on Learning Representations, ICLR (2014)

35. Tsipras, D., Santurkar, S., Engstrom, L., Turner, A., Madry, A.: Robustness may be at odds with accuracy. In: International Conference on Learning Representations, ICLR (2019). https://openreview.net/forum?id=SyxAb30cY7

36. Tsuzuku, Y., Sato, I.: On the structural sensitivity of deep convolutional networks to the directions of Fourier basis functions. In: IEEE/CVF Conference on Computer Vision and Pattern Recognition, CVPR (2019)

37. Yin, D., Gontijo Lopes, R., Shlens, J., Cubuk, E.D., Gilmer, J.: A Fourier perspective on model robustness in computer vision. In: Advances in Neural Information Processing Systems, NeuRIPS (2019). https://proceedings.neurips.cc/paper_files/paper/2019/file/b05b57f6add810d3b7490866d74c0053-Paper.pdf
38. Zhang, R., Isola, P., Efros, A.A., Shechtman, E., Wang, O.: The unreasonable effectiveness of deep features as a perceptual metric. In: IEEE Conference on Computer Vision and Pattern Recognition, CVPR (2018)
39. Zhao, Z., Liu, Z., Larson, M.: Towards large yet imperceptible adversarial image perturbations with perceptual color distance. In: IEEE/CVF Conference on Computer Vision and Pattern Recognition, CVPR (2020)

Certified Robust Models with Slack Control and Large Lipschitz Constants

Max Losch[1]([⊠])[ID], David Stutz[1][ID], Bernt Schiele[1][ID], and Mario Fritz[2][ID]

[1] Max Planck Institute for Informatics, Saarland Informatics Campus,
Saarbrücken, Germany
`{mlosch,dstutz,schiele}@mpi-inf.com`
[2] CISPA Helmholtz Center for Information Security, Saarbrücken, Germany
`fritz@cispa.de`

Abstract. Despite recent success, state-of-the-art learning-based models remain highly vulnerable to input changes such as adversarial examples. In order to obtain certifiable robustness against such perturbations, recent work considers Lipschitz-based regularizers or constraints while at the same time increasing prediction margin. Unfortunately, this comes at the cost of significantly decreased accuracy. In this paper, we propose a Calibrated Lipschitz-Margin Loss (CLL) that addresses this issue and improves certified robustness by tackling two problems: Firstly, commonly used margin losses do not adjust the penalties to the shrinking output distribution; caused by minimizing the Lipschitz constant K. Secondly, and most importantly, we observe that minimization of K can lead to overly smooth decision functions. This limits the model's complexity and thus reduces accuracy. Our CLL addresses these issues by explicitly calibrating the loss w.r.t. margin and Lipschitz constant, thereby establishing full control over slack and improving robustness certificates even with larger Lipschitz constants. On CIFAR-10, CIFAR-100 and Tiny-ImageNet, our models consistently outperform losses that leave the constant unattended. On CIFAR-100 and Tiny-ImageNet, CLL improves upon state-of-the-art deterministic L_2 robust accuracies. In contrast to current trends, we unlock potential of much smaller models without $K = 1$ constraints.

Keywords: Certified robustness · Lipschitz · Large margin · Slack

1 Introduction

The Lipschitz constant K of a classifier specifies the maximal change in output for a given input perturbation. This simple relation enables building models that are certifiably robust to constrained perturbations in the input space, i.e., those with L_2-norm below ϵ. This is because the resulting output distance $K \cdot \epsilon$ can be calculated efficiently (i.e., in a closed form) without expensive test-time randomization, such as randomized smoothing [8], or network bound relaxations,

Supplementary Information The online version contains supplementary material available at https://doi.org/10.1007/978-3-031-54605-1_37.

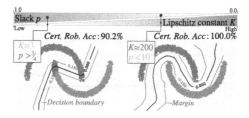

Fig. 1. Existing Lipschitz margin methods control the Lipschitz constant K to be low, yet we observe decision functions becoming overly smooth when K is too low (left) – impairing accuracy. Our CLL loss provides slack control, which we show is inversely proportional to K (see gradients on top). We can control K to be high, avoid the smoothing and achieve improved clean and robust accuracies (right). Incorrect or not robust samples marked red (Color figure online).

e.g. [14,50]. This way of obtaining certifiable robustness is also directly linked to large margin classifiers, as illustrated in Fig. 1, where a training sample free area of radius ϵ is created around the decision boundary. The earliest practical examples implementing Lipschitz margins for certified robustness include [16], which provided first guarantees on deep networks or LMT [38] and GloRo [25] that design Lipschitz margin losses.

A limitation with Lipschitz margin classifiers is their decreased performance, as has been shown on standard datasets like CIFAR-10 or TinyImageNet, both in terms of empirical robustness and clean accuracy. This is emphasized in particular when comparing to approaches such as adversarial training [5,28] and its variants [6,45,49]. Thus, recent work proposed specialized architectures [1,2,7,27,29,30,32,37,42,46,47] to enforce specific Lipschitz constraints, adjusted losses [25,30,32,38,47,48] or tighter upper Lipschitz bounds [10,18,24] to address these shortcomings. Despite existing efforts, clean and robust accuracy still lags behind state-of-the-art empirical results.

We relate this shortcoming to two interlinked properties of used losses: Firstly, logistic based margin losses, including GloRo [25], SOC [32] and CPL [29] do not adjust their output penalties to the output scaling caused by minimization of K. In practice, this results in samples remaining in under-saturated regions of the loss and effectively within margins. And secondly, we identify that controlling the Lipschitz constant K to be too low, may result in overly smooth decision functions – impairing clean and robust accuracy. The result is exemplarily illustrated in Fig. 2b (middle) for GloRo on the two moons dataset. The induced overly smooth decision surface eventually leads to reduced clean and robust accuracy.

Contributions: In this work, we propose Calibrated Lipschitz-Margin Loss (CLL), a loss with improved control over slack and Lipschitz constant K to instrument models with a margin of width 2ϵ. Key to our loss is integrating the scale of the logistic loss with K, allowing calibration to the margin. This calibration endows CLL with explicit control over slack and K, which can improve certified robust accuracy. As a result, the classifier avoids learning an overly smooth decision boundary while obtaining optimal margin, as illustrated for two moons in Fig. 2c. On CIFAR-10, CIFAR-100 and Tiny-ImageNet, our method allows greater Lipschitz constants while at the same time having tighter bounds and yielding competitive certified robust accuracies (CRA). I.e. applying CLL to existing training frameworks consistently improves CRA by multiple percentage points while maintaining or improving clean accuracy.

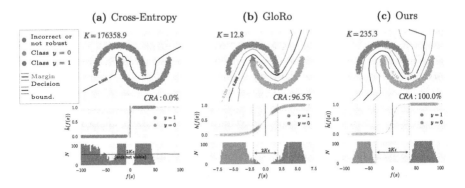

Fig. 2. We illustrate how our loss *calibrates* the logistic function of the loss w.r.t. the margin, leading to improved clean and certified robust accuracy (CRA). (a) Cross-Entropy does not guarantee margins, the Lipschitz constant K is large. (b) Uncalibrated margin losses such as GloRo may produce violated margins (gray) and decision boundaries (black) on the two-moons dataset. (c) In contrast, our calibrated loss is better visually and quantitatively for robust and accurate samples. The middle row plots their output probabilities (Color figure online).

2   Related Work

Lipschitz Classifiers for Robustness. For completeness, we note that many methods exist for certified robustness. For an extensive overview we refer the reader to a recent published summary [26]. Since their discovery in [36], many methods for certified robustness have been published [26]. Among others, Lipschitz regularization was considered as a potential way to improve robustness against adversarial examples. While such regularizers could only improve empirical robustness [7,17,20], local Lipschitz bounds where used to obtain certified robustness in [16] at the expense of additional calculations at inference. The use of global Lipschitz bounds has a key advantage over most other methods: certification at inference is deterministic and cheap to compute. Alas, it was originally considered intractable due to very loose bounds [16,41]. More recently, however, a number of methods allow robustness certification based on global Lipschitz bounds, including [1,2,18,24,25,27,29,30,32,37,38,42,47,48]. These improvements can fundamentally be attributed to two independent developments: (i) preventing gradient norm attenuation by specialized non-linearities to preserve classifier complexity [1,27] and (ii) architectural constraints that guarantee a Lipschitz constant of 1 [2,27,29,30,32,37,42,46]. Additional work investigated the use of tighter bound estimation [10,13,18,21,27,41]. Nevertheless, training deep Lipschitz networks with appropriate expressive power remains an open problem [19,31]. We approach this issue using a novel loss that provides more control over the Lipschitz constant which bounds expressiveness [4].

Large Margin for Deep Learning. Large margin methods have a long standing history in machine learning to improve generalization of learning algorithms, e.g., see [9,39,40]. While margin optimization is actively researched in the context of deep learning, as well [3,12,15,33–35], state-of-the-art deep networks usually focus on improving accuracy and remain vulnerable to adversarial examples [5,28]. This indicates that the obtained margins are generally not sufficient for adversarial robustness. Moreover, the proposed margin losses often require expensive pairwise sample comparison [35], normalization of the spectral norm of weights [3] or linearization of the loss [11,12,43]. Adversarial training can also be viewed as large margin training [11], but does not provide certified robustness. This is the focus of our work.

3   Calibrated Lipschitz-Margin Loss (CLL)

We propose a new margin loss called CLL that calibrates the loss to the width of the margin – a property not explicitly accounted for in existing large margin Lipschitz methods. Specifically, we calibrate the logistic functions at the output (sigmoid and softmax), by integrating the Lipschitz constant K into the definition of the logistic scale parameter. This new formulation reveals two properties important for margin training: (i) the scale parameter controls slackness and (ii) slackness influences classifier smoothness. This slack control allows to trade-off certified robust and clean accuracy. But more importantly, we find that this slackness determines K of the whole model. This is illustrated on the two moons dataset in Fig. 1 (left) with high slack implying small K and right with low slack implying large K. Given this improved control, we train models with large constants that produce new state-of-the-art robust accuracy scores.

3.1   Background

Let $(x, y) \in \mathcal{D}_\mathcal{X}$ be a sample-label pair in a dataset in space $\mathcal{X}$, f be a classifier $f : \mathcal{X} \to \mathcal{S}$ where $\mathcal{S} \subseteq \mathbb{R}^N$ is the logit space with N logits and h be a non-linearity like the logistic function or softmax mapping, e.g. $h : \mathcal{S} \to \mathbb{R}^N$.

Lipschitz Continuity. The Lipschitz continuity states that for every function f with bounded first derivative, there exists a Lipschitz constant K that relates the distance between any two points x_1, x_2 in input space $\mathcal{X}$ to a distance in output space. That is, for any input sample distance $\|x_1 - x_2\|_p$, the resulting output distance $\|f(x_1) - f(x_2)\|_p$ is at most $K \cdot \|x_1 - x_2\|_p$. Consequently, this inequality enables the construction of losses that measure distances in input space: e.g.

the margin width – and importantly: quick input certification. E.g. assume a classifier with two logits f_1, f_2. An input x is certified robust w.r.t. radius ϵ when the Lipschitz bounded distance ϵK is less than the distance between the two logits: $\epsilon K < |f_1(x) - f_2(x)|$. Note that K is not required to be small to allow certification. The inequality also holds when K is large, as long as the distance between logits is greater, as we will see in our experiments in Sect. 4. The exact Lipschitz constant, though, is non-trivial to estimate for highly non-linear functions such as deep networks [41]. Fortunately, it is tractable to calculate an upper bound. For this, it is sufficient to be able to decompose the classifier f, e.g., a (convolutional) neural network, into its L individual layers, i.e. $f = g^{(L)} \circ g^{(L-1)} \circ \cdots \circ g^{(1)}$. Then K is upper bounded by the product of norms [36],

$$K \leq \prod_{l=1}^{L} \|g^{(l)}\|_p =: \hat{K}. \tag{1}$$

In general, this bound is extremely loose without any form of Lipschitz regularization [41], yet recent work has shown substantially improved tightness, rendering uses in losses tractable (e.g. [2, 18, 25, 29, 30, 32, 42]).

Lipschitz Margin Losses. To produce certified robust models, we strive to train models with large margins. This can be achieved by adapting the training objective and specifying a minimal distance ϵ between any training sample and the decision boundary. A typical example is the hinge loss formulation in SVMs [9]:

$$\min_f \mathbb{E}_{(x,y) \sim \mathcal{D}_{\mathcal{X}}} \left[h\left(\epsilon - y f(x)\right) + \lambda \|f\|^2 \right], \tag{2}$$

where $\epsilon = 1$ and $h(\cdot) = \max\{\cdot, 0\}$. $\|f\|$ denotes a generic measure of classifier complexity, which in the linear SVM case is the norm of the weight matrix. This formulation can be generalized to Lipschitz classifiers, e.g., by minimizing $\|f\| = K$ or by multiplying ϵ with its Lipschitz factor ϵK. The latter being used in the GloRo loss [25]. All variants of formulation (2) require strict minimization of K to produce margins. We find these types of losses can be improved when h belongs to the logistic family – as sigmoid and softmax are. Since logistic functions assume a fixed output distribution, we observe that minimizing K can leave samples too close to the decision boundary We present exemplary evidence in Fig. 2b in which red samples remain within the margins. This is specifically true for GloRo, but also for methods that hard constrain K (e.g. [29, 32, 46]). In the following, we address these issues with CLL.

3.2 Binary CLL

We base our construction of CLL on the general margin formulation in Eq. (2). Key is calibrating the output non-linearity h to the margin. In the binary case, it is common practice in deep learning to set h in Eq. (2) to a logistic function $h(x) = [1 + \exp\{-x/\sigma\}]^{-1}$ with fixed $\sigma = 1$ and minimize the binary cross-entropy loss. Yet the underlying logistic distribution assumes a fixed distribution width $\sigma = 1$, which can be detrimental for training Lipschitz classifiers. To demonstrate the limitation of this assumption, we look at Fig. 2 illustrating margin training on the two-moons dataset. Figure 2a illustrates vanilla cross-entropy and no Lipschitz regularization. The decision boundary attains an irregular shape without margin. The Lipschitz constant is very high, the output values attain high probabilities since they are pushed to the tails of the distribution (see $p = h(f(x))$ in middle row). In contrast, a Lipschitz margin loss (GloRo [25], Fig. 2b) produces a margin, yet non-robust samples (red) remain within margin boundaries. This is a consequence of minimizing K, which limits the spread of the distribution. Under this condition, the assumption $\sigma = 1$ is inefficient. Additionally, since σ of the logistic is fixed, the final probability p at the margin $\pm\epsilon$ can only be determined post-hoc, after the Lipschitz constant K finds a minimum. We can be more efficient about this process by calibrating the width to $K\epsilon$ at each training step and requiring p at $\pm\epsilon$ to be a specific value. The result is shown in Fig. 2c which produces the desired margin with no errors. Our proposed loss is defined as follows.

Definition 1 - Binary CLL. *Let* $y \in \{-1, 1\}$, *and* $\mathcal{L}$ *be the binary cross entropy loss* $\mathcal{L}(y, h(f(x))) = -\log h(f(x)) - (1 - y)\log(1 - h(f(x)))^1$. *We propose the* objective:

$$\min_f \mathbb{E}_{(x,y)\sim\mathcal{D}_\mathcal{X}} \left[\mathcal{L}(y, \hat{h}(f(x); y)) + \lambda K^2 \right] \tag{3}$$

$$\text{with } \hat{h}(f(x); y) = h\left(-\frac{y\epsilon}{\sigma_\epsilon(p)} + \frac{1}{\sigma_\epsilon(p)} \frac{f(x)}{K} \right) \tag{4}$$

$$\text{and } \sigma_\epsilon(p) = \frac{2\epsilon}{h^{-1}(1 - p) - h^{-1}(p)}, \tag{5}$$

where $\hat{h}$ is our *calibrated logistic* and h^{-1} is the inverse cdf: $h^{-1}(p) = \log(p/1-p)$. Our proposal follows from calibrating σ to 2ϵ. For its realization we only require 4 values to uniquely determine σ: (i) the two positions of the margin boundaries $\pm\epsilon$ and (ii) the two probabilities $p_{-\epsilon}, p_\epsilon$ that the logistic distribution should attain at these positions. We illustrate these 4 values in Fig. 3, which displays an already calibrated logistic function to $\epsilon = 0.15$ (vertical lines) and $p_{-\epsilon} = p = 10^{-3}$ and $p_\epsilon = 1 - p = 1 - 10^{-3}$. The theoretical derivation follows from the logistic distribution, which we discuss in the supplement sec. A. We denote the calibrated scale as $\sigma_\epsilon(p)$ as it depends on ϵ and a probability p (Eq. (5)). So far, this does not express the integration of the Lipschitz constant K. Recall that the input distance 2ϵ can be related to the corresponding output distance via K, i.e. $2K\epsilon$. We consequently acquire the Lipschitz calibrated version shown in Fig. 3: $f(x)/\sigma_\epsilon(p)K$. Next, we integrate hard margin offsets $\pm\epsilon$ as in formulation (2) to maximize the penalty on samples within the margin. To integrate, we add $\pm\epsilon K$, depending on the class sign: $[-yK\epsilon + f(x)]/[\sigma_\epsilon(p)K]$. This places the probability on the margin to the worst case value 0.5. Note that this does not invalidate

---

[1] Transformation to $y \in \{0, 1\}$ is omitted for readability.

our calibration: the offset is a tool to improve margin training and is removed during inference. CLL is easy to generalize to multinomial classification utilizing softmax. We show its implementation in the supplement, sec. A.

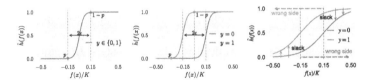

Fig. 3. Calibrated logistic function as key to our CLL loss by parameterizing the scale parameter σ to margin width 2ϵ. Left: without margin offset; middle: with margin offset ϵ; right: slack in CLL is governed by parameter p. That is to increase slack, we increase p which decreases loss for samples on the wrong margin side (indicated by arrows). (Color figure online)

3.3 Discussion

CLL is derived from joining the definition of σ with the Lipschitz inequality while adjusting for the margin distance 2ϵ. By utilizing the Lipschitz constant, this scale parameter can be calibrated to the margin width as if measured in input space. This is feasible because of the normalization by the Lipschitz constant $f(x)/K$ in Eq. (4). This normalization has two additional ramifications. First, it decouples the classifier constant from the loss. K can attain any value, while CLL ensures calibration. And secondly, the Lipschitz constant of the whole model $h(f(x))$ is solely dependent on $\sigma_\epsilon(p)$. That is $K^{(h \circ f)} = K^{(h)} = 1/\sigma_\epsilon(p)$. Below, we discuss the implications of CLL with respect to the tightness of Lipschitz bounds, the interpretation of σ as allowed slack and the classifier's complexity.

Tightness. Tightness dictates the utility of the used Lipschitz bound. To measure, we can estimate a naïve lower bound to K by finding the pair of training samples x_1, x_2 that maximizes the quotient $\|f(x_1) - f(x_2)\|/\|x_1 - x_2\|$. Since the input sample distances remain fixed, tightness can only be increased by increasing output distances *and* bounding K – conceptually bringing the two quantities closer together. Recall that typical losses assume a fixed output distribution $\sigma = 1$. The capacity to push values into the saturated area of the loss is thereby limited. Tightness is thereby mainly achieved by minimizing K because output distances cannot be increased significantly. CLL instead, does not minimize K but bounds it via normalization. Since our loss is calibrated to $K\epsilon$, we can achieve increased tightness by only maximizing output distances. With the difference of increasing output distances much farther than possible with other margin losses (an example is illustrated in Fig. 2 (compare x-axis of (b) and (c))). We find this to converge faster (see figure D1 in supplement) and achieve better robust accuracies than related work, as we present in Sect. 4. However, since increasing output distances has a growth influence on K, we find it necessary to put slight regularization pressure on K via factor λ, as stated on the RHS of Eq. (3).

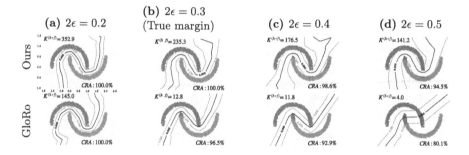

Fig. 4. Our CLL (top row) vs margin loss GloRo (bottom) on two-moons. **Red points** denote incorrect or non-robust samples. GloRos formulation leads to consistently smaller Lipschitz constant $K^{(h \circ f)}$ restricting the classifier complexity. Already for the true margin $2\epsilon = 0.3$ it fits inefficiently. For "too-large" margins, GloRo eventually degenerates to a failure case with a near linear decision boundary. In contrast, our CLL produces a 100% accurate and robust model for the true margin and retains sensible margins for increased ϵ. (Color figure online)

Slack. Since the logistic function has a smooth output transition from 0 to 1, values on the wrong margin side can be interpreted as slackness. We illustrate slack in Fig. 3 which shows a calibrated logistic as in Fig. 3 and indicates wrong margin sides for each class by dashed arrows. Consider class $y = 1$ in green. If a sample falls on the wrong margin side (anywhere along the green arrow at the top) the probability decreases and consequently the loss increases (i.e., negative log-likelihood $\lim_{p \to 0} - \log(p) = \infty$). The governing factor for slack in our loss is the probability p in $\sigma_\epsilon(p)$ of Eq. 4, indicated by the green vertical arrows, which implicitly defines the loss magnitude for samples on the wrong margin side. Note that without calibration, we find the logistic σ or temperature in softmax to have no slack effect. We provide empirical evidence in the supplement, sec. D.

Classifier Complexity. [4] derive complexity bounds for a 2-layered neural network (theorem 18). I.e., given 2 layers with weight norm B and 1 and non-linearity with Lipschitz constant L, the Gaussian complexity of the model is bounded by their product $K = B \cdot L \cdot 1$. This directly applies to hard-constrained $K{=}1$ models, but we find it applies to soft-constrained models as well. Effectively, this bound has implications for training Lipschitz classifiers: if K is too small, it restricts the models ability to fit the data. While theory provides only an upper bound, we find empirical evidence as support. That is, clean and certified robust accuracy can be improved when L of the loss is adjusted – and thus K. We find strongest evidence on two-moons (Fig. 4, bottom row), and consistent support on image data (Sect. 4). With decreasing K (top), the model becomes overly smooth, losing performance. CLL offers direct control over K, simply by adjusting slack. That is, K is inversely proportional to the slack p: $K^{(h \circ f)} = 1/\sigma_\epsilon(p)$. Consequently, for a fixed ϵ, slack bounds the complexity of the model. Models that can separate the data well require little slack, implying a larger $K^{(h \circ f)}$. The next section discusses this in more detail.

4   Evaluation

CLL offers increased control over slack and classifier complexity, discussed in Sect. 3.3. In this section, we present empirical evidence for these claims. We show that decreasing slack leads to models with less smooth decision boundaries, resulting in higher clean and certified robustness. To this end, we present results on the synthetic two-moons dataset by visualizing the produced margins and discuss the application on natural images: CIFAR-10, CIFAR-100 [22] and Tiny-ImageNet [23]. Implementation of our method involves computing the upper Lipschitz bound. We measure the width of the margin with the L_2 distance. Consequently, we implement Eq. (1) with the product of spectral norms [36] and calculate them by performing power iterations. Our training strategy follows the respective method we compare with. That is, we reuse published code (where available) but use our loss. To evaluate, we measure certified robust accuracies (CRA) for three margin widths (36/255, 72/255, 108/255) and Lipschitz bound tightness. CRA represents the average number of accurately classified samples that are also robust (fall outside the margin). The latter is the fraction between empirical lower bound and upper bound. All training and metric details are listed in the supplement, sec. B and C. Our code is made publicly available at github.com/mlosch/CLL.

4.1   Two-Moons Dataset

We start with an analysis on two-moons in order to visualize learned decision boundaries and investigate the connection to the Lipschitz constant. using *uniform* sampled noise of radius 0.1 around each sample. This results in a true-margin of exactly $2\epsilon = 0.3$. In Fig. 4, we exemplarily compare CLL with GloRo, training 7-layered networks for different target margin widths (columns). Individual plots display the decision boundary (black line) and the Lipschitz margin (gray lines). CRAs and Lipschitz constants $K^{(h \circ f)}$ are reported in the corners, non-robust or misclassified training samples are marked red. GloRo already loses CRA at the true margin 2ϵ and the decision boundary becomes very smooth with decreasing $K^{(h \circ f)}$. In contrast, CLL retains 100% CRA for the true margin and only slowly loses CRA beyond. The key is in the control over slack and hence $K^{(h \circ f)}$ – we set $p = 10^{-12}$ in Eq. 4. Our decision functions do not become overly smooth.

4.2   Image Datasets

We continue our discussion on CIFAR-10, CIFAR-100 and Tiny-ImageNet, evaluating multiple architectures: On CIFAR-10/100, we evaluate *6C2F* [24], *4C3F* [44], *LipConv* [32] and *XL* [2,29]. On Tiny-ImageNet, we consider *8C2F* [24], *LipConv*, XL and LBDN [42]. We report Tiny-ImageNet results in table 1 and CIFAR results in table 2, considering CRA for three different margin widths and clean accuracy. Hereby, all values produced with CLL are averages over 9 runs

Table 1. Results on Tiny-ImageNet on clean and certified robust accuracy (CRA) for six different methods using Lipschitz bounds $\overline{K}^{(h \circ f)}$. Applying CLL to existing methods consistently improves certified robust accuracy (CRA). Architectures evaluated: *8C2F* [24], *LipConv* [32], *XL* [2,29] and *Sandwich* [42] ⊤ indicates model is additionally trained with TRADES-loss [49]. †-flagged numbers are reproduced values with our own code. CLL numbers are averaged over 9 runs.

	Method	Model	Clean (%)	CRA $\frac{36}{255}$ (%)	CRA $\frac{72}{255}$ (%)	CRA $\frac{108}{255}$(%)	$\overline{K}^{(f)}$	$\overline{K}^{(h \circ f)}$	Tightness (%)
Tiny-ImageNet	GloRo [25]	8C2F$^\top$	35.5	22.4	-	-		12.5	47
		8C2F$^\top$†	39.5	23.9	14.3	9.0		3.9	53
	Local-Lip-B [18]	8C2F	36.9	23.4	12.7	6.1	–	–	–
	Ours $\epsilon = 0.5, p = 0.01$	8C2F	39.8 (+0.3)	25.9 (+2.0)	16.5 (+2.2)	10.7 (+1.7)	288.3	10.6	64 (+11)
	SOC [32]	LipConv-10	32.1	21.5	12.4	7.5		6.4	85
		LipConv-20	31.7	21.0	12.9	7.5		6.4	81
	Ours	LipConv-20	32.6 (+0.5)	26.0 (+3.5)	20.2 (+7.3)	15.5 (+8.0)	4.9	11.6	84 (+3)
	SLL [2]	XL	32.1	23.2	16.8	12.0	–	–	-
	LBDN [42]	Sandwich	33.4	24.7	18.1	13.4	–	–	–
	Ours $\epsilon = 1.0, p = 0.025$	8C2F	33.5 (+0.1)	25.3 (+0.6)	19.0 (+0.9)	13.8 (+0.4)	24.4	4.4	73

with different random seeds. Standard deviations are reported in the supplement, sec D. Additionally, we report tightness and Lipschitz constants of both the classifier f, as well as the composition with the loss $h \circ f$ – stating the effective complexity of the model. $\overline{K}^{(f)}$ and $\overline{K}^{(h \circ f)}$ state the largest constant between pairs of classes, e.g. $\overline{K}^{(f)} = \max_{i,j} \hat{K}^{(f)}_{i,j}$. Hereby, data scaling factors (e.g. normalization) influence $K^{(h \circ f)}$. E.g. a normalization factor of 5, increases $K^{(h \circ f)}$ by the same factor.

Certified Robust Accuracy. For fair comparison, we adjust ϵ and p of CLL to match or outperform clean accuracy of the respective baseline (details in supplement, sec. D). First, we consider Tiny-ImageNet (Table 1). *8C2F* is used to compare GloRo, *Local-Lip-B* and CLL, *LipConv* is used to compare *SOC* and CLL and *SLL* on *XL* and *LBDN* on *Sandwich* is compared to CLL on *8C2F*. Here, GloRo on *8C2F* achieves 23.9% CRA for $\epsilon = 36/255$ and 39.5% clean accuracy. Trained with CLL, we achieve a substantial increase for the same margin of 25.9%(+2.0) while improving clean accuracy 39.8%(+0.3%). We note that GloRo additionally uses the TRADES-loss [49] on *8C2F* to trade-off clean for robust accuracy. CLL simplifies this trade-off control via slack parameter p, see Sect. 4.3. Regarding *SOC* on *LipConv*, we find 10 layers to perform slightly better than 20 (training setup in supplement, sec B). This is in line with the observation in [32]: adding more layers can lead to degrading performance. CLL, in contrast, clearly outperforms *SOC* on 20 layers with 26.0%(+3.5) CRA ($\epsilon = 36/255$), 15.5%(+8.0) CRA ($\epsilon = 108/255$) and 32.6%(+0.5) clean accuracy on *LipConv-20*. These CRAs outperform the recent best methods *SLL* and *LBDN*. Differently to the AOL loss used in *SLL* and *LBDN* CLL also enables soft-constrained architectures like *8C2F* to achieve sota-performances. I.e., when choosing a lower slack value $p = 0.025$ and $\epsilon_{train} = 1.0$, CLL on *8C2F* out-competes even *LBDN* [42]. I.e., we increase CRAs for $\epsilon = 36/255$ to 25.3%(+0.6) and for $\epsilon = 108/255$ to 13.8%(+0.4) while maintaining clean accuracy 33.5%(+0.1). Interestingly, *8C2F* has fewer parameters than *Sandwich* and *XL*: 4.3M vs 39M vs 1.1B [42],

Table 2. Continuation of Table 1 but on CIFAR-10 and CIFAR-100. Additional architectures evaluated: *4C3F* [44], *6C2F* [24]. Local-Lip-B tightness is estimated by reading values off of Fig. 2a [18].

	Method	Model	Clean (%)	CRA $\frac{36}{255}$ (%)	CRA $\frac{72}{255}$ (%)	CRA $\frac{108}{255}$(%)	$\overline{K}^{(l)}$	$\overline{K}^{(\lambda=l)}$	Tightness (%)
CIFAR-10	Local-Lip-B [18]	6C2F	77.4	60.7	–	-	7.5		≈80
	GloRo [25]	6C2F	77.0	58.4	–	-	15.8		70
		4C3F†	77.4	59.6	40.8	24.8	7.4		71
	Ours	6C2F	**77.6** (+0.6)	61.3 (+2.9)	43.5	27.7	709.3	11.6	**78** (+8)
		4C3F	77.6 (+0.2)	**61.4** (+1.8)	**44.2** (+3.4)	**29.1** (+4.3)	72.1	11.6	**80** (+9)
	SOC [32]	LipConv-20	76.3	62.6	48.7	**36.0**	5.6		86
	Ours	LipConv-20	**77.4** (+1.1)	**64.2** (+1.6)	**49.5** (+0.8)	**36.7** (+0.7)	35.8	14.7	86
	CPL [29]	XL	78.5	64.4	48.0	33.0	$\sqrt{2}$		78
	Ours	XL	**78.8** (+0.3)	**65.9** (+1.5)	**51.6** (+3.6)	**38.1** (+5.1)	34.6	11.8	**80** (+2)
	SLL [2]	XL	**73.3**	**65.8**	**58.4**	**51.3**	$\sqrt{2}$	6.7	88
	Ours	XL	73.0	65.5	57.8	51.0	59.4	10.6	88.0
CIFAR-100	SOC [32]	LipConv-20	47.8	34.8	23.7	15.8	6.5		**85** (+1)
	Ours	LipConv-20	**48.2** (+0.4)	**35.1** (+0.3)	**25.3** (+1.6)	**18.3** (+2.5)	45.4	9.2	84
	CPL [29]	XL	47.8	33.4	20.9	12.6	1.6		74
	Ours	XL	**47.9** (+0.1)	**36.3** (+2.9)	**28.1** (+7.2)	**21.5** (+8.9)	42.0	7.6	**79** (+5)
	SLL [2]	XL	46.5	36.5	29.0	23.3	1.5	6.0	**81**
	Ours	XL	**46.9** (+0.4)	**36.6** (+0.1)	29.0	**23.4** (+0.1)	1.3	6.5	80

Next, we consider CIFAR-10 and CIFAR-100 (Table 2) GloRo applied to *6C2F* and *4C3F* produces a CRA ($\epsilon = 36/255$) of under 60% (58.4% and 59.6% respectively) on CIFAR-10. Note that our reimplementation of GloRo improves CRA to 59.6%(+1.2) upon the reported baseline in [25]. Replaced with CLL, we report gains to 61.3%(+2.9) and 61.4%(+1.8) respectively. Additionally, we increase clean accuracy to 77.6% for both (+0.6 and +0.2 respectively). Thereby, outperforming the local Lipschitz bound extension *Local-Lip-B* [18] (60.7% CRA), which utilizes expensive sample dependent local Lipschitz bounds to increase tightness. We also compare to *SOC* [32], *CPL* [29] and *SLL* [2], which constrain all layers to have Lipschitz constant 1. Here, we consider the *LipConv-20* architecture for *SOC* and the *XL*-architectures for *CPL* and *SLL*. *LipConv-20* contains 20 layers and *XL* 85. *SOC* achieves a clean accuracy of 76.3% on CIFAR-10, which CLL improves to 77.4%(+1.1) while also improving CRA on all tested margins. E.g. for $\epsilon = 36/255$ we report a gain to 64.2%(+1.6) and for $\epsilon = 128/255$ a gain to 36.7%(+0.7). Similarly, when applying CLL to *CPL-XL*, we report CRA gains to 65.9%(+1.5) and 38.1%(+5.1) ($\epsilon = 36/255$ and $\epsilon = 128/255$ respectively) while retaining clean accuracy (+0.3). However, CLL on *SLL-XL* provides no improvements. This is due to *SLL* using the *AOL*-loss [30], which has similar properties to CLL on $K=1$ constrained models. We provide a discussion in the supplement, sec. D. On CIFAR-100 though, CLL provides improvements on all tested models. On *CPL-XL*, we improve CRA on $\epsilon = 108/255$ to 21.5%(+8.9) while retaining clean accuracy 47.9%(+0.1). On *SLL*, we report slight gains in clean accuracy to 46.9%(+0.4) and CRA (+0.1 for both $\epsilon = 36/255$ and $\epsilon = 128/255$).

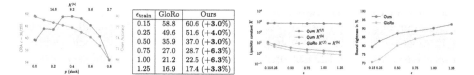

Fig. 5. Left column: Slack governs robust accuracy trade-off in *4C3F* on CIFAR-10. Remaining columns: Under increasing $0.15 \leq \epsilon \leq 1.25$ on CIFAR-10, we compare our method with GloRo on *4C3F*. We report consistently better CRA with at least 3% improvement (left table). Our Lipschitz bounds are less constrained and $K^{(f)}$ is decoupled from the loss (middle figure). And lastly, our method produces tighter bounds (right).

Lipschitz Bound and Tightness. CLL offers increased control over the Lipschitz bound of the model $K^{(h \circ f)}$. Across all datasets, we find CLL to increase the Lipschitz constant $K^{(h \circ f)}$ over the respective baselines (while improving clean and robust accuracies). On soft-constrained models like *8C2F* on Tiny-ImageNet, CLL allows a doubling of the constant over GloRo (7.3 vs 3.9). Similarly, on the hard-constrained model *LipConv-20* on Tiny-Imagenet, we observe another doubling over SOC (11.6 vs 6.4). This is consistent with $K^{(h \circ f)}$ on CIFAR. $K^{(h \circ f)}$ of *LipConv-20* is increased with CLL from 5.6 to 14.7. We note an exception for methods that utilize the *AOL*-loss [30]: SLL and LBDN. On these models, we find the constant $K^{(h \circ f)}$ to be highly similar, e.g. SLL-XL on CIFAR-100 ($K^{(h \circ f)} = 6$ vs 6.5). Importantly, these constant changes come with increased tightness as well. On Tiny-ImageNet, we increase tightness from 53% to 64%(+11) on *8C2F* over GloRo and from 81% to 84%(+3) on *LipConv-20* over SOC. Similarly, on CIFAR-10, we increase tightness from 71% to 80% on *4C3F* over GloRo. In general, we observe the largest tightness improvements on soft-constrained models, although improvements on *CPL* are substantial. Here we gain, +2 and +5 percent points on CIFAR-10 and CIFAR-100 respectively.

4.3   Analysis and Ablation

We considered different design choices when training with CLL. An important aspect being the robust accuracy trade-off, which we investigate in the following by controlling slack. Furthermore, we investigate the bound, tightness and CRA over increasing margin width on CIFAR-10. An extended discussion on selecting ϵ and p is discussed on *8C2F* for Tiny-ImageNet in the supplement, sec D.

Slack. As discussed in Sect. 3.3, we can regard the calibration probability p as slack, which trades-off CRA and clean accuracy. We report both on *4C3F* for $p \in [0.01, 0.8]$ in Fig. 5 (left). An increase in p decreases clean accuracy (green) from 80% to 68% but CRA increases to a peak at $p = 0.4$ with 61.9%.

Increasing Margin Width. In addition to our main results, we compare CLL and GloRo for larger ϵ. We train all experiments on *4C3F*. Different from before, we evaluate not for $\epsilon = 36/255$ but for the trained target, such that $\epsilon_{\text{train}} = \epsilon_{\text{test}}$.

The table in Fig. 5, reports CRA and relative improvement over GloRo. With a minimum of 3%, we report consistent relative improvement for all ϵ. The two right most plots of Fig. 5, display the Lipschitz constants across ϵ and tightness respectively. We see CLL utilizing higher $K^{(h \circ f)}$ throughout while maintaining higher tightness. Note that $K^{(f)}$ remains fairly unconstrained at $\approx 10^3$ with CLL, which is regularized via parameter λ. We analyzed its effect by choosing values from 10^{-15} to 10^{-1} and present results in figure D4a in the supplement. We find the performance of the model to be insensitive within $\lambda \in [10^{-10}, 10^{-3}]$.

5   Conclusion

We proposed a new loss, CLL, for Lipschitz margin training that is calibrated to the margin width. CLL reveals two intriguing properties: (i) the calibrated distribution width can be interpreted as slackness and (ii) slackness governs the smoothness of the model – and thereby the Lipschitz constant. The ramifications are important for improving certified robustness with Lipschitz constants. The constant can be large – implying increased model complexity and accuracy – if the model is capable of separating the data well. We illustrated these mechanics on two-moons, highlighting the implications for Lipschitz margin training and provided additional results on CIFAR-10, CIFAR-100 and Tiny-ImageNet. Applied across a wide range of datasets and methods, CLL consistently improved clean and certified robustness.

References

1. Anil, C., Lucas, J., Grosse, R.: Sorting out Lipschitz function approximation. In: ICML (2019)
2. Araujo, A., Havens, A.J., Delattre, B., Allauzen, A., Hu, B.: A unified algebraic perspective on Lipschitz neural networks. In: ICLR (2023)
3. Bartlett, P.L., Foster, D.J., Telgarsky, M.J.: Spectrally-normalized margin bounds for neural networks. In: NeurIPS (2017)
4. Bartlett, P.L., Mendelson, S.: Rademacher and gaussian complexities: risk bounds and structural results. In: JMLR (2002)
5. Carlini, N., et al.: On evaluating adversarial robustness. In: ICLR (2019)
6. Carmon, Y., Raghunathan, A., Schmidt, L., Duchi, J.C., Liang, P.S.: Unlabeled data improves adversarial robustness. In: NeurIPS (2019)
7. Cisse, M., Bojanowski, P., Grave, E., Dauphin, Y., Usunier, N.: Parseval networks: improving robustness to adversarial examples. In: ICML (2017)
8. Cohen, J., Rosenfeld, E., Kolter, Z.: Certified adversarial robustness via randomized smoothing. In: ICML (2019)
9. Cortes, C., Vapnik, V.: Support-vector networks. Mach. Learn. **20**, 237–297 (1995)
10. Delattre, B., Barthélemy, Q., Araujo, A., Allauzen, A.: Efficient bound of Lipschitz constant for convolutional layers by gram iteration. In: ICML (2023)
11. Ding, G.W., Sharma, Y., Lui, K.Y.C., Huang, R.: MMA training: direct input space margin maximization through adversarial training. In: ICLR (2019)
12. Elsayed, G., Krishnan, D., Mobahi, H., Regan, K., Bengio, S.: Large margin deep networks for classification. In: NeurIPS (2018)

13. Fazlyab, M., Robey, A., Hassani, H., Morari, M., Pappas, G.: Efficient and accurate estimation of Lipschitz constants for deep neural networks. In: NeurIPS (2019)
14. Gowal, S., et al.: Scalable verified training for provably robust image classification. In: ICCV (2019)
15. Guo, Y., Zhang, C.: Recent advances in large margin learning. In: PAMI (2021)
16. Hein, M., Andriushchenko, M.: Formal guarantees on the robustness of a classifier against adversarial manipulation. In: NeurIPS (2017)
17. Hoffman, J., Roberts, D.A., Yaida, S.: Robust learning with Jacobian regularization. arXiv preprint (2019)
18. Huang, Y., Zhang, H., Shi, Y., Kolter, J.Z., Anandkumar, A.: Training certifiably robust neural networks with efficient local Lipschitz bounds. In: NeurIPS (2021)
19. Huster, T., Chiang, C.Y.J., Chadha, R.: Limitations of the Lipschitz constant as a defense against adversarial examples. In: Alzate, C., et al. ECML PKDD 2018 Workshops. ECML PKDD 2018. LNCS, vol. 11329, pp. 16–29. Springer, Cham (2018). https://doi.org/10.1007/978-3-030-13453-2_2
20. Jakubovitz, D., Giryes, R.: Improving DNN robustness to adversarial attacks using Jacobian regularization. In: ECCV (2018)
21. Jordan, M., Dimakis, A.G.: Exactly computing the local Lipschitz constant of Relu networks. In: NeurIPS (2020)
22. Krizhevsky, A., Hinton, G.: Learning multiple layers of features from tiny images. Technical report (2009)
23. Le, Y., Yang, X.: Tiny ImageNet visual recognition challenge. Technical report (2014)
24. Lee, S., Lee, J., Park, S.: Lipschitz-certifiable training with a tight outer bound. In: NeurIPS (2020)
25. Leino, K., Wang, Z., Fredrikson, M.: Globally-robust neural networks. In: ICML (2021)
26. Li, L., Xie, T., Li, B.: SoK: certified robustness for deep neural networks. In: SP (2023)
27. Li, Q., Haque, S., Anil, C., Lucas, J., Grosse, R.B., Jacobsen, J.H.: Preventing gradient attenuation in Lipschitz constrained convolutional networks. In: NeurIPS (2019)
28. Madry, A., Makelov, A., Schmidt, L., Tsipras, D., Vladu, A.: Towards deep learning models resistant to adversarial attacks. In: ICLR (2018)
29. Meunier, L., Delattre, B.J., Araujo, A., Allauzen, A.: A dynamical system perspective for Lipschitz neural networks. In: ICML (2022)
30. Prach, B., Lampert, C.H.: Almost-orthogonal layers for efficient general-purpose Lipschitz networks. In: Avidan, S., Brostow, G., Cissé, M., Farinella, G.M., Hassner, T. (eds.) Computer Vision – ECCV 2022. ECCV 2022. LNCS, vol. 13681, pp. 350–365. Springer, Cham (2022). https://doi.org/10.1007/978-3-031-19803-8_21
31. Rosca, M., Weber, T., Gretton, A., Mohamed, S.: A case for new neural networks smoothness constraints. "I Can't Believe It's Not Better!". In: NeurIPS workshop (2020)
32. Singla, S., Singla, S., Feizi, S.: Improved deterministic l2 robustness on CIFAR-10 and CIFAR-100. In: ICLR (2021)
33. Sokolić, J., Giryes, R., Sapiro, G., Rodrigues, M.R.: Robust large margin deep neural networks. IEEE Trans. Sig. Proces. **65**, 4265–4280 (2017)
34. Sun, S., Chen, W., Wang, L., Liu, T.Y.: Large margin deep neural networks: theory and algorithms. arXiv preprint (2015)
35. Sun, Y., Chen, Y., Wang, X., Tang, X.: Deep learning face representation by joint identification-verification. In: NeurIPS (2014)

36. Szegedy, C., et al.: Intriguing properties of neural networks. In: ICLR (2014)
37. Trockman, A., Kolter, J.Z.: Orthogonalizing convolutional layers with the Cayley transform. In: ICLR (2020)
38. Tsuzuku, Y., Sato, I., Sugiyama, M.: Lipschitz-margin training: scalable certification of perturbation invariance for deep neural networks. In: NeurIPS (2018)
39. Vapnik, V.: Estimation of Dependences Based on Empirical Data. Springer, New York (1982). https://doi.org/10.1007/0-387-34239-7
40. Vapnik, V.N.: An overview of statistical learning theory. IEEE Trans. Neural Netw. **10**, 988–999 (1999)
41. Virmaux, A., Scaman, K.: Lipschitz regularity of deep neural networks: analysis and efficient estimation. In: NeurIPS (2018)
42. Wang, R., Manchester, I.: Direct parameterization of Lipschitz-bounded deep networks. In: ICML (2023)
43. Wei, C., Ma, T.: Improved sample complexities for deep neural networks and robust classification via an all-layer margin. In: ICLR (2019)
44. Wong, E., Schmidt, F., Metzen, J.H., Kolter, J.Z.: Scaling provable adversarial defenses. In: NeurIPS (2018)
45. Wu, D., Xia, S.T., Wang, Y.: Adversarial weight perturbation helps robust generalization. In: NeurIPS (2020)
46. Xu, X., Li, L., Li, B.: Lot: Layer-wise orthogonal training on improving l2 certified robustness. In: NeurIPS (2022)
47. Zhang, B., Cai, T., Lu, Z., He, D., Wang, L.: Towards certifying L-infinity robustness using neural networks with L-inf-dist neurons. In: ICML (2021)
48. Zhang, B., Jiang, D., He, D., Wang, L.: Boosting the certified robustness of L-infinity distance nets. In: ICLR (2022)
49. Zhang, H., Yu, Y., Jiao, J., Xing, E., El Ghaoui, L., Jordan, M.: Theoretically principled trade-off between robustness and accuracy. In: ICML (2019)
50. Zhang, H., et al.: Towards stable and efficient training of verifiably robust neural networks. In: ICLR (2020)

Multiclass Alignment of Confidence and Certainty for Network Calibration

Vinith Kugathasan and Muhammad Haris Khan[✉]

Mohamed bin Zayed University of Artificial Intelligence, Abu Dhabi, UAE
muhammad.haris@mbzuai.ac.ae

Abstract. Deep neural networks (DNNs) have made great strides in pushing the state-of-the-art in several challenging domains. Recent studies reveal that they are prone to making overconfident predictions. This greatly reduces the overall trust in model predictions, especially in safety-critical applications. Early work in improving model calibration employs post-processing techniques which rely on limited parameters and require a hold-out set. Some recent train-time calibration methods, which involve all model parameters, can outperform the post-processing methods. To this end, we propose a new train-time calibration method, which features a simple, plug-and-play auxiliary loss known as multi-class alignment of predictive mean confidence and predictive certainty (MACC). It is based on the observation that a model miscalibration is directly related to its predictive certainty, so a higher gap between the mean confidence and certainty amounts to a poor calibration both for in-distribution and out-of-distribution predictions. Armed with this insight, our proposed loss explicitly encourages a confident (or underconfident) model to also provide a low (or high) spread in the pre-softmax distribution. Extensive experiments on ten challenging datasets, covering in-domain, out-domain, non-visual recognition and medical image classification scenarios, show that our method achieves state-of-the-art calibration performance for both in-domain and out-domain predictions. Our code and models will be publicly released.

Keywords: Network Calibration · Model Calibration · Uncertainty

1 Introduction

Deep neural networks (DNNs) have displayed remarkable performance across many challenging computer vision problems e.g., image classification [7,13,23,45]. However, some recent works [12,35,40,48] have demonstrated that they tend to make over-confident predictions, and so are poorly calibrated. Consequently, the predicted confidences of classes are higher than the actual likelihood of their occurrences. A key reason behind this DNN behaviour is the supervision from zero-entropy signal which trains them to become over-confident. Poorly calibrated models not only create a general suspicion in the model predictions, but more importantly, they can lead to dangerous consequences in many safety-critical applications, including healthcare [8,44], autonomous vehicles [11], and legal research [49]. In such applications, providing a

Supplementary Information The online version contains supplementary material available at https://doi.org/10.1007/978-3-031-54605-1_38.

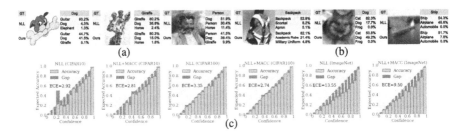

Fig. 1. We propose a new train-time calibration based on a novel auxiliary loss formulation (MACC). We compare between a model trained with NLL loss and ours (NLL+MACC). (a) shows out-of-domain performance (PACS) while (b) displays in-domain performance (Tiny-ImageNet and CIFAR10). NLL+MACC has higher confidence values for correct predictions (Giraffe (PACS)/Backpack (Tiny-ImageNet)) and lower confidence values for incorrect predictions (Dog (PACS)/Dog (CIFAR10)). (c) Reliability diagrams show that NLL+MACC improves bin-wise miscalibration, thereby alleviating under/over-confident predictions.

correct confidence is as significant as providing a correct label. For instance, in automated healthcare, if the control is not shifted to a doctor when the confidence of the incorrect prediction from a disease diagnosis network is high [20], it can potentially lead to disastrous outcomes. We have seen some recent attempts towards improving the network calibration. Among them, a simple technique is based on a post-hoc procedure, which transforms the outputs of a trained network [12]. The parameters of this transformation are typically learned on a hold-out validation set. Such post-hoc calibration methods are simple and computationally efficient, however, they are architecture and data-dependent [31]. Furthermore, in many real-world applications, the availability of a hold-out set is not guaranteed. Another route to reducing miscalibration is train-time calibration which tends to involve all model parameters. A dominant approach in train-time calibration methods proposes auxiliary losses that can be added to the task-specific loss (e.g., NLL) to reduce miscalibration [14,31,35,42]. These auxiliary losses aim at either increasing the entropy of the predictive distribution [31,35,42] or aligning the predictive confidence with the predictive accuracy [14,25].

We take the train-time route to calibration, and propose an auxiliary loss function: Multi-class alignment of predictive mean confidence and predictive certainty (MACC). It is founded on the observation that a model's predictive certainty is correlated to its calibration performance. So, a higher gap between the predictive mean confidence and predictive certainty translates directly to a greater miscalibration both for in-distribution and out-of-distribution predictions. If a model is confident then it should also produce a relatively low spread in the logit distribution and vice versa. Proposed loss function is differentiable, operates on minibatches and is formulated to be used with other task-specific loss functions. Besides showing effectiveness for calibrating in-distribution examples, it is also capable of improving calibration of out-of-distribution examples (Fig. 1). **Contributions: (1)** We empirically observe a correlation between a model's predictive certainty and its calibration performance. **(2)** To this end, we propose a simple, plug-and-play auxiliary loss term (MACC) which attempts to *align the predictive mean confidence with the predictive certainty for all class labels*. It can be used with other task-specific loss functions, such as Cross Entropy (CE), Label Smoothing (LS) [36] and Focal Loss (FL) [35]. **(3)** Besides the predicted class label, it also reduces the gap between the certainty and mean confidence for non-predicted class labels, thereby improving the calibration of non-predicted class labels. **(4)** We carry out extensive experiments on three in-domain scenarios, CIFAR-10/100 [22], and Tiny-ImageNet [4], a class-imbalanced scenario SVHN [38], and four out-of-domain scenarios, CIFAR-10/100-C (OOD) [17], Tiny-ImageNet-C (OOD) [17] and PACS [28]. Results show that our loss is consistently more effective than the existing state-of-the-art methods in calibrating both in-domain and out-of-domain predictions. Moreover, we also show the effectiveness of our approach on non-visual pattern recognition task of natural language classification (20 Newsgroups dataset [27]) and a medical image classification task (Mendeley dataset [21]). Finally, we also report results with a vision transformer-based baseline (DeiT-Tiny [47]) to show the applicability of our method.

2   Related Work

Post-hoc Calibration Methods: A classic approach for improving model calibration, known as post-hoc calibration, transforms the outputs of a trained model [6,12,46,50]. Among different post-hoc calibration methods, a simple technique is temperature scaling (TS) [12], which is a variant of Platt scaling [12]. It scales the logits (i.e. pre-softmax activations) by a single temperature parameter, which is learned on a hold-out validation set. TS increases the entropy of the predictive distribution, which is beneficial towards improving model calibration. However, it decreases the confidence of all predictions, including the correct one. TS which relies on a single parameter for transformation can be generalized to a matrix transform, where the matrix is also learnt using a hold-out validation set. Dirichlet calibration (DC) employs Dirichlet distributions for scaling the Beta-calibration [24] method to a multi-class setting. DC is incorporated as a layer in a neural network on log-transformed class probabilities, which is learnt using a hold-out validation set. Although TS improves model calibration for in-domain predictions, [40] showed that it performs poorly for out-of-domain predictions. To circumvent this, [46] proposed to perturb the validation set before performing the post-hoc calibration. Recently, [33] proposed a ranking model to improve the post-hoc model calibration, and [6] used a regressor to obtain the temperature parameter at the inference stage.

Train-Time Calibration Methods: Brier score is considered as one of the earliest train-time calibration technique for binary probabilistic forecast [3]. Later, [12] demonstrated that the models trained with negative log-likelihood (NLL) tend to be over-confident, and thus, there is a dissociation between NLL and calibration. Several works proposed auxiliary losses that can be used with NLL to improve miscalibration. For instance, [42] penalized the over-confident predictions by using entropy as a regularization term, and [36] showed that label smoothing (LS) can improve model calibration. A similar insight was reported by [35], that Focal loss (FL) implicitly improves model calibration. It minimizes the KL divergence between the predictive distribution and the target distribution, and at the same time increases the entropy of the predictive distribution. These methods establish that implicit or explicit maximization of entropy improves calibration performance. Based on this observation, [31] proposed a calibration technique based on inequality constraints, which imposes a margin between logit distances. Recently, [29] incorporated the difference between confidence and accuracy

(DCA) as an auxiliary loss term with the cross-entropy loss. Similarly, [25] developed an auxiliary loss term (MMCE), for model calibration that is computed with a reproducing kernel in a Hilbert space [10]. Prior methods, such as [25,29], only calibrate the maximum class confidence. To this end, [14] proposed an auxiliary loss term, namely MDCA, that calibrates the non-maximum class confidences along with the maximum class confidence. We also take the train-time calibration route, however, different to existing methods, we propose to minimize the gap between the predictive mean confidence and predictive certainty to improve model calibration.

Other Calibration Methods: Some methods learn to discard OOD samples, either at train-time or post-hoc stage, which reduces over-confidence and leads to improved calibration. Hein et al. [15] demonstrated ReLU makes DNNs provide high confidence for an input sample that lies far away from the training samples. Guo et al. [12] explored the impact of width, and depth of a DNN, batch normalization, and weight decay on model calibration. For more literature on calibrating a DNN through OOD detection, we refer the reader to [5,18,34,41].

Calibration and Uncertainty Estimation in DNNs: Many probabilistic approaches emerge from the Bayesian formalism [1], in which a prior distribution over the neural network (NN) parameters is assumed, and then a training data is used to obtain the posterior distribution over the NN parameters, which is then used to estimate predictive uncertainty. Since the exact Bayesian inference is computationally intractable, several approximate inference techniques have been proposed, including variational inference [2,32], and stochastic expectation propagation [19]. Ensemble learning is another approach for quantifying uncertainty that uses the empirical variance of the network predictions. We can create ensembles using different techniques. For instance, with the differences in model hyperparameters [48], random initialization of weights and random shuffling of training examples [26], dataset shift [40], and Monte Carlo (MC) dropout [9,51]. In this work, we chose to use MC dropout [9] to estimate predictive mean confidence and predictive uncertainty of a given example for all class labels. It provides a distribution of class logit scores and is simple to implement. However, the conventional implementation of MC dropout can incur high computational cost for large datasets, architectures, and longer training schedules. To this end, we resort to an efficient implementation of MC dropout that greatly reduces this computational overhead.

3   Proposed Methodology

Preliminaries: We consider the task of classification where we have a dataset $\mathcal{D} = \langle (\mathbf{x}_i, y_i^*) \rangle_{i=1}^N$ of N input examples sampled from a joint distribution $\mathcal{D}(\mathcal{X}, \mathcal{Y})$, where $\mathcal{X}$ is an input space, and $\mathcal{Y}$ is the label space. $\mathbf{x}_i \in \mathcal{X} \in \mathbb{R}^{H \times W \times C}$ is an input image with height H, width W, and number of channels C. Each image has a corresponding ground truth class label $y_i^* \in \mathcal{Y} = \{1, 2, ..., K\}$. Let us denote a classification model $\mathcal{F}_{cls}$, that typically outputs a confidence vector $\mathbf{s}_i \in \mathbb{R}^K$. Since each element of vector $\mathbf{s}_i$ is a valid (categorical) probability, it is considered as the confidence score of the corresponding class label. The predicted class label $\hat{y}_i$ can be computed as: $\hat{y}_i = \arg\max_{y \in \mathcal{Y}} \mathbf{s}_i[y]$. Likewise, the confidence score of the predicted class $\hat{y}_i$ is obtained as: $\hat{s}_i = \max_{y \in \mathcal{Y}} \mathbf{s}_i[y]$.

3.1 Definition and Quantification of Calibration

Definition: We can define a perfect calibration if the (classification) accuracy for a given confidence score is aligned with this confidence score for all possible confidence scores [12]: $\mathbb{P}(\hat{y} = y^* | \hat{s} = s) = s \quad \forall s \in [0, 1]$, where $\mathbb{P}(\hat{y} = y^* | \hat{s} = s)$ is the accuracy for a given confidence score $\hat{s}$. The expression only captures the calibration of the predicted label i.e. associated with the maximum class confidence score $\hat{s}$. The confidence score of non-predicted classes, also called as non-maximum class confidence scores, can also be calibrated. It provides us with a more general definition of perfect calibration and can be expressed as: $\mathbb{P}(y = y^* | \mathbf{s}[y] = s) = s \quad \forall s \in [0, 1]$.

Expected Calibration Error (ECE): ECE is computed by first obtaining the absolute difference between the average confidence of the predicted class and the average accuracy of samples, that are predicted with a particular confidence score. This absolute difference is then converted into a weighted average by scaling it with the relative frequency of samples with a particular confidence score. The above two steps are repeated for all confidence scores and then the resulting weighted averages are summed [37]:

$\text{ECE} = \sum_{i=1}^{M} \frac{|B_i|}{N} \left| \frac{1}{|B_i|} \sum_{j:\hat{s}_j \in B_i} \mathbb{I}(\hat{y}_j = y_j^*) - \frac{1}{|B_i|} \sum_{j:\hat{s}_j \in B_i} \hat{s}_j \right|$. Where N is the total number of examples. Since the confidence values have a continuous interval, the confidence range $[0, 1]$ is divided into M bins. $|B_i|$ is the number of examples falling in i^{th} confidence bin. $\frac{1}{|B_i|} \sum_{j:\hat{s}_j \in B_i} \mathbb{I}(\hat{y}_j = y_j^*)$ denotes the average accuracy of examples lying in i^{th} bin, and $\frac{1}{|B_i|} \sum_{j:\hat{s}_j \in B_i} \hat{s}_j$ represents the average confidence of examples belonging to i^{th} confidence bin. The ECE metric for measuring DNN miscalibration has two limitations. First, the whole confidence vector is not accounted for calibration. Second, due to binning of the confidence interval, the metric is not differentiable. See description on Maximum calibration error (MCE) in supplementary material.

Static Calibration Error (SCE): SCE extends ECE by taking into account the whole confidence vector, thereby measuring the calibration performance of non-maximum class confidences [39], $\text{SCE} = \frac{1}{K} \sum_{i=1}^{M} \sum_{j=1}^{K} \frac{|B_{i,j}|}{N} \left| A_{i,j} - C_{i,j} \right|$. Where K represents the number of classes and $|B_{i,j}|$ is the number of examples from the jth class and the ith bin. $A_{i,j} = \frac{1}{|B_{i,j}|} \sum_{k:\mathbf{s}_k[j] \in B_{i,j}} \mathbb{I}(j = y_k)$ denotes the average accuracy and $C_{i,j} = \frac{1}{|B_{i,j}|} \sum_{k:\mathbf{s}_k[j] \in B_{i,j}} \mathbf{s}_k[j]$ represents the average confidence of the examples belonging to the jth class and the ith bin. Similar to ECE metric, SCE metric is not differentiable, and so it cannot be used as a loss in gradient-based learning methods.

3.2 Proposed Auxiliary Loss: MACC

Our auxiliary loss (MACC) aims at reducing the deviation between the predictive mean confidence and the predictive certainty for predicted and non-predicted class labels.

Quantifying Mean Confidence and Certainty: Our proposed loss function requires the estimation of *class-wise mean confidence and certainty*. We choose to use the MC dropout method [9] to estimate both of these quantities because it provides a distribution of (logit) scores for all possible classes and only requires the addition of a single dropout layer ($\mathcal{M}$), which in our case, is added between the feature extractor $f(\cdot)$ that generates

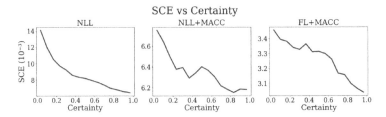

Fig. 2. Left: We investigate if there is a relationship between static calibration error and individual (output) predictive uncertainties. We observe (negative) correlation between a model's predictive certainty and its calibration error (SCE) i.e. as the certainty increases, the calibration error goes down (CIFAR10 trained on ResNet56 model with dropout). Middle & right: Based on this observation, we propose to align predictive mean confidence with the predictive certainty (NLL/FL+MACC), which allow a rapid reduction in the calibration error in comparison to baseline (NLL). See supplementary material for details of the plot.

features and the classifier $g(\cdot)$ that projects the extracted features into class-wise logits vector. The conventional implementation of MC dropout technique requires N MC forward passes for an input example x_i through the model $\mathcal{F}_{cls}$. From the resulting logits distribution, we can then estimate the mean and variance for each class j, which reflects for x_i, its predictive mean logit score $\bar{z}_i[j]$ and the predictive uncertainty in logit scores $u_i[j]$, respectively, where $\bar{z}_i, u_i \in \mathbb{R}^K$. To obtain predictive mean confidence $\bar{s}_i[j]$, we apply softmax to $\bar{z}_i[j] \forall j$. The certainty $c_i[j]$ is obtained from the uncertainty $u_i[j]$ as: $c_i[j] = 1 - \tanh(u_i[j])$. The tanh is used to scale the uncertainty values between 0 and 1.

We resort to an efficient implementation of MC dropout technique aimed at reducing its computational overhead, which is of concern during model training. Specifically, we feed an input example x_i to the feature extractor network only once and obtain the extracted features f_i. These extracted features are then fed to the combination of dropout layer and classifier $(g \circ \mathcal{M}(f_i))$ for N number of MC forward passes. Specifically, $u_i[j] = \frac{1}{N-1} \sum_{m=1}^{M} ([g \circ \mathcal{M}_m(f_i)]_j - \bar{z}_i[j])^2$, where $\bar{z}_i[j]$ represents the mean of the logit distribution given by: $\bar{z}_i[j] = \frac{1}{N} \sum_{m=1}^{M} [g \circ \mathcal{M}_m(f_i)]_j$. This so-called architecture-implicit implementation of MC dropout enjoys the benefit of performing only a single forward pass through the feature extractor f as opposed to N forward passes in the conventional implementation. We empirically observe that, for 10 MC forward passes, the efficient implementation reduces the overall training time by 7 times compared to the conventional implementation (see suppl.). Deep ensembles [26] is an alternate to MCDO, however, it is computationally expensive to be used in a train-time calibration approach. On CIFAR10, training deep ensembles with 10 models require around 7.5 h whereas ours with 10 forward passes, only require around an hour.

MACC: The calibration is a frequentist notion of uncertainty and could be construed as a measure reflecting a network's *overall predictive uncertainty* [26]. So, we investigate if there is a relationship between static calibration error and individual (output) predictive uncertainties. We identify a (negative) correlation between a model's predictive certainty and its calibration error (SCE). In other words, as the certainty increases, the calibration error goes down (Fig. 2). With this observation, we propose to align the predictive mean confidence of the model with its predictive certainty. Our loss function is defined as:

$$\mathcal{L}_{\text{MACC}} = \frac{1}{K} \sum_{j=1}^{K} \left| \frac{1}{M} \sum_{i=1}^{M} \bar{\mathbf{s}}_i[j] - \frac{1}{M} \sum_{i=1}^{M} \mathbf{c}_i[j] \right|, \tag{1}$$

where $\bar{\mathbf{s}}_i[j]$ denotes the predictive mean confidence of the ith example in the mini-batch belonging to the jth class. Likewise, $\mathbf{c}_i[j]$ represents the certainty of the ith example in the mini-batch belonging to the jth class. M is the number of examples in the mini-batch, and K is the number of classes.

Discussion: Given an example, for which a model predicts high mean confidence, our loss formulation forces the model to also produce relatively low spread in logits distribution and vice versa. This alignment directly helps towards improving the model calibration. Figure 2 shows that, compared to baseline, a model trained with our loss allows a rapid decrease in calibration error. Moreover, Fig. 3a, b show that when there are relatively greater number of examples with a higher gap between (mean) confidence and certainty (i.e. the distribution is more skewed towards right), a model's calibration is poor compared to when there are relatively smaller number of examples with a higher gap (Fig. 3c, d). The proposed auxiliary loss is a simple, plug-and-play term. It is differentiable and operates over minibatch and thus, it can be used with other task-specific loss functions to improve the model calibration, $\mathcal{L}_{\text{total}} = \mathcal{L}_{\text{task}} + \beta . \mathcal{L}_{\text{MACC}}$, where β represents the weight with which our $\mathcal{L}_{\text{MACC}}$ is added to the task-specific loss function $\mathcal{L}_{\text{task}}$ e.g., CE, LS [36] and FL [35].

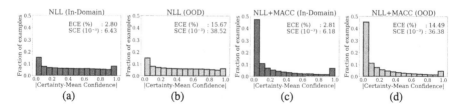

Fig. 3. Empirical distribution of difference between predictive certainty and the predictive mean confidence of all the classes for in-domain examples (CIFAR10), and out-of-domain (OOD) examples (CIFAR10-C). (Left - (a), (b)) When there are relatively greater number of examples with higher gap between the mean confidence and certainty, calibration errors (ECE and SCE) are higher, compared to when there are relatively smaller number of examples (Right - (c), (d)). For (a) and (b), a ResNet56 model with dropout is trained with NLL. For (c) and (d), the same model is trained with NLL+MACC (ours).

4   Experiments

Datasets: To validate in-domain calibration performance, we use four challenging image classification datasets: CIFAR10 [22], CIFAR100 [22], Tiny-ImageNet [4] and Mendeley V2 [21] and a natural language processing dataset: 20 Newsgroups [27]. Tiny-Image-Net is a subset of ImageNet [43] comprising 200 classes. Further, to report calibration performance in out-of-domain scenarios, we show results on four challenging benchmarks: CIFAR10-C [16], CIFAR100-C [16], Tiny-ImageNet-C [16] and PACS [28]. For CIFAR10-C, CIFAR100-C and Tiny-ImageNet-C, we use their corresponding in-domain benchmarks for training and validation. Finally, to evaluate calibration performance under class imbalance, we report results on SVHN [38].

Implementation Details and Evaluation Metrics: We use ResNet [13] and DeiT-Tiny [47] (only for CIFAR10) as the backbone networks in our experiments. For our method, we insert a single dropout layer in between the penultimate feature layer and the final classifier of the ResNet architecture. We also input the predictive mean confidence, obtained for our MACC, to the task-specific loss. We set the number of MC samples to 10 in all experiments. The dropout ratio is sought in the range $p \in \{0.2, 0.3, 0.5\}$ using the validation set. See suppl. material for details. We report the calibration performance with ECE [37] and SCE [39] metrics and the classification performance with top-1 accuracy. The number of bins is $M = 15$ for both the calibration metrics across all the experiments. Moreover, we plot reliability diagrams and report AUROC scores.

Baselines: We evaluate MACC against models trained with CE, LS [36], FL [30], adaptive sample-dependent focal loss (FLSD) [35], brier score (BS) [3] and MMCE [25]. We also compare against the recent auxiliary loss functions: MbLS [31] and MDCA [14]. Hyper-parameters of the compared methods are set based on the values reported in the literature. For both MDCA and our loss (MACC), the relative weight is chosen from $\beta \in \{1, 5, 10, 15, 20, 25\}$ and the most accurate model on the validation set is used to report the calibration performance, following MDCA [14] implementation. Meanwhile, the scheduled γ in FLSD is set to 5 for $s_k \in [0, 0.2)$ and 3 for $s_k \in [0.2, 1)$, where s_k is the confidence score of the correct class. Refer to the supplementary for the detailed description of these hyperparameters.

Experiments with Task-Specific Loss Functions: Our loss (MACC) is developed to be used with a task-specific loss function. We consider CE (NLL), LS and FL as the task-specific losses and report the calibration performance with and without incorporating our MACC. For LS we use $\alpha \in \{0.05, 0.1\}$ and for FL we use $\gamma \in \{1, 2, 3\}$ and the most accurate model on the validation set is used to report the performance. Table 1 shows that our auxiliary loss function (MACC) consistently improves the calibration performance of all tasks-specific losses across six datasets. We also note that FL is a much stronger task-specific loss function in calibration performance in all datasets, except SVHN and 20 Newsgroups. The CE loss performs relatively better than FL loss on SVHN and LS performs better on 20 Newsgroups. We choose to report performance with FL+MACC on all datasets, except SVHN (for which we use CE loss), in all subsequent experiments.

Comparison with State-of-the-Art (SOTA): We compare the calibration performance against recent SOTA train-time calibration methods (Table 2, Table 3). We use NLL+ MbLS to report the performance as it provides better results than FL+MbLS (see suppl.). Our method achieves lower calibration errors in ECE, SCE and AUROC metrics across six datasets. To demonstrate the effectiveness of MACC on natural language classification, we conduct experiments on the 20 Newsgroups dataset (Table 2). Our FL+MACC outperforms others in both SCE and ECE metrics. Experiments with vision-transformer based backbone architecture, namely DeiT-Tiny [47] show that our FL+MACC is capable of improving the calibration performance of DeiT. Note that, DeiT is a relatively stronger baseline in calibration performance compared to ResNet (see Table 2). For training DeiT models, we use the hyperparameters specified by the authors of DeiT.

Table 1. Calibration performance in SCE (10^{-3}) and ECE (%) metrics of our auxiliary loss (MACC) when added to three task-specific losses: CE, LS, and FL. Throughout, the best results are in bold, and the second best are underlined.

Dataset	Model	NLL		NLL+MACC		LS [36]		LS+MACC		FL [30]		FL+MACC	
		SCE	ECE	SCE	ECE	SCE	ECE	SCE	ECE	SCE	ECE	SCE	ECE
CIFAR10	ResNet56	6.50	2.92	6.18	2.81	5.90	1.85	5.51	1.57	_3.79_	_0.64_	**3.04**	**0.59**
CIFAR100	ResNet56	2.01	3.35	_1.99_	2.74	2.08	_0.86_	2.07	0.92	_1.99_	0.89	**1.97**	**0.64**
Tiny-ImageNet	ResNet50	2.06	13.55	1.72	9.50	1.50	2.04	**1.37**	_1.37_	1.50	3.52	_1.44_	**1.33**
SVHN	ResNet56	_1.70_	_0.43_	**1.50**	**0.27**	11.70	4.95	7.72	3.10	7.79	3.55	_1.70_	0.49
20 Newsgroups	GP CNN	23.05	21.11	20.30	18.32	_10.35_	_5.80_	**9.61**	**2.17**	21.30	19.54	13.84	11.28
Mendeley	ResNet50	206.98	16.05	77.12	7.59	133.25	5.32	**57.70**	_4.52_	160.58	5.13	_66.97_	**4.14**

Temperature Scaling (TS): MACC outperforms NLL/FL + TS (Table 3). We report the best calibration obtained for TS with the primary losses of NLL and FL. For TS we follow the same protocol used by the MDCA [14] where 10% of the training data is set aside as the hold-out validation set and a grid search between the range of 0 to 10 with a step-size of 0.1 is performed to find the optimal temperature value that gives the least NLL on the hold-out set. In CIFAR10/100 and SVHN, the obtained metric scores are similar to that of MDCA [14]. For Tiny-ImageNet, MDCA [14] does not report results, and our results are better than MbLS [31], which uses the same protocol as ours.

Class-Wise Calibration Performance and Test Accuracy: Table 4 reports class-wise ECE (%) scores of competing calibration approaches, including MDCA and MbLS, on SVHN and CIFAR10 datasets, with ResNet56. In SVHN, NLL+MACC (ours) achieves the lowest ECE (%) in three classes while demonstrating the second best score in other four. FL+ MACC provides the best values in two classes and the second best values in another two classes. NLL+MbLS also performs well, being the best in five classes. In CIFAR10, FL+MACC (ours) provides the best ECE (%) scores in five classes while showing the second best in all others. Table 2 shows the discriminative performance (top-1 accuracy %) of our loss (MACC) along with the other competing approaches. Our loss shows superior accuracy than most of the existing losses, including MDCA, in CIFAR100 and Tiny-ImageNet. Moreover, it provides the best accuracy in SVHN, Mendeley and 20 Newsgroups.

Out-of-Distribution Performance: Table 5 reports the out-of-domain calibration performance on the CIFAR10-C, CIFAR100-C and Tiny-ImageNet-C benchmarks. In both CIFAR10-C and CIFAR100-C datasets, our loss records the best calibration performance in ECE and SCE metrics. In Tiny-ImageNet-C, our loss shows the lowest ECE score and reveal the second lowest SCE score. We plot calibration performance as a function of corruption level in CIFAR10-C dataset (see Fig. 4 suppl.). Our loss consistently obtains lowest ECE and SCE across all corruption levels. For the OOD evaluation, including CIFAR10-C, CIFAR100- C, and Tiny-ImageNet-C, we follow the same

Table 2. Comparison of calibration performance in SCE (10^{-3}) and ECE (%) metrics with the SOTA train-time calibration methods.

Dataset	Model	BS [3]			MMCE [25]			FLSD [35]			FL+MDCA [14]			NLL+MbLS [31]			FL/NLL+MACC		
		SCE	ECE	Acc.	SCE	ECE	Acc.	SCE	ECE	Acc.	SCE	ECE	Acc.	SCE	ECE	Acc.	SCE	ECE	Acc.
CIFAR10	ResNet56	4.78	1.67	92.46	5.87	1.74	91.75	7.87	3.17	92.37	3.44	0.79	92.92	4.63	1.48	93.41	3.04	0.59	92.86
	DeiT-Tiny	–	–	–	–	–	–	–	–	–	3.63	1.52	97.11	3.01	0.56	96.78	3.02	0.48	96.43
CIFAR100	ResNet56	2.08	4.75	69.64	1.98	2.76	69.71	2.05	1.76	70.97	1.92	0.68	70.34	1.99	0.96	71.33	1.97	0.64	70.50
Tiny-ImageNet	ResNet50	–	–	–	–	–	–	1.50	2.75	60.39	1.44	2.07	60.24	1.42	1.59	62.69	1.44	1.33	61.60
SVHN	ResNet56	2.41	0.51	96.57	12.34	5.88	95.51	17.49	8.59	95.87	1.77	0.32	96.10	1.43	0.37	96.59	1.50	0.27	96.74
20 Newsgroups	GP CNN	21.44	18.64	66.08	17.32	14.76	67.54	14.78	11.62	66.81	17.40	15.47	67.04	17.59	15.55	67.74	13.84	11.28	67.87
Mendeley	ResNet50	224.34	15.73	76.28	199.16	10.98	78.69	146.19	4.16	79.17	177.72	7.85	78.69	176.93	9.70	78.85	66.97	4.14	80.93

Table 3. Calibration performance with Temperature Scaling (TS) & comparison of calibration performance in AUROC metric with SOTA train-time calibration methods.

Dataset	Comparison with TS									SOTA Comparison		
	NLL+MACC		NLL+TS			FL+MACC		FL+TS			MDCA	MbLS	MACC
	SCE	ECE	SCE	ECE	T	SCE	ECE	SCE	ECE	T	AUROC Score		
CIFAR10	6.18	2.81	4.12	0.87	1.4	3.04	0.59	3.79	0.64	1.0	**0.9966**	0.9958	**0.9966**
CIFAR100	1.99	2.74	1.84	1.36	1.1	1.97	0.64	1.99	0.89	1.0	**0.9922**	0.9916	**0.9922**
Tiny-ImageNet	1.72	9.50	2.06	13.55	1.0	1.44	1.33	2.42	18.05	0.6	0.9848	0.9811	**0.9858**
SVHN	1.50	0.27	2.80	1.01	1.2	1.70	49	3.00	0.91	0.8	0.9973	**0.9977**	**0.9977**

Table 4. Class-wise calibration performance in ECE (%) of competing approaches on SVHN and CIFAR10 benchmarks (ResNet56).

Loss	Classes																			
	0	1	2	3	4	5	6	7	8	9	0	1	2	3	4	5	6	7	8	9
	SVHN										CIFAR10									
NLL+MDCA	0.17	0.20	0.34	0.22	_0.13_	_0.16_	0.15	0.17	_0.16_	_0.14_										
NLL+MACC	_0.12_	_0.16_	**0.14**	_0.20_	0.14	**0.14**	**0.10**	0.16	0.19	_0.14_										
FL+MDCA	0.13	0.22	0.21	_0.20_	0.16	0.18	0.16	_0.14_	_0.16_	0.22	_0.33_	**0.32**	0.42	0.72	_0.21_	_0.39_	_0.30_	**0.21**	**0.21**	_0.33_
NLL+MbLS	**0.07**	**0.14**	_0.18_	0.22	**0.11**	0.17	_0.13_	**0.09**	0.18	**0.13**	**0.24**	0.51	_0.33_	_0.68_	0.44	0.51	0.48	0.57	0.46	0.41
FL+MACC	0.17	0.23	_0.18_	**0.18**	0.17	0.19	0.17	_0.14_	**0.10**	0.17	_0.33_	_0.34_	**0.31**	**0.45**	_0.30_	**0.33**	**0.25**	_0.28_	_0.23_	**0.23**

Table 5. Out of Domain (OOD) calibration performance of competing approaches across CIFAR10-C, CIFAR100-C and Tiny-ImageNet-C.

Dataset	Model	FL+MDCA			NLL+MbLS			FL+MACC		
		SCE (10^{-3})	ECE (%)	Acc. (%)	SCE (10^{-3})	ECE (%)	Acc. (%)	SCE (10^{-3})	ECE (%)	Acc. (%)
CIFAR10 (In-Domain)	ResNet56	_3.44_	_0.79_	92.92	4.63	1.48	93.41	**3.04**	**0.59**	92.86
CIFAR10-C (OOD)		29.01	_11.51_	71.30	27.61	12.21	73.75	**23.71**	**9.10**	72.85
CIFAR100 (In-Domain)	ResNet56	**1.92**	_0.68_	70.34	1.99	0.96	71.33	_1.97_	**0.64**	70.5
CIFAR100-C (OOD)		4.09	_12.21_	44.74	_4.03_	12.48	45.60	**4.01**	**12.11**	44.90
Tiny-ImageNet (In-Domain)	ResNet50	1.44	2.07	60.24	**1.42**	_1.59_	62.69	_1.44_	**1.33**	61.60
Tiny-ImageNet-C (OOD)		3.87	22.79	20.74	**3.04**	_18.17_	23.70	_3.46_	**17.82**	21.29

protocol and train/val splits as used for in-domain evaluation. Specifically, we train a model using the training split, and optimize parameters using the validation split and the trained model is then evaluated on the in-domain test set or the corrupted test set.

We also show the OOD calibration performance on the PACS dataset under two different evaluation protocols. In first, following [14], a model is trained on **Photo** domain

Table 6. OOD calibration performance (SCE (10^{-2}) & ECE (%)) on PACS when ResNet18 model is trained on **Photo**, validated on **Art**, and tested on **Sketch** and **Cartoon** [14].

Domain	FL+MDCA			NLL+MbLS			FL+MACC		
	Acc.	SCE	ECE	Acc.	SCE	ECE	Acc.	SCE	ECE
Cartoon	25.34	15.62	44.05	27.69	_12.82_	30.88	32.17	**10.19**	**22.18**
Sketch	29.14	14.82	40.16	26.57	**11.40**	**18.03**	24.94	_12.59_	_28.14_
Average	27.24	15.22	42.10	27.13	_12.11_	**24.45**	28.55	**11.39**	_25.16_

Table 7. Out of Domain (OOD) calibration performance (SCE (10^{-2}) & ECE (%)) on PACS when ResNet18 model is trained on each domain and tested on other 3 domains. Validation set comprises 20% randomly sampled images from the training domain.

FL+MDCA			NLL+MbLS			FL+MACC			FL+MDCA			NLL+MbLS			FL+MACC		
Acc.	SCE	ECE	Acc.	SCE	ECE	Acc.	SCE	ECE	Acc.	SCE	ECE	Acc.	SCE	ECE	Acc.	SCE	ECE
Photo Domain									Art Domain								
38.48	13.59	38.93	35.32	_13.44_	_33.77_	34.75	**9.09**		**14.63**	56.87	_9.33_	24.81	57.46	**8.06**		**15.21**	51.45	9.70	_16.28_
Cartoon Domain									Sketch Domain								
62.68	**5.79**	13.91	59.43	_6.38_	9.62	57.47	6.58	**5.95**	18.31	_17.99_	_54.37_	11.57	19.50	57.17	13.24	**16.68**	45.23
						Average											
			44.09	_11.68_	33.00	40.94	11.83	_28.94_	39.23	**10.51**	20.52						

while **Art** domain is used as the validation set, and the trained model is then tested on the rest of domains. Table 6 shows that the proposed loss obtains the best calibration performance in ECE score, while the second best in SCE. In second, a model is trained on each domain and then tested on all other domains. In this protocol, 20% of images corresponding to the training domain is randomly sampled as the validation set, and the remaining 3 domains form the test set. Table 7 shows that FL+MACC provides improved calibration than all other competing approaches.

Mitigating Under/Over-Confidence: We plot reliability diagrams to reveal the effectiveness of our method in mitigating under/over-confidence (Fig. 1c & 4 (top)). Furthermore, we plot confidence histograms to illustrate the deviation between the overall confidence (dotted line) and accuracy (solid line) of the predictions (Fig. 4 (bottom)). Figure 4a & b show that our method can effectively mitigate the under-confidence of a model trained with LS loss. Figure 4e & f illustrate that our method notably reduces the gap between the overall confidence and accuracy, thereby mitigating the under-confident behaviour. Likewise, Fig. 4c, d, g & h display the capability of our method in mitigating the over-confidence of an uncalibrated model.

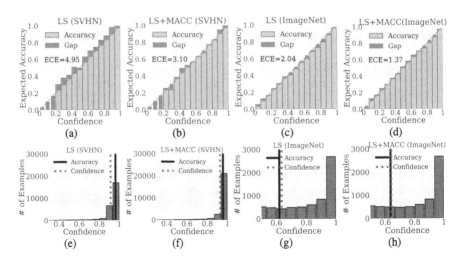

Fig. 4. Reliability diagrams (a, b, c, d) and confidence histograms (e, f, g, h) of (ResNet) models trained with LS and LS+MACC. (a, b, e, f) show that our method is effective in reducing under-confidence, while (c, d, g, h) reveal that it can reduce over-confidence. We refer to the supplementary for similar plots with NLL and FL.

Confidence of Incorrect Predictions: Figure 5 shows the histogram of confidence values for the incorrect predictions. After adding our auxiliary loss (MACC) to CE loss, the confidence values of the incorrect predictions are decreased (see also Fig. 1a & b).

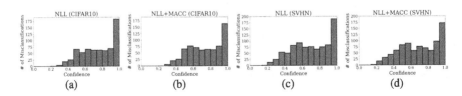

Fig. 5. Confidence histogram of incorrect predictions from CIFAR10 and SVHN (ResNet56).

Calibration Performance Under Class Imbalance: We use SVHN to validate the calibration performance under class imbalance, which has a class imbalance factor of 2.7 [14]. Both Tables 2 and 4 show that, compared to competing approaches, MACC not only improves calibration performance over the (whole) dataset, but also displays competitive calibration performance in each class. This is largely because MACC considers whole confidence/certainty vector, which calibrates even the non-predicted classes.

Comparison of ECE and SCE Convergence with SOTA: Figure 6 shows that the proposed loss function MACC is optimizing both ECE and SCE, better than the current SOTA methods of MbLS and MDCA. Although MACC does not explicitly optimize ECE and SCE, it achieves better ECE and SCE convergence. Moreover, compared to others, it consistently decreases both SCE and ECE throughout the evolution of training.

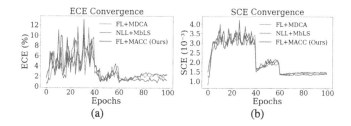

Fig. 6. ECE and SCE convergence plot while training ResNet50 on the Tiny-ImageNet for MDCA, MbLS and ours (MACC). We use the learning rate decay factor of 0.1 and 0.02 at epochs 50 and 70, respectively, while for MDCA and MbLS the factor is 0.1.

Impact of Our Model and Training Settings: Table 8 shows the performance of the task-specific loss functions and the SOTA calibration losses with the same architecture and training settings as in our loss. i.e., ResNet model with dropout is used and the learning rate at the last stage of the learning rate scheduler is reduced. Upon comparing Table 8 with Table 1 and Table 2, we note that with our model architecture and learning rate setting, as such, the calibration of competing losses is poor than our loss. So, the effectiveness of our method is not due to the model architecture or some specific training settings but because of our loss formulation.

Table 8. Calibration performance of different losses with our model (ResNet model as in Table 2 with dropout) and training settings.

Dataset	CE		FL		NLL+MbLS		FL+MDCA	
	SCE	ECE	SCE	ECE	SCE	ECE	SCE	ECE
CIFAR10	6.43	2.80	_3.59_	**0.59**	4.62	1.35	**3.12**	_0.86_
CIFAR100	2.01	4.00	**1.87**	**0.79**	2.12	_0.85_	_2.00_	1.04
SVHN	1.99	**0.27**	7.30	3.30	_1.92_	_0.34_	**1.86**	0.38

5   Conclusion

We propose a new train-time calibration method which is based on a novel auxiliary loss term (MACC). Our loss attempts to align the predictive mean confidence with the predictive certainty and is based on the observation that a greater gap between the two translates to higher miscalibration. It is differentiable, operates on minibatches, and acts as a regularizer with other task-specific losses. Extensive experiments on ten challenging datasets show that our loss consistently shows improved calibration performance over the SOTA calibration methods across in-domain and out-of-domain scenarios.

References

1. Bernardo, J.M., Smith, A.F.: Bayesian Theory, vol. 405. Wiley, New York (2009)
2. Blundell, C., Cornebise, J., Kavukcuoglu, K., Wierstra, D.: Weight uncertainty in neural network. In: International Conference on Machine Learning, pp. 1613–1622 (2015)
3. Brier, G.W., et al.: Verification of forecasts expressed in terms of probability. Mon. Weather Rev. **78**(1), 1–3 (1950)
4. Deng, J., Dong, W., Socher, R., Li, L.J., Li, K., Fei-Fei, L.: ImageNet: a large-scale hierarchical image database. In: Proceedings of the IEEE/CVF Conference on Computer Vision and Pattern Recognition, pp. 248–255 (2009)
5. DeVries, T., Taylor, G.W.: Learning confidence for out-of-distribution detection in neural networks. arXiv preprint arXiv:1802.04865 (2018)
6. Ding, Z., Han, X., Liu, P., Niethammer, M.: Local temperature scaling for probability calibration. In: Proceedings of the IEEE/CVF International Conference on Computer Vision, pp. 6889–6899 (2021)
7. Dosovitskiy, A., et al.: An image is worth 16x16 words: transformers for image recognition at scale. arXiv preprint arXiv:2010.11929 (2020)
8. Dusenberry, M.W., et al.: Analyzing the role of model uncertainty for electronic health records. In: Proceedings of the ACM Conference on Health, Inference, and Learning, pp. 204–213 (2020)
9. Gal, Y., Ghahramani, Z.: Dropout as a Bayesian approximation: representing model uncertainty in deep learning. In: International Conference on Machine Learning, pp. 1050–1059 (2016)
10. Gretton, A.: Introduction to RKHS, and some simple kernel algorithms. In: Advanced Topics in Machine Learning. Lecture Conducted from University College London, vol. 16, p. 5-3 (2013)
11. Grigorescu, S., Trasnea, B., Cocias, T., Macesanu, G.: A survey of deep learning techniques for autonomous driving. J. Field Robot. **37**(3), 362–386 (2020)
12. Guo, C., Pleiss, G., Sun, Y., Weinberger, K.Q.: On calibration of modern neural networks. In: International Conference on Machine Learning, pp. 1321–1330 (2017)
13. He, K., Zhang, X., Ren, S., Sun, J.: Deep residual learning for image recognition. In: Proceedings of the IEEE/CVF Conference on Computer Vision and Pattern Recognition, pp. 770–778 (2016)
14. Hebbalaguppe, R., Prakash, J., Madan, N., Arora, C.: A stitch in time saves nine: a train-time regularizing loss for improved neural network calibration. In: Proceedings of the IEEE/CVF Conference on Computer Vision and Pattern Recognition, pp. 16081–16090 (2022)
15. Hein, M., Andriushchenko, M., Bitterwolf, J.: Why ReLU networks yield high-confidence predictions far away from the training data and how to mitigate the problem. In: Proceedings of the IEEE/CVF Conference on Computer Vision and Pattern Recognition, pp. 41–50 (2019)
16. Hendrycks, D., Dietterich, T.: Benchmarking neural network robustness to common corruptions and perturbations. In: Proceedings of the International Conference on Learning Representations (2019)
17. Hendrycks, D., Gimpel, K.: A baseline for detecting misclassified and out-of-distribution examples in neural networks. arXiv preprint arXiv:1610.02136 (2016)
18. Hendrycks, D., Mazeika, M., Dietterich, T.: Deep anomaly detection with outlier exposure. In: International Conference on Learning Representations (2018)
19. Hernández-Lobato, J.M., Adams, R.: Probabilistic backpropagation for scalable learning of Bayesian neural networks. In: International Conference on Machine Learning, pp. 1861–1869 (2015)

20. Jiang, X., Osl, M., Kim, J., Ohno-Machado, L.: Calibrating predictive model estimates to support personalized medicine. J. Am. Med. Inform. Assoc. **19**(2), 263–274 (2012)
21. Kermany, D., Zhang, K., Goldbaum, M., et al.: Labeled optical coherence tomography (OCT) and chest X-Ray images for classification. Mendeley Data **2**(2), 651 (2018)
22. Krizhevsky, A., Hinton, G., et al.: Learning multiple layers of features from tiny images. Master thesis (2009)
23. Krizhevsky, A., Sutskever, I., Hinton, G.E.: ImageNet classification with deep convolutional neural networks. Commun. ACM **60**(6), 84–90 (2017)
24. Kull, M., Silva Filho, T., Flach, P.: Beta calibration: a well-founded and easily implemented improvement on logistic calibration for binary classifiers. In: Artificial Intelligence and Statistics, pp. 623–631 (2017)
25. Kumar, A., Sarawagi, S., Jain, U.: Trainable calibration measures for neural networks from kernel mean embeddings. In: International Conference on Machine Learning, pp. 2805–2814 (2018)
26. Lakshminarayanan, B., Pritzel, A., Blundell, C.: Simple and scalable predictive uncertainty estimation using deep ensembles. In: Advances in Neural Information Processing Systems, vol. 30 (2017)
27. Lang, K.: NewsWeeder: learning to filter netnews. In: Machine Learning Proceedings, pp. 331–339. Elsevier (1995)
28. Li, D., Yang, Y., Song, Y.Z., Hospedales, T.M.: Deeper, broader and artier domain general-ization. In: Proceedings of the IEEE/CVF International Conference on Computer Vision, pp. 5542–5550 (2017)
29. Liang, G., Zhang, Y., Wang, X., Jacobs, N.: Improved trainable calibration method for neural networks on medical imaging classification. arXiv preprint arXiv:2009.04057 (2020)
30. Lin, T.Y., Goyal, P., Girshick, R., He, K., Dollár, P.: Focal loss for dense object detection. In: Proceedings of the IEEE/CVF International Conference on Computer Vision, pp. 2980–2988 (2017)
31. Liu, B., Ben Ayed, I., Galdran, A., Dolz, J.: The devil is in the margin: margin-based label smoothing for network calibration. In: Proceedings of the IEEE/CVF Conference on Computer Vision and Pattern Recognition, pp. 80–88 (2022)
32. Louizos, C., Welling, M.: Structured and efficient variational deep learning with matrix Gaussian posteriors. In: International Conference on Machine Learning, pp. 1708–1716 (2016)
33. Ma, X., Blaschko, M.B.: Meta-Cal: well-controlled post-hoc calibration by ranking. In: International Conference on Machine Learning, pp. 7235–7245 (2021)
34. Meronen, L., Irwanto, C., Solin, A.: Stationary activations for uncertainty calibration in deep learning. In: Advances in Neural Information Processing Systems, vol. 33, pp. 2338–2350 (2020)
35. Mukhoti, J., Kulharia, V., Sanyal, A., Golodetz, S., Torr, P., Dokania, P.: Calibrating deep neural networks using focal loss. In: Advances in Neural Information Processing Systems, vol. 33, pp. 15288–15299 (2020)
36. Müller, R., Kornblith, S., Hinton, G.E.: When does label smoothing help? In: Advances in Neural Information Processing Systems, vol. 32 (2019)
37. Naeini, M.P., Cooper, G., Hauskrecht, M.: Obtaining well calibrated probabilities using Bayesian binning. In: Twenty-Ninth AAAI Conference on Artificial Intelligence (2015)
38. Netzer, Y., Wang, T., Coates, A., Bissacco, A., Wu, B., Ng, A.Y.: Reading digits in natural images with unsupervised feature learning. In: Advances in Neural Information Processing Systems Workshop on Deep Learning and Unsupervised Feature Learning (2011)
39. Nixon, J., Dusenberry, M.W., Zhang, L., Jerfel, G., Tran, D.: Measuring calibration in deep learning. In: Proceedings of the IEEE/CVF Conference on Computer Vision and Pattern Recognition Workshops, vol. 2 (2019)

40. Ovadia, Y., et al.: Can you trust your model's uncertainty? Evaluating predictive uncertainty under dataset shift. In: Advances in Neural Information Processing Systems, vol. 32 (2019)

41. Padhy, S., Nado, Z., Ren, J., Liu, J., Snoek, J., Lakshminarayanan, B.: Revisiting one-vs-all classifiers for predictive uncertainty and out-of-distribution detection in neural networks. arXiv preprint arXiv:2007.05134 (2020)

42. Pereyra, G., Tucker, G., Chorowski, J., Kaiser, Ł., Hinton, G.: Regularizing neural networks by penalizing confident output distributions. arXiv preprint arXiv:1701.06548 (2017)

43. Russakovsky, O., et al.: ImageNet large scale visual recognition challenge. Int. J. Comput. Vision **115**(3), 211–252 (2015). https://doi.org/10.1007/s11263-015-0816-y

44. Sharma, M., Saha, O., Sriraman, A., Hebbalaguppe, R., Vig, L., Karande, S.: Crowdsourcing for chromosome segmentation and deep classification. In: Proceedings of the IEEE/CVF Conference on Computer Vision and Pattern Recognition Workshops, pp. 34–41 (2017)

45. Simonyan, K., Zisserman, A.: Very deep convolutional networks for large-scale image recognition. arXiv preprint arXiv:1409.1556 (2014)

46. Tomani, C., Gruber, S., Erdem, M.E., Cremers, D., Buettner, F.: Post-hoc uncertainty calibration for domain drift scenarios. In: Proceedings of the IEEE/CVF Conference on Computer Vision and Pattern Recognition, pp. 10124–10132 (2021)

47. Touvron, H., Cord, M., Douze, M., Massa, F., Sablayrolles, A., Jégou, H.: Training data-efficient image transformers & distillation through attention. In: International Conference on Machine Learning, pp. 10347–10357. PMLR (2021)

48. Wenzel, F., Snoek, J., Tran, D., Jenatton, R.: Hyperparameter ensembles for robustness and uncertainty quantification. In: Advances in Neural Information Processing Systems, vol. 33, pp. 6514–6527 (2020)

49. Yu, R., Alì, G.S.: What's inside the black box? AI challenges for lawyers and researchers. Leg. Inf. Manag. **19**(1), 2–13 (2019)

50. Zhang, J., Kailkhura, B., Han, T.Y.J.: Mix-n-Match: ensemble and compositional methods for uncertainty calibration in deep learning. In: International Conference on Machine Learning, pp. 11117–11128 (2020)

51. Zhang, Z., Dalca, A.V., Sabuncu, M.R.: Confidence calibration for convolutional neural networks using structured dropout. arXiv preprint arXiv:1906.09551 (2019)

Drawing the Same Bounding Box Twice? Coping Noisy Annotations in Object Detection with Repeated Labels

David Tschirschwitz[✉][iD], Christian Benz[iD], Morris Florek[iD],
Henrik Norderhus[iD], Benno Stein[iD], and Volker Rodehorst[iD]

Bauhaus-Universität Weimar, Weimar, Germany
david.tschirschwitz@uni-weimar.de

Abstract. The reliability of supervised machine learning systems depends on the accuracy and availability of ground truth labels. However, the process of human annotation, being prone to error, introduces the potential for noisy labels, which can impede the practicality of these systems. While training with noisy labels is a significant consideration, the reliability of test data is also crucial to ascertain the dependability of the results. A common approach to addressing this issue is repeated labeling, where multiple annotators label the same example, and their labels are combined to provide a better estimate of the true label. In this paper, we propose a novel localization algorithm that adapts well-established ground truth estimation methods for object detection and instance segmentation tasks. The key innovation of our method lies in its ability to transform combined localization and classification tasks into classification-only problems, thus enabling the application of techniques such as Expectation-Maximization (EM) or Majority Voting (MJV). Although our main focus is the aggregation of unique ground truth for test data, our algorithm also shows superior performance during training on the TexBiG dataset, surpassing both noisy label training and label aggregation using Weighted Boxes Fusion (WBF). Our experiments indicate that the benefits of repeated labels emerge under specific dataset and annotation configurations. The key factors appear to be (1) dataset complexity, the (2) annotator consistency, and (3) the given annotation budget constraints.

Keywords: Object Detection · Instance Segmentation · Robust Learning

1 Introduction

Data-driven machine learning systems are expected to operate effectively even under "difficult" and unforeseen circumstances. Consider safety-relevant domains such as autonomous driving, medical diagnosis, or structural health monitoring, where system failure sets lives at risk. Robust systems – those capable of reliable

U. Köthe and C. Rother (Eds.): DAGM GCPR 2023, LNCS 14264, pp. 605–623, 2024.
https://doi.org/10.1007/978-3-031-54605-1_39

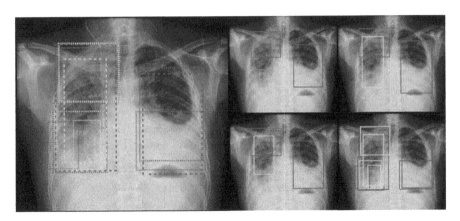

Fig. 1. Comparison between different ground truth aggregation methods, exemplary on the VinDr-CXR dataset [23]. Left: the original image with the repeated labels indicated by the different line types. Right: the four smaller images from top left to bottom right are, MJV+∩, LAEM+μ, LAEM+∪ and WBF.

operation in unseen situations – may encounter several challenges, including domain shifts [5,16,25,36], adversarial attacks [42,43], degrading image quality [7,21,41] and noisy or uncertain labels [9,10,18,37]. Past studies [33] indicate that noisy labels can cause more harm than the three aforementioned sources of input noise. Given this context, our study concentrates on addressing the issue of noisy labels, specifically within noisy test data. Without a unique ground truth, evaluation is unattainable. Therefore, to enhance robustness against label noise, it will be pivotal to first devise methods tailored towards annotation aggregation, which lays the groundwork for potential future integration with multi-annotator learning methods.

The creation of annotated data for supervised learning is a costly endeavor, particularly in cases where experts such as medical professionals or domain experts are needed to annotate the data. To mitigate this issue, crowd-sourcing has emerged as a cost-effective means of generating large datasets, albeit with the disadvantage of potentially lower quality annotations that may contain label noise [30,44,47]. Although the reduced costs of crowd-sourced annotations often justifies their use, deep neural networks have the capacity to memorize noisy labels as special cases, leading to a declining performance and overfitting towards the noisy labeled data [44]. Notably, even expert annotated data is susceptible to label noise, given the difficulty of the data to annotate. A survey by Song et. al.[33] revealed that the number of corrupt labels in real-world datasets ranges between 8.0% to 38.5%. The authors demonstrate that reducing label noise and creating cleaned data can improve the accuracy of models. To address the issue of noisy labels, an approach known as "repeated-labeling" has been proposed. Repeated-labeling means to obtain annotations from multiple annotators/coders for the same data entry, such as an image. More specifically: For a set of images $\{x_i\}_{i=1}^N$ multiple annotators create noisy labels $\{\tilde{y}_i^r\}_{i=1,...,N}^{r=1,...,R}$, with $\tilde{y}_i^r$ being the label assigned from annotator r to image x_i, but without a ground truth label $\{y_i\}_{i=1,...,N}$ [34].

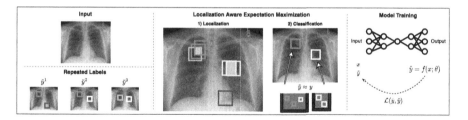

Fig. 2. Left: Original input image featuring three separate annotations by distinct annotators. Center: Application of the LAEM aggregation method to the three annotations, yielding an approximate ground truth. Right: Aggregated ground truth utilized during the training process.

Methods for mitigating the negative effect of label noise via repeated labeling can be divided into two categories [18,34]: (a) *two-stage* approaches [8,39] and (b) *one-stage* or *simultaneous* approaches [11,12,15]. Two-stage approaches aim to approximate the ground truth prior to training, a process known as ground truth estimation or ground truth inference [45], as depicted in Fig. 2; a straightforward approach is to compute a majority vote. Following label aggregation, the model is trained in a regular fashion. Two-stage approaches offer the benefit of being compatible with commonly used model architectures. On the other hand, simultaneous approaches attempt to integrate repeated labels directly into the training process. In any case, the primary objective of both strategies is to achieve robust and accurate results by leveraging the repeated labeled data to the fullest extent possible. Doing so is crucial to justify the additional annotation efforts. Lastly, to enable the use of established performance metrics, such as those employed in the COCO object detection dataset (mAP) [20], a ground truth estimation step is essential for the validation and test sets. While simultaneous approaches can more effectively utilize repeated labels, they are not intended to execute the necessary aggregation step required to generate the unique ground truth estimate [34]. Consequently, reliable approximation methods are indispensable for evaluation purposes.

Object detection and instance segmentation require both localization and classification, which means that existing methods for repeated labels that are used for classification tasks such as image classification or named entity recognition are not applicable [28]. That is, the available selection of ground truth inference methods is limited. Furthermore, the creation of bounding box or polygonal annotations is expensive [10] and reduces the number of datasets with repeated labels available for evaluating ground truth inference methods [23,35]. However, we deliberately avoid using synthetic data and focus on real datasets. Our contributions are as follows:

1. We propose a localization algorithm that enables the use of existing ground truth estimation methods such as majority voting or expectation maximization for instance-based recognition tasks and evaluate it extensively with existing methods [18,32].
2. We introduce a comparative analysis of ground truth inference methods that highlights their properties and limits.
3. We conduct ablation studies to analyze the costs associated with creating repeated annotations, and what to do when the amount of available annotated data is limited.
4. We introduce an extension for the TexBiG dataset [35] in the form of a test subset, wherein each of the 200 test images has been annotated by five expert annotators. Utilizing our aggregation method, we establish a unique approximation of the ground truth, which will serve as the unknown reference standard on an evaluation server. This approach allows the TexBiG dataset to be used for evaluation of robust learning methods addressing the challenge of noisy labels.

Once released, the link to the evaluation server will be posted on the GitHub repository where the code is hosted: https://github.com/Madave94/gtiod.

2 Related Work

To approximate the ground truth, estimation methods make assumptions about the data and task properties as well as the annotation process. Majority Voting (MJV) [14,26,29] assumes correct labels for the majority of training samples and aggregates the labels accordingly:

$$\tilde{y}_i = \begin{cases} 1 \text{ if } (1/R) \sum_r^R = y_i^r > 0.5 \\ 0 \text{ if } (1/R) \sum_r^R = y_i^r < 0.5 \end{cases} \tag{1}$$

In case of a tie, the label is chosen randomly between the tied ones or selected by a super-annotator. On data with high inter-annotator agreement, majority voting can be a straightforward approach to obtain ground truth estimates reasonable quality.

Numerous methods for inferring ground truth rely on the Expectation-Maximization (EM) approach, first introduced by Dawid and Skene [8]. This approach estimates annotator confidence and integrates it into a weighted voting procedure for determining the true label. By considering annotator performance, these methods address the limitations of majority voting, thereby avoiding potential outliers. One notable advancement in this area is the GLAD [39] method, which not only attempts to identify the most probable class but also assesses image difficulty, additional to the annotator confidence. It should be noted, however, that this approach is limited to binary classification tasks [31].

In addition to classification tasks, pixel-wise classification (semantic segmentation) also has existing ground truth inference methods, such as STAPLE [38], SIMPLE [17], and COLLATE [1]. Recent developments in this field have led to approaches that incorporate data difficulty into the estimation process, as seen in a newly developed simultaneous method [11]. Although there are numerous variations of ground truth estimation methods for classification and segmentation tasks, this discussion will focus on methods applicable to object detection and instance segmentation, rather than diving deeper into this area.

For instance-based recognition tasks like object detection and instance segmentation, there is an additional issue to consider – the localization step. During training, methods consisting of a combination of thresholds and non-maximum suppression are used to solve the localization problem and then focus on classification accuracy. While this may work during training, repeated labeling is likely to have more than just a prediction and ground truth pair to match, since multiple annotators might have created multiple labels. Hence, existing methods are not applicable. An existing approach to aggregate annotations for object detection is called Weighted Boxes Fusion (WBF) [18,32], which was used for the VinDr-CXR dataset [23]. WBF focuses on the weighted aggregation within each class, ignoring inter-class disagreements and also not discarding any annotations even with low agreement. This is beneficial in cases where missing a possible case is far more severe then finding too many, such as a task that requires high recall. Apart from this single existing instance-based recognition approach, we are not aware of any other aggregation methods for object detection or instance segmentation.

3   Method

In the following section we introduce a novel adaptation of the EM algorithm, *localization-aware expectation maximization* (LAEM), for instance-based recognition tasks. The same localization algorithm can also be used with majority voting, which therefore functions as a baseline. Additionally, we expand the existing weighted boxes fusion technique to encompass weighted mask fusion, which enables its use in instance segmentation and facilitates benchmarking on a broader range of datasets. As extending weighted boxes fusion is not our core contribution it can be found in Appendix 1.

3.1   Localization-Aware Expectation-Maximization

Our novel approach adds a localization stage to existing methods like majority voting and expectation maximization, enabling the use of these established methods for instance-based recognition tasks. Thus, the proposed label aggregation process consists of two stages: (1) *localization-stage* and (2) *classification-stage*. Assuming that R annotators have created noisy instance-based labels $\tilde{y}_{ij}^r$ for image x_i. Subscript $j = 0, ..., M_r$ refers to the single instances annotated by annotator r for image x_i. M_r can be zero if no instances were labeled by r. Each instance contains a class $c \in C$ denoted $\tilde{y}_{ijc}^r$. Furthermore, $\tilde{y}_{ijb}^r$ refers to the respective bounding box and $\tilde{y}_{ijs}^r$ to the optional pixel-wise segmentation mask.

Algorithm 1. Outline of the localization algorithm used for LAEM

Require:

$X = \{x_i\}_{i=1,\ldots,N}$ ▷ Set of images

$\tilde{Y} = \{\tilde{Y}_i\}_{i=1,\ldots,N}$ ▷ Set of noisy labels per image

$S = \{S_i\}_{i=1,\ldots,N}$ ▷ Set of annotators per image

θ ▷ IoU threshold

for $i \in X$ **do**   ▷ Loop over images

     $\tilde{Y}_i = \{\tilde{y}_{i1}^1, \tilde{y}_{i2}^1, \ldots, \tilde{y}_{iM_1}^1, \tilde{y}_{i1}^2, \tilde{y}_{i2}^2, \ldots, \tilde{y}_{iM_2}^2, \ldots, \tilde{y}_{i1}^R, \tilde{y}_{i2}^R, \ldots, \tilde{y}_{iM_R}^R\}$

     $\tilde{Y}_i^{\mathrm{LAEM}} = \emptyset$

     $Q = \{U_k | U_k \in \mathcal{P}(S_i) \wedge |U_k| \geq |U_{k+1}| \wedge \lceil |S_i|/2 \rceil \leq |U_k|\}$ ▷ Ordered set of annotator combinations

     for $U \in Q$ **do**   ▷ Loop over annotator combinations

         $\mathrm{L} = \{\tilde{Y}_{i:}^{k_1} \times \cdots \times \tilde{Y}_{i:}^{k_n} | k_1, \ldots, k_n \in U \wedge n = |U|\}$ ▷ Possible combinations of labels

         $F = \{u_k | u_k \in L \wedge \theta \leq IoU(u_k) \wedge IoU(u_k) \geq IoU(u_{k+1})\}$ ▷ Filtered and ordered L

         for $k \in N$ **do**   ▷ Loop over label combinations

             $K = \{k_1, k_2, \ldots, k_n\}$

             if $K \cap \tilde{Y}_i = \emptyset$ **then**   ▷ Check for label availability

                 $\tilde{Y}_i = \tilde{Y}_i \setminus K$ ▷ Remove labels from available labels

                 $\tilde{Y}_i^{\mathrm{LAEM}} = \tilde{Y}_i^{\mathrm{LAEM}} \cup aggregate(K)$ ▷ Add aggregated label to accepted labels

             end if

         end for

     end for

end for

Algorithm 1 outlines the LAEM approach. The algorithm requires image set X, a set of noisy labels $\tilde{Y}$, a set of annotators S, and a threshold θ. Looping over the images of the dataset, the power set $\mathcal{P}(\mathcal{S})$ over the annotators is computed. Subsets containing less than half the number of annotators are removed and a descending order is enforced onto the set. It subsequently iterates through the remaining ordered subsets of annotators and computes the Cartesian product between the respective annotators. Each tuple is then ordered and filtered according to threshold θ based on the intersection over union in its generalized form:

$$IoU = \frac{\bigcap_{r=1}^{R} \tilde{y}_{ijb}^r}{\bigcup_{r=1}^{R} \tilde{y}_{ijb}^r} \tag{2}$$

The remaining set of tuples ordered by descending IoU forms the set of candidate solutions F. In case all labels from a candidate tuple are still available, they are aggregated according to an aggregation function and added to the inferred solutions $\tilde{Y}_i^{\mathrm{LAEM}}$. The aggregation function comprises two steps: (1) all classes contained in the original tuple $\tilde{y}_{ijc}^r$ are appended to a list serving as input for expectation maximization or majority voting and (2) the areas of the different candidates $\tilde{y}_{ijb}^r$ are combined according to the union, intersection, or average area of all boxes involved. The average operation is based on the WBF algorithm [32] with uniform weights. If available, the same procedure (for details cf. Appendix 1) is applied to the segmentation masks $\tilde{y}_{ijs}^r$. This concludes the localization stage. In the subsequent classification-stage existing ground truth inference methods can be applied such as majority voting or expectation maximization [8].

3.2   Algorithmic Design Choices

Our algorithm is designed in a divide-and-conquer manner. Firstly, we prioritize localization, effectively reducing the problem to a classification task for each matched instance after localization. This strategy consequently facilitates the application of established methods for ground truth inference developed in other fields. We always prefer a localization match with more annotators to maximize consensus. If a localization match involving all available annotators cannot be found given the threshold value θ, we ensure successive reduction to potentially prefer the next largest number of annotators. This approach first guarantees localization quality, and only upon establishing matched areas based on their localizations do we aggregate the classes. The algorithm is parameterized by the threshold value θ, which can be adjusted to enforce stricter localization quality and also control the order in which instances are matched. Though this heuristic solution may not provide an optimal outcome for larger problem sizes (e.g., numerous instances on a single image), when an image exhibits high agreement among annotators, a consensus area can be aggregated, and the class of this area can be unambiguously determined.

One advantage of the Expectation-Maximization (EM) approach is that assignment is unambiguous. The confidence calculated during the EM algorithm serves as a tie-breaker, a benefit not present with Majority Voting (MJV). Furthermore, fitting the EM algorithm is efficient; following localization matching, no further areas are calculated, and only the solutions $\tilde{Y}_i^{\mathrm{LAEM}}$ are considered along with their classes.

While localization fusion functions, such as union or intersection, are available and applicable for training data, the intended use for test data within the context of LAEM (Localization-Aware Expectation-Maximization) primarily involves the averaging fusion function. This approach enables a balanced aggregation of areas across different annotators. Additionally, this method is also utilized to aggregate test data as required for the TexBiG dataset [35].

3.3   Comparative Analysis

In Table 1, we present a comparative analysis of the four available ground truth inference methods for instance-based recognition tasks, distinguished by their respective characteristics and properties. Each method is described based on eight distinct features relevant to ground truth estimation methods. A noteworthy difference between LAEM and MJV, as compared to WBF and its adaptation (detailed in Appendix 2), is the handling of instances that lack consensus among annotators. Figure 1 and Appendix 3 illustrates the aggregation processes of MJV, LAEM, and WBF on a few specific images, serving as practical examples. This illustrations reveal that MJV and LAEM tend to find consensus instances, resulting in a final image that appears as if a single annotator has labelled the image. In contrast, the WBF image is relatively cluttered with overlapping instances. This discrepancy arises because WBF merges areas of the same class that significantly overlap but does not discard any annotation. This

Table 1. Comparison table for the characteristics and properties of the different ground truth inference methods. MJV and LAEM both use the novel localization algorithm.

Methods	LAEM	MJV	WBF	WBF+EM
Assignment	1) Localization 2) Classification	1) Localization 2) Classification	Localization only	Localization only
Low agreement	Discard annotation	Discard annotation	Keep annotation	Keep annotation
Edge cases	Use confidence	Randomized	–	–
Localization fusion	Union/average/intersection	Union/average/intersection	Averaging	Weighted averaging
Annotator confidence	✓	✗	✗	✓
Handling missing data	✓	✓	✓	✓
Dataset characteristic	Balanced	Precision oriented	Recall oriented	Recall oriented
Data dependence	✗	✗	✗	✗

is also the case, for instances where two annotators found the same instance area but disagreed on the class, resulting in more instances overall. Although this property might be beneficial for a high-recall scenario – where missing an instance is more detrimental than detecting multiple false positives – it is not ideal for many applications. It's important to note that none of the current methods incorporate data dependence, a feature described in several state-of-the-art ground truth estimation methods for semantic segmentation [1,17,38].

4   Experimental Results

In our preliminary experiment, we scrutinized the influence of annotation budget size by exploring scenarios in which repeated labels might be preferred over single labels. This ablation study was designed to determine the optimal use of a restricted annotation budget, i.e., whether it is more beneficial to train with a larger volume of noisy labels or a reduced set of refined labels. This experimental analysis was conducted using two separate datasets.

In our subsequent investigation, we assessed the effect of annotator selection on model performance by deliberately excluding certain annotators from the labeling process. This enabled us to emulate the potential impact of annotator selection on model performance and to probe the influence of proficient and suboptimal annotators on model output.

Our final experiment, which is detailed in Appendix 2, was actually conducted first since it influenced the choice of the aggregation method used for the training data. However, this experiment is not the main focus of this publication.

4.1   Set-Up

To the best of our knowledge, there are only two datasets available that contain repeated labels for object detection and instance segmentation, respectively: the VinDr-CXR [18,23] dataset and the TexBiG [35] dataset. We focus solely on these two datasets and do not make use of any synthetic data.

VinDr-CXR Dataset. This dataset comprises 15,000 training and 3,000 test chest X-ray images, each of which was annotated by three annotators and five annotators, respectively. With a total of 36,096 instances in the training dataset, the dataset can be considered sparsely annotated, with in average 0.8 instances per image[1]. The dataset consists of 14 different classes that were annotated by 17 radiologists [22]. Using the agreement evaluation method presented in [35] describing the data quality, the K-α (Krippendorff's alpha) is 0.79. However, since only 29.3% of the images in the dataset contains any annotations at all, another K-α was calculated for this reduced subset, resulting in a K-α value of 0.29. This indicates that while annotators largely agree in cases where no anomaly is present, there is significant disagreement in cases that contain instances.

TexBiG Dataset. Recently published [35], the TexBiG provides labels for document layout analysis, similar to the PubLayNet [46] or DocBank [19] datasets. It covers 19 classes for complex document layouts in historical documents during a specific time period, and in the version used here, the training data contains 44,121 instances, the validation data 8,251 instances and the test data 6,678 instances. While the total number of instances is larger as in the VinDr-CXR dataset, there are only 2,457 images in total, 1,922 in the training set, 335 in the validation set and 200 in the test set. Due to the iterative creation process of the dataset, the number of repeated labels is different depending on the sample. An agreement value was used per image to evaluate which samples were to be annotated again. For each image, two annotators were assigned, and in case the agreement value was low after the first iteration, an additional annotator was added to that specific sample. This was done until a maximum of four annotators per sample. In the combined validation and training set, 34 images were annotated by 4 annotators, 336 by at least 3 annotators (including the 34 from before), and 2,257 by at least 2 annotators. We created an additional test set with 5 annotators for 200 newly selected images from the same domain, in accordance with the guideline provided by the authors [35]. We plan to publish this test-set for benchmarking purposes on an evaluation server. The TexBiG dataset is more densely annotated, with 10.7 instances per image, which is 13 time more than the VinDr-CXR dataset. Furthermore, the K-α for the TexBiG training dataset is higher with 0.93.

Comparing the two datasets we find that they represent two opposing marginal cases with one dataset having high-agreement and dense annotations, while the other one has a low-agreement and sparse annotations. However, a more balanced dataset is missing.

Architecture Choice. Regarding the architecture choice, we aimed to find a well-performing and stable choice, rather than aiming for state-of-the-art results since we wanted to focus on comparing the ground truth inference methods and ablation studies on different tasks. For the VinDr-CXR dataset, we tested various architectures including different anchor-based two-stage detectors like Faster R-CNN [27], Cascade R-CNN [2] and Double Head R-CNN [40], and

---

[1] Computed by dividing the number of instances by the product of the number of images and the number of annotators.

additionally, the transformer-based Detection Transformer (DETR) [3]. After thorough investigation, we found that the Double Head R-CNN performs stably and with reasonable results. Therefore, we selected this architecture for our experiments. On the TexBiG dataset, we tried several instance segmentation models like Mask R-CNN [13], Cascade Mask R-CNN [2] and DetectorRS [24], as well as the Mask2Former [6] as a transformer-based architecture. In this case, DetectoRS yielded the most stable performance, and we continued our experiments with this model. We extended MMDetection [4] with our implementation, and the code is available on GitHub under https://github.com/Madave94/gtiod.

4.2 Annotation Budget Ablation

When working on a deep learning project, data is often a limiting factor, and resources must be carefully allocated to create task-specific data. Even when there are ample resources, maximizing the value of those resources is important. In the context of human-annotated data, this concept is referred to as the "annotation budget", which represents the available number of images or instances that can be labeled by a pool of annotators within their available time. The question then becomes, "How can a limited annotation budget be best utilized?" One approach is to prioritize annotating as many different images as possible to cover a broad range of cases within the application domain. However, this approach comes with the risk of introducing more noisy labels due to the inherent variability in annotator performance. Alternatively, creating repeated labels may be more beneficial to improve the quality of the annotations. Ultimately, the decision between prioritizing *quantity versus quality* of labels must be carefully weighed and considered in the context of the project goals and available resources.

In the two ablation studies presented in Table 2 and 3, we compare the performance of different annotation budgets, which refer to the available number of images or instances that can be labeled with the pool of annotators and their available time. The splits used in the studies represent three different cases: (1) Only single annotated labels are available, which are more prone to label noise. (2) A mix of repeated labels and single annotated labels is available. Multiple splits may have this property. (3) Maximum label repetition, where no or very few single annotated labels are available, resulting in significantly less training data. To reduce randomization effects, we create five different random versions for each split and compute their mean and maximum results.

Our results show that the TexBiG dataset quickly reached a data saturation point, suggesting potential benefits from employing multi-annotator learning methods to better utilize repeated labels. Conversely, the VinDr-CXR dataset showed improved performance with higher budgets, indicating that more data helps performance in scenarios with noisy, low-agreement labels.

Both datasets demonstrate that moderate inclusion of repeated labels does not adversely impact performance, with mixed splits achieving peak results at their lowest budgets. These findings highlight the value of repeated annotations,

Table 2. Ablation study on the TexBiG dataset using a limited annotation budget. The results are in $mAP@[.5 : .95]$, show that multi annotator learning methods are required to justify repeated labels. However, even without multi annotator methods the performance loss using repeated annotations is marginal.

Split	Budget		Averaged		Maximum	
	rel.	abs.	AP	AP^{bb}	AP	AP^{bb}
1922 × 2	100%	3844	41.9	47.5	43.3	48.7
966 × 2 966 × 1	75%	2883	42.4	47.9	42.8	48.4
1922 × 1	50%	1922	**42.7**	**48.3**	43.4	**48.8**
641 × 2 640 × 1	50%	1922	42.4	47.7	**43.9**	**48.8**
966 × 2	50%	1922	41.1	46.2	42.8	47.8
30 × 4 243 × 3 1073 × 1	50%	1922	41.9	47.3	43.0	48.2
30 × 4 243 × 3 536 × 2 1 × 1	50%	1922	39.7	45.0	41.0	46.5

Table 3. Ablation study on the VinDr-CXR dataset using a limited annotation budget. The results are in mAP_{40} as provided by the leaderboard.

Split	Budget		Avg. AP	Max. AP
	rel.	abs.		
15,000 × 2	66.6%	30,000	14.8	15.0
10,000 × 3	66.6%	30,000	14.7	14.9
15,000 × 1	33.3%	15,000	13.4	13.9
10,000 × 1 2,500 × 2	33.3%	15,000	**13.6**	14.1
7,500 × 2	33.3%	15,000	13.5	13.8
3,000 × 3 3,000 × 2	33.3%	15,000	**13.6**	**14.3**
5,000 × 3	33.3%	15,000	13.4	14.0

which not only increase label reliability, but also allow for efficient use of multi-annotator learning methods. Remarkably, the opportunity costs for creating such repeated labels seem negligible.

Our findings suggest that higher fragmentation in annotator splits could lead to reduced performance, possibly due to enhanced intracoder consistency. Moreover, the influence of split distribution appears prominent only when the annotation budget is limited. Identifying a systematic relationship between split distribution and performance, thereby suggesting optimal splits before the annotation process, could be a promising future research direction.

The overall takeaway is that multiple annotations may not always yield significant advantages, yet in scenarios with a constrained annotation budget, they could prove beneficial. Determining which cases fall into each category remains an open challenge.

4.3 Leave-One-Out Annotator Selection

Table 4 displays the results of a final experiment conducted on the TexBiG dataset. To create four groups of annotators, each group consisting of one to three individuals, annotations were distributed unevenly among them, resulting in groups of different sizes. Subsequently, each group was left out of the training process, while the remaining three groups were used to train the model. This approach led to a smaller training set. Surprisingly, the experiment showed that when the largest group, denoted as **B**, was excluded, leaving only 61.6% of the annotations available, the model's performance reached its peak. This outcome underscores the importance of selecting precise annotators in the training process, since less precise ones may introduce noisy labels that can hinder performance. However, it is challenging to identify precise annotators before the annotation process, as there is no data available to determine their level of precision.

Table 4. Choosing the right annotator? If annotators are not in the group what would happen to the results? Splits are unequal, due to the annotation distribution.

Left out group	Left out images		Left out annotations		Performance	
	rel.	abs.	rel.	abs.	AP	AP^{bb}
Group A	25.1%	1,040	26.8%	11,810	42.4	47.1
Group B	29.5%	1,225	38.4%	16,932	**44.1**	**49.8**
Group C	25.7%	1,067	18.2%	8,017	42.6	48.1
Group D	19.7%	815	16.7%	7,362	43.1	48.3

5   Conclusion

Our results indicate the potential benefits of repeated labels which seem to be contingent on several factors. The identified key factors are the balance between (1) the complexity or variation in the dataset and its corresponding task difficulty, (2) the variability in annotation depending on inter-annotator consistency and annotator proficiency, and (3) the constraints of the annotation budget. This interaction suggests the existence of an 'optimal range' for image annotation strategy. For instance, datasets with high variance and low annotator consistency may benefit from multiple annotations per image, while in cases with low image variation and high annotator consistency, many images annotated once might suffice. This balancing act between data and annotation variation could guide decisions when choosing between single or multiple annotators per image, given a fixed annotation budget.

However, the utility of repeated labels is substantially hampered due to the lack of multi-annotator-learning approaches for object detection and instance segmentation. Thus, future work should concentrate on developing methods that bridge this gap between these areas and other computer vision domains like image classification or semantic segmentation.

Lastly, a significant challenge remains regarding the availability of suitable datasets. With limited datasets in the domain and disparities among them, our findings' generalizability remains constrained to the two domains covered in this study. A larger dataset with repeated labels and balanced agreement would be valuable for future research. Synthetic data could be beneficial but pose the risk that models trained on these data may only learn the distribution used to randomly create repeated labels from the original annotations. Thus, creating a suitable dataset remains a formidable task.

Acknowledgment. This work was supported by the Thuringian Ministry for Economy, Science and Digital Society/Thüringer Aufbaubank (TMWWDG/TAB).

Appendix 1

This section presents our adaptation of the weighted box fusion (WBF) technique, tailored specifically for instance segmentation as a weighted mask fusion (WMF).

In their study, [18] propose a method for combining annotations from multiple annotators using a weighted box fusion [32] approach. In this method, bounding boxes are matched greedily only with boxes of the same class, and no annotations are discarded. The WBF algorithm fuses boxes that exceed a specified overlap threshold, resulting in new boxes that represent the weighted average of the original boxes. The approach also allows for inclusion of box confidence scores and prior weights for each annotator.

To extend the WBF method for instance segmentation, we introduce an option to fuse segmentation masks, which involves four steps: (1) calculating the weighted area and weighted center points from the different masks, (2) compute the average center point and average area from the selected masks, (3) determining the closest center point of the original masks to the weighted center point and selecting this mask, and (4) dilating or eroding the chosen mask until the area is close to the averaged area. The resulting mask is used as the aggregated segmentation mask and is also used as the averaging operation during the aggregation for LAEM and MJV with uniform weight.

Moreover, we integrate the WBF approach with LAEM, yielding WBF+EM. This integration involves assessing annotator confidence using LAEM, and subsequently incorporating it into the WBF method to produce weighted average areas instead of simply averaged areas. While the differences between LAEM and WBF might seem subtle, WBF+EM offers a more thorough approach to annotator fusion. This modification is relatively minor, and its impact is modest, as corroborated by our experiments delineated in Appendix 2.

Appendix 2

In this experiment, we carried out a comparative analysis of different ground truth inference methods. To do this, we separated the annotations for training and testing, and created various combinations of train-test datasets using the available ground truth estimation methods. Afterward, a model was trained on these combinations. The results from this experiment reveal how aggregation methods can impact the performance of the trained models and show how these outcomes can vary based on the specific combination of training and testing aggregation used.

Tables 5 and 6 present the application of various ground truth estimation methods on repeated labels. In the TexBiG dataset, each method is employed to aggregate the labels of both training and test data, and all possible train-test combinations are learned and tested to perform a cross comparison of the different ground truth inference methods, as shown in Table 5. The hyperparameter for the area combination is denoted as $\cup$ for union, μ for averaging and $\cap$ for

Table 5. Cross-Validation of ground truth inference combinations between training and test data, for the DetectoRS with a ResNet-50 backbone on the TexBiG dataset. Showing the $mAP@[.5 : .95]$ for instance masks and bounding boxes. Union is represented by $\cup$, intersection by $\cap$ and averaging by μ. RL denotes training conducted on un-aggregated noisy labels. The two rows on the bottom show how the training methods perform on average.

DetectoRS TexBiG			RL	MJV $\cup$	MJV μ	MJV $\cap$	LAEM $\cup$	LAEM μ	LAEM $\cap$	WBF base	WBF EM
	MJV $\cup$	AP	32.5	34.5	30.4	25.5	**35.1**	29.1	28.4	30.2	30.7
		AP^{bb}	34.7	36.6	34.0	29.9	**37.5**	32.7	33.4	34.4	33.5
	MJV μ	AP	41.9	**43.9**	39.9	35.8	43.6	40.8	35.0	41.5	41.9
		AP^{bb}	45.6	**48.2**	44.6	41.4	47.9	44.5	40.2	45.5	46.2
	MJV $\cap$	AP	44.2	41.7	**46.6**	45.0	43.2	45.3	45.2	46.0	44.9
		AP^{bb}	49.6	47.9	**51.4**	49.9	49.3	50.6	49.5	51.0	49.2
	LAEM $\cup$	AP	31.5	34.9	**44.4**	25.9	33.6	30.5	26.8	29.8	31.1
		AP^{bb}	33.6	36.5	**48.9**	30.5	35.8	33.8	31.4	33.0	34.6
	LAEM μ	AP	41.1	42.5	40.5	34.9	**43.6**	40.2	35.9	40.7	40.4
		AP^{bb}	44.8	46.8	44.6	41.9	**47.7**	44.3	41.7	45.5	45.1
	LAEM $\cap$	AP	43.5	40.8	43.0	45.0	41.6	44.1	44.0	45.0	**45.1**
		AP^{bb}	49.8	46.0	48.5	49.5	46.9	48.9	48.0	49.5	**50.3**
WBF base		AP	36.1	**38.0**	34.8	33.4	37.3	30.3	32.7	34.9	36.9
		AP^{bb}	38.8	**41.6**	38.0	37.4	40.2	33.6	37.8	38.5	40.3
WBF EM		AP	38.1	**39.9**	34.9	32.4	39.8	36.5	32.8	36.3	35.9
		AP^{bb}	40.6	**42.8**	38.3	36.4	42.8	40.2	37.6	40.0	39.3
Mean		AP	38.6	39.5	39.3	34.7	**39.7**	37.1	35.1	38.1	38.4
		AP^{bb}	42.2	43.3	**43.5**	39.6	**43.5**	41.1	40.0	42.2	42.3

intersection. Additionally, the plain repeated labels, without any aggregation, are compared with the different aggregated test data. Our findings reveal that on a high-agreement dataset, weighted boxes fusion does not perform well. This could be attributed to the inclusion of most annotations by WBF, whereas in cases with high agreement, it is more desirable to exclude non-conforming instances. Majority voting and localization-aware expectation maximization perform similarly; however, LAEM provides a more elegant solution for addressing edge cases. Calculating the annotator confidence, as performed in LAEM, is highly advantageous. However, in rare cases, spammer annotators could potentially circumvent annotation confidence by annotating large portions of simple examples correctly but failing at hard cases. Such cases would result in a high confidence level for the spammer, potentially outvoting the correct annotators on challenging and crucial cases.

Table 6. Comparing results with the private Kaggle leaderboard [22] for the VinDr-CXR dataset using the double headed R-CNN at mAP_{40}. Union is represented by $\cup$, intersection by $\cap$ and averaging by μ. RL denotes training conducted on un-aggregated noisy labels.

Double Head R-CNN VinDr-CXR	RL	Training							
		MJV			LAEM			WBF	
		$\cup$	μ	$\cap$	$\cup$	μ	$\cap$	base	EM
private LB	**16.2**	15.2	14.6	14.3	14.9	15.0	14.7	13.7	14.3

The main performance differences between MJV and LAEM arise due to the application of the three different combination operations – union, averaging, and intersection. Combining areas by taking their union results in larger areas, making it easier for a classifier to identify the respective regions. Analysis of the mean results of the training methods reveals that both MJV+$\cup$ and LAEM+$\cup$ exhibit the highest performance across various test configurations. On the contrary, methods parameterized with intersection $\cap$ yield the lowest mean results. Training with repeated labels without any aggregation yields results similar to training with aggregated labels. However, while it may be generally feasible to train with noisy labels, the performance is slightly dampened. Since the test data aggregation method is LAEM-μ as described in Sect. 3.2, the best performing training method LAEM-$\cup$ is chosen as the aggregation method for the training data in the experiments shown in Sect. 4.2 and 4.3.

For the VinDr-CXR dataset, a smaller, similar experiment is performed as shown in Table 6. As the Kaggle leaderboard already provides an aggregated ground truth and labels are unavailable, only the training data are aggregated. Our findings indicate that training with plain repeated labels leads to higher results. Given the low agreement of the dataset, training with repeated labels may be seen as a form of "label augmentation." Interestingly, the methods used to aggregate the test data, such as WBF, do not outperform the other methods. However, ground truth estimation methods are not designed to boost performance but rather to provide a suitable estimation for the targeted outcome. Based on these results, the following experiments on VinDr-CXR will be run with the repeated labels for training.

Appendix 3

This section shows three more comparisons between different ground truth aggregation methods, exemplary on the VinDr-CXR dataset [23]. All of them follow the same structure. Left: the original image with the repeated labels indicated by the different line types. Right: the four smaller images from top left to bottom right are, MJV+$\cap$, LAEM+μ, LAEM+$\cup$ and WBF (Fig. 3).

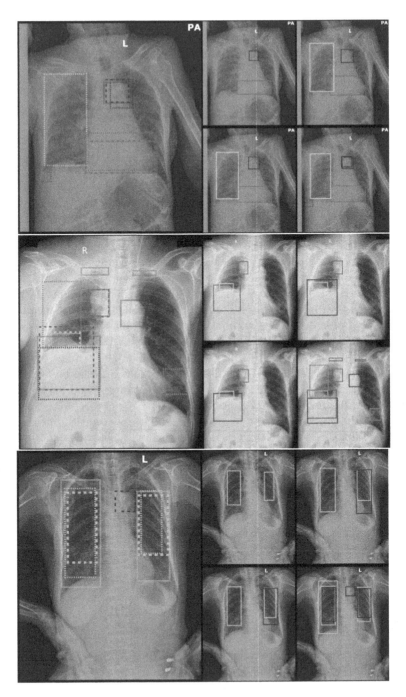

Fig. 3. Qualitative results on three test images from the VinDr-CXR. Left: the original image with the repeated labels indicated by the different line types. Right: the four smaller images from top left to bottom right are, MJV+∩, LAEM+μ, LAEM+∪ and WBF.

References

1. Asman, A.J., Landman, B.A.: Robust statistical label fusion through consensus level, labeler accuracy, and truth estimation (collate). IEEE Trans. Med. Imaging **30**(10), 1779–1794 (2011)

2. Cai, Z., Vasconcelos, N.: Cascade R-CNN: high quality object detection and instance segmentation. IEEE Trans. Pattern Anal. Mach. Intell. 1 (2019). https://doi.org/10.1109/tpami.2019.2956516. https://dx.doi.org/10.1109/tpami.2019.2956516

3. Carion, N., Massa, F., Synnaeve, G., Usunier, N., Kirillov, A., Zagoruyko, S.: End-to-end object detection with transformers. In: Vedaldi, A., Bischof, H., Brox, T., Frahm, J.-M. (eds.) ECCV 2020. LNCS, vol. 12346, pp. 213–229. Springer, Cham (2020). https://doi.org/10.1007/978-3-030-58452-8_13

4. Chen, K., et al.: MMDetection: open MMLab detection toolbox and benchmark. arXiv preprint arXiv:1906.07155 (2019)

5. Chen, Y., Li, W., Sakaridis, C., Dai, D., Van Gool, L.: Domain adaptive faster R-CNN for object detection in the wild. In: Proceedings of the IEEE Conference on Computer Vision and Pattern Recognition, pp. 3339–3348 (2018)

6. Cheng, B., Misra, I., Schwing, A.G., Kirillov, A., Girdhar, R.: Masked-attention mask transformer for universal image segmentation. In: Proceedings of the IEEE/CVF Conference on Computer Vision and Pattern Recognition, pp. 1290–1299 (2022)

7. Cheng, Y., et al.: Flow: a dataset and benchmark for floating waste detection in inland waters. In: Proceedings of the IEEE/CVF International Conference on Computer Vision, pp. 10953–10962 (2021)

8. Dawid, A.P., Skene, A.M.: Maximum likelihood estimation of observer error-rates using the EM algorithm. J. Roy. Stat. Soc.: Ser. C (Appl. Stat.) **28**(1), 20–28 (1979)

9. Feng, D., et al.: Labels are not perfect: inferring spatial uncertainty in object detection. IEEE Trans. Intell. Transp. Syst. **23**(8), 9981–9994 (2021)

10. Gao, J., Wang, J., Dai, S., Li, L.J., Nevatia, R.: Note-RCNN: noise tolerant ensemble RCNN for semi-supervised object detection. In: Proceedings of the IEEE/CVF International Conference on Computer Vision, pp. 9508–9517 (2019)

11. Gao, Z., et al.: Learning from multiple annotator noisy labels via sample-wise label fusion. In: Avidan, S., Brostow, G., Cissé, M., Farinella, G.M., Hassner, T. (eds.) ECCV 2022. LNCS, vol. 13684, pp. 407–422. Springer, Cham (2022). https://doi.org/10.1007/978-3-031-20053-3_24

12. Guan, M., Gulshan, V., Dai, A., Hinton, G.: Who said what: modeling individual labelers improves classification. In: Proceedings of the AAAI Conference on Artificial Intelligence, vol. 32 (2018)

13. He, K., Gkioxari, G., Dollár, P., Girshick, R.: Mask R-CNN. In: Proceedings of the IEEE International Conference on Computer Vision, pp. 2961–2969 (2017)

14. Karimi, D., Dou, H., Warfield, S.K., Gholipour, A.: Deep learning with noisy labels: exploring techniques and remedies in medical image analysis. Med. Image Anal. **65**, 101759 (2020)

15. Khetan, A., Lipton, Z.C., Anandkumar, A.: Learning from noisy singly-labeled data. arXiv preprint arXiv:1712.04577 (2017)

16. Khodabandeh, M., Vahdat, A., Ranjbar, M., Macready, W.G.: A robust learning approach to domain adaptive object detection. In: Proceedings of the IEEE/CVF International Conference on Computer Vision, pp. 480–490 (2019)

17. Langerak, T.R., van der Heide, U.A., Kotte, A.N., Viergever, M.A., Van Vulpen, M., Pluim, J.P.: Label fusion in atlas-based segmentation using a selective and iterative method for performance level estimation (simple). IEEE Trans. Med. Imaging **29**(12), 2000–2008 (2010)

18. Le, K.H., Tran, T.V., Pham, H.H., Nguyen, H.T., Le, T.T., Nguyen, H.Q.: Learning from multiple expert annotators for enhancing anomaly detection in medical image analysis. arXiv preprint arXiv:2203.10611 (2022)

19. Li, M., Xu, Y., Cui, L., Huang, S., Wei, F., Li, Z., Zhou, M.: DocBank: a benchmark dataset for document layout analysis. arXiv preprint arXiv:2006.01038 (2020)

20. Lin, T.-Y., et al.: Microsoft COCO: common objects in context. In: Fleet, D., Pajdla, T., Schiele, B., Tuytelaars, T. (eds.) ECCV 2014. LNCS, vol. 8693, pp. 740–755. Springer, Cham (2014). https://doi.org/10.1007/978-3-319-10602-1_48

21. Michaelis, C., et al.: Benchmarking robustness in object detection: autonomous driving when winter is coming. arXiv preprint arXiv:1907.07484 (2019)

22. Nguyen, D.B., Nguyen, H.Q., Elliott, J., KeepLearning, Nguyen, N.T., Culliton, P.: VinBigData chest X-ray abnormalities detection (2020). https://kaggle.com/competitions/vinbigdata-chest-xray-abnormalities-detection

23. Nguyen, H.Q., et al.: VinDr-CXR: an open dataset of chest X-rays with radiologist's annotations. Sci. Data **9**(1), 429 (2022)

24. Qiao, S., Chen, L.C., Yuille, A.: Detectors: detecting objects with recursive feature pyramid and switchable atrous convolution. In: Proceedings of the IEEE/CVF Conference on Computer Vision and Pattern Recognition, pp. 10213–10224 (2021)

25. Ramamonjison, R., Banitalebi-Dehkordi, A., Kang, X., Bai, X., Zhang, Y.: Sim-ROD: a simple adaptation method for robust object detection. In: 2021 IEEE/CVF International Conference on Computer Vision (ICCV), Montreal, QC, Canada, pp. 3550–3559. IEEE, October 2021. https://doi.org/10.1109/ICCV48922.2021.00355. https://ieeexplore.ieee.org/document/9711168/

26. Raykar, V.C., et al.: Supervised learning from multiple experts: whom to trust when everyone lies a bit. In: Proceedings of the 26th Annual International Conference on Machine Learning, pp. 889–896 (2009)

27. Ren, S., He, K., Girshick, R., Sun, J.: Faster R-CNN: towards real-time object detection with region proposal networks. In: Advances in Neural Information Processing Systems 28 (2015)

28. Rodrigues, F., Pereira, F.: Deep learning from crowds. In: Proceedings of the AAAI Conference on Artificial Intelligence, vol. 32 (2018)

29. Sheng, V.S., Provost, F., Ipeirotis, P.G.: Get another label? Improving data quality and data mining using multiple, noisy labelers. In: Proceedings of the 14th ACM SIGKDD International Conference on Knowledge Discovery and Data Mining, pp. 614–622 (2008)

30. Sheng, V.S., Zhang, J.: Machine learning with crowdsourcing: a brief summary of the past research and future directions. In: Proceedings of the AAAI Conference on Artificial Intelligence, vol. 33, pp. 9837–9843 (2019)

31. Sinha, V.B., Rao, S., Balasubramanian, V.N.: Fast Dawid-Skene: a fast vote aggregation scheme for sentiment classification. arXiv preprint arXiv:1803.02781 (2018)

32. Solovyev, R., Wang, W., Gabruseva, T.: Weighted boxes fusion: ensembling boxes from different object detection models. Image Vis. Comput. **107**, 104117 (2021)

33. Song, H., Kim, M., Park, D., Shin, Y., Lee, J.G.: Learning from noisy labels with deep neural networks: a survey. IEEE Trans. Neural Netw. Learn. Syst. **34**, 8135–8153 (2022)

34. Tanno, R., Saeedi, A., Sankaranarayanan, S., Alexander, D.C., Silberman, N.: Learning from noisy labels by regularized estimation of annotator confusion. In: Proceedings of the IEEE/CVF Conference on Computer Vision and Pattern Recognition, pp. 11244–11253 (2019)

35. Tschirschwitz, D., Klemstein, F., Stein, B., Rodehorst, V.: A dataset for analysing complex document layouts in the digital humanities and its evaluation with Krippendorff's alpha. In: Andres, B., Bernard, F., Cremers, D., Frintrop, S., Goldlücke, B., Ihrke, I. (eds.) DAGM GCPR 2022. LNCS, vol. 13485, pp. 354–374. Springer, Cham (2022). https://doi.org/10.1007/978-3-031-16788-1_22

36. Wang, X., et al.: Robust object detection via instance-level temporal cycle confusion. In: Proceedings of the IEEE/CVF International Conference on Computer Vision, pp. 9143–9152 (2021)

37. Wang, Z., Li, Y., Guo, Y., Fang, L., Wang, S.: Data-uncertainty guided multi-phase learning for semi-supervised object detection. In: Proceedings of the IEEE/CVF Conference on Computer Vision and Pattern Recognition, pp. 4568–4577 (2021)

38. Warfield, S.K., Zou, K.H., Wells, W.M.: Simultaneous truth and performance level estimation (staple): an algorithm for the validation of image segmentation. IEEE Trans. Med. Imaging **23**(7), 903–921 (2004)

39. Whitehill, J., Wu, T.F., Bergsma, J., Movellan, J., Ruvolo, P.: Whose vote should count more: optimal integration of labels from labelers of unknown expertise. In: Advances in Neural Information Processing Systems 22 (2009)

40. Wu, Y., et al.: Rethinking classification and localization for object detection. In: Proceedings of the IEEE/CVF Conference on Computer Vision and Pattern Recognition, pp. 10186–10195 (2020)

41. Wu, Z., Suresh, K., Narayanan, P., Xu, H., Kwon, H., Wang, Z.: Delving into robust object detection from unmanned aerial vehicles: a deep nuisance disentanglement approach. In: Proceedings of the IEEE/CVF International Conference on Computer Vision, pp. 1201–1210 (2019)

42. Xie, C., Wang, J., Zhang, Z., Zhou, Y., Xie, L., Yuille, A.: Adversarial examples for semantic segmentation and object detection. In: Proceedings of the IEEE International Conference on Computer Vision, pp. 1369–1378 (2017)

43. Zhang, H., Wang, J.: Towards adversarially robust object detection. In: 2019 IEEE/CVF International Conference on Computer Vision (ICCV), Seoul, South Korea, pp. 421–430. IEEE, October 2019. https://doi.org/10.1109/ICCV.2019. 00051. https://ieeexplore.ieee.org/document/9009990/

44. Zhang, Z., Zhang, H., Arik, S.O., Lee, H., Pfister, T.: Distilling effective supervision from severe label noise. In: Proceedings of the IEEE/CVF Conference on Computer Vision and Pattern Recognition, pp. 9294–9303 (2020)

45. Zheng, Y., Li, G., Li, Y., Shan, C., Cheng, R.: Truth inference in crowdsourcing: is the problem solved? Proc. VLDB Endow. **10**(5), 541–552 (2017)

46. Zhong, X., Tang, J., Yepes, A.J.: PubLayNet: largest dataset ever for document layout analysis. In: 2019 International Conference on Document Analysis and Recognition (ICDAR), pp. 1015–1022. IEEE (2019)

47. Zhu, X., Wu, X.: Class noise vs. attribute noise: a quantitative study. Artif. Intell. Rev. **22**(3), 177 (2004)

An Evaluation of Zero-Cost Proxies - from Neural Architecture Performance Prediction to Model Robustness

Jovita Lukasik[1]([✉])(iD), Michael Moeller[1](iD), and Margret Keuper[1,2](iD)

[1] University of Siegen, Siegen, Germany
{jovita.lukasik,michael.moeller,margret.keuper}@uni-siegen.de
[2] Max Planck Institute for Informatics, Saarland Informatics Campus,
Saarbrücken, Germany

Abstract. Zero-cost proxies are nowadays frequently studied and used to search for neural architectures. They show an impressive ability to predict the performance of architectures by making use of their untrained weights. These techniques allow for immense search speed-ups. So far the joint search for well-performing and robust architectures has received much less attention in the field of NAS. Therefore, the main focus of zero-cost proxies is the clean accuracy of architectures, whereas the model robustness should play an evenly important part. In this paper, we analyze the ability of common zero-cost proxies to serve as performance predictors for robustness in the popular NAS-Bench-201 search space. We are interested in the single prediction task for robustness and the joint multi-objective of clean and robust accuracy. We further analyze the feature importance of the proxies and show that predicting the robustness makes the prediction task from existing zero-cost proxies more challenging. As a result, the joint consideration of several proxies becomes necessary to predict a model's robustness while the clean accuracy can be regressed from a single such feature.

Keywords: neural architecture search · zero-cost proxies · robustness

1 Introduction

Neural Architecture Search (NAS) [7,34] seeks to automate the process of designing high-performing neural networks. This research field has gained immense popularity in the last years, with only a few NAS papers in 2016 to almost 700 in 2022 [34]. The ability of NAS to find high-performing architectures, capable of outperforming hand-designed ones, notably on image classification [39], makes this research field highly valuable. However, classical approaches like reinforcement learning [18,39] or evolutionary algorithms [26] are expensive, which

---

Supplementary Information The online version contains supplementary material available at https://doi.org/10.1007/978-3-031-54605-1_40.

led to a focus-shift towards improving the search efficiency. Therefore different approaches such as one-shot methods [20] or performance prediction methods [35] were introduced. Recently, zero-cost proxies (ZCP) [23], as part of performance prediction strategies, were developed. These proxies build upon fast computations, mostly in one single forward and backward pass on an untrained model, and attempt to predict the accuracy that the underlying architecture will have after training. In recent years, several zero-cost proxies were introduced [1,23], including simple architectural baselines as FLOPS or the number of parameters. NAS-Bench-Suite-Zero [14] provides a more in-depth analysis and evaluates 13 different ZCPs on 28 different tasks to show the effectiveness as a performance prediction technique.

So far, the main focus of NAS research was the resulting performance of the architectures on a downstream task. Another important aspect of networks, namely their robustness, has been less addressed in NAS so far. Most works targeting both high accuracy and a robust network rely on one-shot methods [12,24]. However, using only ZCPs as a performance prediction model for the multi-objective has not been addressed. The search for architectures that are robust against adversarial attacks is especially important for computer vision and image classification since networks can be easily fooled when the input data is changed using slight perturbations that are even invisible to the human eye. This can lead to networks making false predictions with high confidence.

This aspect is particularly important in the context of NAS and ZCPs because the search for robust architectures is significantly more expensive: an the architecture's robustness is to be evaluated on trained architectures against different adversarial attacks [4,8,16].

In this paper, we therefore address the question: How transferable are the accuracy-focused ZCPs to the architecture's robustness? A high-performing architecture is not necessarily robust. Therefore, we analyze which ZCPs perform well for predicting clean accuracy, which are good at predicting robustness, and which do well at both. For our evaluation, we leverage the recently published robustness dataset [13] which allows for easily accessible robustness evaluations on an established NAS search space [6]. Since every ZCP provides a low-dimensional (scalar) measure per architecture, we understand each ZCP as a feature dimension in a concatenated feature vector and employ random forest regression as a predictor of clean and robust accuracy. This facilitates not only the evaluation of the performance or correlation of the different measures with the prediction target but also to gain direct access to every proxy's feature importance compared with all others.

Our evaluation of all ZCPs from NAS-Bench-Suite-Zero allows us to make the following observations:

- While the correlation of every single ZCP with the target is not very strong, the random forest regression allows predicting the clean accuracy with very good and the robust accuracy with good precision.

- As a result, we expect that leveraging several ZCPs simultaneously will allow for NAS with the aim to find robust architectures, while every single ZCP will likely not provide the needed information.
- When analyzing the feature importance, ZCPs using Jacobian-based information generally carry the most employed information.
- The analysis of the feature importance for robust model accuracy prediction confirms that various ZCPs contribute strongly to the overall prediction.

2   Related Work

2.1   Zero-Cost Proxies for NAS

NAS is the process to automate the design of neural architectures with the goal to find a high-performing architecture on a particular dataset. In the last few years, this research field gained immense popularity and is able to surpass hand-designed neural architectures on different tasks, especially on image classification. See [34] for a survey. For fast search and evaluation of found architectures, many NAS methods make use of performance prediction techniques via surrogate models. The surrogate model predicts the performance of an architecture, without the need of training the architecture, with the goal to keep the query amount (i.e. the amount necessary training data to train the surrogate model) low. Each query means one full training of the architecture, therefore, successful performance prediction-based NAS methods are able to use only a few queries. [22,27,32,33,36] show improved results using surrogate models keeping the query amount low. However, these methods use the validation or test accuracy of the architecture as a target and require high computation time. In order to predict the performance of an architecture without full training, zero-cost proxies (ZCPs), measured on untrained architectures, can be used [23]. The idea is that these ZCPs, which often require only one forward and one backward pass on a single mini-batch, are somehow correlated with the resulting performance of the architecture after full training. [23] originally used ZCPs for NAS by analyzing the linear regions and how well they are separated. In contrast, [1] uses pruning-at-initialization techniques [17,29,31] as ZCPs. The best performing ZCP in [1] synflow is data-independent, which does not consider the input data for the proxy calculation. Another data-independent architecture was proposed by [19]. Other approaches use the neural tangent kernel for faster architecture search [2].

The recent benchmark NAS-Bench-suite zero [14] compares different ZCPs on different NAS search spaces and shows how they can be integrated into different NAS frameworks. Other works include ZCPs into Bayesian optimization NAS approaches (as for example [28,35]) and one-shot architecture search [37]. In contrast, this paper evaluates how well ZCPs can predict the robust accuracy of a model under adversarial attacks, and demonstrates (surprising) success in combining different ZCP features in a random-forest classifier.

2.2 Robustness in NAS

Compared to searching for an architecture with the single objective of having a high performance, including the architecture's robustness results in an even more challenging task that requires a multi-objective search. Recent works that search for both high-performing and robust architectures combine both objectives in one-shot search approaches [5,9,12,24]. [5] includes a parameter constraint in the supernet training in order to reduce the Lipschitz constant. Also [12] adds additional maximization objectives, the certified lower bound and Jacobian norm bound, to the supernet training. [24] includes the loss landscape of the Hessian into the bi-level optimization approach from [20]. In contrast to these additional objectives, [9] proposes adversarial training of the supernet training for increased network robustness. The recent robustness dataset [13] facilitates this research area. All 6 466 unique architectures in the popular NAS cell-based search space, NAS-Bench-201 [6], are evaluated on four different adversarial attacks (FGSM [8], PGD [16], APGD and Square [4]) with different attack strengths on three different image datasets, CIFAR-10 [15], CIFAR-100 [15], and ImageNet16-120 [3].

3 Background on Zero-Cost Proxies

As presented in NAS-Bench-Suite-Zero [14], we can differentiate the proxies into different types: Jacobian-based (★), pruning-based (♦), baseline (■), piecewise-linear (▼), and also Hessian-based (●) zero-cost proxies. In the following, we will provide more information about the ZCPs, which we evaluate in this paper.

3.1 Jacobian-Based

Mellor et al. [23] were the first to introduce ZCPs into NAS, by analyzing the network behavior using local linear operations for each input $\mathbf{x}_i \in \mathbb{R}^D$ in the training data mini-batch, which can be computed by the Jacobian of the network for each input. The idea is based on the fact that a resulting well-performing untrained network is supposed to be able to distinguish the local linear operations of different data points. For that, the metric `jacov` was introduced, which is using the correlation matrix of the Jacobian as a Gaussian kernel. The score itself is the Kullback-Leibler divergence between a standard Gaussian and a Gaussian with the mentioned kernel. Therefore, the higher the score, the better the architecture is likely to be.

Building on that, [23] further introduced `nwot` (Neural Architecture Search without Training), which forms binary codes, depending on whether the rectified linear unit is active or not, which define the linear region in the network. Similar binary codes for two input points indicate that it is more challenging to learn to separate these points. [21] developed `nwot` even further by introducing `epe-nas` (Efficient Performance Estimation Without Training for Neural Architecture Search). The goal of epe-nas is to evaluate if an untrained network is able to distinguish two points from different classes and equate points from the same class. This is measured by the correlation of the Jacobian (jacov) for input data being from the same class. Therefore, the resulting correlation matrix can be used to analyze how the network behaves for each class and thus may indicate if this network can also distinguish between different classes.

As an alternative to these methods, [1] proposed a simple proxy, grad-norm, which is simply the sum of the Euclidean norm of the weight gradients.

So far, these Jacobian-based measurements focused on the correlation with the resulting clean performance of architectures. In this paper, we are also interested in the correlation and influence on the robust accuracy of the architecture. As also used in [12,13] combined the search for a high-performing architecture that is also robust against adversarial attacks, by including the Frobenius norm of the Jacobian (jacob-fro) into the search. As introduced in [11] the change of the network output, when a perturbed data point $\mathbf{x}_i + \epsilon, \epsilon \in \mathbb{R}^D$ is the input to the network instead of the clean data point $\mathbf{x}_i$, can be used as a measurement for the robustness of the architecture: the larger the change, the more unstable is the network in case of perturbed input data. This change can be measured by the square of the Frobenius norm of the difference of the network's prediction on perturbed and unperturbed data.

3.2 Pruning-Based

Pruning-based ZCPs are based on network pruning metrics, which identify the least important parameters in a network at initialization time. [17] introduced a measurement, snip (Single-shot Network Pruning), which uses a connection sensitivity metric to approximate the change in the loss, when weights with a small gradient magnitude are pruned. Based on that, [31] improves snip by approximating the change in the loss after weight pruning in their grasp (Gradient Signal Preservation) metric. Lastly, [29] investigated these two pruning-based metrics in terms of layer collapse, and proposes synflow, which multiplies all absolute values of the parameters in the network, which is independent of the training data.

In contrast to that, [30] obtains and aggregates the Fisher information fisher for all channels in a convolution block, to identify the channel with the least important effect on the network's loss.

3.3 Piecewise Linear

[19] proposes the zen score, motivated the observation that a CNN can be also seen as a composition of piecewise linear functions being conditioned on activation patterns. Therefore, they propose to measure the network's ability to express complex functions by its Gaussian complexity. This score is data-independent since both the network weights and the input data are sampled from a standard Gaussian distribution.

3.4 Hessian-Based

As mentioned in Sect. 3.1, the goal for ZCP research was mainly motivated by finding a measurement, which is correlated with the network's performance after training. In this paper, we want to shift the focus towards the robustness of architectures, which is also a crucial aspect of neural architectures. [24] also included the robustness as a target for architecture search, by considering the smoothness of the loss landscape of the architecture. [38] investigated the connection between the smoothness of the loss landscape of a network and its robustness, and shows that the adversarial loss is correlated with the biggest eigenvalue of the Hessian. A small Hessian spectrum implies a flat minimum, whereas a large Hessian spectrum, implies a sharp minimum, which is more sensitive to changes in the input and therefore can be more easily fooled by adversarial attacks.

3.5 Baselines

In addition to the above mentioned developed ZCPs, basic network information have also been successfully used as ZCPs [1,25]. The most common baseline proxies are the number of FLOPS (`flops`) as well as the number of parameters (`params`). In addition to these, [1] also considers the sum of the L2-norm of the untrained network weights, `l2-norm`, and the multiplication of the network weights and its gradients, `plain`.

4 Feature Collection and Evaluation

In the following, we are going to describe our evaluation setting.

4.1 NAS-Bench-201

NAS-Bench-201 [6] is a cell-based search space [34], in which each cell has 4 nodes and 6 edges. The node represents the architecture's feature map and each edge represents one operation from a predefined operation set. This operation set contains 5 different operations: 1×1 convolution, 3×3 convolution, 3×3 avg.pooling, skip $-$ connection, zero. The cells are integrated into a macro-architecture. The overall search space has a size of $5^6 = 15\,625$ different architectures, from which $6\,466$ architectures are unique and non-isomorphic. Isomorphic architectures have the same information flow in the network architecture, resulting in similar outcomes and only differ due to numerical reasons. All architectures are trained on three different image datasets, CIFAR-10 [15], CIFAR-100 [15], and ImageNet16-120 [3].

4.2 Neural Architecture Design and Robustness Dataset

The dataset by [13] evaluated all the unique architectures in NAS-Bench-201 [6] against three white-box attacks, i.e., FGSM [8], PGD [16], APGD [4], as well as one black-box attack, Square Attack [4] to evaluate the adversarial robustness of the architectures, given by the different topologies. In addition, all architectures were also evaluated on corrupted image datasets, CIFAR-10C and CIFAR-100-C [10]. Along with these evaluations, the dataset also shows three different use cases, on how the data can be used: evaluation of ZCPs for robustness, NAS on robustness, and an analysis of how the topology and the design of an architecture influence its resulting robustness. This dataset also provides evaluations for the Frobenius norm from Sect. 3.1 and the biggest eigenvalue of the Hessian from Sect. 3.4 as two zero-cost proxies for their first use case. Note, the latter proxy, the Hessian, was only evaluated on the CIFAR-10 image data [15].

4.3   Collection

Both datasets [13,14] provide us with the necessary proxies for the NAS-Bench-201 [6] search space evaluations. Therefore we will analyze 15 different proxies for 6 466 architectures on three different image datasets. Note, the ZCPs in [14] were evaluated on the validation accuracy, while [13] provide test accuracy information. We will focus here on the test accuracies.

5   Evaluations of Zero-Cost Proxies

As presented in Sect. 4, we can directly gather all proxies. Having these at hand allows us to evaluate the correlation, influence and importance of each proxy not only on the clean test accuracy of the architectures but also on their robust accuracy.

5.1   Correlation

Figure 1 shows the Kendall tau rank correlation in absolute values between each ZCP and all available accuracies, from clean test accuracy to all adversarial attack test accuracies (fgsm, pgd, aa-apgd-ce, aa-square) on CIFAR-10. For the correlation plots on CIFAR-100 and ImageNet16-120 we refer to the supplementary material. The Jacobian-based proxies (especially jacov and nwot) and the baseline proxies show the highest correlation over all datasets, especially for the FGSM attack. Furthermore, the large correlation within the same attack over different strengths of ϵ values stays steady. However, the more difficult the attack gets, from FGSM over PGD to APGD, the larger is the correlations decrease. Interestingly, the zen proxy has the lowest correlation with each test accuracy.

5.2   Feature Importance

In the following we want to analyze the ability of ZCPs to be used as features to predict the robust accuracy as a single objective target, as well as the multi-objective target, for both clean and robust accuracy.

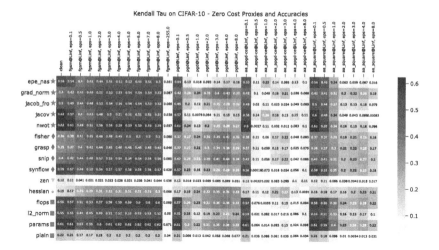

Fig. 1. Kendall tau rank correlation in **absolute values** between all zero-cost proxies computed on all architectures given in the robustness dataset [13] to the test accuracy and adversarial attacks for CIFAR-10.

For that we split the architecture dataset (6 466 architectures from [13]) into 80% training and 20% test data to train a random forest regression model, that takes as input a feature vector of all concatenated ZCPs. We use the default regression parameters, with 100 numbers of trees and the mean squared error as the target criterion. For a better overview, we will consider the attack ϵ value of $1/255$ for all the following experiments. We first analyze the prediction ability itself in Table 1 by means of the R^2 score of the prediction model on the test dataset. As we can see, the random forest prediction model is able to predict the single accuracy (clean and robust) and the multi-objective accuracies in a proper way, while the prediction of the clean accuracy seems to be the easiest task, where R^2 values of 0.93 to 0.97 are reached.

Next, we are interested in the feature importance of individual ZCPs. So far the ZCPs in NAS-Bench-Suite-Zero are motivated by their correlation with the resulting clean accuracy of the architectures. Yet, how well can they be transferred to the more challenging task of robust accuracy and even more challenging than that, the multi-objective task? High clean accuracy does not necessarily mean that a network is also robust. Therefore we use all ZCPs from NAS-Bench-Suite-Zero [14] and the robustness dataset [13], which we already presented in Sect. 3 as feature inputs for the random forest prediction model and calculate their importance as the mean variance reduction (Gini importance). Note that in this measure, the comparison of correlated features needs to be considered with caution. Figure 2 visualizes the feature importance on the CIFAR-10 image datasets for all adversarial attacks with $\epsilon = 1/255$ for all three use cases: clean test accuracy, robust test accuracy, both test and robust accuracy. The latter one is used as the bar plot alignment. As we can see, `jacov` is the most important

Table 1. Test R^2 of the random forest prediction model for both single objective and multi objectives on the clean test accuracy and the robust test accuracy for $\epsilon = 1/255$.

Dataset	Test Accuracy $\epsilon = 1/255$								
	Single Objective					Multi Objective			
	Clean	FGSM	PGD	APGD	Squares	Clean-FGSM	Clean-PGD	Clean-APGD	Clean-Squares
CIFAR-10	0.97	0.88	0.65	0.66	0.75	0.92	0.81	0.82	0.86
CIFAR-100	0.96	0.75	0.69	0.73	0.68	0.86	0.83	0.85	0.82
ImageNet16-120	0.93	0.65	0.84	0.87	0.76	0.78	0.88	0.90	0.85

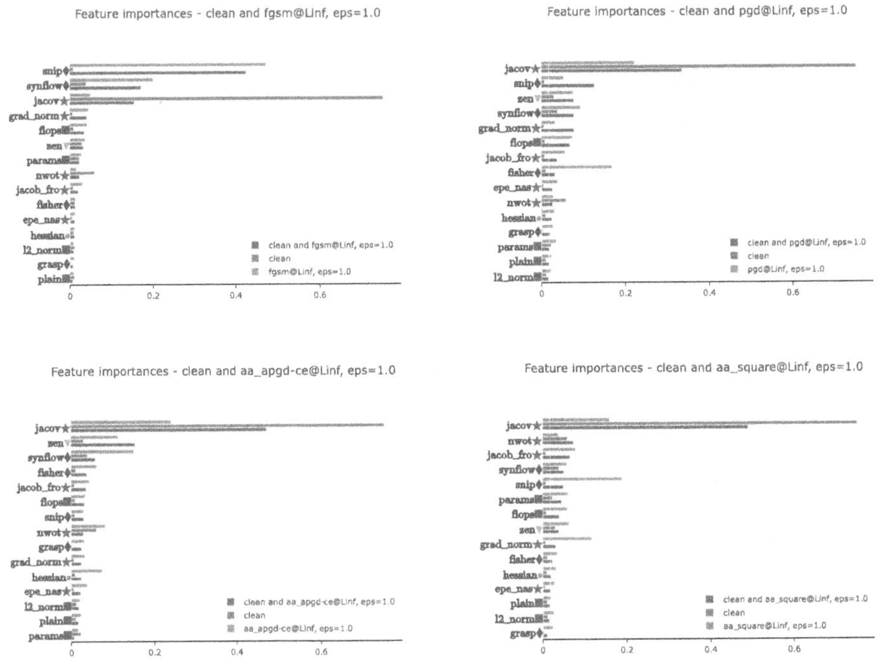

Fig. 2. Feature importance of the random forest prediction model trained on 80% of the data provided in [13] with all zero-cost proxies as features and multi targets being clean test accuracy and different adversarial accuracies on **CIFAR-10**.

feature for both the clean test accuracy and the multi-objective task, except for FGSM. Interestingly, the Top 5 most important ZCPs are all different for all considered adversarial attacks.

If we look at the feature importance for CIFAR-100 (Fig. 3), we can see that the Top 4 most important features for clean and robust accuracy are always the same, with the Jacobian-based ZCP nwot being the most important one. Note here, for CIFAR-100 the rank correlation decreases the most for more difficult attacks.

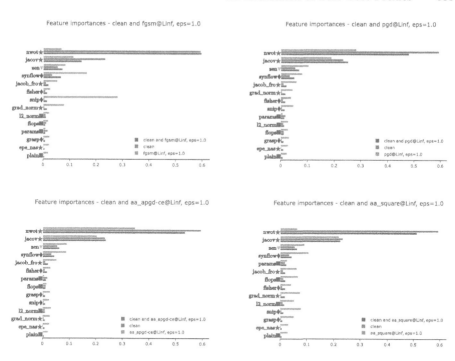

Fig. 3. Feature importance of the random forest prediction model trained on 80% of the data provided in [13] with all zero-cost proxies as features and multi targets being clean test accuracy and different adversarial accuracies on **CIFAR-100**.

Table 2. Test R^2 of the random forest prediction model using the **most important feature** for both single objectives and multi objectives on the clean test accuracy and the robust test accuracy for $\epsilon = 1/255$.

Dataset	Test Accuracy $\epsilon = 1/255$								
	Single Objective					Multi Objective			
	Clean	FGSM	PGD	APGD	Squares	Clean-FGSM	Clean-PGD	Clean-APGD	Clean-Squares
CIFAR-10	jacov 0.84	snip 0.41	jacov -0.31	jacov 0.002	snip 0.16	snip 0.37	jacov 0.26	jacov 0.42	jacov 0.54
CIFAR-100	nwot 0.74	snip 0.12	nwot 0.09	nwot 0.28	jacov -0.004	nwot 0.42	nwot 0.42	nwot 0.51	nwot 0.31
ImageNet16-120	jacov 0.61	jacov -0.003	jacov 0.58	jacov 0.64	jacov 0.44	jacov 0.31	jacov 0.60	jacov 0.63	jacov 0.52

When we turn now to ImageNet16-120, the ranking of the feature importance is the same for all considered attacks. Also there, a Jacobian-based ZCP, in this case `jacov`, is the most important feature.

We can see, that the most important features for clean accuracy are also important for the architecture's robust accuracy. In total, Jacobian-based ZCPs, especially `jacov` and `nwot`, seem to be the considerable measures for all different prediction tasks, ranging from single clean and robust accuracy prediction to the multi-objective prediction task. Noticeable is the high feature importance of `snip` for the single robust accuracy prediction task for both CIFAR datasets.

Interestingly, we can see that the task of robust accuracy prediction becomes more difficult on all three image datasets and attacks (see smaller R^2 values in

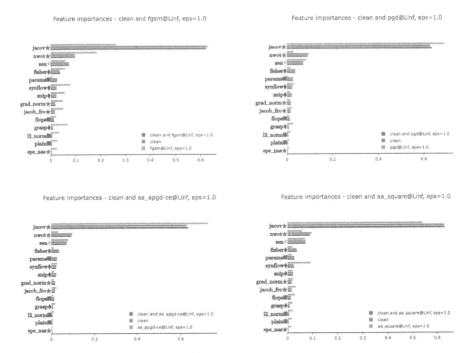

Fig. 4. Feature importance of the random forest prediction model trained on 80% of the data provided in [13] with all zero-cost proxies as features and multi targets being clean test accuracy and different adversarial accuracies on **ImageNet16-120**.

Table 3. Test R^2 of the random forest prediction model for the multi-objective task for $\epsilon = 1/255$ **without the most important feature** for the FGSM and PGD, respectively.

Dataset	Test Accuracy $\epsilon = 1/255$	
	Multi Objective	
	Clean-FGSM	Clean-PGD
CIFAR-10	0.92	0.79
CIFAR-100	0.87	0.83
ImageNet16-120	0.72	0.81

Table 1) in comparison to the multi-objective task. In addition, Figs. 2, 3, and 4 give the impression that solely the most important feature could be used to predict the clean accuracy.

Therefore, we analyze in Table 2 the prediction ability using only the most important feature for all considered tasks, respectively. As we can see the reduced R^2 values show that the joint consideration of several proxies is necessary to predict a model's robustness, while the clean accuracy can be regressed from only one such feature. Concluding, considering only one ZCP for the more difficult

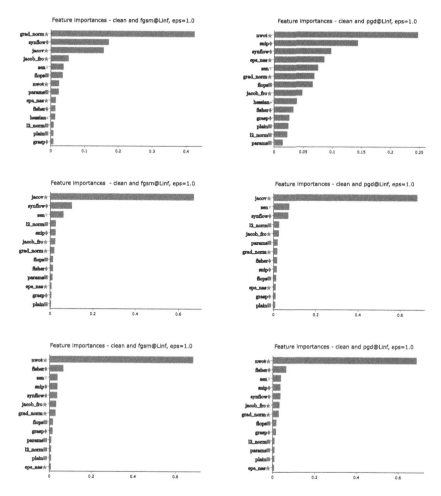

Fig. 5. Feature importance of the random forest prediction model trained on 80% of the data provided in [13] **without the most important feature** from Tables 2, 3, 4 for FGSM, and PGD at $\epsilon = 1/255$. **(top)**: CIFAR-10, **(middle)**: CIFAR-100, **(bottom)**: ImageNet16-120.

task of robust accuracy prediction (single and multi-objective) hinders the prediction ability.

5.3 Feature Importance Excluding Top 1

From the previous section it became clear that using one zero cost proxy as a feature is not sufficient to predict the robustness of an architecture. This leads to the next question if the regression model can still make good predictions, using all ZCPs **except** the most important one.

The comparison of Table 1 with Table 3 presents only a slight decrease in R^2 values. The prediction ability for the clean accuracy and FGSM robust accuracy on CIFAR-10, as well as for the clean accuracy and PGD accuracy on CIFAR-100 even remained the same.

We also plot the updated feature importances in Fig. 5 for all ZCPs without the most important one from the previous section for FGSM and PGD. CIFAR-100 (middle) and ImageNet16-120 (bottom) show a new most distinctive important feature, which is in both cases a Jacobian-based one. If we turn towards CIFAR-10 (top) there is no such distinctive important feature and rather a steady decrease in importance from one feature to the other.

6   Conclusion

In this paper, we presented an analysis of 15 zero-cost proxies with regard to their ability to act as performance prediction techniques for architecture robustness using a random forest. We made use of two provided datasets, NAS-Bench-Suite-Zero and a robustness dataset, which allows fast evaluations on the here-considered NAS-Bench-201 search space. Commonly, these zero-cost proxies are targeting the clean accuracy of architectures. Therefore, our analysis shows that the prediction of robustness is a more difficult task. Additionally, we investigated the feature importance of these zero-cost proxies. We found that, although the correlation of single zero-cost proxies with the robust accuracy of neural networks is quite weak, the signal contained in several such proxies considered simultaneously provides strong indication of a network's robustness. Thus, we conclude that (1) zero-cost proxies can, in principle, be used for NAS to search for robust architectures, and (2) unlike NAS for best clean accuracy, which usually employs a single proxy, NAS for robust architectures will need to leverage a multitude of zero-cost proxies in practice. At the same time, we see that the use of multiple proxies is beneficial even when regressing a network's clean accuracy. Future directions using zero-cost proxies in the NAS research should therefore consider the usage of several proxies with different underlying information instead of focusing only on one best proxy which should fit all tasks.

Acknowledgment. The authors acknowledge support by the DFG research unit 5336 Learning to Sense.

References

1. Abdelfattah, M.S., Mehrotra, A., Dudziak, L., Lane, N.D.: Zero-cost proxies for lightweight NAS. In: Proceedings of the International Conference on Learning Representations (ICLR) (2021)
2. Chen, W., Gong, X., Wang, Z.: Neural architecture search on ImageNet in four GPU hours: a theoretically inspired perspective. In: Proceedings of the International Conference on Learning Representations (ICLR) (2021)
3. Chrabaszcz, P., Loshchilov, I., Hutter, F.: A downsampled variant of ImageNet as an alternative to the CIFAR datasets. arXiv:1707.08819 (2017)

4. Croce, F., Hein, M.: Reliable evaluation of adversarial robustness with an ensemble of diverse parameter-free attacks. In: Proceedings of the International Conference on Machine Learning (ICML) (2020)

5. Dong, M., Li, Y., Wang, Y., Xu, C.: Adversarially robust neural architectures. arXiv:2009.00902 (2020)

6. Dong, X., Yang, Y.: NAS-Bench-201: extending the scope of reproducible neural architecture search. In: Proceedings of the International Conference on Learning Representations (ICLR) (2020)

7. Elsken, T., Metzen, J.H., Hutter, F.: Neural architecture search: a survey. J. Mach. Learn. Res. **20**, 55:1-55:21 (2019)

8. Goodfellow, I.J., Shlens, J., Szegedy, C.: Explaining and harnessing adversarial examples. In: Proceedings of the International Conference on Learning Representations (ICLR) (2015)

9. Guo, M., Yang, Y., Xu, R., Liu, Z., Lin, D.: When NAS meets robustness: in search of robust architectures against adversarial attacks. In: Proceedings of the IEEE Conference on Computer Vision and Pattern Recognition (CVPR) (2020)

10. Hendrycks, D., Dietterich, T.: Benchmarking neural network robustness to common corruptions and perturbations. In: Proceedings of the International Conference on Learning Representations (ICLR) (2019)

11. Hoffman, J., Roberts, D.A., Yaida, S.: Robust learning with Jacobian regularization. arXiv:1908.02729 (2019)

12. Hosseini, R., Yang, X., Xie, P.: DSRNA: differentiable search of robust neural architectures. In: Proceedings of the IEEE Conference on Computer Vision and Pattern Recognition (CVPR) (2021)

13. Jung, S., Lukasik, J., Keuper, M.: Neural architecture design and robustness: a dataset. In: Proceedings of the International Conference on Learning Representations (ICLR) (2023)

14. Krishnakumar, A., White, C., Zela, A., Tu, R., Safari, M., Hutter, F.: NAS-Bench-suite-zero: accelerating research on zero cost proxies. In: Advances in Neural Information Processing Systems (NeurIPS) (2022)

15. Krizhevsky, A.: Learning multiple layers of features from tiny images. Technical report, University of Toronto (2009)

16. Kurakin, A., Goodfellow, I.J., Bengio, S.: Adversarial machine learning at scale. In: Proceedings of the International Conference on Learning Representations (ICLR) (2017)

17. Lee, N., Ajanthan, T., Torr, P.H.S.: SNIP: single-shot network pruning based on connection sensitivity. In: Proceedings of the International Conference on Learning Representations (ICLR) (2019)

18. Li, Y., Vinyals, O., Dyer, C., Pascanu, R., Battaglia, P.W.: Learning deep generative models of graphs. arXiv:1803.03324 (2018)

19. Lin, M., et al.: Zen-NAS: a zero-shot NAS for high-performance image recognition. In: Proceedings of the IEEE International Conference on Computer Vision (ICCV) (2021)

20. Liu, H., Simonyan, K., Yang, Y.: DARTS: differentiable architecture search. In: Proceedings of the International Conference on Learning Representations (ICLR) (2019)

21. Lopes, V., Alirezazadeh, S., Alexandre, L.A.: EPE-NAS: efficient performance estimation without training for neural architecture search. In: International Conference on Artificial Neural Networks (ICANN) (2021)

22. Lukasik, J., Jung, S., Keuper, M.: Learning where to look - generative NAS is surprisingly efficient. In: Avidan, S., Brostow, G., Cissé, M., Farinella, G.M., Hassner, T. (eds.) ECCV 2022. LNCS, vol. 13683, pp. 257–273. Springer, Cham (2022). https://doi.org/10.1007/978-3-031-20050-2_16

23. Mellor, J., Turner, J., Storkey, A.J., Crowley, E.J.: Neural architecture search without training. In: Proceedings of the International Conference on Machine Learning (ICML) (2021)

24. Mok, J., Na, B., Choe, H., Yoon, S.: AdvRush: searching for adversarially robust neural architectures. In: Proceedings of the IEEE International Conference on Computer Vision (ICCV) (2021)

25. Ning, X., et al.: Evaluating efficient performance estimators of neural architectures. In: Advances in Neural Information Processing Systems (NeurIPS) (2021)

26. Real, E., Aggarwal, A., Huang, Y., Le, Q.V.: Regularized evolution for image classifier architecture search. In: Proceedings of the Conference of Artificial Intelligence (AAAI) (2019)

27. Ru, B., Wan, X., Dong, X., Osborne, M.: Interpretable neural architecture search via Bayesian optimisation with Weisfeiler-Lehman kernels. In: Proceedings of the International Conference on Learning Representations (ICLR) (2021)

28. Shen, Y., et al.: ProxyBO: accelerating neural architecture search via Bayesian optimization with zero-cost proxies. arXiv:2110.10423 (2021)

29. Tanaka, H., Kunin, D., Yamins, D.L.K., Ganguli, S.: Pruning neural networks without any data by iteratively conserving synaptic flow. In: Advances in Neural Information Processing Systems (NeurIPS) (2020)

30. Turner, J., Crowley, E.J., O'Boyle, M.F.P., Storkey, A.J., Gray, G.: BlockSwap: fisher-guided block substitution for network compression on a budget. In: Proceedings of the International Conference on Learning Representations (ICLR) (2020)

31. Wang, C., Zhang, G., Grosse, R.B.: Picking winning tickets before training by preserving gradient flow. In: Proceedings of the International Conference on Learning Representations (ICLR) (2020)

32. Wen, W., Liu, H., Chen, Y., Li, H., Bender, G., Kindermans, P.-J.: Neural predictor for neural architecture search. In: Vedaldi, A., Bischof, H., Brox, T., Frahm, J.-M. (eds.) ECCV 2020. LNCS, vol. 12374, pp. 660–676. Springer, Cham (2020). https://doi.org/10.1007/978-3-030-58526-6_39

33. White, C., Neiswanger, W., Savani, Y.: BANANAS: Bayesian optimization with neural architectures for neural architecture search. In: Proceedings of the Conference of Artificial Intelligence (AAAI) (2021)

34. White, C., et al.: Neural architecture search: insights from 1000 papers. arXiv:2301.08727 (2023)

35. White, C., Zela, A., Ru, B., Liu, Y., Hutter, F.: How powerful are performance predictors in neural architecture search? In: Advances in Neural Information Processing Systems (NeurIPS) (2021)

36. Wu, J., et al.: Stronger NAS with weaker predictors. In: Advances in Neural Information Processing Systems (NeurIPS) (2021)

37. Xiang, L., Dudziak, L., Abdelfattah, M.S., Chau, T., Lane, N.D., Wen, H.: Zerocost proxies meet differentiable architecture search. arXiv:2106.06799 (2021)

38. Zhao, P., Chen, P., Das, P., Ramamurthy, K.N., Lin, X.: Bridging mode connectivity in loss landscapes and adversarial robustness. In: Proceedings of the International Conference on Learning Representations (ICLR) (2020)

39. Zoph, B., Le, Q.V.: Neural architecture search with reinforcement learning. In: Proceedings of the International Conference on Learning Representations (ICLR) (2017)

Author Index

Printed in the United States
by Baker & Taylor Publisher Services